THE
LYLE
OFFICIAL
ANTIQUES
REVIEW 1983

All prices quoted in this book are obtained from a variety of auctions in various countries during the twelve months prior to publication and are converted to dollars at the rate of exchange prevalent at the time of sale.

DRAWINGS BY

PETER KNOX
PETER TENCH
DENISE FREEMAN

THE
LYLE
OFFICIAL
ANTIQUES
REVIEW 1983

COMPILED BY MARGOT RUTHERFORD
EDITED BY TONY CURTIS

INTRODUCTION

This year over 100,000 Antique Dealers and Collectors will make full and profitable use of their Lyle Official Antiques Review. They know that only in this one volume will they find the widest possible variety of goods — illustrated, described and given a current market value to enable them to BUY RIGHT AND SELL RIGHT throughout the year of issue.

They know, too, that by building a collection of these immensely valuable volumes year by year, they will equip themselves with an unparalleled reference library of facts, figures and illustrations which, properly used, cannot fail to help them keep one step ahead of the market.

In its thirteen years of publication, Lyle's has gone from strength to strength and has become without doubt the pre-eminent book of reference for the antique trade throughout the world. Each of its fact filled pages are packed with precisely the kind of profitable information the professional Dealer needs — including descriptions, illustrations and values of thousands and thousands of individual items carefully selected to give a representative picture of the current market in antiques and collectables — and remember all values are prices actually paid, based on accurate sales records in the twelve months prior to publication from the best established and most highly respected auction houses in Europe and America.

This is THE book for the Professional Antiques Dealer. 'The Lyle Book' — we've even heard it called 'The Dealer's Bible'.

Compiled and published afresh each year, the Lyle Official Antiques Review is the most comprehensive up-to-date antiques price guide available. THIS COULD BE YOUR WISEST INVESTMENT OF THE YEAR!

TONY CURTIS

The publishers wish to express their sincere thanks
to the following for their kind help and assistance
in the production of this volume:

JANICE MONCRIEFF
NICOLA PARK
JENNIFER KNOX
MAY MUTCH
KAREN KILGOUR
CHRISTINE O'BRIEN
JOSEPHINE McLAREN
TANYA FAIRBAIRN
MARION McKILLOP
ELAINE HARLAND

S.B.N. 0 - 86248 - 028 - 0

Printed and bound by R. J. Acford , Chichester , Sussex.

CONTENTS

Acknowledgements

Abbots, *The Hill, Wickham Market, Suffolk*
Ader Picard Tajan, *12 Rue Favart, 75002, Paris*
Aldridge's, *130-132 Walcot Street, Bath, Avon*
Allen & May, *18 Bridge Street, Andover*
Anderson & Garland, *Anderson House, Market Street, Newcastle*
Gilbert Baitson, *194 Anlaby Road, Hull, Yorks.*
Richard Baker & Thomson, *9 Hamilton Street, Birkenhead, Merseyside*
T. Bannister & Co., *7 Calbourne, Haywards Heath, W. Sussex*
Barber's, *Town Mill, Bagshot Road, Chobham, Surrey*
Biddle & Webb, *Ladywood, Middleway, Birmingham*
Boardman's, *Station Road Corner, Haverhill, Suffolk*
Bonhams, *Montpelier Galleries, Montpelier Street, London*
Bonsor Penningtons, *82 Eden Street, Kingston-on-Thames*
Richard A. Bourne, *P.O. Box 141, Hyannis Port, Mass.*
Brogden & Co., *38 & 39 Silver Street, Lincoln*
Wm. H. Brown, *31 St. Peter's Hill, Grantham, Lincs.*
Bruton, Knowles & Co., *Albion Chambers, 55 Barton Street, Gloucester*
Buckell & Ballard, *49 Parsons Street, Banbury, Oxfordshire*
Burrows & Day, *39/41 Bank Street, Ashford, Kent*
Burtenshaw Walker, *66 High Street, Lewes, Suffolk*
Butler & Hatch Waterman, *86 High Street, Hythe, Kent*
Butterfield & Butterfield, *1244 Sutter Street, San Francisco*
Button, Menhenitt & Mutton, *Belmont Auction Rooms, Wadebridge*
Capes, Dunn & Co., *The Auction Galleries, 38 Charles Street, Manchester*
Michael Capo Antiques Ltd., *831 Broadway, New York, 10003*
Chancellor's, *31 High Street, Ascot, Berks.*
H. C. Chapman & Son, *The Auction Mart, North Street, Scarborough*
C. B. Charles Galleries, *825 Woodward Avenue, Pontiac, Michigan*
Christie's, *8 King Street, St. James's, London*
Christie's East, *219 East 67th Street, New York, NY 10021*
Christie's & Edmiston's, *164-166 Bath Street, Glasgow*
Christie's Geneva, *8 Place de la Taconnerie, 1204 Geneva*
Christie's, *502 Park Avenue, New York, NY 10022*
Christie's S. Kensington, *85 Old Brompton Road, London*
Christie's Zurich, *Steinwiesplatz, 8032, Zurich*
Clarke Gammon, *45 High Street, Guildford, Surrey*
Clements, *Box 747, Forney, Texas 75126*

Coles, Knapp & Kennedy, *Georgian Rooms, Ross-on-Wye*
Cooper Hirst, *Goldway House, Parkway, Chelmsford*
Crystals Auctions, *Athol Street, Douglas, I.O.M.*
Dacre, Son & Hartley, *1-5 The Grove, Ilkley, Yorks.*
Dee & Atkinson, *The Exchange, Driffield, Yorks.*
Dickinson, Davy & Markham, *10 Wrawby Street, Brigg, S. Humberside*
Wm. Doyle Galleries Inc., *175 East 87th Street, New York*
Drewatt, Watson & Barton, *Donnington Priory, Newbury, Berks.*
Hy. Duke & Son, *40 South Street, Dorchester, Dorset*
Du Mouchelle Art Galleries, *409 East Jefferson Avenue, Detroit*
John Edelmann Galleries, *123 East 77th Street, New York, NY 10021*
Edwards, Bigwood & Bewlay, *The Old School, Tiddington, Stratford-on-Avon*
Robert C. Eldred, *Route 6a, Box 796a, East Dennis, Mass.*
Elliott & Green, *40 High Street, Lymington, Hants.*
Farrant & Wightman, *2/3 Newport Street, Old Town, Swindon*
John Francis, Thomas Jones & Sons, *King Street, Carmarthen*
Frank H. Fellows & Sons, *Bedford House, 88 Hagley Road, Birmingham*
John D. Fleming & Co., *Melton House, High Street, Dulverton*
Fletcher Galleries, *2119 Westheimer, Houston, Texas*
Fox & Sons, *5 & 7 Salisbury Street, Fordingbridge, Hants.*
Galerie Moderne, *Rue Caroly 31, 1040 Brussels*
Garrett's, *1800 Irving Boulevard, Dallas, Texas 75207*
Garrod Turner, *50 St. Nicholas Street, Ipswich, Suffolk*
Garth's Auctions, *2690 Stratford Road, Delaware, Ohio*
Geering & Colyer, *Highgate, Hawkhurst, Kent*
Andrew Grant, *59-60 Foregate Street, Worcester*
Graves, Son & Pilcher, *38 Holland Road, Hove, Sussex*
Gribble, Booth & Taylor, *West Street, Axminster, Devon*
Arthur G. Griffiths & Sons, *57 Foregate Street, Worcester*
Rowland Gorringe, *15 North Street, Lewes, Sussex*
Hall Wateridge & Owen, *Welsh Bridge, Shrewsbury*
James Harrison, *35 West End, Hebden Bridge, W. Yorks.*
Heathcote Ball & Co., *47 New Walk, Leicester*
John Hogbin & Son, *53 High Street, Tenterden, Kent*
Honiton Galleries, *High Street, Honiton, Devon*
Edgar Horn, *47 Cornfield Road, Eastbourne, Sussex*
Jackson-Stops & Staff, *Fine Art Dept., 14 Curzon Street, London W1*

G. A. Key, *Market Place, Aylesham*
Lacy Scott & Sons, *3 Hatter Street, Bury St. Edmunds*
Lalonde Bros. & Parham, *Station Road, Weston-Super-Mare*
W. H. Lane & Son, *Morrab Road, Penzance, Cornwall*
Langlois, *10 Waterloo Street, Jersey, C.I.*
Laurin, Guilloux, Buffetaud, Tailleur, *Paris, France*
Lawrence Fine Art, *South Street, Crewkerne*
James & Lister Lea, *11 Newhall Street, Birmingham*
Locke & England, *Walton House, 11 The Parade, Leamington Spa*
Love's, *St. John's Place, Perth*
Mallams, *24 St. Michael's Street, Oxford*
May, Whetter & Grose, *Cornubia Hall, Par, Cornwall*
John Milne, *9-11 North Silver Street, Aberdeen*
Milwaukee Galleries, *4747 West Bradley Road, Milwaukee*
Moore, Allen & Innocent, *33 Castle Street, Cirencester*
Morphets, *4-6 Albert Street, Harrogate, Yorks.*
Morris, Marshall & Poole, *2 Short Bridge Street, Newtown, Powys.*
Mortons Auction Exchange, *643 Magazine Street, New Orleans*
Alfred Mossop & Co., *Kelsick Road, Ambleside, Cumbria*
McCartney, Morris & Barker, *Corve Street, Ludlow, Salop*
Neales, *192 Mansfield Road, Nottingham*
D. M. Nesbit & Co., *7 Clarendon Road, Southsea, Hants.*
Northampton Auction Galleries, *33-39 Sheep Street, Northampton*
Olivers, *23-24 Market Hill, Sudbury, Suffolk*
Osmond, Tricks, *Regent Street Auction Rooms, Clifton, Bristol*
Outhwaite & Litherland, *Kingsway Galleries, Fontenoy Street, Liverpool*
J. R. Parkinson, Son & Hamer, *14 Bolton Street, Bury, Lancs.*
Parsons, Welch & Cowell, *129 High Street, Sevenoaks, Kent*
Pattison Partners & Scott, *Ryton*
Pearsons, *Walcote Chambers, High Street, Winchester*
Phillips, *7 Blenheim Street, New Bond Street, London*
Phillips, *867 Madison Avenue, New York, NY 10021*
Phillips & Brooks, *39 Park End Street, Oxford*
Phillips & Jolly's, *The Auction Rooms, Old King Street, Bath*
John H. Raby & Son, *St. Mary's Road, Bradford*
Samuel Rains & Son, *Trinity House, 114 Northenden Road, Sale, Manchester*
Renton & Renton, *16 Albert Street, Harrogate, Yorks.*
Riddetts, *Richmond Hill, The Square, Bournemouth*

Russell, Baldwin & Bright, *Ryelands Road, Leominster*
Sandoe, Luce Panes, *Chipping Manor Salerooms, Wotton-under-Edge*
Schrader Galleries, *211, 3rd St. South, St. Petersburg, Florida*
M. Philip H. Scott, *East View, Bedale, Yorks.*
Shouler & Son, *43 Nottingham Street, Melton Mowbray*
Robert W. Skinner Inc., *Bolton Gallery, Mass.*
Smith-Woolley & Perry, *43 Castle Hill Avenue, Folkestone*
Sotheby's, *34-35 New Bond Street, London*
Sotheby's, *980 Madison Avenue, New York*
Sotheby Bearne, *Rainbow, Torquay, Devon*
Sotheby's Belgravia, *19 Motcomb Street, London*
Sotheby Beresford Adams, *Booth Mansion, Chester*
Sotheby's Chester, *Watergate Street, Chester*
Sotheby, King & Chasemore, *Station Road, Pulborough*
Spear & Sons, *The Hill, Wickham Market, Suffolk*
H. Spencer & Sons Ltd., *20 The Square, Retford, Notts.*
Stalker & Boos, *280 N. Woodward Avenue, Birmingham, Michigan*
Stride & Son, *Southdown House, St. John's Street, Chichester*
David Symonds, *High Street, Crediton, Devon*
Taylor, Lane & Creber, *Western Auction Rooms, Plymouth*
Laurence & Martin Taylor, *63 High Street, Honiton, Devon*
Louis Taylor & Sons, *Percy Street, Hanley, Stoke-on-Trent*
Terry Antiques, *175 Junction Road, London N19*
Theriault, *P.O. Box 151, Annapolis, Maryland, 21404*
Trosby, *Tower Place Suite 200, 3340 Peach Tree Road, NE Atlanta*
Turner, Rudge & Turner, *29 High Street, East Grinstead*
V. & V's., *The Memorial Hall, Shiplake-on-Thames*
Vernon's, *1 Westgate, Chichester*
Vidler & Co., *Auction Offices, Cinque Ports St., Rye, Sussex*
Warren & Wignall, *113 Towngate, Leyland, Lancs.*
Way, Riddett & Co., *Town Hall Chambers, Lind Street, Ryde, I.O.W.*
J. M. Welch & Son, *The Old Town Hall, Great Dunmow, Essex*
Whitehead's, *111-113 Elm Grove, Southsea, Hants.*
Whitton & Laing, *32 Okehampton Street, Exeter*
Richard Withington, *Hillsboro, New Hampshire 03244*
Woolley & Wallis, *The Castle Auction Mart, Salisbury*
Eldon E. Worrall & Co., *15 Seel Street, Liverpool*
Wyatt & Son with Whiteheads, *59 East Street, Chichester, Sussex*

ANTIQUES
REVIEW 1983

How things have changed! Little more than two years after they were riding the top of the wave, the 'big three' auction houses' fortunes have declined and prosperity has passed to smaller auction houses in the provinces.

It would be simple to say that the buyer's premium controversy was the cause of this reversal as far as Sotheby's and Christie's were concerned. It undoubtedly plays a part in the story of decline, if not fall, but there are other factors to be taken into account. When the going was good there was too profligate spending, especially at Sotheby's, and it seems as if the forecasters there failed to read the auguries quickly enough.

Of course the drop in fortunes of the best known names would not have come if the art and antiques market had remained buoyant but the fact is that 1981 was a very bad year for business for saleroom and dealer alike. If a dealer cannot sell, he cannot buy, and in spite of saleroom protestations that they draw the private buyer as well as the professional, figures have shown that the Trade is the backbone of the saleroom business.

The first signs that the Trade might well recover from its serious set back began to appear in November 1981 and it was a cause for rejoicing on all fronts that business was well and truly back at the

British International Antiques Dealers' Fair at the National Exhibition Centre at Birmingham in the spring of 1982. The patient was obviously going to live after all.

It will however take some time and a great deal of soul searching before the biggest auction houses regain anything like the old predominance. Much of the clout has passed to small provincial houses who have consistently avoided charging buyer's premium. The survey of the year highlights the fact that many items of first class quality have been turning up in out-of-town houses and making good prices . . . a Tang horse sold for £8,000 at Wingetts; an amazing American Wootton desk with almost 100 drawers and compartments made £3,500 at Dacre, Son & Hartley of Ilkley. These are only two examples of what has been a fairly general trend. The eyes of sellers have turned away from the big London auctioneers and of course buyers will go where they know good quality goods are to be found. It is cheering to think that the day of the country auction may be coming back.

The long running and still unresolved saga of the buyer's premium is too well known to rehash from the beginning but the 1982 developments have pointed up the differences between Sotheby's and

Christie's. This means that while Sotheby's are still in the doldrums up to the waist, Christie's have escaped with only getting their feet wet.

In January 1982, Christie's announced that they had cut their buyer's premium from 10% to 8%. Vendor commission on lots below £1,000 however increased from 10% to 12.5%. Sotheby's remained resolutely determined to retain their buyer's premium. It stays at 10% – but they did increase the vendor's commission on lots under £500 to 15%.

Christie's buyer's premium was also only applicable in King Street, South Kensington and their provincial outlets charge no buyer's premium. This may explain the excellent business returned by South Kensington this year. It was the only one of Christie's departments to show a profit and to increase the turnover. The overall turnover of South Kensington rose from £5.7m. to £7.5m. King Street's turnover fell slightly to £22.8m. The overseas turnover was also marginally down to £37.6m. On the whole 1981 was the worst year ever for Christie's and the pre-tax profits dropped from £7 million to £5.3 million. When this announcement was made it said that the second half of the year was the slackest time for business. The reasons given for this were 'inflation, competition and slackening of demand.' In October Christie's had taken the long planned move into Amsterdam to completion when they opened a permanent gallery opposite the Maritime Museum there. This must have taken a large bite of the profits at a bad time for the firm.

Sotheby's however would have been happy if they had been able to announce even such marginally loss making figures. In an uncharacteristic show of coyness, the autumn trading figures were not made public – because, it was explained, they were 'not representative'. For the year ended August 1981 however Sotheby's pre-tax profits were down by almost 14% to just over £7 million. During that period of time there had been a 36% increase in turnover.

A month after the announcement of this disappointing year, the company then released the news that their Belgravia salerooms were going to close. This, it was said, was not so much a cut back as a relocation. Sotheby's were planning to integrate the Belgravia departments in the Steinway building off Bond Street which they recently bought. Nevertheless, the Belgravia closure has meant that 70 staff were made redundant. Added to that, 10 people from the Torquay branch and another 7 from Chester also lost their jobs. In America the purge was even larger – 200 people went. Much of the work of the redundant American staff is to be replaced by a computer.

In spite of the board's assurances that this thinning out was only in the interests of increased efficiency, there was still uncertainty about Sotheby's future – and who ten years ago would have believed we would ever be able to say that? Rothschilds, who at one time held a 20% stake in the country, gradually withdrew their money till they now have only a half percent share. There was also a huge board shake-up. Lord Westmoreland resigned and publishing chief Gordon Thomson of the International Thomson Organisation was appointed non-executive chairman with art expert Julian Thompson as Chairman. Both of these new brooms are young. Rumours were rife of a U.S.

takeover bid with references being made by the board to 'American predators'. Warner Brothers were suspected of being among them.

As well as pruning the staff – around 350 in all will go – the company intends to save around £300,000 on catalogue printing. Till now the Sotheby's printing was contracted out unlike Christie's, who do their own and save much money as a result. Sotheby's also intend to dispose of surplus property both in Britain and in the U.S.A. Shipping and framing firms have been shed. The Bourlet shipping line is to be sold and the Bourlet framing service which Sotheby's bought ten years ago has been sold to its 14 members of staff for a nominal £1 – a unique and enterprising Job Ownership scheme.

The other two smaller auction houses in London – Phillips and Bonhams – have escaped the bad times with slightly less trauma.

Bonhams had their worst time in 1980 when they closed some departments and cut back on their spending. The result has been very satisfactory for the company. One of their ploys to attract business this year has been to hold a series of special sales timed to coincide with events on the London calendar. This attracts a large number of out of town customers and private collectors. For example, their sale of antiques with a flower theme, to coincide with the Chelsea Flower Show, was a great success.

Phillips whose worldwide turnover increased by 2% to £33.5 million in the past year is concentrating on presenting themselves as a viable alternative to Sotheby's and Christie's. The recently appointed Managing Director of Phillips, Robert Saunders, said that his company planned 'a massive marketing push' for the coming year to consolidate their position. The fight is on.

One of the factors which seems to have cost Sotheby's dear was their recent move to America. When the company made its big move to expand in the U.S.A. it was confidently asserted that London had lost its place as the auction house capital of the world. Even the august 'Connoisseur' magazine which has been published in London for 80 years followed the trend and switched its main office to New York. But almost immediately the American market began to slump and that slump is still prevailing although the European market has shown definite signs of an upturn.

The European revival has been helped by a series of fiscal measures – or in some cases, like France, by the lack of them. In Britain the spring Budget of 1982 raised the level for Capital Gains Tax from £3,000 to £5,000. It was also announced that from 1983, the level would be indexed to take account of inflation.

The French market, which looked as if it was about to disappear entirely because of planned Wealth Tax moves on the part of the Mitterand government, was given a last minute reprieve at the end of 1981 when the government decided to exempt works of art from the tax.

Since that reassurance was given to French collectors, the art market there has boomed. February figures showed that Parisian auction house figures had overtaken London becuase they increased by 12%. Although the turnover was still less than London's, the growth rate was much bigger. All over France too, antique shops are opening and doing good business. French buyers are also out in force in London.

At the same time as France was given her reprieve from Wealth Tax on works of art, the Germans also had their reassurance. The German government also had plans to raise an increased value added tax which was pegged at 6.5% on works of art and antiques to 13%. In the end it was decided to allow the lower level to remain for high quality goods only.

Another cheering sign that recovery might be round the corner in Europe was the news that in order to maintain its tax free status the J. Paul Getty Museum of California must spend 85% of the income from its $1.3 billion capital over a five year period. This can only bring a boost to the art and antiques market and much of the money will be spent in Europe and London.

The Gulf area too, which for a few years contributed to the London boom before dropping off, has once again appeared as a big buying area for antiques. Board of Trade figures for the 12 months to the end of June 1981 showed that 4,500 items worth more than £73 million had been exported and London shippers Pitt and Scott said that much of the increase in their shipping trade had gone to the Gulf.

A good thing about bad times is the way it forces people to concentrate their minds and to come up with new ideas. Fine Art Funding Ltd. announced a financial scheme to help dealers who had been suffering from lack of liquid funds. The Fine Art scheme in association with

First National Securities Ltd. was to give vendors at certain selected UK auction houses, advances of up to 50% of the estimated value of high quality, easily assessable goods which they consigned for sale. Interest at a rate of 75p per £100 is charged every week and repayment is deducted from the sale returns.

Other schemes that can only benefit the trade are two 'computer based' ideas which have been launched by separate 'find an antique' companies. Compute Antique was opened in May as a computerised location service. Dealers buy space and customers are given quick read outs of the location and price of the sort of item they are looking for.

About the same time as the Compute Antique idea was begun, another Antique Dealers' and Collectors' Service — ADACS — for short — and operating on similar lines, was started by a retiring Army officer. He was a keen collector of china and had always been frustrated by the sometimes fruitless searches he had made for special pieces. His scheme is intended to help searchers like himself to locate their quarry with the minimum trouble.

Other people that seem to have little trouble locating their quarry however this year have been burglars. The volume of antique theft has grown alarmingly. Some of the thefts have been cunningly planned — like the man who went to a viewing of a house sale to look over the goods on offer. That night the best items were cleaned out. Collectors are continually being warned by the police and insurance companies to take photographs or make drawings of their cherished possessions. Judging by the sort of things that are being stolen, the

17

antique thieves are very knowledgeable indeed. Churches are often the object of the thief's attention and furniture, statues and figures as well as silver and brass are being plundered. Many country churches now have to be securely locked outside services and this is regarded as a sad sign of modern times by people who were able to go into a church to pray or look around at any time they chose.

Other signs of the times can be seen in areas of the market that continue to be depressed. Jewellery has had a dull year because the price of precious stones has dropped considerably — they are down by as much as £30,000 to £40,000 a carat in some cases. Diamonds, which were once popularly believed to be a girl's best friend, are sometimes found to be almost unsaleable when their optimistic owners try to cash them in.

The gold and silver market has also shown the fallibility of old favourites. The market has had a series of ups and downs for the whole year. At the end of 1981, 22 carat gold sold for £214.57p an ounce. By March, 1982, it was below its 1979 level at £155.20p. A month later it had climbed back to £182.88p but another reversal came in June when it was back down to £162.04p an ounce.

Silver has been even more shaky, swinging between £4.49p an ounce for 925 standard hallmarked to £2.74p over the same period. The lowest price was in June, 1982. When silver reached £3.74p an ounce it was then selling at less than the price it took to produce. In auction, silver sales have been unremarkable except for a few rare or specialised items.

A fine five-piece Victorian silver tea and coffee set by John Wilmin Figg and Edward Barnes, 84oz. (Sotheby, King & Chasemore)   *£880*

Art Deco furniture has had a boom year in Monaco where it seems that almost any interesting item from the period finds eager bidders.

Another market which Britain shared with France has been in bronzes where there has been keen interest on both sides of the Channel. Animalia figures

A sought after Hododa earthenware jardiniere, 47cm. diameter, circa 1870. (Sotheby's Belgravia) £880

But the picture is not all gloom. Even when the going was bad, there were areas of the market that were healthy and since recovery has begun, they are now booming.

Oriental art and antiques have appreciated in value because of the renewed interest of Japanese buyers. This interest has also been in evidence in French auction rooms.

A bronze figure of the Dromadaire Harnache D'Egypt after Antoine Louis Barye, 1870's. (Sotheby's Belgravia) £385

A dark stained pine and wrought iron side table designed for the Argyle Street Tearooms by Charles Rennie Mackintosh. (Christie's)

have attracted high prices — a 19th century pair of racehorses sold for £1,080; an equestrian group by Russian sculptor Yevgen Alexandrovitch Lanceray made £8,000.

A 20th century bronze figure of silent film star Will Rogers sold for £450 and an even earlier stage idol, Sir Henry Irving caught the limelight again when a bust of him by E. Onslow Ford was sold at Sotheby's for £1,950. At Phillips in Edinburgh a lifesize pair of Japanese deer sold for £5,000 in spite of one of the figures having been repaired. An erotic bronze statuette of a young woman with a riding whip by Bruno Zack made the very high price of £9,200. It was bought by an American bidder at the provincial saleroom of Locke & England of Leamington Spa . . not the sort of place you might expect Bruno Zack's young lady to turn up.

Dealers all over the country have commented that Edwardian furniture which has been attracting a certain amount of interest for some years has at last hit the big time. And even more surprising, the wardrobe is back. Gone are the days when wardrobes had to be sold for firewood because they were a drag on the market. The most eagerly sought after are elegant Edwardian wardrobes with veneered designs and plenty of drawers and shelves inside. A wardrobe of this type was in a bedroom suite which Anderson & Garland of Newcastle sold for £1,400 this year. It bore the label of Goodall's of Manchester and had been made for a municipal visit of Queen Alexandra. Triple section Victorian wardrobes on their own — not part of a suite — make around £600 and smaller Edwardian ones for prices between £250 and £400.

Bronze statuette of a young woman with a whip, by Bruno Zach. (Locke & England) £9,200

An Edwardian mahogany and crossbanded desk, circa 1910. (Sotheby , King & Chasemore) £700

A good quality George III mahogany and crossbanded serpentine-fronted side-board, circa 1790. (Sotheby, King & Chasemore) £2,860

A Dutch marquetry and mahogany bureau, 3ft.5in. wide, circa 1760. (Sotheby, King & Chasemore)£2,750

Good quality furniture has done well and here too the age bracket has advanced to the Edwardian era and even to the 1920's. A Maple & Co. bookcase made about the turn of the century sold for £1,900. A cane bergere suite of the 1920's sold for £500 in Manchester and another of the same time made £2,000 in Birmingham.

Also among the 'new' antiques is the pottery of Clarice Cliff which is enjoying a huge vogue. It was made during the '20's and '30's and many pieces are still around in private houses. Clarice Cliff prices have been on a steady spiral

A fine mahogany breakfront wardrobe with satinwood stringing, 8ft.1in. wide, circa 1815. (Sotheby, King & Chasemore) £1,350

Two breakfast sets designed by Clarice Cliff, circa 1930. (Sotheby's Belgravia) £462

and when Sotheby's sold a selection of her pieces this spring most of the lots exceeded their estimates, some by as much as four times.

Specialist sales have always attracted interest and it is there that significant price rises have been seen.

For example there does not seem to be any height to which the price of toy soldiers cannot soar. When Phillips in London sold the L. W. Richards' toy soldier collection in late 1981, the 17,000 lots made an astonishing £69,000 with not a single one unsold.

A world record price of £260 for a Britain's figure of a trooper riding a camel was returned. There were figures in the sale by Britains, by the French maker Mignot and the German makers Heyde. Bids came in by telex for the toy soldiers and the strength of the market can be shown by the sale bid of £920 for a motor cycle combination that cost its first purchaser 11½d. in 1939.

The toy boom did not end with miniature armies. Sotheby, King &

A British Camel Corps. figure from the Richards' Collection, circa 1910. (Phillips) £260

Chasemore of Pulborough sold a 1930's Hornby train for £600 and a clockwork battleship made in 1922 for £380. Sotheby's in Belgravia sold a 1930 Disney toy model of Felix the Cat for £500. The market for dolls of course continues to be solid — bisque headed French dolls are much in demand and a good specimen can make between £1,100 and £1,500 . . . 'There's nothing childish about the doll market today,' said a dealer.

Russian Cossacks in the original box from the Richards' Collection sold at Phillips.

A rare Steiner talking doll, circa 1890.
(Sotheby's Belgravia)   *£1,045*

A Wedgwood Fairyland lustre Malfrey
pot, 16cm. high, circa 1920. (Sotheby's
Belgravia)   *£550*

In the field of china it has proved to be most profitable to look around for the off beat items. One of the latest fads is for 1920's Wedgwood Fairyland pottery – vases, plates and bowls painted with a high lustre finish and decorated with twee pictures of elves and fairies disporting themselves by sliding down rainbows or flirting with rabbits. This may not be to everyone's taste but a Fairyland lustre vase recently made £1,200 and a bowl with cover sold for £380.

Just to show that the old rule – 'nothing chipped or broken is worth collecting' no longer holds good, a collection of English blue and white pottery in which there was hardly one undamaged piece made an astonishing price at Christie's at the end of 1981. There were 335 lots in the sale and the total was £57,662. Among the top prices were £1,100 for a teapot and £820 for a Worcester sauceboat.

Asked what they would tip as good buys for the coming year two London dealers came up with longcase clocks and patchwork quilts or samplers. Longcase clocks have had a revival of interest over the past few months and many of them are once again breaking the £1,000 barrier.

As far as patchwork quilts are concerned, the market has been strengthened by much interest from abroad. At a recent sale of quilts in Christie's in London buyers were there from Switzerland, Germany, USA and Britain. Almost every lot made more than its estimate – a Pennsylvania Dutch quilt of the 1860's was bought for £500; a 20th century Amish quilt made £250 and another American quilt made in the 1950's sold for £300 – youth was no deterrent to its price.

'Even at those prices a patchwork quilt bought in auction is still a better buy than a new one,' said a dealer. 'People are snapping them up because they are so lovely and make a marvellous addition to a modern home. Besides they are proving to be investments.'

William IV sampler by Fanney Wood, aged 13, April 1831. (Sotheby's Chester) £99

Samplers are also doing well and their prices keep rising. Today a 17th century sampler can fetch between £750 and £820.

But the strongest money making tip was — buy cigarette cards or postcards. Sale after sale has proved that cards are big money. The interest in cards is vast and because it is such a huge market people are able to specialise with ease. There are several books on the market advising what buyers should look for and what sort of prices they can expect to pay.

'Cards are becoming another currency in a way,' said a happy dealer.

The survey of the past year shows that it began in gloom but is ending up with much more optimism. Buyers are out again, proceeding with caution it is true but with more confidence than they have shown for some time.

'I'm not saying boom times are back but I am saying things are much better,' said a well known London dealer, 'from now on it looks as if the only way to go is up.'

LIZ TAYLOR

An early 18th century walnut and oak longcase clock by James Atfield. (Sotheby, King & Chasemore) £1,155

Alabaster jar of Necho II, barrel-shaped with twin handles, 13¼in. high, circa 610-595 B.C. (Christie's)$7,275 £3,850

Mid 17th century alabaster statue of the Virgin and Child, 68.5cm. high. (Christie's)$8,450 £4,400

Early 15th century Nottingham alabaster relief of the Adoration of the Kings, 16¾in. high. (Sotheby's) $14,000 £8,000

19th century Italian alabaster and marble statue of Beatrice, inscribed P. Bazzanti Firenze, 69.5cm. high.(Christie's)$580 £324

15th century Nottingham alabaster panel of The Trinity, 46cm. high. (Christie's)$9,715 £5,060

Gilt bronze and alabaster figure entitled 'Nature unveiling herself', circa 1893, 42in. high. (Wm. Doyle Galleries Inc.) $12,000 £6,520

Early 17th century English kneeling alabaster figure, 20in. high. (Sotheby's) $1,245 £660

15th century Nottingham alabaster plaque carved in high relief with the head of St. John the Baptist, 8 x 5in. (Sotheby's) $3,740 £1,980

Scmidtcassel alabaster and ivory figure 'Tanzlegende', signed, circa 1910-20, 23.25cm. high. (Sotheby's Belgravia) $800 £440

27

Coin-operated automaton 'The Drunkard's Dream', circa 1935, 66½in. high. (Sotheby's Belgravia) $1,020 £528

Ahrens football game, coin-operated, in oak casing with glazed upper section, circa 1930, 43¾in. wide.(Sotheby's Belgravia) $850 £440

English coin-operated automaton 'The Burglar', circa 1935, 67in. high. (Sotheby's Belgravia) $745 £385

Mutoscope by the International Mutoscope Reel Co., circa 1905, 74in. high. (Sotheby's Belgravia) $710 £385

Great Race game, coin-operated, in oak casing with glazed upper section, 47in. wide, circa 1925. (Sotheby's Belgravia) $850 £440

'Pussy Shooter' amusement machine by British Automatic Co. Ltd., circa 1935, 76in. high. (Sotheby's Belgravia) $635 £330

Zodiac fortune teller, coin-operated machine, circa 1940, 24½in. high.(Sotheby's Belgravia)$235 £121

Allwin De Luxe amusement machine in oak case with glazed front, 27in. high, circa 1935. (Sotheby's) $100 £55

'Laughing Sailor' amusement machine bearing Ruffler & Walker plaque, circa 1935, 68½in. high. (Sotheby's Belgravia) $1,020 £528

English coin-operated automaton 'The Haunted House', circa 1935, 70½in. high. (Sotheby's Belgravia) $890 £462

American 'Twenty-one' gambling machine in cast alloy and oak casing, circa 1930, 13½in. wide. (Sotheby's Belgravia) $210 £110

English coin-operated automaton 'The Night Watchman', by the British Automatic Co. Ltd., circa 1935, 66½in. high. (Sotheby's Belgravia) $1,020 £528

American coin-operated mutoscope 'Death Dive', circa 1915, 50in. high. (Sotheby's Belgravia) $680 £352

Early Rowland Pier Head amusement machine 'The Racer', circa 1900, 19in. wide. (Sotheby's) $395 £220

English Green Ray 'television' amusement machine with glass dome above, circa 1945, 75in. high. (Sotheby's Belgravia) $635 £330

Green Ray 'television' amusement machine in wooden casing, circa 1945, 75in. high. (Sotheby's Belgravia) $405 £209

Auto-stereoscope in oak casing with viewer and coin slot at top, circa 1930, 22½in. high. (Sotheby's Belgravia) $320 £165

English 'Pussy Shooter' amusement machine with glazed window, circa 1935, 76in. high. (Sotheby's Belgravia) $595 £308

Automaton of a young girl seated at a piano, doll with French bisque head, 41cm. high, restored. (Phillips) $2,880 £1,500

Continental floral chased and embossed musical singing bird box. (Christie's S. Kensington) $895 £480

Singing bird in cage, in inlaid rosewood case, 18in. high. (Robert W. Skinner Inc.) $750 £395

19th century French magician automaton with plaster head and glass eyes, 28in. high. (Phillips) $2,870 £1,595

Rare musical tightrope dancer automaton, French, circa 1840, under glass cover. (Sotheby's Belgravia) $985 £550

French ballerina automaton with bisque head impressed SFBJ 801, Paris, circa 1900, 23in. high. (Sotheby's) $1,975 £1,045

Large French singing bird automaton, 18½in. high, circa 1900. (Sotheby's Belgravia) $610 £330

Automaton magician, 52½in. high, 36½in. wide. (Robert W. Skinner Inc.) $450 £240

French lady conjuror automaton with bisque head and musical movement, circa 1905, 26in. high. (Sotheby's Belgravia) $1,810 £990

French sleeping doll automaton with clockwork and musical movement, 14in. long, circa 1910. (Sotheby's Belgravia) $845 £462

Automaton gum machine in upright oak case, 11½in. wide. (Robert W. Skinner Inc.) $1,200 £635

Early 20th century German singing bird box with timepiece, 10.2cm. long. (Sotheby's Belgravia) $635 £330

Rare French mid 19th century singing bird automaton, 21½in. high. (Sotheby's Belgravia) $10,065 £5,500

Mid 19th century American dancing negress toy, 7¾in. long, with key. (Sotheby's Belgravia) $130 £71

Dancing negress automaton with key wound mechanism, in good condition, 10½in. high. (Sotheby's) $230 £121

Large magician automaton on ebonised wooden glass-fronted base, 42in. high, circa 1930.(Sotheby's Belgravia) $1,015 £550

Monkey artist automaton with Manievelle musical movement, circa 1900, 13½in. wide. (Sotheby's Belgravia) $915 £495

Automaton 'The Conjuror', of bisque head doll before a pedestal table, 16½in. high. (Robert W. Skinner Inc.) $1,800 £950

Bank of Poyais, unissued One Dollar, at St. Joseph 182-, by W. H. Lizars, rare, some foxing. (Christie's)
$110 £60

Bank of England 2/6, signed K. O. Peppiatt 1941, very rare.(Christie's)
$925 £500

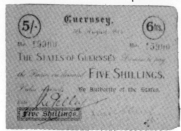

The States of Guernsey Five Shillings or Six Francs, 5th August 1914, rare. (Christie's) $1,575 £850

Union Bank £5 proof on card by Perkins, Bacon & Petch. (Christie's)
$185 £100

Sir William Forbes, James Hunter & Company £1, 181-. (Christie's)
$185 £100

Bank of England 5/-, signed K. O. Peppiatt 1941, very rare. (Christie's)
$1,145 £620

Union Bank £100 dated August 1877 but unissued, in black with red. (Christie's) $185 £100

Western Bank £10 proof on card by W. H. Lizars, engraved. (Christie's)
$280 £150

Douglas Heron & Company £1 dated 6th November 1769. (Christie's) $1,200 £650

Banking Company of Aberdeen 5/- issued in 1799, very rare. (Christie's) $1,295 £700

John McAdam & Company 5/- note issued in 1763, bearing portrait of George III, damaged, extremely rare. (Christie's) $1,330 £720

Government of India, One Thousand Rupees, 2nd June 1913, Bombay, scarce. (Christie's) $335 £180

Dundee Banking Company £1 of 1824, torn on right side. (Christie's) $590 £320

Union Bank £1 proof in green and blue on unwatermarked paper, dated 1864. (Christie's) $260 £140

National Bank £20 proof on paper dated 1889. (Christie's) $185 £100

National Bank £1 proof on card, some staining. (Christie's) $405 £220

Perth Banking Co. £1 proof by W. H. Lizars. (Christie's) $445 £240

Royal Bank of Scotland £1 dated 9th Feb. 1750, on watermarked paper, rare. (Christie's) $2,500 £1,350

The Central Bank of Scotland £1 proof on card engraved by W. H. Lizars. (Christie's) $350 £190

Bank of Scotland proof £100 note in black and white, by Bradbury & Evans. (Christie's) $280 £150

Montrose Bank One Guinea dated 16th December 1814, very rare.(Christie's) $1,390 £750

Greenock Bank Company £1 issued 15th May 1830. (Christie's) $260 £140

Thistle Bank £1 1770, on unwatermarked paper. (Christie's) $1,515 £820

North of Scotland Bank Ltd. £1 overprinted with the Town and Country Bank.(Christie's) $300 £160

Paisley Banking Co. One Guinea dated 2nd May 1826. (Christie's)$390 £210

British Linen Company £100 issued 1905, issue lasted only 2 years, very rare. (Christie's) $1,330 £720

City of Glasgow £100 printed by Perkins, Bacon & Petch, very rare. (Christie's) $740 £400

Bank of Scotland proofs of the One Guinea of 1825. (Christie's)$370 £200

Glasgow Bank Company £1 1823, torn. (Christie's) $740 £400

Bank of Scotland proof of £1 on card, engraved by W. H. Lizars on copper. (Christie's) $335 £180

The Caledonian Banking Company £20 proof on card circa 1838.(Christie's) $370 £200

Ship Bank £1 proof by Joseph Swan, cracked in two places. (Christie's) $280 £150

Mahogany inlaid stick barometer by Curtis & Horsepool, Leicester. (Honiton Galleries) $460 £250

Early 18th century Regency mahogany wheel barometer by Antoni Pilatt, Nottingham, 42in. high. (Sotheby Beresford Adams) $410 £220

Mid 18th century oak stick barometer by F. L. West, London, trunk applied with thermometer, 38in. high.(Sotheby Beresford Adams) $370 £200

Victorian mahogany wheel barometer with hygrometer thermometer, dial signed T. Bedwell, London, 37in. high. (Christie's) $525 £280

19th century mahogany wheel barometer by A. Gallatti, Glasgow, inlaid with marquetry, 98cm. high. (Phillips) $370 £200

Early 19th century mahogany stick baromater by Newman, London, 39in. high. (Sotheby, King & Chasemore) $1,785 £980

19th century mahogany stick barometer by F. Pastorelli, London, 94cm. high. (Phillips) $460 £250

William IV rosewood bow-fronted stick barometer, signed Gardener & Co., Glasgow, 40in. high. (Christie's)$655 £350

Antique mahogany five dial banjo barometer. (Honiton Galleries) $370 £200

19th century mahogany stick barometer by Jno. Gally & Co., Exeter, silvered plate incorporating a thermometer, 96cm. high. (Phillips) $550 £300

Mid Victorian banjo-shaped barometer by J. Amadio, London, in rosewood case with mother-of-pearl inlay, 40¼in. high. (Sotheby Bearne) $465 £250

Victorian walnut stick barometer signed J. Bassnett & Son, Liverpool, 2ft.10in. high. (Sotheby, King & Chasemore) $1,080 £580

Victorian mahogany stick barometer signed F. W. Clarke, London, with ivory register plates, 38in. high.(Christie's) $635 £340

18th century French Louis XVI carved, gessoed and gilt barometer/thermometer, 37½in. high. (Robert W. Skinner Inc.) $350 £190

Late 18th/early 19th century George III mahogany stick barometer by G. Monolla, London, 38in. high. (Sotheby Beresford Adams)$630 £340

Mid 19th century rosewood wheel barometer by Adie, Liverpool, restored, 38½in. high. (Sotheby Beresford Adams) $445 £240

37

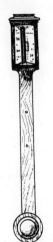

Early 19th century rosewood stick barometer with ivory register plate, 36in. high. (Sotheby, King & Chasemore) $530 £280

Banjo-shaped and shell inlaid mahogany barometer by Lione & Co. (Worsfolds) $430 £240

18th century mahogany stick barometer/thermometer by Adams, London, 42in. long. (W. H. Lane & Son) $1,330 £740

Early 19th century wheel barometer by J. M. Ronketti, London, 93cm. high. (Phillips) $470 £250

Mahogany wheel barometer in the form of a longcase clock, by J. Hallifax, Barnsley, 45in. high.(Christie's) $2,805 £1,500

George II walnut stick barometer with arched portico cresting and ribbed bowed base, 42in. high. (Christie's) $2,290 £1,200

Antique walnut banjo barometer and thermometer by D. Fagioli & Son, Clerkenwell. (Butler & Hatch Waterman) $205 £115

19th century rosewood ship's barometer by Jones, Dublin, 93cm. high. (Phillips) $805 £430

George III banjo barometer by Ortelli & Co., Carmarthen, in mahogany case. (Osmond, Tricks) $580 £320

Oak cased aneroid wheel barometer, circa 1930. (David Symonds)$70 £40

Late Georgian mahogany bow-fronted stick barometer by G. & C. Dixey. (Stride & Son) $1,535 £820

Mid 19th century mahogany wheel barometer by F. Houghton, Chester, 47½in. long. (Sotheby's) $1,065 £580

Mid 19th century mahogany wheel barometer, signed A. Martinelli, London, 37½in. long. (Sotheby's) $295 £160

George III mahogany stick barometer, signed Aliano Fecit, 1800, 95cm. high. (Phillips) $750 £400

19th century mahogany wheel barometer by A. Pastorelli, London, 98cm. high. (Phillips) $505 £270

Late Georgian mahogany bow-fronted stick barometer by Davis of Arbroath. (Stride & Son) $1,665 £890

BRONZE

Large Lorenzl bronze dancing girl, signed, 1920's, 69cm. high, on marble base. (Sotheby's Belgravia) $1,560 £858

Austrian bronze figure of a young woman, inscribed Sautner, 24.5cm. high.(Christie's) $455 £250

Bronze and ivory figure 'Sonny Boy' by F. Preiss, inscribed, 21.4cm. high, on green onyx base. (Christie's) $1,830 £1,000

One of a pair of bronze koros and covers, inlaid in gold, silver and copper, circa 1900, 9.5cm. high. (Sotheby's Belgravia) $805 £440

Bronze and ivory figure, inscribed A. Gilbert, 21.5cm. high. (Christie's)$915 £500

Gilt bronze figure of a snake charmer, on marble base, 1920's, 28cm. wide. (Sotheby's Belgravia) $800 £440

Bronze figure of a girl holding a ball, inscribed B. Zach, on marble base, 42cm. high. (Christie's) $2,930 £1,600

Gyoko bronze figure of an oni supporting a gong, circa 1900, 77cm. high.(Sotheby's Belgravia) $885 £484

Seiya bronze Bijin dressed in a kimono, engraved Seiya, circa 1900, 39.5cm. high.(Sotheby's Belgravia) $300 £165

Bronze and ivory figure of a dancer inscribed Lorenzl, on onyx base, 36.5cm. high. (Christie's) $1,190 £650

Bronze and ivory figure 'Hoop Girl' cast and carved by F. Preiss, 20.6cm. high. (Christie's) $1,465 £800

Bronze figure of a young girl as an Egyptian dancer, by Cl. J. R. Colinet, 43cm. high.(Christie's) $1,005 £550

French bronze statue of a horse and a dog, signed P. J. Mene, circa 1860, 19in. long. (Robert W. Skinner Inc.) $1,300 £720

Art Deco bronze figure of a young woman in harem trousers, 56cm. high. (Christie's) $585 £320

17th/18th century splashed gilt bronze compressed globular tripod censer, 23cm. wide, with dragon handles. (Christie's)$1,275 £660

One of a pair of Japanese bronze bulbous vases, 3ft.9in. high. (Butler & Hatch Waterman) $1,700 £950

Bronze and ivory figure of a young woman holding a viola, by P. Philippe, 30.5cm. high. (Christie's) $4,025 £2,200

Bronze and ivory figure of a dancer holding a hoop, by E. Seger, 36cm. high. (Christie's) $1,465 £800

41

Late 19th century Japanese bronze group of an eagle and a snake, 14¼in. high. (Sotheby's) $210 £110

Alliot bronze nude study of a woman, 47.5cm. wide, 1930's, signed. (Sotheby's Belgravia) $635 £350

Small Chiparus and ivory figure of a young girl, 1920's, 24.75cm. high. (Sotheby's Belgravia) $1,245 £700

Lorenzl bronze dancing figure, nude, holding a drape, 1920's, signed. (Sotheby's Belgravia) $675 £380

Roland Paris bronze and ivory group of the Devil and a girl accomplice, 40cm. high, 1920's. (Sotheby's Belgravia) $2,135 £1,200

Preiss bronze and ivory dancer on green marble tray, 1930's, 29cm. high, signed. (Sotheby's Belgravia) $2,135 £1,200

Bronze figure of a lady with an asp, signed Phillipe, Ru. M., 19in. high. (R. H. Ellis & Sons) $545 £300

Two 19th century bronze busts, 9in. high. (J. M. Welch & Son) $155 £85

Oriental bronze vase with two handles, 13in. high. (J. M. Welch & Son) $545 £300

Late 19th century Chinese bronze of Guanyin, 18¾in. high.(Sotheby's) $705 £374

Bouraine silvered bronze figure of an Amazon warrior, signed, 1920's, 37cm. wide. (Sotheby's Belgravia) $1,870 £1,050

One of a pair of Japanese bronze vases with dragon head handles, circa 1900, 25in. high. (Sotheby's)$580 £308

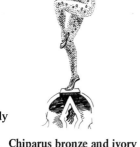

Dyson Smith bronze study of a nude dancer, 1926, 30.5cm. high. (Sotheby's Belgravia) $1,245 £700

Chiparus bronze and ivory dancing girl on brown marble base, 1920's, signed, 56.75cm. high.(Sotheby's Belgravia) $7,655 £4,300

Bronze figure of a young woman, signed E. Villanis, 80cm. high. (Christie's) $2,055 £1,100

Sabatier bronze study of a woman carrying flowers, circa 1905, 39.75cm. high. (Sotheby's Belgravia) $855 £480

Japanese bronze figure of an eagle, perched on a rock, 21in. high. (J. M. Welch & Son) $620 £340

Small Preiss bronze and ivory figure of a girl, 14.75cm. high, signed, 1930's. (Sotheby's Belgravia) $500 £280

43

Regency bronze and glass girandole, with triple candle sconces and pendant drops, 21in. high. (John Hogbin & Son)
$460 £250

19th century bronze figure of Cupid, 10½in. high, on rouge marble base. (Burrows & Day)
$205 £110

Bronze model of a bird of prey, 14in. high. (Sotheby, King & Chasemore)
$310 £170

19th century bronze figure of a Roman lady, on square base, 39in. high. (Edwards, Bigwood & Bewlay)
$1,830 £1,000

Early 20th century bronze figure by Bruno Zach, 34½in. high. (Locke & England)
$17,020 £9,200

Art Deco silvered bronze and ivory figure 'Con Brio' by F. Preiss, signed, 15in. high. (Morphets)
$4,650 £2,500

Late 19th century bronze figure of a young warrior, symbolising 'Victory', signed E. Picault, 33½in. high.(Sotheby Beresford Adams)
$595 £320

Mid 19th century gilt bronze and ivory figure of a young girl by Matheau Moireau, signed, 20in. high. (Sotheby Beresford Adams)
$1,265 £680

Bronze model of an Egyptian vulture, perched on the head of a Sphinx, by A. Cain, 6½in. high. (Sotheby, King & Chasemore)
$130 £70

19th century bronze classical figure of a cymbal player, 13¾in. high. (Burrows & Day)$225 £125

One of a pair of gilt bronze lamps, circa 1880, 21½in. high. (Sotheby's Belgravia)
$470 £260

Bronze classical figure of a nude man with a goatskin on his shoulder, 15in. high. (Burrows & Day)
$145 £80

Small Chiparus bronze and ivory figure 'The Starfish Girl', on shaped marble base, 1920's, 37cm. high. (Sotheby's Belgravia)
$2,300 £1,265

Bronze group of Aeneas, rescuing his father from Troy. (Sotheby, King & Chasemore)
$1,130 £620

Art Deco bronze figure of Pierrot on two-tier marble plinth, signed Bouraine, 11in. high.(Burtenshaw Walker)
$745 £400

Gilt bronze figure of a naked girl, inscribed F. Quillon-Carrere, 1919, 55cm. high. (Phillips)
$535 £300

45

16th century Paduan bronze candlestick of a kneeling satyr, 22.5cm. high. (Christie's) **$3,800 £1,980**

Large bronze figure of the Huntsman's Horse after J. Willis Good, 12½in. wide. (Boardman's) **$1,360 £720**

French gilt bronze bust of a young man, 19cm. high. (Christie's) **$1,480 £770**

Florentine bronze statuette of Bacchus, 17.5cm. high. (Christie's) **$1,690 £880**

Bronze and ivory figure of a dancer, inscribed Godard, on brown marble base. (Christie's) **$2,260 £1,210**

Late 16th/early 17th century Venetian bronze statuette of Cupid seated, 6.5cm. high. (Christie's) **$360 £187**

Bronze figure of an Edwardian lady, inscribed I. Blanchot, 32cm. high. (Christie's) **$535 £286**

Bronze figure of a horse, circa 6th century B.C., 7.5cm. high. (Christie's) **$875 £462**

Bronze group of Mephistopheles with a girl, inscribed Roland Paris, 40cm. high. (Christie's) **$1,645 £880**

Bronze figure of a coquette, inscribed Bruno Zach, Austria, 34cm. wide. (Christie's) $1,440 £770

Rare 16th century Venetian bronze statuette of the Young Jupiter, 16cm. high. (Christie's) $1,690 £880

Late 16th century Florentine bronze model of a walking bull, 23cm. high. (Christie's) $7,180 £3,740

Bronze and ivory figure 'Starfish', inscribed D. H. Chiparus, slightly damaged, 38.5cm. high. (Christie's) $2,365 £1,265

Late 16th century North Italian bronze statuette of Hercules Pomarius, 20cm. high. (Christie's) $8,450 £4,400

Bronze and ivory figure of a dancer, inscribed J. Philippe, 42cm. high. (Christie's) $2,055 £1,100

Bronze and ivory figure 'Hoop Girl', by F. Preiss, on marble base, 20.5cm. high. (Christie's) $1,070 £572

17th century Roman gilt bronze group of Marcus Aurelius on horseback, 25.5cm. high. (Christie's) $12,730 £7,150

Gallo-Roman bronze figure of a Lar, circa 2nd century A.D., 4¾in. high. (Christie's) $1,245 £660

Bronze model of a running hare. (Sotheby, King & Chasemore) $110 £60

Viennese cold-painted bronze model of a woodcock, 6¾in. high. (Sotheby, King & Chasemore) $100 £55

19th century Austrian bronze figure of a whippet, signed H. Muller, 7¼in. long. (Robert W. Skinner Inc.) $300 £165

One of a pair of mid 19th century gilt bronze and porcelain candelabra, 20in. high. (Sotheby Beresford Adams) $335 £180

Pair of spelter figures of warriors in full armour, circa 1900, 20¾in. high. (Sotheby's Belgravia) $220 £120

Bruno Zach bronze figure of a young girl, on square marble base, 46.5cm. high, inscribed Zach. (Phillips) $1,165 £650

One of a pair of ormolu three-branch wall lights, fitted for electricity, 29in. high. (Christie's) $1,105 £600

Bronze group, signed Ch. Raphael Peyre, of a young girl and a dog, 23.5cm. high. (Phillips) $575 £320

One of a pair of gilt bronze mounted urns with curved handles, circa 1870, 8½in. high. (Sotheby's Belgravia) $610 £340

BRONZE

Bronze model of a horse, cast by Morris Singer, after a model by Gainsborough, 9in. long. (Sotheby, King & Chasemore) $275 £150

Mid 19th century bronze figure of Pan, after Eutrope Bouret, 10½in. high. (Sotheby Beresford Adams) $240 £130

Bronze study of a bear, 8¼in. long. (Sotheby, King & Chasemore) $120 £65

One of a pair of parcel gilt bronze candelabra, on pierced rococo bases, 1870's, 22in. high. (Sotheby's Belgravia) $470 £260

Pair of Directoire ormolu busts of Voltaire and Rousseau, 12½in. high. (Christie's) $955 £520

One of a pair of early 19th century parcel gilt bronze candlesticks, 13in. high. (Sotheby's Belgravia) $145 £80

Mid 19th French bronze figure of Pomona, 14in. high. (Sotheby Beresford Adams) $410 £220

Gilt bronze and ivory figure of a girl in pantaloons, possibly by Colinet, 45cm. high. (Phillips) $1,255 £700

Bronze figure of a seated hound, by Emmanuel Fremiet, signed, 10in. high. (Sotheby, King & Chasemore) $410 £220

49

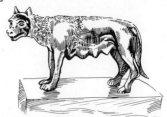

Bronze group of a standing coursing grey-hound with a hare in its mouth, by P. J. Mene, 5in. high. (Sotheby, King & Chasemore) $280   £150

16th century Paduan bronze model of The Capitoline Wolf, by Severo da Ravenna, 14cm. wide. (Christie's) $3,380   £1,760

Bronze figure of a charging elephant by Barye, 7½in. wide. (Sotheby, King & Chasemore) $1,080   £580

Bronze group of three dogs by Pierre Jules Mene, 1870's, 15in. wide, signed. (Sotheby, King & Chasemore)$805   £460

Bronze figure of a stallion by P. J. Mene, signed, 8½in. long. (Sotheby, King & Chasemore) $930   £500

Bronze and ivory group 'Towards the Unknown', signed Cl. J. R. Colinet, 41cm. wide. (Christie's) $7,200   £3,850

Bronze figure of a donkey, circa 6th-4th century B.C., 4.2cm. high, sold with another. (Christie's)$540   £286

Pair of ormolu chenets of Louis XV design, stamped Morisot, 13½in. high. (Christie's) $955   £520

16th century Paduan bronze inkstand of a crab attacking a frog, 16cm. wide. (Christie's) $3,380 £1,760

Japanese bronze model of a crawling monkey, 18in. long. (Hall Wateridge & Owen) $445 £240

Bronze model of a stretching dog, 7½in. long. (Sotheby, King & Chasemore) $485 £260

Bronze figure of a grazing goat by Antoine Louis Barye, 3¾in. long, signed. (Sotheby, King & Chasemore) $520 £280

Bronze figure of a stag and hind by Pierre Jules Mene, 7¼in. wide. (Sotheby, King & Chasemore) $930 £500

Bronze model of the Lion and Serpent, by A. L. Barye, 6¼in. high. (Sotheby, King & Chasemore) $890 £480

Pair of Regency bronze figures of a poodle and a cat on ormolu cushion bases, 14in. high. (Russell, Baldwin & Bright) $2,970 £1,650

Bronze model of a bull by Rosa Bonheur, signed, 11in. long. (Sotheby, King & Chasemore) $315 £170

BRONZE

Mid 19th century gilt bronze and porcelain encrier, 16in. wide. (Sotheby's) $305 £209

Romano-British bronze lampstand, circa 4th century A.D., 24in. high. (Christie's) $1,290 £682

Late 16th century Nuremberg gilt bronze miniature casket, 7cm. wide. (Christie's) $3,170 £1,650

Gilt bronze champleve and glass vase with trumpet stem, circa 1880, 15¾in. high. (Sotheby's Belgravia) $275 £154

19th century French cast bronze quail, signed J. Moigniez, 9in. high. (Robert W. Skinner Inc.) $270 £145

One of a pair of late 19th century spelter figures, signed Rancoulet, 19½in. high. (Sotheby's Belgravia) $455 £242

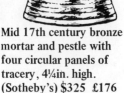

Antique Benin bronze miniature hip mask with pierced headdress, 7¼in. high. (Burrows & Day) $90 £50

Bronze group of a mare fighting off a wolf, 13½in. long, by Christoph Fratin. (Sotheby, King & Chasemore) $2,065 £1,400

Mid 17th century bronze mortar and pestle with four circular panels of tracery, 4¼in. high. (Sotheby's) $325 £176

52

BRONZE

Charles II bronze mortar and pestle with two loop handles, circa 1676. (Sotheby's) $1,380 £638

One of a pair of mid 18th century George II bell metal candlesticks, 6½in. high. (Sotheby's) $335 $176

Mid 17th century bronze mortar, cast with two bands of rosehead prunts, 3¾in. diam. (Sotheby's) $285 £154

19th century bronze group of Pan and Syrinx, 13in. high. (Burrows & Day) $475 £260

One of a pair of parcel gilt bronze candelabra of two cherubs, circa 1860, 18½in. high. (Sotheby's Belgravia) $535 £286

Late 19th century Austrian bronze rug merchant, 7in. high. (Robert W. Skinner Inc.) $700 £375

Late 19th century Austrian bronze worshipper, 5in. high. (Robert W. Skinner Inc.) $700 £375

Russian bronze figural group, 1870, damaged, 9½in. wide. (Robert W. Skinner Inc.) $1,100 £590

Late 16th century Elizabethan bronze mortar with moulded lip and foot, 4½in. high. (Sotheby's) $345 £187

Bronze figure of a crouching dog by P. J. Mene, 5¼in. high. (Sotheby, King & Chasemore) $315 £170

American bronze inkwell in the form of a crab, circa 1900, 10½in. long.(Robert W. Skinner Inc.)$325 £180

One of a pair of Japanese bronze models of elephants with ivory tusks, signed, 5½in. high. (Sotheby, King & Chasemore) $480 £260

Unusual gilt bronze model of a winged maiden, signed Adolph, 33cm. high. (Phillips) $1,110 £620

Green patinated bronze figure of a dancer on brown marble base, unsigned, 49cm. high. (Phillips) $465 £260

Stylish bronze figure of a nude girl holding a robe, signed Motto, 46cm. high. (Phillips) $535 £300

Bronze Roman warrior by Gotthilf Jaeger, Germany, born 1871, 26¼in. high. (Robert W. Skinner Inc.) $500 £280

Bronze group of two kittens playing, 7in. wide. (Sotheby, King & Chasemore) $155 £85

Late 19th century French bronze of a seated Breton woman holding an umbrella, 5¾in. high. (Robert W Skinner Inc.) $200 £11(

BRONZE

Cold-painted bronze model of a seated bulldog, 3¾in. high. (Sotheby, King & Chasemore) $185 £100

French cast bronze rabbit on black marble base, signed F. Pautrot, circa 1861, 5½in. long. (Robert W. Skinner Inc.) $600 £335

Viennese cold-painted bronze model of a cat, 6½in. long. (Sotheby, King & Chasemore) $45 £25

Colinet gilt bronze figure of a naked girl, signed Cl. J. R. Colinet, 49.5cm. high. (Phillips) $895 £500

Prof. Poertzel figure 'Snake Dancer', in painted bronze and ivory, signed, 52.5cm. high. (Phillips) $6,800 £3,800

Frederick Leighton bronze figure of a man 'The Sluggard', signed, 52cm. high. (Phillips) $4,655 £2,600

Bronze figure of a seated hare by Barye, 3¼in. high. (Sotheby, King & Chasemore) $240 £130

Bronze group of a bull and a recumbent cow, 16in. long. (Sotheby, King & Chasemore) $770 £420

Striking Polish bronze abstract model of an eagle, 1930, 44cm. high. (Phillips) $750 £420

Mid 16th century Venetian bronze figure of a winged putto, 5in. high. (Sotheby's)
$2,495 £1,320

Late 16th century Italian gilt bronze furniture mount in the shape of a lion's head, 3¼in. high. (Sotheby's) $375 £198

Lorenzl cold-painted bronze dancing girl, 1920's, signed, 40.5cm. high.(Sotheby's Belgravia)
$1,240 £682

Hagenauer ebonised wood and bronze gondola, Vienna, circa 1910-20, 44.75cm. wide. (Sotheby's Belgravia)
$400 £220

Rosenberg bronze dish, oval, signed Rosenberg 1902, 35cm. wide. (Sotheby's Belgravia) $320 £180

Ouillon Carrere bronze nude study, dated 1919, 54.5cm. high, signed. (Sotheby's Belgravia)
$880 £484

Florentine bronze group of the Rape of the Sabines, circa 1690, 20½in. high. (Sotheby's) $1,245 £660

Large gilt bronze figure by Bruno Zach 'The Cigarette', on black marble base, 72.5cm. high. (Christie's)$5,305 £2,900

French painted bronze
statue, of mid-Eastern
girl, circa 1898, signed
E. Le Guillemin,
26½in. high. (Robert
W. Skinner Inc.)
$1,800 £995

Early 17th century Flemish
bronze mortar with flared
lip and base, 5in. high.
(Sotheby's) $830 £440

Large Lorenzl bronze
dancing girl, signed,
1920's, 69cm. high,
on marble base.
(Sotheby's Belgravia)
$1,560 £858

19th century Japanese bronze figure of
a tiger, 20in. long. (J. M. Welch & Son)
$380 £210

White metal figure of a partially draped
nude, inscribed D. H. Chiparus, 74.5cm.
wide. (Christie's) $915 £500

Bronze and ivory group
of Cupid and Psyche by
G. Omerth, with fitment
for electricity, 39.3cm.
high. (Christie's)
$1,190 £650

One of two similar Gyoko
bronze archers, circa 1900,
on wood stands. (Sotheby's
Belgravia) $1,650 £902

Mid 19th century gilt
bronze mounted cela-
don vase, 22in. high.
(Sotheby's Belgravia)
$825 £440

One of a rare pair of 17th century Dutch bell-metal pricket candlesticks, 16in. high. (Christie's) $4,025 £2,200

Limousin Art Deco group in cold painted bronze, ivory and marble, inscribed, central figure 14½in. high. (Lawrence Fine Art) $320 £170

18th/19th century bronze tripod censer with applied dragon handles, wood cover and jade finial, 43cm. wide. (Christie's) $680 £352

Bronze and ivory group 'Les Amis de Toujours', by D. H. Chiparus, inscribed, 64.2cm. wide. (Christie's) $17,385 £9,500

Bronze figure of a standing nymph, inscribed Pierre Laurel, 58.5cm. high. (Christie's) $785 £432

Oriental bronze group of an elephant being attacked by two tigers. (T. Bannister & Co.) $365 £200

Late 19th century Japanese bronze figure of a falconer, 32cm. high, signed. (H. Spencer & Sons Ltd.) $1,480 £840

16th century Flemish bronze mortar with inscription round rim, 6¼in. high. (Sotheby's) $2,855 £1,595

Bronze and ivory figure of 'Sonny Boy', inscribed F. Preiss, 8in. high. (Lawrence Fine Art) $1,060 £560

BRONZE

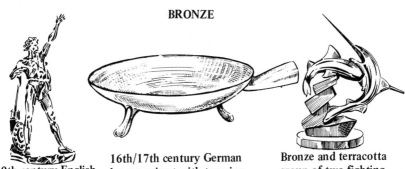

19th century English bronze statuette of The Norseman, 79cm. high. (Christie's)
$1,835 £1,026

16th/17th century German bronze grisset with tapering handle, 9in. diam. (Christie's)
$1,200 £648

Bronze and terracotta group of two fighting swordfish by Gaston Lachaise, 81.5cm. wide. (Christie's)
$7,320 £4,000

Bronze and ivory figure 'Hoop Girl' inscribed F. Preiss, 8in. high. (Lawrence Fine Art)
$1,135 £600

Bronze figure of Amazon inscribed M. Bouraine, Etling, Paris, 58.5cm. wide. (Christie's) $2,950 £1,620

Gilt bronze figural lamp of Loie Fuller by Raoul Larche, 34cm. high. (Christie's)
$5,490 £3,000

Bronze bell with cast pierced crown, 1633, 12in. diam. (Sotheby's)
$355 £198

Late 19th century Maruki bronze hawk with detailed plumage, 28cm. wide. (Sotheby's Belgravia)
$925 £506

Tokyo School bronze peasant with a lantern, circa 1900, 58cm. high, with wood stand. (Sotheby's Belgravia)
$1,485 £770

One of a pair of George III brass bound mahogany bottle carriers, 11¼in. high.(Christie's) $3,420 £1,850

Large 19th century copper bucket with brass swing handle, 13in. diam. (Dickinson, Davy & Markham) $120 £70

One of a pair of George III mahogany plate buckets with brass bands, 14in. diam. (Lawrence Fine Art) $1,505 £840

George III mahogany boat-shaped oyster bucket with brass banding liner and handle, 14in. high, circa 1790. (Sotheby, King & Chasemore) $1,470 £800

Dutch tole-peinte tea bucket decorated with chinoiserie, circa 1800, 1ft.1in. wide. (Sotheby's) $805 £418

Dutch floral marquetry oyster bucket with brass banding and handle, circa 1760, 13in. diam. (Sotheby, King & Chasemore) $1,065 £580

Antique leather fire bucket with coat of arms on front. (J. M. Welch & Son) $75 £40

George III brass bound bucket with swing handle. (Christie's S. Kensington) $835 £480

Gustav Stickley oak waste bucket, banded together with iron, 12in. diam. (Robert W. Skinner Inc.) $950 £530

Early 17th century Jacobean oak casket, lid with crowned Tudor rose, 12½in. long. (Sotheby's) $1,350 £715

Early 19th century American carved and painted trinket box in pine, 10in. wide. (Robert W. Skinner Inc.) $750 £405

Early 19th century American decorated tin document box with domed cover, 13½in. long. (Robert W. Skinner Inc.) $275 £150

Late 17th century carved oak bible box with lock. (J. M. Welch & Son) $210 £115

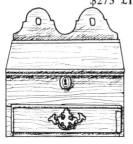

18th century American pine hanging wall candle box with double tombstone crest, 15in. wide. (Robert W. Skinner Inc.) $800 £440

Early 19th century Federal mahogany wall box with scrolled crest, 7¼in. wide. (Robert W. Skinner Inc.) $1,200 £660

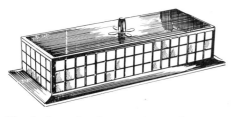

Ebonised wood and marquetry pen box and cover inset with mother-of-pearl, 24.7cm. long. (Christie's)$5,460 £3,000

Mahogany and inlaid sewing box, 9 x 18in. (J. M. Welch & Son) $110 £60

Papier-mache letter casket, curved top inlaid with mother-of-pearl, circa 1840, 6¼in. wide. (Sotheby's Belgravia) $145 £80

George III ivory veneered tea caddy of oval shape, lid with pineapple finial, circa 1790. (Sotheby, King & Chasemore)
$350   £190

Gilt metal jewel casket with pierced hinged lid and sides, 1880's, 16.5cm. long. (Sotheby's Belgravia) $480 £260

19th century mahogany domestic medicine chest with rising top, 30cm. high. (Phillips)
$480 £260

Late 18th century George III cutlery urn of ovoid form in mahogany with boxwood and ebony lines, 27in. high. (Sotheby Beresford Adams)
$315 £170

Burr-satin birch scent box, containing four scent bottles and stoppers, circa 1850, 5½in. wide. (Sotheby's Belgravia) $315 £175

Mid 19th century Tunbridgeware coromandel box by Thos. Barton, enclosing three graduated drawers, 8in. wide. (Sotheby's Belgravia)
$115 £65

One of a pair of George III mahogany knife boxes with fitted interiors and plated mounts, circa 1780, 9in. wide. (Sotheby, King & Chasemore)
$1,105 £600

Electroplated parcel gilt copper electrotype jewel casket by Elkington, Mason & Co., circa 1855, 17cm. long. (Sotheby's Belgravia) $495 £270

Tunbridgeware rosewood bookstand with serpentine support, 14in. wide, circa 1860. (Sotheby's Belgravia) $250 £140

George III mahogany and harewood tea caddy, crossbanded in rosewood, 5½in. wide, circa 1790. (Sotheby, King & Chasemore) $230 £125

Regency tortoiseshell two-division tea caddy with serpentine front, 7½in. wide, circa 1820. (Sotheby, King & Chasemore) $315 £170

Mid 19th century papier-mache decanter case of square form, containing four glass scent decanters, 5in. square. (Sotheby Beresford Adams) $165 £90

Mid 19th century coromandel cigar box by Edmund Nye, 8in. wide. (Sotheby's Belgravia) $405 £225

Adjustable Tunbridgeware bookshelf with two arched ends, circa 1870, 11½in. wide, closed. (Sotheby's Belgravia) $235 £130

George III mahogany and boxwood string-banded tea caddy with Tunbridgeware band. (Sotheby, King & Chasemore) $150 £80

Tunbridgeware coromandel box by Thos. Barton, circa 1870, 9½in. wide. (Sotheby's Belgravia) $450 £250

Early 19th century covered oval quill work box with ivory finial, 5½in. long. (Robert W. Skinner Inc.) $170 £90

63

Rosewood Tunbridgeware box with floral mosaic lid and fitted interior, circa 1870, 9½in. wide. (Sotheby's Belgravia) $305 £170

Mid 19th century Tunbridgeware ash box with floral mosaic borders, 9½in. wide. (Sotheby's Belgravia)$325 £180

Mid 19th century papier-mache sewing casket, fitted with lift-out tray, 13in. wide. (Sotheby's Belgravia) $325 £180

Tunbridgeware rosewood work box with inlaid top and mosaic border, circa 1840, 10½in. wide.(Sotheby's Belgravia) $740 £410

Mid 19th century rosewood table writing box inlaid with mother-of-pearl, 14in. wide. (Sotheby Beresford Adams) $110 £60

Mid 19th century rosewood Tunbridgeware tea caddy by William Upton, inlaid with cube marquetry, 12½in. wide. (Sotheby's Belgravia) $360 £200

18th century Japanese mother-of-pearl inlaid lacquer, dome topped casket, 9in. wide. (Sotheby, King & Chasemore) $1,340 £720

Tunbridgeware rosewood tea caddy with fitted interior, circa 1840, 13½in. wide. (Sotheby's Belgravia) $665 £370

Mid 19th century Tunbridgeware rosewood pen box by William Upton, 9¾in. long. (Sotheby's Belgravia) $360 £200

Mid 19th century rosewood Tunbridgeware casket with domed top, 10½in. wide. (Sotheby's Belgravia) $245 £135

Regency Tunbridgeware box inlaid with cube pattern, circa 1820, 12in. wide. (Sotheby's Belgravia) $305 £170

Tunbridgeware rosewood box, top inlaid with a view of Penshurst Place, circa 1870, 9in. wide. (Sotheby's Belgravia) $270 £150

Double papier-mache tea caddy, moulded top inlaid with mother-of-pearl, 8¼in. wide. (Sotheby's Belgravia) $125 £70

Late 18th/early 19th century satinwood and mahogany tea caddy with two canisters and a mixing bowl, 11½in. wide. (Sotheby Beresford Adams) $130 £70

Papier-mache box by Jennens & Bettridge, circa 1850, 11in. wide. (Sotheby's Belgravia) $180 £100

Rosewood Tunbridgeware writing slope with a view of Hever Castle, circa 1870, 12in. wide. (Sotheby's Belgravia) $485 £270

Regency Tunbridgeware tea caddy of octagonal shape, circa 1820, 6in. wide. (Sotheby's) $470 £253

Mid 19th century French gilt metal jewel casket with five porcelain panels, 20.5cm. long. (Sotheby's Belgravia) $550 £297

Rare George III embroidered tea caddy of hexagonal shape, circa 1775, 7½in. wide. (Sotheby's) $305 £165

Early 19th century English apothecary's chest in rosewood case with boxwood stringing, 6¼in. high. (Sotheby's Belgravia) $140 £75

Red tole painted tea caddy and writing box, circa 1790, 8in. wide. (Robert W. Skinner Inc.) $300 £165

One of a pair of George III mahogany knife boxes, circa 1780, 8¾in. high. (Sotheby's) $1,240 £660

Georgian satinwood inlaid tea caddy. (Christie's S. Kensington) $185 £100

Regency tortoiseshell-veneered tea caddy with engraved plaque, circa 1820, 7¼in. wide. (Sotheby's) $175 £95

Late 16th century French leather covered casket mounted with crowns and studs, 21½in. wide. (Christie's) $3,295 £1,800

Regency mother-of-pearl inlaid tortoiseshell veneered tea caddy, circa 1820, 6¾in. wide. (Sotheby's) $430 £231

Gilt metal mounted oval ebonised wood jewel casket by Charles Asprey, London, circa 1860. (Sotheby's Belgravia) $345 £187

Mid 19th century American painted wooden folk art box with hinged cover, 12in. long. (Robert W. Skinner Inc.) $275 £150

Victorian coromandel brass bound vanity case with silver mounted bottles, 12in. wide. (Locke & England) $300 £160

Set of three late 18th century George III knive boxes in mahogany, with inlaid lids.(Robert W. Skinner Inc.) $1,550 £845

One of a pair of mahogany cutlery vases in George III style, 28in. high. (Burrows & Day) $360 £200

George III rolled paperwork tea caddy, circa 1785, 6¼in. wide, slightly chipped.(Sotheby's) $370 £200

Canteen of Old English pattern table cutlery by Martin Hall & Co., Sheffield, in oak case. (Dickinson, Davy & Markham) $350 £200

Rare George III maplewood and tortoiseshell tea caddy, 6in. wide, circa 1780. (Sotheby's) $815 £440

Mid 19th century French
tulipwood jewel box
with metal mounts, 8½in.
wide. (Sotheby's)
$135 £71

Early 19th century painted and
decorated wall box, 11½in. wide.
(Robert W. Skinner Inc.)
$615 £325

Regency tortoiseshell
tea caddy with silver
escutcheon and ivory
mounted lid, circa
1820, 6¾in. wide.
(Sotheby, King &
Chasemore)
$290 £160

Early 19th century straw-
work casket with parque-
try and floral marquetry
borders, 12½in. wide.
(Sotheby's) $385 £203

Early 19th century apothecary's
chest in mahogany case, 15in.
high. (Sotheby Bearne)$560 £300

Late 19th/early 20th
century oak writing
compendium with
fall front, 16½in.
wide.(Sotheby's)
$295 £154

George III maho-
gany cutlery box
inlaid with box-
wood lines, 15½in.
high. (Sotheby's)
$155 £82

Mid 19th century ivory Anglo-
Indian work box with gadrooned
top and sides, 13½in. wide.
(Sotheby Beresford Adams)
$410 £220

George III fruitwood
tea caddy in the form
of a gourd with stalk,
circa 1800, 5½in. high.
(Sotheby, King &
Chasemore)$525 £290

Mid 19th century Anglo-Indian ivory workbox, 10½in. wide. (Sotheby's) $250 £132

Mid 19th century Anglo-Indian ebony and ivory table writing box with domed superstructure, 16½in. wide. (Sotheby's) $280 £148

Mid 19th century tortoiseshell two-division tea caddy with fluted front, 7½in. wide. (Sotheby's)$165 £88

Unusual George IV brass inlaid rosewood medicine cabinet, circa 1825, 11½in. wide. (Sotheby's) $1,160 £616

Mid 19th century Austrian walnut cigar cabinet with carved top and front, 14in. square. (Sotheby's)$135 £71

Mid 19th century Anglo-Indian ebony and ivory stationery rack and encrier, 14in. wide. (Sotheby's) $175 £93

One of two late 19th century covered French boxes. (Robert W. Skinner Inc.) $350 £190

Regency tortoiseshell single compartment tea caddy with silver mounts, circa 1820, 5½in. high. (Sotheby, King & Chasemore) $290 £160

Mid 17th century Charles II oak bible box with foliate carved front, 27in. wide. (Sotheby's) $195 £104

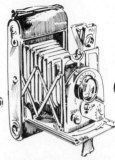

Newman & Guardia Nydia folding plate camera with detachable bellows, circa 1900, 4¼in. high. (Sotheby's Belgravia) $275 £150

Newman & Guardia New Ideal Sibyl folding camera, circa 1925.(Sotheby's Belgravia) $145 £80

Marion's metal miniature camera, 1¼in. high, circa 1884, in mahogany case. (Sotheby's Belgravia) $2,575 £1,400

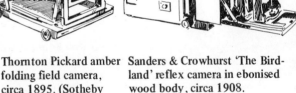

Thornton Pickard amber folding field camera, circa 1895. (Sotheby Beresford Adams) $115 £60

Sanders & Crowhurst 'The Bird-land' reflex camera in ebonised wood body, circa 1908. (Sotheby's Belgravia)$295 £160

Newman & Guardia Nydia folding plate camera, 4¼in. high, in original leather case, circa 1905. (Sotheby's Belgravia) $310 £170

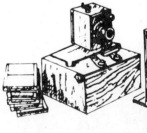

Japanese Canon Model 7 35mm. camera and filter, in leather case, circa 1962. (Sotheby's Belgravia) $550 £300

Mahogany cased stereo-scopic camera and six plates by Negretti & Zambra. (Christie's S. Kensington) $7,135 £3,900

Mid 19th century English sliding box camera, 7½in. square, in mahogany body with brass fittings. (Sotheby's Belgravia) $700 £380

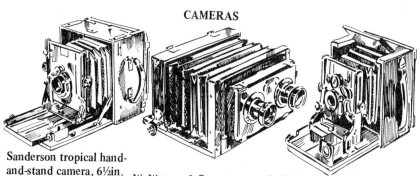

Sanderson tropical hand-and-stand camera, 6½in. high, circa 1910, in teak body with brass fittings. (Sotheby's Belgravia) $590 £320

W. Watson & Sons stereo tailboard camera, 6¾in. wide, circa 1900. (Sotheby's Belgravia) $440 £240

Early Sinclair Una hand-and-stand camera in black leather-covered mahogany body, circa 1905, 4¼in. high. (Sotheby's Belgravia) $165 £90

Ensign tropical special reflex camera in teak body with brass fittings, circa 1930, 4¼in. high. (Sotheby's Belgravia) $275 £150

ICA universal juwel 440 folding plate camera with Zeiss Tessar lens, circa 1925, 18cm. high. (Sotheby's Belgravia) $310 £170

Voigtlander prominent folding camera in original leather case, German, circa 1933. (Sotheby's Belgravia) $405 £220

Postcard-size tropical Soho stereoscopic reflex camera. (Christie's S. Kensington) $6,440 £3,700

English wet-plate camera by W. Rouch, London, circa 1864, in mahogany body. (Sotheby's Belgravia) $1,290 £700

Zeiss Ikon contaflex twin lens reflex camera, 36mm. high, circa 1935. (Sotheby's Belgravia) $830 £450

French gold parasol
handle set with a watch,
by Cartier, 2¾in. high.
(Christie's)$2,805 £1,485

Walking stick with wood
shaft and handle and horn
ferrule, circa 1900, 88.4cm.
long. (Sotheby's Belgravia)
$265 £143

Austrian silver gilt walking cane handle, Vienna,
1753, 14.2cm. long.
(Sotheby's) $855 £462

Late 19th century mala-
cca walking cane with
scrimshaw ball grip set
with a compass, 81.5cm.
long. (Sotheby's Belgravia)
$245 £132

Early 18th century German
gilt metal finial from a jester's stick, 4¾in. high.
(Sotheby's) $2,285 £1,210

Gold, silver and enamel
mounted parasol handle,
initial set with rose-cut
diamonds, 2¾in. high.
(Christie's) $935 £495

Ebonised wood walking
stick with carved ivory
handle, circa 1900,
90.3cm. long.(Sotheby's
Belgravia) $305 £165

Japanese carved ivory cane
top. (Robert W. Skinner
Inc.) $75 £40

Silver mounted whip with
engraved collar and grip,
London, 1864, 92.5cm.
long. (Sotheby's Belgravia)
$350 £187

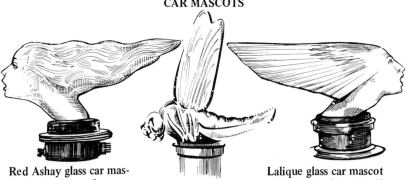

Red Ashay glass car mascot in the form of a woman's head, 23cm. wide, 1930's.(Sotheby's Belgravia) $625 £330

Lalique moulded glass car mascot 'Libellule', in the shape of a dragon-fly. (Woolley & Wallis) $1,265 £700

Lalique glass car mascot 'The Spirit of the Wind', in original chromed metal mount, 25.5cm. wide, circa 1925. (Sotheby's Belgravia) $1,985 £1,045

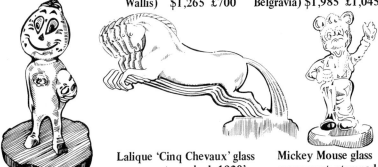

A standing figure of the Esso man, 5½in. high. (Vernons) $240 £125

Lalique 'Cinq Chevaux' glass car mascot, marked, 1920's, 16.5cm. wide. (Sotheby's Belgravia) $1,215 £638

Mickey Mouse glass car mascot, stamped Walt Disney Productions, circa 1940, 5¼in. high. (Sotheby's Belgravia)
$140 £77

Lalique glass dragon-fly car mascot, 20.5cm. long, 1920's, signed. (Sotheby's Belgravia) $1,360 £748

Lalique glass hawk mascot, engraved, 1920's, 16.5cm. high. (Sotheby's Belgravia)$500 £275

A nickel plated Minerva car mascot. (Sotheby's Belgravia) $290 £150

19th century American wooden butter stamp, carved with a ram, 4½in. diam. (Robert W. Skinner Inc.) $350 £190

19th century American butter stamp, carved with a lamb, 3in. diam. (Robert W. Skinner Inc.) $275 £150

19th century American wooden butter stamp showing a bird on a branch, 3in. diam. (Robert W. Skinner Inc.) $225 £120

19th century Japanese carved, gessoed and painted Oriental deity, 29½in. high. (Robert W. Skinner Inc.) $200 £110

Early 18th century Norwegian peg tankard, 8in. high. (Sotheby, King & Chasemore) $310 £170

Fine 14th century French walnut group of the Virgin and Child, 42.5cm. high. (Christie's) $8,450 £4,400

American pine candle box with carved decoration on all sides, 9¾in. long. (Robert W. Skinner Inc.) $800 £435

One of a pair of Venetian rococo blackamoors, painted and parcel gilt, 4ft. 10in. high. (Sotheby's) $18,000 £9,735

19th century Scandinavian carved and painted butter tub with flat cover, 13in. diam. (Robert W. Skinner Inc.) $1,450 £790

19th century American wooden handleless butter stamp with incised anchor, 3½in. diam. (Robert W. Skinner Inc.) $75 £40

Early 18th century English fruitwood relief of two cherub heads flanking a chalice, 30cm. high. (Christie's)$505 £264

19th century American wooden butter stamp carved with a cow, 3½in. diam. (Robert W. Skinner Inc.) $150 £80

15th century Umbrian wood statue of St. Sebastian, damaged, 120cm. high.(Christie's) $5,280 £2,750

Early 16th century French polychrome wood relief of the road to Calvary, 81.5cm. wide. (Christie's) $4,855 £2,530

17th century Spanish polychrome wood figure of St. John, 12½in. high. (Robert W. Skinner Inc.) $150 £80

19th century American wooden butter stamp carved with a running fox, 2½in. diam. (Robert W. Skinner Inc.) $150 £80

17th century Scandinavian carved burl tankard, thumbpiece in the form of a lion, 8in. high. (Robert W. Skinner Inc.) $700 £380

19th century American wooden butter stamp with incised deer, 4in. diam. (Robert W. Skinner Inc.) $300 £165

19th century American wooden butter stamp of shell design, 3½in. diam. (Robert W. Skinner Inc.) $100 £55

Late 19th century lesser yellowleg in original paint, 10½in. high. (Robert W. Skinner Inc.) $475 £260

Scandinavian burrwood peg tankard with carved lid, 8¼in. high. (Burrows & Day) $435 £240

Pair of Elizabethan boxwood nutcrackers, 1583, 4½in. high. (Lawrence Fine Art) $810 £420

19th century Scandinavian painted bride's box of plywood strips, 17½in. long. (Robert W. Skinner Inc.) $450 £245

One of a pair of early George III rococo giltwood wall brackets, circa 1750, 1ft.wide. (Sotheby's) $3,605 £1,950

One of a pair of antique giltwood candle sconces. (J. M. Welch & Son) $345 £190

17th century Flemish boxwood relief of Adam and Eve in the Garden of Eden, 14.5cm. wide. (Christie's) $2,745 £1,430

Well-carved 19th century figurehead in the form of a maiden, with twisted iron chains, 42cm. high. (Osmond, Tricks) $545 £300

Old oak wool winder with spindle and folding arm. (Butler & Hatch Waterman) $90 £50

Early 20th century American painted and carved wood seagull, mounted on a board, 16½in. high. (Robert W. Skinner Inc.) $225 £125

North American Indian carved wooden rattle, 1ft. long. (Stride & Son) $6,360 £3,400

One of a pair of modern painted blackamoor torcheres on moulded bases, 41in. high. (Sotheby's Belgravia) $925 £495

One of a pair of 19th century carved carousel horses with brass harnesses and saddles, 46in. long. (Robert W. Skinner Inc.) $850 £465

Scandinavian carved and painted mangling board, circa 1803, 26¼in. long.(Robert W. Skinner Inc.) $100 £55

Adam period carved pine fire surround from Hemsworth Hall. (Phillips) $2,400 £1,250

19th century American wooden oval butter stamp with carved eagle standing on a globe, initials on either side, 5½in. long. (Robert W. Skinner Inc.) $350 £190

'Swiss Chalet' decanter case with hinged roof, circa 1900, 25½in. wide. (Sotheby's Belgravia) $105 £55

15th century North Italian polychrome oak group of St. Christopher and a child, 25½in. high. (Sotheby's) $1,455 £770

Pair of early 18th century Liege fruitwood plaques, inscribed in ink on the back J. Vognoulle, 10¾in. wide. (Sotheby's) $3,430 £1,815

Mid 17th century Flemish life-size figure of Cupid, in oak, 29¾in. high, sold with an oak column. (Sotheby's)$2,080 £1,100

Cherrywood snuff rasp by Bagard of Nancy, circa 1687, 8in. high, grater missing. (Sotheby's)$1,350 £715

Three late 17th century South German polychrome wood Nativity figures dated 1681. (Sotheby's) $1,975 £1,045

16th century Malines oak group of Anna Selbdritt, 11½in. high, on later base.(Sotheby's) $2,080 £1,100

One of two 17th century vertical carved wood panels, 16in. and 18½in. high. (Lawrence Fine Art) $305 £170

Continental carved wood figure of a girl, on Victorian carved wood plinth. (Lawrence Fine Art) $1,075 £600

One of three 17th/18th century carved oak panels, 17¾in. high. (Lawrence Fine Art) $195 £110

18th century English cast brass chandelier of six arms, 17in. high. (Robert W. Skinner Inc.)
$1,050 £570

Early 19th century or-molu and cut-glass chandelier hung from a gilt metal corona, 44in. high.(Christie's)
$4,785 £2,600

18th/early 19th century wood and iron painted chandelier, 38in. wide. (Robert W. Skinner Inc.)
$2,600 £1,430

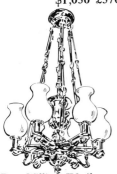

Rare William IV gilt brass kolza oil lantern of six lights, circa 1830, 2ft.1in. diam. (Sotheby's)
$1,850 £1,000

Modern 'Louis XIV' gilt bronze chandelier, 36¼in. wide. (Sotheby's Belgravia)
$720 £385

Edwardian gilt bronze and glass chandelier in late 18th century style, fitted for electricity. (H. Spencer & Sons Ltd.)
$1,285 £680

Georgian gilt metal mounted cut-glass twelve-light chandelier, 43in. high. (Christie's)
$18,910 £9,900

Gilt bronze chandelier of twenty-four lights, 42in. wide, circa 1840-60. (Sotheby's Belgravia)
$410 £220

Georgian cut-glass eighteen-light chandelier with baluster stem, 58in. high. (Christie's)
$13,655 £7,150

Newcomb pottery vase in blue, artist Leona Nicholson, circa 1903, 10½in. high. (Robert W. Skinner Inc.)
$2,100 £1,185

19th century American Rogers group 'Why Don't You Speak For Yourself John?' (Wm. Doyle Galleries Inc.) $550 £290

Weller Sicardo vase, Fultonham, Ohio, circa 1905, 10½in. high. (Robert W. Skinner Inc.)
$400 £225

Newcomb pottery vase, New Orleans, circa 1910, signed A.S.F., 6in. high. (Robert W. Skinner Inc.)
$200 £105

19th century American glazed redware pottery jar with cover, 10in. high. (Robert W. Skinner Inc.)
$130 £70

Mid 19th century American stoneware decorated water cooler with domed cover, Pennsylvania, 21½in. high. (Robert W. Skinner Inc.) $500 £275

Dedham pottery experimental vase, Massachusetts, circa 1895, 7½in. high. (Robert W. Skinner Inc.) $600 £340

Wheatley pottery vase, Cincinnati, Ohio, circa 1880, 9in. high. (Robert W. Skinner Inc.)$175 £100

19th century American glazed redware pottery jug with handle, 9in. high. (Robert W. Skinner Inc.) $160 £90

Glazed earthenware musical jug, circa 1935, 10in. high. (Sotheby's Belgravia) $205 £110

American double stoneware jug, 1830, with single handle. (Robert W. Skinner Inc.)$1,250 £685

19th century stoneware decorated crock by Fulper Bros., Flemington, N.J., 10in. high. (Robert W. Skinner Inc.) $350 £190

ANSBACH

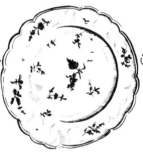

Ansbach slop-bowl with trailing sprigs of leaves and flowers, circa 1770, 17cm. wide. (Sotheby's) $675 £374

Ansbach shaped circular plate with Ozier rim, circa 1775, 23cm. diam. (Christie's) $590 £320

Ansbach two-handled seau crenelle with gilt dentil rim, circa 1770, 17.5cm. wide. (Christie's) $1,570 £850

ATTIC

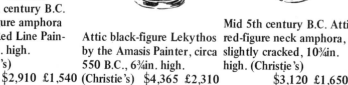

Late 6th century B.C. black-figure amphora by the Red Line Painter, 11in. high. (Christie's) $2,910 £1,540

Attic black-figure Lekythos by the Amasis Painter, circa 550 B.C., 6¾in. high. (Christie's) $4,365 £2,310

Mid 5th century B.C. Attic red-figure neck amphora, slightly cracked, 10¾in. high. (Christie's) $3,120 £1,650

Royal Bayreuth figural milk jug in the form of an eagle, circa 1900, 6¼in. high. (Robert W. Skinner Inc.)
$350 £195

Royal Bayreuth sunbonnet baby's hair receiver, Germany, circa 1900, 2¾in. diam. (Robert W. Skinner Inc.) $100 £55

Royal Bayreuth figural cream and sugar, circa 1900, 3½in. and 4½in. high. (Robert W. Skinner Inc.) $425 £235

BELLARMINE

Small 17th century tigerware bellarmine bottle with grey beard mask and circular seal, 8½in. high. (Boardman's)
$275 £150

17th century bellarmine flask with plain loop handle, 9¼in. high. (Sotheby, King & Chasemore)
$390 £210

17th century Rhenish saltglaze bellarmine in mottled brown, 9¾in. high. (Sotheby's) $335 £176

BELLEEK

Early Belleek sweetmeat dish in the form of a clam shell, 9.5cm. high. (Sotheby, King & Chasemore) $55 £30

Belleek flower holder in the form of a flying fish, 18.5cm. high. (Sotheby, King & Chasemore)
$185 £100

Belleek hexagonal basket with trelliswork body, 1891-1926, 28.4cm. wide. (Sotheby's Belgravia)
$530 £286

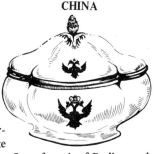

Early 18th century Berlin silver mounted white enamel snuff box, 2½in. wide, in the form of a tricorn hat.(Christie's) $1,350 £715

One of a pair of Berlin royal presentation armorial quatrefoil sauce tureens and covers, circa 1775, 16.5cm. wide. (Christie's) $4,070 £2,200

Berlin named view plate decorated with harvest scene, 9¾in. diam. (Sotheby's)$560 £297

Mid 18th century Berlin pewter mounted faience tankard, with portrait of Frederick the Great, 23.5cm. high.(Sotheby's) $1,880 £1,045

Pair of Berlin blackamoor sweetmeat dishes and covers, 18cm. high, late 19th century. (Sotheby, King & Chasemore) $770 £420

Unusual K.P.M. Berlin biscuit porcelain figure 'The Blue Boy', 19in. high. (W. H. Lane & Son) $110 £60

One of a pair of mid 19th century Berlin pot pourri vases and covers, 28cm. high. (Sotheby, King & Chasemore) $520 £290

One of three Berlin armorial shaped circular dishes, circa 1775, 24cm. diam.(Christie's) $2,960 £1,600

Late 19th century Continental plaque, probably Berlin, 16.5cm. high. (H. Spencer & Sons Ltd.) $675 £360

One of a pair of rare Bow 'grotto' candle-stick groups, circa 1765-70, 8¾in. high. (Sotheby's)$820 £440

Early Bow group of a ewe and a lamb, circa 1750, 13.5cm. wide. (Sotheby, King & Chasemore) $295 £160

Early Bow figure of a seated monk, circa 1755. (Sotheby, King & Chasemore) $165 £90

Bow figure of a negress in Turkish dress, circa 1760, 18.5cm. high, hand slightly chipped. (Christie's)$1,015 £550

One of a pair of Bow 'Birds in Branches' candlesticks, circa 1755-60, 9in. high. (Sotheby's) $2,645 £1,430

Rare Bow flower vase and arrangement, circa 1765-70, 7¼in. high. (Sotheby's)$345 £187

Bow figure of Harlequin in chequered suit, circa 1753, 12cm. high. (Christie's)$2,455 £1,320

One of two Bow white groups of 'Birds in Branches', circa 1755-60, 6¼in. high. (Sotheby's) $775 £418

Bow figure of a dancing girl in yellow hat, circa 1760, 18.5cm. high. (Christie's) $775 £418

Bow figure of a pug dog, circa 1755, 6.5cm. high, (Sotheby, King & Chasemore) $485 £260

Early white Bow figure of 'Hearing', circa 1755-60, 15cm. high. (Sotheby, King & Chasemore)
$410 £220

Bow triple salt painted in famille rose style, circa 1753, 13.5cm. wide. (Christie's)
$650 £352

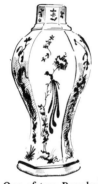

One of two Bow hexagonal baluster vases painted in Kakiemon style, circa 1760, 24cm. high. (Christie's)$3,255 £1,760

Early Bow cream jug with sparrow-beak spout, 3½in. high, circa 1755. (Sotheby's) $285 £154

One of a pair of Bow figures of seated musicians, circa 1765, 18.5cm. high. (Christie's)$1,225 £660

Signed Bow mug of bell shape, circa 1765, 3¾in. high. (Sotheby's)
$610 £330

Ormolu mounted Bow figure of a girl flanked by bullrushes, circa 1765, 21.5cm. high. (Christie's)$860 £462

Bow white figure of a girl emblematic of Smell, circa 1755, 13cm. high. (Christie's)$735 £396

Four Bow figures of the Seasons, circa 1755, 5in. high, Summer and Spring restored. (Sotheby's) $995 £550

Early Bow shell-bowl with ribbed body, circa 1752, 8½in. wide. (Sotheby's) $315 £176

Bow bell-shaped mug with grooved loop handle, circa 1760, 6in. high. (Sotheby's) $795 £440

Bow leaf-shaped dish, moulded with ribbing and veining, circa 1760, 11¾in. long. (Sotheby's) $490 £275

Bow mug of cylindrical shape with slightly flared base, circa 1755-60, 5¾in. high. (Sotheby's) $275 £154

Rare Bow garniture of three frill vases and covers, circa 1765, slightly chipped. (Sotheby, King & Chasemore) $1,340 £750

Early Bow coffee pot and cover of the 'Golfer and Caddy' pattern, circa 1752-55, 9in. high, slightly cracked. (Sotheby's) $2,985 £1,650

English delft bough pot, probably Bristol, 8in. diam., circa 1765-70. (Sotheby's) $935 £506

Bristol oval sauceboat with scroll handle, from Benjamin Lund's factory, 1749-51, 20.5cm. wide. (Christie's) $2,965 £1,620

Bristol leaf-shaped pickle dish from Benjamin Lund's factory, 1749-51, 10cm. wide. (Christie's) $2,765 £1,512

Bristol delft Adam and Eve charger with triangle pattern rim, circa 1730, 34cm. wide. (Christie's) $3,665 £1,980

Bristol delft blue and white inscribed and dated oviform jug, 1730, 23.5cm. high. (Christie's) $2,660 £1,430

Bristol delft blue and white plate with brick pattern rim, circa 1730, 21.5cm. diam. (Christie's) $385 £209

One of a pair of Bristol pearlware documentary spirit barrels, 1834, 12cm. high.(Christie's) $975 £528

Bristol delft plate with scalloped rim, 9in. diam., circa 1760. (Sotheby's) $205 £110

Bristol delft tea caddy of octagonal form, circa 1760-70, 4¼in. high. (Sotheby's)$1,730 £935

87

Rare jar for Hill and Ledger, showing Windsor Castle, chipped and stained. (Phillips) $1,155 £620

English porcelain whistle, circa 1820-30, 4.5cm. wide. (Sotheby King & Chasemore) $240 £130

Rare Lloyd, Shelton, figure of Queen Victoria and the Princess Royal, circa 1841, 17cm. high. (Sotheby's Belgravia) $245 £132

Early 19th century sporting mug with foliate handle, 5¾in. high. (Sotheby Beresford Adams) $350 £190

Dated creamware box and cover of circular shape, 1773, 3¼in. diam. (Sotheby's) $650 £352

Documentary Billingsley Mansfield jug with two named views, signed, 6¾in. high. (Neales) $1,665 £900

Late 19th century porcelain basket on pedestal, 8¼in. high. (Robert W. Skinner Inc.)$250 £140

'Marriage Pattern' coffee cup, teacup and saucer of fluted form, circa 1775. (Phillips) $465 £250

One of a pair of club-shaped ironstone vases with flared mouths, 15in. high. (Russell Baldwin & Bright)$935 £520

Figure of M. Lind from the Alpha factory, circa 1847, 20cm. high. (Sotheby's Belgravia) $430 £231

Early 19th century English porcelain whistle, 4.5cm. wide. (Sotheby, King & Chasemore) $205 £110

18th century English creamware leech jar and cover, 40.5cm. high. (Phillips) $1,045 £560

Early 18th century English wet-drug jar, 7¼in. high, slightly chipped. (Christie's)$530 £286

Charger from an English iron-stone dinner service of fifty-three pieces, circa 1810. (Sotheby, King & Chasemore) $760 £410

English stoneware silver mounted tankard with grooved handle, circa 1710, 14.5cm. high. (Christie's) $860 £462

Early English delft bowl, probably London, circa 1710-20, 10in. diam., slightly cracked. (Sotheby's) $975 £528

One of a pair of English bough pots, circa 1800, on bun feet, 9½in. high. (Robert W. Skinner Inc.) $900 £495

English delft tulip charger with blue-dash rim, 35.5cm. diam. (Phillips) $890 £480

Tureen from a late 19th century ironstone dinner service by Ashworth, forty-three pieces in all. (Sotheby Beresford Adams) $350 £190

Slipware puzzle jug with pear-shaped body, 14cm. high. (Phillips)$535 £290

James Walford hand modelled pottery group of two figures, 26cm. wide. (Christie's) $350 £190

Part of a thirty-eight-piece Ridgway dessert service painted with figures in country landscapes. (Phillips) $4,625 £2,500

Victorian tea urn with floral decoration, 55cm. high, on quadruple scroll feet. (Jackson-Stops & Staff) $510 £280

Dublin delftware meat dish, Delamain's factory, circa 1760, 43cm. high.(Sotheby, King & Chasemore) $250 £140

James Walford slab-built stoneware figure of a vulture, contemporary, 19.3cm. high. (Christie's) $120 £65

Adams silver mounted blue and white mug with angular handle, London, 1802, 12.5cm. high. (Christie's) $365 £198

19th century Newcastle cow creamer and cover, 8in. high. (Sotheby's) $510 £275

Astbury brown-ground miniature teapot and cover with faceted spout, circa 1745, 13cm. wide. (Christie's) $1,220 £660

Pearlware ornithological part dessert service of fourteen pieces. (Phillips) $2,220 £1,200

Rare 'Thin Man' Toby jug with gaunt toper seated in cream coloured chair, circa 1770, 9¾in. high.(Sotheby's) $1,395 £770

Interesting and documentary Donyatt pottery fuddling cup of three linked vessels, 4¾in., circa 1733. (Sotheby's) $1,355 £748

English mediaeval jug, 14th century, probably Nottingham or Cambridge, 33cm. high. (Phillips) $1,110 £600

Rare Parian group of 'Union Refugees', 1861, 46cm. high. (Sotheby's Belgravia) $505 £280

Late 18th century Porto-bello cow creamer and cover, 6¼in. long. (Sotheby's) $385 £209

Ralph Wood Toby jug, figure in grey coat and yellow breeches, 1770's, 10½in. high. (Sotheby Beresford Adams) $795 £430

Part of a thirty-eight-piece Ridgway dessert service, circa 1820, painted with fruit and flowers. (Sotheby's) $4,090 £2,200

Walton figure of Diana holding a bow and quiver, circa 1820, 11½in. high. (Sotheby's) $245 £132

Coalbrookdale kettle on stand with flower encrust-ing. (Christie's S. Kensing-ton) $1,190 £650

Rare finely modelled English porcelain figure, of the Duke of Welling-ton, circa 1800, 29cm. high. (Sotheby, King & Chasemore) $445 £250

One of a pair of Canton famille rose baluster vases with lion mask handles, mid 19th century, 35cm. high. (Christie's)$1,315 £682

19th century Chinese Canton shallow bowl with flat rim, 13in. diam. (Robert W. Skinner Inc.)$750 £410

One of a pair of late 19th century Cantonese vases of pear shape, 14¼in. high. (Sotheby's) $665 £352

Mid 19th century Cantonese porcelain part dessert service of thirteen pieces. (Locke & England) $625 £350

One of a pair of Canton famille rose slender pear-shaped vases, 45cm. high. (Christie's) $685 £380

Guangxu Canton bowl painted with panels of courtiers and birds, 40.5cm. diam. (Sotheby's Belgravia) $845 £462

Late 19th century Cantonese bulb pot and cover of flared form, 9½in. high. (Sotheby's) $375 £198

93

Large 18th century Canton blue and white basin, mounted, 28¼in. diam. (Wm. Doyle Galleries Inc.)
$2,900 £1,535

One of a pair of near matching 19th century Canton candlesticks of inverted trumpet shape, 8½in. high. (Robert W. Skinner Inc.) $1,600 £875

Canton porcelain bowl decorated in famille rose manner, 16in. diam. (Gilbert Baitson)
$605 £320

One of a pair of 19th century Canton vases of flattened baluster form, 31cm. high. (H. Spencer & Sons Ltd.)
$780 £420

One of a pair of 19th century Chinese Canton jars of hexagonal section, 11in. high. (W. H. Lane & Son) $210 £120

One of a pair of Canton vases and covers with domed lids and lion handles, 52cm. high. (Sotheby's Belgravia)
$1,650 £902

Cantonese vase of ovoid form with buddhist lion handles, 25½in. high. (Sotheby's) $810 £429

One of a pair of Canton candlesticks with self tapering columns, 24.5cm. high. (Sotheby's Belgravia)
$405 £220

One of a pair of Canton vases painted with warriors, 35cm. high. (Sotheby's Belgravia)
$465 £260

Set of four late 19th century Capodimonte figures of the seasons, 13¼in. high. (Sotheby, King & Chasemore) $780 £420

Capodimonte (Carlo III) figure of a Callot dwarf in peaked hat, circa 1750, 8cm. high. (Christie's) $1,665 £900

Capodimonte circular sugar bowl and cover, circa 1758, 10.5cm. diam. (Christie's) $8,165 £4,536

Large Capodimonte porcelain table lamp with four dancing figures on base. (Honiton Galleries) $315 £170

CAUGHLEY

Part of a Caughley part tea and coffee service of thirty-two pieces, painted in grey black and gilt. (H. Spencer & Sons Ltd.) $670 £360

Part of a thirty-four-piece Caughley dessert service in underglaze blue and gold. (Phillips) $1,445 £780

95

Chelsea leaf dish moulded as two lettuce leaves, circa 1755, 25.5cm. wide. (Christie's) $450 £286

Chelsea baluster coffee cup and saucer with gilt dentil rims, circa 1760. (Christie's) $855 £462

Chelsea fluted leaf-shaped cream jug, red anchor mark, circa 1753, 11cm. wide. (Christie's) $5,290 £2,860

Chelsea gold mounted baluster scent bottle and butterfly stopper, circa 1755, 9cm. high. (Christie's) $650 £352

Pair of Chelsea sweetmeat dishes in the form of a gallant and his companion, 17.5cm. high. (Sotheby, King & Chasemore) $1,685 £920

Chelsea figure of a begging pug bitch, gold anchor mark, circa 1760, 9cm. high. (Christie's) $1,730 £935

Chelsea moulded plate painted with an exotic bird, circa 1758, 22cm. diam. (Christie's) $530 £286

One of a pair of Chelsea candlestick figures, circa 1760-65, 11¾in. high. (Sotheby's) $775 £418

Chelsea plate painted with a border of birds, circa 1760, 21.5cm. diam. (Christie's) $530 £286

One of a pair of Chelsea fluted beakers with chocolate line rims, circa 1752, 6.5cm. high. (Christie's)
$4,475 £2,420

Chelsea silver-shaped oval dish, red anchor mark, circa 1753, 21cm. wide. (Christie's)
$1,465 £792

One of a pair of Chelsea Derby porcelain shaped circular shallow dishes, 7¾in. diam. (Geering & Colyer) $590 £320

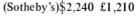

Chelsea 'sunflower' dish, 9in. wide, circa 1752-56. (Sotheby's) $530 £286

Chelsea figure of Pu-Tau Ho-Shang, 1746-49, 8cm. high. (Christie's) $3,070 £1,650

Chelsea botanical dish painted with a leafy branch, circa 1755, 10½in. diam. (Sotheby's) $2,240 £1,210

Chelsea lobed botanical dish painted with leaves and insects, circa 1755, 20.5cm. diam. (Christie's)
$1,740 £935

Chelsea chinoiserie group of a lady and child scribe, circa 1758, 17.5cm. high. (Christie's) $2,150 £1,155

Rare Chelsea famille rose fluted dish, 7in. diam., circa 1745-52. (Sotheby's)
$1,140 £616

Chelsea double handled cup and saucer, circa 1760-65, minor chips, slight rubbing. (Sotheby's) $280 £154

Chelsea gold mounted scent bottle and stopper modelled as a bunch of yellow flowers, circa 1758, 8cm. high. (Christie's) $1,420 £777

One of a pair of Chelsea plates of oval shape, red anchor marks, circa 1755, 12¼in. wide. (Sotheby's) $395 £220

Pair of Chelsea Derby candlestick figures, circa 1770, 11½in. high. (Sotheby's) $1,730 £935

Pair of Chelsea vases of small size with double scroll handles, 6in. high, circa 1765. (Sotheby's) $380 £209

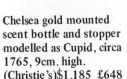

Rare Chelsea dish of silver shape, circa 1752-56, 10¾in. wide. (Sotheby's) $770 £407

Chelsea gold mounted scent bottle and stopper modelled as Cupid, circa 1765, 9cm. high. (Christie's) $1,185 £648

Chelsea plate with lobed rim, gold anchor mark, circa 1760-70, 8½in. diam. (Sotheby's) $315 £176

Doucai jardiniere with plain interior, slightly everted rim, 27cm. diam. (Christie's) $805 £418

One of a pair of Chinese armorial octagonal dishes with mazareens, 15¾in. wide. (Lawrence Fine Art) $2,270 £1,200

One of a pair of Chinese armorial sauce tureens, covers and stands, 7¾in. wide. (Lawrence Fine Art) $2,080 £1,100

One of a pair of late 17th century Chinese blue and white bottles, 10in. high. (Sotheby's) $1,415 £748

Jiaqing yellow-ground vase, one of a pair, with double vertically set tubular handles, 29.3cm. high. (Sotheby's) $5,760 £3,080

Late 18th century heavily potted blanc-de-chine standing figure of Guanyin, 50cm. high. (Christie's) $1,700 £880

Late 19th century Chinese rose medallion garden seat of barrel form, 19½in. high. (Robert W. Skinner Inc.) $1,700 £935

Late Qing dynasty blue and white oviform jardiniere, 46cm. diam. (Christie's) $1,680 £858

One of a pair of 18th century Chinese blue-ground hexafoil baluster vases, 41.5cm. high. (Christie's) $1,350 £750

One of two Tongzhi blue and white saucer dishes on wood stands, 15.5cm. diam. (Christie's)
$340 £190

19th century Chinese rose medallion teapot with high domed cover, 10in. high. (Robert W. Skinner Inc.)
$500 £265

Chinese Wanli plate decorated with dragons and flowers, 8in. diam. (J. M. Welch & Son)
$14,105 £7,700

Mid 19th century rose medallion garden seat of barrel form, 18in. high. (Robert W. Skinner Inc.)
$2,500 £1,365

One of a pair of 19th century Chinese export porcelain, teak framed panels, 13¾in. square. (Robert W. Skinner Inc.) $900 £490

19th century Chinese garden seat of hexagonal form, sides and top with pierced medallions, 18½in. high. (Robert W. Skinner Inc.) $1,700 £930

19th century Chinese rose medallion vase with flaring top, 13½in. high. (Robert W. Skinner Inc.)$375 £205
100

Large Doucai dish, encircled Yongzheng six-character mark, 48cm. diam.(Christie's)
$1,350 £750

19th century Chinese Mandarin temple vase with shaped rim, 24½in. high.(Robert W. Skinner Inc.)
$500 £275

One of a pair of late Qing dynasty inlaid black lacquer boxes and covers, 35.5cm. diam. (Christie's) $1,530 £850

One of a pair of antique Chinese containers of flattened gourd shape. (Butler & Hatch Waterman) $380 £205

One of a pair of early 19th century blue and white cache-pots on pedestal bases, 14½in. diam. (Locke & England)$1,020 £560

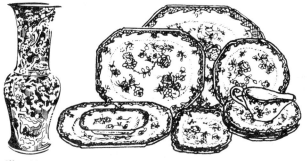

Famille noire vase painted with birds flying amongst flowers, 57cm. high. (Sotheby's Belgravia) $2,685 £1,500

Fifteen pieces of late 18th/ early 19th century Chinese porcelain. (Lacy Scott) $1,035 £540

19th century Chinese porcelain temple vase of baluster form with flared rim, 24in. high. (Robert W. Skinner Inc.) $650 £355

19th century Chinese pottery garden seat on hexagonal panelled base, 19¾in. high. (Robert W. Skinner Inc.) $150 £80

Tang dynasty unglazed buff pottery figure of a guardian, 40cm. high. (Christie's)$935 £520

Transitional blue and white oviform jar, circa 1640, 24cm. high. (Christie's) $575 £320

CHINESE

18th century Chinese blue
and white bowl, 12in. diam.
(J. M. Welch & Son)
$255 £140

18th century Chinese
hexagonal tureen and
cover, 23cm. high.
(Osmond, Tricks)
$580 £320

Kangxi Doucai bowl on
high, slightly tapering
foot, 18.4cm. diam.
(Sotheby's) $720 £385

Transitional blue and
white flaring beaker,
circa 1640, 20cm. high,
chipped. (Christie's)
$775 £432

19th century Chinese rose medallion pitcher and bowl decorated
on gold ground.(Robert W. Skinner Inc.) $775 £425

Rare Sui dynasty
'chicken head'
ewer with double
lug handles, 44cm.
high.(Sotheby's)
$34,970 £18,700

18th/19th century tur-
quoise-glazed pilgrim
bottle applied with scroll
handles, 29cm. high.
(Christie's) $810 £453

Wucai dragon and phoenix
saucer dish with foot rim,
32.1cm. diam., decorated
in famille verte.(Sotheby's)
$3,910 £2,090

Qianlong celadon glazed
barrel-shaped jar with
two mask and ring han-
dles, 16.2cm. high.
(Sotheby's)$3,085 £1,650

Newport pottery 'bizarre' crocus vase by Clarice Cliff, 31cm. high, 1930's.(Sotheby's Belgravia)$150 £82

Newport pottery 'Fantasque' two-person breakfast set, designed by Clarice Cliff, 1930's. (Sotheby's Belgravia) $1,280 £720

Newport pottery vase designed by Clarice Cliff, 1930's, 29cm. high.(Sotheby's Belgravia)$260 £143

Newport pottery 'bizarre' two-person breakfast set, designed by Clarice Cliff, 1930's. (Sotheby's Belgravia)$535 £300

Newport pottery 'bizarre' one-person breakfast set, designed by Clarice Cliff, 1930's. (Sotheby's Belgravia) $500 £280

Wilkinson Ltd. 'bizarre' lemonade set of seven pieces, 1930's, designed by Clarice Cliff.(Sotheby's Belgravia)$720 £396

Part of an eighteen-piece table set by Wilkinson Ltd., 1930's, designed by Clarice Cliff. (Sotheby's Belgravia)
                    $400 £220

Newport pottery 'bizarre' coffee pot, designed by Clarice Cliff, 1930's, 19cm. high. (Sotheby's Belgravia)
                    $200 £110

Coalport Election jug, commemorating the Shropshire General Election, of 1841, 23cm. high.(Phillips)$580 £320

Part of a Coalport part dessert service of twenty-one pieces, circa 1910. (Sotheby Beresford Adams) $775 £420

Coalport lamp base, circa 1900, 5½in. high. (Sotheby's Belgravia) $280 £150

One of a pair of Coalport named view vases and covers, circa 1910, 17½in. high. (Sotheby Beresford Adams) $445 £240

Garniture of three English bone china vases in Empire style, probably Coalport. (H. Spencer & Sons Ltd.) $600 £320

One of a pair of Coalport two-handled vases of ovoid pedestal form, 31cm. high. (H. Spencer & Sons Ltd.) $730 £420

Part of a Coalport sea-green-ground part dessert service, circa 1820. (Christie's) $2,850 £1,540

Teapot from an early Coalport tea and coffee service, early 19th century, twenty-two pieces in all. (Sotheby's) $425 £225

Coalport blue-ground part dessert service painted with flowers, circa 1820. (Christie's) $3,055 £1,650

Unusual 'Albert' plate moulded in light relief, circa 1840, 18.1cm. diam. (Sotheby's Belgravia) $220 £121

'Queen Caroline' jug bat-printed in black with two portraits, circa 1820, 8.8cm. high. (Sotheby's Belgravia) $255 £143

'Queen Caroline' plaque of rectangular shape, circa 1820, 11.2cm. wide. (Sotheby's Belgravia) $305 £165

Rare 'Victoria R.' jug, possibly Scottish, with faceted body, circa 1838, 17.5cm. high. (Sotheby's Belgravia) $255 £143

One of a rare pair of commemorative children's plates, circa 1840, 13.2cm. diam. (Sotheby's Belgravia) $430 £231

Commemorative mug made for the Coronation of Queen Victoria, 1838, restored, 8.8cm. high. (Sotheby's Belgravia) $890 £495

Mug made to commemorate the Coronation of Queen Victoria. (Sotheby's Belgravia) $1,090 £600

Very rare commemorative bowl made for Seven Incorporations of Dumfries, circa 1820-25, 18.3cm. diam. (Sotheby's Belgravia) $140 £77

Unusual commemorative mug showing Queen Victoria and Prince Albert, 1840, 12.5cm. wide. (Sotheby's Belgravia) $295 £165

18th century Staffordshire slipware dish with dark-brown-ground, 43.5cm. wide. (Sotheby, King & Chasemore)$1,040 £580

Rare Staffordshire pearlware commemorative bowl, circa 1793, 8¾in. diam. (Sotheby's)
$435 £231

Commemorative mug made for the Coronation of Queen Victoria, 1838, 8cm. high. (Sotheby's Belgravia)
$980 £528

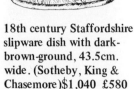

Rare late 18th century American commemorative earthenware dish, 14¾in. diam. (Sotheby's)
$235 £132

Coalport jug, commemorating the Shropshire Election of 1841, 29cm. high. (Phillips)
$580 £320

Rare Dutch commemorative plate with portraits of William IV, Princess Anne and Princess Caroline, 1747, 22.5cm. diam. (Phillips) $1,545 £850

Rare and very large commemorative punchbowl, 1743, 15½in. diam. (Sotheby's) $690 £374

Very rare commemorative shaving bowl and stand, 1840, for the marriage of Victoria and Albert. (Sotheby's Belgravia)
$530 £286

Pearlware teapot and cover depicting the Battle of Trafalgar, circa 1806-10, 4¾in. high. (Sotheby's)
$305 £165

Mid 19th century Copeland plaque painted with a view of the Bay of Naples, 30cm. wide. (Sotheby's Belgravia) $345 £190

Copeland cow creamer, date code for 1884, 14.5cm. high. (Sotheby, King & Chasemore) $390 £210

Copeland commemorative tyg painted with panels of Queen Victoria, Britannia, etc., 1900, 14cm. high. (Sotheby's Belgravia) $285 £154

Late 19th century Copeland parian figure of 'Corinna, the Lyric Muse', 55cm. high, slightly cracked. (Sotheby, King & Chasemore) $215 £120

Part of a large 19th century Copeland late Spode dinner service of eighty-three pieces. (Dickinson, Davy & Markham) $195 £105

COPER

Hans Coper stoneware vase of oval section, circa 1970, 21cm. high. (Christie's) $3,660 £2,000

Hans Coper stoneware vase with spade-shaped body in stone-grey glaze, circa 1968, 49.8cm. high. (Christie's) $12,810 £7,000

Hans Coper stoneware vase of rectangular oval section, in milky white glaze, 23cm. high. (Christie's) $4,575 £2,500

107

Daoguang dragon bowl with green enamel decoration, 12cm. diam. (Sotheby's Belgravia) $445 £242

One of a pair of Daoguang famille rose vases, 21.8cm. high. (Sotheby's Belgravia) $375 £200

One of a pair of Daoguang famille rose bowls, 13.7cm. diam. (Sotheby's) $1,335 £715

Daoguang small drum-shaped garden seat in famille rose enamels, 21.5cm. high.(Sotheby, King & Chasemore) $610 £340

Attractive Daoguang cloisonne bowl on blue-ground, 28cm. diam. (Sotheby's Belgravia) $382 £209

Rare Daoguang dated blue and white water jar and cover in bucket shape, 23.2cm. high. (Sotheby's) $14,400 £7,700

DAVENPORT

Early 19th century Davenport stone china dessert set. (Lacy Scott)$665 £360

One of a pair of Davenport oviform vases with caryatid handles, circa 1820, 24.5cm. high. (Christie's) $935 £506

Part of a Davenport pearlware botanical part dessert service, circa 1815, sixteen pieces in all. (Christie's)$2,850 £1,540

18th century Dutch Delft plate with blue rim, 9in. diam. (Robert W. Skinner Inc.) $100 £55

Dutch Delft tobacco jar painted in blue, circa 1750, 10¾in. high. (Sotheby's) $520 £275

18th century Dutch Delft charger with central reserve of cornflower and fern spray, 13¾in. diam. (Robert W. Skinner Inc.) $325 £175

19th century Dutch Delft bulb pot with blue, yellow and green decoration, 9¾in. long. (Robert W. Skinner Inc.) $375 £205

Mid 18th century Dutch Delft 'peacock pattern' dish, 13½in. diam., slightly chipped. (Sotheby's) $165 £88

Mid 18th century Dutch Delft plaque of shaped oval form, 23.5cm. wide. (Sotheby's) $870 £484

One of a pair of Dutch Delft plates in Wanli style, 10in. diam., early 18th century. (Sotheby Beresford Adams) $295 £160

18th century Dutch Delft tobacco jar decorated in blue, 36.5cm. high. (Sotheby's) $695 £385

18th century Dutch Delft charger, 13¼in. diam. (Robert W. Skinner Inc.) $425 £230

109

DELLA ROBBIA

Della Robbia vase with three tubular loop handles, galleon D. R. and artist's initials on base, 32cm. high. (Phillips) $250 £140

Della Robbia vase of pear shape with two loop handles, circa 1898, 14¼in. high. (Sotheby's) $605 £319

Della Robbia pottery vase decorated by Cassandia Ann Walker, 1903, 10in. high. (Phillips) $660 £360

DE MORGAN

De Morgan dish painted by Charles Passenger in crimson and mushroom, 39.7cm. diam.(Sotheby's Belgravia) $515 £275

De Morgan two-handled oviform vase with garlic neck, 44cm. high. (Christie's) $60 £33

De Morgan jardiniere, bell body with twin lug handles, 21.5cm. high. (Sotheby's Belgravia) $540 £286

Unusual De Morgan vase, incised by Farini, 1890, 21.3cm. high. (Sotheby's Belgravia) $455 £242

Late Fulham period De Morgan lustre dish painted in ruby and salmon pink, circa 1900, 36.6cm. diam.(Sotheby's Belgravia) $295 £160

William De Morgan oviform vase painted by Joe Juster, 15cm. high. (Phillips) $660 £360

Rare Royal Derby miniature coal scuttle of helmet shape, dated for 1912, 2¼in. high. (Sotheby Beresford Adams) $220 £120

Derby circular basket with pierced trellis sides and rope-twist handles, circa 1758, 6¾in. wide.(Sotheby's) $1,355 £748

Royal Crown Derby miniature teapot and cover, 2in. high, dated for 1913. (Sotheby Beresford Adams) $205 £110

Set of four Derby porcelain figures of the Four Seasons attributed to Pierre Stephan, circa 1780, 16 to 17cm. high. (Sotheby, King & Chasemore)
$930 £500

Bloor Derby cow creamer, 15cm. high. (Sotheby, King & Chasemore) $390 £210

One of a pair of Derby ice pails and covers with campana-shaped bodies, circa 1815, 40cm. high. (Sotheby, King & Chasemore) $645 £360

Derby plate, painted by William Slater Snr., circa 1825, 23cm. diam. (Sotheby, King & Chasemore) $465 £250

One of a pair of Derby
two-handled vases deco-
rated by Richard Dodson,
18cm. high. (Phillips)
$925 £500

Early 19th century Derby
whistle, 4.5cm. wide.
(Sotheby, King & Chase-
more) $370 £200

Fine Derby sucrier of
deep U-shape, circa 1790,
2¾in. high. (Sotheby's)
$1,560 £825

Derby plate, decorated
with a view of Worcester.
(Christie's S. Kensington)
$275 £150

Derby crested mask jug,
spout modelled as Admi-
ral Rodney, circa 1770,
24.5cm. high.(Christie's)
$735 £396

Derby documentary oval
plaque with portrait of
Shakespeare, 1839,
10.5cm. high, in giltwood
frame. (Christie's)
$815 £440

Early 19th century Derby
cow creamer, 16cm. high.
(Sotheby, King & Chase-
more) $370 £200

Pair of Derby figures of a
gallant and companion,
circa 1760, 22cm. high.
(Christie's) $735 £396

Royal Derby Imari min-
iature vase of pear shape,
4in. high, dated for
1908. (Sotheby Beres-
ford Adams)$240 £130

One of a pair of Derby oval sauce tureens and covers, circa 1813, 7.5cm. wide.(Christie's) $1,015 £550

Bloor Derby cylindrical mug decorated with flowers, circa 1815, 12.5cm. high.(Christie's) $755 £407

One of a pair of oval Derby two-handled Monteiths with shell handles, circa 1790, 26.5cm. wide. (Christie's) $915 £495

Derby figure of a street vendor modelled as girl with a basket, circa 1760, 22cm. high. (Christie's) $895 £484

Early Derby figure of a wild boar, circa 1755, 12.7cm. wide. (Sotheby, King & Chasemore) $160 £85

Derby blue and white shell centrepiece by Wm. Duesbury & Co., circa 1770, 21.5cm. high. (Christie's) $820 £440

Derby centrepiece and stand surmounted by a figure of Neptune, 43.5cm. high, circa 1768. (Christie's) $1,535 £825

Pair of Derby figures of a shepherd and his companion, circa 1765, 23cm. high. (Christie's) $1,630 £880

Unusual Crown Derby pierced vase and cover, 13½in. high. (Hall Wateridge & Owen) $445 £240

113

DERBY

Part of a sixty-three-piece Crown Derby dessert service, circa 1815-30. (W. H. Lane & Son) $2,115 £1,150

DOUCAI

Rare Doucai vase of compressed baluster form, 21.8cm. high.(Sotheby's)
$3,700 £1,980

Early 18th century Doucai saucer dish, encircled Chenghua character mark, 15.5cm. diam. (Christie's)
$680 £352

Fine Doucai vase of well potted pear shape, with tall narrow neck, 28.6cm. high. (Sotheby's)
$74,050 £39,600

DOULTON

Doulton stoneware beaker, showing golfers, circa 1900, 4¾in. high. (Sotheby's) $185 £99

Royal Doulton and Rix patent 'marqueterie' bowl with lobed rim, circa 1900, 30.8cm. diam. (Sotheby's Belgravia) $350 £190

Doulton stoneware figure of a merry musician by G. Tinworth, circa 1895, 12cm. high. (Sotheby, King & Chasemore) $500 £270

Doulton pottery study of Adam and Eve by Mark V. Marshall, signed and dated 1878, 17in. high.(Sotheby's) $3,700 £2,000

Royal Doulton 'flambe' shallow circular bowl on pedestal foot, 18cm. diam. (Christie's) $275 £150

Doulton stoneware loving cup with cricketing subject, 1882, 6in. high. (Sotheby's) $875 £462

Royal Doulton stoneware slender oviform vase by Frank A. Butler, 41cm. high. (Christie's)$275 £150

Rare Doulton character jug of Field Marshall Smuts, circa 1946-48. (Dee & Atkinson) $980 £540

Rare Royal Doulton Titanianware figure of 'Blighty', 1920's, 29cm. high. (Sotheby, King & Chasemore)$745 £400

One of a pair of Doulton stoneware baluster vases by Hannah Barlow and Francis Lee, 30.5cm. high. (Christie's) $695 £380

Royal Doulton 'flambe' carp, painted by Noke, 31cm. high.(Christie's) $510 £280

One of a pair of Doulton stoneware beakers showing cricketers, circa 1900, 4¾in. high. (Sotheby's)$520 £275

115

Royal Doulton 'flambe' model of a sparrow, 5.5cm. high, roundel mark. (Phillips) $195 £110

Unusual Royal Doulton 'Sung' vase, painted by Arthur Charles Eaton, 25cm. high, impressed 6-25. (Phillips) $1,345 £750

Doulton stoneware figure of a merry musician modelled by George Tinworth, circa 1895, 10cm. high. (Sotheby, King & Chasemore) $1,490 £800

Royal Doulton earthenware vase by Florence Barlow, on muddy brown ground, circa 1910, 20.5cm. high. (Sotheby, King & Chasemore) $220 £120

Doulton figure of Folly, circa 1929-38, 22.5cm. high. (Phillips) $715 £400

One of a pair of 19th century Royal Doulton vases, decorated by Hannah Barlow, 10¼in. high. (Sotheby Beresford Adams) $630 £340

Royal Doulton group 'The Return of Persephone', dated for 1919, 16½in. high. (Sotheby Beresford Adams) $1,480 £800

Royal Doulton figure of Annabella designed by L. Harradine, dated for 1939, 13.5cm. high. (Phillips) $285 £160

Rare Royal Doulton figure 'The Prince of Wales', 19cm. high, dated for 1936. (Phillips) $715 £400

Royal Doulton twin-hand-led loving cup 'The Three Musketeers', 25cm. high. (Phillips) $395 £220

Royal Doulton 'flambe' model of an alsation sitting upright, 9cm. high, roundel mark. (Phillips) $320 £180

Doulton Lambeth stone-ware group 'The Cockneys at Brighton', as a family of brown mice, 14cm. long, 1886. (Phillips)$570 £320

Doulton Lambeth vase by Mary Mitchell, 1881, unsigned, 27cm. high. (Phillips) $270 £150

Royal Doulton figure of Lady Anne Nevill, design-ned by Margaret Davies, 1948, 25cm. high. (Phillips) $500 £280

One of a pair of late 19th century Royal Doulton vases in Art Deco style, 18¾in. high. (Sotheby Beresford Adams) $575 £310

Royal Doulton 'Sung' vase, painted by Arthur Charles Eaton, 33cm. high. (Phillips) $535 £300

Early Doulton stoneware can-dlestick group, 1879, 16cm. high. (Sotheby, King & Chase-more) $485 £260

Rare Royal Doulton character jug of Field-Marshall Smuts, 1946, 17cm. high. (Phillips) $1,110 £620

117

One of a pair of Dresden vases by Carl Thierne, 22½in. high. (Sotheby's) $1,000 £525

Pair of Dresden candlestick figures of a gardener and a laundry maid, 11½in. high. (Dickinson, Davy & Markham) $295 £160

Late 19th century Dresden gilt metal mounted tankard, 25cm. high. (Sotheby's Belgravia) $390 £200

Dresden plaque painted with 'The German Bride', circa 1880, framed, 20.8 x 16cm. (Sotheby's Belgravia) $2,570 £1,375

One of a pair of late 19th century Dresden 'schneeballen' vases and covers, 57cm. high. (Sotheby's Belgravia) $1,540 £825

Late 19th century Dresden plaque, framed, 24 x 14.4cm. (Sotheby's Belgravia) $1,235 £660

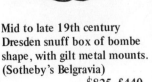

Tall Dresden comport with pierced and shaped circular bowl on a slender stem, 18½in. high. (Dickinson, Davy & Markham) $370 £200

Mid to late 19th century Dresden snuff box of bombe shape, with gilt metal mounts. (Sotheby's Belgravia) $825 £440

Dresden 'Naples' sedan chair, sides and door inset with bevelled glass windows, circa 1900, 28cm. high. (Sotheby's Belgravia) $495 £264

Glazed earthenware garden seat modelled as an elephant, in polychrome enamels, 21in. high. (Edgar Horn) $150 £80

Nishida earthenware bowl, interior painted with warriors, circa 1870's, 31cm. diam. (Sotheby's Belgravia) $500 £280

Fine Sylvestrie pottery figure of an eagle owl, 37in. long. (Sotheby, King & Chasemore) $955 £520

Earthenware vase with baluster body, circa 1900, 24.5cm. high. (Sotheby's Belgravia) $240 £132

Hododa Kinkozan earthenware vase in the form of a phoenix, 1890, 14.5cm. high. (Sotheby's Belgravia) $395 £220

One of a pair of earthenware vases, painted and gilt with panels of Samurai, 37cm. high, circa 1900. (Sotheby's Belgravia) $1,040 £580

Mid 19th century Unzan koro and cover in earthenware, with hexagonal body, 13cm. high. (Sotheby's Belgravia) $215 £120

Earthenware kettle and cover painted with panels of Samurai in gardens, circa 1900, 13cm. high. (Sotheby's Belgravia) $325 £180

Amphora earthenware vase with shaped neck, 40.25cm. high, circa 1900. (Sotheby's Belgravia) $260 £143

119

Copenhagen stoneware figure of a child with a cat, modelled by Knud Kyhn. (Christie's)
$165 £88

Rare Bottger porcelain bowl decorated in Holland in Kakiemon manner, early 18th century, 21cm. diam. (Sotheby's) $4,790 £2,660

European majolica covered cheese dish, circa 1880, in the form of a grass hut, 13½in. high. (Robert W. Skinner Inc.)
$340 £190

Late 19th century European hand-painted porcelain plate with cobalt blue rim, 15in. diam. (Robert W. Skinner Inc.)
$200 £110

Small pair of 19th century Continental porcelain candlesticks depicting Summer and Winter. (May, Whetter & Grose)
$340 £190

One of a pair of Companiedes-Indes blue and white plates, painted with a tree peony. (Sotheby, King & Chasemore) $275 £150

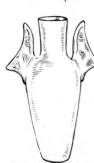

One of a pair of large vases by Clement Massier. (Phillips)
$35 £20

One of two European porcelain figural groups playing music, 20th century, 7 and 7½in. high. (Robert W. Skinner Inc.)
$250 £140

Austrian pottery figure of a young boy, in the manner of Michael Powolny, 31.5cm. high. (Phillips) $180 £100

Late 19th century Austrian porcelain plaque, in brass frame, 10in. high. (Robert W. Skinner Inc.) $325 £180

Mid 18th century European tinglazed tureen and cover in the form of a bunch of asparagus, 16.5cm. wide. (Sotheby, King & Chasemore) $680 £380

Early 19th century Continental porcelain chocolate pot with angular handle, 8in. high. (Wm. Doyle Galleries Inc.) $350 £185

Continental amphora jardiniere, circa 1900, 16½in. high. (Sotheby Beresford Adams) $150 £80

Pair of Hochst figures of a boy and a girl, circa 1780, 13.5cm. high.(Sotheby's) $1,685 £935

Late 19th century European porcelain ewer with applied figures, 26½in. high. (Robert W. Skinner Inc.) $500 £285

Large Continental vase painted by T. Leroy, signed, 1890's, 87.5cm. high. (Sotheby's Belgravia) $700 £374

One of a pair of oval Berlin dishes with gilt athemion wells, circa 1820, 45cm. wide. (Christie's) $1,200 £650

One of a pair of late 19th century Samson 'Derby' candlesticks, 26cm. high, chipped. (Sotheby's Belgravia) $660 £352

FAMILLE NOIRE

Qing dynasty famille noire square tapering vase, enamelled on a black ground, 49cm. high. (Christie's) $735 £410

18th century famille noire porcelain vase of baluster form, 52cm. high. (Sotheby's Belgravia) $565 £308

19th century famille noire baluster vase with flaring neck, 59.5cm. high. (Christie's) $695 £388

FAMILLE ROSE

Famille rose lemon-ground globular vase with detachable neck, 27.5cm. high. (Christie's) $1,910 £990

19th century famille rose yellow-ground fish bowl, with wood stand, 46cm. diam. (Christie's) $485 £270

One of a pair of Canton famille rose baluster vases and domed covers, 50.5cm. high. (Christie's) $1,160 £648

One of a pair of famille rose garden seats of hexagonal section, 47cm. high, wood stands. (Sotheby's Belgravia) $1,485 £770

One of a pair of famille rose armorial soup plates, circa 1750, 22.5cm. diam. (Christie's) $635 £330

One of a pair of famille rose vases and covers, enamelled with flowers and foliage, 28cm. high. (Sotheby's Belgravia) $595 £308

FAMILLE VERTE

Large Kangxi famille verte saucer dish, damaged and repaired, 52cm. diam. (Christie's) $1,255 £702

Continental famille verte vase on wood stand, circa 1900, 54cm. high. (Sotheby's Belgravia) $805 £418

FAMILLE VERTE

Famille verte jardiniere painted with storks among reeds, 50.5cm. diam., on wood stand.(Christie's) $3,500 £1,815

FRANKENTHAL

Frankenthal mythological figure of the Rape of Prosperine, modelled by J. F. Luck, circa 1756, 28cm. high.(Christie's) $2,035 £1,100

Rare Frankenthal figure of a poultry girl, by Adam Bauer, 13.5cm. high. (Phillips) $1,000 £550

Rare Frankenthal group of musicians, modelled by J. F. Luck, circa 1755-59, 23cm. high. (Sotheby's) $4,750 £2,640

Frankenthal ornithological plate painted with a grouse, circa 1756-59, 24cm. diam. (Christie's) $1,185 £605

Early Frankenthal arched rectangular tea caddy and cover painted with large birds, circa 1756, 16cm. high. (Christie's) $830 £450

Frankenthal cup and saucer decorated with landscapes, 1781. (Sotheby's) $405 £220

FRENCH

CHINA

19th century French plate on blue and gilt ground, Paris, 1823, 9¼in. diam. (W. H. Lane & Son)$110 £60

Rare Chantilly figure of a Chinaman, circa 1735-40, 14cm. high, damaged. (Sotheby's) $4,950 £2,750

One of a pair of French porcelain cache pots, late 19th century, 16cm. high. (H. Spencer & Sons Ltd.) $745 £400

19th century Sevres pedestal ovoid vase with ormolu top, 71cm. high. (H. Spencer & Sons Ltd.) $680 £390

Late 19th century Limoges porcelain tea service with gilt floral details. (Robert W. Skinner Inc.) $200 £105

Late 18th century French faience wine cistern. (Sotheby's) $4,225 £2,200

One of a pair of Second Empire green fluorspar vases with ormolu mounts, circa 1870, 14½in. high. (Sotheby, King & Chasemore) $1,395 £750

Pair of French figures of a young man and woman, circa 1900, 67.5 and 65.5cm. high. (Sotheby's Belgravia) $1,890 £1,012

Vincennes jug with elaborate gilt border, circa 1750-55, 23.5cm. high. (Sotheby's) $990 £550

One of a pair of late 19th century French vases, 19in. high, slightly damaged. (Sotheby's)$310 £165

Rare mid 18th century Chantilly double salt and pepper box in three sections, 25cm. wide. (Sotheby's) $595 £330

French Art Pottery vase of bulbous form, circa 1910, 10¼in. high. (Robert W. Skinner Inc.) $325 £185

Galle faience seated cat with black glazed body, 33cm. high. (Christie's) $1,340 £715

FUKAGAWA

20th century French porcelain covered urns with domed tops, 13¼in. high. (Robert W. Skinner Inc.) $125 £70

French Doccia figure of a girl on a rock, damaged, circa 1780, 15cm. high.(Sotheby's) $845 £462

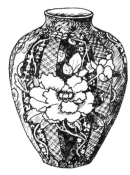

One of a pair of Fukagawa vases with coloured enamels, circa 1900, 13in. high. (Sotheby's) $665 £352

Fukagawa bowl of squat form, circa 1900, 9½in. high. (Sotheby's) $560 £297

One of a pair of Fukagawa Imari bottle vases with red grounds, circa 1900, 30cm. high. (Sotheby's) $405 £220

125

One of two Loosdrecht shaped oval quatrefoil trencher salts, circa 1770, 9.5cm. wide. (Christie's)$350 £190

Pair of German biscuit figures, 1873, 17in. high. (Sotheby's) $460 £242

One of a pair of late 19th century Helena Wolfsohn seaux crenelles, 27.5cm. wide. (Sotheby's Belgravia) $355 £187

Large late 19th century Potschappel vase, cover and stand, applied with nymphs, 82cm. high. (Sotheby's Belgravia) $1,130 £605

Mid 19th century German plaque painted with two ladies, framed, 17.5 x 13.5cm. (Sotheby's Belgravia) $1,440 £770

Mid 19th century German porcelain egg supported on three scrolled feet, 5in. high. (Robert W. Skinner Inc.) $475 £255

Late 19th century German porcelain epergne, embossed with flowers, 18in. high, damaged. (J. M. Welch & Son) $365 £200

Late 19th century German figure of a seated Maltese terrier, decorated in shades of brown, 19cm. high. (H. Spencer & Sons Ltd.) $595 £320

Late 19th century German porcelain figural piece, slightly damaged, 5½in. high. (Robert W. Skinner Inc.) $350 £190

126

German sweetmeat dish divided into six sections with ruffled rim, 10¼in. wide. (Robert W. Skinner Inc.) $50 £30

Amstel circular sugar bowl and cover with acorn finial, circa 1780, 11cm. high. (Christie's) $175 £95

19th century German inlaid panel depicting Abraham and Isaac, 61cm. high. (Osmond, Tricks) $220 £120

Mennecy figure of a Turk carrying a cap and two bags, circa 1750, 16cm. high. (Christie's) $740 £400

Plaue-on-Havel frog band of six pieces, circa 1900. (Sotheby's Belgravia) $580 £308

Plaue centrepiece with pierced detachable bowl on a tree trunk stem, circa 1900, 40.5cm. high.(Sotheby's Belgravia) $270 £150

Late 18th century German enamelled pocket telescope, 2in. diam.(Christie's) $720 £380

Part of a Furstenberg part coffee service of twelve pieces decorated with flowers, circa 1775. (Sotheby's) $1,880 £1,045

German stoneware jardiniere and stand. (Allen & May) $615 £325

127

GOLDSCHEIDER

CHINA

One of two pottery figures of negro musicians, probably by Goldscheider. (Phillips) $3,170 £1,750

Goldscheider earthenware figure after a model by Lorenzl, 1920's, 24.25cm. (Sotheby's Belgravia) $240 £132

Goldscheider cold-painted low-fired figure of a fairy, modelled by E. Tell, circa 1900, 76.25cm. high. (Sotheby's Belgravia) $640 £360

Goldscheider pottery figure of a young girl with flowers, 39.8cm. high. (Christie's) $785 £432

Small Goldscheider earthenware 'bat girl', 1920's, 21.5cm. high. (Sotheby's Belgravia) $320 £176

Goldscheider earthenware nude figure holding a blue cloak, 1930's, 41.75cm. high. (Sotheby's Belgravia) $620 £341

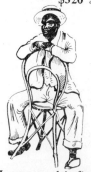

Goldscheider earthenware mask, modelled as a woman, 1920's, 30.5cm. high. (Sotheby's Belgravia) $195 £110

Large porcelain figure by Friedrich Goldscheider of a young man seated on a chair, 21in. high. (Phillips & Jolly) $1,765 £960

Goldscheider 'bat girl' with winged cape, 1930's, 46.25cm. high. (Sotheby's Belgravia) $1,040 £572

Goss model of the birthplace of Thomas Hardy, 4in. long. (Lawrence Fine Art)
$395 £220

Late 19th century Goss parian figure of 'The Devil Looking Over Lincoln', 14.5cm. high. (Sotheby's Belgravia)
$105 £55

Early 20th century Goss model of the Feathers Hotel, Ledbury, 11.6cm. wide. (Sotheby's Belgravia) $1,065 £572

Goss bust 'My Beautiful Duchess', colour decoration, restored. (Phillips)
$985 £540

Rare Goss parian bust of 'The Veiled Bride', circa 1865, 26cm. high. (Sotheby's Belgravia)
$475 £264

Rare late 19th century Goss figure of Lady Betty with flowers and a shawl, 6¾in. high. (Sotheby's) $125 £71

Early 20th century Goss model of Thomas Hardy's birthplace, 9.9cm. (Sotheby's Belgravia)
$285 £154

Early 20th century Goss model of John Bunyan's House, unglazed, 6cm. (Sotheby's Belgravia)
$1,025 £550

Early 20th century Goss model of Portman Lodge, 8.5cm. (Sotheby's Belgravia) $325 £176

129

Early 20th century Goss oven, unglazed, 7.6cm., slightly discoloured. (Sotheby's Belgravia) $225 £121

Goss coloured parian bust of 'Peeping Tom of Coventry', 11.4cm. high, dated 1893. (Sotheby's Belgravia) $165 £88

Early 20th century Goss model of Dove Cottage, Grasmere, 10.1cm. (Sotheby's Belgravia) $470 £253

Goss parian bust of General Gordon, square base titled, dated 1885, 18.5cm. high. (Sotheby's Belgravia) $185 £99

Early 20th century Goss model of Izaak Walton's birthplace, Shallowford, 9.1cm. wide. (Sotheby's Belgravia)$530 £286

Goss parian bust of Queen Victoria, dated 1881, 15.4cm. high. (Sotheby's Belgravia) $145 £77

Early 20th century Goss oven with red brick and slate roof, green details, 7.4cm. long. (Sotheby's Belgravia) $235 £132

Rare Goss model of The Round Tower, Windsor, 14.4cm., circa 1900.(Sotheby's Belgravia)$695 £374

Early 20th century Goss model of The Abbot's Kitchen, Glastonbury, 8.4cm. high.(Sotheby's Belgravia) $900 £484'

One of a pair of Guangxu famille rose bowls with central panels, 16.5cm. diam. (Sotheby's Belgravia) $485 £264

Guangxu blue and white jar and cover with panels of flowers, 34cm. high, slightly chipped. (Sotheby's Belgravia) $605 £330

Gaungxu blue and white jardiniere painted with He He erxian, 18in. high. (Sotheby, King & Chasemore) $4,090 £2,200

One of a pair of Guangxu period blue and white jars and covers, 34cm. high. (Sotheby's Belgravia) $845 £462

Guangxu blue and white fish bowl with wave border, slightly cracked, 42cm. high.(Sotheby's Belgravia) $885 £484

One of a pair of Guangxu blue and white moon flasks painted with boys, 45.5cm. high.(Sotheby's Belgravia) $1,410 £770

HAN

Rare Han dynasty green glazed hill jar and cover on tripod feet, 22.8cm. (Sotheby's)$4,525 £2,420

Han dynasty green glazed granary jar with cylindrical body, 25.4cm. high. (Sotheby's) $1,750 £935

Rare Han dynasty green glazed pottery cauldron and cover, 20.2cm. wide. (Sotheby's)$14,400 £7,700

131

HOCHST

Hochst white figure of a nymph, emblematic of Smell, circa 1765, 14.5cm. high. (Christie's)$260 £140

Hochst figure of a young boy modelled by J. P. Melchior, circa 1770, 12cm. high. (Christie's) $705 £380

Hochst figure of a bird-nester by Joh. P. Melchior, 18cm. high, circa 1765-75. (Sotheby's)$1,385 £770

IMARI

One of a pair of rare Chinese Imari bottles with chamfered corners, 27cm. high. (Sotheby, King & Chasemore)$630 £340

One of a set of five late 19th century Imari dishes of shaped octagonal outline, 27cm. diam. (Sotheby's Belgravia) $300 £165

One of a fine pair of heavy bottle-shaped antique Imari vases, richly gilded and decorated, 14¼in. high. (Butler & Hatch Waterman) $280 £150

19th century Japanese Imari vase with ribbed baluster body, 18in. high. (Robert W. Skinner Inc.) $775 £425

One of a set of four late 19th century Imari bowls with pierced rims, 15cm. diam. (Sotheby's Belgravia) $485 £264

19th century large Japanese Imari vase of baluster form, 25¼in. high. (Robert W. Skinner Inc.) $1,200 £655

Late 19th century Imari jardiniere with panels of vases of flowers, 35cm. wide. (Sotheby's Belgravia) $705 £385

19th century Japanese Imari vase with cylindrical neck, 12¾in. high. (Robert W. Skinner Inc.) $475 £260

Imari charger painted in four colours and gilt, 18in. diam. (Russell, Baldwin & Bright) $325 £180

One of a pair of Imari vases and covers, circa 1900, 39cm. high, with ribbed bodies. (Sotheby's Belgravia) $705 £385

Large 19th century Japanese Imari charger, 18½in. diam. (Robert W. Skinner Inc.) $225 £125

Late 19th century Imari jardiniere painted and gilt, 31cm. high. (Sotheby's Belgravia) $360 £198

Late 19th century Japanese Imari charger decorated with cranes, 21in. diam. (Robert W. Skinner Inc.) $375 £205

Late 17th/early 18th century black-ground Imari vase and cover, cracked, 37cm. high. (Sotheby, King & Chasemore) $135 £75

One of a pair of 19th century Imari meat dishes of octagonal form. (J. M. Welch & Son) $325 £180

133

Dated Italian faenza basket of oval shape, 1613, 23cm. wide. (Sotheby's)
$645 £352

Late 19th century Crown Milano cracker jar with plated silver fittings, 7¾in. high. (Robert W. Skinner Inc.)$275 £155

Late 17th century Montelupo dish painted in bright colours, 13in. diam. (Lawrence Fine Art)
$1,135 £600

17th century Caltagirone waisted albarello painted with a classical bust, 11in. high. (Lawrence Fine Art)
$380 £200

Late 17th century Gubbic lustred vase with waisted neck, 21cm. high, damaged. (Sotheby's)
$965 £528

Late 16th century Castel Durante drug jar with strap handle, 21cm. high. (Sotheby's)$1,425 £792

Late 17th century Montelupo dish painted with a man and a banner, 12¾in. diam. (Lawrence Fine Art)
$1,360 £720

Early Ginori armorial beaker and saucer, circa 1745.(Christie's)
$2,220 £1,200

Late 17th/early 18th century Castelli plaque of circular shape, 26cm. diam. (Sotheby's) $1,285 £715

Faenza tureen and cover, circa 1760, 29cm. wide, sold with another. (Sotheby's)$1,610 £880

Rare Doccia white glazed figure of a lion, 10cm. high. (Sotheby, King & Chasemore) $295 £160

Vezzi flattened oviform teapot and cover with loop handle, circa 1725, 15cm. wide. (Christie's) $31,450 £17,000

Naples dancing group of a young man and a girl, circa 1780, 19.5cm. high. (Christie's) $1,665 £900

Early 17th century North Italian drug jar with scrolling grooved handle, 21.5cm. high, damaged. (Sotheby's) $405 £220

Rare Cozzi milk jug and cover with unusual scrolling handle, circa 1767, 12.5cm. high.(Sotheby's) $5,940 £3,300

One of a pair of Venice puce scale tea bowls and saucers, circa 1770, with shaped borders. (Christie's)$2,035 £1,100

Venice two-handled beaker vase on spreading foot, circa 1770, 10cm. high. (Christie's) $775 £420

Early 18th century Castelli plate decorated with Fortitude sitting on a tomb, 19cm. diam. (Sotheby's) $1,625 £902

135

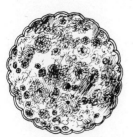

Large late 19th century Japanese cloisonne potiche and cover on three knop feet, 26.5cm. high. (Sotheby, King & Chasemore) $180 £100

19th century Japanese export covered jar with cobalt blue decoration, 13in. high. (Robert W. Skinner Inc.) $125 £70

Japanese earthenware bowl, signed, circa 1900, 9¾in. diam. (Sotheby's) $415 £220

19th century Japanese porcelain vase decorated with peacocks and flowers, 24in. high. (Robert W. Skinner Inc.) $300 £165

Japanese earthenware vase and cover in the form of a rope-tied bag, 22cm. high, circa 1880. (Sotheby's Belgravia) $260 £143

19th century Japanese Imari temple vase with flared top, 24in. high. (Robert W. Skinner Inc.) $650 £355

One of a pair of antique Japanese jars and covers, 19in. high. (Butler & Hatch Waterman) $650 £350

Japanese lacquer circular bowl applied with mother-of-pearl, 21¼in. diam. (Burrows & Day) $224 £120

Chinoiserie hexagonal tea caddy and cover painted with six scenes, circa 1725, 9.75cm. high. (Christie's) $22,200 £12,000

Hododa earthenware bowl painted and gilt, circa 1900, 31cm. diam. (Sotheby's Belgravia)
$645 £352

One of a pair of Japanese earthenware vases, circa 1900, 22¼in. high, one damaged. (Sotheby's)$310 £165

Late 19th century Japanese charger painted in coloured enamels, 22¼in. diam. (Sotheby's) $560 £297

One of a pair of 19th century Japanese Imari vases with flared tops and handles at necks, 16in. high. (Robert W. Skinner Inc.)
$650 £355

One of a pair of Japanese earthenware flasks, 1880's, 28cm. high. (Sotheby's Belgravia) $240 £132

One of a pair of Japanese earthenware vases gilt with panels, circa 1900, 30.5cm. high. (Sotheby's Belgravia)
$765 £418

19th century Japanese celadon vase with pierced neck, 23in. high. (Robert W. Skinner Inc.) $300 £165

Late 19th century Kyoto earthenware bowl in the form of a shell, 42.5cm. wide. (Sotheby's Belgravia) $665 £363

Kinkozan earthenware kettle and cover painted and gilt on a blue ground, circa 1900, 13cm. high. (Sotheby's Belgravia) $285 £160

137

CHINA

One of a pair of George Jones & Sons wall plaques, signed Schenek, circa 1875. (Robert W. Skinner Inc.) $600 £335

George Jones jug in Oriental taste, circa 1850, 7½in. high. (Sotheby's)$60 £33

Plate from a sixteen-piece George Jones apple-green-ground dessert service, circa 1900. (Sotheby's Belgravia) $550 £297

KAKIEMON

Arita porcelain bottle in Kakiemon style, circa 1700.(Sotheby's) $1,800 £1,000

Kakiemon decorated Meissen bottle of unusual form, circa 1730. (Bonhams) $2,495 £1,300

One of a pair of late 17th century Dutch-decorated Japanese Kakiemon square bottle vases, 20.5cm. high.(Christie's) $830 £450

KANGXI

Kangxi blue and white beaker vase, 45cm. high. (Christie's)$1,200 £625

Kangxi famille verte saucer dish painted with cranes, 34.5cm. diam., slightly chip-ped. (Christie's)$1,065 £594

Kangxi blue and white stem cup, 13.5cm. high. (Christie's)$490 £250

Large Kangxi famille verte dish painted with a four-clawed dragon, 39cm. diam. (Christie's)
$1,275 £660

Kangxi moulded celadon glazed stemcup with wide flaring bowl, 14.7cm. wide. (Sotheby's)
$2,055 £1,100

One of a pair of Kangxi famille verte dishes with central roundels, 37.5cm. diam. (Christie's)
$1,165 £605

Kangxi famille verte bowl, decorated in blue, orange, green and yellow, slightly cracked. (W. H. Lane & Son) $720 £380

Kangxi blue and white gu-shaped beaker vase, 45.5cm. high. (Christie's)
$1,620 £900

Rare celadon-ground bowl of Kangxi period, enamelled in famille verte, 11.8cm. diam. (Sotheby's)
$1,850 £990

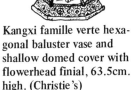

Kangxi famille verte vase of tapering square section, 40cm. high. (Sotheby's Belgravia) $460 £253

One of a pair of Kangxi famille rose dishes decorated with dragons, 37.5cm. diam. (Sotheby's Belgravia)
$360 £198

Kangxi famille verte hexagonal baluster vase and shallow domed cover with flowerhead finial, 63.5cm. high. (Christie's)
$4,245 £2,200

139

One of two Kangxi famille verte furniture bricks, one cracked, 26cm. wide. (Christie's) $1,060 £550

Kangxi blue and white vase of gu form, 14½in. high. (Sotheby, King & Chasemore) $745 £400

Kangxi bowl with everted rim, decorated in blue and white, 8¼in. diam. (W. H. Lane & Son) $795 £420

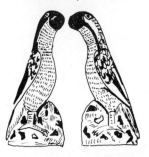

Kangxi blue and white baluster vase and domed cover, 55cm. high, cover restored. (Christie's) $775 £432

Pair of brightly painted Kangxi parrots. (Christie's S. Kensington) $1,080 £580

One of two Kangxi blue and white flattened pear-shaped ewers and covers, 17.5cm. high. (Christie's) $685 £380

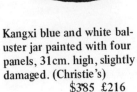

One of a pair of Kangxi famille verte saucer dishes, 25cm. diam. (Christie's) $2,125 £1,100

Kangxi blue and white baluster jar painted with four panels, 31cm. high, slightly damaged. (Christie's) $385 £216

Kangxi famille verte dish painted at the centre with a deer pulling a chariot, 31.5cm. diam. (Christie's) $975 £506

Kutani bijin adjusting her hair, circa 1900, 33cm. high. (Sotheby's Belgravia) $380 £198

One of a pair of late 19th century Kutani tureens and covers in the shape of partridges, 12cm. wide. (Sotheby's Belgravia) $750 £420

Kutani figure of a bijin dressed in a kimono and holding a drum, circa 1900, 31cm. high. (Sotheby's Belgravia) $380 £198

One of a pair of late 19th century Kutani bottle vases with long necks, 31cm. high. (Sotheby's Belgravia) $645 £352

One of a pair of Kutani dishes, circa 1860, 37cm. diam., within diaper borders. (Sotheby's Belgravia) $785 £419

Kutani group of a mother and child, circa 1900, 39cm. high, glaze chipped. (Sotheby's Belgravia) $240 £132

LAMBETH

Lambeth delft polychrome bowl, circa 1710, 30.6cm. diam. (Christie's) $610 £330

Rare dated Lambeth fuddling cup, 1639, slightly chipped, 4¾in. high. (Sotheby's) $5,290 £2,860

Lambeth delft blue and white ballooning bowl of shallow form, circa 1784, 22cm. diam. (Christie's) $1,015 £550

St. Ives preserve pot and cover decorated by Bernard Leach, 11.5cm. high. (Christie's) $275 £150

Bernard Leach stoneware vase with cylindrical body and narrow neck, 34cm. high. (Christie's)$1,465 £800

Bernard Leach stoneware vase of bulbous form, circa 1935, 18.5cm. high. (Christie's) $355 £194

Bernard Leach stoneware circular dish, centre incised with an antelope, circa 1968, 34cm. diam. (Christie's) $405 £220

Bernard Leach stoneware vase of oviform, with everted rim, 34cm. high. (Christie's)
$1,830 £1,000

St. Ives stoneware deep bowl decorated by Bernard Leach, 31.5cm. diam., centre showing an owl. (Christie's)
$1,465 £800

Bernard Leach vase with pinch foot and narrow neck, 8in. high. (W. H. Lane & Son) $350 £190

St. Ives stoneware bowl, decorated by Bernard Leach, 31cm. diam. (Christie's) $585 £320

Bernard Leach stoneware slab bottle with narrow neck, 19.4cm. high. (Christie's) $915 £500

Leeds creamware bonbonniere in the form of a lady's head, circa 1780-90, 3¼in. high. (Sotheby's) $455 £260

Very rare Leeds creamware commemorative plate, 1821, 22.7cm. diam. (Sotheby's Belgravia) $735 £396

Leeds pearlware group of Venus and Cupid, late 18th century. (Sotheby's) $190 £100

LE NOVE

Antonibon period Le Nove polychrome group of a shepherd serenading his companion, circa 1770, 15cm. high.(Christie's) $1,570 £850

Pair of Le Nove figures of a lady and a gentleman, circa 1790, 15cm. high. (Christie's) $2,035 £1,100

White Le Nove pastoral group on detached stand, circa 1770, 22cm. high. (Christie's) $830 £450

Le Nove group of two boys and a girl round a tree stump, circa 1780, 18cm. high. (Christie's) $1,295 £700

One of three Le Nove tea-bowls and saucers painted with famille rose flowers, circa 1770. (Christie's) $925 £500

Le Nove figure of a girl, emblematic of Spring, circa 1775, 13cm. high. (Christie's) $830 £450

143

Liverpool blue and white lobed oval sauceboat, Wm. Reid's factory, 1755-61, 23cm. wide.(Christie's)
$895 £484

Liverpool teabowl in 'cannonball' pattern, with saucer, circa 1765-70. (Sotheby's)
$160 £88

Liverpool hexagonal creamboat with angular handle, circa 1758, 14.5cm. wide. (Christie's)
$2,765 £1,512

Large Liverpool delft plate, circa 1760, 13in. diam., slightly chipped. (Sotheby's) $935 £506

Liverpool figure of Minerva on circular mound base, 1754-61, 14cm. high. (Christie's) $1,185 £648

Liverpool delft polychrome tile, circa 1760, 13cm. wide, slightly chipped. (Christie's)
$265 £143

Liverpool delft octagonal pill slab, mid 18th century, 10½in. square. (Sotheby's)
$2,240 £1,210

Rare Liverpool spoon tray of oval shape, 6in. wide, circa 1770. (Sotheby's) $510 £275

Early 19th century Liverpool Washington memorial pitcher with black transfer printed scene, 9in. high. (Robert W. Skinner Inc.) $700 £380

London delft plate decorated in blue, circa 1710-20, 8½in. diam. (Sotheby's) $860 £462

Rare London 'apollo' drug jar with shouldered ovoid body, 1710-30, 10¾in. high. (Sotheby's) $830 £440

One of a pair of London delft plates painted with cockerels, 6½in. diam., circa 1750. (Sotheby's) $1,730 £935

London delft dated plate, centre with initials LIM and date 1688, 21cm. diam. (Christie's) $1,630 £880

Late 17th century London delft charger with cracked rim, 13¾in. diam. (Sotheby's) $305 £165

London delft blue and white plate, circa 1685, 21.5cm. diam., rim slightly chipped. (Christie's) $650 £352

London delftware Royal portrait bowl with deep interior, circa 1690, 22cm. diam. (Sotheby, King & Chasemore) $985 £550

Rare mid 17th century London blue and white flower vase, 6¼in. high. (Sotheby's) $2,035 £1,100

London delft plate with border pattern, 8½in. diam., circa 1710-20. (Sotheby's) $345 £187

LONGTON HALL

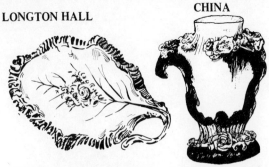

One of a pair of Longton Hall leaf-dishes, moulded as cabbage leaves, circa 1755, 9¼in. wide. (Sotheby's) $815 £440

One of a pair of early Longton Hall vases with double ogee bodies, 6¼in. high. (Sotheby's) $375 £198

Longton Hall blue and white teabowl and saucer, circa 1755. (Christie's) $855 £462

LOWESTOFT

Lowestoft blue and white dated birth-tablet, 1793, 7cm. diam. (Christie's) $2,250 £1,210

Small Lowestoft teapot and cover, circa 1770-80, 4in. high. (Sotheby's) $425 £231

Rare Lowestoft cylindrical tankard with scrolling handle, circa 1770-80, 4½in. high. (Sotheby's) $490 £264

LUDWIGSBURG

Ludwigsburg ornithological shaped circular plate, circa 1765, 23cm. diam. (Christie's) $430 £220

Ludwigsburg group of Haymakers from a set of the Months, 12.5cm. high, circa 1760-70. (Sotheby's)$1,585 £880

Ludwigsburg figure of a peasant, modelled by Adam Bauer, 11.5cm. high, circa 1760-70. (Sotheby's) $1,030 £572

CHINA

Ludwigsburg oval tea caddy with metal cover, circa 1770, 13.5cm. high. (Christie's) $335 £180

Ludwigsburg porcelain teapot, spherical shape tapering to base, circa 1775, 4¾in. high. (Robert W. Skinner Inc.) $875 £475

Ludwigsburg arched rectangular tea caddy with Ozier border, circa 1765, 12.5cm. high. (Christie's) $685 £370

Ludwigsburg figure of a fish seller modelled by J. J. Louis, circa 1770, 12.5cm. high.(Christie's) $740 £400

Ludwigsburg two-handled ecuelle, cover and stand with Ozier borders, circa 1765. (Christie's) $1,200 £650

Ludwigsburg figure of a huntsman with a dead deer, circa 1765, 16.5cm. high. (Christie's) $1,665 £900

Ludwigsburg figure of a butcher carrying meat on his shoulder, circa 1765, 11.5cm. high. (Christie's) $925 £500

Ludwigsburg group of fruit-pickers from a set of the Months, modelled by Adam Bauer, circa 1760-70, 13.5cm. high. (Sotheby's)$1,190 £660

Ludwigsburg figure of a dancer modelled by J. Nees & C. Fr. Riedel, circa 1765, 14.5cm. high. (Sotheby's) $715 £396

147

Pilkington's Royal Lancastrian lustre vase, painted by R. Joyce, 16cm. high. (Christie's) $275 £150

Large silver-resist lustre jug, decoration depicting fox hunting and hare coursing, 7½in. high. (Russell, Baldwin & Bright) $360 £200

Pilkington's Royal Lancastrian lustre vase, decorated by R. Joyce, 18cm. high. (Christie's) $330 £180

Lancastrian lustre vase of baluster form, decorated by R. Joyce, circa 1910, 9in. high. (Sotheby Beresford Adams) $335 £180

Royal Lancastrian lustre vase of globular shape, dated for 1912, 7¼in. high. (Sotheby Beresford Adams) $140 £75

Lancastrian lustre vase decorated by R. Joyce, circa 1910, 9in. high. (Sotheby Beresford Adams) $165 £90

Pilkington's Royal Lancastrian lustre waisted cylindrical vase, designed by Wm. S. Mycock, dated 1922, 19.5cm. high. (Christie's) $255 £140

Rare Lancastrian lustre alms dish painted by Charles Cundall, 1908, 22in. diam. (Sotheby's) $1,350 £715

Lancastrian lustre vase of slender ovoid form, circa 1912, 8in. high. (Sotheby Beresford Adams) $110 £60

148

Martinware terracotta gro-
tesque, signed, 1898, 32cm.
wide. (Phillips)
         $4,800 £2,500

Small Martinware
jug of flattened ovi-
form shape with loop
handle, signed, 9.5cm.
high. (Phillips)
      $275 £150

Martin Brothers stoneware
double-face jug with angular strap handle, 1911,
16.5cm. high. (Christie's)
      $825   £453

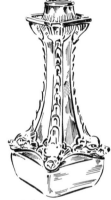

Martin Brothers vase with
tapered body, dated 1-
1900, 22.4cm. high.
(Sotheby's Belgravia)
         $775 £420

One of a pair of Martin
Bros. candlesticks, signed,
4-1902, 20.5cm. high.
(Phillips) $255 £140

Martinware vase of slen-
der oviform shape, with
tall cylindrical neck, signed, 24.75cm. high.
(Phillips) $255 £140

Small Martin Bros. vase
decorated in green and
brown with fish, signed,
10.5cm. high.(Phillips)
      $310 £170

Martinware terracotta gro-
tesque, signed, 1898, 27cm.
wide. (Phillips)
         $3,650 £1,900

Martin Bros. bird vase,
in the form of two birds
standing back to back,
24.2cm. high. (Sotheby,
King & Chasemore)
      $4,375 £2,500

149

Martin Brothers vase
with globular body,
dated 1-1891, 21.5cm.
high. (Sotheby's Bel-
gravia) $480 £260

Rare Martin Brothers figure
of a pike, by Wallace Martin,
circa 1890, 49.3cm. long.
(Sotheby, King & Chasemore)
$1,930 £1,050

Martin Brothers gourd
vase with ovoid body,
speckled in olive, dated
7-1904, 26.2cm. high.
(Sotheby's Belgravia)
$2,390 £1,300

Martin Brothers Art Pottery
bottle vase of twin-handled
ovoid form, 7½in. high.
(W. H. Lane & Son)
$245 £135

Martinware figure of a
bird with large talons,
signed on rim, 29cm.
high. (Phillips)
$5,370 £3,000

Martin Brothers jug with
ovoid body incised with
a goat's head, dated
1-1896, 26.3cm. high.
(Sotheby's Belgravia)
$955 £520

Martin Brothers Art Pottery
vase with flared rim and
narrow neck, circa 1899.
(Robert W. Skinner Inc.)
$275 £155

Martin Brothers stone-
ware bird with wide
beak, inscribed, 1906,
21.7cm. high.(Christie's)
$1,555 £850

One of a pair of Martin
Brothers gourd and
lobed shaped vases,
1901, 25.5cm. high.
(Christie's)
$3,085 £1,650

One of a pair of Martin Brothers gourd vases with hexagonal feet, dated 6-1904, 27cm. high. (Sotheby's Belgravia) $1,690 £920

Martin Brothers jardiniere with bell body, dated 3-1886, 21.8cm. high. (Sotheby's Belgravia) $955 £520

Martin Brothers oviform vase, body with five panels, 1900, 16cm. high. (Christie's) $535 £286

Unusual 'experimental' Martin Brothers flask, signed, 16cm. high. (Phillips) $70 £40

Martin Brothers stoneware bird in mottled russet glaze, inscribed, 22.5cm. high. (Christie's) $4,025 £2,200

Martinware jug incised with fish, 1886, 8½in. high. (Sotheby Beresford Adams) $740 £400

Martin Brothers ewer of flattened oviform with loop handle, 25cm. high. (Christie's) $905 £484

Rare Martin Brothers stoneware bird with long neck, incised, 41cm. high. (Christie's) $8,235 £4,500

Martin Brothers vase of tapering rectangular form, 29.1cm. high, 1900. (Christie's) $265 £143

151

MASON'S

Four-piece set of Mason's Ironstone toiletware of octagonal shape, with serpent handles. (Russell, Baldwin & Bright) $360 £200

Mid 19th century plate from a Mason's Ironstone part service of ten pieces. (Sotheby, King & Chasemore) $645 £360

MEISSEN

Meissen figure of a flower seller, by J. J. Kaendler, circa 1745, 20cm. high.(Sotheby's) $1,030 £572

Mid 18th century Meissen group 'The Impetuous Lover' by J. J. Kaendler, 16.5cm. (Sotheby's) $9,110 £5,060

Late 19th century Meissen vase painted with roses, incised E116, 39cm. high. (Sotheby's Belgravia) $575 £308

One of a pair of late 19th century Meissen cake-stands of three tiers, 33 and 32cm. high.(Sotheby's Belgravia) $1,810 £968

Late 19th century Meissen vase painted with sprays of flowers, 39.5cm. high. (Sotheby's Belgravia) $825 £440

Mid 19th century Meissen two-light candelabrum, chipped, 23cm. high. (Sotheby's Belgravia) $660 £352

Early Meissen tea caddy of hexagonal form with gilt grooved edges, 9.1cm. high, circa 1725-80. (Sotheby's) $1,625 £902

Rare Meissen sugar box and cover of stepped octagonal shape, 1723-24, 11.2cm. (Sotheby's) $9,900 £5,500

Meissen milk jug and cover with strawberry knop, 14cm., circa 1745. (Sotheby's) $1,090 £605

Meissen figure of a Harlequin by J. J. Kaendler, circa 1750, 12.5cm. high. (Sotheby's) $2,575 £1,430

One of two mid 18th century Meissen figures of Chinese boys, 25cm. high.(Sotheby's) $3,960 £2,200

Rare mid 18th century Meissen chinoiserie group with ormolu base, 39cm. high. (Sotheby's) $26,730 £14,850

Meissen group of a gardener and his companion, 15.5cm. high, circa 1750. (Sotheby's) $1,386 £770

One of a pair of Meissen figures of squirrels modelled by J. J. Kaendler, 21cm. high, circa 1760.(Sotheby's) $2,770 £1,540

Early 19th century Marcolini Meissen vase and cover, vertically fluted, 32cm. high.(Sotheby, King & Chasemore) $360 £200

19th century Meissen figure of a cockatoo by J. J. Kaendler, 23cm. high. (Sotheby, King & Chasemore) $180 £100

Meissen chinoiserie miniature globular teapot with scroll handle, circa 1730, 14.5cm. wide. (Christie's)$1,385 £750

Mid 18th century Meissen figure of a sheep, by Paul Reinicke, 10cm. high. (Sotheby, King & Chasemore)$810 £440

19th century Meissen figure of a swan by J. J. Kaendler, 30.5cm. high. (Sotheby, King & Chasemore) $535 £300

Late Meissen tete-a-tete of twelve pieces, crossed swords in blue. (Phillips) $2,590 £1,400

Rare Meissen Hausmalerei pipe bowl with silver mount and carved wood and antler stem. (Phillips)$775 £420

Late 19th century Meissen group of two sea nymphs and two putti, 31cm. high. (Sotheby, King & Chasemore) $895 £500

Early Meissen teabowl and saucer, painted with quatrelobed panels. (Phillips) $1,850 £1,000

Part of a late 19th century Meissen part coffee service of eighteen pieces. (Sotheby's) $2,495 £1,320

154

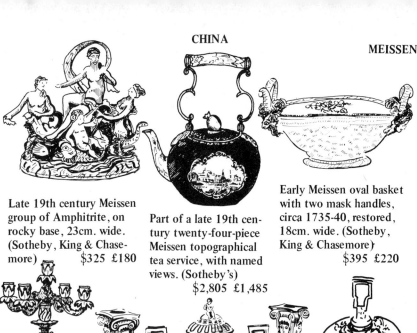

Late 19th century Meissen group of Amphitrite, on rocky base, 23cm. wide. (Sotheby, King & Chasemore) $325 £180

Part of a late 19th century twenty-four-piece Meissen topographical tea service, with named views. (Sotheby's)
$2,805 £1,485

Early Meissen oval basket with two mask handles, circa 1735-40, restored, 18cm. wide. (Sotheby, King & Chasemore)
$395 £220

One of a pair of late 19th century Meissen candelabra, 18¼in. high. (Sotheby's)
$1,495 £792

19th century three-piece Meissen garniture of an urn and two candlesticks. (Robert W. Skinner Inc.)
$600 £325

Late Meissen table bell. (Christie's S. Kensington)
$270 £140

Early Meissen teabowl and saucer, crossed swords in blue marks. (Phillips)
$960 £520

Pair of late 19th century Meissen figures, 7½in. high. (J. M. Welch & Son)
$530 £290

One of a set of twelve mid 19th century Meissen dessert plates, 21.5cm. diam. (Christie's) $1,120 £600

Meissen arched rectangular tea caddy and cover, borders edged with gilt, circa 1765, 12cm. high. (Christie's) $1,015 £550

Pair of late 19th century Meissen figures of girls, 11.8cm. high. (Sotheby's Belgravia) $790 £418

White Meissen figure of the 'Magic Lantern Carrier', by Kaendler & Reinicke, 15cm. high, circa 1745. (Sotheby, King & Chasemore) $405 £220

One of a set of eight Meissen plates in two sizes, circa 1880, decorated in underglaze blue. (Sotheby's Belgravia) $760 £420

Early 20th century Meissen porcelain urn on stand, 16½in. high. (Robert W. Skinner Inc.) $175 £95

Meissen tea bowl and saucer gilt with chinoiserie figure, birds and plants, circa 1730. (Christie's) $925 £500

Late 19th century Meissen group of two children and a dog, 10¼in. high. (Sotheby Beresford Adams) $795 £430

One of a pair of Meissen figures of prancing horses modelled by J. J. Kaendler, circa 1745, 20.5cm. wide. (Christie's) $1,015 £550

Late 19th century Meissen group of Europa and the Bull, 8¾in. high. (Sotheby Beresford Adams) $705 £380

Early 20th century
Meissen figure of a
shepherdess and
lamb, 24cm. high.
(Sotheby's Belgravia)
$290 £160

Meissen chinoiserie small
baluster teapot and cover
painted by Herold, 14cm.
wide. (Christie's)
$1,940 £1,050

Meissen chinoiserie hexa-
gonal baluster tea caddy
and silver gilt cover,
9.5cm. high. (Christie's)
$2,960 £1,600

Meissen chinoiserie hot
milk jug and cover pain-
ted by C. F. Herold,
circa 1725, 15cm. high.
(Christie's) $830 £450

One of a pair of Meissen
blue and white tea bowls
and saucers painted in
the manner of Ferner,
circa 1735. (Christie's)
$775 £420

Mid 18th century Meissen
swan service jug and cover,
by J. J. Kaendler, 17cm.
high. (Sotheby, King &
Chasemore)$2,140 £1,150

Meissen chinoiserie rect-
angular tea caddy painted
by C. F. Herold. (Christie's)
$1,850 £1,000

Meissen circular two-handled
tureen and cover with Ozier
borders, circa 1745, 32cm.
wide. (Christie's)
$1,295 £700

Mid 18th century later
decorated Meissen
group of dancers,
14cm. high. (Sotheby's
Belgravia) $305 £170

Meissen blue and white octagonal baluster tea caddy and cover, circa 1725-30, 9.5cm. high. (Christie's) $890 £480

Meissen brocade pattern circular butter tub and cover with pine cone finial, circa 1735, 12.5cm. wide. (Christie's) $2,960 £1,600

Meissen arched rectangular tea caddy and cover decorated with scrolls, shells and foliage, circa 1755, 12.5cm. high. (Christie's) $520 £280

Meissen group of apple pickers, 27cm. high, crossed sword mark. (Sotheby, King & Chasemore) $660 £360

Meissen figure of a Sultan riding an elephant, modelled by J. J. Kaendler, circa 1745, 28cm. wide. (Christie's) $27,750 £15,000

Meissen white figure of a goddess, circa 1741, 30.5cm. high. (Christie's) $405 £220

Meissen oviform jug with pewter mounts and hinged cover, circa 1759, 29cm. high. (Christie's) $925 £500

Meissen Grunes Watteau armorial plate painted in panels, circa 1741, 21cm. diam. (Christie's) $12,950 £7,000

Mid 18th century Meissen white glazed 'Commedia Dell'Arte' figure of Pantaloon, 12.5cm. high. (Sotheby, King & Chasemore) $835 £450

Meissen arched rectangu-
lar tea caddy and cover,
circa 1740-50, 13cm.
high. (Christie's)
$445 £240

Meissen figure of a recumbent sheep modelled by P.
J. Reinicke, circa 1750,
17cm. wide. (Christie's)
$260 £140

Meissen arched rectangu-
lar tea caddy and cover,
stippled with cupids,
circa 1755, 11cm. high.
(Christie's) $520 £280

Meissen figure of a Pan-
dur modelled by J. J.
Kaendler, circa 1750,
23cm. high. (Christie's)
$4,810 £2,600

Meissen pot pourri vase
and cover with loop han-
dles. (Sotheby, King &
Chasemore) $365 £200

Meissen group of three putti
emblematic of the Liberal
Arts, circa 1760, 30cm. high.
(Christie's) $405 £220

Meissen baluster coffee
pot and cover with knob
finial, circa 1770,
24.5cm. high.(Christie's)
$370 £200

Meissen crinoline group of
the gout sufferer, modelled
by J. J. Kaendler, circa 1742,
19.5cm. wide. (Christie's)
$18,500 £10,000

Meissen rococo scent
flask with silver mount
and stopper, circa
1750, 13.5cm. high.
(Christie's)$645 £350

159

METTLACH

Mettlach earthenware vase, tapering at base and neck, circa 1905, 25.25cm. high.(Sotheby's Belgravia) $445 £250

One of a pair of Mettlach plaques, signed J. Stahl, 18¼in. diam. (Sotheby Beresford Adams) $945 £510

Mettlach stein with tapering cylindrical body, circa 1910, 22.8cm. high, cover with pewter hinge.(Sotheby's Belgravia) $430 £231

Mettlach flagon of two litres, Germany, 1909, with pewter thumbpiece, 14¾in. high. (Robert W. Skinner Inc.)$525 £275

One of a pair of Mettlach vases decorated with classical maidens, 34.5cm. high, circa 1910. (Sotheby's Belgravia) $515 £275

Large Mettlach ewer decorated with central frieze, 46cm. high, circa 1900. (Sotheby's Belgravia) $370 £198

MING

Late Ming blue and white 'kraak porselein' dish with eight panels, Wanli period, 35.5cm. diam. (Christie's) $580 £324

Late Ming/early Qing dynasty figures of Buddhistic lions in deep aubergine glaze, 19cm. high. (Christie's) $485 £270

Early 17th century Ming blue and white 'kraak porselein' dish, 36.5cm. diam. (Christie's) $345 £194

Late Ming blue and white 'kraak porselein' dish of Wanli period, 50cm. diam.(Christie's) $2,015 £1,045

Late Ming blue and white box of slender rectangular form, 33cm. long. (Sotheby's) $1,540 £825

Late Ming blue and white broad oviform jar, Wanli, 12.5cm. high. (Christie's) $575 £320

Ming dynasty Cizhou type slender vase painted in brown on white ground, 57.5cm. high. (Christie's)$1,080 £600

One of two late Ming blue and white foliate dishes decorated with hares, 12.5cm. diam. (Christie's) $430 £220

Late Ming dynasty carved jade ewer and cover with pear-shaped body, 21.3cm. high.(Sotheby's) $6,580 £3,520

One of a pair of Ming dynasty tilemaker's pottery figures of mounted warriors, 33cm. high.(Christie's) $1,440 £800

Rare Ming Wucai box of square section, 13.2cm., with wood cover and stand. (Sotheby's) $5,760 £3,308

Early 17th century Ming blue and white octagonal baluster jar with short neck, 21.5cm. high. (Christie's)$380 £210

Minton pate-sur-pate plate with pierced border, 23cm. diam., dated for 1902. (Phillips) $590 £320

One of a pair of Minton secessionist candlesticks with two loop handles, circa 1889, 52cm. high. (Christie's) $880 £480

One of ten rare Minton tiles from the Elfin series, 15.5cm. square. (Phillips) $205 £115

Unusual Minton's model of a puma covered in ruby-red glaze, 16cm. high. (Phillips) $130 £70

Minton 'Dresden New Vase' and cover of campana form, circa 1840, 45cm. high. (Sotheby's Belgravia) $1,330 £715

Rare Minton 'malachite' ewer with loop handle, 35cm. high, dated for 1862. (Sotheby's Belgravia) $265 £143

One of a pair of Minton vases and covers in Sevres style, 12¼in. high, circa 1850. (Sotheby's) $730 £385

Minton 'globe pot-pourri' vase, cover and stand, painted with a scene of Hereford, circa 1825-30, 24.5cm. high. (Sotheby's Belgravia) $615 £330

One of a pair of Minton vases with elephant's head and ring handles, dated for 1875, 42cm. high. (Sotheby's Belgravia) $450 £242

Moorcroft Hazledene
biscuit jar and cover
painted in Moonlit
Blue pattern, 17cm.
high. (Christie's)
$330 £176

Moorcroft punch bowl with
rolled foot, circa 1911,
14½in. wide, slightly damaged. (Robert W. Skinner Inc.)
$250 £140

Unusual Moorcroft
vase with lightly ribbed
body, circa 1935, 31cm.
high. (Sotheby's
Belgravia) $495 £270

Moorcroft slender balu-
ster vase, signed, 1914,
30.5cm. high, painted
in Claremont pattern.
(Christie's)$475 £260

One of a pair of Moorcroft
Macintyre vases with gilt
details and high loop handles, circa 1900, 12.5cm.
high. (Sotheby's Belgravia)
$590 £320

One of a pair of Moor-
croft Macintyre Florian-
ware vases of double
gourd shape, signed,
28cm. high. (Phillips)
$320 £180

Moorcroft Art Pottery
vase in red brown flo-
ral motif, signed and
dated, circa 1911,
11¾in. high. (Robert
W. Skinner Inc.)
$450 £255

Moorcroft loving cup of
broad cylindrical shape,
flaring at rim, signed, 19cm.
high. (Phillips) $215 £120

One of a pair of William
Moorcroft vases, signed
and numbered, 12in.
high. (Geering & Colyer)
$505 £270

163

NANTGARW

Stand from a pair of Nantgarw London-decorated sauce tureens, covers and stands, circa 1820, 19cm. wide.(Christie's) $10,275 £5,616

Nantgarw shaped oval centre dish from the Mackintosh service, circa 1820, 35.5cm. wide. (Christie's)$1,730 £935

Nantgarw lobed oval dish painted with flower sprays, 1817-20, 29.5cm. wide. (Christie's) $1,015 £550

NYMPHENBURG

Nymphenburg figure of a Chinese archer modelled by Franz Anton Bustelli, circa 1765, 21.5cm. high.(Christie's) $4,810 £2,600

Nymphenburg figure of Anselmo or L'Abbe, modelled by Franz Anton Bustelli, circa 1760, 20cm. high. (Christie's) $11,100 £6,000

Rare Nymphenburg nightlight in the shape of a jug, 19cm. high, circa 1765.(Sotheby's) $1,585 £880

Nymphenburg teacup and saucer with gilt and iron-red scrollwork borders, 1755-65. (Sotheby's) $1,095 £609

One of a pair of Nymphenburg white equestrian figures, 8½in. high. (Coles, Knapp & Kennedy) $270 £150

Nymphenburg snuff box with shaped oval body moulded with basketwork, circa 1755-65, 6.5cm. wide. (Sotheby's) $845 £462

One of a pair of Oriental pottery ducks, standing on rocks. (Honiton Galleries) $105 £55

Transitional Jiajing blue and white bowl of hemispherical form, 14.3cm. diam.(Sotheby, King & Chasemore)$610 £340

One of a pair of large Oriental decorated pot pourri vases and covers, on padouk stands. (Gilbert Baitson) $320 £170

Late 16th/early 17th century Swatow polychrome truncated jar, 23cm. high. (Sotheby, King & Chasemore) $295 £160

Sang-de-boeuf vase of baluster form and square section, 30.5cm. high. (Sotheby's Belgravia) $645 £352

One of a pair of modern blue and white garden seats, one cracked, 48cm. high. (Sotheby's Belgravia) $525 £286

Transitional blue and white oviform vase, 17.2cm. high.(Sotheby, King & Chasemore) $860 £480

One of a pair of 18th century clobbered blue and white tureens, covers and stands, 33cm. wide. (Sotheby's Belgravia) $965 £528

19th century Chinese Oriental porcelain bottle with bulbous body and slender neck, 11in. high. (Robert W. Skinner Inc.) $50 £25

165

Paris bowl decorated in gilt with birds and flowers, 6½in. diam. (Burrows & Day) $3,740 £2,000

Rare Paris veilleuse modelled as an 18th century woman, torso detaching to form a teapot, circa 1840, 35cm. high. (Sotheby's Belgravia) $700 £374

Mid to late 19th century Paris oval dish with bleu-celeste-ground, 63cm. wide. (Sotheby's Belgravia) $740 £396

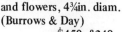

Paris baluster chocolate pot with domed lid and gilt metal thumbpiece, 6½in. high. (Burrows & Day) $7,480 £4,000

Paris Napoleon portrait coffee can and saucer, circa 1805, saucer repaired. (Sotheby's) $790 £440

One of two Paris jardinieres painted with birds and flowers, 4¾in. diam. (Burrows & Day)

$450 £240

PLYMOUTH

One of a pair of Plymouth white figures of seated musicians, 1768-70, 14cm. and 15.5cm. high. (Christie's) $820 £440

Plymouth sauceboat with ribbed scroll handle, circa 1770, 14cm. wide. (Christie's) $1,585 £858

Important Plymouth figure of 'Winter' in the form of a naked boy with a robe, in mint condition. (W. H. Lane & Son) $755 £420

'The Trysting Place' a small lid with plain margin. (Sotheby's Belgravia) $185 £88

Large pot lid showing the Exhibitions Buildings, 1851. (Sotheby's Belgravia) $165 £88

'Bear Hunting' a small pot lid with retailer's inscription and gilt line border. (Sotheby's Belgravia) $325 £176

Large pot lid showing Pegwell Bay, by S. Banger Shrimp Sauce Manufacturer. (Sotheby's Belgravia) $355 £198

Small pot lid 'Bears at School', with base. (Sotheby's Belgravia) $110 £60

Small lid with well-defined print of Bear, Lion and Cock, with base. (Sotheby's Belgravia) $120 £66

Rare medium pot lid 'The Tower of London', in good condition. (Sotheby's Belgravia) $635 £352

'Shooting Bears', a small lid with a clear pring and plain border. (Sotheby's Belgravia) $150 £82

'Shooting Bears' a small pot lid in good condition, with base. (Sotheby's Belgravia) $110 £60

Unusual Prattware figure of Lucretia, lying on a couch, circa 1790, 11in. long. (Sotheby's) $460 £253

Late 18th century Prattware Toby jug, shaped base with brown line-border, 9½in. high. (Sotheby's) $405 £230

Comport from an eleven-piece Prattware part dessert service printed with Tyrolean views. (Sotheby's) $355 £198

Rare late 18th/early 19th century 'Collier' Toby jug with Prattware style colours, 10¼in. high. (Sotheby's) $675 £374

Prattware teapot and cover modelled as a lady in a chair, circa 1785-90, 8¾in. high. (Sotheby's) $715 £396

One of a pair of pot-pourri vases and covers of baluster form, circa 1865, 70cm. high. (Sotheby's Belgravia) $820 £440

Late 18th century Prattware Toby jug, toper seated and holding a tankard of ale, 9½in. high. (Sotheby's) $515 £286

Early 19th century rare Prattware cradle of oval form, 30.5cm. long, cracked. (Sotheby, King & Chasemore) $750 £420

Late 18th/early 19th century Prattware Toby jug in traditional style, 9½in. high, hat restored.(Sotheby's) $440 £242

Early Qianlong famille rose dish painted with a lady beneath a tree, 37cm. diam.(Christie's) $680 £352

One of four Qianlong famille rose deep wine cups, 1776, 6.5cm. diam. (Christie's) $505 £280

Qianlong famille rose deep dish painted with a lady and two small boys, 37.5cm. diam. (Christie's)$805 £418

19th century Qianlong blue and white octagonal vase, 47cm. high. (Sotheby, King & Chasemore)$890 £480

Qianlong famille rose oblong twelve-sided tureen and cover, 34cm. wide.(Christie's) $1,260 £700

Qianlong blue and white ewer with long strap handle, 33.3cm. high. (Sotheby's) $9,255 £4,950

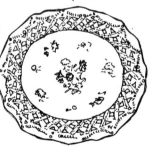

Qianlong blue and white deep dish with complex brocade border, 37.7cm. diam. (Sotheby, King & Chasemore) $230 £130

One of a pair of Qianlong ormolu mounted famille rose beaker vases, 40cm. high. (Christie's) $1,350 £750

One of a set of four late Qianlong Companies-des-Indes dishes of shaped oval form, 23.3cm. wide. (Sotheby, King & Chasemore) $1,110 £620

169

Early earthenware bowl by Lucie Rie, 17cm. diam., dated 1931. (Phillips) $715 £400

Lucie Rie porcelain vase with cylindrical neck and flared rim, 24.8cm. high. (Christie's) $1,100 £600

Lucie Rie porcelain bowl with mustard lime-green glaze, circa 1968, 21.2cm. diam. (Christie's) $640 £350

Early Lucie Rie porcelain deep bowl with crossed linear decoration, circa 1957, 20.8cm. diam. (Christie's) $375 £205

Lucie Rie stoneware bulbous bottle with narrow flattened neck and flared rim, 1979, 30cm. high. (Christie's) $3,145 £1,728

Lucie Rie porcelain bowl with slightly flattened sides, exterior in dark copper manganese, 14.5cm. wide. (Christie's) $255 £140

Lucie Rie porcelain shallow conical bowl with two concentric bands, 17cm. diam. (Christie's) $880 £480

Early Lucie Rie earthenware vase of slightly flared form, 1932, damaged, 19.7cm. high. (Christie's) $1,005 £550

Lucie Rie porcelain bowl on cylindrical foot, signed, 25.2cm. diam. (Christie's) $1,645 £900

Rockingham leaf-moulded basket with overhead twig handle, circa 1830-35, 9in. wide. (Sotheby's)
$635 £352

Stand from a twenty-nine-piece Rockingham dessert service, circa 1826-30. (Sotheby's)$2,800 £1,600

Very rare Rockingham fox mask stirrup cup in plain white glaze, 11.5cm. long. (H. Spencer & Sons Ltd.)
$505 £280

One of a pair of Rockingham two-handled vases with flared rims, 4in. high. (Burrows & Day)
$75 £42

Part of a Rockingham tea and coffee service of forty-two pieces, early 19th century. (Sotheby Beresford Adams)
$925 £500

Rockingham table napkin ring, unmarked, decorated with flowers. (Burrows & Day)
$12 £7

Rockingham violeteer of teapot form, circa 1831-42, 2¾in. wide. (Sotheby's) $775 £418

Rare early 19th century Rockingham group of a shepherdess and a sheep, 7in. high.(Sotheby Beresford Adams) $815 £440

Superb Rockingham rococo-shaped porcelain teapot and cover, circa 1830. (John Hogbin & Son)
$105 £55

171

ROOKWOOD

Rookwood pottery iris glaze vase, Ohio, circa 1908, 10½in. high, cracked. (Robert W. Skinner Inc.) $475 £260

Rookwood sterling overlay standard glaze jardiniere, Ohio, circa 1907, 5½in. high. (Robert W. Skinner Inc.) $1,500 £845

Rookwood pottery vellum glaze plaque, Ohio, circa 1919, 8¾in. high. (Robert. W. Skinner Inc.)
$1,600 £905

Rookwood scenic vellum glaze vase, Ohio, circa 1919, 14½in. high. (Robert W. Skinner Inc.)
$1,300 £735

Rookwood bisque Spanish water jug, Ohio, circa 1883, 9½in. high. (Robert W. Skinner Inc.) $1,250 £705

Rookwood pottery iris glaze jar, Ohio, circa 1914, probably by Sara Alice Toohey, 7in. high. (Robert W. Skinner Inc.)
$400 £225

Rookwood pottery ewer in sage green clay, Ohio, 1900, 8½in. high. (Robert W. Skinner Inc.)
$425 £235

Rookwood standard glaze vase, signed A. R. Valentien, circa 1897, 11½in. high. (Robert W. Skinner Inc.)
$1,050 £585

Rookwood pottery standard glaze mug, signed for Kataro Shirayamadani, circa 1887. (Robert W. Skinner Inc.)$550 £310

Rosenberg 'eggshell' porcelain cup and saucer by Samuel Schellink, 1903. (Christie's) $825 £450

Rosenberg 'eggshell' bowl and cover, decorated by Roelof Sterken, 12cm. high, 1901. (Sotheby's Belgravia) $410 £230

Rosenberg 'eggshell' vase with basket handle. (Bonham's)$1,410 £800

Rosenberg 'eggshell' porcelain two-handled vase, 1904, 24.5cm. high. (Christie's)$1,830 £1,000

Rosenberg 'eggshell' beaker and saucer, decorated by Sam Schellink, 1904. (Sotheby's Belgravia) $320 £180

Rosenberg 'eggshell' vase decorated by Sam Schellink, 1908, 22.5cm. high, with flared neck. (Sotheby's Belgravia)$260 £143

Rosenberg 'eggshell' vase, decorated by R. Sterken, 1903, 10cm. high.(Sotheby's Belgravia)$320 £176

Rosenberg 'eggshell' vase, decorated by Sam Schellink, 1904, 21.5cm. high. (Sotheby's Belgravia) $1,880 £990

Rosenberg 'eggshell' vase decorated by Sam Schellink, 1904, 34cm. high. (Sotheby's Belgravia) $1,440 £792

Late 19th century Royal Dux céntrepiece with figurine, 12¼in. high. (Robert W. Skinner Inc.) $225 £125

Royal Dux camel group, applied pink triangle, circa 1910, 45.5cm. high. (Sotheby's Belgravia) $780 £418

Royal Dux figure group of a family, circa 1880, 25in. high. (Robert W. Skinner Inc.)$375 £210

Royal Dux earthenware mirror, circa 1900, 54.5cm. high, with scoop dish below. (Sotheby's Belgravia) $800 £440

Royal Dux figure of a boy at a spring filling pitchers, circa 1880, 24in. high. (Robert W. Skinner Inc.)$300 £165

20th century Royal Dux mirror frame, 53cm. high, applied and impressed pink triangle. (Sotheby's Belgravia) $615 £330

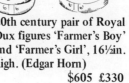

20th century Royal Dux figure of a Turkish street vendor, one of a pair, 50.5cm. high. (Sotheby's Belgravia) $985 £528

20th century pair of Royal Dux figures 'Farmer's Boy' and 'Farmer's Girl', 16½in. high. (Edgar Horn) $605 £330

Royal Dux figure of a naked girl on a stool, circa 1920, 14½in. high. (Sotheby's) $290 £154

CHINA

Ruskin high-fired porcelain vase of baluster form, dated 1928, 36cm. high. (Phillips) $550 £300

Ruskin 'high-fired' porcelain shallow bowl and stand, 26cm. diam. (Phillips) $385 £200

Ruskin high-fired porcelain vase, impressed 'Ruskin, England', 36cm. high. (Phillips) $730 £400

RUSSIAN

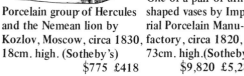

Biscuit group of a mother and child by Gardner, Moscow, circa 1880-90, 23.5cm. high. (Sotheby's) $550 £297

Biscuit group of a laundress and child by Gardner, Moscow, circa 1880-90, 11cm. high.(Sotheby's) $655 £352

Biscuit group of a woman playing blindman's buff, by Gardner, Moscow, circa 1880-90, 24.5cm. high. (Sotheby's)$410 £220

Porcelain group of Hercules and the Nemean lion by Kozlov, Moscow, circa 1830, 18cm. high. (Sotheby's) $775 £418

One of a pair of urn-shaped vases by Imperial Porcelain Manufactory, circa 1820, 73cm. high.(Sotheby's) $9,820 £5,280

Biscuit figure of a man playing an accordion by Gardner, Moscow, circa 1880-90, 18cm. high. (Sotheby's) $655 £352

175

One of a pair of Samson nodding mandarins, late 19th century, slightly damaged. (Sotheby's Belgravia) $1,070 £572

One of a pair of late 19th century ormolu mounted Samson 'Meissen' figures of a Shepherd and Shepherdess, 15.8cm. high. (Sotheby's Belgravia) $535 £286

Late 19th century Samson group of putti celebrating the harvest, 36cm. high. (Sotheby's Belgravia) $865 £462

Late 19th century Samson famille rose vase, one of a pair, on wood stands, 29cm. high. (Sotheby's Belgravia) $1,005 £550

Late 19th century Samson tete-a-tete, tray 26.5cm. wide. (Sotheby's Belgravia)$325 £180

Large Samson vase and cover painted in famille verte, 1870's, 60cm. high. (Sotheby's Belgravia) $2,800 £1,452

Samson 'Chelsea' group modelled as Diana bathing in a stream, circa 1880, 38cm. high. (Sotheby's Belgravia) $455 £242

Samson 'Meissen' comport and stand in the shape of an elephant carrying a basket, circa 1880, 35.5cm. wide. (Sotheby's Belgravia) $1,030 £550

One of a pair of late 19th century Samson 'Derby' candlesticks, 26cm. high, chipped.(Sotheby's Belgravia) $660 £352

One of a pair of Satsuma vases of tapering square section, circa 1900, 38.5cm. high. (Sotheby, King & Chasemore) $445 £250

Late 19th century Japanese Satsuma plate, signed, 8¾in. diam. (Robert W. Skinner Inc.) $300 £160

Large Satsuma koro and cover on three oni supports, 21in. high, slightly damaged. (Lawrence Fine Art) $905 £480

Late 19th century Japanese Satsuma vase of baluster form, 12in. high. (Robert W. Skinner Inc.) $800 £430

Late 19th century barrel-shaped Satsuma vase, 59cm. high, slightly cracked. (Sotheby, King & Chasemore) $145 £80

One of a pair of early 20th century Japanese Satsuma vases with wide necks, 15½in. high. (Robert W. Skinner Inc.) $600 £325

Late 19th century Japanese Ko-Satsuma vase, signed Koto-Togiki Gaisha, 12¼in. high. (Robert W. Skinner Inc.) $1,300 £705

Late 19th century Satsuma figure of a crane with head back, 34.5cm. high. (Sotheby, King & Chasemore) $205 £115

19th century Japanese Satsuma pottery vase with embossed decoration, 12¾in. high. (Robert W. Skinner Inc.) $150 £80

Sevres deep green-ground eventail jardiniere, painted by Charles Tandart, 1756-60, 28.5cm. wide. (Christie's) $5,605 £2,860

Unusual champleve mounted Sevres dish painted and gilt by Hete, signed, circa 1900, 22.5cm. diam.(Sotheby's Belgravia) $215 £120

Sevres bleu-celeste-ground ice pail and cover, painted with scenes of lovers after Watteau, 25cm. high. (Sotheby, King & Chasemore) $730 £400

Rare Sevres shaped circular plate from the service made for Catherine the Great, 23.5cm. diam., dated for 1782. (Christie's) $3,700 £2,000

One of a pair of Sevres pattern blue-ground ormolu mounted vases, 48.5cm. high. (Christie's) $1,725 £918

Sevres rose pompadour cup and saucer painted with flowers, dated for 1757. (Christie's) $1,200 £650

One of a pair of ormolu and Sevres porcelain vases of Louis XVI design, 20½in. high. (Christie's) $2,760 £1,500

Sevres hexafoil two-handled seau a verre from the Du Barry service, 16.5cm. wide. (Christie's) $705 £380

Late 18th century Sevres urn of footed baluster form, 17in. high. (Robert W. Skinner Inc.) $1,000 £545

178

Sevres salad bowl with lobed and shaped border, dated for 1759, 9¼in. diam. (Lawrence Fine Art) $455 £240

Sevres pink-ground cylindrical miniature teapot and cover, circa 1775, 9.5cm. high. (Christie's) $240 £130

Sevres oval jardiniere of lobed outline, 1759, 9in. wide, painted with flowers. (Lawrence Fine Art) $550 £290

Sevres pear-shaped cream jug painted with exotic birds, circa 1755, 10cm. high. (Christie's) $260 £140

One of a pair of Sevres pattern blue-ground ormolu mounted two-handled vases, 42cm. high. (Christie's) $610 £324

Sevres coffee cup and saucer with paintings of landscapes and birds, circa 1760. (Christie's) $175 £95

One of a pair of large Sevres vases and covers, circa 1860, one knop glued, 49cm. high. (Sotheby, King & Chasemore) $1,465 £820

One of a pair of Sevres green-ground shaped rectangular jardinieres, 19.5cm. wide. (Christie's) $5,605 £2,860

One of a pair of Sevres metal mounted vases, late 19th century, 15¾in. high. (Sotheby's) $435 £231

Part of a Spode's 'New Stone' part dinner service decorated in Imari palette, with gilding. (Christie's) $6,290 £3,400

Tureen from a Spode 'New Stone' dinner service, circa 1820. (Sotheby's) $2,645 £1,430

Spode 'New Stone' blue and white part dinner service decorated in Oriental style. (Christie's) $3,450 £1,836

Spode's Imperial covered teapot with gadrooned and leaf mouldings, circa 1810. (John Hogbin & Son) $35 £20

Plate from a Spode part dessert service painted with flowers and shrubs, circa 1820.(Christie's) $2,570 £1,404

Teapot from an early 19th century Spode tea service of thirty-three pieces. (Sotheby Beresford Adams) $405 £220

Rare pair of figures of a stag and hind at lodge, circa 1750-55, 17cm. wide. (Sotheby, King & Chasemore) $930 £500

Staffordshire white salt-glaze 'house' teapot and cover, circa 1740-50, 6¼in. high.(Sotheby's)
$650 £352

Early 19th century Staffordshire hound's head stirrup cup, 5½in. wide. (Sotheby's)
$175 £99

Very rare complete set of First World War pottery Toby jugs by Wilkinsons Ltd. (Locke & England)$2,865 £1,600

18th century Staffordshire slipware dish with dark-brown-ground, 43.5cm. wide.(Sotheby, King & Chasemore)
$1,040 £580

Staffordshire saltglaze shaped oval dish, circa 1755, 31.5cm. wide. (Christie's)$1,525 £825

Rare pair of Thomas Parr equestrian figures of the Prince and Princess of Wales, circa 1862, 19.5cm. high. (Sotheby, King & Chasemore)
$840 £450

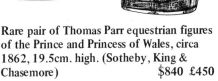

Staffordshire figurine of
Jumbo, large moulded
elephant, 10¾in. high.
(Robert W. Skinner Inc.)
$300 £165

Pair of unusual 19th century Staffordshire
commemorative jugs, 6½in. and 5¾in. high,
slightly chipped. (W. H. Lane & Son)
$795 £420

18th century Staffordshire
slipware dish, 13¼in. diam.
(Sotheby's) $1,320 £715

Staffordshire saltglaze
pectin-shell moulded
teapot and cover with
loop handle, circa 1755,
15.5cm. wide.(Christie's)
$610 £330

Staffordshire slipware dish
by William Simpson, circa
1700, 34cm. diam.
(Christie's) $6,545 £3,520

Pair of late 18th/early 19th century Staffordshire figures of a lion and lioness, 8¼in. and
8in. (Sotheby's) $1,180 £638

Staffordshire pottery group,
circa 1820, 20cm. high.
(Sotheby, King & Chasemore)
$670 £360

Staffordshire washbowl and jug showing Lafayette at Franklin's tomb, circa 1825, 12in. diam. (Robert W. Skinner Inc.)
$900 £490

Staffordshire saltglaze polychrome teapot and cover, with crabstock handle, circa 1755, 20.5cm. wide. (Christie's) $1,015 £550

19th century Staffordshire 'barge' teapot, 13in. high. (J. M. Welch & Son)
$165 £90

Pair of Staffordshire pottery figures of The Cobbler and his Wife, restored. (Honiton Galleries) $60 £32

One of a pair of Staffordshire furniture rests, late 18th/early 19th century, 6in. high. (Sotheby's)
$205 £110

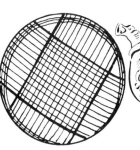

Two of a set of thirteen mid 19th century Staffordshire carpet bowls. (Sotheby's Belgravia) $490 £264

Staffordshire white salt-glaze 'house' teapot and cover, 4½in. high, circa 1740-50. (Sotheby's)
$570 £308

Staffordshire covered vegetable dish with high domed cover, circa 1825, 12¼in. long. (Robert W. Skinner Inc.) $750 £410

Obadiah Sherratt group 'The Red Barn', 8½in. high. (Edwards, Bigwood & Bewlay) $1,500 £820

Staffordshire pottery box and cover in the form of a tortoise, circa 1820, 13cm. wide. (Sotheby, King & Chasemore) $355 £190

Staffordshire pottery figure of C. H. Spurgeon in straight-sided pulpit, 12in. high. (Russell, Baldwin & Bright) $65 £35

Very rare pair of Staffordshire equestrian figures of Gholab and Ranbir Singh, circa 1846, 22cm. high. (Sotheby, King & Chasemore) $520 £280

Staffordshire pottery figure of John Wesley in scroll-edged pulpit, 11in. high. (Russell, Baldwin & Bright) $115 £65

Staffordshire solid agate model of a cat, circa 1740-50, 4¾in. high. (Sotheby's) $705 £380

Large Staffordshire coffee pot, circa 1825, 11in. high, with C-scrolled handle. (Robert W. Skinner Inc.) $800 £435

Early 19th century Staffordshire pearlware watch stand, 23.2cm. high. (Sotheby, King & Chasemore) $355 £190

Large Staffordshire platter with wide floral border, circa 1825, 19in. wide. (Robert W. Skinner Inc.) $375 £205

Staffordshire pastille burner in the form of a rustic cottage, 7in. high. (Edwards, Bigwood & Bewlay)$455 £250

Early 19th century Staffordshire pearlware pointer by Wood & Caldwell, 11.5cm. wide. (Sotheby, King & Chasemore) $120 £65

Staffordshire equestrian figure of Sir Robert Peel, circa 1850, 31.5cm. high. (Sotheby, King & Chasemore) $560 £300

Staffordshire pottery group of a family, circa 1820, 20cm. high. (Sotheby, King & Chasemore) $670 £360

Rare Staffordshire equestrian figure of Lady Godiva, circa 1870, 25.5cm. high.(Sotheby, King & Chasemore)$855 £460

Two Staffordshire portrait figures of Queen Victoria and Prince Albert, 18in. high. (Edwards, Bigwood & Bewlay) $730 £400

Staffordshire group of the elephant of Siam and Mr Hemming as Prince Almansor, 15.7cm. high, circa 1840-50. (Sotheby, King & Chasemore) $315 £170

Rare Staffordshire porcelain figure of Van Amburgh, 15.5cm. high. (Sotheby, King & Chasemore) $2,945 £1,600

185

Henry Hammond stoneware bowl with flared body, circa 1977, 22cm. diam. (Sotheby's Belgravia) $175 £100

Rare dated German stoneware tankard, probably Creussen, 1654, 12.5cm. diam. (Sotheby's) $6,040 £3,300

Rare Reginald Wells stoneware model of a carthorse, 1930's, 14.5cm. wide. (Sotheby's Belgravia) $300 £170

Burgundian limestone relief of St. James and a donor, circa 1460, 19½in. high. (Sotheby's) $23,910 £12,650

Tall stoneware flagon with broad strap handle, stamped R. Merkelbach, Grenzhausen, 37.5cm. high.(Phillips) $430 £240

Unusual stoneware vase of hu form, 49cm. high, decorated with imitate bronze. (Sotheby's Belgravia) $1,445 £825

Small Tang dynasty stone head of Buddha, 10.8cm. high. (Sotheby's) $1,645 £880

18th century carved stone bust of Minerva, on black stone plinth, 5¾in. high. (Burrows & Day)$120 £65

Michael Cardew Wenford Bridge stoneware stool, 1970's, 30.8cm. diam. (Sotheby's Belgravia) $265 £150

Miniature Swansea taper-stick, circa 1814-22, 3in. high. (Sotheby's) $345 £187

One of a pair of Swansea creamware sauce tureens, covers and stands, 18.5cm. high. (Phillips) $1,665 £900

Swansea fluted oval two-handled centre dish, 35.5cm. wide.(Christie's) $4,475 £2,420

Circular Swansea dish, impressed mark, 23.5cm. diam. (Christie's) $1,425 £770

Swansea cabinet cup and saucer, painted by Wm. Pollard, circa 1820. (Sotheby, King & Chasemore) $1,210 £650

One of a pair of Swansea deep plates of lobed silver shape, 18.5cm. diam. (Phillips) $1,260 £680

Swansea plate decorated by William Pollard, circa 1820-22, 8¼in. diam. (Sotheby's) $570 £308

Swansea cabinet cup painted by Wm. Billingsley, circa 1820, 12.2cm. high. (Sotheby, King & Chasemore) $520 £280

One of a pair of Swansea square dishes, impressed marks, 24cm. wide. (Christie's)$4,070 £2,200

187

Small Tang dynasty chestnut glazed jar and cover on solid splayed foot, 17.1cm. high. (Sotheby's)$4,115 £2,000

Large Tang dynasty cream glazed figure of an unsaddled horse, 59cm.(Sotheby's) $26,740 £14,300

Sui/early Tang dynasty Changsha glazed stoneware vase and cover with cup-shaped mouth, 13.1cm. high.(Sotheby's) $2,880 £1,540

Marbled Tang dynasty pottery tray of circular shape, 13.4cm. diam. (Sotheby's)$2,880 £1,540

Tang dynasty Sancai pottery figure of a court dignitary on pierced plinth, 76cm. high.(Sotheby's) $5,140 £2,750

Tang dynasty glazed pottery figure of a lady, on wooden stand, 27.3cm. high. (Sotheby's) $2,675 £1,430

Tang dynasty glazed stoneware jar and cover in colourless glaze, 20.4cm. high. (Sotheby's) $3,700 £1,980

Tang dynasty glazed pottery figure of a groom, wood stand, 27.9cm. high. (Sotheby's) $1,235 £660

Small Tang dynasty splash glazed pottery jar with short waisted neck, 14cm. high. (Sotheby's) $9,875 £5,280

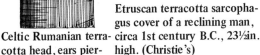

Celtic Rumanian terracotta head, ears pierced, circa 1st century B.C., 2¾in. high. (Christie's)$415 £220

Etruscan terracotta sarcophagus cover of a reclining man, circa 1st century B.C., 23½in. high. (Christie's)
$9,145 £4,840

Late 19th/early 20th century Austrian cold-painted terracotta figure of a negro street vendor, 31in. high. (Sotheby Beresford Adams)
$335 £180

18th century English terracotta bust of a girl on a marble plinth, 29cm. high. (Christie's) $635 £330

6th century B.C. Greek terracotta figure of a woman, neck repaired, 11in. high. (Robert W. Skinner Inc.)$175 £95

18th century Flemish terracotta group of two putti by Laurent Delvaux, 39.5cm. high. (Christie's)$5,490 £2,860

One of a pair of terracotta vases and stands with gadrooned bodies, circa 1900, 50in. high. (Sotheby's Belgravia)
$680 £370

Roman terracotta oscillum in the form of a theatre mask, circa 1st-2nd century A.D., 4¼in. high. (Christie's) $1,080 £572

Late 19th century Austrian cold-painted terracotta figure of a Arab street vendor, 38in. high. (Sotheby Beresford Adams) $225 £120

One of a set of six Tournai soup plates with moulded borders, 9¼in. diam. (Woolley & Wallis) $325 £180

Rare Tournai tankard, cover and saucer in the form of a hooped barrel, circa 1760, 13.5cm. high. (Sotheby, King & Chasemore) $3,130 £1,750

One of a pair of Tournai white figures of a boy and his companion, circa 1770, 14cm. high. (Christie's) $1,510 £770

One of a pair of Tournai pot-pourri vases and covers, mid 18th century, 25.5cm. high. (Sotheby's) $1,685 £935

Tournai spirally gadrooned shaped circular plate, circa 1765, 24cm. diam. (Christie's) $335 £180

Tournai white group of two boys collecting flowers, circa 1770, 18.5cm. high. (Christie's) $646 £330

Tournai spirally gadrooned soup plate painted in the manner of Lindemann, circa 1765, 24cm. diam. (Christie's) $1,295 £700

Tournai white group of a young woman and a pack horse, circa 1765, 13cm. high. (Christie's) $1,080 £550

Tournai lobed circular soup plate painted in the manner of Fidelle Duvivier, circa 1765, 24cm. diam. (Christie's) $705 £380

19th century Vienna porcelain cabinet plate with tooled gilt and blue border, 7¼in. diam. (Locke & England) $180 £100

Vienna Du Paquier tall slender beaker, probably by Carl Wendelin Anreiter von Zirnfeld, circa 1725. (Christie's) $1,295 £700

Early Vienna Du Paquier famille rose globular two-handled pot and cover, 1720-25, 22.5cm. high. (Christie's) $25,150 £19,000

Very rare figure of the Buddha, perhaps by Du Paquier, circa 1740, 13.25cm. high.(Christie's) $1,665 £900

Large Vienna Du Paquier lobed and fluted saucer dish painted in Imari style, circa 1730, 39.5cm. diam. (Christie's) $13,875 £7,500

Vienna Du Paquier beaker and saucer with silvered rims, circa 1730-35. (Christie's) $3,700 £2,000

Late 19th century Vienna plate with wavy ribbon border, 9½in. diam. (Sotheby Beresford Adams)$335 £180

One of a pair of early 19th century Vienna porcelain vases, 10½in. high. (W. H. Lane & Son) $690 £380

Vienna Du Paquier plate with lobed rim, circa 1730, 22cm. diam. (Christie's) $2,035 £1,100

Fine Viennese porcelain sixteen-piece cabaret set, signed Sibl, in mint condition. (Morphets) $4,230 £2,300

Part of a late 18th century seven-piece Vienna porcelain part service of a dish and six plates. (Wm. Doyle Galleries Inc.) $500 £265

VYSE

Glazed figure by Chas. Vyse, 'The Lavender Seller', signed and dated 1922, 8½in. high. (Geering & Colyer) $370 £200

Charles Vyse stoneware vase of compressed spherical form, incised 1934, 22cm. diam. (Christie's) $640 £350

Charles Vyse figure 'Market Day, Boulogne', 1931, 25cm. high. (Sotheby, King & Chasemore) $560 £300

Charles Vyse pottery figure of a flower seller, signed, 25cm. high. (Christie's)$535 £286

Rare Charles Vyse figure of a shire horse, circa 1920, 28.5cm. (Sotheby, King & Chasemore) $820 £440

Charles Vyse pottery figure 'The Madonna of World's End Passage', dated 1921, 23.5cm. high. (Phillips)$295 £160

192

Wedgwood Fairyland lustre bowl, printed in gilding, circa 1920, 9in. diam. (Sotheby's) **$580 £308**

Wedgwood & Bentley white jasper oval portrait medallion of Wm. Shakespeare, circa 1775, 8.5cm. high. (Christie's) **$610 £330**

Fairyland lustre chalice bowl on pedestal foot, 1920's, 10½in. diam. (Sotheby's)**$1,350 £715**

Wedgwood blue and white jasper oval desk set with central taperstick, circa 1790, 15cm. wide. (Christie's) **$650 £352**

Wedgwood blue and white oval medallion, circa 1800, 7cm. wide. (Christie's) **$140 £77**

Wedgwood three-colour jasper circular salt, marked Z. & H., circa 1790, 6.5cm. diam. (Christie's) **$735 £396**

Wedgwood creamware charger lustred in platinum by Louise Powell, 41.5cm. diam. (Christie's) **$365 £198**

Wedgwood blue and white jasper oviform scent bottle with cut glass stopper and gold mount, circa 1785, 9.5cm. high. (Christie's) **$815 £440**

Wedgwood & Bentley blue and white jasper circular plaque showing Medusa, circa 1780, 13cm. diam. (Christie's) **$935 £506**

193

Wedgwood Fairyland lustre bowl and cover. (Christie's S. Kensington) $695 £380

Mid 18th century Wedgwood basalt covered sugar bowl with two handles, 4¾in. diam. (Robert W. Skinner Inc.) $50 £25

Wedgwood Fairyland lustre vase of flaring square section, 19cm. high. (Phillips) $665 £360

One of a pair of Wedgwood and Bentley vases in black basaltes, circa 1775, 9½in. high. (Sotheby's) $3,460 £1,870

Wedgwood Fairyland lustre candlemas vase, 23cm. high. (H. Spencer & Sons Ltd.) $710 £380

Wedgwood and Bentley 'Porphyry' vase and cover, circa 1775, 15½in. high. (Sotheby's) $2,240 £1,210

Wedgwood 'Oriental' Fairyland lustre vase and cover, 9½in. high. (Morphets) $1,200 £650

Plate from a Wedgwood part dinner service of twenty-seven pieces, circa 1815-20. (Sotheby's) $1,535 £825

Wedgwood Fairyland lustre vase, early 1920's, 16½in. high. (Phillips) $2,170 £1,200

Wedgwood basalt covered bowl of spherical shape, silver encaustic borders, circa 1793, 4¼in. high. (Robert W. Skinner Inc.)　$50 £25

Tureen from a Wedgwood pottery dinner and dessert set of ninety-one pieces, circa 1883, signed.(Sotheby Beresford Adams)$390 £210

Wedgwood Fairyland lustre octagonal bowl, 22.5cm. high. (Phillips) $1,075 £580

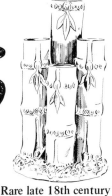

One of a pair of late 19th century Wedgwood blue jasper vases, 8½in. high. (Sotheby's) $610 £330

Wedgwood encaustic-decorated two-handled bell krater, circa 1820, 35cm. wide. (Christie's)　$2,045 £1,100

Rare late 18th century Wedgwood caneware quadruple bamboo flower vase, 10¾in. high. (Sotheby's) $1,525 £825

Wedgwood Fairyland lustre vase, of baluster form, circa 1920, 26cm. high. (Sotheby, King & Chasemore)　　$295 £160

Mid to late 19th century Wedgwood blue jasperware oval plaque, 39cm. wide. (Sotheby's Belgravia)　　$255 £140

One of a pair of Wedgwood Fairyland lustre vases of slender ovoid form, 1920's, 8in. high. (Sotheby Beresford Adams)$925 £500

CHINA

Wedgwood Fairyland lustre bowl, interior painted with the 'Woodland Bridge' pattern, 1920's, 28.5cm. diam. (Sotheby's Belgravia)
$1,145 £616

Wedgwood oviform pepper pot with pierced top, circa 1790, 6cm. high. (Christie's) $530 £286

Part of a late 18th century Wedgwood creamware dinner service, some pieces damaged. (Woolley & Wallis) $445 £250

Rare Wedgwood 'Queen's ware' argyle and cover, circa 1780-90, 6¼in. high. (Sotheby's) $630 £352

Wedgwood Fairyland lustre vase and cover, 28.8cm. high, 1920's. (Sotheby's Belgravia) $1,430 £770

Wedgwood Fairyland lustre octagonal bowl, 1920's, 22cm. wide. (Sotheby's Belgravia) $1,145 £616

Wedgwood Fairyland lustre bowl, 1920's, 9in. diam. (Sotheby's) $460 £242

Rare Wedgwood Fairyland lustre plaque decorated with the 'Bubbles' design, 29cm. wide, framed, 1920's. (Sotheby's Belgravia) $1,840 £990

Wedgwood creamware cruet painted by Emile Lessore, circa 1865, 22cm. high.(Christie's) $1,060 £572

Westerwald mug of cylindrical form with chequer pattern, 11cm. high. (Phillips)$260 £140

Mid 18th century Westerwald inkstand of rectangular shape, 19cm. wide. (Sotheby's) $530 £275

Large Westerwald jug of ovoid form, 31cm. high. (Phillips) $465 £250

Mid 17th century Westerwald pewter mounted jug, neck applied with lion's mask, 41cm. high. (Sotheby, King & Chasemore) $895 £500

Rare 18th century Westerwald part writing set modelled as lions, 17.7cm. high. (Sotheby's) $1,105 £605

Westerwald jug with flattened globular body, 1641, with replacement metal handle, 31.5cm. high.(Sotheby's) $1,880 £1,045

Late 18th century Westerwald stoneware jug applied with the monogram G.R., 25.5cm. high. (Sotheby, King & Chasemore) $250 £140

Rare 18th century Westerwald tankard, inscribed 'London', 18.5cm. high. (Sotheby's) $1,285 £715

Rare Westerwald pewter mounted humpen, circa 1650, 25cm. high. (Sotheby, King & Chasemore) $680 £380

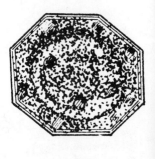

Whieldon oviform teapot and cover with crabstock spout and handle, circa 1755, 19cm. wide. (Christie's) $650 £352

Whieldon lobed globular bottle with garlic neck, circa 1760, 24.5cm. high. (Christie's) $1,260 £682

Mid 18th century Whieldon creamware pot with tortoiseshell glaze, slightly damaged, 4in. high. (Robert W. Skinner Inc.) $175 £95

Whieldon model of a ram lying on a grassy base, circa 1760-70, 5½in. wide. (Sotheby's) $1,065 £572

Rare mid 18th century Whieldon type bust of a man, covered with a grey, ochre and manganese glaze, 5¼in. high. (Sotheby's)$1,085 £605

Whieldon octagonal plate in tortoiseshell sponged decoration, 9in. (Edwards, Bigwood & Bewlay) $175 £95

Whieldon teapot and cover with crabstock handle, decorated in tortoiseshell glaze, 4½in. high. (Edwards, Bigwood & Bewlay) $385 £210

Mid 18th century Whieldon model of a swan, 3½in. high, slightly chipped. (Sotheby's) $700 £400

Small Whieldon teapot and cover with crabstock handle and spout, circa 1770, 6½in. diam. (Sotheby's) $470 £253

WOOD

Late 18th century model of a squirrel in the style of Ralph Wood. (Sotheby's) $875 £450

Ralph Wood or Prattware 'Fox and Swan' sauceboat, circa 1770, 6¾in. long. (Sotheby's) $490 £264

Ralph Wood Toby jug of traditional type, circa 1770-80, 9in. high, hat restored. (Sotheby's)$635 £352

Ralph Wood Toby jug, seated, wearing a reddish-brown coat and yellow breeches, 25cm. high. (H. Spencer & Sons Ltd.) $785 £450

Ralph Wood group of St. George and the Dragon, circa 1770, restored, 10¾in. high. (Sotheby's)$905 £506

Late 18th century Ralph Wood Toby jug, 24.5cm. high. (Sotheby, King & Chasemore) $575 £310

Ralph Wood figure of 'The Lost Sheep Found', circa 1775, 21cm. high. (Christie's) $920 £495

Enoch Wood figure of a roaring lion, circa 1790, 12¾in. wide. (Sotheby's)$510 £275

Figure of Mars modelled as a Roman Emperor, by Enoch Wood, circa 1780-90, 9½in. high. (Sotheby's) $305 £165

199

WORCESTER

Chamberlain's Worcester yellow-ground chamber candlestick with gilt leaf handle, circa 1815, 10cm. diam. (Christie's) $815 £440

One of a pair of Worcester blue and white lobed oval sauceboats, circa 1770, 17.5cm. wide. (Christie's) $865 £464

One of a pair of Chamberlain's Worcester named view plaques, circa 1800, 7in. wide. (Sotheby's) $830 £440

Unusual Royal Worcester claret jug with gilt briar handle, dated for 1899, 8¾in. high. (Woolley & Wallis) $45 £24

Part of a Chamberlain's Worcester part dinner service of one hundred and one pieces. (Pearsons) $2,790 £1,500

Worcester vase of slender shouldered form, 1765-70, 8in. high. (Sotheby's) $875 £462

Mid 18th century Worcester porcelain reticulated bowl with two handles, 9in. diam. (Wm. Doyle Galleries Inc.) $550 £290

One of a pair of Worcester green-ground ice pails, covers and liners, circa 1820, 27.5cm. high. (Christie's) $3,055 £1,650

18th century Worcester Blind Earl plate decorated with foliage, 7½in. diam. (Wm. Doyle Galleries Inc.) $650 £345

Rare Worcester vase and cover by J. Stinton, signed, 10¾in. high. (Woolley & Wallis) $395 £220

Worcester basket of large oval shape with rope-twist handles, circa 1770, 11¼in. wide. (Sotheby's) $695 £374

Royal Worcester spherical vase by J. Stinton, signed, dated for 1916, 6in. high. (Woolley & Wallis) $555 £310

Royal Worcester cylindrical vase with pierced foot, dated for 1921, 10¼in. high.(Woolley & Wallis) $715 £400

Worcester garniture of three cachepots by Flight, Barr & Barr, 12cm. and 14.5cm. high. (Sotheby, King & Chasemore) $770 £420

Royal Worcester centrepiece, stem supported by four cherubs, 14½in. high. (J. M. Welch & Son) $1,490 £820

Model of a giraffe by Grainger, Lee & Co., 4½in. high, on oval gilt base. (Christie's S. Kensington) $465 £250

One of a pair of first period Worcester plates with shaped edged borders, 8½in. diam. (Woolley & Wallis)$250 £140

Worcester herringbone moulded coffee pot and domed cover, circa 1760, 25cm. high. (Christie's) $6,510 £3,250

201

Chamberlain's Worcester reticulated cup and saucer, 1846-50. (Sotheby Beresford Adams) $685 £370

One of a pair of Royal Worcester shell-shaped fruit dishes, decorated by H. Ayrton, 26cm. diam. (H. Spencer & Sons Ltd.)$395 £220

One of a pair of Worcester chinoiserie bowls, circa 1760-65, 9in. high. (Sotheby, King & Chasemore) $200 £110

Late Victorian Royal Worcester porcelain figure 'The Turkish Water Carrier', 18in. high. (Geering & Colyer) $370 £200

Rare set of three Chamberlain's Worcester hunting figures, circa 1820-30, 12cm. and 9cm. high. (Sotheby, King & Chasemore) $1,155 £620

Royal Worcester table lamp as a young girl perched on a tree trunk, 39cm. high. (H. Spencer & Sons Ltd.) $415 £230

Fine Chamberlain's Worcester ice pail, cover and liner, on square marble base, 35cm. wide. (Sotheby, King & Chasemore) $2,195 £1,200

Royal Worcester 'shot enamel' spill holder, date letter for 1881, 17cm. high.(Sotheby, King & Chasemore) $150 £80

Royal Worcester vase and cover dated for 1919, 7¼in. high. (Sotheby Beresford Adams) $405 £220

Worcester comport after Dr.
Flight, Barr & Barr Worces- One of a pair of Royal Wall, of shaped oval pede-
ter fruit bowl of fluted Worcester ovoid two- stal design, 13½in. wide. (W.
oval form, 14in. wide. (W. handled vases by C. H. Lane & Son) $585 £310
H. Lane & Son)$455 £240 Baldwyn, 27cm. high.
(H. Spencer & Sons
Ltd.) $1,115 £620

Royal Worcester pot pourri
vase and cover painted and Pair of Royal Worcester Grainger's Worcester vase
signed by J. Stinton, 12in. classical female figures, and cover, dated for 1901,
high, dated for 1924. supported on square gilt 9¾in. high. (Sotheby
(Sotheby Beresford Adams) socles, 37cm. high. (H. Beresford Adams) $335
            $1,590 £860 Spencer & Sons Ltd.)   £180
                        $485 £270

Royal Worcester bowl painted by Jas. Stinton, signed,
1924, 22cm. diam. Grainger's Worcester fig- Royal Worcester vase
(Sotheby's Belgravia) ure of a giraffe, 11cm. and cover with ovoid
            $360 £200 high. (Sotheby, King & body and mask handles,
                        Chasemore)$295 £160 1896, 26cm. high.
                        (Sotheby's Belgravia)
                                    $325 £180

203

Worcester thistle-shaped cup painted in Imari style, circa 1770. (Christie's) $715 £385

One of three Worcester cups and saucers of double ogee shape, circa 1765-70. (Sotheby's) $900 £484

Large Royal Worcester ovoid vase with two handles, decorated by C. Baldwyn, 45cm. high.(H. Spencer & Sons Ltd.) $790 £440

Large Royal Worcester figure of 'The Bather Surprised', 65.5cm. high, 1911. (H. Spencer & Sons Ltd.) $560 £300

Worcester kidney-shaped dish, circa 1775, 26cm. wide. (Christie's) $3,680 £1,980

Worcester cream jug with grooved loop handle, 3¾in. high, circa 1765-70. (Sotheby's) $550 £297

Worcester blue and white shell salt, circa 1770, 20.5cm. wide. (Christie's)　$570 £308

Worcester blue scale pear-shaped cream jug and cover, circa 1770, 12.5cm. high. (Christie's) $1,185 £638

Early Worcester 'Blind Earl' pattern plate, circa 1780. (Northampton Auction Mart)$885 £480

One of a pair of Royal Worcester moon flasks, enamelled in the Japanese style. (Sotheby, King & Chasemore) $570 £310

Flight, Barr & Barr candlestick of hexagonal shape, by Barker, 4in., circa 1820-25.(Sotheby's) $1,120 £605

One of a set of eight Worcester dishes, signed A. Shuck, 1916. (Hall Wateridge & Owen) $1,480 £800

One of a pair of Royal Worcester vases painted by Harry Stinton, 15in. high, dated for 1909. (H. Spencer & Sons Ltd.) $1,815 £970

Worcester kidney-shaped dish painted with sprays of fruit, circa 1775, 26cm. wide. (Christie's) $3,680 £1,980

Rare Worcester 'King of Prussia' vase of Chinese shape, dated 1757, 8¼in. high. (Sotheby's) $3,885 £2,090

One of a pair of Worcester 'scale-blue' wine coolers, of U-shape, circa 1770-75, 7½in. high. (Sotheby's) $3,865 £2,090

One of a pair of Flight, Barr & Barr vases of urn shape, circa 1813-20, 3½in. high. (Sotheby's) $530 £286

Small Worcester mug of cylindrical shape with loop handle, 2¼in. high, circa 1760-65. (Sotheby's) $345 £187

205

Royal Worcester cracker jar with squat bulbous gadrooned body, 1888, 7in. high. (Robert W. Skinner Inc.) $175 £95

Royal Worcester ewer with squat domed body, 1887, 4½in. high. (Robert W. Skinner Inc.) $225 £125

Royal Worcester vase, circa 1880, with moulded woven body, 8in. high. (Robert W. Skinner Inc.) $400 £225

Rare Worcester figure 'The Bather Surprised', modelled by Sir Thos. Brock, 10in. high, 1919. (Sotheby Beresford Adams) $275 £150

Part of a Flight, Barr & Barr period Worcester tea and coffee service. (H. Spencer & Sons Ltd.) $1,225 £660

Royal Worcester cylindrical vase painted and signed by A. Shuck, 1909, 9in. high. (Sotheby Beresford Adams) $220 £120

Worcester Dr. Wall period tea caddy and cover decorated with flowers and insects, 4¾in. tall. (T. Bannister & Co.) $470 £260

One of a pair of Chamberlain Worcester ice pails, covers and liners, circa 1820-30, 37cm. wide. (Sotheby, King & Chasemore) $2,195 £1,200

Royal Worcester pot pourri vase and cover, 5½in. high, date for 1921, signed G. A. Stinton. (Sotheby Beresford Adams) $370 £200

Royal Worcester jug with lion's profile, circa 1880, 9in. high. (Robert W. Skinner Inc.) $325 £180

Royal Worcester basket in the form of a bird's nest, circa 1890, 6in. high. (Robert W. Skinner Inc.) $250 £140

Royal Worcester ewer with gilt reptile handle, 1881, 11½in. high. (Robert W. Skinner Inc.) $550 £305

Royal Worcester figurine of a woman in 12th century costume, 9in. high, circa 1890. (Robert W. Skinner Inc.) $450 £250

Royal Worcester elephant in gold coloured harness and carrying a jardiniere, circa 1882, 6in. high. (Robert W. Skinner Inc.) $150 £85

Royal Worcester vase and cover, signed and painted by H. Stinton, 10½in. high, dated for 1915. (Sotheby Beresford Adams) $515 £280

One of two Royal Worcester vases, circa 1880, 4in. and 6in. high. (Robert W. Skinner Inc.) $200 £110

Royal Worcester squat pot pourri vase and cover, painted and signed by Ricketts, 5in. high, dated for 1926. (Sotheby Beresford Adams) $315 £170

Royal Worcester vase of tankard form, 9in. high. (Robert W. Skinner Inc.) $300 £165

Early Worcester bowl decorated in coloured enamels, 5in. diam., circa 1752-55. (Sotheby's) $1,635 £880

One of a pair of Royal Worcester vases with 'old ivory' ground, 28cm. high, 1885. (Phillips)$685 £370

Worcester teacup and saucer decorated in floral festoons, circa 1775. (Phillips) $295 £150

Worcester cabbage leaf mask jug printed in underglaze blue, circa 1770, 29.5cm. high. (Phillips) $425 £230

Rare Worcester teabowl and saucer in underglaze blue, circa 1757-60. (Sotheby's) $570 £308

Worcester cylindrical mug printed in red by Robert Hancock, circa 1765, 13cm. high. (Phillips) $1,295 £700

Royal Worcester reticulated chalice of campana shape, dated for 1877, 19.5cm. high. (Phillips)$1,260 £680

Worcester dessert dish of fluted oval shape, circa 1770, 12¾in. long. (Sotheby's) $730 £395

Royal Worcester vase of globular form, by Chas. Deakins, 1884, 28cm. high. (Phillips)$280 £150

Worcester yellow-ground basket with pierced and interlaced handles, circa 1765-70, 8in. diam. (Sotheby's) $1,810 £979

Royal Worcester vase, one of a pair, painted by Charley Baldwyn, 1902, 15cm. high. (Phillips) $1,575 £850

Worcester yellow-ground basket of ovoid shape, circa 1765, 27.5cm. wide. (Phillips) $1,515 £820

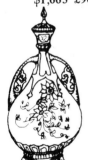

Royal Worcester teapot and cover by George Owen, outer shell pierced, dated for 1876, 12cm. high. (Phillips) $1,665 £900

Early Worcester cream jug of pear shape, circa 1751-52, 6.7cm. high.(Phillips) $5,365 £2,900

Early Worcester teapot and cover, circa 1754-55, 12cm. high. (Phillips) $1,480 £800

Royal Worcester Persian style vase and pierced cover, 1893, 40.5cm. high. (Phillips) $445 £240

Worcester oval butter tub and cover with stand, circa 1770-80, 7¼in. wide. (Sotheby's) $900 £484

Shield-shaped Royal Worcester vase, painted by Charley Baldwyn, 1905, 22cm. high. (Phillips) $1,110 £600

Tureen, cover and stand from a Chamberlain's Worcester pink-ground part dessert service, circa 1825. (Christie's) $1,580 £864

Early Worcester sauceboat of shallow oval form, circa 1754, 6¼in. wide. (Sotheby's)　$995 £550

Early Worcester/Lunds Bristol shell-shaped dish with central flower spray, circa 1752, 3¼in. high. (Sotheby's) $995 £550

Worcester teapot, cover and stand painted with 'Bengal Tiger Pattern', circa 1775, 21.5cm. wide. (Christie's) $950 £518

Royal Worcester slender oviform vase with tall neck, painted by A. Lewis, 27cm. high. (Christie's) $385 £205

Royal Worcester two-handled oviform vase and cover, painted by F. Roberts, 56cm. high. (Christie's)$1,725 £918

Worcester blue and white bough pot of bombe shape, circa 1765-70, 9in. diam. (Sotheby's)　$670 £374

Royal Worcester orange-ground two-handled oviform vase and cover, painted by H. Davis, 22cm. high.(Christie's)$530 £281

One of a pair of Worcester lobed oval dishes, circa 1770, 27cm. wide. (Christie's)　$990 £540

Yongzheng Companie-des-Indes blue and white dish with flanged rim, 35cm. diam. (Sotheby, King & Chasemore) $170 £95

Yongzheng period celadon vase with two pairs of loop handles, 13.6cm. high. (Sotheby's) $3,085 £1,650

Yongzheng famille rose bowl of double ogee form, wood stand, 17.2cm. diam. (Sotheby's) $4,115 £2,200

YORKSHIRE

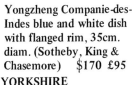

Yorkshire figure of a sportsman, circa 1780, 20cm. high. (Christie's) $490 £264

Yorkshire figure of a cockerel splashed in brown, ochre, yellow and blue, circa 1780, 16.5cm. high. (Christie's) $820 £440

Late 18th/early 19th century Yorkshire Toby jug, face coloured deep red, 10in. high, restored. (Sotheby's) $555 £308

Unusual Yorkshire jug and cover, probably Rothwell pottery, circa 1770, 5½in. high. (Sotheby's) $550 £297

Early 19th century Yorkshire Pratt type group of an elephant and rider, 20cm. wide. (Sotheby, King & Chasemore) $3,220 £1,750

Yorkshire pottery watch-holder, modelled as a man and woman on either side of a clock, 9in. high. (Christie's S. Kensington) $930 £500

BRACKET CLOCKS

Mahogany bracket clock in broken arched case with brass fret sides, 16½in. high. (Lawrence Fine Art) $960 £500

Early 18th century bracket clock by Andrew Moran, London, with inverted bell top, 18in. high. (Boardman's) $2,225 £1,250

Early 19th century ebonised bracket clock, 1ft. 6½in. high. (Sotheby's) $1,450 £750

Late 18th century mahogany bracket clock, dial inscribed Joseph Ismay, London, 22in. high. (Sotheby, King & Chasemore) $1,050 £600

Black lacquer bracket clock signed Marwick Markham, London, 20¾in. high. (Lawrence Fine Art) $1,825 £950

19th century mahogany striking and chiming bracket clock, inscribed Thos. Lace, 24in. high. (Sotheby, King & Chasemore) $2,625 £1,500

George III ebonised bracket clock by Jno. Starey, London, sides with sunburst grilles, 20in. high. (Sotheby, King & Chasemore) $1,165 £640

Small repeating ebonised bracket clock by J. & W. Mitchell, Glasgow, circa 1850, 8¾in. high. (Sotheby's Belgravia) $2,360 £1,320

Early 18th century ebonised bracket clock, signed Fromanteel, London. (Christie's) $3,310 £1,800

Satinwood repeating bracket clock by Desbois & Wheeler, London, 1830's, 16in. high. (Sotheby's Belgravia) $845 £451

Early 19th century bracket clock by John Agar, Malton, in mahogany case, 58cm. high. (Osmond, Tricks) $785 £430

Ebonised bracket clock, signed Barraud, Cornhill, London, 17in. high. (Lawrence Fine Art) $1,150 £600

Small early George III ebonised bracket clock by William Allam, London, 15in. high. (Sotheby's) $4,575 £2,420

Chain fusee repeating ebonised bracket clock, 1880's, 18in. high. (Sotheby's Belgravia) $1,520 £814

German lacquered bracket clock, case painted with chinoiserie on green-ground, 24in. high, circa 1900. (Sotheby's Belgravia) $825 £440

Early 19th century bracket clock in ornate case, 25in. high. (J. M. Welch & Son) $1,275 £700

Late 19th century bracket clock in ebonised case, retailer's mark of W. H. Collins, Ipswich, 23in. high. (Olivers) $1,430 £800

Late 18th century Continental bracket clock with brass finials. (J. M. Welch & Son) $545 £300

Early 19th century maho-
gany brass inlaid bracket
clock by George Miles,
with double fusee move-
ment. (T. Bannister & Co.)
$1,265 £700

Quarter repeating bracket clock
by Thos. Tompion, London,
signed, on ebonised wall bracket,
12½in. high. (Christie's)
$22,440   £12,000

Regency ebonised strik-
ing bracket clock with
chamfered top, case
with brass inlay, 14in.
high. (Christie's)
$1,685 £900

Ebonised bracket clock
by James McCabe, Lon-
don, case with brass in-
lay, 16in. high.(Christie's)
$1,870   £1,000

George III mahogany
striking bracket clock,
dial signed Wm. Storr,
London, 19in. high.
(Christie's)$3,555 £1,900

Late 17th century yew-
wood striking bracket
clock, signed Jno. Snow,
London, 14½in. high.
(Christie's)$4,300 £2,300

George III mahogany striking bracket clock, dial signed James Tregent, Lon-
don, 15½in. high.
(Christie's)$1,495 £800

Fruitwood striking brac-
ket clock, signed Henry
Massy, London, case with
scroll carrying handle,
17½in. high. (Christie's)
$4,490 £2,400

Late George III fruitwood
bracket timepiece alarm,
dial signed Duncan, St.
James's Street, London,
9½in. high. (Christie's)
$1,215 £650

214

Ebonised bracket clock by Abel Panchaud, London, with brass handles and feet, 16in. high. (Locke & England) $1,790 £1,000

Walnut bracket clock by A. Miller, Brighton, with enamel dial and Roman numerals. (T. Bannister & Co.) $310 £170

South German ebonised striking bracket clock, dial signed Fr. Hav. Gegenreiner Augsburg, 10¾in. high. (Christie's) $1,495 £800

Early George III chiming bracket clock with automaton, dial signed Thozon Fitter, London, 20in. high. (Christie's) $6,360 £3,400

George II fruitwood striking bracket clock with inverted bell-top case, dial signed John Fladgate, London, 18½in. high. (Christie's) $2,620 £1,400

Austrian ebonised quarter striking bracket clock in bell-top case, 19in. high. (Christie's) $1,870 £1,000

Dark green lacquer striking bracket clock, dial signed Gio. Batta Callin Genoua, mid 18th century, 26in. high. (Christie's) $3,365 £1,800

Garrard Silver Jubilee clock, designed by F. W. Elliott, 1977. (T. Bannister & Co.) $1,630 £900

Late 17th century ebonised striking bracket clock, signed Wm. Speakman, London, 14½in. high. (Christie's) $5,235 £2,800

215

Early 19th century late Regency rosewood bracket clock by John Moore & Son, Clerkenwell, 16in. high. (Sotheby Beresford Adams) $670 £360

George III fruitwood bracket timepiece, dial signed Allam & Caithness, London, 22cm. high.(Phillips)$2,175 £1,150

19th century bracket clock in heavily carved mahogany case.(Burtenshaw Walker) $1,370 £725

Late George II mahogany bracket clock by Thos. Chappell, London, 55cm. high. (Phillips) $1,700 £900

19th century oak and ormolu bracket clock, 29in. high, with pierced oak wall bracket. (Morphets) $1,185 £640

George III mahogany cased bracket clock by Thos. Wagstaffe, London, 24½in. high. (Burrows & Day) $4,525 £2,500

Ebonised bracket timepiece by Johan Meyer, Steyer, in glazed case, 15in. high. (Burrows & Day)$450 £250

Tortoiseshell and gilt metal musical bracket clock by G. Prior, London, for the Turkish market.(Sotheby's) $6,550 £3,600

Georgian mahogany bracket clock with brass and steel dial by Mudge, London, on ogee feet.(Burtenshaw Walker)$1,170 £620

Architectural designed walnut striking bracket clock, marked Frank Giles & Co., Kensington. (Allen & May) $330 £175

18th century Bohemian ebonised quarter striking bracket clock, 19¼in. high. (Sotheby's) $2,600 £1,375

Late 19th century oak chiming bracket clock in carved case, 28in. high. (Sotheby Beresford Adams) $1,005 £540

Mahogany bracket clock by Thos. Wagstaffe, London, in bell-top case, 19in. high. (Sotheby's) $1,975 £1,045

19th century bracket clock, painted dial inscribed Thwaites & Reed, London, 37cm. high. (Phillips) $1,360 £720

George III ebonised bracket clock by Matthew Dutton, London, 15in. high. (Sotheby, King & Chasemore) $3,840 £2,000

Ebonised quarter repeating bracket clock by Marmaduke Storr, London, 18in. high. (Sotheby's) $3,745 £1,980

George III ebonised bracket clock by S. & C. Joyce, London, 13½in. high. (Sotheby, King & Chasemore) $1,185 £650

Early 19th century Regency mahogany bracket timepiece, enamel dial inscribed Sheppery & Pearce, Nottingham, 16in. high. (Sotheby Beresford Adams) $500 £270

Brass timepiece carriage clock with enamel dial, in one-piece case with hinged rear door, 4¼in. high.(Christie's)$450 £240

English walnut cased chronometer carriage clock, 10in. high. (Christie's)$1,400 £750

Early gilt brass striking chronometer carriage clock by Bolviller, Paris, 7in. high. (Christie's) $2,620 £1,400

Miniature ivory cased carriage timepiece with enamel dial, 3¼in. high. (Christie's) $335 £180

Early 19th century French brass capucine clock with carrying handle above the bell, 10in. high.(Christie's) $1,400 £750

Large lacquered brass grande sonnerie carriage clock, stamped D. C., in wood travelling case, 8½in. high. (Christie's) $4,115 £2,200

Miniature lacquered brass carriage timepiece, stamped Payne & Co., Paris, 3in. high. (Christie's) $560 £300

French gilt metal and porcelain mounted striking carriage clock in 'bamboo' case, 6¾in. high.(Christie's) $1,870 £1,000

Brass carriage clock with Sevres porcelain dial and in gorge case, 6in. high. (Christie's) $1,495 £800

19th century French carriage clock with repeat and alarm, 6½in. high. (Sotheby Bearne) $975 £520

Gilt metal porcelain mounted striking carriage clock, 6¾in. high. (Christie's) $2,245 £1,200

Miniature silver and enamel carriage clock with porcelain mask and side panels, 3in. high. (Christie's) $1,590 £850

Lacquered brass miniature carriage clock with enamel dial, 3in. high. (Christie's) $260 £140

Gilt metal timepiece carriage clock by Arnold's/Chas. Frodsham, in engraved case, circa 1860, 5in. high. (Christie's) $2,620 £1,400

Gilt metal porcelain mounted grande sonnerie carriage clock by Drocourt, 5¾in. high. (Christie's) $5,425 £2,900

Gilt metal petite sonnerie carriage clock, backplate stamped Grohe, London, 5½in. high. (Christie's) $2,805 £1,500

Brass quarter striking carriage clock, dial signed Leroy et Fils, 5in. high. (Christie's) $970 £520

Gilt metal and champleve enamel striking carriage clock with lever platform, 6in. high. (Christie's) $1,215 £650

Silver-cased boudoir clock by William Comyns, London, 1896, 9.5cm. high. (Sotheby's Belgravia) $505 £264

Miniature French brass carriage clock, stamped E. White, Paris, 3¾in. high. (Lawrence Fine Art) $300 £155

Rare silver-cased carriage clock, handle set with shield with coat-of-arms, 6¼in. high. (Christie's) $2,055 £1,100

Early 20th century gilt brass carriage clock by Russells Ltd., Paris, in red leather case, 6¼in. high. (Sotheby Beresford Adams) $410 £220

Unusual brass carriage clock in the shape of a padlock, 6½in. high. (Lawrence Fine Art) $250 £130

Mid 19th century gilt brass alarm carriage clock by Leroy et Fils, Paris, 6¼in. high. (Sotheby Beresford Adams) $595 £320

Gilt metal miniature carriage clock with enamel side panels, 2½in. high. (Christie's) $4,300 £2,300

Early 20th century gilt brass carriage clock by A. W. Butt, Chester, 7½in. high. (Sotheby Beresford Adams) $370 £200

French brass carriage clock in gorge type case, 6¼in. high. (Lawrence Fine Art) $595 £310

Enamel mounted carriage clock, signed R. & W. Sorley, Paris, 5¼in. high. (Sotheby's) $1,415 £748

Very rare double striking alarm carriage clock with enamel dial, 5½in. high. (Sotheby's) $4,575 £2,420

French brass carriage clock dated 1886, 7in. high. (Lawrence Fine Art) $385 £200

Enamel mounted carriage clock with ivorine dial, 6¼in. high. (Sotheby's) $1,455 £770

Gilt metal striking carriage clock in the manner of Thos. Cole, 6¾in. high. (Christie's) $1,870 £1,000

French brass and porcelain miniature carriage timepiece, in a case, 10cm. high. (Phillips) $2,835 £1,500

English petite sonnerie brass carriage clock, 31cm. high, signed Edw. Funnell, Brighton. (Phillips) $5,670 £3,000

French brass carriage clock inscribed Mappin & Webb, French Make, 5½in. high. (Lawrence Fine Art) $190 £100

Good late 19th century French carriage clock with blue enamel dial and side panels, 7¼in. high.(Sotheby Bearne) $1,495 £800

221

Gilt brass hour repeating carriage clock, dial signed Connell, London, circa 1890, 6¾in. high. (Sotheby's Belgravia) $1,030 £550

Ornate French carriage clock with serpentine-shaped front and hinged handle. (Butler & Hatch Waterman) $660 £360

19th century French carriage clock by Magraine in brass oval case, 7in. high. (Dacre, Son & Hartley) $725 £390

Miniature French gilt, brass and enamel carriage clock, 2¾in. high, with canted corners. (Phillips) $1,665 £900

Large French brass repeating carriage clock with day and date dials. (M. Philip H. Scott) $2,864 £1,600

Gilt bronze and enamel carriage clock, with painted sides, surmounted by a gallery, circa 1890, 4½in. high. (Sotheby's Belgravia) $4,215 £2,255

Plain faced French brass carriage clock with repeat and alarm. (M. Philip H. Scott) $1,520 £850

French brass carriage clock with alarm, side panels, face and rear door painted. (M. Philip H. Scott) $2,900 £1,620

Parcel gilt silver miniature carriage clock by Asprey, London, 2½in. high. (Christie's) $655 £350

Miniature French brass carriage timepiece with enamel dial, 4in. high. (Lawrence Fine Art) $325 £170

Gilt bronze carriage clock, signed Lucien, Paris, circa 1870, 7¼in. high. (Sotheby's Belgravia) $780 £418

Late 19th century French enamelled repeater carriage clock with Sevres face, 5¾in. high. (Robert W. Skinner Inc.) $1,800 £995

English repeating carriage clock by E. White, London, circa 1850. (Bonhams) $7,295 £3,800

Ebony bracket clock by Thomas Boxell, Brighton, circa 1840, 15½in. high, with key. (Sotheby's Belgravia) $1,440 £770

Fine French gilt metal striking and repeating alarm carriage clock by Leroy et Fils, Paris. (Andrew Grant) $1,090 £600

Small French carriage clock in case with filigree decoration and Corinthian columns. (Butler & Hatch Waterman) $575 £315

Ebony cased striking alarm carriage clock, 7in. high. (Andrew Grant) $475 £260

Large bow-sided brass carriage clock by Elkington & Co. Ltd., in original case. (Worsfolds) $885 £460

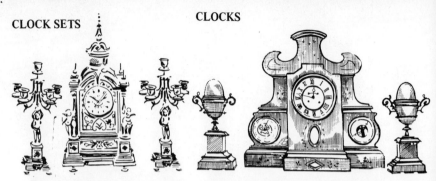

French gilt bronze and champleve enamel clock garniture, stamped Japy Freres, 21¼in. high. (Lawrence Fine Art) $1,825 £950

Black and red marble calendar clock garniture, signed Brush & Drummond, circa 1870, clock 23in. high. (Sotheby's Belgravia) $825 £440

Gilt bronze and 'jewelled' Sevres clock garniture by Leroy & Fils, mid 19th century, clock 20in. high. (Sotheby Beresford Adams) $3,535 £1,900

Gilt spelter and porcelain clock garniture, circa 1890, clock 20½in. high. (Sotheby's Belgravia) $1,130 £605

Mid 19th century composed gilt bronze and porcelain clock garniture by J. Mayer. (Sotheby Beresford Adams) $1,155 £620

Gilt bronze, onyx and champleve clock garniture, signed Mellington Cleton, Boulogne. (Sotheby's Belgravia) $1,400 £748

Three-piece slate garniture de cheminee with urn-shaped vases. (J. M. Welch & Son) $145 £80

Late 18th century clock garniture by Antide Janvier, Paris. (Robert W. Skinner Inc.) $2,000 £1,085

French parcel gilt green patinated bronze three-piece clock garniture, signed Hry. Marc, Paris. (Sotheby, King & Chasemore) $545 £300

Late 19th century carved walnut sculptural clock garniture, movement stamped Leuenberger Interlaken. (Sotheby's Belgravia) $1,030 £550

19th century French Louis XVI style champleve enamel garniture, clock by Japy Freres. (Robert W. Skinner Inc.) $1,100 £600

Louis XVI style Sevres three-piece clock garniture by Ph. Maurey, France, circa 1870. (Robert W. Skinner Inc.) $1,450 £790

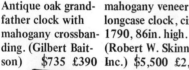

Antique oak grandfather clock with mahogany crossbanding. (Gilbert Baitson) $735 £390

Federal cherry and mahogany veneer longcase clock, circa 1790, 86in. high. (Robert W. Skinner Inc.) $5,500 £2,910

Grandfather clock with walnut case and brass face, burrwalnut panels in door and base. (Gilbert Baitson) $2,175 £1,150

Oak longcase clock with brass dial inscribed M. Thomas, Caernarvon, 84in. high. (Sotheby Beresford Adams) $1,080 £580

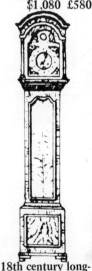

Walnut and marquetry longcase clock, signed Tho. Grimes, London, 78in. tall. (T. Bannister & Co.) $8,145 £4,500

Late 18th century oak longcase clock by Hines, Needham, 81in. high. (Lacy Scott) $1,250 £650

Mahogany longcase clock inlaid and with painted dial, by Wm. Foster, Whitehaven. (Alfred Mossop & Co.) $1,020 £530

18th century longcase clock by Thos. Bridge, Wigan, in mahogany case. (Edwards, Bigwood & Bewlay) $2,560 £1,400

Oak longcase clock
by Foden, Congle-
ton, 77in. high.
(Sotheby Beresford
Adams) $595 £320

Oak longcase clock
by Thos. Brown,
Chester, 86in. high.
(Sotheby Beresford
Adams) $1,525 £820

Early 19th century
mahogany longcase
clock, enamel dial
inscribed Thos.
Morgan, Edinburgh,
84in. high.(Sotheby
Beresford Adams)
$1,450 £780

Early 19th century
oak and mahogany
longcase clock, ena-
mel dial signed Ste-
venson, Nottingham,
86in. high.(Sotheby
Beresford Adams)
$560 £300

Early 19th century
mahogany longcase
clock with enamel
dial, signed Wilson,
87in. high.(Sotheby
Beresford Adams)
$1,265 £680

18th century Dutch
longcase clock by B.
Vermeulen of Am-
sterdam, in walnut
case, 93in. high.
(Sotheby, King &
Chasemore)
$13,985 £7,600

Spring-driven walnut
eight-day chiming
grandmother clock,
inscribed Irvine
Hindle, Halifax, 5ft.
4in. high. (Woolley
& Wallis)$500 £280

Georgian longcase
clock by J. Capen,
Ulveston, in maho-
gany case. (Hall
Wateridge & Owen)
$815 £440

227

GRANDFATHER CLOCKS

19th century long-
case regulator in
bird's-eye maple
case with brass face.
(Lewes Auction
Rooms)
$3,440 £1,850

George III black
lacquered and chin-
oiserie longcase
clock by Thos.
Hawting, 97in.
high. (T. Bannister
& Co.) $1,540 £850

Georgian eight-day
longcase clock in
mahogany case,
arched dial by Sam.
Davy, Norwich.
(Burtenshaw Wal-
ker)$3,070 £1,650

18th century oak
longcase clock by
John Buntin,
Long Buckby, 6ft.
8in. high.(Dickin-
son, Davy & Mark-
ham) $560 £300

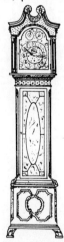

Faded mahogany
longcase clock,
dial signed Vul-
liamy, London,
7ft.1in. high.
(Christie's)
 $7,480 £4,000

George III quarter
striking, chiming,
calendar maho-
gany longcase clock,
signed Shakeshalft,
Preston, 8ft. high.
(Christie's)
 $9,350 £5,000

Rare George III
mahogany long-
case regulator
by Thos. Earn-
shaw, London,
6ft.4½in. high.
(Christie's)
 $14,960 £8,000

Late 19th cen-
tury mahogany
longcase clock
by W. Cranbrook,
88in. high.(Lacy
Scott)
 $2,960 £1,600

Oak longcase clock by J. Roberts, Wrexham., with swan neck pediment, 92in. high. (Sotheby Beresford Adams)$1,580 £850

Thirty-hour oak longcase clock with brass dial signed Chr. Gould, London, 76in. high. (Sotheby Beresford Adams) $1,210 £650

Eight-day longcase clock by C. Vibert, Penzance, with arched painted dial 98in. high, in mahogany and satinwood case. (Sotheby Bearne) $785 £420

Mahogany longcase clock, circa 1830, 93in. high. (Sotheby's Belgravia) $1,200 £600

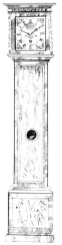

Charles II walnut longcase clock, signed Joseph Knibb, London, circa 1682-85, 7ft. high. (Christie's) $28,050 £15,000

Late 18th century mahogany longcase clock by Brand, Hull, 7ft.6in. high. (Russell, Baldwin & Bright)$1,530 £850

17th century William and Mary japanned longcase clock, works by J. Metzell, London, 77½in. high (Robert W. Skinner Inc.) $1,800 £980

Late 18th century oak longcase clock with 19th century carving, signed Clifton, Liverpool, 89in. high. (Sotheby Beresford Adams) $1,525 £820

CLOCKS

Oak grandmother longcase clock inscribed Tempus Fugit, 5ft.3in. high. (Lawrence Fine Art) $805 £420

Oak longcase clock with square hood surmounted by three brass balls. (Butler & Hatch Waterman) $775 £425

Longcase clock by Anthony Charles. (Cooper Hirst) $3,135 £1,650

18th century red lacquer and chinoiserie longcase clock by George Washbourne, 2.38m. high. (Phillips) $1,700 £900

18th century walnut veneered and seaweed marquetry longcase clock by Wm. Sellers, Long Acre, 2.16m. high.(Phillips) $7,180 £3,800

Early provincial walnut longcase clock, signed John Greenhill, Maidstone, 6ft. 11in. high.(Sotheby's) $3,745 £1,980

Oak longcase clock, signed John Knapp, Reading Fecit, 6ft. 9¼in. high. (Lawrence Fine Art) $1,440 £750

Mahogany eight-day longcase clock with pagoda pediment. (Dee & Atkinson) $740 £400

230

Grandfather clock in mahogany with domed hood, restored. (Butler & Hatch Waterman) $1,720 £940

George III mahogany striking longcase clock by Isaac Hewlett, Bristol, 7ft.9in. high. (Woolley & Wallis) $2,590 £1,400

Rare William IV mahogany equation of time clock, dial signed Wm. Dutton, London, 2.30m. high. (Phillips) $3,305 £1,750

Carved oak quarter chiming longcase clock, signed Wm. Ferrar, Dundee, 7ft.4½in. high. (Lawrence Fine Art) $1,575 £820

Late 18th century green lacquered longcase clock by John Harris, London, 2.32m. high. (Phillips) $1,285 £680

Oak longcase clock, signed Wm. Graham, London, 6ft.9½in. high. (Lawrence Fine Art) $1,765 £920

Small and rare George III oak regulator, dial signed Wm. Allam, London, 6ft.1in. high. (Sotheby's) $5,200 £2,750

Mahogany grandmother clock, signed Thos. Hunter, 56½in. high. (Lawrence Fine Art) $1,650 £860

231

GRANDFATHER CLOCKS

Oak and mahogany longcase clock by Enoch of Warwick, circa 1810. (Locke & England) $665 £360

Early 18th century longcase clock by T. Bacon, Tewkesbury, circa 1720, 79½in. high. (Sotheby, King & Chasemore) $1,315 £720

American Chippendale style mahogany tall cased musical clock, circa 1880, 98in. high. (Robert W. Skinner Inc.) $1,300 £725

Georgian mahogany longcase clock, painted dial signed Robson, N. Shields, 7ft. 9in. high. (Christie's) $2,055 £1,100

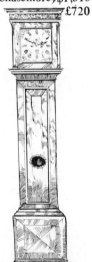

Inlaid mahogany longcase clock with panelled plinth, signed Wm. Evill, Bath, 7ft.11in. high. (Christie's) $2,990 £1,600

18th century Dutch walnut longcase clock, signed Fromanteel & Clarke, 6ft.8½in. high. (Christie's) $3,740 £2,000

Longcase clock by T. Mudge, London, in later mahogany case, 6ft.9in. high. (Christie's) $2,150 £1,150

Late 17th century marquetry longcase clock with concave mouldings, 6ft.8½in. high. (Christie's) $7,105 £3,800

Fine mahogany long-case clock, by T. Mudge, London, 7ft. 4in. high. (Christie's) $5,235   £2,800

Mahogany longcase clock with brass face, by T. Meakings, Dublin. (John Hogbin & Son) $315   £170

Dutch striking marquetry longcase clock signed Daniel Quare, London, 6ft. 8½in. high. (Christie's) $21,505   £11,500

Charles II style simulated tortoiseshell grandmother longcase clock, 6ft. high.(Christie's) $1,685   £900

Victorian mahogany longcase clock with panelled plinth, dial signed 1003 Barrauds, London, 6ft. 3in. high.(Christie's) $4,115   £2,200

Late 17th century marquetry longcase clock, dial signed Gerrard OverZee Isleworth, 6ft.5in. high. (Christie's) $5,425   £2,900

Early 19th century eight-day regulator clock by J. Bell, Bath, in mahogany case, 84in. high. (Sotheby Bearne) $2,710   £1,450

19th century mahogany longcase clock with swan neck pediment, 7ft.3in. high. (Dickinson, Davy & Markham)$735   £400

GRANDFATHER CLOCKS

Early 18th century floral marquetry longease clock by Andrew Dunlop, London. (Locke & England) $9,100 £5,000

Mid 18th century black japanned longcase clock with chinoiserie decoration, 86½in. high.(Sotheby, King & Chasemore) $1,260 £720

Federal mahogany inlaid longcase clock, dial inscribed S. Willard, Roxbury, circa 1790, 87in. high. (Robert W. Skinner Inc.) $4,000 £2,185

Black japanned longcase clock, dial signed Wm. Allam, London, 6ft.1in. high. (Sotheby's) $5,200 £2,750

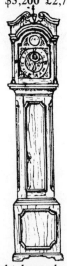

Walnut and marquetry longcase clock by Stephen Wilmot, London, 6ft.9in. high. (Phillips) $4,255 £2,300

18th century Dutch marquetry longcase clock by Steven Hoogendyk, Rotterdam, 110in. (Wm. Doyle Galleries Inc.) $12,000 £6,350

German giltwood and porcelain longcase clock, circa 1880, 63½in. high. (Sotheby's Belgravia) $4,730 £2,530

Eight-day mahogany longcase clock by Hunt of Ludgate Hill. (J. M. Welch & Son) $1,590 £875

18th century walnut cased longcase clock, inscribed John Pursel de Tocester, 197cm. high. (H. Spencer & Sons Ltd.)
$2,550 £1,400

George III mahogany longcase clock by James Lawson, Liverpool, 97in. high. (Sotheby, King & Chasemore)
$1,665 £950

18th century burr-walnut longcase clock by James Snelling, London, 91in. high.(Boardman's)
$2,760 £1,550

Walnut and marquetry cased month going longcase clock by J. Barnett, London. (Sotheby's)
$7,310 £4,200

18th century French walnut longcase clock with moulded arched pediment, 8ft.8in. high.(Phillips) $2,035 £1,100

Mahogany longcase clock with quarter striking on eight chimes, circa 1910, 85in. high.(Sotheby's Belgravia)
$1,220 £682

Early 18th century walnut and herringbone longcase clock by John Wrench, Chester. (Locke & England)
$2,910 £1,600

Mahogany longcase clock with fret carved hood, 95in. high, circa 1910. (Sotheby's Belgravia)$3,940 £2,200

235

LANTERN CLOCKS

19th century, late 17th century style brass lantern clock by Thos. Speakman, London, 15½in. high. (Sotheby Beresford Adams) $520 £280

Wing alarm lantern clock, dial signed J. Windmills, London, circa 1700, 15½in. high. (Sotheby's) $2,080 £1,100

Late 19th century French lantern clock in brass-sided case, 14½in. high. (Robert W. Skinner Inc.) $325 £175

English brass lantern clock, dial plate signed Edward Stanton, London, 17in. high. (Christie's) $2,805 £1,500

German brass lantern clock, stamped W. H. Sch., circa 1900, 15in. high. (Sotheby's Belgravia) $615 £330

Small brass lantern clock by Tho. Tompion, London, signed, 6in. high. (Christie's) $7,480 £4,000

18th century French alarm lantern clock, signature erased, 9in. high. (Sotheby's) $1,765 £935

18th century Continental lantern clock, 27cm. high, with carved walnut bracket. (Phillips) $945 £500

18th century lantern clock, dial signed Step. Harris, Seven Oakes, 13½in. high. (Sotheby's) $1,560 £825

236

Unusual mid 19th century mahogany cased bracket chiming clock, 17in. high. (Sotheby, King & Chasemore) $545 £300

Gilt bronze porcelain mounted mantel clock by Japy Freres, circa 1870, 17in. high. (Sotheby's Belgravia) $845 £451

20th century coppered brass Atmos clock by Jaeger le Coultre, 9¼in. high. (Sotheby's Belgravia) $370 £198

Gilt bronze mantel clock with enamel dial, circa 1870, 15in. high. (Sotheby's Belgravia) $390 £209

Marble and ormolu clock by Achille Brocot, Paris, 23in. high, circa 1850. (Robert W. Skinner Inc.) $1,300 £700

Mid 19th century brass alarm mantel timepiece with glass dome, 9in. high. (Sotheby's Belgravia) $780 £418

Oak quarter chiming bracket clock, signed Pearce & Co., Leeds and Huddersfield, 30½in. high.(Lawrence Fine Art) $940 £490

French Empire ormolu and bronze mantel clock, 54cm. high. (Phillips)$1,170 £620

Mahogany bracket clock, signed Turner, London, in pagoda topped case, 24¼in. high. (Lawrence Fine Art) $540 £280

237

French ormolu mounted enamel faced striking mantel clock. (John Hogbin & Son) $375 £200

Floating-turtle mystery clock, signed Planchon Palais Royale, on ebonised square base, 10in. (Christie's) $2,055 £1,100

Rococo revival walnut mantel clock, Ansonia, Connecticut, circa 1875, 23½in. high. (Robert W. Skinner Inc.) $175 £100

French Empire mantel clock in ormolu and black painted case, 12½in. wide. (Sotheby Bearne) $560 £300

Late 19th century French enamel and jewelled clock with semi-precious stone and pearl decoration, 8¼in. high. (Robert W. Skinner Inc.) $1,700 £925

Liberty & Co. 'Tudric' pewter timepiece in almost rectangular case and with brass hands, 33.5cm. high.(Phillips) $285 £160

Unusual Art Deco Smith's electric mantel clock on raised black backed glass panel, 15in. high.(Sotheby Bearne) $860 £460

Louis XV style ormolu and boulle bracket clock, signed Courtois a Paris, 34in. high. (Sotheby, King & Chasemore) $1,580 £850

Late 19th century French brass and glass mantel clock in bevelled case, 12in. high. (Robert W. Skinner Inc.)$450 £250

Thomas Cole gilt brass cake basket clock with concave dial, 6¼in. diam. (Christie's) $2,430 £1,300

Mid 19th century brass and ormolu French mantel clock with white enamel dial. (T. Bannister & Co.) $290 £160

Thomas Cole gilt metal strut clock, case signed London & Ryder, London, circa 1859, 4¾in. high. (Christie's) $485 £260

Exotic English silver gilt quarter striking carriage clock, movement signed Hunt & Roskell, London, 11¾in. high. (Christie's) $5,610 £3,000

French gilt metal mantel clock with perpetual calendar, signed Leroy & Fils, 20in. high.(Christie's) $2,055 £1,100

Gilt metal and marble mantel clock, stamped J.B.D., with perpetual calendar dial, 18½in. high. (Christie's) $2,805 £1,500

Stylish Cartier timepiece case of semi-circular shaped on waisted and stepped base, signed, 25cm. high. (Phillips) $2,865 £1,600

Unusual Liberty & Co. 'Tudric' timepiece, designed by Archibald Knox, 30.5cm. high. (Phillips)$1,575 £880

French black marble astrological mantel clock with thermometer, calendar dial and barometer, circa 1870, 19¾in. high. (Robert W. Skinner Inc.) $750 £420

18th century Friesland table clock, signed Augustin Linder and Melchior Bruner. (Sotheby, King & Chasemore) $1,690 £920

Ormolu mantel clock by Chas. Frodsham, 18in. high. (Hall Wateridge & Owen) $735 £400

Mid 19th century gilt bronze and porcelain mantel clock, dial inscribed JB Delettrez, Paris, 20in. high. (Sotheby Beresford Adams) $1,155 £620

19th century French clock in boullework case, 2ft.6in. high. (Lacy Scott) $1,060 £580

Late 19th century gilt spelter and porcelain mantel clock by S. Wartenberg, Paris, 14in. high.(Sotheby Beresford Adams) $370 £200

Late 19th century Meissen clock case with movement by Morley, 24½in. high. (Sotheby, King & Chasemore) $3,035 £1,650

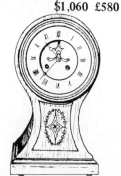

Mahogany cased Edwardian 'balloon' mantel clock. (Alfred Mossop & Co.) $345 £180

French gilt metal four-glass mantel clock by Hry. Marc, Paris, 14in. high.(Sotheby, King & Chasemore) $580 £320

Gilt bronze four-glass battery mantel timepiece, dated 1906, and marked 'Made in England', 12¾in. high. (Sotheby Beresford Adams) $1,040 £560

French gilt metal mantel clock with porcelain mounts, 23½in. high. (Sotheby, King & Chasemore) $805 £420

Regency rosewood mantel clock, silvered dial signed Jas. Tupman, Bloomsbury, 8¾in. high. (Christie's S. Kensington)$1,860 £1,000

Paris clock case and stand, circa 1840, 43.3cm. high, slightly chipped.(Sotheby's Belgravia) $875 £462

Mid 19th century French red boulle and brass inlaid bracket clock.(Lacy Scott) $1,075 £580

Viennese white metal watch stand, movement inscribed Claydon. (Christie's S. Kensington) $2,380 £1,300

Gilt metal mounted mantel clock, dial signed Seth Thomas, U.S.A., 13¾in. high. (Sotheby, King & Chasemore)$185 £100

Late George III inlaid mahogany bracket clock with painted dial, 23½in. high. (Sotheby's) $1,665 £880

French gilt and ormolu striking mantel clock. (Alfred Mossop & Co.) $330 £170

19th century red boulle mantel clock signed Martinot, Paris, 15in. high. (Sotheby, King & Chasemore) $780 £410

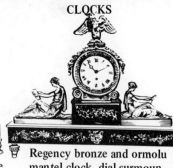

Gilt bronze and marble clock with silvered dial, circa 1850, 19in. high. (Sotheby's Belgravia) $495 £264

Regency bronze and ormolu mantel clock, dial surmounted by a displayed eagle, 14½in. wide. (Christie's) $2,100 £1,100

Gilt bronze mantel clock in inlaid case, with key and pendulum, circa 1870, 15¼in. high. (Sotheby's Belgravia) $350 £187

Gilt bronze and porcelain mantel clock, sides flanked with simulated bamboo columns, circa 1870, 14½in. high. (Sotheby's Belgravia) $555 £297

Early Louis XV ormolu mounted boulle bracket clock, signed Dufour a Paris, 44in. high, with bracket.(Christie's) $2,110 £1,100

Gilt brass mantel clock in bevel-glazed case with pierced columns, circa 1890, 12½in. high. (Christie's) $430 £231

Eight-day mantel chronometer, dial signed Harris, late Hatton & Harris, London, 35cm. high. (Phillips) $1,890 £1,000

Parcel gilt bronze automaton mantel clock, circa 1860, 17¼in. high. (Sotheby's Belgravia) $1,235 £660

Gilt bronze mantel clock with half-hour striking, in rococo case, 16½in. high, circa 1900. (Sotheby's Belgravia) $640 £341

Ebony mantel clock by Thomas Boxell, Brighton, circa 1840, 15½in. high, with key. (Sotheby's Belgravia) $1,440 £770

German beechwood bracket clock, dial signed T. Maury, Lisboa, circa 1880, 20in. high. (Sotheby's Belgravia)$635 £341

Gilt bronze and porcelain mantel clock with painted dial, circa 1880, 17in. high. (Sotheby's Belgravia) $1,440 £770

Mahogany mantel timepiece with gilt bronze mounts, circa 1870, 14in. high. (Sotheby's Belgravia) $330 £176

Coalbrookdale neo-rococo clock case, 30cm. high, circa 1820, movement by Bennet, Holborn.(Sotheby, King & Chasemore) $500 £280

Architectural champleve enamel mantel clock with movement by Japy Freres, circa 1870, 21in. high.(Sotheby's Belgravia) $1,955 £1,045

Gilt bronze and porcelain 'Gothic' mantel clock with Roman numerals, circa 1880, 23in. high. (Sotheby's Belgravia)$1,005 £539

Louis XVI mantel clock in brass and ormolu with enamel dial, 20in. high. (Sotheby, King & Chasemore) $385 £220

Mid 19th century mantel clock by James McCabe, London, 9½in. high. (Phillips) $1,665 £900

Brass skeleton clock on marble base with wood plinth, 13in. high. (Dickinson, Davy & Markham) $445 £240

Rare three-train brass skeleton clock by J. Defries & Sons, London, 22in. high. (Boardman's)$5,340 £3,000

Brass skeleton clock on white marble base, circa 1860, 16in. high. (Sotheby's Belgravia) $845 £451

Brass skeleton 'one at the hour' timepiece, 13½in. high, on mahogany and velvet plinth. (Sotheby's) $775 £420

Rare quarter striking skeleton clock by James Condliff. (Sotheby's) $6,265 £3,600

Timepiece skeleton clock, supported on two Tuscan columns flanking a thermometer scale.(Christie's) $3,555 £1,900

Brass skeleton clock surmounted by a bell, 16in. high, with glass dome. (Sotheby's Belgravia) $845 £451

Small brass skeleton clock under glass dome. (Honiton Galleries) $185 £100

Skeleton clock by Brooking, Clifton, on white marble base and under glass dome, 20½in. high. (Sotheby Bearne) $1,495 £800

Lantern alarm wall clock, face signed Zac Mount-fort, St. Albans, 13in. high. (Sotheby, King & Chasemore) $930 £500

18th century blue lacquered Act of Parliament clock by Thos. Watts, Lavenham, 56in. high. (Boardman's) $1,460 £820

Gilt bronze strut time-piece by R. & S. Gar-rard & Co., London, circa 1870, 4½in. high. (Sotheby's Belgravia) $515 £275

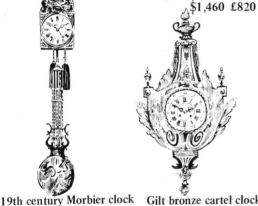

19th century Morbier clock with brass harp pendulum, maker's name M. N. Brecha A Redon. (T. Bannister & Co.) $385 £210

Gilt bronze cartel clock, stamped A. Chapuis A La Gerbe D'Or, Paris, 25in. high, circa 1880. (Sotheby's Belgravia) $865 £462

Friesland wall clock, Holland, circa 1800, 26in. high. (Robert W. Skinner Inc.) $600 £335

Late 19th century French kingwood and ormolu mounted wall clock, 4ft. 7in. high. (Phillips) $2,775 £1,500

'Regency' gilt bronze car-tel clock with enamel dial, 1870's, 29in. high. (Sotheby's Belgravia) $1,480 £792

Walnut wall regulator by E. Howard & Co., 56in. high. (Robert W. Skinner Inc.) $4,500 £2,570

245

WALL CLOCKS

CLOCKS

Victorian rosewood trunk wall clock with white dial, 2ft.2in. high. (Dickinson, Davy & Markham) $185 £100

Mid Victorian papier-mache and mother-of-pearl inlaid wall clock, 29in. high. (Coles, Knapp & Kennedy) $325   £180

American mahogany wall acorn timepiece with painted tin dial, 28in. high. (Robert W. Skinner Inc.) $1,200 £655

Late 19th/early 20th century Swiss wall clock in chalet style case, 40in. high. (Sotheby Beresford Adams) $2,140 £1,150

Friesian oak staartklok surmounted by three brass ball finials, 54in. high. (Lawrence Fine Art) $1,845 £960

Georgian Act of Parliament clock by Thos. Thwaites of Mitcham, in black japanned case, 150cm. high. (H. Spencer & Sons Ltd.) $1,675   £900

Eight-day striking Vienna regulator clock. (J. M. Welch & Son) $545 £300

Drop-dial wall clock in carved case, circa 1840. (J. M. Welch & Son) $435 £240

American Federal mahogany banjo clock, 46½in. high. (Wm. Doyle Galleries Inc.)$2,000 £1,060

Weight-driven rosewood veneer double dial calendar wall clock, Connecticut, circa 1865, 32in. high. (Robert W. Skinner Inc.) $800 £440

Mid 19th century painted wood automaton wall clock, case painted with flowers, 19in. high. (Sotheby's Belgravia) $3,700 £1,980

Vienna regulating wall clock, circa 1900. (J. M. Welch & Son) $275 £150

18th century marquetry cased Friesland staartklok. (Anderson & Garland) $1,720 £940

Antique wall clock with fret carving to base and bracket, by Samuel Porter, London. (Butler & Hatch Waterman) $340 £190

Japanese padouk stick clock, trunk with brass chapters, 42cm. high. (Phillips) $755 £400

American Victorian walnut clock, circa 1875, 29½in. high. (Robert W. Skinner Inc.) $500 £280

Pressed wood advertising figure-eight wall clock by Edward P. Baird & Co., New York circa 1880, 31in. long. (Robert W. Skinner Inc.) $450 £240

Victorian inlaid walnut trunk wall clock, dial inscribed 'Fowler', 2ft. 11in. high. (Dickinson, Davy & Markham) $225 £120

247

Quarter repeating verge pair-cased watch by Benjamin Sidey, hallmarked 1776. (Sotheby Bearne) $785 £420

Lady's Hampden hunting-cased dress watch with white enamel dial and in gold case. (Sotheby Bearne) $580 £310

Silver-cased keyless free sprung reversed escape wheel lever pocket watch, unsigned, 44mm. diam. (Christie's) $300 £160

George III gold lever watch, hallmarked 1816, with diamond end stone. (Sotheby Bearne) $450 £240

Gold hunter-cased minute repeating lever watch, movement signed Falconer & Co., Hong Kong, 52mm. diam. (Christie's) $3,180 £1,700

Silver pair-cased verge watch movement signed I. Tudham, London, 57mm. diam. (Christie's) $750 £400

Silver pair-cased half quarter repeating verge watch, signed Joseph Martineau Senr., London, 58mm. diam. (Christie's) $1,125 £600

Silver pair-cased verge watch, movement signed George Etherington, London. (Christie's) $895 £480

Silver pair-cased Sun and Moon false pendulum verge watch, signed Regn. Westwood, London, 57mm. diam. (Christie's) $2,055 £1,100

Gold pair-cased quarter repeating cylinder watch, signed Chas. Haley, London, 1785, 50mm. diam. (Christie's) $2,245 £1,200

French gold and enamel verge watch, signed Lepaute a Paris, 40mm. diam. (Christie's) $1,400 £750

Silver and gold case lever pocket watch, movement signed W. Ehrhardt, Birmingham, 45mm. diam. (Christie's) $410 £220

George III quarter repeating verge watch by John Ellicott, London, silver case hallmarked 1781. (Sotheby Bearne) $1,125   £680

Swiss gold hunter-cased minute repeating keyless lever calendar chronograph, 55mm. diam. (Christie's) $4,115 £2,200

French centre-seconds chronometer by R. Laurent Jouvenat & Cie, London, in silver case. (Sotheby Bearne) $505   £270

Gold-cased English cylinder pocket watch, cover signed Rundell, Bridge & Rundell, London, 1811, 38mm. diam. (Christie's) $840 £450

Fine gold and enamel duplex watch, signed Vaucher Fleurier, 58mm. diam. (Christie's) $12,155 £6,550

Silver-cased free sprung lever pocket watch, movement signed Chas. Frodsham, London, 45mm. diam. (Christie's) $390 £210

249

Open-faced quarter repeating cylinder watch in engine-turned case, 53mm. diam. (Sotheby's Belgravia) $555 £297

14ct. gold hunter pocket watch by the Deutsche Uhrenfabrikation Glashutte. (Sotheby, King & Chasemore) $8,465 £4,600

Glass calendar desk watch, case with magnifying rear bezel forming the stand, 67mm. diam. (Sotheby's Belgravia) $700 £374

Mid 18th century silver repousse pair-cased 'pendulum' watch by Wolf Burqui, Middleburg, 54mm. diam. (Phillips) $1,510 £800

Late 18th century gilt and enamel calendar verge watch by Joseph Buchegger, Scharnstein, 46mm. diam.(Phillips) $905 £480

Swiss gold and enamel cased cylinder watch, cuvette signed Henry Capt, Geneve, 31mm. diam. (Phillips) $565 £300

Gold hunting cased duplex watch by Barwise, London, 1806, 53mm. diam. (Sotheby's) $1,664 £880

18ct. yellow gold hunter-cased keyless lever pocket watch, movement dated 1888. (Sotheby, King & Chasemore) $690 £380

Silver and horn pair-cased verge alarm watch, signed Conyers Dunlop, London, 53mm. diam. (Lawrence Fine Art) $960 £500

Silver pair-cased verge
watch by Nathaniel
Chamberlain, circa 1720,
58mm. diam. (Sotheby's)
$1,245 £660

Silver hunting cased duplex
watch by Barwise, London,
1820, 55mm. diam.
(Sotheby's Belgravia)
$370 £198

22ct. gold pair-cased
lever watch, signed
Geo. Graham, London,
1734, 49mm. diam.
(Phillips)$1,135 £600

Gold keyless lever dress
watch, dial signed for
Cartier, 45mm. diam.,
with gold and platinum
guard chain. (Phillips)
$1,135 £600

Victorian 18ct. gold case
hunter keyless watch,
London, 1867. (Geering
& Colyer) $2,335 £1,250

Gold and enamel triple
cased verge watch by
Geo. Prior, London,
1833, 40mm. diam.
(Phillips)$5,480 £2,900

Gold and enamel verge watch
by Leroy, Paris, circa 1830,
44mm. diam. (Phillips)
$1,665 £880

Cartier gold wrist
watch, signed Cartier,
London, 22 x 38mm.,
in presentation box.
(Sotheby's Belgravia)
$2,260 £1,210

19th century gold and enamel quarter repeating cy-
linder watch, inscribed
Breguet, 47mm. diam.
(Phillips) $3,685 £1,950

251

Swiss chronograph with enamel dial, in 18ct. gold case. (Hy. Duke & Son) $345 £180

William IV 18ct. gold open-faced key-wound lever watch, by J. & G. Benford, London. (Sotheby Beresford Adams) $335 £180

Slim 18ct. gold open-faced keyless lever watch, movement inscribed Paul Ditisheim, 48mm. diam. (Sotheby Beresford Adams) $355 £190

Slim gold and enamel open-faced key-wound cylinder watch, 40mm. diam. (Sotheby Beresford Adams) $445 £240

Gold half hunting cased keyless lever watch by James McCabe, London, 1878, 52mm. diam. (Sotheby's) $1,415 £748

18ct. gold open-faced verge watch by Grayhurst & Harvey, London, 1810, 45mm. diam. (Sotheby Beresford Adams) $1,080 £580

18ct. gold verge watch by Pilkington, Dublin, 43mm. diam., with engine-turned gold dial. (Sotheby Beresford Adams) $485 £260

18ct. gold hunting cased keyless lever centre-seconds watch, Chester, 1898, 57mm. diam. (Sotheby Beresford Adams) $520 £280

18ct. gold open-faced keyless lever watch by Lund & Blockley, London, 1886. (Sotheby Beresford Adams) $335 £180

Early silver keyless watch by John Roger Arnold, 1823, 55mm. diam. (Sotheby's) $1,290 £682

Gilt metal watch and pedometer by Ralph Gout of London, circa 1800, 55mm. diam. (Sotheby's) $1,040 £550

18ct. half hunting cased keyless lever fob watch, signed R. Curtis, Hull, 38mm. diam. (Sotheby Beresford Adams) $335 £180

Enamel and simulated pearl keyless fob watch suspended from ribbon bow. (Lawrence Fine Art) $240 £125

Keyless lever centre-seconds half hunter watch by Dent, London, numbered 50425, 18ct. gold case. (Sotheby Bearne) $560 £300

14ct. gold five-minute repeating pocket watch by The American Watch Co., Waltham. (Hy. Duke & Son) $2,880 £1,500

Silver pair-cased verge watch, signed Josephson, London, mid 18th century, 50mm. diam. (Sotheby Beresford Adams) $485 £260

Swiss gold hunter-cased keyless lever minute repeating watch, 54mm. diam. (Christie's) $1,870 £1,000

Silver pair-cased alarm verge watch by Thos. Tompion, late 17th century, 58mm. diam. (Sotheby's) $1,870 £990

WATCHES

CLOCKS

Gilt metal pair-cased verge watch by Wightwick & Moss, London, 54mm. diam. (Phillips)$150 £80

Gold and enamel half-hunting cased keyless lever watch, 45mm. diam. (Sotheby's Belgravia) $615 £330

Gold open-faced keyless lever chronograph with Swiss movement, 53mm. diam. (Sotheby's Belgravia) $475 £253

18ct. gold half hunting cased keyless lever watch by Barrauds & Lunds, London, 1919, 48mm. diam. (Sotheby's Belgravia) $530 £297

Rare ivory commemorative watch and ivory Albert, 50mm. diam. (Christie's)$2,055 £1,100

Gold hunting cased keyless lever watch, case applied with a monogram J. L., 54mm. diam. (Sotheby's Belgravia) $535 £286

18ct. gold half hunting cased lever watch by J. & A. Jump, London, 49mm. diam. (Sotheby's Belgravia) $570 £319

18ct. gold open-faced lever watch by Richd. Hornby & Son, Liverpool, 1851, 40mm. diam. (Sotheby's Belgravia) $925 £517

18ct. gold half hunting cased keyless lever watch by Chas. Frodsham, London, 47mm. diam. (Sotheby's Belgravia) $730 £407

Early 19th century French silver cased open-faced clock watch, signed Michaud a Montelmard. (Sotheby, King & Chasemore) $365 £200

Late George III 18ct. gold cased pocket chronometer, signed Barraud, London, 1816, 54mm. diam. (Phillips) $3,330 £1,800

English pair-cased silver open-faced pocket watch, signed, May, London, 1783. (Sotheby, King & Chasemore) $365 £200

18ct. gold half hunting cased keyless lever watch by Jn. Jones, London, 1876. (Sotheby's Belgravia) $635 £341

Fine French silver chaise calendar watch, signed Pierre Joseph van Rickstall a Paris, 90mm. diam. (Lawrence Fine Art) $1,000 £520

18ct. gold lever watch by J. Penlington, Liverpool, 47mm. diam. (Phillips) $1,110 £600

Gold and enamel hunting cased cylinder watch with matching buckle brooch. (Sotheby's Belgravia) $1,005 £539

18ct. gold open-faced centre-seconds lever watch, London, 1876, 53mm. diam. (Sotheby's Belgravia) $335 £187

18ct. gold open-faced quarter-repeating keyless lever watch by Hunt & Roskell, 47mm. diam. (Sotheby's Belgravia) $1,005 £539

Qianlong cloisonne enamel tripod broad globular censer, 11.5cm. high. (Christie's) $810 £450

Silver gilt and cloisonne enamel cigarette case, Moscow, 1886, 8.6cm. wide. (Sotheby's) $550 £297

One of a pair of Japanese cloisonne vases decorated in bright colours, circa 1900, 7¾in. high. (Sotheby's) $705 £374

Small 19th century Ota Tamasiro cloisonne vase with hexalobed body, 15.2cm. high. (Sotheby, King & Chasemore) $250 £140

Slightly cracked cloisonne vase, with full body enamelled with cranes, circa 1900, 13cm. high. (Sotheby's Belgravia) $300 £165

Late 19th century Japanese cloisonne vase with baluster body, 24.8cm. high, signed. (Sotheby, King & Chasemore) $575 £320

Late 19th century Japanese cloisonne opaque and transparent enamel on copper jar, 3½in. high. (Robert W. Skinner Inc.) $150 £80

Late 19th century Chinese cloisonne opaque enamel on copper vase of baluster form, 6in. high. (Robert W. Skinner Inc.) $80 £45

Polish silver gilt and cloisonne enamel cigarette case, circa 1915, 10.2cm. wide. (Sotheby's) $550 £297

18th/early 19th century large cloisonne enamel lobed baluster vase, one of a pair, 72.5cm. high. (Christie's)
$3,395 £1,760

Silver gilt and cloisonne enamel cigarette case by G.P., St. Petersburg, 1908-1917, 10.7cm. wide. (Sotheby's)
$595 £319

One of a pair of cloisonne enamel jardinieres with blue grounds, 7¾in. diam. (Burrows & Day)
$355 £190

One of a pair of cloisonne vases with silver wire decoration, circa 1900, 25.5cm. high. (Sotheby's Belgravia)
$1,085 £594

One of a pair of cloisonne enamel pilgrim bottles, late 18th/early 19th century, 29.5cm. high. (Christie's)$1,260 £700

Late 19th century Chinese cloisonne opaque and transparent enamel on copper vase, 9¼in. high. (Robert W. Skinner Inc.)
$100 £55

16th century cloisonne enamel censer and cover of squat bombe shape, 15.3cm. (Sotheby's) $740 £396

Cloisonne enamel baluster vase, fitted as an electric lamp, 23cm. high. (Christie's)
$990 £550

Silver gilt and cloisonne enamel bowl by P. Ovchinnikov, Moscow, 12cm. diam., 1899-1908. (Sotheby's)$940 £506

Kosen Kyoto cloisonne bowl with ribbed body, 15.5cm. diam., circa 1900, signed. (Sotheby's Belgravia)
$465 £242

18th/early 19th century cloisonne enamel globular bottle vase, slightly pitted, 39cm. high. (Christie's)
$635 £330

Silver gilt and cloisonne enamel cigarette case, Moscow, 1899-1908, 9.7cm. wide. (Sotheby's) $530 £286

Cloisonne vase with enamelled shouldered body on midnight-blue-ground, 19cm. high, signed Kitsuzan, circa 1900.(Sotheby's Belgravia)
$340 £176

Early 20th century Inaba cloisonne vase with beige-ground, silver rim and foot, 16cm. high.(Sotheby's Belgravia) $170 £88

One of a pair of cloisonne vases decorated with birds and branches, 52cm. high. (Sotheby's Belgravia)
$2,230 £1,155

16th/17th century Ming cloisonne enamel censer with bronze lion handles, 12cm. wide.(Christie's)
$580 £324

One of a pair of 19th century Japanes deep-blue-ground cloisonne enamel vases, 13in. high. (Lawrence Fine Art)
$265 £140

16th/early 17th century late Ming cloisonne enamel two-handled bowl, 13cm. wide across handles. (Christie's)
$735 £410

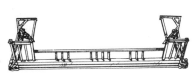

Mid 17th century brass salver with gadrooned edge, 11in. diam. (Sotheby's) $185 £99

Victorian brass fender with shell corners and railed gallery, 4ft. 5in. wide. (Dickinson, Davy & Markham) $125 £67

19th century copper eagle weathervane, from Massachusetts, 30in. long. (Robert W. Skinner Inc.) $600 £330

One of a pair of 17th century Dutch brass candlesticks on stepped and domed bases, 12¼in. high. (Sotheby's) $1,040 £550

Brass electric kettle designed by Peter Behrens, circa 1920, 22.75cm. high. (Sotheby's Belgravia) $240 £132

Pair of tall brass temple candlesticks from Bangkok, 38in. high. (Butler & Hatch Waterman) $115 £65

Italian black fossil limestone gilt brass bound circular table top, 27in. diam. (Christie's) $2,485 £1,350

One of a pair of brass fire iron rests, by Christopher Dresser, 1880's, 21.75cm. wide. (Sotheby's Belgravia) $80 £44

18th century famille noire porcelain vase of baluster form, 52cm. high. (Sotheby's Belgravia) $565 £308

Brass Imperial bushel measure by Pontifex & Wood, circa 1842, 19in. diam. (Sotheby's Belgravia) $645 £350

Mid 17th century German brass alms dish with engraved rim, 17in. diam. (Sotheby's) $565 £297

Early 19th century English copper bath on wheels, with brass rim, 54in. long. (Sotheby's Belgravia) $625 £340

One of a pair of late 18th century turned brass candlesticks, 9½in. high. (Woolley & Wallis) $100 £55

Late 19th century European cast brass hand mirror decorated with enamel, 8in. long, in fitted case. (Robert W. Skinner Inc.) $175 £100

One of a pair of late 19th century cast brass bear candlesticks, 7¼in. high. (Robert W. Skinner Inc.) $250 £135

One of two copper jugs and cover, 12in. and 18in. high. (Lawrence Fine Art) $65 £35

19th century brass footman, pierced with cabriole shaped front supports, 12½in. high. (Lawrence Fine Art) $185 £100

Early 19th century two-gallon copper measure of circular form, 15in. high. (Sotheby's) $135 £71

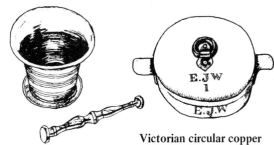

Dutch copper milk pail with snap-over cover, 16in. high. (Lawrence Fine Art) $200 £110

Antique brass mortar with pestle. (Woolley & Wallis) $110 £60

Victorian circular copper picnic saucepan with lid initialled, 5in. diam. (Woolley & Wallis)$80 £44

One of a pair of late 19th century brass medieval revival candlesticks, 38½in. high. (Sotheby's Belgravia) $295 £154

18th century English brass inkstand on trefoil-shaped tray. (Robert W. Skinner Inc.) $700 £380

One of a pair of English 18th century brass candlesticks, 11¾in. high.(Robert W. Skinner Inc.) $400 £215

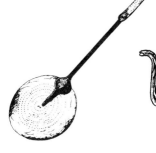

Early 19th century four-gallon copper and brass measure inscribed R. Cain. (Sotheby's) $146 £77

18th century brass skimmer with iron handle. (Woolley & Wallis) $160 £85

One of two large copper kettles and covers, 12½in. high. (Lawrence Fine Art) $165 £90

16th century German or French gilt brass circlet, 11cm. diam. (Christie's) $465 £242

One of a pair of late 17th/ early 18th century brass andirons with downswept supports and ball feet, 18½in. high. (Sotheby's) $375 £198

Silvered copper ewer and bowl, ewer with riveted curved handle, circa 1904. (Christie's) $2,910 £1,600

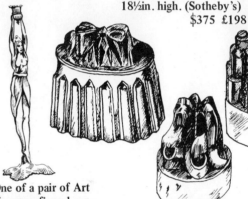

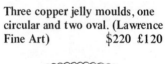

One of a pair of Art Nouveau figural candlesticks, in brass plated white metal, circa 1920, 18½in. high. (Robert W. Skinner Inc.) $325 £170

Three copper jelly moulds, one circular and two oval. (Lawrence Fine Art) $220 £120

Large brass witch's hat phonograph horn, 31½in. high, circa 1908. (Sotheby's) $110 £59

Brass 'student's' candlestick on square base. (J. M. Welch & Son) $85 £47

Hagenauer pierced and hammered brass box with flat cover, 1920's, 47.5cm. wide. (Sotheby's Belgravia) $1,780 £1,000

Victorian brass and gilt metal cotton reel holder with pin cushion. (Butler & Hatch Waterman) $165 £90

19th century globe-shaped copper tea urn. (J. M. Welch & Son) $230 £125

20th century wrought iron and copper pea fowl weathervane, American, 30½in. wide. (Robert W. Skinner Inc.) $700 £380

Antique copper kettle with domed lid and wooden handle. (Alfred Mossop & Co.) $100 £55

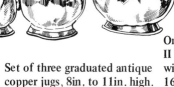

Mid 15th century Persian base brass candlestick, one of a pair, 9½in. high.(Sotheby's) $2,160 £1,155

Set of three graduated antique copper jugs, 8in. to 11in. high. (J. M. Welch & Son)$235 £130

One of a pair of Charles II brass candlesticks with ribbed stems, circa 1660, 7½in. high. (Sotheby's) $3,395 £1,815

Late 19th century sheet metal butterfly weathervane, American, in copper. (Robert W. Skinner Inc.) $1,100 £605

Art Deco brass sparkguard carved with a peacock. (J. M. Welch & Son) $90 £50

One of a pair of early 19th century American Federal brass George Washington figural andirons, 21in. high. (Robert W. Skinner Inc.) $500 £270

263

Brass mounted copper coal helmet. (Morris, Marshall & Poole) $190 £105

One of three American copper plaques, signed Raymond Averill Porter, circa 1913-19.(Robert W. Skinner Inc.) $250 £140

One of a pair of 17th century French brass candlesticks, 20in. high. (Boardman's) $1,245 £670

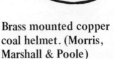

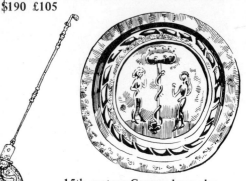

15th century German brass alms dish with slightly flaring rim, 10½in. diam. (Robert W. Skinner Inc.) $1,650 £895

One of a pair of brass candlesticks, European, circa 1870, 10¼in. high. (Robert W. Skinner Inc.) $250 £135

Dutch brass warming pan with pierced lid, dated 1619, 44in. long.(Sotheby, King & Chasemore) $220 £120

19th century circular copper kettle with ringed cover and acorn finial, 11in. high. (Dickinson, Davy & Markham)$110 £60

Large 19th century seamed copper kettle with cover, cast iron handle and brass tap, 12in. high. (Dickinson, Davy & Markham) $75 £42

19th century Japanese patinated brass teapot of bulbous form with wrapped handle grip, 6in. diam.(Robert W. Skinner Inc.)$80 £45

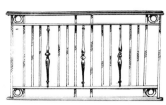

Large 19th century sea-
med copper kettle with
cover and curving han-
dle, 1ft.1in. high.
(Dickinson, Davy &
Markham)   ✝
$75 £40

One of a set of seven brass railings,
circa 1910, each 50in. wide.
(Sotheby's Belgravia) $845 £460

One of a pair of 16th
century Flemish tur-
ned brass candlesticks,
16in. high. (Board-
man's) $2,420 £1,300

Jewelled and enamelled gilt
copper monstrance, designed
by John Francis Bentley,
circa 1864, 65.8cm. high.
(Sotheby's Belgravia) $2,590
£1,400

Limoges enamelled
copper dish with trans-
parent red border, circa
1870, 6¾in. long.
(Robert W. Skinner Inc.)
$300 £165

Benham & Froud copper
and brass kettle, designed
by Christopher Dresser,
77cm. high. (Phillips)
$230 £130

American Art Deco cop-
per water jug with sphe-
rical body, circa 1930,
12in. high. (Robert W.
Skinner Inc.) $45 £25

Pair of early 19th century
Federal brass and wrought
iron steeple-top andirons,
21in. high.(Robert W.
Skinner Inc.)$1,150 £630

Georgian copper choco-
late pot with fitted tur-
ned fruitwood side han-
dle, 18cm. high. (Sotheby,
King & Chasemore)
$205 £110

Late 19th century Kesi informal robe on saxe-blue ground, bordered with indigo and white. (Sotheby's Belgravia) $820 £440

Pair of early 17th century gauntlets of white kid, cuff applied with ivory silk and sequins. (Phillips)$335 £180

Rare late 19th century Kesi formal robe woven with coloured silks on indigo ground. (Sotheby's Belgravia) $2,045 £1,100

Black georgette dress with vertical lines of black beads and red plastic 'gems', 1920's. (Sotheby's Belgravia) $205 £110

Paisley pattern shawl with central lobed medallion, circa 1860, 106 x 134½in.(Sotheby's Belgravia) $250 £132

Red beaded georgette dress bordered with trailing scrolls, 1920's. (Sotheby's Belgravia) $370 £198

Chinese robe of midnight blue silk, deep sleeves lined with cream and beige Afghan fox. (Phillips) $1,015 £550

Early 17th century uncut velvet fragment with initials 'CR' surmounted by a crown.(Phillips) $185 £100

Early 19th century Chinese robe of midnight blue silk, embroidered with coloured silks, lined. (Phillips) $405 £220

19th century lady's Kesi informal robe on rose-pink ground. (Sotheby's Belgravia) $615 £330

Pair of late 18th century stays of white linen with silk binding, circa 1790. (Phillips) $1,075 £580

20th century Moroccan Pasha's robe edged with heavy gold braid. (Sotheby's Belgravia) $615 £330

Silver and white beaded georgette dress, sold with a suede bag, 1920's. (Sotheby's Belgravia) $185 £99

19th century Norwich shawl with ivory silk ground, fringed, 1.46m. square. (Phillips) $205 £110

Gold, white and black beaded dress and jacket, 1920's. (Sotheby's Belgravia) $570 £308

Late 19th century Algerian silk scarf with embroidered ends, on lemon ground.(Sotheby's Belgravia) $100 £55

Kid jerkin with overlay of late 17th century French brocade, silk and cotton lined. (Phillips)$150 £80

Finely embroidered silk shawl in polychrome silks on a black ground, circa 1900, 48 x 51in. (Sotheby's Belgravia) $185 £99

Christian Dior two-piece evening dress, labelled, circa 1950. (Sotheby's Belgravia) $125 £66

Gold, black, silver and white beaded dress with V-neck, 1920's. (Sotheby's) $580 £308

Printed silk two-piece bodice and skirt, with purple violet sprigs, circa 1895.(Sotheby's Belgravia) $205 £110

Unusual polychrome and gold thread long satin evening dress with cross-over bodice, 1920's. (Sotheby's Belgravia) $455 £242

Gold sequinned and beaded black strapless satin evening dress, probably by C. Dior, circa 1960. (Sotheby's Belgravia) $115 £60

Maroon and black shot silk dress, circa 1865, with later lace collar. (Sotheby's Belgravia) $105 £55

Nini Ricci full-length black velvet evening dress, labelled, 1940's. (Sotheby's Belgravia) $205 £110

Shaded blue and silver beaded dress probably by Chanel, circa 1923, on a black satin ground. (Sotheby's Belgravia)$205 £110

268

Black, white and eau-de-nil beaded dress with overlapping leaf design, 1920's.(Sotheby's Belgravia) $580 £308

Painted and printed brown chiffon dress and cape painted by Elaine Bodley, 1920's. (Sotheby's Belgravia)$175 £93

Fortuny 'Delphos' dress of black satin, circa 1920, unlabelled. (Sotheby's Belgravia)$580 £308

Coco Chanel black satin and tulle evening dress, labelled, circa 1930.(Sotheby's Belgravia) $730 £385

Gold lace long evening dress and jacket with roses down the side, 1930's.(Sotheby's Belgravia) $355 £187

Chanel sequinned long evening dress, labelled, circa 1930, zip and bodice added. (Sotheby's Belgravia) $625 £330

French beaded dress with slate blue muslin ground, 1920's, skirt with vandyked hem. (Sotheby's Belgravia) $625 £330

Black taffeta short evening dress by Christian Dior, 1950's. (Sotheby's Belgravia) $70 £38

269

Woven shawl of Paisley design, 64 x 137in., circa 1870. (Sotheby's Belgravia) $305 £165

19th century Chinese triangular panel of yellow silk, designed with a dragon, 2.30 x 1.15m. (Phillips) $520 £280

Unusual printed cockade fan, 1876, Viennese, 24.5cm. long. (Sotheby's Belgravia) $290 £154

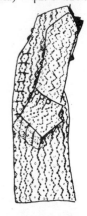

Mid 19th century dress of printed cotton in check pattern, circa 1840's. (Phillips) $295 £160

19th century Paisley shawl of 'moon shawl' design, with ivory cashmere ground, circa 1840's, 1.60 x 1.72m. (Phillips) $85 £45

Coat from an 18th century French gentleman's three-piece suit, in moire silk. (Sotheby's Belgravia) $1,245 £660

Chinese mandarin's coat of turquoise silk with orange lining, embroidered in gilt thread. (Woolley & Wallis) $140 £80

Two-piece green and cream silk jacket and trained skirt, sold with belt and bag, circa 1867. (Sotheby's Belgravia) $115 £60

Late 19th century lady's embroidered informal robe with indigo satin ground. (Sotheby's Belgravia) $540 £286

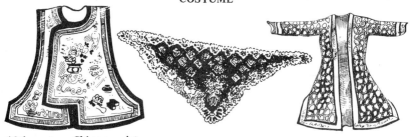

19th century Chinese waistcoat of grey silk embroidered in coloured and ivory silks, lined. (Phillips) $370 £200

19th century Brussels triangular shawl of bobbin and needlepoint applique.(Phillips) $445 £240

Late 18th century Persian jacket of stamped brocade, sleeves with loop fastenings, lined. (Phillips) $665 £360

Length of mid 17th century gros point de Venise designed with curled flowers, 0.09 x 1m. (Phillips) $350 £190

19th century Russian priest's vestment and robe in brocade with metallic thread.(Robert W. Skinner Inc.) $425 £230

Cheruit evening coat of bright yellow, edged with black velvet, circa 1920. (Sotheby's Belgravia) $105 £55

19th century Paisley shawl of striped design, circa 1840's, fringed, 1.55m. square. (Phillips)$350 £190

Clear beaded black georgette dress with fringed panels, 1920's. (Sotheby's)$165 £88

19th century Paisley shawl of 'moon shawl' design, with olive green cashmere ground, 1.62m. square. (Phillips) $390 £210

271

Leon Bakst costume design for the Negro Dancer from Le Dieu Bleu, 1922, 25½ x 18½in.(Sotheby's) $34,650 £19,250

Costume design for the Coster Girls from My Fair Lady, by C. Beaton, 19 x 17in. (Sotheby's) $545 £297

Leon Bakst costume design for Andre from La Boutique Fantasque, 1918, 17¼ x 11in. (Sotheby's) $5,545 £3,080

Alexandre Benois costume design for Von Rothbart as an owl, dated 1946, signed, 9½ x 6½in.(Sotheby's) $715 £396

Design for a Pioneer's outfit, 1926, 13½ x 8¾in. (Sotheby's) $1,620 £880

Alexandre Benois costume design for Parpagnol, 1946, 12½ x 9½in.(Sotheby's) $435 £242

One of six costume designs for girls in evening dress and Spanish style costume, 13 x 10in.(Sotheby's)$395 £220

Costume design by Cecil Beaton for My Fair Lady, signed, 13½ x 5¾in. (Sotheby's)$705 £385

Costume design by F. Leger, for Goliath, dated Dec. '36, 12 x 10in. (Sotheby's) $4,050 £2,200

A. Benois costume design for a court lady from Le Bourgeois Gentilhomme, 1932, 11¾ x 9in.(Sotheby's) $395 £220

Costume design for a Grenadier from Le Regiment qui Passe, 15¼ x 7in.(Sotheby's) $315 £176

One of three costume designs for La Baronne Sandore from L'Argent, 14 x 10¾in. (Sotheby's)$255 £143

A. Benois costume design for a young girl, dated '52, 9 x 6¼in.(Sotheby's) $375 £209

Costume design by B. Bilinsky for the prison watchman in La Princesse Cygne, 19¼ x 12¼in.(Sotheby's) $445 £242

One of six costume designs by I. Segalle for Dick Whittington, 1935, 15 x 10½in. (Sotheby's) $30 £16

Leon Bakst costume design for one of the Boy Brigands, signed, 10½ x 7¼in. (Sotheby's) $1,030 £572

Alexandra Exter design for two Duelling Figures, signed, circa 1926, 21½ x 18½in. (Sotheby's) $6,730 £3,740

Alexandre Benois costume design for a jester from Sadko, signed, dated 1930, 12½ x 9in. (Sotheby's) $830 £462

Rare French shoulder bisque fashion doll, circa 1860, 17½in. high, sold with a selection of clothes, (Sotheby's Belgravia) $1,585 £858

French bisque 'Parisienne' doll with gusseted kid body, circa 1870, 15in. high. (Sotheby's Belgravia) $1,060 £572

Rare Armand Marseille top-knot 'googly-eyed' doll with curved limb body, 11in. high. (Sotheby's Belgravia) $610 £330

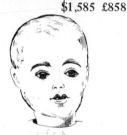

Unusual S.F.B.J. bisque character boy doll with felted-on hair, 15in. high. (Sotheby's Belgravia) $490 £264

Poured shoulder-waxed doll possibly by Montanari in original pink satin dress, 22in. high. (Sotheby Beresford Adams) $335 £180

Rare Gebruder Heubach black bisque character boy doll, left toes chipped, 14in. high.(Sotheby's Belgravia) $915 £495

German shoulder china doll with kid body, original jacket and skirt, circa 1865, 13in. high. (Sotheby's Belgravia) $550 £297

Shoulder bisque doll with painted features, dressed in original fairy costume, 13in. high. (Sotheby Beresford Adams) $250 £135

German bisque 'walking' doll in purple silk dress, 20in. high. (Sotheby's Belgravia) $405 £220

A. Lanternier 'favorite' bisque doll, with ermine stole and green suit, 17in. high. (Sotheby's Belgravia) $345 £187

Large Jumeau bisque Bebe doll, circa 1885, 31in. high, in white lace-trimmed cotton coat and bonnet. (Sotheby's Belgravia) $2,035 £1,100

Jumeau bisque Bebe doll marked Tete Jumeau, 23in. high, wig replaced. (Sotheby's Belgravia) $1,015 £550

Kammer & Reinhardt/Simon & Halbig 'My Darling' bisque doll in white dress and kid shoes, 17½in. high.(Sotheby's Belgravia) $3,050 £1,650

Fine 'long face' Jumeau Bebe doll, 28in. high, circa 1870. (Sotheby's Belgravia)$3,560 £1,925

S.F.B.J. bisque character boy doll, 21in. long, in white cotton robe. (Sotheby's Belgravia) $1,015 £550

Biedermeier shoulder papier-mache doll with kid body, circa 1840, 11in. high. (Sotheby's Belgravia) $530 £286

Catterfelder Puppenfabrik bisque doll, with navy blue velvet suit, 30in. high. (Sotheby's Belgravia)$405 £220

Good Steiner clockwork walking/talking doll with papier-mache and kid body, 18in. high.(Sotheby's Belgravia)$975 £528

Heubach bisque head doll, Germany, circa 1900, 15½in. high, original dress and hat. (Robert W. Skinner Inc.) $175 £95

Kammer & Reinhardt bisque head character baby doll, Germany, circa 1900, 17in. long. (Robert W. Skinner Inc.) $350 £185

20th century Heubach dusky bisque character doll, with glass eyes, 6¾in. long. (Robert W. Skinner Inc.) $80 £42

German yellow plush teddy bear with elongated body, circa 1925, 20½in. high. (Robert W. Skinner Inc.) $60 £35

Victorian waxed shoulder composition doll in original ivory satin and lace bridal dress, 24in. high. (Sotheby Beresford Adams) $280 £150

Bisque doll, stamped Jumeau d'Or Paris, 20in. high, lacking wig, in original navy blue and wine red peasant costume. (Sotheby Beresford Adams) $2,525 £1,350

Armand Marseille bisque 'My Dream Baby' doll in original ensemble. (Sotheby's Belgravia) $235 £121

Bisque character doll, possibly by Heubach, 13½in. high, with moulded hair. (Sotheby Beresford Adams) $335 £180

Simon & Halbig bisque headed doll, Germany, circa 1880, 12½in. high. (Robert W. Skinner Inc.) $950 £502

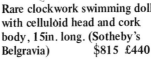

S.F.B.J. bisque headed doll, Paris, early 20th century, stamped Made in France, 15¼in. high. (Robert W. Skinner Inc.)
$170 £90

Rare clockwork swimming doll with celluloid head and cork body, 15in. long. (Sotheby's Belgravia)
$815 £440

Kammer & Reinhardt bisque headed character baby doll, Germany, 1909, 11in. long. (Robert W. Skinner Inc.)
$200 £105

German bisque head doll with composition body, circa 1900-10, 24in. long, thumb missing. (Robert W. Skinner Inc.)
$300 £160

Fine French bisque fashion doll, impressed F, circa 1870, 18in. high. (Sotheby's Belgravia)
$2,750 £1,430

German bisque head character doll, circa 1900, 15in. long, slightly chipped. (Robert W. Skinner Inc.)
$375 £200

Early 20th century German lithographed tin wind-up newsboy, 7¼in. high. (Robert W. Skinner Inc.)
$80 £42

Large Kestner bisque head doll, circa 1900, 32in. long, with sleeping glass eyes. (Robert W. Skinner Inc.)
$475 £250

Late 19th century German beige bisque head doll, 11¼in. high, with glass eyes. (Robert W. Skinner Inc.)$350 £185

Armand Marseille bisque headed doll with kid body, 13in. high. (Burrows & Day) $260 £140

Late Victorian wax doll in pink silk dress and leather shoes. (Woolley & Wallis) $485 £260

Rare mid 19th century German triple faced bisque headed doll with fabric body, 13½in. high. (Locke & England) $1,260 £680

Rare Heubach 'Whistling Jim' character boy doll with cloth body, 15in. high. (Sotheby's Belgravia) $890 £462

Kammer & Reinhardt/Simon & Halbig 'My Darling' doll with jointed body, 22in. high. (Sotheby's Belgravia) $3,355 £1,815

Bruno Schmidt 'Tommy Tucker' bisque character doll, circa 1910, 13in. high. (Sotheby's Belgravia) $890 £462

Barr & Proschild bisque character doll with curved limb body, 13in. high. (Sotheby's Belgravia) $340 £176

Armand Marseille bisque 'Oriental' baby doll in printed 'Japanese' robe, 8in. high. (Sotheby's Belgravia) $680 £352

Good French bisque 'Parisienne' doll with gusseted kid body, circa 1875, 16in. high. (Sotheby's Belgravia) $610 £330

Bisque character headed baby doll marked K*R, S. & H., 114/A, 18in. high. (Christie's S. Kensington) $2,325 £1,250

Late Victorian wax doll in pale blue silk dress and straw hat. (Woolley & Wallis) $485 £260

Victorian china doll in cream silk dress. (Woolley & Wallis) $150 £80

French bisque 'Parisienne' doll with gusseted kid body, 16in. high, in original white cotton dress. (Sotheby's Belgravia) $1,165 £605

Ges. Gesch shoulder bisque character boy doll with cloth body, 14in. high. (Sotheby's Belgravia) $510 £264

Kammer & Reinhardt/ Simon & Halbig bisque doll with jointed body, 26in. high. (Sotheby's Belgravia) $635 £330

Simon & Halbig walking/ talking doll with jointed body, 20in. high. (Sotheby's Belgravia) $635 £330

Alt. Beck & Gottschalck bisque doll, 24in. high, with jointed body. (Sotheby's Belgravia) $340 £176

Tinplate somersaulting figure, probably by F. Martin, France, circa 1905, 7½in. high. (Sotheby's Belgravia) $405 £219

French cloth doll, circa 1920's, 2ft.3in. high. (Sotheby's Belgravia) $65 £35

Bisque 'Bald' head doll with perished lambswool wig, in original dress, circa 1880, 10½in. high. (Sotheby's Belgravia) $725 £396

Simon & Halbig doll with jointed body and opening eyes, 5in. high. (Woolley & Wallis) $115 £65

Kammer & Reinhardt bisque character doll with painted blue eyes, circa 1915, 16½in. high. (Sotheby's Belgravia) $2,820 £1,540

Victorian waxed shoulder-papier-mache pumpkin head doll, 20in. high, circa 1860, in box. (Sotheby's Belgravia) $360 £198

George III wooden doll with pink kid arms, 18½in. high, in original dress. (Sotheby's) $1,400 £742

Wax shoulder doll with stuffed fabric body, 18in. high, in white cotton dress. (Sotheby's) $415 £220

China headed Nanny doll with original clothes and child doll, 5in. high. (Woolley & Wallis) $115 £65

Jumeau bisque doll, head marked, with glass eyes and blonde wig, 16½in. high. (Sotheby's Belgravia) $1,410 £770

Ernst Heubach boy doll with bisque head and composition body, 18in. high, in pyjamas. (Sotheby's) $250 £132

Large early 19th century female Hina festival doll, right hand detached, 16in. high. (Sotheby's Belgravia) $260 £143

Kammer & Reinhardt character bisque doll, 15in. high, head repaired, in white cotton dress. (Sotheby's Belgravia) $525 £286

Mid 19th century poured shoulder wax lady doll, possibly by Pierotti, 18in. high. (Sotheby's) $415 £220

Pair of Armand Marseille bisque 'Red Indian' dolls, 9in. high, in original costumes. (Sotheby's Belgravia) $405 £220

Fine Bru bisque doll with original clothing and shoes, circa 1875, 21in. high.(Christie's) $7,650 £4,180

Strobel & Wilken 'googly-eyed' bisque doll, in green cotton dress, 7in. high.(Sotheby's Belgravia)$440 £242

S.F.B.J. Bebe doll with jointed body, 26in. high, in red silk dress. (Sotheby's Belgravia) $565 £308

'Googly-eyed' bisque doll by JDK Ges. Gesch, 11in. high, in knitted pullover and cap. (Sotheby's Belgravia) $1,610 £880

Model doll's house of 'Harethorpe Hall' with painted brick front, 47in. long. (Sotheby's Belgravia) $725 £396

Late 19th/early 20th century wooden model of a stable with two papier-mache horses, 23in. wide. (Robert W. Skinner Inc.) $250 £140

Early 20th century American wooden gabled roof doll's house with glass windows, 24¾in. high. (Robert W. Skinner Inc.) $200 £115

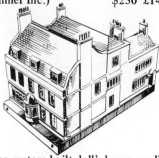

Triang custom built doll's house, replica of 45 Kensington Square, London, 51in. wide, complete with accessories. (Sotheby's) $605 £319

Late Victorian wooden doll's house, circa 1890, 33in. wide, with hinged front. (Sotheby's Belgravia)$850 £440

Late 19th century doll's house with opening front, 47in. high x 37in. wide. (Woolley & Wallis) $385 £220

American diorama of an early 19th century hallway, circa 1950, fitted with dolls and furniture, 19½in. wide. (Robert W. Skinner Inc.) $125 £70

19th century wooden Mansard roof doll's house with painted brick front, 23¾in. high. (Robert W. Skinner Inc.) $200 £115

Liberty & Co., silver and enamel frame, 29cm. high, Birmingham, 1905. (Sotheby's Belgravia) $1,030 £580

German enamel snuff box decorated with hunting scenes, circa 1760, 8.5cm. wide. (Sotheby's) $610 £330

17th century Limoges enamel hexalobate dish by Jacques Laudin, 6½in. wide.(Sotheby's) $1,245 £660

Unusual circular German enamel snuff box with lobed bombe-shaped sides, circa 1750, 7.5cm. diam. (Sotheby's) $3,460 £1,870

Mid 19th century enamelled double-handled vase with gilt handles, 48.5cm. high. (Sotheby's Belgravia) $300 £165

Late 19th century French enamel dish with dark-blue-ground, 9in. diam. (Sotheby's) $890 £495

German enamel snuff box painted by Andreas Bech-dolff of Ellwangen, 1763, 7.5cm. wide. (Sotheby's) $4,475 £2,420

Mid 18th century German gold and enamel mounted walking stick with mush-room-shaped handle. (Christie's) $1,355 £734

German enamel comme-morative snuff box with portrait of Frederick the Great, circa 1760, 8cm. wide. (Sotheby's) $2,035 £1,100

19th century Swiss gold and enamel box formed as a barrel, 1¾in. high. (Christie's) $5,820 £3,080

Continental rectangular enamel snuff box, probably Vienna, circa 1760, 3¼in. wide. (Christie's)$960 £520

Bilston green-ground mustard pot with loop handle and detachable cover, circa 1770, 3½in. high. (Christie's) $455 £242

Late 18th century Bilston enamel frog bonbonniere, 2in. diam. (Christie's) $665 £360

Late 19th century small Viennese enamel standing cup and cover, 16cm. high. (Sotheby's Belgravia)$730 £396

17th century Limoges grisaille and polychrome enamel fluted bowl by Jean Laudin, 14.5cm. across. (Christie's) $380 £198

Birmingham fine enamel tea caddy of oval form, circa 1765, 4¾in. wide.(Christie's) $6,235 £3,300

17th century Limoges polychrome enamel water stoup by Pierre Nouailher, 27.5cm. high. (Christie's) $950 £495

Late 19th/early 20th century small Viennese enamel bowl with fluted oval body, 12.3cm. wide. (Sotheby's Belgravia) $580 £308

Early 20th century Norwegian plique-a-jour cup and saucer decorated with enamel. (Sotheby's Belgravia) $995 £528

Chinese rectangular famille rose porcelain snuff box, circa 1760, with silver gilt mounts, 3in. wide. (Christie's) $1,295 £700

Swiss jewelled gold and enamel vinaigrette with split pearl border, early 19th century, 3.8cm. wide.(Sotheby's) $1,910 £990

Modern Limoges enamel vase designed by Camille Faure, 27.2cm. high. (Sotheby's Belgravia) $605 £330

One of a pair of Bilston enamel cassolettes on plinth bases, circa 1770. (Christie's)$4,575 £2,420

Late 19th century Viennese enamel nef with gilt metal mounts, 14cm. high. (Sotheby's Belgravia) $825 £440

Framed enamel on copper plaque of Neptune, signed E. Sieffert, circa 1910, 36½in. high. (Robert W. Skinner Inc.) $1,900 £1,050

Louis XVI oval gold and enamel snuff box by Joseph Etienne Blerzy, Paris, 1776, 3¼in. wide. (Christie's) $20,790 £11,000

Large pair of French or Swiss enamelled opera glasses, 11.5cm. high, circa 1875. (Sotheby's Belgravia) $660 £352

Late 19th century Japanese ivory fan decorated in Shibayama style, 38cm. long. (Sotheby's Belgravia) $195 £88

French mother-of-pearl fan with pierced sticks, circa 1860, signed Mabel, 26.8cm. long. (Sotheby's Belgravia) $265 £143

Fan painted with a watercolour and with gilt and mother-of-pearl sticks, 1895, 34cm. long. (Sotheby's Belgravia) $370 £198

Late 18th century ivory fan with pierced and carved sticks with chinoiserie figures, 23cm. long. (Sotheby's Belgravia) $130 £71

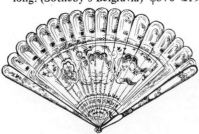

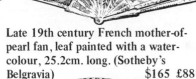

18th century chinoiserie 'peep-hole' fan decorated with mother-of-pearl, 29cm. long. (Sotheby's Belgravia) $370 £198

Late 19th century French mother-of-pearl fan, leaf painted with a water-colour, 25.2cm. long. (Sotheby's Belgravia) $165 £88

Mid 19th century lacquered Chinese brise fan, 23.5cm. long. (Sotheby's Belgravia) $270 £143

Framed Chinese ivory brise fan with finely pierced and draped central shield, circa 1795, 19in. wide. (Robert W. Skinner Inc.) $160 £85

Lace fan with mother-of-pearl sticks, circa 1890, 27cm. long. (Sotheby's Belgravia) $125 £66

Early 18th century Vernis Martin brise fan, 21cm. long. (Sotheby's Belgravia) $1,345 £605

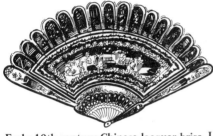

Early 19th century Chinese lacquer brise fan, black sticks painted in shades of blue, red and green, 20cm. long. (Sotheby's Belgravia) $1,135 £605

Unusual asymmetrical Chinese export fan with black lacquered sticks, circa 1860, 30.5cm. long. (Sotheby's Belgravia) $225 £121

Late 19th century Chinese ivory brise fan with carved bead, 28cm. long. (Sotheby's Belgravia) $405 £220

Mid 19th century Chinese parcel gilt filigree brise fan, 19.5cm. long. (Sotheby's Belgravia) $660 £352

Mid 19th century Chinese silver filigree and enamel fan, slightly damaged, 28.5cm. long. (Sotheby's Belgravia) $455 £242

Chinese ivory and feather fan with pierced and carved sticks and guards, 23cm. long, circa 1830. (Sotheby's Belgravia) $185 £99

287

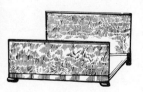

19th century Chinese red-wood day bed with carved frame, 214cm. wide. (H. Spencer & Sons Ltd.)
$1,380 £750

Late 19th century bed from a Renaissance revival walnut suite of five pieces. (Robert W. Skinner Inc.)
$1,050 £585

Bed from a three-piece set of Art Deco burl and ash bedroom suite, American, circa 1930. (Robert W. Skinner Inc.) $250 £130

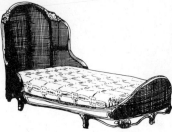

Hepplewhite four-poster with domed top and fluted and carved pillars, 6ft. wide. (Russell, Baldwin & Bright)
$2,970 £1,650

Late 19th/early 20th century giltwood double bed with caned headboard and carved toprail, 54in. wide. (Sotheby's Belgravia)
$985 £528

Early 17th century James I oak tester bed with leaf-carved panels, 4ft.8in. wide. (Sotheby's)
$4,320 £2,310

Oak four-poster bed made from Jacobean timbers, with triple panelled head-board, 57in. wide.(Locke & England) $1,275 £700

Bed from a late 19th cen-tury American Renais-sance revival walnut bed-room suite, with burl panels. (Robert W. Skin-ner Inc.) $1,900 £1,075

American Renaissance revival walnut and burl veneer bed with carved arch, sold with a match-ing commode, circa 1870. (Robert W. Skin-ner Inc.) $1,500 £835

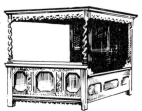

Oak swinging cradle
with carved side
panels. (Dee & Atkinson)　　$160 £90

Brass and mother-of-pearl
three-sided double bed,
circa 1880, 75¼in. wide.
(Sotheby's Belgravia)
　　　　$740 £396

17th century German oak
four-poster bed with
panelled canopy, and footboard. (Boardman's)
　　$2,685 £1,450

Bed from a late 19th
century American
three-piece walnut
bedroom set. (Robert
W. Skinner Inc.)
　　$900 £510

Superbly carved Spanish walnut four-poster bed on carved
animal feet. (John Hogbin &
Son)　　　　$3,600 £2,000

Early 17th century
Jacobean carved oak
tester bed with carved arcading, 4ft.9in.
wide. (Sotheby's)
　　$3,085 £1,650

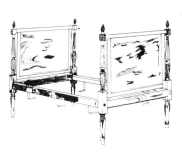

Mahogany Hepplewhite
style four-poster bed
with carved arcaded frieze. (Edward, Bigwood
& Bewlay)$1,645 £900

19th century American bed
frame with panelled ends,
3ft.11½in. wide.(Sotheby's)
　　　　$1,455 £792

Four-poster bed of Hepplewhite style, with finely
reeded front pillars and
cornice, 4ft.6in. wide.
(Butler & Hatch Waterman)　　$1,850 £1,000

Late 19th century mahogany secretaire library bookcase. (Biddle & Webb) $4,850 £2,650

One of a pair of Regency satinwood veneered open bookcases, 30in. wide. (Woolley & Wallis) $3,160 £1,700

Gustav Stickley oak bookcase, New York, circa 1912, 53½in. wide. (Robert W. Skinner Inc.) $1,600 £905

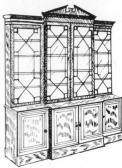

Walnut breakfront bookcase of Chippendale style with satinwood inlay, 90in. high. (Hy. Duke & Son) $2,975 £1,550

Late 19th century mahogany bookcase of Adam style with pierced trellis, 3ft.6in. wide. (Sotheby, King & Chasemore) $3,905 £2,100

Mid 19th century mahogany library bookcase with moulded pediment, 75in. wide. (Sotheby Beresford Adams) $3,070 £1,650

George III mahogany bookcase with moulded cornice, 55in. wide. (Christie's) $2,980 £1,595

George III mahogany double breakfront library bookcase with broken scrolled pediment, 157in. wide. (Christie's) $11,840 £6,400

George IV mahogany cabinet bookcase, circa 1825, 3ft.2in. wide. (Sotheby, King & Chasemore) $650 £350

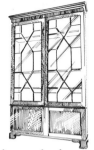

Gustav Stickley oak book-
case, New York, circa
1912, 39in. wide.(Robert
W. Skinner Inc.)
$1,550 £875

Mahogany bookcase on
French bracket feet, top
with glazed tracery doors,
4ft.6in. wide. (Gilbert
Baitson) $710 £375

Eastern United States Re-
naissance revival walnut
bookcase, circa 1870,
46in. wide, with two gla-
zed doors. (Robert W.
Skinner Inc.)$425 £240

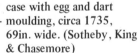

George III mahogany
bookcase with moulded
cornice, 40in. wide.
(Burrows & Day)
$1,265 £700

Mid 19th century William IV
mahogany breakfront library
bookcase with moulded pediment, 95in. wide. (Sotheby
Beresford Adams)
$2,510 £1,350

George II mahogany book-
case with egg and dart
moulding, circa 1735,
69in. wide. (Sotheby, King
& Chasemore)
$6,990 £3,800

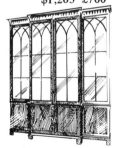

Mahogany breakfront book-
case, top with four glazed
Gothic tracery doors, 6ft .
wide. (Gilbert Baitson)
$1,700 £900

William IV mahogany breakfront bookcase with decorated cornice, 108in. wide.
(Boardman's)$4,345 £2,300

George III mahogany breakfront bookcase, 9ft.3in.
wide, circa 1770.(Edwards,
Bigwood & Bewlay)
$12,810 £7,000

291

Regency mahogany break-front library bookcase with ball-encrusted cornice, 122½in. wide. (Christie's)$5,985 £3,200

William IV rosewood bookcase with raised back portion having a brass gallery, 65in. wide. (Lawrence Fine Art) $2,505 £1,400

American Arts & Crafts oak bookcase, circa 1900, with three doors, 54in. wide. (Robert W. Skinner Inc.)$200 £110

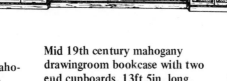

'George III' mahogany bookcase with swan-neck cresting, circa 1910, 33½in. wide. (Sotheby's Belgravia)$1,725 £924

Mid 19th century mahogany drawingroom bookcase with two end cupboards, 13ft.5in. long. (Russell, Baldwin & Bright) $2,160 £1,200

Early 20th century burr-walnut display cabinet/bookcase. (Warren & Wignall) $520 £290

'George III' mahogany breakfront bookcase with blind fret frieze, circa 1880, 91in. wide. (Sotheby's Belgravia) $5,140 £2,750

Late 19th century carved oak bookcase, 9ft. wide. (R. H. Ellis & Sons) $1,890 £1,000

Georgian mahogany breakfront bookcase with moulded pediment, by M. Wilson, 8ft.8in. wide. (W. H. Lane & Son) $4,550 £2,500

Burr-walnut breakfront bookcase with central mirror-back compartment, late 1840's, 78in. wide. (Sotheby's Belgravia) $1,070 £572

Edwardian mahogany revolving bookcase on brass castors. (J. M. Welch & Son)$280 £155

Mahogany open shelved library bookcase with galleried top, 8ft.5in. wide. (Lawrence Fine Art) $3,495 £1,900

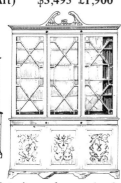

Regency bookcase with scrolled and pierced cornice, 45¼in. wide. (Christie's) $5,110 £2,808

Late Georgian mahogany breakfront bookcase, 15ft. long. (Dee & Atkinson)$5,180 £2,800

Victorian mahogany bookcase of George III style with pierced fretwork pediment, stamped Edwards and Roberts, 75½in. wide. (Christie's) $5,800 £3,240

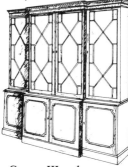

George III mahogany breakfront bookcase with glazed doors, 7ft. 10in. wide. (Lawrence Fine Art)$3,310 £1,800

Regency mahogany breakfront library bookcase with moulded cornice, 98½in. wide. (Christie's) $10,810 £5,940

George III mahogany breakfront bookcase with four glazed doors. (Sotheby Bearne) $9,385 £5,100

BUREAUX

Georgian mahogany bureau with oval brass handles, 36in. wide. (Lawrence Fine Art) $715 £390

George III tambour top writing table with raised gallery, 36in. wide. (Edwards, Bigwood & Bewlay)$1,315 £720

George I figured walnut bureau on bracket feet, 37in. wide. (Lawrence Fine Art) $1,750 £950

Mahogany and satinwood clerk's desk, stamped Bertram & Son, London, 32½in. wide, 1890's. (Sotheby's Belgravia) $955 £495

Fine early walnut bureau with decorative stringing and crossbanding, 3ft.2in. wide. (Butler & Hatch Waterman) $1,205 £670

Maple's mahogany and painted bureau, labelled, 1890's, 29in. wide. (Sotheby's Belgravia) $850 £440

Small early 18th century style oak bureau on cabriole legs and pad feet, 2ft.1in. wide. (Russell, Baldwin & Bright) $4,140 £2,300

Mid 19th century Dutch mahogany and walnut bureau with bombe-shaped flap, 36in. wide. (Sotheby's Belgravia) $1,870 £1,001

Georgian oak bureau of small size, 31in. wide, with steel side carrying handles. (Lawrence Fine Art) $1,380 £750

Georgian style mahogany bureau on bracket feet, 36in. wide. (Hall Wateridge & Owen)
$1,280 £680

George III mahogany cylinder bureau, circa 1780, 3ft.6½in. wide. (Sotheby's)$1,615 £858

George I walnut bureau with crossbanded flap, on bracket feet, 40½in. wide. (Christie's)
$2,710 £1,450

George III mahogany bureau with crossbanded front, 101cm. wide. (H. Spencer & Sons Ltd.)
$965 £520

Queen Anne tiger maple slant front desk, circa 1760, 36in. wide. (Robert W. Skinner Inc.)
$24,570 £13,000

Georgian mahogany bureau on cut down splayed feet, 3ft.4in. wide. (Dickinson, Davy & Markham) $425 £230

Mahogany bureau on bracket feet, with brass handles and ivory escutcheons. (Gilbert Baitson) $1,085 £575

Chippendale cherry and pine slant front desk, circa 1780, 37½in. wide. (Robert W. Skinner Inc.) $4,250 £2,250

George I walnut bureau, circa 1720, 2ft.7½in. wide. (Sotheby's)
$5,730 £3,080

Early George II mahogany bureau with gilt bronze rococo handles, 43in. wide. (Christie's) $3,235 £1,750

Satinwood cylinder bureau with three short drawers above, 55¼in. wide. (Christie's) $1,590 £880

Early 18th century South German or Austrian walnut bureau with raised superstructure, 50in. wide. (Christie's) $4,970 £2,700

Rosewood and marquetry cylinder bureau by James Shoolbred & Co., circa 1890, 38in. wide. (Sotheby's Belgravia) $1,475 £820

Mid 18th century Louis XV kingwood bureau de dame, 3ft. wide, with ormolu mounts. (Sotheby, King & Chasemore) $16,370 £8,800

Unusual oak standing desk with fall flap enclosing fitted interior, 3ft. wide, circa 1720. (Sotheby, King & Chasemore) $2,415 £1,300

Chippendale maple and birch slant top desk, New England, circa 1780, 39¼in. wide. (Robert W. Skinner Inc.) $1,900 £1,040

Dutch floral marquetry bombe bureau with four drawers, 44in. wide. (Christie's) $5,520 £3,000

George III mahogany bureau, inlaid with oval shell and stringings, 42in. wide. (Burrows & Day) $2,220 £1,200

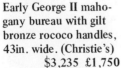

Early Georgian walnut bureau with oyster veneered sloping flap, 36in. wide. (Christie's)
$2,590 £1,400

Dutch tulipwood and marquetry bombe bureau with solid cylinder, 47½in. wide. (Christie's) $4,785 £2,600

Late 18th century George III mahogany bureau on bracket feet, with swan neck carrying handles, 30in. wide.(Sotheby Beresford Adams)
$1,210 £650

George I walnut bureau inlaid with herringbone stringing and crossbanded, 30in. wide. (Locke & England)$3,515 £1,900

Early 19th century Dutch marquetry cylinder bureau with brass gallery, 40in. wide. (Boardman's)
$3,700 £2,000

George I walnut and burr-walnut bureau, on later ogee bracket feet, 39in. wide. (Christie's)
$2,775 £1,500

Mahogany bureau with brass drop handles and escutcheons, on ogee feet, 39in. wide. (Dee & Atkinson)
$1,115 £600

Mid 18th century North Italian serpentine walnut bureau with ebonised upper section, 46in. wide. (Christie's)
$19,320 £10,500

18th century Dutch walnut bureau of bombe shape, with four drawers. (John Hogbin & Son)
$3,240 £1,800

297

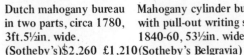

Dutch mahogany bureau in two parts, circa 1780, 3ft.5½in. wide. (Sotheby's)$2,260 £1,210

Mahogany cylinder bureau with pull-out writing slide, 1840-60, 53½in. wide. (Sotheby's Belgravia) $660 £352

18th century Massachusetts Chippendale reverse-serpentine mahogany bureau, 43½in. wide. (Wm. Doyle Galleries Inc.) $4,750 £2,515

Late George I walnut bureau, flap inlaid with chequered lines, on ogee bracket feet, 32½in. high. (Christie's) $6,290 £3,400

Small Edwardian banded mahogany bureau with floral marquetry panel to lid, 2ft.6in. wide.(Russell, Baldwin & Bright) $1,170 £650

George I walnut bureau with brass handles, 37in. wide. (Sotheby, King & Chasemore)$2,210 £1,200

Georgian oak fall-front bureau with brass handles and escutcheons. (J. M. Welch & Son)$765 £420

Sheraton rosewood tambour front bureau, outlined with boxwood stringing, 36in. wide. (Wm. Doyle Galleries Inc.) $5,750 £3,040

German marquetry cylinder bureau, lowest drawer inlaid with parquetry, circa 1780, 3ft.5½in. wide. (Sotheby's) $3,085 £1,650

Lombard walnut bureau with three graduated serpentine drawers, circa 1740, 3ft.6in. wide. (Sotheby's)$3,395 £1,815

18th century New England Chippendale reverse-serpentine birchwood bureau, 41in. wide. (Wm. Doyle Galleries Inc.) $5,500 £2,910

Wall fall-front bureau with fitted interior and brass drop handles. (Alfred Mossop & Co.) $835 £460

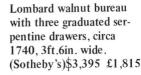

Federal cherry inlaid slant top desk, circa 1790, 40½in. wide. (Robert W. Skinner Inc.) $4,250 £2,250

19th century rosewood cylinder top writing desk, 32in. wide. (J. M. Welch & Son) $875 £480

American Chippendale mahogany slant top bureau on bracket feet, circa 1780, 41¼in. wide. (Robert W. Skinner Inc.) $2,400 £1,305

George III mahogany and crossbanded bureau with brass drop handles and ivory escutcheons, 42in. wide. (Dacre, Son & Hartley) $1,640 £900

Painted satinwood cylinder bureau with oval medallion, circa 1900, 23in. wide. (Sotheby's Belgravia) $785 £440

Georgian walnut fall-front bureau on bracket feet, 38in. wide. (J. M. Welch & Son) $1,400 £770

Sheraton design mahogany bureau inlaid with satinwood and ebony herringbone stringing, 42in. wide. (Morphets) $1,050 £600

Georgian oak bureau on bracket feet, 3ft. wide. (J. M. Welch & Son) $1,055 £580

George II mahogany cylinder bureau with tambour front and oval-panelled doors, 47in. wide. (Christie's) $5,615 £2,970

Early 18th century walnut and burr-walnut slope front well bureau, 36in. wide. (W. H. Lane & Son) $3,915 £2,150

Dutch seaweed marquetry small bureau, circa 1920, 27½in. wide. (Sotheby's Belgravia) $845 £451

George I walnut and featherbanded bureau on later shaped bracket feet, circa 1720, restored, 3ft. wide.(Sotheby, King & Chasemore) $2,235 £1,250

Mahogany bureau with bracket feet, original brass fittings, 3ft. wide. (Honiton Galleries) $875 £490

Mid 18th century George III oak bureau on later bracket feet, 40in. wide. (Sotheby's) $985 £550

George III mahogany bureau with fitted interior, on bracket feet, 33in. wide. (Lawrence Fine Art) $1,265 £660

18th century bureau in mahogany and oak with oval brass drop handles, 42in. wide. (Butler & Hatch Waterman)
$665 £370

Edwardian mahogany and crossbanded inlaid bureau, circa 1910, 2ft.9in. wide. (Sotheby, King & Chasemore) $1,275 £700

Early 18th century walnut and marquetry bureau with brass escutcheons. (Edgar Horn)
$2,195 £1,200

Late 17th/early 18th century oak bureau on stand, 33in. wide. (Christie's)
$2,560 £1,400

Oak and elm bureau applied with geometric mouldings, remodelled in 20th century, 30in. wide. (Sotheby's)
$510 £286

Vernis Martin bureau a cylindre with brass galleried superstructure, 1880-1900, 30½in. wide. (Sotheby's Belgravia)
$605 £330

Rosewood and marquetry bureau de dame with serpentine flap, circa 1880, 28in. wide. (Sotheby's Belgravia) $770 £418

18th century mahogany bureau with lacquered interior and brass handles. (Graves, Son & Pilcher) $1,860 £1,000

William and Mary walnut marquetry bureau in two parts, 2ft.8in. wide. (Sotheby, King & Chasemore) $9,215 £4,800

Queen Anne oak bureau bookcase with double domed cornice, circa 1710, 3ft. wide.(Sotheby, King & Chasemore) $3,145 £1,700

18th century South German walnut bureau cabinet. (Sandoe, Luce Panes) $11,400 £6,200

Queen Anne walnut and featherbanded bureau bookcase, circa 1710, 3ft.3in. wide.(Sotheby, King & Chasemore) $6,005 £3,300

Walnut bureau bookcase with moulded cornice, doors inlaid with herringbone bands, 80in. high. (Christie's)$2,715 £1,500

Dutch bleached mahogany bureau bookcase with domed pediment, with silvered metal handles and escutcheons, 4ft.3in. wide. (Geering & Colyer) $3,145 £1,700

Mahogany bureau bookcase with swan neck cresting, fall front with beaded moulding, circa 1880, 44in. wide.(Sotheby's Belgravia) $3,310 £1,800

Dutch walnut and floral marquetry bureau cabinet with double domed cornice, 43in. wide. (Christie's)$14,720 £8,000

Early George III mahogany bureau bookcase with broken pediment having centre shell finial, 39in. wide. (Locke & England) $10,415 £5,600

Walnut and featherbanded Queen Anne bureau cabinet, circa 1710, slightly damaged, 3ft.3in. wide. (Sotheby, King & Chasemore)$6,070 £3,300

Dutch walnut and marquetry bureau cabinet with bombe base, 53in. wide. (Christie's) $16,930   £9,200

Queen Anne figured walnut bureau bookcase, on a later stand. (Anderson & Garland) $9,700 £5,300

Queen Anne walnut bureau bookcase with mirror glazed doors, 40in. wide. (Christie's) $7,400 £4,000

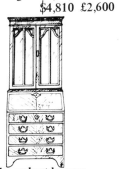

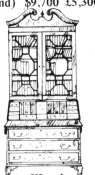

Early 18th century walnut, crossbanded and feather inlaid bureau bookcase on bracket feet, 3ft.2in. wide. (Geering & Colyer) $4,810 £2,600

George III mahogany bureau bookcase with swan neck pediment, on ogee bracket feet, 44in. wide. (Sotheby, King & Chasemore) $4,970 £2,700

George I walnut bureau cabinet with moulded cornice and two panelled and fielded doors, 37½in. wide. (Christie's) $9,990 £5,400

Maples walnut bureau bookcase with arched astragal doors, on bracket feet. (T. Bannister & Co.) $1,355 £750

American Chippendale style mahogany secretaire bookcase, circa 1920, 37in. wide. (Robert W. Skinner Inc.) $1,100 £620

Mahogany and oak bureau bookcase with moulded dentilled cornice, 79½in. wide. (Christie's) $2,775 £1,500

303

FURNITURE

American Chippendale veneer secretary bookcase, circa 1770, 41in. wide. (Robert W. Skinner Inc.)
$5,500 £2,990

George III mahogany bureau cabinet with shaped cornice and lancet frieze, circa 1790, 3ft.9in. wide. (Sotheby's) $7,030 £3,800

18th century New England tiger maple secretaire bookcase with bonnet top, 38½in. wide. (Wm. Doyle Galleries Inc.)
$20,000 £10,580

Late 19th century bureau bookcase in Sheraton manner with astragal glazed doors.(Pearson)
$1,765 £950

Mahogany bureau cabinet with two glazed cupboard doors, 34in. wide. (Christie's) $2,995 £1,674

Queen Anne burr-walnut bureau cabinet with moulded double domed cornice, 41½in. wide. (Christie's)
$9,620 £5,200

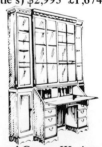

Small George II mahogany bureau bookcase on bracket feet, circa 1755, 2ft.8½in. wide. (Sotheby's)
$2,455 £1,320

Unusual George III pine breakfront bureau bookcase, 6ft.9in. wide, circa 1765, restored.(Sotheby's)
$6,410 £3,410

George I walnut bureau bookcase with broken arched pediment, 38in. wide. (Lawrence Fine Art)
$8,450 £4,400

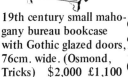

19th century small mahogany bureau bookcase with Gothic glazed doors, 76cm. wide. (Osmond, Tricks) $2,000 £1,100

George III mahogany bureau cabinet on bracket feet, circa 1770, 4ft.1½in. wide. (Sotheby's) $3,515 £1,870

18th century German walnut and fruitwood bureau cabinet with brass knob handles, 32½in. wide. (Wm. Doyle Galleries Inc.) $6,250 £3,305

Early 20th century George III style mahogany cylinder bureau bookcase, 44in. wide. (Sotheby Beresford Adams) $1,155 £620

German mid 18th century rococo walnut parquetry bureau cabinet, 47½in. wide. (Robert W. Skinner Inc.) $7,500 £4,075

Queen Anne style burr-walnut bureau bookcase, top with single mirror panelled door, 34in. wide. (Wm. Doyle Galleries Inc.) $9,500 £5,025

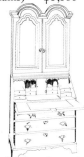

Early Georgian oak double-domed bureau cabinet with shaped base apron. (Graves Son & Pilcher) $1,860 £1,000

Late Georgian bureau bookcase with glazed trellis doors, moulded cornice and broken pediment, 45in. wide. (Locke & England) $2,275 £1,250

George III mahogany bureau bookcase, circa 1800, 3ft.8in. wide. (Sotheby, King & Chasemore) $1,920 £1,000

305

19th century mahogany bureau bookcase with glazed doors. (Graves Son & Pilcher) $2,325 £1,250

Mahogany and satinwood crossbanded bureau bookcase, 1900, 43in. wide. (Sotheby's Belgravia) $1,235 £660

Mid Georgian mahogany bureau cabinet with broken scrolled pediment, 39in. wide. (Christie's) $7,590 £4,104

Mid 18th century Dutch walnut and marquetry bureau bookcase with shaped cornice, 3ft.6in. wide. (Sotheby's) $7,900 £4,180

Black and gold lacquer bureau cabinet with double domed cornice and gilt metal hinges, 39in. wide. (Christie's)$10,810 £5,720

Mid 18th century Dutch fruitwood bureau cabinet, 44in. wide. (Wm. Doyle Galleries Inc.) $12,000 £6,350

George I walnut bureau cabinet with double domed cornice, 37¾in. wide. (Christie's) $9,150 £4,840

George I walnut and featherbanded bureau bookcase, circa 1720, 2ft.7½in. wide. (Sotheby, King & Chasemore) $4,835 £2,700

George I walnut bureau bookcase with two arched bevelled cupboard doors, 41in. wide. (Christie's) $10,395 £5,500

Victorian burr-walnut side cabinet inlaid with satinwood and with ormolu mounts, 32½in. wide. (Morphets) $755 £420

19th century lacquer and chinoiserie cabinet, 15in. wide. (J. M. Welch & Son) $290 £160

Late 19th century rosewood veneered writing table with inlaid decoration, 40in. wide. (W. H. Lane & Son) $830 £460

Satinwood and marquetry display cabinet on stand by Edwards & Roberts, circa 1900, 45in. wide. (Sotheby's Belgravia)$1,750 £935

Bronze mounted Louis Philippe inlaid whatnot-cabinet. (Wm. Doyle Galleries Inc.) $2,300 £1,250

George I burr-walnut cabinet with cavetto frieze drawer, 41¼in. wide. (Christie's) $5,820 £3,080

One of a pair of walnut and marquetry side cabinets with grained tops, circa 1870, 33½in. wide. (Sotheby's Belgravia) $2,160 £1,155

Edwardian satinwood breakfront cabinet with burr-walnut inlay, 74in. wide. (Dee & Atkinson) $1,075 £600

Walnut and marquetry side cabinet with bowfront, circa 1870, 46½in. wide. (Sotheby's Belgravia) $2,015 £1,078

307

Mid 19th century ebony and ivory inlaid cabinet on stand, 33in. wide, probably Spanish. (Sotheby Beresford Adams) $1,395 £750

17th century Flemish tortoiseshell and ebonised cabinet with later hinged top, 24in. wide. (Christie's) $2,210 £1,200

Swedish walnut serpentine bombe voting box on carved legs and ball and claw feet, 34in. wide. (Christie's) $1,325 £720

Late 17th century carved oak standing cabinet. (Lacy Scott) $1,370 £740

Small 16th century German oak stollenschrank, probably Westfalian, 37in. wide. (Boardman's) $4,070 £2,200

Walnut and ebonised Renaissance cabinet, late 17th century, 33in. wide. (Lacy Scott) $2,110 £1,100

17th century Flemish rosewood, walnut and marquetry cabinet on stand, 76in. wide. (Christie's) $3,496 £1,900

17th century Flemish silver mounted ebony and tortoiseshell cabinet on scrolled legs and paw feet, 55½in. wide. (Christie's) $9,200 £5,000

17th century Goanese ivory and tortoiseshell inlaid rosewood table cabinet, 20½in. wide. (Christie's) $1,235 £660

17th century Dutch oak cabinet on stand with ebony inlay, 57in. wide. (Edwards, Bigwood & Bewlay) $5,215 £2,850

Regency rosewood dwarf cabinet with brass gallery, 44½in. wide. (Christie's) $5,965 £3,190

Arts & Crafts music cabinet. (Capes, Dunn & Co.) $1,040 £560

18th century German scarlet and gold lacquer cabinet on chest with broken scrolled pediment, 46½in. wide. (Christie's) $1,840 £1,000

William and Mary oyster veneered chest on stand, late 17th century with later stand, 32½in. wide. (Sotheby Beresford Adams) $1,860 £1,000

Dutch carved marquetry cabinet on chest, circa 1790, 6ft. wide. (Sotheby, King & Chasemore) $3,990 £2,100

Writing cabinet on stand in satinwood and harewood with marquetry inlay, 19th century, by A. Chalmers, 20in. wide. (Morphets) $1,860 £1,000

Fine late 19th century Sheraton design silver cabinet veneered in amboyna with satinwood banding, 2ft.7in. wide. (Locke & England) $930 £500

Late 17th century Dutch cabinet on stand with marquetry medallions, 6ft. 3in. wide. (Phillips & Jolly's) $7,320 £4,000

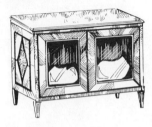

Early 19th century Louis XVI influence two-door cabinet in mahogany with mottled marble top. (Robert W. Skinner Inc.) $750 £405

Rosewood side cabinet, superstructure with pierced gallery and mirror panel, circa 1840, 57in. wide. (Sotheby's Belgravia) $740 £410

Walnut side cabinet with central cupboard door inlaid with flowers, circa 1870, 59in. wide. (Sotheby's Belgravia) $1,170 £650

Giltwood cabinet on stand, door applied with a mid 18th century Soho tapestry, 40in. wide.(Sotheby's Belgravia) $920 £500

19th century Spanish vargueno in mahogany and mahogany veneer, 14in. wide. (Robert W. Skinner Inc.) $150 £80

Ebonised wooden cabinet by Gillows & Co., Lancaster, dated for 1871, 138cm. wide. (Phillips) $805 £450

Burr-walnut and marquetry side cabinet with D-shaped top, cupboard door inlaid with flowers, circa 1870, 67in. wide. (Sotheby's Belgravia) $2,070 £1,150

One of a pair of 19th century French Napoleon III boulle mounted meubles a hauteur d'appui, 33in. wide. (Robert W. Skinner Inc.) $4,500 £2,445

Burr-walnut porcelain mounted side cabinet with gilt bronze mounts, circa 1870, 71½in. wide. (Sotheby's Belgravia) $3,680 £2,000

Ebonised burr-walnut small side cabinet, door with Wedgwood plaque, circa 1870, 49in. wide.(Sotheby's Belgravia) $790 £430

Late 18th/early 19th century Japanese lacquered travelling cabinet on stand, 3ft.2in. wide. (Dickinson, Davy & Markham) $2,115 £1,150

19th century Georgian style two-door cabinet, painted black with gilt decoration, 40in. wide. (Robert W. Skinner Inc.) $600 £325

Victorian bamboo cabinet with gilt black lacquered panels and open undertier, 17½in. wide. (John Hogbin & Son)$130 £70

Marquetry side cabinet with carara marble top, circa 1860, 89in. wide. (Sotheby's Belgravia) $2,520 £1,400

Art Nouveau mahogany cabinet with gallery top and railed sides, 3ft. 4½in. wide.(Dickinson, Davy & Markham) $660 £360

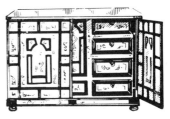

Breakfront walnut side cabinet applied with five Sevres plaques, circa 1870, 65½in. wide. (Sotheby's Belgravia) $1,690 £920

19th century boulle cabinet, ebonised with simulated tortoiseshell and brass, 29in. wide. (Locke & England) $465 £260

17th century South German ebony and bone marquetry table cabinet, 27in. wide. (Boardman's)$1,945 £1,050

Good mid Victorian walnut and marquetry side cabinet with gilt metal mounts, 147.5cm. wide. (H. Spencer & Sons Ltd.) $1,450 £780

Walnut and marquetry serpentine display cabinet, 35½in. wide, circa 1860. (Sotheby's Belgravia) $2,165 £1,122

Ebony veneered side cabinet with inlaid frieze, circa 1880, 84¼in. wide. (Sotheby's Belgravia) $1,655 £858

Mid 18th century Dutch walnut veneered and oak cabinet on chest, 4ft. wide. (Woolley & Wallis) $3,160 £1,700

Regency mahogany side cabinet with well-figured crossbanded bowed breakfront top, 52½in. wide. (Christie's) $4,810 £2,600

One of a pair of walnut and marquetry side cabinets, circa 1870, 31in. wide. (Sotheby's Belgravia) $1,955 £1,012

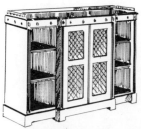

William IV rosewood breakfront side cabinet, circa 1830, 5ft.3½in. wide. (Sotheby's) $2,035 £1,100

Rosewood side cabinet with mirrored back, 1890's, 24½in. wide. (Sotheby's Belgravia) $510 £265

Late Regency painted and parcel gilt breakfront side cabinet, 5ft. wide, circa 1820. (Sotheby's) $1,200 £650

Mid 19th century tulipwood, gilt bronze, porcelain and marquetry side cabinet, 72in. wide. (Sotheby Beresford Adams) $3,905 £2,100

Aesthetic movement mahogany hanging cabinet, signed CWM, dated 1888, 44cm. wide. (Christie's)
$370 £198

17th century Goanese ivory and tortoiseshell inlaid rosewood table cabinet, 20½in. wide. (Christie's)
$1,235 £660

Early 18th century Chinese black lacquer cabinet on stand, 3ft.2½in. wide. (Sotheby's)$3,310 £1,760

Edwardian walnut glazed back display cabinet. (Alfred Mossop & Co.) $405 £210

Mid 19th century Italian Renaissance ebony and ivory cabinet with broken arch pediment, 38in. wide. (Sotheby Beresford Adams) $1,675 £900

17th century style Flemish carved oak cabinet, 4ft.9in. high, circa 1860. (Sotheby, King & Chasemore)
$920 £480

William and Mary black and gold lacquer cabinet on chest, 23½in. wide. (Christie's)$8,025 £4,290

Regency rosewood side cabinet with three-quarter brass gallery, circa 1810, 2ft.6½in. wide.(Sotheby's)
$3,825 £2,035

Victorian walnut side cabinet with glazed bowed ends and gilt metal mounts, 60in. wide. (Lawrence Fine Art) $1,575 £820

George IV brass inlaid rosewood side cabinet with grille-fronted doors, circa 1825, 2ft.5in. wide. (Sotheby's) $2,150 £1,155

One of a pair of Regency pier cabinets with marble tops, 3ft.6in. wide. (Lawrence Fine Art)
$3,865 £2,100

17th century oak spice cupboard inlaid with bone and mother-of-pearl, 22in. wide. (Lawrence Fine Art)
$690 £360

Walnut side cabinet with oval glazed doors, 45in. wide, circa 1870. (Sotheby's Belgravia)
$730 £396

Walnut side cabinet with rosewood cross-banded interior, 16in. wide. (Lawrence Fine Art) $3,865 £2,100

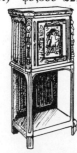

Mid 18th century George II black-japanned cabinet on stand, 3ft.3in. wide. (Sotheby's) $1,665 £900

Marquetry cabinet on chest with ogee cornice, circa 1690, on bracket feet, 4ft. wide. (Sotheby's)$4,090 £2,200

Oak aumbry with moulded cornice and panelled door, 27in. wide.(Lawrence Fine Art)
$330 £180

Walnut side cabinet with serpentine front, circa 1870, 75in. wide. (Sotheby's Belgravia) $3,500 £1,815

Burr-walnut side cabinet with breakfront, 71in. wide, circa 1870. (Sotheby's Belgravia) $3,185 £1,650

Ebony and porcelain mounted side cabinet with gilt bronze moulding, circa 1870, 71in. wide. (Sotheby's Belgravia) $3,290 £1,705

George II mahogany apothecary's cabinet, circa 1740, 5ft. high by 2ft.8in. wide. (Sotheby's) $2,070 £1,100

Dutch parquetry cabinet crossbanded with satinwood and kingwood, circa 1790, 3ft.0½in. wide. (Sotheby's) $1,110 £594

Charles II walnut cabinet on stand, inlaid with seaweed marquetry, circa 1670, 3ft.4in. wide. (Sotheby's) $4,500 £2,420

Dutch marquetry bow-fronted cabinet with tambour shutters, 29in. wide. (Lawrence Fine Art) $735 £400

Victorian amboynawood pier cabinet of bow-fronted shape, 73in. wide. (Lawrence Fine Art) $1,380 £750

Late William IV mahogany side cabinet, circa 1830, 37½in. wide, with three-quarter brass gallery. (Sotheby's Belgravia) $350 £187

315

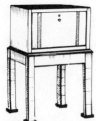

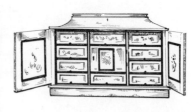

Mirror glass cocktail cabinet, bordered in blue and pink, 1930's, 133cm. high.(Sotheby's Belgravia)
$1,000 £550

Late 17th century Flemish rosewood and walnut table cabinet, 1ft.6in. wide. (Sotheby's)
$1,955 £1,045

George IV rosewood side cabinet with mirror-backed super-structure, circa 1830, 3ft.3in. wide. (Sotheby's)
$2,630 £1,430

Pietra dura ebonised writing cabinet with three-quarter gallery, legs joined by a cross-stretcher, 1870's. (Sotheby's Belgravia)
$1,540 £825

Adam Galt mahogany 'quaint' side cabinet, circa 1910, 66in. wide. (Sotheby's Belgravia)
$1,480 £792

Late 17th century oak side cabinet with recessed doors, circa 1690, 5ft.1in. wide. (Sotheby's) $2,285 £1,210

Open cabinet with adjustable height shelf, designed by Marcel Breuer, 1920's, 36cm. wide. (Sotheby's Belgravia)
$410 £230

Mid 19th century papier-mache table cabinet, fitted with ivory and mother-of-pearl bobbins, 12½in. high. (Sotheby Beresford Adams)
$205 £110

Mid 19th century padoukwood side cabinet with carved and pierced panels. (T. Bannister & Co.)$260 £145

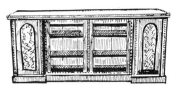

James I oak table cabinet with floral marquetry, dated 1623, 18in. wide. (Christie's) $2,470 £1,350

William IV rosewood and bird's eye maple side cabinet with three-quarter gallery, 7ft. wide. (Coles, Knapp & Kennedy) $1,255 £700

Partly 16th century oak cabinet of Gothic design with single panelled door, 48in. wide. (Christie's) $3,295 £1,800

Amboyna and thuya-wood writing cabinet, circa 1870, 36¼in. wide, with raised superstructure. (Sotheby's Belgravia) $2,440 £1,265

Charles II oak press with carved cornice, dated 1679, 64in. wide. (Christie's) $2,835 £1,550

Flemish walnut cabinet on stand with giltwood cresting, circa 1670, 3ft.8in. wide. (Sotheby's) $6,105 £3,410

Mid 17th century oak cabinet, doors carved with quatrefoil guilloche, 47in. wide. (Christie's) $1,740 £950

Chinese hardwood cabinet with two carved panel doors above two drawers, 40in. wide. (Lawrence Fine Art) $625 £350

Mid 17th century ivory inlaid kingwood veneered table cabinet, 2ft. 5½in. wide. (Sotheby's) $2,160 £1,155

FURNITURE

William IV mahogany canterbury with four divisions, circa 1835, 21in. wide.(Sotheby's Belgravia) $685 £380

Fine Regency rosewood music canterbury of four compartments. (Dee & Atkinson) $645 £360

Mid 19th century mahogany canterbury of three divisions, 22½in. square. (Sotheby Beresford Adams)$895 £480

Simulated rosewood canterbury with three compartments, circa 1840, 20½in. wide. (Sotheby's Belgravia) $640 £341

Mid 19th century walnut canterbury, top tier with fretwork pierced gallery, 25in. wide. (Sotheby's) $1,015 £550

Early Victorian rosewood canterbury of four compartments, 43cm. wide. (H. Spencer & Sons Ltd.) $805 £430

Walnut canterbury in well-figured wood, circa 1850, 19in. wide. (Sotheby's Belgravia) $505 £280

Walnut canterbury with pierced gallery, circa 1860, 24in. wide.(Sotheby's Belgravia) $765 £396

Early 19th century bird's eye maple canterbury, circa 1825, 1ft.8in. wide. (Sotheby's) $850 £460

William and Mary banister back side chair, America, circa 1720, 43in. high. (Robert W. Skinner Inc.) $140 £75

One of a set of six mid 19th century unusual country-made chairs with spade-shaped backs, restored. (Sotheby's) $735 £396

One of a pair of 18th century Chippendale mahogany side chairs with pierced splats. (Wm. Doyle Galleries Inc.) $1,600 £845

One of a pair of early 18th century mahogany chairs with shaped backs. (W. H. Lane & Son) $400 £220

One of a pair of walnut side chairs with leather seats and backs, circa 1680. (Sotheby's) $800 £429

Ebonised hall chair, back with horizontal splats and with rush seat, by Chas. Rennie Mackintosh, circa 1903. (Christie's) $4,370 £2,400

One of an early 19th century set of ten elmwood and beechwood children's school-room chairs. (Sotheby's) $1,425 £770

One of a set of six William IV mahogany dining chairs, circa 1835. (Sotheby's Belgravia) $1,195 £638

One of a set of six rosewood framed chairs with squab seats. (Arthur G. Griffiths & Sons) $1,090 £590

One of a set of four mahogany dining chairs with carved, arched toprails, circa 1870. (Sotheby's Belgravia) $325 £180

One of a pair of Renaissance revival side chairs in ebonised wood, walnut and burl veneer, circa 1865, 34½in. high. (Robert W. Skinner Inc.) $175 £95

One of a set of five mid 19th century walnut drawingroom chairs with balloon backs. (Sotheby's Belgravia) $685 £380

American Queen Anne child's ladder back side chair with rush seat, circa 1765. (Robert W. Skinner Inc.)$300 £165

Mid Georgian mahogany dining chair with pierced splat and wavy toprail. (Christie's)$1,450 £800

One of a set of eight 19th century baroque style carved side chairs in oak, backs 53in. high. (Robert W. Skinner Inc.) $800 £435

One of a set of four walnut dining chairs with pierced and carved backs, circa 1860, on cabriole legs. (Sotheby's Belgravia) $810 £450

One of a set of four mid 18th century George III mahogany dining chairs.(Sotheby Beresford Adams) $485 £260

New England Queen Anne maple Spanish foot side chair with vase-shaped splat, circa 1730, back of chair 41½in. high. (Robert W. Skinner Inc.) $700 £380

One of a set of twelve late William IV mahogany dining chairs with drop-in seats. (Sotheby Beresford Adams)
$1,210 £650

One of a set of three thumb back side chairs, signed H. Cook, New England, circa 1820. (Robert W. Skinner Inc.)
$650 £355

·One of a set of six Georgian Chippendale style dining chairs with pierced splats. (Dickinson, Davy & Markham)
$1,240 £675

One of a set of six early George III mahogany dining chairs with pierced waved ladder backs. (Christie's)$5,365 £2,900

One of a pair of antique black papier-mache chairs with mother-of-pearl inlay, and cane seats. (John Hogbin & Son) $590 £320

One of a set of eleven 18th century mahogany dining chairs with cane seats, possibly Anglo-Chinese. (Christie's)
$1,755 £950

Gustav Stickley oak side chair, New York, circa 1905, back 39in. high. (Robert W. Skinner Inc.)
$140 £80

One of a set of ten mahogany dining chairs with pierced Gothic pattern baluster splats and needlework seats. (Christie's)
$5,550 £3,000

One of a set of six George III provincial mahogany dining chairs with Gothic pierced vase splats. (H. Spencer & Sons Ltd.)
$1,955 £1,050

Two from a set of eight carved mahogany chairs in Chippendale style, circa
1900. (Sotheby, King & Chasemore)
$3,240 £1,750

Two from a set of six American 20th
century Chippendale style mahogany
chairs with pierced splats. (Robert W.
Skinner Inc.) $1,300 £735

Two from a set of eight late 18th century George III mahogany dining chairs,
with reeded stick splats. (Sotheby
Beresford Adams) $12,460 £6,700

Two from a set of five Georgian mahogany dining chairs with rope twist
splats. (Dickinson, Davy & Markham)
$1,240 £675

Two from a set of six George III carved
mahogany chairs, circa 1770, stamped
W.B. (Sotheby, King & Chasemore)
$7,770 £4,200

Two from a set of eight Edwardian
carved mahogany chairs in Chippendale style, circa 1910. (Sotheby, King
& Chasemore) $1,630 £880

Two from a set of seven unusual mahogany dining chairs on tapered square
legs. (Graves, Son & Pilcher)
$2,260 £1,250

Two from a set of four 20th century
American Queen Anne mahogany din-
ing chairs, chair back 40in. high.
(Robert W. Skinner Inc.)
$2,500 £1,265

Two from a set of five Stickley Brothers
oak chairs, circa 1915. (Robert W.
Skinner Inc.) $100 £55

Two from a set of twelve Federal style
mahogany chairs, 20th century, with
pierced splats. (Robert W. Skinner Inc.)
$650 £365

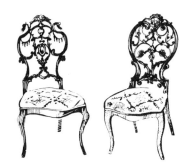

Two rococo revival side chairs, American, circa 1865, with carved backs.
(Robert W. Skinner Inc.) $375 £210

Two from a set of eight George II walnut dining chairs, circa 1730, with
tapestry covered seats. (Sotheby, King
& Chasemore) $33,120 £18,000

DINING CHAIRS

One of a set of seven Dutch marquetry dining chairs with solid vase-shaped splats, sold with a settee. (Christie's) $5,150 £2,800

Two of a set of six Hepplewhite period mahogany fluted frame carved back dining chairs, circa 1785. (Neales) $2,140 £1,150

One of a set of eight 18th/19th century French Provincial side chairs, 42½in. high. (Robert W. Skinner Inc.) $1,500 £815

One of a set of six 19th century oak Jacobean style high back chairs, heavily carved. (Dickinson, Davy & Markham) $1,120 £620

Two of a set of eight late Victorian mahogany dining chairs in Chippendale style. (H. Spencer & Sons Ltd.) $1,955 £1,050

One of a pair of Regency ebonised mahogany dining chairs with cane seats and sabre legs. (John Hogbin & Son) $240 £130

Victorian mother-of-pearl inlaid papier-mache occasional chair with cane seat. (Hy. Duke & Son) $220 £115

Two of a set of twelve late 19th century 'George III' mahogany dining chairs with shield backs. (Sotheby's Belgravia) $2,790 £1,550

18th century French transitional Louis XV chaise with canted rectangular back, 43½in. high. (Robert W. Skinner Inc.) $150 £80

One of a set of six
Victorian mahogany
balloon back dining
chairs on shaped
reeded legs.(Burten-
shaw Walker) $1,395
£750

Two of a set of eight Chippendale
style dining chairs with pierced
splats, and leather covered seats.
(Locke & England)$1,850 £1,000

One of a pair of Chip-
pendale period maho-
gany single chairs
with pierced splats.
(Edwards, Bigwood &
Bewlay) $785 £430

One of a pair of Dutch
walnut and marquetry
chairs with baluster-
shaped splats and cab-
riole legs. (Christie's)
$2,945 £1,600

Two of a set of ten carved oak
and inlaid Elizabethan style chairs,
20th century. (Sotheby, King &
Chasemore) $2,310 £1,250

19th century Ger-
man carved oak
hall chair.
(Christie's S. Ken-
sington) $560 £300

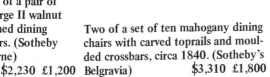

One of a pair of
George II walnut
framed dining
chairs. (Sotheby
Bearne)
$2,230 £1,200

Two of a set of ten mahogany dining
chairs with carved toprails and moulded crossbars, circa 1840. (Sotheby's
Belgravia) $3,310 £1,800

George I walnut
dining chair with
solid splat.
(Sotheby, King &
Chasemore)
$255 £140

DINING CHAIRS

One of a set of four walnut dining chairs with oval backs, circa 1860.(Sotheby's Belgravia) $865 £480

One of a set of three late 18th century fan back Windsor chairs with shaped crest rails. (Robert W. Skinner Inc.) $3,800 £2,075

One of a set of six walnut dining chairs with balloon backs and serpentine seats, circa 1860. (Sotheby's Belgravia) $1,655 £900

One of a set of six Regency simulated rosewood beech-framed chairs, circa 1810. (Sotheby, King & Chasemore) $1,630 £880

One of a set of eight mahogany dining chairs of mid Georgian design with pierced and carved splats. (Christie's) $8,140 £4,400

One of a set of six George III mahogany dining chairs with arched toprails and pierced bar-shaped splats. (Christie's) $1,630 £880

One of a pair of late 18th century Chippendale period Gothic design chairs with pierced lancet backs. (Locke & England) $360 £200

One of a set of six walnut dining chairs with waisted balloon backs, circa 1860. (Sotheby's Belgravia) $1,080 £600

One of a set of eight William IV rosewood dining chairs with leaf-carved crossbar, circa 1835. (Sotheby's Belgravia) $3,060 £1,700

326

One of a set of four mid 19th century walnut dining chairs with moulded oval backs. (Sotheby Beresford Adams) $855 £460

One of a set of six early 19th century George III mahogany dining chairs, moulded splats centred by vases. (Sotheby Beresford Adams) $1,525 £820

One of a set of six mid 19th century William IV rosewood dining chairs with drop-in seats. (Sotheby Beresford Adams) $595 £320

One of a set of seven George III provincial mahogany dining chairs with Gothic pierced vase splats. (H. Spencer & Sons Ltd.) $2,230 £1,200

One of a set of six Gillows ebonised dining chairs designed by Bruce J. Talbert. (Phillips) $715 £400

One of a set of six Heal's walnut dining chairs, 1914, with curved lattice backs. (Phillips) $1,255 £700

One of a pair of early 19th century Regency mahogany hall chairs with carved and moulded shell backs. (Sotheby Beresford Adams) $520 £280

One of a set of twelve mahogany dining chairs of George III design with pierced splats. (Christie's) $6,290 £3,400

Viennese beech chair, designed by Josef Hoffmann, with fluted toprail. (Phillips) $215 £120

327

DINING CHAIRS

One of a set of five early 19th century painted side chairs, 35½in. high. (Robert W. Skinner Inc.) $1,000 £530

Two from a set of eight Chippendale style mahogany dining chairs with vase-shaped splats. (Jackson-Stops & Staff) $4,850 £2,650

One of a set of four mid 19th century rosewood drawing-room chairs, on cabriole legs.(Sotheby's Belgravia)$720 £374

One of a set of four mid 19th century beechwood drawing-room chairs. (Sotheby's Belgravia) $425 £220

Two from a set of eight carved mahogany dining chairs, circa 1910. (Sotheby, King & Chasemore) $2,225 £1,160

One of a set of eight red painted and gilded dining chairs in early Georgian style. (Christie's) $2,990 £1,600

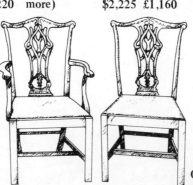

One of a set of ten Regency simulated rosewood and parcel gilt dining chairs. (Christie's) $4,320 £2,310

Two of a set of ten Reproduction dining chairs in Chippendale style. (Hall Wateridge & Owen) $3,420 £1,850

One of a set of eight walnut balloon-back dining chairs with carved toprails, circa 1870.(Sotheby's Belgravia)$1,870 £968

One of a set of four early 18th century Dutch walnut marquetry chairs. (Edwards, Bigwood & Bewlay) $1,830   £1,000

Two of a set of eight George III Hepplewhite design chairs with camel-shaped backs. (Boardman's) $3,215 £1,700

One of a set of six George III mahogany dining chairs with X-pattern splats. (Christie's) $2,470 £1,320

One of a set of ten 'George III' mahogany dining chairs with three-stick splats, circa 1880. (Sotheby's Belgravia) $1,805 £935

Two from a set of eight 19th century mahogany framed Hepplewhite style dining chairs with carved frames. (W. H. Lane & Son) $1,585 £880

One of a set of eight 'George II' dining chairs, circa 1900. (Sotheby's Belgravia) $1,590 £825

One of four Victorian mahogany dining chairs with open backs. (Dickinson, Davy & Markham) $205 £110

Two of a set of twelve mahogany dining chairs in Sheraton style. (Hall Wateridge & Owen) $3,385 £1,800

One of a pair of Victorian papier-mache chairs with mother-of-pearl inlay and cane seats. (Dee & Atkinson) $560 £300

One of a set of four 19th century rosewood dining chairs with shaped toprails. (J. M. Welch & Son) $525 £290

Two of a set of eight mahogany dining chairs, 19th century, with carved and pierced backs. (Lawrence Fine Art) $2,880 £1,500

One of a set of four 19th century mahogany dining chairs. (J. M. Welch & Son) $500 £275

One of a set of five Charles II oak North Country chairs, circa 1660. (Sotheby's) $3,560 £1,925

Two from a set of eight Regency mahogany chairs, circa 1815. (Sotheby, King & Chasemore) $3,275 £1,800

One of a set of six Art Nouveau dining chairs with rush seats. (J. M. Welch & Son) $420 £230

One of a pair of unusual William and Mary oak chairs with pierced strapwork toprails, circa 1690. (Sotheby's) $1,220 £660

Two from a set of twelve Victorian oak dining chairs with leather seats. (Hall Wateridge & Owen) $1,130 £600

One of a set of four rosewood chairs with serpentine toprails, circa 1850. (Sotheby's Belgravia) $720 £385

One of a set of six 19th century balloon-back mahogany dining chairs. (J. M. Welch & Son) $930 £510

Two of a set of eight Sheraton period mahogany dining chairs with square moulded backs. (Woolley & Wallis) $2,415 £1,350

One of a set of five balloon-backed rosewood chairs, 19th century. (J. M. Welch & Son) $580 £320

One of six Art & Crafts oak side chairs, Gustav Stickley, New York, circa 1912. (Robert W. Skinner Inc.) $300 £160

Two from a set of seven Essex chairs on turned front legs. (J. M. Welch & Son) $525 £290

Chippendale mahogany side chair with serpentine crest rail, Massachusetts, circa 1770. (Robert W. Skinner Inc.) $1,700 £930

One of a set of six rosewood dining chairs, circa 1840. (J. M. Welch & Son) $1,275 £700

Two from a set of eight German mahogany dining chairs, mid 19th century. (Sotheby, King & Chasemore) $4,650 £2,500

One of a set of six Victorian mahogany dining chairs with upholstered backs. (J. M. Welch & Son) $620 £340

DINING CHAIRS

One of a set of twelve Victorian walnut cabriole leg dining chairs with oval backs. (Boardman's) $3,780 £2,000

Two from a set of six carved mahogany dining chairs and one carver, with openwork splats. (Brogden & Co.) $630 £340

One of a set of six Regency mahogany hall chairs, circa 1805, with squab cushions. (Sotheby's) $1,200 £650

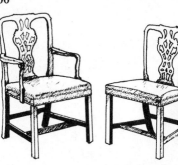

William and Mary carved side chair, early 18th century New England, 47½in. high. (Robert W. Skinner Inc.) $4,000 £2,115

Two from a set of ten George III mahogany dining chairs, circa 1775, on square moulded legs. (Sotheby's) $5,320 £2,860

Early 19th century Dutch walnut standard chair with carved frame, with paw feet.(Jackson-Stops & Staff) $550 £300

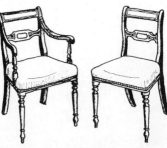

One of a set of six George III mahogany dining chairs with pierced vase-shaped splats, circa 1760. (Sotheby's)$2,045 £1,100

Two from a set of eight Georgian mahogany dining chairs with reeded bar backs. (Lawrence Fine Art) $2,390 £1,300

One of a set of five late George II mahogany side chairs, circa 1760. (Sotheby's) $5,375 £2,860

One of a set of eight Hepplewhite dining chairs with shield-shaped backs. (Messenger, May & Baverstock)
$7,680 £4,000

Two of a set of six Hepplewhite style dining chairs with shield backs. (Lawrence Fine Art)
$1,435 £780

One of a pair of mahogany dining chairs on fluted tapering legs. (Gilbert Baitson)
$170 £90

One of a set of four Flemish beechwood and walnut side chairs with carved and pierced toprails. (Sotheby's) $1,150 £605

Two of a set of six Hepplewhite mahogany dining chairs on sabre legs. (Lawrence Fine Art)
$1,750 £950

One of a set of twelve mahogany dining chairs with three-stick splats. (Sotheby's)
$1,570 £850

One of a set of six George III mahogany dining chairs with buttoned backs and seats. (Sotheby's)
$4,550 £2,420

Two of a set of ten Chippendale style mahogany dining chairs with pierced and waved ladder-backs. (Lawrence Fine Art)
$2,945 £1,600

One of a set of five George III mahogany chairs with stick backs, circa 1785. (Sotheby's)
$1,330 £715

One of a set of four Regency rosewood dining chairs with carved cresting rails. (Butler & Hatch Waterman)·
$520 £290

Early 18th century mahogany framed chair with waisted hoop back and shaped cresting rail. (W. H. Lane & Son)$155 £85.

One of a pair of early 19th century Russian painted chairs with carved toprails. (Sotheby's)$805 £418

Two of a set of six Chippendale style dining chairs on ball and claw feet. (Burtenshaw Walker) $1,745 £975

Two of a set of ten late 19th century 'George II' mahogany dining chairs. (Sotheby's Belgravia) $3,495 £1,870

One of a set of eight 17th century oak dining chairs with partly caned backs and caned seats. (Christie's) $2,795 £1,512

One of a set of six Dutch walnut parquetry side chairs with inlaid frames, circa 1800. (Sotheby's) $2,545 £1,320

One of a set of six mid 18th century Dutch and walnut marquetry chairs with bent vase-shaped splats. (Sotheby's) $6,005 £3,300

One of a set of five Victorian dining chairs with kidney-shaped backs. (Butler & Hatch Waterman)
$520 £290

Early occasional chair in carved frame, with cane seat and back, on barley-twist front legs. (Butler & Hatch Waterman) $465 £260

One of a pair of Italian oak chairs with tall serpentine-topped backs, circa 1750.(Sotheby's)
$1,530 £792

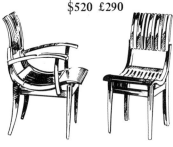

Two from a set of five chairs with outcurved slatted backs and seats. (Christie's) $1,185 £650

Two of a set of eight late 19th century mahogany dining chairs in Sheraton style. (H. Spencer & Sons Ltd.)
$2,210 £1,200

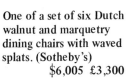

One of a set of six Dutch walnut and marquetry dining chairs with waved splats. (Sotheby's)
$6,005 £3,300

One of a set of six late 17th/early 18th century oak and fruitwood 'Derbyshire' dining chairs. (Sotheby's) $1,065 £594

One of a set of four mid 18th century Portuguese beechwood dining chairs with pierced vase-shaped splats. (Christie's)
$1,400 £756

335

EASY CHAIRS

One of a pair of mahogany armchairs with padded backs and wing sides, circa 1900. (Sotheby's Belgravia) $550 £300

Early Victorian period ornately carved walnut salon chair with spoon back. (Locke & England) $1,340 £750

Queen Anne red walnut wing arm easy chair on cabriole legs, circa 1710. (Sotheby, King & Chasemore) $2,115 £1,150

One of a pair of carved giltwood and Aubusson tapestry bergeres. (Sotheby, King & Chasemore) $7,810 £4,200

17th century Queen Anne high-backed open armchair with turned front legs and stretchers. (Butler & Hatch Waterman) $650 £350

One of a pair of mid 19th century carved giltwood bergeres of Louis XVI style, covered in Aubusson tapestry. (Sotheby, King & Chasemore) $4,090 £2,200

Mid 19th century European oak campaign chair on collapsible and adjustable frame. (Sotheby's Belgravia) $250 £140

One of a set of two walnut chairs, one an armchair, with padded oval backs, circa 1860. (Sotheby's Belgravia) $1,620 £900

Mid 19th century carved giltwood bergere, covered in Aubusson tapestry. (Sotheby, King & Chasemore) $2,790 £1,500

Mid 18th century George III wing armchair with padded back, sides and seats, 42in. high. (Sotheby Beresford Adams) $315 £170

Superb Victorian walnut lounge chair with buttoned back, upholstered in tapestry. (Allen & May) $700 £370

Modern George II style wing armchair with slightly arched padded back. (Sotheby Beresford Adams) $175 £95

One of a pair of library armchairs with padded backs and arm supports, circa 1770. (Sotheby's) $2,695 £1,450

Late 17th/early 18th century walnut wing armchair on cabriole legs with hoof feet. (Christie's) $1,850 £1,000

Late 17th century walnut armchair with curved and moulded arms, Flemish. (Sotheby, King & Chasemore) $1,490 £800

Mid 19th century George II elm wing armchair with tall padded back, arms and serpentine seat, 42in. high.(Sotheby Beresford Adams) $595 £320

20th century early George III style mahogany cockfighting chair with adjustable writing slope. (Sotheby Beresford Adams) $425 £230

Late 18th century George III armchair with out-turned arms, back 46in. high. (Robert W. Skinner Inc.) $1,650 £895

Early George III maho-
gany elbow chair with
carved arm supports.
(Lawrence Fine Art)
$1,000 £520

Leather upholstered reclining
armchair by J. Foot, London,
1880-1900. (Sotheby's Belgravia) $1,070 £572

Arts & Crafts lady's oak
spindle Morris chair by
Gustav Stickley, circa
1905. (Robert W. Skin-
ner Inc.) $2,300 £1,215

17th century Flemish
walnut armchair with
X-stretcher. (Sotheby,
King & Chasemore)
$550 £300

Pair of walnut framed Victorian
grandfather and mother chairs
with scroll feet. (Worsfolds)
          $2,055 £1,070

Victorian rosewood
button back lady's
chair upholstered in
velvet. (Honiton
Galleries)$445 £240

One of a pair of French
'Louis XVI' beechwood
armchairs on stop-fluted
turned tapering legs, circa
1880. (Sotheby's Belgravia)
          $660 £352

Victorian walnut spoon back
lady's chair with carved top
and cabriole legs. (Dickinson,
Davy & Markham)$630 £340

Queen Anne walnut arm-
chair with shaped wings
and out-curved arms,
circa 1710.(Sotheby's)
          $1,945 £1,045

Victorian mahogany framed tub chair on turned front legs. (J. M. Welch & Son) $115 £62

Swedish laminated plywood chaise longue, by Bruno Mattsson, 1930's, 82cm. high. (Sotheby's Belgravia) $605 £340

Carved mahogany armchair upholstered in green hide. (Brogden & Co.) $185 £100

Victorian carved rosewood framed easy chair on cabriole legs. (Geering & Colyer) $820 £440

Two rococo Revival walnut chairs, America, circa 1860, with carved crests, 45in. and 40½in. high. (Robert W. Skinner Inc.) $550 £290

19th century rosewood lady's chair with carved frame. (J. M. Welch & Son) $475 £260

One of a pair of rosewood button-upholstered armchairs, circa 1860. (Sotheby's Belgravia) $1,170 £627

19th century rosewood framed lady's chair. (J. M. Welch & Son) $690 £380

Mid 19th century walnut lady's chair with button-back and carved legs. (T. Bannister & Co.) $560 £310

339

Victorian rosewood lady's chair with button back. (Honiton Galleries)
$520 £280

18th century English open armchair with mahogany frame, circa 1750. (W. H. Lane & Son) $2,710 £1,450

Victorian spoon back nursing chair with scrolling arms and cabriole legs. (Lawrence Fine Art) $425 £230

George III mahogany armchair, stamped B. Harmer, circa 1770, with bow-fronted seatrail. (Sotheby's)
$980 £528

Victorian gentleman's chair in mahogany frame with button back. (Alfred Mossop & Co.) $810 £420

Chair from a three-piece suite of drawingroom furniture, circa 1870. (Sotheby's Belgravia)
$1,050 £561

Georgian style library armchair with shaped top and wings. (Lawrence Fine Art) $590 £320

One of a pair of French 18th century Louis XV style fauteuil en cabriolet, in fruitwood, 34in. high. (Robert W. Skinner Inc.) $1,450 £790

One of a pair of mahogany framed Gainsborough armchairs. (Gilbert Baitson)
$225 £120

George III mahogany
library armchair, legs
with blind Chinese fret,
circa 1770. (Sotheby's)
$2,560 £1,375

One of a pair of Victorian
grandfather chairs with
mahogany frames. (Hall
Wateridge & Owen)
$715 £380

William IV tulipwood reclining armchair, circa 1835.
(Sotheby, King & Chase-
more) $800 £420

George II mahogany
armchair in French
style, circa 1750, with
carved front legs.
(Sotheby's) $980 £528

Queen Anne walnut and up-
holstered chair on pad feet,
circa 1715. (Sotheby, King
& Chasemore) $1,730 £900

Victorian lady's button
back chair in mahogany
frame. (Alfred Mossop
& Co.) $885 £460

Victorian walnut carved
spoon back chair with
serpentine-fronted seat
and cabriole legs. (John
Hogbin & Son)$380 £210

One of a pair of 19th century
French Louis XV style fau-
teuils a la Reine, 38in. high.
(Robert W. Skinner Inc.)
$650 £350

Queen Anne walnut
wing frame easy chair,
circa 1710. (Sotheby,
King & Chasemore)
$2,945 £1,600

One of a pair of Dutch mahogany armchairs with horseshoe-shaped toprails, circa 1790. (Sotheby's) $2,865 £1,485

Herman Miller lounge chair designed by Charles Eames, 1956, 81cm. high.(Sotheby's Belgravia) $1,040 £572

Victorian spoon-back chair in carved walnut frame, upholstered in brown tapestry. (Butler & Hatch Waterman) $610 £340

One of a pair of 17th century restored walnut open armchairs. (Christie's) $1,800 £972

Chair from an eleven-piece suite of bamboo porch furniture, circa 1930, 30in. high. (Robert W. Skinner Inc.) $5,900 £3,260

One of four oak hall chairs with carved and pierced backs, on scroll form supports. (Outhwaite & Litherland) $830 £460

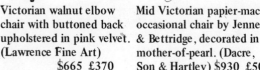

Victorian walnut elbow chair with buttoned back upholstered in pink velvet. (Lawrence Fine Art) $665 £370

Mid Victorian papier-mache occasional chair by Jennens & Bettridge, decorated in mother-of-pearl. (Dacre, Son & Hartley) $930 £500

Victorian elbow chair, walnut frame with oval back, upholstered in orange velvet.(Lawrence Fine Art) $555 £310

Oak turner's chair, back with pierced horizontal and vertical baluster splats. (Christie's) $1,425 £780

Regency mahogany library step chair with cane seat, folding to reveal four baize covered steps. (Lawrence Fine Art)$1,575 £880

18th century elm, oak and beechwood Windsor arm-chair with pierced Gothic pattern splats.(Christie's) $620 £340

Early 18th century maho-gany, beech and oak fra-med elbow chair with vase-shaped splat. (W. H. Lane & Son) $275 £150

Rare mid 17th century wainscot armchair with shaped cresting above a panelled back.(Sotheby's) $490 £275

Late 18th century Wind-sor armchair in elm, ash and beech, with shaped pierced splat. (W. H. Lane & Son)$290 £160

One of a set of six Dutch marquetry chairs with pierced splats, circa 1765. (Sotheby's) $1,800 £990

Late 18th century Windsor stick-back armchair in elm, ash and beech, with crino-line stretchers. (W. H. Lane & Son) $125 £70

Early 18th century country-made beech and oak framed elbow chair with vase-sha-ped splat. (W. H. Lane & Son) $255 £140

343

American Art Nouveau laminated mahogany and maple armchair, circa 1910, back 44½in. high. (Robert W. Skinner Inc.) $350 £200

One of a pair of 'George III' satinwood armchairs with Prince of Wales's feathers carved on backs, 1910-20. (Sotheby's Belgravia) $1,510 £820

Laminated mahogany armchair by the Paine Furniture Co., Boston, circa 1920, back 45in. high. (Robert W. Skinner Inc.) $250 £140

One of a set of twelve Regency mahogany open armchairs with reeded frames. (Christie's) $6,660 £3,600

French carved walnut 'caqueteuse' chair upholstered in rose red velvet. (Butler & Hatch Waterman) $520 £280

One of a pair of Regency mahogany armchairs with reeded toprails, circa 1805. (Sotheby's) $2,420 £1,300

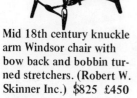

Mid 18th century knuckle arm Windsor chair with bow back and bobbin turned stretchers. (Robert W. Skinner Inc.) $825 £450
344

One of a set of eight late Regency mahogany dining chairs with concave rails and padded seats. (Sotheby Beresford Adams) $2,230 £1,200

Late 19th century Japanese carved oak armchair with serpentine cloud form apron, 34½in. high.(Robert W. Skinner Inc.) $375 £20?

One of a set of eight mid 20th century George III style mahogany dining chairs by Waring & Gillow Ltd. (Sotheby Beresford Adams) $1,580 £850

19th century French Empire armchair with barrel-shaped backrail and with cast brass mounts, 31½in. high. (Robert W. Skinner Inc.) $500 £270

Federal mahogany lolling chair with serpentine back, Massachusetts, circa 1780. (Robert W. Skinner Inc.) $9,500 £5,190

One of a set of eight George IV mahogany dining chairs, circa 1820, with pierced scroll crossbars. (Sotheby's) $3,535 £1,900

Early 18th century Dutch East Indies Colonial burgomaster's armchair, back flanked by mask finials. (Sotheby Beresford Adams) $1,860 £1,000

One of a set of seven early 20th century Queen Anne style mahogany dining chairs, with vase-shaped splats. (Sotheby Beresford Adams) $1,765 £950

American Elizabethan revival walnut platform rocker, New York, circa 1884. (Robert W. Skinner Inc.) $275 £155

American Arts & Crafts oak armchair with corniced rail, circa 1900, back 51in. high. (Robert W. Skinner Inc.) $175 £100

Gustav Stickley oak Morris chair with slanted arms, New York, circa 1906, 33in. wide. (Robert W. Skinner Inc.) $10,000 £5,650

One of a pair of Chinese padouk framed armchairs with
carved backs and arms. (W.
H. Lane & Son) $935 £500

Arts & Crafts oak
armchair with padded
back rest and pierced
apron, 83cm. high.
(Christie's) $225 £121

One of a pair of Regency
painted armchairs with
cane seats, circa 1805.
(Sotheby's)
$2,130 £1,150

One of a set of seven mahogany elbow chairs of Hepplewhite design with wheel
backs. (Jackson-Stops &
Staff) $2,760 £1,500

Walnut corner chair on
slight cabriole legs and
pad feet. (Alfred Mossop
& Co.) $365 £190

One of a set of eight mahogany dining chairs. (Row-
land Gorringe)
$4,115 £2,200

One of a set of eight
'George I' mahogany
dining chairs with solid
splats, circa 1900.
(Sotheby's Belgravia)
$3,290 £1,705

19th century elm high back
Windsor chair with turned
legs and stretcher.
(Dickinson, Davy & Markham)
$230 £125

One of a set of eight
early 18th century ash
and oak ladderback
dining chairs. (Lacy
Scott) $2,540 £1,340

One of a pair of Hepple-
white design mahogany
wheel back dining chairs.
(Jackson-Stops & Staff)
$505 £275

One of a pair of Regency
painted and parcel gilt
caned bergeres, circa 1815.
(Sotheby's) $3,410 £1,815

Late Victorian mahogany
occasional elbow chair.
(Gilbert Baitson)
$190 £100

One of a set of eight Hepplewhite design mahogany dining chairs. (Woolley &
Wallis) $2,510 £1,350

Hepplewhite style carver
chair in mahogany frame
with floral upholstery.
(Alfred Mossop & Co.)
$270 £140

One of a set of four late
George II mahogany din-
ing chairs with vase-sha-
ped splats, circa 1755.
(Sotheby's)
$1,850 £1,000

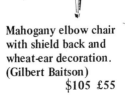

Mahogany elbow chair
with shield back and
wheat-ear decoration.
(Gilbert Baitson)
$105 £55

Small 19th century high back
Windsor chair with pierced
splat and crinoline stretcher.
(Dickinson, Davy & Mark-
ham) $295 £160

One of a set of eight
mahogany ladderback
dining chairs in Chip-
pendale style, with
leather seats. (Woolley
& Wallis)$1,490 £800

Mahogany elbow chair with inlaid back panel, on square tapering legs. (Gilbert Baitson) $130 £70

Edwardian corner chair with slatted back and cross stretcher. (Honiton Galleries) $130 £70

18th century yewwood low back Windsor chair with pierced splat and elm seat. (Dickinson, Davy & Markham) $355 £190

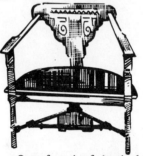

Late 19th century American Victorian oak hall tree, top with bevelled glass mirror, 38½in. wide. (Robert W. Skinner Inc.) $550 £310

One of a pair of ebonised mahogany armchairs with half-moon seats, on hexagonal legs jointed by turned stretchers, 1870's. (Sotheby's Belgravia) $295 £160

One of a pair of American chrome plated spring steel armchairs with fabric seats, circa 1930, back 42in. high. (Robert W. Skinner Inc.) $550 £310

Late Georgian child's mahogany high armchair with scroll crest rail. (Burrows & Day) $315 £170

Antique high winged comb back chair with saddle seat. (Butler & Hatch Waterman) $270 £150

One of a set of four Regency ebonised and painted open armchairs with pierced splats.(Christie's) $4,525 £2,420

348

Mahogany elbow chair with stuffed seat, on square tapering legs in Hepplewhite manner. (Gilbert Baitson)
$150 £80

17th century oak armchair with plain panel back and seat, stretchers of a later date. (Edwards, Bigwood & Bewlay) $340 £185

Elm low back Windsor chair with crinoline stretcher. (Dickinson, Davy & Markham)
$240 £130

One from a set of nine American William and Mary style armchairs, circa 1900, back of chair 49in. high. (Robert W. Skinner Inc.) $475 £270

George I walnut reading chair with U-shaped top-rail, and pierced solid splat. (Christie's)
$1,480 £800

Antique ladder back rush-seated open armchair. (Butler & Hatch Waterman)
$170 £95

One of a set of seven ladder back chairs with original rush seats re-seated in seagrass. (Butler & Hatch Waterman) $970 £540

One of six antique elm Windsor stick back armchairs with crinoline stretchers. (Butler & Hatch Waterman)
$1,330 £740

Early George III mahogany open armchair with serpentine seat. (Christie's)
$3,700 £1,980

ELBOW CHAIRS

19th century Scandinavian carved and painted arm-chair on spiral supports. (Lawrence Fine Art)
$700 £380

Russian poplar armchair, heavily carved, circa 1900. (Sotheby's Belgravia)
$455 £242

One of a set of six George III mahogany dining chairs with arched toprails, circa 1780. (Sotheby's)
$2,220 £1,200

18th century armchair in fruitwood and beech with pierced crest, 45in. high. (Robert W. Skinner Inc.)
$225 £125

Second Empire armchair, France, circa 1855, with carved arms and legs. (Robert W. Skinner Inc.)
$850 £460

One of a set of eight Regency mahogany din-ing chairs with rope-twist toprails, circa 1805. (Sotheby's)
$4,765 £3,410

One of a set of eight Regency mahogany dining chairs with bowed toprails, circa 1810. (Sotheby's)
$4,705 £2,530

One of a set of four Charles II beechwood armchairs, circa 1660, with carved top-rail and backs. (Sotheby's)
$5,350 £2,860

Late George II maho-gany armchair with carved toprail, circa 1755. (Sotheby's)
$735 £396

One of a pair of Regency armchairs with caned seats and black and gilt decoration. (J. M. Welch & Son) $290 £160

One of a set of six late 19th/early 20th century mahogany dining chairs with shield backs. (Sotheby's Belgravia) $660 £352

One of a set of four Georgian period mahogany elbow chairs with pierced splat backs. (Woolley & Wallis) $16,655 £9,100

High-back Essex elbow chair on square legs. (J. M. Welch & Son) $290 £160

Flemish carved walnut armchair with gadrooned scrolled back, circa 1690, legs joined by waved X-stretchers. (Sotheby's) $1,480 £792

Spindle-backed 19th century rocking chair with rush seat. (J. M. Welch & Son) $90 £45

One of a set of ten George III mahogany dining chairs

Small early 19th century comb-back chair on turned legs. (J. M. Welch & Son) $335 £185

Edwardian Art Nouveau satinwood armchair with slender padded back, circa 1910. (Sotheby's Belgravia) $865 £462

One of a set of ten George III mahogany dining chairs including two armchairs, circa 1765. (Sotheby's) $5,170 £2,750

351

18th century comb-back elbow chair with shaped toprail. (J. M. Welch & Son) $565 £310

Painted satinwood arm-chair with caned back and sides, circa 1900. (Sotheby's Belgravia) $265 £143

One of a set of eight Charles II style oak dining chairs, six single and two carvers. (J. M. Welch & Son) $1,275 £700

Chippendale style elbow chair with pierced splat. (J. M. Welch & Son) $245 £135

One from a set of eight country style rail and wheel back dining chairs. (Butler & Hatch Waterman) $455 £245

One of a rare pair of late George II mahogany corner armchairs, circa 1760, with pierced Gothic splats. (Sotheby's) $1,580 £858

One of a set of six late 19th century 'George III' mahogany dining chairs. (Sotheby's Belgravia) $430 £231

Late 19th century carved oak elbow chair with cane seat and back. (J. M. Welch & Son) $455 £250

One of a set of eight mahogany dining chairs, including two armchairs, circa 1880. (Sotheby's Belgravia) $1,400 £748

19th century yew-backed child's Windsor chair. (J. M. Welch & Son)
$180 £100

19th century child's high chair with tray and foot rest. (J. M. Welch & Son)
$125 £70

Early 17th century yew-wood Turner's chair with T-shaped back. (Sotheby's)
$3,190 £1,705

Mid 18th century George III oak and elm wainscot armchair with solid seat. (Sotheby's) $440 £231

Antique open armchair with carved splat and apron, with squab cushion. (J. M. Welch & Son)
$300 £165

One of a pair of formerly caned Guangxu rosewood armchairs. (Sotheby's Belgravia) $505 £275

George II mahogany corner armchair with arched upholstered back, circa 1735. (Sotheby's)
$786 £419

French giltwood fauteuil with reeded legs and upholstered seat and back. (J. M. Welch & Son) $290 £160

One of a pair of 'George III' armchairs with serpentine backs, circa 1920. (Sotheby's Belgravia)
$615 £330

English Colonial solid camphorwood and ebony military secretaire chest in two parts, 42in. wide, circa 1840. (Sotheby's Belgravia)
$2,250 £1,250

George III serpentine mahogany chest of drawers, circa 1780, 3ft. wide.(Sotheby's)
$4,340 £2,310

Early Georgian mahogany chest of five drawers with brass handles, 3ft. wide. (Allen & May)$605 £320

Chinese export camphorwood military secretaire chest with brass fittings, circa 1900, 36in. wide. (Sotheby's Belgravia) $1,655 £920

New England Chippendale tiger maple tall chest of drawers with applied moulded cornice, 36in. wide, circa 1760. (Robert W. Skinner Inc.) $2,200 £1,200

Charles II oak chest of four long drawers on stand with a ball turned frame, 40in. wide. (Sotheby, King & Chasemore) $900 £490

Late 17th century William and Mary walnut chest, on four ball feet. (Robert W. Skinner Inc.) $950 £515

Chest of four short and two long drawers with turned wood handles. (Honiton Galleries) $300 £160

Early 18th century herringbone walnut chest of four long drawers with brass knob handles, 30in. wide. (Burtenshaw Walker) $1,635 £8

Late 18th/early 19th century Dutch rosewood and marquetry chest of three long drawers, 32in. wide. (Sotheby Beresford Adams) $820 £440

Mid 19th century camphorwood military chest of drawers with brass bindings, 44in. wide. (Eldon E. Worrall & Co.)$1,730 £950

Georgian mahogany chest of five drawers with brass drop handles and escutcheons, on ogee bracket feet. (John Hogbin & Son) $340 £190

Charles II oak chest with applied mouldings and panelled ends, 29in. wide. (Burrows & Day) $460 £250

Charles II oak chest of drawers with walnut veneered drawer fronts. (H. C. Chapman & Son) $1,900 £1,050

Edwardian style inlaid mahogany chest of five drawers with brass ring handles and on bracket feet. (John Hogbin & Son) $215 £120

Sheraton mahogany bow-fronted chest of four drawers, 35in. wide. (Hall Wateridge & Owen) $1,090 £580

Louis XV kingwood parquetry chest of drawers with ormolu mounts, 4ft.3in. wide, with red marble top. (Turner, Rudge & Turner) $9,100 £5,000

George III mahogany serpentine chest of four drawers, circa 1775, 3ft.5½in. wide. (Sotheby's) $3,620 £1,925

Mahogany and ebony banded chest of five drawers with brass drop handles. (John Hogbin & Son)
$130 £70

American Federal maple inlaid chest with rectangular top and bow front, circa 1790, 38½in. wide. (Robert W. Skinner Inc.)
$1,200 £655

George II mahogany chest of four long drawers, circa 1750, 2ft.6in. wide. (Sotheby's)
$1,700 £950

18th century George II walnut commode with brass handles and escutcheons, 38in. wide. (Robert W. Skinner Inc.)$950 £515

19th century French Empire semainier in mahogany and mahogany veneer, 61in. high. (Robert W. Skinner Inc.)$1,200 £650

Late 19th century walnut chest with herringbone inlay to top, drop loop handles and bracket feet. (T. Bannister & Co.)
$1,175 £650

Early Georgian walnut chest, top inset with a panel of burr-maple, 37½in. wide. (Christie's) $2,080 £1,150

19th century French ebonised boullework chest with tortoiseshell and brass drawer fronts, 2ft.2in. wide.(Dickinson, Davy & Markham)
$440 £240

Regency mahogany dressing chest with bowed top crossbanded with rosewood 39½in. wide. (Christie's)
$2,405 £1,300

George I walnut chest of four long drawers and quartered crossbanded top, 31½in. wide. (Christie's) $2,775 £1,500

Mid 19th century square front mahogany chest of drawers with shaped apron. (T. Bannister & Co.) $305 £170

George III gentleman's plum pudding mahogany dressing chest, circa 1790, 37in. wide. (Sotheby, King & Chasemore)
    $1,920 £1,050

American Chippendale pine two drawer blanket chest, with simulated five drawer front, circa 1765, 37in. wide. (Robert W. Skinner Inc.) $1,500 £820

Country Chippendale tiger maple chest of drawers, 48in. high, circa 1770, on dovetailed bracket feet. (Robert W. Skinner Inc.) $1,800 £985

American Queen Anne pine lift-top blanket chest with simulated drawer front, circa 1740, 38¾in. wide. (Robert W. Skinner Inc.)
    $10,500 £5,735

Country William and Mary pine and maple painted chest of drawers, Deerfield, Massachusetts, 1700-1715, 40in. wide. (Robert W. Skinner Inc.)$14,000 £7,650

19th century Louis XVI style five drawer chiffonier with marble top, 43½in. high. (Robert W. Skinner Inc.) $425 £230

Late 18th century serpentine-fronted mahogany dressing chest, circa 1770, 43½in. wide. (Sotheby, King & Chasemore)
    $11,345 £6,200

357

CHESTS OF DRAWERS

Charles II walnut chest of drawers with dentil moulding, circa 1680, 3ft.2in. wide.(Sotheby's) $1,260 £682

Mid 19th century teak military chest of five drawers, in two sections, 39in. wide. (Lawrence Fine Art) $590 £320

Late Georgian mahogany bow-fronted chest of three graduated drawers, 36in. wide. (Lawrence Fine Art) $590 £320

Small chest of drawers, designed by Marcel Breuer, 1920's, 30cm. wide. (Sotheby's Belgravia) $1,425 £800

19th century Far Eastern five drawer chest, 55in. long. (Robert W. Skinner Inc.) $850 £460

William IV mahogany Wellington chest of eight drawers, 24in. wide. (Lawrence Fine Art) $590 £320

Late 17th century oak chest of four long drawers, restored, 37in. wide. (Sotheby's) $670 £352

Mid 17th century oak chest of four long drawers, 2ft. 10in. wide. (Sotheby's) $855 £462

Georgian mahogany chest of drawers with ivory escutcheons and brass handles, 33in. wide. (Lawrence Fine Art) $625 £340

18th century Massachusetts mahogany chest of drawers with brass handles and escutcheons. (Wm. Doyle Galleries Inc.) $21,000 £10,700

Charles II chest of drawers in oak with walnut veneered front, circa 1670, feet later, 3ft.8in. wide. (Sotheby's)$2,340 £1,265

Jacobean oak chest of four long drawers, 36in. wide, in need of restoration. (J. M. Welch & Son) $800 £440

18th century figured walnut chest of five drawers, 37in. wide. (Lawrence Fine Art) $2,210 £1,200

Early 19th century black lacquer and chinoiserie chest of drawers, 3ft.6in. wide. (J. M. Welch & Son) $420 £230

Mid 18th century Dutch walnut and marquetry chest with moulded top, 3ft.2in. wide.(Sotheby's) $4,730 £2,530

'George III' serpentine-fronted chest of drawers in mahogany, circa 1880, 54in. wide. (Sotheby's Belgravia) $1,530 £792

Queen Anne walnut chest of six drawers on bracket feet, 36in. wide. (J. M. Welch & Son)$400 £220

18th century George III oak chest on ogee bracket feet, 33½in. wide. (Sotheby's)$1,045 £550

359

CHESTS OF DRAWERS

Late 18th century New England Chippendale tiger maple chest of drawers, 40in. wide, restored.(Wm. Doyle Galleries Inc.) $4,100 £2,170

Charles II oak chest of drawers, on later turned feet, 35½in. wide. (Christie's) $1,555 £850

American Chippendale serpentine-fronted chest of drawers, circa 1780, 43¾in. wide. (Robert W. Skinner Inc.) $1,900 £1,045

American Chippendale maple and pine tall chest of drawers, circa 1780, 41in. wide. (Robert W. Skinner Inc.) $2,500 £1,375

Lombard bone-inlaid walnut chest of drawers, circa 1710, 4ft.9½in. wide. (Sotheby's) $6,500 £3,630

Victorian walnut Wellington chest of seven drawers, 22in. wide. (Lawrence Fine Art) $550 £300

Early 18th century burr-walnut and veneered chest of five drawers, inlaid with marquetry borders, 39½in. wide. (W. H. Lane & Son) $1,230 £675

Mid 18th century George III pollard oak chest of four drawers, crossbanded in mahogany, 29in. wide. (Sotheby's) $1,360 £715

17th century oak Commonwealth panelled chest of four drawers, 38in. wide. (W. H. Lane & Son) $765 £420

Charles II oak chest with four panelled and coffered drawers, 38in. wide. (Christie's) $880 £480

Church style lacquer chest of drawers from the momoyama period. (Christie's) $8,640 £4,500

Antique walnut chest of five drawers, on bracket feet, with brass handles. (Alfred Mossop & Co.) $245 £135

American Chippendale mahogany serpentine-fronted chest of drawers, circa 1770, 38¾in. wide. (Robert W. Skinner Inc.)$4,000 £2,175

American Chippendale tiger maple chest of drawers, 37½in. wide. (Robert W. Skinner Inc.) $3,000 £1,640

Dark oak chest of three drawers with geometric moulding, with pear-drop handles, 38in. wide. (Butler & Hatch Waterman) $465 £260

Late 18th century Connecticut Chippendale reverse-serpentine cherrywood chest of drawers, 42in. wide. (Wm. Doyle Galleries Inc.) $3,400 £1,800

18th century flat-fronted chest of drawers with brass drop handles and escutcheons, 36in. wide. (Butler & Hatch Waterman) $305 £170

Victorian mahogany bow-fronted chest of four drawers, 36in. wide. (J. M. Welch & Son) $345 £190

361

CHESTS ON CHESTS

Georgian walnut tallboy with oak crossbanding, brass plate handles and moulded cornice, 41in. wide. (Lawrence Fine Art) $1,010 £550

George III provincial chest on chest veneered in mahogany, 100cm. wide. (Osmond, Tricks)
    $1,090 £600

Georgian mahogany tallboy with moulded cornice, 47in. wide. (Lawrence Fine Art)
    $3,130 £1,700

18th century walnut tallboy with brass handles and bracket feet, 3ft.4in. wide. (Dickinson, Davy & Markham) $2,990 £1,650

George I walnut tallboy with cavetto cornice, circa 1720, 3ft.5in. wide. (Sotheby's)$4,225 £2,310

Queen Anne walnut and chevronbanded chest on chest, circa 1710, restored, 3ft.5in. wide. (Sotheby, King & Chasemore) $2,595 £1,450

George I black japanned tallboy, circa 1725, 3ft. wide. (Sotheby's)
    $2,895 £1,540

Early 18th century walnut and burr-walnut chest on chest with contemporary brass handles, 42in. wide. (W. H. Lane & Son)
    $1,365 £750

George I walnut secretaire tallboy with cavetto cornice, restored, circa 1720, 3ft.8in. wide. (Sotheby's)
    $2,455 £1,320

18th century American Chippendale cherrywood bonnet top chest on chest, 53in. wide. (Wm. Doyle Galleries Inc.) $5,250 £2,775

Late 18th/early 19th century George III provincial walnut and fruitwood chest on chest, 41in. wide. (Sotheby Beresford Adams) $820 £440

Mid 18th century Chippendale tiger maple chest on chest, New Hampshire, 36in. wide. (Robert W. Skinner Inc.) $4,500 £2,460

Mahogany tallboy chest of eight drawers, with turned wood handles. (J. M. Welch & Son) $525 £290

Late 19th century walnut chest on chest with brass key plates and drop loop handles, on bracket feet. (T. Bannister & Co.) $2,760 £1,525

American Chippendale maple chest on chest, 40in. wide, circa 1780. (Robert W. Skinner Inc.) $2,500 £1,360

Late 18th century Queen Anne maple chest on chest, 38in. wide, with original brasses. (Robert W. Skinner Inc.) $18,000 £9,785

Early 18th century American Queen Anne walnut bonnet top highboy, 39in. wide. (Robert W. Skinner Inc.) $6,000 £3,280

18th century mahogany two-section tallboy with brass swan neck handles, 42in. wide. (W. H. Lane & Son) $520 £290

363

CHESTS ON STANDS

19th century William and Mary style black lacquered chest on stand, 38in. wide. (Dee & Atkinson) $1,300 £700

German walnut veneered chest inlaid with ivory and boxwood, 3ft.5in. wide. (Woolley & Wallis) $2,605 £1,400

George II mahogany chest on stand on cabriole legs, circa 1740, 3ft.0½in. wide. (Sotheby's) $2,070 £1,100

American Chippendale style mahogany bonnet top highboy, circa 1930, 38½in. wide. (Robert W. Skinner Inc.) $800 £445

George II oak chest on stand with cavetto cornice, 39in. wide. (Lawrence Fine Art) $1,345 £700

Queen Anne walnut, mahogany and cherrywood highboy, circa 1770, 38¾in. wide. (Robert W. Skinner Inc.) $15,000 £8,195

American Queen Anne maple highboy, circa 1760, 38¼in. wide, with flat moulded cornice. (Robert W. Skinner Inc.) $5,250 £2,885

Late 18th century black lacquer and chinoiserie chest on stand, 3ft.6in. wide. (J. M. Welch & Son) $2,910 £1,600

Queen Anne tiger maple chest on stand, late 18th century, 38in. wide. (Robert W. Skinner Inc.) $4,100 £2,240

Late 17th century walnut marquetry chest on stand on five barley-sugar twist legs, 42in. wide.(Edwards, Bigwood & Bewlay)
$6,405 £3,500

Reproduction Jacobean chest of five drawers, on stand with five pear-shaped feet, 39in. wide. (Gilbert Baitson)
$455 £240

Mid 18th century George III chest on stand with moulded pediment, 44in. wide. (Sotheby's)
$1,880 £990

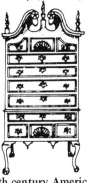

20th century American Chippendale style mahogany tallboy with broken arch top, 39in. wide. (Robert W. Skinner Inc.)
$1,650 £930

Queen Anne walnut chest on stand, drawers framed by herringbone bands, 39in. wide. (Christie's)
$4,015 £2,145

18th century New Jersey Queen Anne stained wood chest on stand on cabriole legs, 42in. wide. (Wm. Doyle Galleries Inc.)
$10,000 £5,290

Early Georgian oak chest on stand on later short baluster supports, 40in. wide. (Lawrence Fine Art) $690 £360

Queen Anne cherrywood highboy, American, circa 1730, 36in. wide. (Robert W. Skinner Inc.)$8,000 £4,395

Late 17th century Portuguese chest on stand with elaborately panelled fronts, 3ft.10½in. wide. (Sotheby's)$3,820 £1,980

Victorian black lacquered and japanned chiffonier with plate glass top, 48in. wide. (Dee & Atkinson) $1,955 £1,050

One of a pair of Regency mahogany chiffoniers with pleated silk panels, 33in. wide. (Boardman's) $1,890 £1,000

William IV rosewood veneered chiffonier, with mirrored galleried top, circa 1830, 3ft.9½in. wide. (Sotheby's) $2,480 £1,320

George III Sheraton design chiffonier with shaped gallery and silk-lined glazed panel doors, 31in. wide. (Locke & England) $3,220 £1,800

Regency ormolu mounted rosewood chiffonier with raised superstructure, 36in. wide. (Christie's) $3,990 £2,090

Regency ormolu mounted rosewood and parcel gilt chiffonier, 41½in. wide, with three-quarter galleried top.(Christie's) $3,330 £1,800

19th century chiffonier with carved back, 44in. wide. (W. H. Lane & Son) $420 £225

Dutch mahogany chiffonier inlaid with fan medallions, circa 1790, 3ft.3in. wide.(Sotheby's) $1,275 £682

Unusual mid 19th century Colonial satinwood chiffonier on gadrooned turned feet, 40in. wide. (Sotheby Beresford Adams) $745 £400

18th century mahogany bedside cupboard with tray top, on square legs, 1ft.11in. wide. (Jackson-Stops & Staff)$185 £100

Georgian mahogany boudoir cabinet with tray top and tambour front, on bracket feet. (Gilbert Baitson) $815 £440

Georgian mahogany tray top commode with shaped apron. (Cooper Hirst) $325 £180

One of a pair of satinwood petite commodes with marble tops, 17½in. wide. (Christie's) $3,590 £1,870

A George III mahogany tray top commode with sliding drawer. (Phillips) $575 £300

Early 19th century Georgian mahogany pot cupboard, top with three-quarter gallery, 14in. wide. (Sotheby's) $155 £85

Late 19th century Georgian mahogany pot cupboard with serpentine-shaped door, 16in. wide. (Sotheby's)$920 £500

Antique mahogany tray top pot cupboard on square legs. (Farrant & Wightman) $175 £100

Victorian fluted mahogany pot stand with inset marble top.(Phillips) $190 £100

367

Italian style rosewood, walnut and marquetry inlaid serpentine commode chest, 4ft.8½in. wide. (Geering & Colyer) $2,300 £1,250

Mid 18th century South German pewter inlaid walnut serpentine commode, 48in. wide. (Christie's) $8,280 £4,500

One of a pair of late 18th century fruitwood and parquetry commodes, Italian or Austrian, 40½in. wide. (Christie's) $2,945 £1,600

Louis XV provincial walnut commode with serpentine moulded top, 53in. wide. (Christie's) $6,255 £3,400

Early 19th century provincial Louis XV commode in serpentine case, 36in. wide. (Robert W. Skinner Inc.) $1,350 £735

Louis XV transitional marquetry breakfront commode with moulded white marble top, circa 1775, 3ft. wide. (Sotheby, King & Chasemore) $2,230 £1,200

One of a pair of 'Chippendale' mahogany commodes with serpentine-shaped tops, circa 1900, 28¼in. wide. (Sotheby's Belgravia) $2,390 £1,300

19th century provincial oak three drawer commode with applied moulding, 34in. wide. (Robert W. Skinner Inc.) $625 £340

George III serpentine-fronted mahogany commode chest, on ogee bracket feet, 42in. wide, circa 1780. (Sotheby, King & Chasemore) $5,890 £3,200

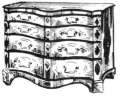 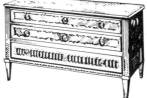 

Dutch mahogany serpentine commode, inlaid with mother-of-pearl roundels, 51½in. wide. (Christie's)
$4,230 £2,300

18th century Italian Louis XVI three-drawer commode in mahogany and other veneers, 48in. wide. (Robert W. Skinner Inc.)
$1,500 £815

18th century North Italian rosewood commode with moulded serpentine top, 48½in. wide. (Christie's)
$6,990 £3,800

Mid 18th century Italian tulipwood and rosewood bombe commode with marble top, 50½in. wide. (Christie's)
$5,890 £3,200

19th century French Louis XVI style bombe commode in mahogany and burl veneers, 38in. wide. (Robert W. Skinner Inc.)
$1,250 £680

Mid 18th century Swedish kingwood bombe commode with moulded marble top, 41½in. wide. (Christie's)
$7,360 £4,000

18th century French Louis XV provincial commode in fruitwood, with overhanging serpentine top, 47in. long. (Robert W. Skinner Inc.) $3,000 £1,630

Late Louis XVI mahogany commode with eared rectangular marble top, 51½in. wide. (Christie's)
$2,390 £1,300

18th century Italian Louis XVI two drawer commode with grey marble top, 46½in. wide. (Robert W. Skinner Inc.)
$1,500 £815

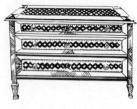

18th century North Italian walnut commode, inlaid with rosewood banding, 48in. wide. (Wm. Doyle Galleries Inc.) **$15,000 £7,935**

18th century Swiss parquetry commode with three long drawers, in zig-zag pattern.(Graves, Son & Pilcher) **$3,185 £1,750**

Hungarian 'transitional' mahogany parquetry commode with marble top, circa 1930, 45¾in. wide. (Sotheby's Belgravia) **$1,050 £561**

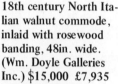
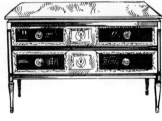

William IV mahogany commode with raised back and carved decoration, 2ft.9in. wide. (Butler & Hatch Waterman) **$695 £380**

18th century Louis XVI two-drawer marquetry commode in harewood and fruitwood, 41in. long. (Robert W. Skinner Inc.) **$1,700 £925**

Late 18th/early 19th century double serpentine-fronted burr-walnut and crossbanded Continental commode, 36in. wide. (Locke & England) **$2,885 £1,550**

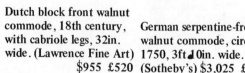

Dutch block front walnut commode, 18th century, with cabriole legs, 32in. wide. (Lawrence Fine Art) **$955 £520**

German serpentine-fronted walnut commode, circa 1750, 3ft.10in. wide. (Sotheby's) **$3,025 £1,700**

George III serpentine mahogany commode chest, circa 1775, 3ft. 8½in. wide.(Sotheby's) **$5,115 £2,750**

18th century Continental walnut serpentine commode on short cabriole legs. (Graves, Son & Pilcher) $965 £520

Neapolitan parquetry commode in quarter veneered kingwood, with serpentine front, circa 1770, 4ft.6in. wide. (Sotheby's) $3,025 £1,700

Continental bow-fronted mahogany commode, 18th century, 49½in. wide. (Lawrence Fine Art) $3,130 £1,700

Mid 18th century Dutch walnut commode chest of four drawers, on bracket feet, 2ft.9½in. wide. (Sotheby's) $2,865 £1,485

Hepplewhite mahogany serpentine-fronted commode with reeded pilaster corners, circa 1790, 3ft.2½in. wide.(Sotheby, King & Chasemore) $2,455 £1,350

North Italian walnut parquetry commode with serpentine top, circa 1760, 3ft.11½in. wide. (Sotheby's) $11,930 £6,380

Mid 18th century Louis XV provincial walnut commode with inverted serpentine top, 4ft.2in. wide. (Sotheby's) $3,705 £1,980

One of a pair of 18th century Italian walnut commodes on bracket feet. (Capes, Dunn & Co.) $5,795 £3,100

18th century French provincial walnut commode, 4ft.1in. wide, with serpentine front. (Turner, Rudge & Turner) $3,310 £1,800

CORNER CUPBOARDS

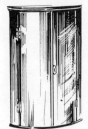

Late 18th century bow-fronted corner cupboard, 2ft. wide. (Dickinson, Davy & Markham) $295 £160

Louis XV kingwood and marquetry encoignure with serpentine marble top, 38in. wide. (Christie's) $1,730 £900

Late 18th century American Chippendale basswood corner cupboard, 45in. wide. (Robert W. Skinner Inc.)$1,400 £760

Good late 18th century Dutch walnut and marquetry encoignure with bowed front, 72cm. wide. (H. Spencer & Sons Ltd.) $670 £360

George III mahogany corner cupboard with moulded cornice and canted corners, circa 1770, 4ft. 2½in. wide.(Sotheby's) $1,210 £650

George III mahogany standing corner cabinet in two parts, circa 1760, 3ft.10in. wide.(Sotheby, King & Chasemore) $2,955 £1,650

Dutch walnut bow-fronted corner cabinet, top inlaid with harewood, 37½in. high. (Lawrence Fine Art) $955 £520

Late 18th century oak standing corner cupboard with plain pediment, 4ft.3in. wide. (Dickinson, Davy & Markham)$680 £370

One of a pair of Louis XV black and gold lacquer encoignures with marble tops, 28in. wide. (Christie's) $9,505 £4,950

18th century oak corner cupboard with double panelled doors, with brass key escutcheons, 40in. wide. (Gilbert Baitson) $285 £150

Mahogany corner cabinet by Wright & Mansfield, door crossbanded in tulipwood, 1880's, 27½in. wide. (Sotheby's Belgravia) $1,510 £820

Mid 18th century George III oak corner cupboard with fluted canted sides, 36in. wide. (Sotheby's) $835 £440

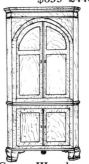

18th century Dutch architectural double corner cupboard with dentil cornice, 55in. wide. (Boardman's) $1,780 £1,000

Mid 18th century Dutch walnut and marquetry corner cupboard with ogee-fronted base, 3ft.5in. wide. (Sotheby's) $10,830 £6,050

George III mahogany corner cupboard in well-figured wood, circa 1780, 3ft.10in. wide. (Sotheby's) $1,475 £792

Late 19th century mahogany and inlaid double corner cupboard on bracket feet, 36in. wide. (Lacy Scott) $2,305 £1,200

George III Chippendale mahogany corner cupboard with scroll-shaped pediment, 43in. wide. (Boardman's) $4,345 £2,300

Late 18th/early 19th century George III oak standing corner cupboard with glazed doors, 42in. wide. (Sotheby's) $960 £506

Mid 17th century oak buffet with carved frieze and doors, 56in. wide. (Christie's)
$2,560 £1,400

Late 17th century carved oak court cupboard with recessed top cupboard, 5ft.4in. wide. (Russell, Baldwin & Bright)
$990 £550

Mid 17th century oak cupboard with recessed upper section, 56in. wide. (Edwards, Bigwood & Bewlay)
$3,295 £1,800

Heavily carved 19th century oak court cupboard, 4ft.9in. wide. (J. M. Welch & Son) $730 £400

17th century oak buffet with carved frieze and doors, 48½in. wide. (Christie's)
$4,390 £2,400

Early 18th century oak court cupboard with pendant finials, 59in. wide. (Sotheby's)
$1,800 £990

George II oak tridarn with moulded cornice, 4ft.4½in. wide. (Sotheby's)
$3,105 £1,595

Mid 17th century Charles II oak court cupboard, 5ft.5in. wide, probably Westmorland. (Sotheby's) $3,120 £1,650

Mid 17th century oak court cupboard with fluted frieze, 60in. wide. (Sotheby's)
$1,360 £715

Italian Renaissance walnut credenza, heavily carved, basically 16th century, 70in. wide. (Boardman's) $3,700 £2,000

Victorian burr-walnut and kingwood banded ormolu mounted credenza, 3ft. 10½in. wide, circa 1865. (Sotheby, King & Chasemore) $3,170 £1,650

Early 17th century Tuscany Provincial walnut credenza with canted ends, 59in. wide. (Robert W. Skinner Inc.) $3,000 £1,630

Victorian burr-walnut credenza with marquetry panels in kingwood surround, 65in. wide. (Boardman's) $2,405 £1,350

Victorian walnut credenza with inlaid satinwood stringing and ormolu beading, 5ft.5in. wide. (Dickinson, Davy & Markham) $2,160 £1,200

Mid Victorian ebonised and ormolu mounted credenza with burr-walnut frieze, 65in. wide. (Dacre, Son & Hartley) $735 £420

Victorian walnut credenza crossbanded in rosewood, 70in. wide. (Dee & Atkinson) $1,860 £1,000

Mid Victorian ebonised and ormolu mounted credenza with inlaid frieze, 54in. wide. (Dacre, Son & Hartley) $820 £450

George II oak wall cupboard with shaped panel doors, circa 1730, 2ft. 5¼in. wide. (Sotheby's) $405 £220

Partly 17th century carved oak cupboard in two parts, 48in. wide. (Lawrence Fine Art) $1,805 £940

George I oak press cupboard with panelled cornice and front, circa 1725, 4ft.11in. wide.(Sotheby's) $4,070 £2,200

Small mid 17th century North Holland oak four door cupboard on pearshaped bun feet, 47in. wide. (Boardman's) $4,625 £2,500

Unusual Regency mahogany clothes press in the manner of George Smith, 55in. wide. (Christie's) $4,255 £2,300

19th century Louis XI style chinoiserie decorated lingere, in mahogany with marble top, 38in. wide. (Robert W. Skinner Inc.) $1,800 £980

Georgian oak press cupboard with moulded cornice, 57in. wide. (Lawrence Fine Art) $1,565 £850

17th century oak zeeuwschekast, doors inlaid with a marquetry of palisander, 63in. wide. (Boardman's) $4,070 £2,200

Joined oak press cupboard, circa 1670, 5ft. 5in. wide, on stile feet. (Lawrence Fine Art) $2,485 £1,350

17th century German walnut schrank with original pewtered lock and keys, 81in. wide. (Boardman's) $3,235 £1,750

Mid 18th century George III oak wall cupboard with two arched fielded panelled doors, 41in. wide. (Sotheby's) $355 £187

Rare West Country painted and carved oak cupboard with moulded cornice, circa 1640, 5ft. 3½in. wide.(Sotheby's) $5,350 £2,860

Chinese Chippendale mahogany linen press with dentil cornice, on ogee feet, 3ft. 8in. wide. (Gilbert Baitson) $630 £340

Early 18th century South German serpentine walnut kommodenschrank with domed top, 55in. wide. (Boardman's) $3,795 £2,050

19th century Anglo-Indian padoukwood cupboard with gadroon panelled doors, 46in. wide. (Sotheby Beresford Adams) $705 £380

Large 19th century Continental oak hall cupboard with wrought iron hinges and handles. (Butler & Hatch Waterman) $925 £500

18th century oak breakfront linen press with brass handles and escutcheons. (J. M. Welch & Son) $1,600 £880

Early 18th century Namuroise oak armoire with breakfront pediment, 6ft. 3in. wide. (Boardman's) $2,960 £1,600

CUPBOARDS

Mid 17th century oak hanging cupboard with arcaded upper section, 33¾in. wide. (Christie's) $1,280 £700

Early 18th century oak hanging cupboard with triangular pediment, 50in. wide. (Christie's) $560 £302

17th century press with overhanging moulded cornice, on block feet, 60in. wide. (Christie's) $1,370 £750

Mid 17th century oak press with overhanging cornice carved with lozenges and rosettes, 55½in. wide. (Christie's) $2,470 £1,350

Fine North German oak cupboard, doors applied with octagonal moulded panels, 65½in. wide. (Christie's)$3,795 £2,052

17th century oak food cupboard with moulded cornice, 49in. wide. (Christie's) $1,190 £650

South German or Swiss walnut and fruitwood veneered cupboard with serpentine cornice, 1760, 3ft.9in. wide.(Sotheby's) $3,740 £2,090

Early 17th century Tuscan walnut cupboard with moulded projecting top, 4ft.6in. wide. (Sotheby's) $3,645 £2,035

Swiss pewter-inlaid walnut standing cupboard, circa 1700, 1ft.9½in. wide. (Sotheby's) $1,180 £660

Victorian inlaid walnut Davenport with carved 'dolphin' supports, 23in. wide. (Burtenshaw Walker)
$1,255 £700

Rococo revival rosewood Davenport desk with pierced brass gallery, 22½in. wide. (Robert W. Skinner Inc.) $500 £275

Late Regency rosewood . Davenport with galleried top, 19in. wide. (Christie's)$2,260 £1,242

Unusual walnut Davenport in well-figured and burr-wood, circa 1870, 22½in. wide.(Sotheby's Belgravia) $1,335 £715

Early 19th century George III mahogany Davenport with three-quarter gilt metal gallery, 20in. wide. (Sotheby's) $4,785 £2,600

Victorian walnut Davenport with shaped front and finely moulded supports. (M. Philip H. Scott)
$2,430 £1,300

Burr-walnut Harlequin Davenport, superstructure with pierced gallery, circa 1860, 23in. wide. (Sotheby's Belgravia) $1,750 £935

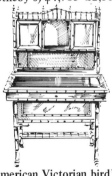

American Victorian bird's-eye maple veneer bamboo Davenport desk, circa 1870, 32in. wide. (Robert W. Skinner Inc.)
$1,800 £1,030

Victorian walnut piano top Davenport with wood gallery, 22in. wide. (Woolley & Wallis) $1,520 £850

379

Walnut Davenport, circa 1860's, 22¼in. wide, on moulded cabriole legs. (Sotheby's Belgravia) $945 £506

William IV mahogany Davenport with galleried top, circa 1830, 1ft.9in. wide. (Sotheby's) $2,035 £1,100

Early Victorian burr-walnut Davenport with boxwood stringing, 1ft.10in. wide. (Capes, Dunn & Co.) $1,160 £620

Victorian inlaid walnut Davenport. (Honiton Galleries) $880 £475

Victorian walnut Davenport with pierced fret gallery, 2ft. 3in. wide, circa 1855. (Sotheby, King & Chasemore) $1,385 £750

Burr-walnut Harlequin Davenport with sprung superstructure, circa 1870, 22in. wide. (Sotheby's Belgravia) $1,485 £770

Mid 19th century walnut Davenport with gallery, 22in. wide. (Locke & England) $800 £440

Unusual japanned Davenport with waisted top and pierced gallery, circa 1900, 27in. wide. (Sotheby's Belgravia) $1,280 £715

Victorian Davenport in inlaid burr-walnut, in good condition. (Way, Ridet & Co.) $980 £550

Burr-maple and ebonised wood Davenport with leather surface, circa 1870, 22¾in. wide. (Sotheby's Belgravia) $595 £319

Mid 19th century Anglo-Indian walnut Davenport with irregular black graining, 49½in. wide. (Sotheby's Belgravia) $925 £495

Walnut Davenport with hinged stationery compartment, circa 1870, 21in. wide. (Sotheby's Belgravia) $1,195 £638

Mid 19th century mahogany pedestal desk with inset writing surface, 62in. wide, restored. (Sotheby's Belgravia) $1,295 £720

English Renaissance revival bird's-eye maple veneer and inlaid Davenport desk, circa 1870, 22in. wide. (Robert W. Skinner Inc.) $750 £420

19th century walnut Davenport desk with raised superstructure. (J. M. Welch & Son) $490 £270

Mahogany Davenport, superstructure with hinged lid, 1880's, 22½in. wide. (Sotheby's Belgravia) $460 £250

19th century walnut Davenport desk on turned legs. (J. M. Welch & Son) $435 £240

Walnut Harlequin Davenport with secret rising section, in very good condition. (Allen & May) $1,700 £900

Double-domed walnut display cabinet, 19th century, 45in. wide. (Lawrence Fine Art) $2,390 £1,300

Dutch walnut display cabinet, circa 1760, with moulded serpentine cornice, 5ft.6½in. wide. (Sotheby's) $3,290 £1,760

Mahogany and marquetry small display cabinet, circa 1900, 26in. wide. (Sotheby's Belgravia) $740 £396

Late 19th century Chippendale style display cabinet on stand. (J. M. Welch & Son)$475 £260

Mid 18th century Portuguese rosewood display cabinet on stand, 39½in. wide.(Christie's) $1,590 £850

One of a pair of late 19th century French vitrines with pierced brass galleries and ormolu mounts, 2ft.2in. wide.(Sotheby, King & Chasemore) $5,395 £2,900

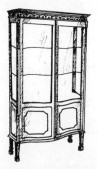

Display cabinet of Hepplewhite design in mahogany frame, 39in. wide. (W. H. Lane & Son) $770 £420

Giltwood Vernis Martin display cabinet in Louis XV style, circa 1900, 44in. wide. (Sotheby's Belgravia) $2,230 £1,155

Edwardian 'Sheraton' display cabinet framed in mahogany with satinwood inlay, 36in. wide. (W. H. Lane & Son) $735 £400

382

Mid 19th century walnut and marquetry display cabinet with gilt metal mounts, 75in. wide. (Sotheby Beresford Adams) $1,860 £1,000

Early 19th century Dutch mahogany and boxwood inlaid display cabinet, 73in. wide. (Boardman's) $1,985 £1,050

Late 19th century mahogany and giltwood bronze display cabinet in the manner of Francois Linke, 50in. wide. (Sotheby Beresford Adams) $1,395 £750

'William and Mary' burr-walnut display cabinet with double-domed top, circa 1900, 53in. wide. (Sotheby's Belgravia) $1,700 £880

20th century Louis XV style French vitrine in harewood and other veneers, 49in. wide. (Robert W. Skinner Inc.) $1,500 £815

Art Nouveau mahogany breakfront display cabinet on tapering octagonal legs, 169cm. wide. (Christie's) $2,055 £1,100

Mahogany display cabinet with glazed astragal doors and running frieze, 3ft.9in. wide. (Brogden & Co.) $665 £360

Dutch oak and marquetry display cabinet with moulded cornice, 85½in. wide. $8,830 £4,800

Art Nouveau mahogany display cabinet inlaid with mother-of-pearl, 135cm. wide. (Christie's) $2,880 £1,540

383

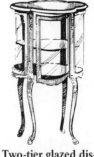

Burr-walnut display cabinet with domed top above a glazed door, 19in. wide. (Hy. Duke & Son)
$480
£250

Satinwood display cabinet, superstructure with a pierced gallery, circa 1890, 58in. wide. (Sotheby's Belgravia)
$1,195 £650

Two-tier glazed display cabinet, on cabriole legs.
(Honiton Galleries)
$205 £110

Mid 19th century satinwood display cabinet with moulded cornice, crossbanded with rosewood, 38in. wide. (Sotheby's Belgravia)
$1,190 £660

18th century Dutch marquetry vitrine, cornice rising to carved centre, 35in. wide. (Boardman's)$4,440 £2,400

Mid 20th century 'Charles II' giltwood rectangular cabinet on stand with glazed top, 43in. wide. (Sotheby's Belgravia)
$1,655 £920

Dutch walnut display cabinet with scrolled pediment and bombe base, 84in. wide. (Christie's)
$11,040 £6,000

Mahogany and marquetry Art Nouveau display cabinet with bow-fronted glazed doors, circa 1900, 55in. wide. (Sotheby's Belgravia) $645 £350

Mahogany display cabinet with arched top frieze and open mirror back, 58½in. high. (Locke & England)
$1,200 £650

19th century French kingwood small display cabinet with coloured marble top, 2ft.2½in. wide. (Dickinson, Davy & Markham) $2,850 £1,550

Early 20th century Edwardian mahogany and marquetry display cabinet with gilt metal gallery, 49in. wide. (Sotheby Beresford Adams) $930 £500

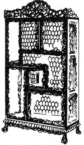

Carved and stained hardwood display cabinet with open shelves. (Phillips) $810 £440

One of a pair of satinwood display cabinets with bowed-fronts, circa 1900, 29in. wide. (Sotheby's Belgravia) $4,050 £2,250

Early 20th century satinwood display cabinet with bow-front, 46in. wide. (Sotheby Beresford Adams) $930 £500

19th century French vitrine in Louis XV style, with serpentine-front and bow sides. (John Milne) $1,840 £1,000

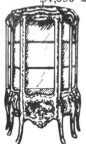

19th century French kingwood vitrine with serpentine-fronted glass door, 3ft.9in. wide. (Edwards, Bigwood & Bewlay) $5,305 £2,900

Large 18th century Dutch walnut and marquetry vitrine with dome-shaped top, 80in. wide. (Boardman's) $8,510 £4,600

Mahogany display cabinet with gilt bronze mouldings, circa 1880-1900, 46½in. wide. (Sotheby's Belgravia) $885 £480

385

Chinese carved padouk-wood display cabinet with simulated bamboo frame, 3ft.3in. wide, circa 1900. (Sotheby, King & Chasemore)
$730 £400

19th century German provincial hanging vitrine in walnut, 45in. wide. (Robert W. Skinner Inc.)
$600 £325

Edwardian Art Nouveau display cabinet with inlaid doors, circa 1910, 36in. wide. (Sotheby's Belgravia)$575 £297

'Chinese Chippendale' mahogany display cabinet with pagoda cresting, 1880's, 26in. wide. (Sotheby's Belgravia)
$905 £484

Early 20th century fruitwood moon cabinet on an X-frame with rectangular plinth, 206cm. high. (Sotheby's Belgravia)
$3,020 £1,650

Late 19th century satinwood and painted display cabinet with elliptically glazed doors, 34in. wide. (Sotheby's Belgravia) $4,115 £2,200

Edwardian carved rosewood and satinwood inlaid display cabinet with moulded and pierced top, 45in. wide. (Dacre, Son & Hartley)
$760 £410

Unusual William and Mary yewwood display cabinet on stand, 53in. wide. (Christie's) $6,860 £3,630

'George I' walnut display cabinet on stand, circa 1900, 41in. wide. (Sotheby's Belgravia)
$1,700 £880

Reproduction mahogany display cabinet with pierced pediment, 68in. wide. (Outhwaite & Litherland) $1,350 £750

French mahogany and floral marquetry serpentined bijouterie table with hinged top, circa 1900, 2ft. 1in. wide.(Sotheby, King & Chasemore) $510 £280

One of a pair of Edwardian china display cabinets in mahogany with floral decoration, 3ft. 3in. wide. (Russell, Baldwin & Bright) $1,710 £950

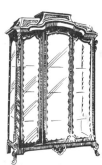

French ormolu mounted kingwood vitrine with shaped and arched pediment, 67in. high. (Lawrence Fine Art) $5,370 £3,000

19th century inlaid kingwood vitrine with ormolu mounts and shaped glass door. (John Milne) $1,880 £1,000

French kingwood and ormolu mounted marble top vitrine, circa 1890, 2ft.2in. wide. (Sotheby, King & Chasemore) $2,365 £1,300

Unusual mahogany and marquetry table display cabinet with bowed glazed lid, circa 1900, 28in. wide. (Sotheby's Belgravia) $700 £374

Small French display cabinet, 1920's, 110cm. high. (Sotheby's Belgravia) $680 £374

Victorian figured walnut cabinet with glazed door and galleried superstructure, 84cm. wide. (H. Spencer & Sons Ltd.) $1,055 £580

18th century Welsh oak
dresser with baluster turned front supports, 5ft.
6in. wide, with potboard
below. (Russell, Baldwin
& Bright) **$3,060 £1,700**

18th century Normandy dresser
with canted corners and carved
mouldings. (Locke & England)
$1,430 £800

18th century oak Shrop-
shire dresser with brass
swan neck handles and
pierced carved canopy.
(Burtenshaw Walker)
$1,550 £820

Queen Anne oak tri-
darn, dated 1722, 4ft.
6in. wide. (Sotheby,
King & Chasemore)
$1,940 £1,050

18th century oak dresser with
brass handles and lockplates.
(Sotheby, King & Chasemore)
$1,455 £800

Early 19th century
oak dresser with
ogee pediment,
80in. wide.(Sothe-
by's)**$2,715 £1,430**

Georgian oak high dres-
ser with divided open
shelves and shaped
apron, 82in. wide.
(Lawrence Fine Art)
$3,650 £1,900

17th/18th century oak dresser
base with three Gothic panelled doors and iron hinges, 51in.
wide. (Andrew Grant)
$3,625 £1,950

Late 18th century
American pine cup-
board with flat cor-
nice, 48in. wide.
(Robert W. Skinner
Inc.) **$1,400 £765**

George III three drawer oak dresser with shaped apron, 6ft.11in. wide. (Wyatt & Sons with Whitehead's) **$1,820 £1,000**

Oak Shropshire dresser on cabriole legs, 63in. wide. (Hall Wateridge & Owen) **$1,940 £1,050**

Partly 18th century oak dresser with wavy pediment and apron, 88in. wide. (Sotheby's) **$1,045 £550**

Antique oak dresser base, three deep drawers fitted with brass swan neck handles, on four turned legs with shaped frieze. (Butler & Hatch Waterman) **$230 £130**

Early 20th century James I style oak dresser base, 72in. wide. (Sotheby's) **$795 £418**

19th century oak dresser with cyma recta pediment and bracket feet, 74in. wide. (Sotheby's) **$1,360 £715**

Charles II oak and elm dresser, circa 1680, 5ft. wide, restored. (Sotheby, King & Chasemore) **$1,730 £900**

George I oak dresser on stem feet, 5ft.6in. wide, circa 1725. (Sotheby, King & Chasemore) **$1,445 £780**

18th century oak Welsh dresser with plain pediment, triple delft rack and panelled back, 5ft. 8in. wide. (Dickinson, Davy & Markham) **$2,575 £1,400**

389

DRESSERS & BUFFETS

Georgian oak high dresser with brass handles, 68in. wide. (Lawrence Fine Art) $1,510 £820

Charles II oak dresser with brass pear-drop handles, moulded understretchers, 75in. wide. (Dacre, Son & Hartley) $1,820 £1,000

Georgian oak high dresser with shaped frieze, 55in. wide. (Lawrence Fine Art) $2,575 £1,400

George II oak dresser with ogee top, circa 1740, 4ft.8½in. wide, later cornice. (Sotheby's) $8,315 £4,400

18th century open back oak dresser with scalloped frieze and lower pot shelf, 70in. wide. (W. H. Lane & Son) $1,090 £600

Late Elizabethan oak buffet, circa 1600, 4ft.10½in. wide. (Sotheby's) $5,820 £3,080

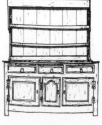

Oak dresser with raised solid back with moulded top, 5ft. wide. (Coles, Knapp & Kennedy) $535 £300

George II oak and pollard elm dresser with shaped apron, circa 1740, 7ft. 8in. wide. (Sotheby, King & Chasemore) $4,650 £2,500

Early oak dresser with plain canopy and wrought iron hinges, 5ft.1in. wide. (Butler & Hatch Waterman) $1,965 £1,075

19th century French pro-
vincial oak dresser base,
56in. wide, on cabriole
legs. (Lawrence Fine Art)
$1,140 £620

Late Georgian oak dresser
with brass handles and
escutcheons. (Biddle &
Webb) $1,395 £750

George II oak and elm
dresser with three-quar-
ter gallery, circa 1740,
5ft.9½in. wide.
(Sotheby's)
$1,730 £935

18th century oak dresser
on square legs united by
pot board, original iron
hooks, 61in. wide.
(Locke & England)
$1,185 £650

Georgian oak joined
dresser with inlaid
frieze, 63in. wide.
(Lawrence Fine Art)
$2,025 £1,100

Early 19th century
Welsh dresser on
cabriole legs.
(V. & V's.)
$1,730 £900

Late 18th century Geor-
gian oak joined dresser
with brass knob handles,
60in. high. (Lawrence
Fine Art) $1,195 £650

Late 17th/early 18th century
oak dresser base on turned
supports and feet, 79in. long.
(Sotheby's) $1,880 £990

Oak dresser with later
rack and moulded
cornice above an ogee-
cut frieze, 6ft.2½in.
wide. (Sotheby's)
$1,670 £902

DUMB WAITERS

Regency mahogany two-tier dumb waiter with graduated shelves, 25in. diam. (Christie's) $1,110 £594

One of a pair of George III mahogany dumb waiters on tripod bases, circa 1800, 1ft.11in. diam. (Sotheby's) $1,585 £825

Regency mahogany two-tier dumb waiter on moulded tripod base, 25½in. diam. (Christie's) $910 £486

Unusual William IV mahogany concertina whatnot on reeded column, circa 1835, 20¾in. wide. (Sotheby's Belgravia) $515 £275

George III mahogany three-tier circular dumb waiter with ebony stringing, circa 1800, 30in. diam. (Edwards, Bigwood & Bewlay) $1,060 £580

Satinwood three-tier tea table with leaf-cast bronze handle, circa 1920. (Sotheby's Belgravia) $330 £180

Modern George III style mahogany dumb waiter with two foliate moulded tiers, 24in. diam. (Sotheby's) $405 £220

Satinwood dumb waiter with circular top and four further trays, circa 1900, 22in. diam. (Sotheby's Belgravia) $905 £506

Hepplewhite period mahogany three-tier dumb waiter on three cabriole legs, 24in. high. (Woolley & Wallis) $4,900 £2,800

George II red walnut lowboy, circa 1750, 2ft.4in. wide. (Sotheby, King & Chasemore) $1,825 £950

Queen Anne oak lowboy with moulded edged top, shaped apron and square cabriole legs, 36in. wide. (Dacre, Son & Hartley) $490 £270

Georgian oak lowboy, top with moulded edge, 30in. wide. (Lawrence Fine Art) $1,290 £700

One of two similar late George II mahogany lowboys, circa 1755, 2ft. 10in. wide. (Sotheby's) $1,570 £850

Mid 18th century oak lowboy with brass handles. (Lacy Scott) $1,405 £760

William and Mary lowboy in mahogany and mahogany veneer, 30½in. wide. (Robert W. Skinner Inc.) $850 £460

George II oak lowboy, crossbanded borders and inlaid stringing, pierced brass loop handles, circa 1730, 31½in. wide. (Neales) $1,860 £1,000

George I mahogany lowboy with brass butterfly plates and swan-neck handles, 83.5cm. wide. (Jackson-Stops & Staff) $915 £500

Queen Anne cherrywood dressing table with central fan carved drawer, 30in. wide, circa 1760. (Robert W. Skinner Inc.) $14,000 £7,610

393

PEDESTAL & KNEEHOLE DESKS

Mid 19th century mahogany pedestal desk with inset writing surface, 62in. wide, restored. (Sotheby's Belgravia) $1,295 £720

Victorian solid mahogany roll-top desk on bracket feet. (Parkinson, Son & Hamer) $1,455 £790

18th century walnut kneehole desk with crossbanded and featherbanded top, 31in. wide. (Hy. Duke & Son) $2,590 £1,350

Mid 19th century mahogany pedestal desk with leather-lined top, 60in. wide. (Sotheby's Belgravia) $1,010 £560

Mid 20th century mahogany pedestal desk with rope-carved moulded edge, 60in. wide. (Sotheby's Belgravia) $700 £363

George III mahogany kneehole writing table on bracket feet, circa 1770, 3ft. 7in. wide. (Sotheby's) $835 £450

Mahogany chest of drawers with moulded top, circa 1770, 3ft.3½in. wide. (Sotheby's) $3,145 £1,700

George III mahogany double-sided writing table with crossbanded top, circa 1790, 4ft.7in. wide. (Sotheby's) $2.480 £1,320

Desk by Howard & Sons on four bamboo legs with brass castors, mid 19th century, 49½in. wide. (Sotheby's Belgravia) $700 £380

George III mahogany partner's desk with nine drawers, 56½in. wide. (Christie's) $4,440 £2,400

Victorian mahogany cylinder front desk with maplewood drawers, 5ft. wide. (Capes, Dunn & Co.) $1,045 £560

Queen Anne walnut kneehole desk with crossbanded top, 31in. wide. (Christie's) $2,245 £1,200

Mahogany secretaire desk with leather-lined interior, circa 1850. (Sotheby's Belgravia) $1,045 £580

George III mahogany kneehole pedestal writing table with leather top, circa 1770, 3ft.8in. wide. (Sotheby's) $4,135 £2,200

Mid 19th century mahogany pedestal desk stamped T. Willson, London, 54in. wide. (Sotheby Beresford Adams) $1,080 £580

George III satinwood kneehole desk with oval inlaid top, 32in. wide. (Christie's) $2,150 £1,150

Pedestal kneehole desk in mahogany, with leather top, circa 1880, 72in. wide. (Sotheby's Belgravia) $1,955 £1,045

George III mahogany kneehole writing desk, 3ft.3in. wide. (Sotheby's) $2,250 £1,210

20th century mahogany pedestal desk with green leather top, 60in. wide. (Sotheby's Belgravia) $825 £440

Victorian satinwood bow-fronted desk, cupboards with panels of maidens, 44in. wide. (Morphets) $1,755 £975

19th century walnut Wootton Patent Office desk with galleried top, 58in. wide. (Dacre, Son & Hartley) $6,370 £3,500

19th century Georgian mahogany desk of kneehole shape, with oak linings, 38½in. wide. (Lawrence Fine Art) $995 £540

Late 18th century mahogany twin pedestal kneehole desk, 37½in. wide. (W. H. Lane & Son) $625 £340

Chippendale style partner's desk with red leather top, inset with fan corners. (Coles, Knapp & Kennedy) $1,255 £700

George II mahogany kneehole writing desk, top with canted corners, circa 1750, 3ft. 1½in. wide.(Sotheby's) $5,115 £2,750

Mid 19th century oak Jacobean revival pedestal desk, 84in. wide. (Sotheby's Belgravia) $3,395 £1,815

Walnut and marquetry pedestal desk, 48in. wide. (J. M. Welch & Son) $1,345 £740

Mid 19th century oak partner's desk with red tooled leather top, 68in. wide. (Sotheby's) $1,255 £660

George III mahogany library writing table of kneehole form, 46in. wide. (Wm. Doyle Galleries Inc.)
          $4,400 £2,330

George III mahogany kneehole writing and toilet chest, circa 1775, 3ft.1in. wide. (Sotheby's)
          $1,385 £750

Dutch or German inlaid mahogany writing desk, circa 1790, 4ft.4in. wide. (Sotheby's)
          $1,195 £638

William IV rosewood partner's desk, top inset with red American cloth. (Woolley & Wallis)
          $4,115 £2,300

Victorian mahogany rolltop pedestal desk with writing slope. (J. M. Welch & Son)$910 £500

Mid 18th century mahogany kneehole writing desk with centre cupboard, 32in. wide. (Lacy Scott) $2,590 £1,350

PEDESTAL & KNEEHOLE DESKS

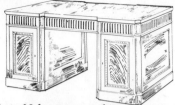

Early 20th century mahogany partner's desk with red leather top, 60in. wide. (Sotheby's Belgravia) $2,230 £1,155

Late 19th century mahogany partner's desk with leather writing surface, 60in. wide. (Sotheby's Belgravia)
$3,185 £1,650

Early George III mahogany kneehole desk with leather-lined top, 47½in. wide. (Christie's) $6,290 £3,456

George III satinwood secretaire kneehole desk, top crossbanded in tulipwood, 33in. wide. (Christie's) $1,575 £864

Late Victorian mahogany and floral marquetry inlaid kidney-shaped desk, 4ft. wide. (Woolley & Wallis)
$1,575 £900

Rare George III mahogany kneehole architect's desk, circa 1775. (Graves, Son & Pilcher) $4,280 £2,300

George IV mahogany double-sided pedestal desk with red leather top, 5ft. wide, circa 1820. (Sotheby's) $5,635 £3,080

Late Georgian mahogany pedestal desk, doors inlaid with burr-walnut ovals, 48in. wide. (Christie's) $1,510 £800

Berlin woolwork and Italian firescreen of Queen Victoria's pets, circa 1840, 51 x 31in. (Sotheby's Belgravia) $410 £220

Mid 19th century papier-mache firescreen of shaped oval outline, 41.5cm. long. (Sotheby's Belgravia) $415 £220

Mid 18th century Queen Anne mahogany pole screen, 56in. high. (Robert W. Skinner Inc.) $2,500 £1,360

One of a set of four embroidered panels in silk, with carved frames, circa 1900, 55cm. wide. (Sotheby's Belgravia) $2,820 £1,540

Walnut firescreen, central panel showing a mother and three children, circa 1860, 33in. wide. (Sotheby's Belgravia) $650 £360

Mahogany pole screen with brass stem, base with cabriole legs, circa 1860, 60½in. high. (Sotheby's Belgravia) $380 £210

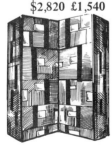

Four-panel lacquer screen, adapted from door panels, circa 1925. (Sotheby's Belgravia) $2,135 £1,200

Stained glass firescreen with painted central panel, circa 1880, 32in. high. (Sotheby's Belgravia) $425 £220

Six-fold painted leather screen, circa 1760, 9ft. 5½in. high. (Sotheby's) $4,115 £2,200

18th century Dutch black and gold lacquer six-leaf screen decorated in raised gilt, 95½in. high. (Christie's) $7,565 £3,960

Large Chinese screen inlaid in ivory and hardstones, circa 1900, 130cm. wide. (Sotheby's Belgravia) $3,850 £2,200

Guangxu four-fold embroidered screen with carved frame, 70cm. high. (Sotheby's Belgravia) $5,435 £2,970

Shibayama two-fold table screen, each leaf divided into two panels, 10½in. high.(Phillips)$865 £484

19th century Chinese six-panel Oriental screen, 67½in. high. (Robert W. Skinner Inc.) $7,750 £4,210

Late 18th/early 19th century Chinese Export black and gold lacquer eight-leaf screen, 95in. high. (Christie's) $5,455 £2,916

Two mid 19th century Burmese carved wood panels from a screen, each 23½in. wide. (Sotheby's)$790 £440

17th century four-leaf screen formed from an oil painting in the style of P. Snayers, 72in. high. (Christie's) $3,955 £2,160

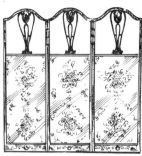

Three-fold lacquer screen by M. Lattry, Paris, circa 1930, 165.5cm. high. (Sotheby's Belgravia) $1,000 £550

18th century painted Flemish four-fold screen. (Andrew Grant) $1,920 £1,000

Satinwood three-fold screen, each fold with arched glazed top, circa 1900, 69in. high. (Sotheby's Belgravia) $700 £380

19th century six-fold Chinese screen showing a junk. (Robert W. Skinner Inc.) $7,750 £4,120

'Moorish' four-fold polychrome and parcel gilt screen in walnut, 1890's, 73¾in. high. (Sotheby's Belgravia) $2,560 £1,430

Very rare three-fold Regency screen of nine japanned panels on copper, circa 1810, 81in. wide. (Sotheby, King & Chasemore) $19,215 £10,500

Early 20th century painted three-fold screen in mahogany frames, 71in. high. (Sotheby's Belgravia) $205 £110

Early 19th century Chinese Export lacquer eight-leaf screen decorated in black and gold, 85in. high. (Christie's) $8,480 £4,536

Georgian mahogany secretaire chest, 45in. wide. (J. M. Welch & Son) $675 £370

Unusual Georgian mahogany secretaire with pierced brass gallery, 3ft.8in. wide. (Lawrence Fine Art) $1,195 £650

Mahogany secretaire chest of three drawers with brass drop handles. (John Hogbin & Son) $1,890 £1,050

Georgian walnut secretaire a abattant with pear drop handles, 41in. wide. (Lawrence Fine Art) $955 £520

Continental mahogany escritoire with pierced gallery back, on turned and reeded trestle ends and stretcher. (Locke & England) $965 £540

Mahogany secretaire a abattant with raised superstructure, 1840's, 42in. wide. (Sotheby's Belgravia) $595 £319

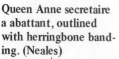

Queen Anne secretaire a abattant, outlined with herringbone banding. (Neales) $7,135 £3,900

William and Mary walnut secretaire cabinet on later bun feet, circa 1700, 3ft. 5in. wide. (Sotheby's) $3,930 £2,090

Late Georgian mahogany secretaire with turned wood handles, 30in. wide. (Lawrence Fine Art) $810 £440

Mahogany secretaire Wellington chest, circa 1880, 28in. wide. (Sotheby's Belgravia) $1,540 £825

Late Georgian mahogany secretaire chest of drawers with brass handles. (J. M. Welch & Son) $1,600 £880

Gustav Stickley oak fall front desk with pine compartments, New York, circa 1905, 31¾in. wide. (Robert W. Skinner Inc.) $550 £310

Mid/late 19th century French walnut and marquetry inlaid secretaire a abattant. (Lacy Scott) $3,935 £2,050

Late 19th century American Victorian walnut butler's desk, 40in. wide. (Robert W. Skinner Inc.) $1,000 £565

Regency black and gold lacquer secretaire, fitted with Bramah lock, 33½in. wide. (Christie s) $1,030 £550

Dutch satinwood secretaire a abattant with crossbanded mahogany top, 35in. wide. (Christie's) $2,025 £1,100

George I period burr-elm and crossbanded secretaire tallboy chest, 3ft. 6¼in. wide. (Geering & Colyer) $2,335 £1,250

Fine Sino-Dutch Lac Burgaute secretaire a abattant, circa 1820, 3ft. 2in. wide. (Sotheby's) $3,705 £1,980

Early George III mahogany secretaire cabinet with waved three-quarter gallery, 34½in. wide. (Christie's) $1,530 £842

19th century Dutch marquetry secretaire on block feet, 42in. high. (Olivers)$1,890 £1,000

Late Louis XVI mahogany, rosewood and boulle secretaire with galleried top, 20in. wide. (Christie's)
$3,170 £1,650

George I walnut secretaire on chest with moulded cornice and convex frieze drawer, 42½in. wide. (Christie's) $2,700 £1,430

German mahogany secretaire a abattant, circa 1760, 38½in. wide, by Abraham Roentgen. (Christie's)
$18,240 £9,500

Louis XVI mahogany and brass inlaid secretaire with galleried top, 31in. wide. (Christie's)
$6,335 £3,300

Italian marquetry secretaire a abattant, inlaid on rosewood ground, circa 1835, 37½in. wide. (Sotheby's Belgravia)
$4,935 £2,640

Regency camphorwood military secretaire chest on turned knob feet, 36in. wide. (Burtenshaw Walker)
$1,385 £775

Mahogany secretaire tallboy with brass handles and side carrying handles, circa 1800. (J. M. Welch & Son)
$2,365 £1,300

George III mahogany
secretaire bookcase,
circa 1790, 4ft. wide.
(Phillips)
$2,685 £1,500

Late George III mahogany
secretaire bookcase, circa
1820, 4ft.1½in. wide.
(Sotheby's)$2,935 £1,595

Mid Georgian mahogany
secretaire cabinet with
dentilled cornice, 50in.
wide. (Christie's)
$2,390 £1,265

Late Georgian maho-
gany secretaire book-
case with reeded astra-
gal glazed doors, 45½in.
wide. (Lawrence Fine
Art) $2,865 £1,600

Large Victorian mahogany
bookcase-secretaire with
three glazed doors, circa
1860, 61in. wide. (Neales)
$2,805 £1,550

George III secretaire
bookcase in mahogany
and satinwood, circa
1770, later cresting,
3ft.3½in. wide.(Sothe-
by's) $7,245 £3,960

Regency mahogany and
calamanderwood secre-
taire cabinet with narrow
cornice, 31¼in. wide.
(Christie's)$6,460 £3,456

Antique secretaire book-
case with adjustable
bookshelves, 3ft.5in.
wide. (Brogden & Co.)
$4,440 £2,400

George III mahogany
secretaire bookcase,
circa 1770, 3ft.1in.
wide. (Sotheby's)
$4,540 £2,365

405

Mahogany tallboy with secretaire, brass fittings, 3ft.6in. wide. (Gilbert Baitson) $1,135 £600

George III mahogany secretaire tallboy, circa 1780, 50in. wide. (Sotheby, King & Chasemore)$4,050 £2,200

Mid 19th century mahogany secretaire bookcase with two arched glazed doors, 58in. wide. (Sotheby Beresford Adams) $1,490 £800

George III mahogany secretaire bookcase, circa 1790, 3ft.7½in wide. (Sotheby's) $2,325 £1,265

Tall 19th century secretaire bookcase with glazed astragal doors, 3ft.9in. wide. (Dickinson, Davy & Markham) $1,105 £600

Late Regency mahogany secretaire cabinet with moulded ribbed cornice, 50in. wide. (Christie's) $2,960 £1,600

George III mahogany secretaire cabinet, circa 1785, 3ft.8½in. wide. (Sotheby's) $3,720 £1,980

Pollard oak secretaire bookcase, heavily carved, 3ft.9in. wide. (Gilbert Baitson) $1,560 £825

Regency mahogany secretaire bookcase, circa 1810, 3ft.5¼in. wide. (Sotheby, King & Chasemore) $1,090 £600

Late 18th century mahogany secretaire bookcase with swan-neck cresting, 4ft. wide. (Sotheby's) $1,455 £770

Wellington secretaire chest of drawers with fitted interior. (Butler & Hatch Waterman) $825 £450

George III secretaire cabinet, circa 1800, 3ft.7in. wide, with dentil cornice. (Sotheby's)$2,035 £1,100

Mahogany secretaire bookcase with double glazed doors, 35½in. wide, 1840's. (Sotheby's Belgravia) $1,620 £900

Sheraton style mahogany secretaire bookcase with satinwood crossbanding. (Phillips)$8,370 £4,500

Late 18th/early 19th century mahogany secretaire bookcase with satinwood veneered frieze, 44½in. wide. (Sotheby Beresford Adams) $1,860 £1,000

Gothic mahogany secretaire bookcase with glazed doors, 19th century, 50in. wide. (Lawrence Fine Art) $1,010 £550

Georgian style mahogany secretaire bookcase with astragal doors, 37½in. wide. (Lawrence Fine Art) $1,140 £620

William IV mahogany secretaire bookcase, circa 1830, 55in. wide, plinth remade.(Sotheby's Belgravia) $2,160 £1,155

FURNITURE

Superb mid 19th century American settee by John H. Belter of New York, in laminated rosewood frame. (Edwards, Bigwood & Bewlay) $38,430 £21,000

18th century curved oak settle with panel seat and high panelled back, 6ft.1in. wide. (Edwards, Bigwood & Bewlay) $935 £510

One of a pair of matching rosewood chaise longues, circa 1840, 84in. long. (Sotheby's Belgravia) $1,980 £1,100

Small late Victorian mahogany two-seat settee, on cabriole legs, 4ft.6in. wide. (Dickinson, Davy & Markham)
$515 £280

Walnut sofa with padded back, upholstered in 18th century gros and petit point needlework, 52in. wide.(Christie's)
$2,775 £1,500

19th century German Provincial carved oak settle with hinged seat, 70in. wide. (Robert W. Skinner Inc.) $450 £245

Fine 17th century oak four panel settle on baluster turned supports, 6ft. wide. (Andrew Grant) $1,115 £600

Walnut settee with button back, circa 1860, 87in. wide. (Sotheby's Belgravia)
$560 £310

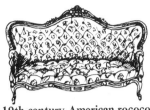

Mid 19th century American rococo revival walnut sofa with carved arm supports and apron. (Robert W. Skinner Inc.) $600 £340

18th century Portuguese jacarandawood settee with triple chair back, 69in. wide. (Christie's) $4,970 £2,700

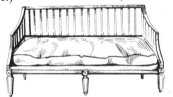

18th century French Provincial Louis XVI canape on square moulded frame, 50½in. wide. (Robert W. Skinner Inc.) $800 £435

Walnut settee on moulded frame carved with flowers, 1860's, 73in. long. (Sotheby's Belgravia) $1,225 £680

19th century Japanese carved teak settle, 65in. long. (Robert W. Skinner Inc.) $850 £460

One of a pair of early 19th century Regency hall benches in the manner of Thos. Tatham, 54in. long. (Sotheby Beresford Adams) $1,710 £920

One of a pair of late 19th century American rococo revival rosewood reclamiers, 51in. long. (Robert W. Skinner Inc.) $1,150 £650

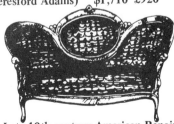

Late 19th century American Renaissance revival finger carved walnut sofa, 68in. long. (Robert W. Skinner Inc.) $300 £170

SETTEES & COUCHES

'George III' painted small settee with arched padded back, circa 1890, 44in. wide. (Sotheby's Belgravia)$445 £231

Early George III mahogany day bed, 6ft.11in. long, circa 1765. (Sotheby's) $3,070 £1,650

Mid 20th century 'Louis XV' parcel gilt and caned settee from a suite, 46in. wide. (Sotheby's Belgravia) $410 £220

'George II' mahogany settee with triple chair back, circa 1880, 59in. wide. (Sotheby's Belgravia) $1,655 £858

19th century George III style 'satyr and mask' settee, in mahogany, 51in. long. (Robert W. Skinner Inc.)$3,600 £1,955

Settee from a mahogany inlaid Edwardian seven-piece drawingroom suite, with carved backs and brocade seats. (Outhwaite & Litherland)$1,800 £1,000

19th century French Louis XVI style tapestry covered canape, 67in. long. (Robert W. Skinner Inc.) $600 £325

Mid 18th century George III elm settle with panelled concave back, 68in. wide. (Sotheby's) $1,880 £990

19th century Chinese carved rosewood settee with triple panelled back, 76in. long. (Robert W. Skinner Inc.)
$800 £435

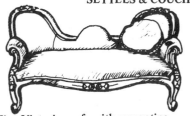

Fine Victorian sofa with serpentine front in walnut frame. (Butler & Hatch Waterman) $2,745 £1,500

Victorian rosewood framed small couch with single scroll end, 154cm. long. (H. Spencer & Sons Ltd.) $700 £380

George II walnut and parcel gilt day bed with scrolled arm supports, 76in. long. (Christie's) $1,605 £858

Rare Queen Anne walnut double chair settee. (Bonham's) $14,510 £7,800

Rosewood conversation settee with three padded chair backs, 54in. wide, 1880's. (Sotheby's Belgravia)$730 £396

Victorian walnut framed chaise longue, on short cabriole legs. (J. M. Welch & Son) $675 £370

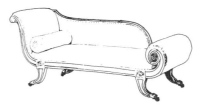

Early 19th century Regency painted day bed with scroll end, 8ft. long. (Sotheby's) $1,415 £770

411

Silk upholstered and beechwood chaise longue by Betty Joel, of gondola form, circa 1930, 194cm. long. (Christie's) $1,185 £650

American Renaissance revival walnut and burl walnut settee, circa 1870, 61in. wide. (Robert W. Skinner Inc.) $325 £180

Victorian walnut small settee with pierced and carved frame, 50in. wide. (Lawrence Fine Art) $1,255 £700

One of a pair of George III blue painted and gilded hall seats, 55in. wide. (Christie's) $3,845 £2,035

Early 20th century rosewood and fruitwood settle with rush matted seat, 98cm. wide. (Sotheby's Belgravia) $1,740 £902

Walnut centre seat of three addorsed chairs, 44in. wide, approx., 1870's. (Sotheby's Belgravia) $680 £363

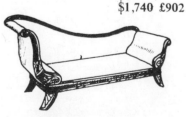

Regency simulated rosewood and white painted day bed, 85in. wide. (Christie's) $985 £540

Mid 19th century cast-iron and brass campaign bed with hinged back. (Sotheby's Belgravia) $410 £220

One of a pair of D-shaped mahogany shelf-sofa ends, 1930's, 69cm. high. (Sotheby's Belgravia) $300 £165

Regency ebonised and parcel gilt set of shelves, circa 1815, 4ft.4in. wide. (Sotheby's) $2,585 £1,375

Early 19th century mahogany cartonnier with carrying handles, 41cm. wide. (H. Spencer & Sons Ltd.) $605 £330

One of a pair of Regency bookcases with two shelves, two cupboard doors and a drawer each. (Capes, Dunn & Co.) $9,350 £5,000

Rococo revival walnut etagere, American, circa 1865, with pierced, carved crest, 45½in. wide. (Robert W. Skinner Inc.) $1,500 £855

Ebonised and mahogany hanging shelf by Carlo Bugatti, 101cm. high. (Christie's) $730 £400

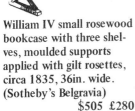

William IV small rosewood bookcase with three shelves, moulded supports applied with gilt rosettes, circa 1835, 36in. wide. (Sotheby's Belgravia) $505 £280

Early George III pine chimney-piece with later carved shelf, 66in. wide. (Christie's) $6,765 £3,780

Late 19th century mahogany book trough. (J. M. Welch & Son) $200 £110

413

Georgian mahogany breakfront sideboard, 68in. wide, with satinwood
crossbanding. (Lawrence Fine Art)
$1,565 £850

George III semi-lunar sideboard inlaid
with harewood, 89in. wide. (Lawrence
Fine Art) $2,390 £1,300

Late 18th century George III demi-lune
sideboard in mahogany, 71in. long.
(Robert W. Skinner Inc.) $1,650 £895

'George III' ebonised bow-front sideboard with a superstructure, 58in.
wide, applied with Sevres panels.
(Sotheby's Belgravia) $625 £340

Sheraton sideboard in figured mahogany
with shell inlay, 5ft. wide, top with brass
rail and curtain. (Gilbert Baitson)
                              $2,835 £1,500

Late George IV mahogany breakfront
sideboard with tambour-fronted superstructure, circa 1825, 4ft.11½in. wide.
(Sotheby's) $890 £480

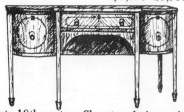

Late 18th century Sheraton design mahogany and boxwood inlaid breakfront
sideboard, 66in. wide. (Locke &
England) $1,835 £1,025

George III serpentine-fronted mahogany sideboard on square tapering legs.
78in. wide, circa 1790. (Sotheby, King
& Chasemore) $1,470 £800

Pollard oak sideboard with carved panels on cupboards and drawers, 6ft. wide. (Gilbert Baitson) $815 £440

George III Sheraton mahogany sideboard with ebony inlay, 84in. wide. (Boardman's) $2,930 £1,550

Regency mahogany bow-fronted sideboard with inlaid blackwood stringing, 6ft.4½in. wide. (Jackson-Stops & Staff) $1,380 £750

George III apsidal sideboard in 'plum-pudding' mahogany, circa 1780, 5ft.4in. wide. (Sotheby's) $5,320 £2,860

George III mahogany serpentine-fronted sideboard, top set with an oval, circa 1790, 6ft.1in. wide. (Sotheby's) $6,290 £3,400

Mid 19th century William IV mahogany sideboard with arched and carved back panel, 96in. wide. (Sotheby Beresford Adams) $445 £240

Late 18th/early 19th century George III bow-front mahogany sideboard, 72in. wide. (Robert W. Skinner Inc.) $1,500 £815

American Federal style mahogany inlaid sideboard with bowed front, circa 1920, 45½in. wide. (Robert W. Skinner Inc.) $950 £520

'Italian 1950's upright mahogany sideboard, with vellum-covered upper cabinet, 139.5cm. high. (Sotheby's Belgravia) $320 £176

George III mahogany and kingwood crossbanded sideboard of Sheraton design, 5ft.10in. wide, circa 1800. (Sotheby, King & Chasemore) $1,315 £750

Unusual small George III serpentine mahogany sideboard, circa 1790, 2ft.11½in. wide. (Sotheby's) $1,950 £1,045

American Louis XV influence rosewood and rosewood veneer sideboard, circa 1930, 50in. wide. (Robert W. Skinner Inc.) $800 £450

Gustav Stickley oak sideboard with rectangular top and ledge back, 178cm. wide.(Christie's) $1,820 £1,000

One of a pair of American custom oak sideboards with galleried cornice top, circa 1920, 43½in. wide. (Robert W. Skinner Inc.) $1,350 £760

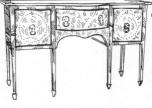

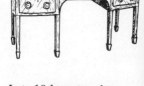

George III mahogany breakfront sideboard with brass curtain rails, 4ft.11½in. wide. (Lawrence Fine Art) $1,655 £900

Mahogany Sheraton sideboard with inlay and serpentine front, 5ft. wide. (Brogden & Co.)$555 £300

Late 18th century bow-fronted sideboard framed and veneered in mahogany, 66½in. wide. (W. H. Lane & Son) $920 £500

American Federal mahogany and mahogany veneer sideboard, circa 1790, 68¾in. wide. (Robert W. Skinner Inc.)
$1,800 £990

Late Georgian mahogany and string and shell inlaid serpentine-fronted sideboard, 84½in. wide. (Dacre, Son & Hartley)
$910 £500

Chinese carved teak sideboard, circa 1930, 56in. wide, with glazed centre door. (Robert W. Skinner Inc.) $400 £220

Eastlake cherry sideboard with carved bee and brickwork, circa 1875, 45in. wide. (Robert W. Skinner Inc.) $650 £365

American baroque style oak sideboard with carved crest, circa 1900, 64½in. wide. (Robert W. Skinner Inc.)
$1,150 £640

Victorian oak sideboard, American, with mirror back, circa 1900, 48in. wide. (Robert W. Skinner Inc.) $250 £140

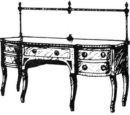

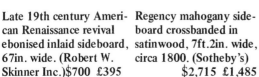

Late 19th century American Renaissance revival ebonised inlaid sideboard, 67in. wide. (Robert W. Skinner Inc.)$700 £395

Regency mahogany sideboard crossbanded in satinwood, 7ft.2in. wide, circa 1800. (Sotheby's)
$2,715 £1,485

17th century oak sideboard with panelled cupboard doors and brass handles, 3ft. 9in. wide. (J. M. Welch & Son) $1,865 £1,025

George III mahogany sideboard with brass oval handles, crossbanded in satinwood, 168cm. wide. (H. Spencer & Sons Ltd.) $785 £420

Late George III mahogany sideboard with break bow-front, 229cm. wide. (H. Spencer & Sons Ltd.) $825 £440

Early 19th century George III sideboard in mahogany and mahogany veneer, 71½in. wide. (Robert W. Skinner Inc.) $780 £425

Sheraton design mahogany sideboard with brass gallery back, 96in. wide. (Locke & England) $1,455 £800

Georgian style mahogany sideboard of breakfront outline, inlaid with stringing, 54in. wide. (Lawrence Fine Art) $1,110 £620

American rococo revival walnut and burled veneered sideboard, circa 1870, 49in. wide. (Robert W. Skinner Inc.) $600 £345

Federal mahogany and mahogany veneer sideboard, circa 1790, 72½in. wide. (Robert W. Skinner Inc.)$2,500 £1,375

Inlaid mahogany Sheraton sideboard with serpentine front and two tambour doors, 79in. wide.(John Hogbin & Son) $2,160 £1,200

18th century American
decorated pine spoon
rack, 12¾in. long.
(Robert W. Skinner Inc.)
$850 £465

Decorative hall stand by
Carlo Bugatti, circa 1890,
120cm. wide. (Sotheby's
Belgravia) $4,805 £2,700

19th century marble-top-
ped stand by George
Bullock, 3ft. high. (J. M.
Welch & Son)
$4,915 £2,700

George II walnut wig stand.
(J. M. Welch & Son)
$380 £210

Bugatti stand with square
top and lower shelf, circa
1900, inlaid with pewter,
112cm. high. (Sotheby's
Belgravia) $680 £374

One of a pair of stained
beechwood plant stands,
by Josef Hoffman,
110.5cm. high.
(Christie's) $820 £450

Rare early 18th century
turned maple lighting
stand on three tapering
legs, 43in. high. (Robert
W. Skinner Inc.)
$2,400 £1,305

One of a matching pair of
Victorian burr-walnut
pedestals with ormolu galleries, 23in. wide. (Hy.
Duke & Son)$1,055 £550

18th century American
oak screw post lighting
device, 47in. high.
(Robert W. Skinner
Inc.) $700 £385

Chinese carved teak and marble stand with lobed top, 33in. high, circa 1880. (Robert W. Skinner Inc.)
　　　　$375 £210

Mid 19th century papier-mache book or music stand inlaid with mother-of-pearl, 12¼in. wide. (Sotheby's Belgravia)
　　　　$160 £90

Sheraton style inlaid mahogany urn stand with shell inlay to lower shelf. (Gilbert Baitson) $225 £120

One of a pair of Regency rosewood pedestal music stands with lyre-shaped insets. (Worsfolds)
　　　　$1,535 £800

Walnut jardiniere in well-figured wood with re-movable lid and liner, 1860's, 26in. wide. (Sotheby's Belgravia)
　　　　$575 £320

William and Mary tri-pod stand with octa-gonal top, circa 1680, 1ft.2½in. wide. (Sotheby's)$895 £484

Early 18th century American pine and maple cross stretcher base candlestand, 27in. high. (Robert W. Skinner Inc.) $425 £230

George II bottle rack on walnut stand, circa 1750, 2ft.2in. wide. (Sotheby's) $1,570 £836

One of a pair of 19th century French ebon-ised pedestal cabinets with marble tops. (J. M. Welch & Son)
　　　　$1,820 £1,000

One of a pair of Regency burr-yew diningroom pedestals on bronze paw feet, 19½in. wide. (Christie's) $1,645   £880

Late Empire French jardiniere stand on cabriole legs. (J. M. Welch & Son) $275 £150

Folding circular telescopic lectern table with swivel action, by Swan & Milligan. (Butler & Hatch Waterman) $430 £235

One of a pair of mid 19th century giltwood and burr-walnut torcheres, 52in. high. (Sotheby's Belgravia) $2,545 £1,320

William IV mahogany folio stand with railed adjustable sides, 28in. wide. (Christie's) $1,355 £750

William and Mary oak tripod stand with spiral-twist stem and baluster base, circa 1680, 1ft. 1½in. wide. (Sotheby's) $935 £506

17th century Flemish ebony and rosewood press on spirally turned legs and cross stretcher, 32in. wide. (Christie's) $2,390 £1,300

Early 19th century Empire planter with copper insert, 44in. wide. (Robert W. Skinner Inc.) $350 £190

Edwardian mahogany shaving stand on square tapering legs. (J. M. Welch & Son) $125 £70

Chinese hardwood urn stand with marble top, 18in. diam. (Lawrence Fine Art) $205 £110

One of a pair of Irish Georgian mahogany lecterns with sloping tops, 26½in. wide. (Christie's)
$1,560 £825

One of a pair of Chinese hardwood urn stands with marble tops, 23in. high. (Lawrence Fine Art)
$285 £150

Antique fruitwood spinning wheel. (Honiton Galleries) $350 £190

Early 19th century Dutch mahogany tea kettle stand with cover or cellarette, 26in. high. (Lawrence Fine Art)
$700 £390

17th century Spanish walnut lectern with moulded book-rest, 44in. high.(Christie's)
$360 £194

George IV mahogany reading table with adjustable top, 2ft.11½in. wide, circa 1820. (Sotheby's)
$1,010 £550

18th century elm candlestand with circular top and splayed pine legs, 17¼in. diam.(Christie's)
$600 £324

Fine quality beechwood spinning wheel. (J. M. Welch & Son)
$635 £350

Regency style rosewood X-framed stool with tapestry seat. (J. M. Welch & Son) $235 £130

Victorian 12in. foot stool, with copper warmer inside. (J. M. Welch & Son) $90 £50

Herman Miller stool, designed by Charles Eames, 41cm., 1956. (Sotheby's Belgravia) $340 £187

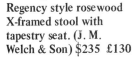

One of a pair of early George II fruitwood stools with drop-in seats in floral needlework, 21½in. wide. (Christie's) $9,250 £5,000

Rare set of late George III mahogany bed steps, circa 1805, 2ft. 10in. long. (Sotheby's) $1,475 £792

One of a pair of late 16th century Gothic oak stools, 1ft.10in. wide. (Sotheby's) $1,645 £880

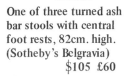

George III mahogany window seat with scroll ends, circa 1765, 2ft. 10in. wide. (Sotheby's) $2,380 £1,265

One of three turned ash bar stools with central foot rests, 82cm. high. (Sotheby's Belgravia) $105 £60

Dressing stool with petit point seat and carved cabriole legs in mahogany. (John Hogbin & Son) $160 £90

Victorian mahogany framed piano stool with revolving top. (Vernons) $100 £50

One of a pair of mid 19th century rosewood footstools with cut plush tops, 13½in. wide. (Sotheby's) $170 £95

19th century mahogany framed stool on turned and fluted legs. (Vernons) $45 £20

One of a pair of Swedish giltwood stools with slightly dipped padded tops, 1ft.10in. wide, circa 1805. (Sotheby's) $2,865 £1,485

Oak coffin stool with carved frieze and reeded legs. (Butler & Hatch Waterman) $985 £550

Late 19th century elm stool on turned legs. (Vernons) $35 £15

One of a pair of 17th century oak joint stools with moulded rectangular tops, 18in. wide. (Christie's) $730 £400

Pair of Regency period stools with dish-shaped seats, on turned and fluted mahogany legs, 18in. wide. (Woolley & Wallis) $980 £560

17th century design oak joint stool. (Biddle & Webb) $295 £160

Bugatti vellum and beaten metal on wood stool, circa 1900, 43cm. high. (Sotheby's Belgravia) $570 £320

19th century French Empire banquette in mahogany with upholstered seat, 32in. wide. (Robert W. Skinner Inc.) $750 £405

One of a pair of early George III giltwood stools with serpentine seats, 21in. wide. (Christie's) $5,465 £2,860

Early Georgian Chippendale mahogany stool on four boldly carved cabriole legs, 23in. wide. (Boardman's) $2,250 £1,250

Victorian rosewood piano stool on carved legs. (Phillips) $135 £60

Victorian rosewood square stool on cabriole legs, 1ft. 7in. square. (Dickinson, Davy & Markham)$125 £70

American William and Mary joint stool, circa 1700, 26in. wide, on stretcher base. (Robert W. Skinner Inc.) $3,000 £1,705

One of a pair of late 16th century Gothic oak stools, 1ft.10in. wide. (Sotheby's) $1,645 £880

Charles II walnut stool with needlework upholstered seat, 15in. wide. (Boardman's)$660 £370

FURNITURE

Part of a 20th century French Louis XVI giltwood parlour set of five pieces in tapestry upholstery. (Robert W. Skinner Inc.) $3,900 £2,205

Part of a mid 19th century walnut drawingroom suite of thirteen pieces covered with floral ivory damask. (Sotheby Beresford Adams)
$3,625 £1,950

Part of a ten-piece drawingroom suite with oval carved backs, circa 1860. (Sotheby's Belgravia) $5,705 £3,100

Three-piece bergere lounge suite with front cabriole legs. (Allen & May)
$700 £370

Part of a four-piece walnut drawingroom suite, circa 1860, in gold upholstery.
(Sotheby's Belgravia) $4,245 £2,200

Part of a six-piece Victorian rosewood salon suite with oval backs and floral
upholstery. (Dickinson, Davy & Markham) $1,860 £1,000

Part of a seven-piece walnut drawingroom suite, circa 1860. (Sotheby's
Belgravia) $3,395 £1,815

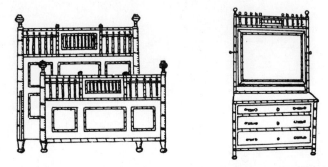

Victorian birch and bird's-eye maple bed by R. J. Horner & Co., New York,
circa 1870, 74in. long, sold with dressing table. (Robert W. Skinner Inc.)
                                               $1,800 £995

Part of a seven-piece Edwardian mahogany drawingroom suite in Hepplewhite
manner, upholstered in striped patterned plush. (Burtenshaw Walker)
                                               $1,345 £750

Part of a seven-piece Edwardian mahogany and ivory satinwood inlaid boudoir suite, upholstered in silk damask. (Dacre, Son & Hartley)
$1,545 £850

Part of a three-piece walnut and burr-walnut drawingroom suite including a chaise longue, circa 1870. (Sotheby's Belgravia) $1,105 £650

19th century French Empire mahogany exhibition bedroom suite of a double bed, a gentleman's wardrobe and a dressing table. (Locke & England)
$3,045 £1,700

Three-piece Art Nouveau fruitwood parlour set, France, circa 1910, with carved crests. (Robert W. Skinner Inc.) $600 £315

FURNITURE

19th century French walnut fold-over card table with inlaid shaped top, 3ft.1½in. wide. (Dickinson, Davy & Markham) $1,215 £660

Ebony and rosewood envelope card table, swivel top inlaid with boxwood and ivory motifs, circa 1900, 21¾in. wide. (Sotheby's Belgravia) $535 £290

Rosewood card table by Gillows, top with beaded border, circa 1840, 36in. wide. (Sotheby's Belgravia) $755 £410

Marquetry card table with serpentine top on kingwood ground, circa 1870, 32½in. wide. (Sotheby's Belgravia) $1,655 £900

One of a pair of mid 19th century rosewood tea tables with hinged tops, 39in. wide. (Sotheby's Belgravia) $1,330 £740

Chippendale mahogany serpentine-fronted tea table with fold-over top and blind fret carving to frieze, 36in. wide, circa 1760. (Sotheby, King & Chasemore) $2,850 £1,550

George III demi-lune tea table on tapering fluted legs. (Capes, Dunn & Co.) $935 £500

20th century American Federal style mahogany card table with shaped top, 35in. wide. (Robert W. Skinner Inc.) $350 £200

George III satinwood card table, top crossbanded with tulipwood and inlaid with a lunette, 38in. wide. (Christie's) $2,265 £1,250

One of a pair of Victorian shaped rosewood folding top tea tables on quadruple supports, 36in. wide. (Lewes Auction Rooms)
$2,325 £1,250

Early 20th century Maple & Co., mahogany and marquetry envelope card table, crossbanded in satinwood, 22in. wide.(Sotheby Beresford Adams) $855 £460

One of a pair of fairly plain Regency card tables with fold-over tops. (Stride & Son)
$3,035 £1,650

Burr-walnut games table with hinged swivelling top, circa 1860, 35in. wide. (Sotheby's Belgravia) $990 £550

George II folding top tea table in red walnut, on slender cabriole legs, shell carved at knees. (Christie's & Edmiston's)
$8,235 £4,500

Early Victorian burr-walnut card table with boxwood string inlay and folding flap top. (Capes, Dunn & Co.)
$1,215 £650

New England Federal mahogany inlaid card table, top with ovolu corners, circa 1700, 34¾in. wide.(Robert W. Skinner Inc.)
$1,600 £875

George II red walnut triple flap card and tea table with lobed top, 36in. wide. (Christie's)
$4,255 £2,300

Federal mahogany card table with demi-lune top on square tapered legs, 35in. wide.(Robert W. Skinner Inc.)
$400 £220

FURNITURE

Victorian walnut card table of serpentine shape with fold-over swivel top, 36in. wide. (Lawrence Fine Art) $1,035 £540

Rosewood card table on central octagonal-shaped pillar on shaped platform with bun feet, 35½in. wide. (Butler & Hatch Waterman) $450 £250

Chinese Chippendale fold-over top card table with carved frieze. (Morris, Marshall & Poole) $1,410 £780

One of a pair of late George III mahogany card tables, circa 1805, 2ft.10in. wide. (Sotheby's)$1,850 £1,000

Regency rosewood tea table inlaid with brass stringing, on quadruple splay feet, 3ft. wide. (Jackson-Stops & Staff) $955 £540

One of a pair of George III mahogany D-shaped breakfront card tables, 3ft. wide. (Sotheby's) $4,625 £2,500

Small George II mahogany tea or games table on cabriole legs, circa 1740, 2ft.1in. wide. (Sotheby's) $4,295 £2,310

Late 18th century George III mahogany demi-lune tea table with satinwood crossbanding, 39in. wide. (Sotheby Beresford Adams) $965 £520

Early Georgian solid mahogany circular tea table, 30in. diam. (Hall Wateridge & Owen) $1,110 £600

432

Regency rosewood and brass parquetry card table on four turned supports, 36in. wide. (Boardman's) **$1,360 £720**

Victorian figured mahogany fold-over breakfast table on gun barrel stem. (Gilbert Baitson) **$470 £250**

One of a pair of George III semi-circular mahogany card tables, circa 1785, 3ft. wide. (Sotheby's) **$2,310 £1,250**

Victorian walnut French style card table, top crossbanded in kingwood, 36in. wide. (Hy. Duke & Son) **$1,380 £720**

George I walnut games table with rounded corners, circa 1725, 2ft. 8in. wide. (Sotheby's) **$980 £528**

Mid 18th century George III satinwood card table with fold-over top and tulipwood crossbanding, 37in. wide. (Sotheby Beresford Adams) **$1,265 £680**

Regency coromandel card table, circa 1815, 3ft. wide, with hinged top.(Sotheby's) **$825 £440**

George III mahogany tea table on chamfered square legs, circa 1760, 2ft.11in. wide. (Sotheby's) **$1,040 £550**

One of a pair of William IV rosewood-veneered card tables with burr-elm scroll feet, circa 1830, 3ft. wide. (Sotheby's) **$925 £500**

433

George II walnut card table with squared out-set corners, 34in. wide. (Wm. Doyle Galleries Inc.) $6,000 £3,175

Sheraton period fold-over top card table in mahogany, veneered and crossbanded in walnut and kingwood, 3ft. wide. (Edgar Horn) $690 £370

Regency rosewood and palisanderwood cross-banded card table, circa 1810, 3ft. wide.(Sotheby, King & Chasemore) $3,310 £1,850

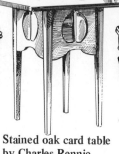

Marquetry card table, Damascus, circa 1900, 28in. wide, with hinged top. (Sotheby's Belgravia) $515 £275

Stained oak card table by Charles Rennie Mackintosh, circa 1897, with overhang top, 81.2cm. wide.(Christie's) $12,740 £7,000

19th century French card table, marquetry inlaid with flowers and scrolls, 2ft.9¾in. wide.(Geering & Colyer) $860 £460

Early 19th century mahogany fold-over card table with paw feet. (J. M. Welch & Son) $345 £190

American Federal mahogany and mahogany veneer card table with shaped top, 36in. wide, circa 1810. (Robert W. Skinner Inc.)$2,900 £1,575

Walnut serpentine card table on baluster gad-rooned stem and cabriole legs, circa 1860, 33½in. wide.(Sotheby's Belgravia) $865 £462

Georgian figured mahogany semi-circular card table, inlaid with satinwood and harewood, 39½in. wide.(Morphets) $540 £300

19th century mahogany fold-over card table on pedestal stem and quadruple base. (J. M. Welch & Son) $55 £29

George III satinwood fold-over tea table, 3ft.3in. wide, open. (J. M. Welch & Son) $2,365 £1,300

Regency rosewood and cut brass inlaid card table with crossbanded top, circa 1815, 3ft.wide. (Sotheby, King & Chasemore) $1,455 £800

Fold-over tea table on carved tripod pillar supports in oak. (Alfred Mossop & Co.) $425 £220

Victorian mahogany fold-over pillar tea table with scroll feet. (Alfred Mossop & Co.) $320 £175

George II mahogany card table with lobed top and pointed pad feet, 33in. wide. (Lawrence Fine Art) $2,850 £1,550

American Queen Anne card table, circa 1765, with mahogany top, 32½in. wide. (Robert W. Skinner Inc.) $1,000 £550

Sheraton style fold-over card table with square tapering legs. (Alfred Mossop & Co.) $400 £220

Louis XVI console table with serpentine marble top, on pierced scroll supports, 51½in. wide. (Christie's)$2,485 £1,350

One of a pair of George III console tables in satinwood veneers, 33in. long. (Robert W. Skinner Inc.) $2,400 £1,305

German giltwood serpentine-fronted console table with carved cabriole legs, circa 1750, 3ft.9½in. wide. (Sotheby's) $3,085 £1,650

Regency console table with mottled grey marble top, circa 1815, 2ft.9¼in. wide. (Sotheby's) $1,685 £902

One of a pair of 18th century giltwood pier glasses with matching side tables, 3ft.10in. wide.(Dickinson, Davy & Markham) $1,520 £825

20th century American Federal style mahogany console table with inlaid edge, 35in. wide.(Robert W. Skinner Inc.)$125 £70

One of a pair of George IV rosewood and grained rosewood console tables, circa 1820, 2ft.0½in. wide. (Sotheby's) $635 £350

George III console table with Carrara marble top, circa 1775, 4ft.6½in. wide. (Sotheby's) $2,585 £1,375

Louis XV giltwood console table with serpentine rosso Levanto marble top, 27in. wide. (Christie's) $2,050 £1,045

Regency rosewood and amboyna breakfast table with rectangular top, 51in. wide. (Boardman's) $2,455 £1,300

Regency mahogany circular dining table on arched sabre legs. (Lawrence Fine Art) $7,175 £3,900

Rosewood veneered circular tip-top breakfast table on paw feet, 1840's, 48in. diam. (Sotheby's Belgravia) $850 £440

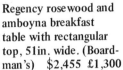

German mahogany centre table with grey veined marble top, circa 1840. (Sotheby's Belgravia) $845 £451

19th century mahogany breakfast table with oval top. (J. M. Welch & Son) $345 £190

Late Georgian mahogany revolving drum table on turned column and four swept legs, 41in. diam. (Locke & England) $1,820 £1,000

Rosewood and marquetry breakfast table, top inlaid with satinwood border, circa 1840, 48in. diam. (Sotheby's Belgravia) $3,085 £1,650

19th century Regency tilt-top breakfast table in mahogany, 59in. long. (Robert W. Skinner Inc.) $850 £460

Mid Victorian walnut and inlaid loo table with boxwood and amboyna top, 52in. wide. (Dacre, Son & Hartley) $655 £360

Rectangular mahogany breakfast table with moulded top, circa 1850, 45in. wide. (Sotheby's Belgravia) $735 £400

Burr-walnut centre table with quarter-veneered moulded top, circa 1860, 48in. wide. (Sotheby's Belgravia)

    $665 £370

Walnut oval breakfast table with tip-top, circa 1870, 46½in. wide. (Sotheby's Belgravia) $770 £420

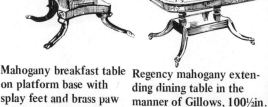

Walnut dining table with oval quarter-veneered top, 1860's, 52in. long. (Sotheby's Belgravia)

    $660 £360

Mahogany breakfast table on platform base with splay feet and brass paw castors, 3ft.6in. wide. (Allen & May) $720 £380

Regency mahogany extending dining table in the manner of Gillows, 100½in. wide. (Christie's)

    $9,620 £5,200

Burr-walnut centre table with oval top on four fluted columns, 1860's, 42in. wide. (Sotheby's Belgravia) $560 £310

Flemish oak and walnut centre table with parquetry inlaid motifs, on bulbous-shaped legs, 43¾in. wide. (Geering & Colyer)

    $570 £310

Pollard oak and parcel gilt breakfast table, circular tip-top inlaid with flowers, 53¼in. diam., 1840's. (Sotheby's Belgravia) $2,150 £1,200

Walnut loo table in well-figured and burr-wood, top inlaid with stringing, circa 1860, 51in. long. (Sotheby's Belgravia) $1,115 £620

George IV mahogany and rose-wood crossbanded circular tilt-top pedestal table, 4ft. diam., circa 1825. (Sotheby, King & Chasemore) $1,570 £850

Mid 19th century rose-wood breakfast table on faceted baluster stem, 48in. diam. (Sotheby Beresford Adams) $595 £320

20th century walnut and parcel gilt breakfast table in well-figured wood with dolphin supports, 50in. diam. (Sotheby's Belgravia) $1,840 £1,000

Regency rosewood and satin-wood crossbanded library table with ebonised and reeded border, circa 1800, 4ft.3in. diam.(Sotheby's) $860 £480

William IV rosewood break-fast table with circular tip-top, circa 1835, 52½in. diam. (Sotheby's Belgravia) $1,380 £750

Mid 19th century rosewood breakfast table, 49in. diam. (Sotheby Beresford Adams) $630 £340

Oak coaching table with oval folding top, 3ft.6in. wide, circa 1800. (Sotheby, King & Chasemore) $930 £500

Walnut and rosewood mar-quetry centre table with circular tip-top, circa 1850, 39in. diam. (Sotheby's Belgravia) $2,340 £1,300

439

Rosewood circular breakfast table with moulded border, circa 1850, 53in. diam. (Sotheby's Belgravia) $1,485 £770

Large oval George IV mahogany breakfront or dining table, 5ft.4in. diam., circa 1820. (Sotheby's) $3,930 £2,090

George IV mahogany two pedestal dining table of unusual form, circa 1820, 3ft.5in. wide. (Sotheby's)$1,385 £750

Regency rosewood and cut brass inlaid pedestal table, circa 1810. (Sotheby, King & Chasemore)
$2,375 £1,250

Victorian walnut centre table on carved pillar and quadruple scroll legs. (Hall Wateridge & Owen) $600 £320

George IV mahogany three pillar extended dining table, circa 1820, 11ft.4in. wide. (Sotheby's) $7,240 £3,850

Georgian mahogany triple pedestal dining table with reeded edge, 11ft.6in. wide, open. (Jackson-Stops & Staff)
$1,885 £1,025

Victorian walnut loo table with oval top inlaid with birds, on quadruple base. (Hall Wateridge & Owen) $770 £420

Georgian mahogany D-end dining table with extending leaf, 9ft.3½in. wide extended. (Dickinson, Davy & Markham) $1,100 £585

Victorian burr-walnut and marquetry centre table, 54in. wide. (Boardman's) $4,535 £2,400

Circular Regency brass inlaid rosewood snap-top breakfast table, 48in. diam. (Burtenshaw Walker) $3,025 £1,600

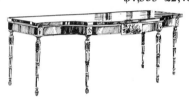

Large George III serpentine-fronted dining-room side table, circa 1785, 9ft.1½in. wide. (Sotheby's) $1,665, £900

Early 20th century 'George III' mahogany dining table with intersection, 112in. long extended. (Sotheby's Belgravia) $1,805 £935

Early Victorian walnut breakfast table with oval top veneered in well-figured wood, 152.5cm. wide. (H. Spencer & Sons Ltd.) $1,210 £650

Rare George III drop-leaf pedestal dining table with circular top, 3ft.11in. diam., circa 1805. (Sotheby's) $2,560 £1,375

William IV four-pedestal dining table, circa 1835, 13ft.2in. wide.(Sotheby's) $9,000 £4,840

441

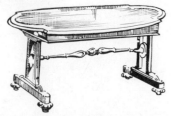

Rosewood centre table with tooled leather top, circa 1840, 60in. wide. (Sotheby's Belgravia) $2,055 £1,100

Regency rosewood breakfast table in the manner of George Bullock, on concave triangular base, 48in. diam. (Christie's) $4,445 £2,376

Regency rosewood centre table with crossbanded top, 48in. diam. (Christie's) $2,425 £1,296

Late 17th/early 18th century Dutch marquetry centre table, 3ft.7½in. wide. (Sotheby's) $3,495 £1,870

Walnut expanding table of serpentine outline, circa 1900, 76in. long.(Sotheby's Belgravia) $555 £297

Late Regency rosewood breakfast table with octagonal tip-top, 57in. wide. (Christie's) $1,815 £972

Regency mahogany breakfast table, tiptop crossbanded with calamanderwood and satinwood, 66¼in. wide.(Christie's) $2,425 £1,296

Rosewood pedestal table, circa 1820, 51in. diam. (J. M. Welch & Son) $1,135 £625

Mahogany dining table with two D-ends, circa 1870, 108in. wide, extended. (Sotheby's Belgravia) $1,695 £968

Victorian walnut oval table with quartered top inlaid with foliate design, 54in. wide. (Lawrence Fine Art)
           $1,000 £520

Late 18th century George III oak tripod table on vase-turned stem. (Sotheby's) $295 £165

18th century Alpine walnut and oak dining table with plank top, drawer inlaid with parquetry, 42½in. wide. (Christie's) $2,595 £1,404

Regency mahogany dining table with fifth leg, 13ft.2in. long, extended. (David Symonds) $1,970 £1,125

George II red walnut drop-leaf table with plain oval top, circa 1740, 4ft. 9in. wide, open. (Sotheby's)
          $2,970 £1,650

'George III' mahogany dining table in three parts, circa 1900, 147in. long. (Sotheby's Belgravia) $1,280 £715

17th century Provincial oak draw table on ring turned legs, 50in. wide. (Robert W. Skinner Inc.) $1,550 £840

FURNITURE

One of a pair of Regency mahogany dressing tables with galleried tops, 39in. wide. (Lawrence Fine Art) $1,380 £750

Rococo revival walnut mirrored bureau, circa 1860, with arched top mirror, 47½in. wide. (Robert W. Skinner Inc.) $475 £250

American rococo revival rosewood and rosewood veneer dressing table, circa 1860, 24½in. wide. (Robert W. Skinner Inc.) $600 £335

19th century dressing table veneered in thuyawood with tulipwood crossbanding, 48in. wide. (W. H. Lane & Son) $1,635 £875

George V lady's toilet cabinet, fitted with silver brushes, bottles and manicure implements. (Locke & England) $340 £190

Dressing table from a satinwood bedroom suite in six pieces, circa 1910. (Sotheby's Belgravia) $1,080 £600

Regency mahogany dressing table in the manner of Gillows, 48in. wide. (Christie's) $3,700 £2,000

Hindley & Wilkinson painted satinwood dressing table with shield mirror, circa 1890, 40¼in. wide. (Sotheby's Belgravia) $4,935 £2,640

19th century mahogany and inlaid dressing table, 38in. wide. (J. M. Welch & Son) $890 £490

Late 18th century George III mahogany and satinwood dressing table with opening folding top, 25in. wide. (Sotheby Beresford Adams) $895 £480

George III bow-fronted mahogany dressing chest with boxwood inlay, 39in. wide. (Boardman's) $1,625 £860

Amboynawood and parcel gilt decorated Art Deco dressing table by W. & T. Lock Ltd., 63in. wide. (Boardman's)$1,435 £760

Late Victorian/early Edwardian Sheraton design oval dressing table surmounted by an oval mirror. (Locke & England) $750 £420

Renaissance revival walnut and burl veneer princess bureau with carved crest, circa 1870, 63½in. wide. (Robert W. Skinner Inc.) $950 £530

Victorian bamboo writing desk/dressing table, lacquered with birds and flowers, with brass drop handles. (John Hogbin & Son) $295 £160

19th century French Louis XVI transitional style marquetry poudreuse, in harewood, mahogany and other woods, 32in. wide. (Robert W. Skinner Inc.)$950 £515

Late 18th century German Directoire mahogany dressing table with arched swing mirror plate, 21in. wide. (Sotheby Beresford Adams) $670 £360

Mid 19th century mahogany Sheraton revival dressing table with satinwood crossbanded top, 35in. wide. (Sotheby Beresford Adams) $595 £320

19th century oak Sutherland table on turned legs. (J. M. Welch & Son) $155 £85

George III D-end mahogany dining table with centre portion, restored, 106in. wide, extended. (Lawrence Fine Art) $2,325 £1,300

Gustav Stickley oak drop-leaf table, circa 1909, 32in. diam., open. (Robert W. Skinner Inc.) $1,100 £615

Cherrywood inlaid dining table with drop leaves, circa 1790, 48in. wide. (Robert W. Skinner Inc.) $1,800 £985

Early 18th century William and Mary butterfly table, 38½in. diam. (Robert W. Skinner Inc.)$3,970 £2,100

Rare George II solid yewwood drop-leaf table with one flap, 2ft.3½in. wide, circa 1755. (Sotheby's) $2,240 £1,210

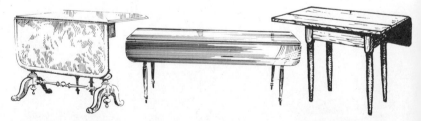

Rare Victorian bird's-eye maple Sutherland table on bobbin turned supports, 22in. wide. (Locke & England) $475 £260

Federal painted harvest table, New England, circa 1810, 72in. long. (Robert W. Skinner Inc.) $4,725 £2,500

Early 19th century Shaker cherrywood drop-leaf table, 29in. wide. (Robert W. Skinner Inc.) $3,000 £1,640

Early 19th century maho-
gany writing table on
quadruple turned pillars
and four sabre legs, 56in.
wide. (W. H. Lane & Son)
$540 £295

Late George III mahogany
Cumberland-action drop-
leaf dining table, circa
1810, 5ft.5½in. wide.
(Sotheby's)$1,880 £1,012

George II mahogany
drop-leaf table with D-
shaped flaps, circa 1740,
6ft. wide extended.
(Sotheby's)$2,865 £1,600

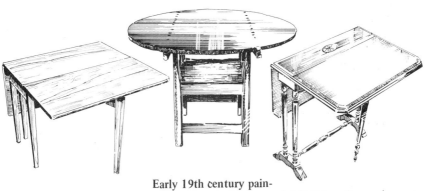

George III mahogany drop-
leaf dining table on tapering legs. (Warren & Wignall)
$445 £250

Early 19th century pain-
ted maple and pine
hutch table, 41in. diam.
(Robert W. Skinner Inc.)
$1,900 £1,005

Inlaid Edwardian maho-
gany Sutherland table, top
with inlaid oval. (Warren &
Wignall) $305 £170

Irish Georgian mahogany
supper table with two-flap
top, 52½in. wide extended.
(Lawrence Fine Art)
$865 £470

Rare George II oak gate-
leg table with unusual
hipped legs on paw feet,
circa 1730, 5ft.4½in. wide.
(Sotheby's)$7,935 £4,290

Early 19th century maho-
gany drop-leaf dining
table with tapering legs
on pad feet. (T. Bannister
& Co.) $380 £210

447

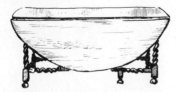

Early 19th century oval gateleg table in solid walnut, fitted with a single drawer. (Edwards, Bigwood & Bewlay) $4,970 £2,700

William and Mary oak gateleg table, late 17th century, 4ft.6in. wide. (Sotheby's) $1,665 £880

Late 17th century oak gateleg table with oval top, 57in. wide, extended. (Sotheby's) $1,465 £770

17th century oak gateleg table with later oval twin-flap, 71in. wide, open. (Christie's) $2,105 £1,150

17th century oak eight/ten seater gateleg dining table with oval top, 68in. wide, open. (Boardman's)$2,590 £1,400

Oval gateleg table in oak on baluster turned legs, 5ft. wide, extended. (Andrew Grant) $1,535 £825

William and Mary walnut gateleg table with oval top, circa 1690, 4ft.10in. wide. (Sotheby's) $1,000 £528

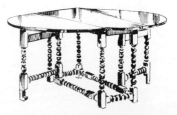

Charles II oval oak gateleg table on bobbin-turned legs, circa 1670, 5ft. 4in. wide, open. (Sotheby's) $2,775 £1,485

Late 19th century oak gateleg table with oval top. (J. M. Welch & Son) $345 £190

Small oval dining table with turned legs and stretchers in oak. (Alfred Mossop & Co.) $540 £280

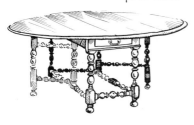

Mid 17th century oak gateleg dining table with moulded apron, 62½in. long. (Dacre, Son & Hartley) $1,820 £1,000

Late 17th century oak gateleg table on columnar supports, 52in. wide, extended. (Sotheby's) $670 £352

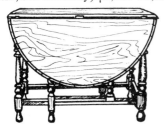

Late 17th century oak gateleg table with oval top, 63in. wide, extended. (Sotheby's) $1,545 £814

18th century George III walnut gateleg table on block and baluster turned supports, 30in. wide. (Robert W. Skinner Inc.) $3,000 £1,630

Early Georgian period red walnut oval twin flap top gateleg table, 3ft.8in. wide. (Woolley & Wallis) $1,280 £700

17th century Charles II oak gateleg table with oval top, on turned baluster supports, 58in. wide, extended. (Sotheby's) $1,715 £902

Georgian mahogany D-end dining table on turned supports, 9ft.4in. long extended. (Dickinson, Davy & Markham) $1,700 £925

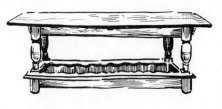

17th century German oak refectory table with two-plank top and four turned legs. (Boardman's) $2,220 £1,200

Walnut and oak banded dining table, 4ft. 4in. wide, legs carved with figures of lions. (Allen & May) $2,835 £1,500

Walnut dining table of elongated rectangular form, mid 1960's, 90in. long. (Sotheby's Belgravia) $830 £450

17th century Flemish oak drawleaf table, 90in. wide, open. (Sotheby, King & Chasemore) $2,850 £1,550

Early 20th century George III style mahogany three-pillar dining table, 147in. long open. (Sotheby Beresford Adams) $2,140 £1,150

Early 19th century convertible mahogany dining table. (Clarke Gammon) $8,830 £4,800

17th century oak side table with four-plank top, 98in. long, on six turned tapering legs. (Edwards, Bigwood & Bewlay) $3,385 £1,850

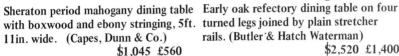

Sheraton period mahogany dining table with boxwood and ebony stringing, 5ft. 11in. wide. (Capes, Dunn & Co.) $1,045 £560

Early oak refectory dining table on four turned legs joined by plain stretcher rails. (Butler & Hatch Waterman) $2,520 £1,400

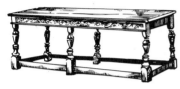

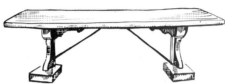

Early 17th century oak refectory table with four-plank top, 8ft.2in. long. (Edgar Horn) $3,660 £2,000

16th century Gothic walnut and oak trestle table with plank top, 120in. wide. (Boardman's) $6,290 £3,400

Unusual late Victorian mahogany patent extending dining table, 68in. diam., closed. (Christie's S. Kensington) $22,320 £12,000

Oak refectory table with rectangular plank top on bulbous cup and cover legs, 74in. wide. (Christie's) $915 £500

Oak serving table on turned baluster supports, 8ft. long. (Sotheby, King & Chasemore) $2,605 £1,400

Period oak side table on carved and bulbous stretcher supports, 52in. wide. (John Hogbin & Son) $250 £140

Mahogany D-end extending dining table,
mid 19th century, 12ft. long.
(Sotheby's) $1,650 £902

Joined oak dining table with two-plank
top, 78in. wide. (Lawrence Fine Art)
                         $1,750 £950

Oak joined long dining table of faded
colour with lunette carved frieze,
11ft.1½in. long. (Lawrence Fine Art)
              $3,865 £2,100

Mid 17th century oak refectory table
with three-plank top, 11ft.5½in. wide,
re-constructed. (Sotheby's)
              $6,375 £3,410

Mahogany two-pedestal dining table with
tip-tops, circa 1880, 73in. wide.
(Sotheby's Belgravia) $2,980 £1,595

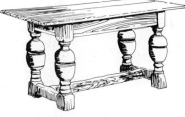

Oak refectory table with two-plank top,
on cup and cover legs, 6ft.2in. long.
(Sotheby's) $1,665 £880

Large Charles I oak refectory table,
circa 1640, 9ft.10in. long. (Sotheby's)
                 $11,225 £5,940

Rare oak refectory table with three-
plank top on stepped bases, 8ft.4½in.
long. (Sotheby's) $3,700 £1,980

Dutch oak dining table with plain edge, 88in. wide. (Lawrence Fine Art) $1,380 £750

Early 17th century Charles I oak refectory table with three-plank top, 5ft.8in. wide. (Sotheby's) $2,775 £1,485

17th century oak refectory table with five-plank top, 96in. wide. (Christie's) $8,050 £4,400

Oak refectory table with triple-plank top and gadrooned frieze, 84in. long, with plate glass top. (Christie's) $2,930 £1,600

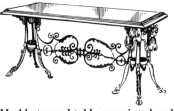

Early 20th century walnut centre table, top with ogee apron, 76in. long. (Sotheby's Belgravia) $640 £343

Marble-topped table on painted and decorated iron frame, in need of restoration. (J. M. Welch & Son) $1,090 £600

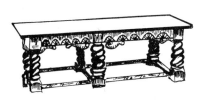

Large refectory table in oak, with turned legs. (Russell, Baldwin & Bright) $3,840 £2,000

Early 20th century Cromwellian style oak refectory table with three-plank top, 84in. long. (Sotheby's) $1,085 £572

William and Mary yew-
wood table on spiral-
twist legs, 2ft.7in. wide,
circa 1690. (Sotheby's)
$3,155 £1,705

Satinwood and marquetry display table with hinged glazed
top, circa 1890, 48in. wide.
(Sotheby's Belgravia)
$1,275 £660

Walnut centre display
table with lobed ser-
pentine top, circa
1850, 50in. wide.
(Sotheby's Belgravia)
$535 £285

Late George II maho-
gany tripod table,
circa 1750, 2ft.1in.
wide. (Sotheby's)
$955 £506

Mid 18th century George III
elm cricket table, top 25in.
diam. (Sotheby's)$545 £283

Well-carved George III
tilt-top table, top with
Bath rim, 84cm. diam.
(Osmond, Tricks)
$910 £500

William IV small drum
table in satin-birch,
circa 1820, 2ft.4½in.
diam. (Sotheby's)
$5,115 £2,750

Early 19th century Irish George
III style wine tasting table with
attachable tray. (Robert W.
Skinner Inc.) $3,300 £1,795

Early 19th century
amboynawood occa-
sional table with oct-
agonal top, 2ft.4in.
wide. (Whitton &
Laing)$1,515 £790

454

Mid 19th century satin-wood occasional table with lobed tray top, 26in. wide.(Sotheby's Belgravia) $615 £330

Qing dynasty marbled lacquer low table, 48.5cm. wide. (Christie's) $430 £240

William IV calamander occasional table, circa 1835, 31½in. diam. (Sotheby's Belgravia) $575 £308

Late 18th century George III tea table with piecrust top, 26in. diam.(Robert W. Skinner Inc.) $650 £355

Late 17th/early 18th century William and Mary one drawer table on turned legs, 29¼in. wide. (Robert W. Skinner Inc.) $800 £430

19th century French Louis XV style table in fruitwood with gallery top, 18¼in. wide. (Robert W. Skinner Inc.) $550 £300

William and Mary oak table on spiral-twist legs with waved X-stretchers, circa 1690, 3ft.4in. wide.(Sotheby's) $1,060 £572

18th century provincial painted table with single gate, 42in. long. (Robert W. Skinner Inc.) $850 £460

George II serpentine mahogany silver table with incurved top, 2ft.7½in. wide, circa 1740. (Sotheby's) $5,320 £2,860

455

OCCASIONAL TABLES

19th century French kingwood and marquetry centre table on cabriole legs, 2ft.11in. wide. (Dickinson, Davy & Markham) $370 £200

Set of three satinwood tea tables on four fluted turned supports joined by trestle bases, circa 1920.(Sotheby's Belgravia) $550 £300

Georgian mahogany circular tilt-top occasional table on triple splay support, 3ft. diam. (Geering & Colyer) $590 £320

One of a pair of mid 19th century rosewood tripod tables with gadrooned borders. (Sotheby Beresford Adams) $1,675 £900

Octagonal-shaped drum-top table in mahogany, with tooled leather inset, 36in. wide. (Sotheby, King & Chasemore) $830 £450

Late 19th century French tulipwood parquetry gueridon, on tapering cabriole legs, 1ft.11in. wide. (Sotheby, King & Chasemore)$1,025 £550

Rosewood and marquetry occasional table, with circular top, circa 1830, 22½in. diam. (Sotheby's Belgravia) $450 £250

456

Regency mahogany reading table on easel support and quadripartite base, 34in. wide. (Christie's) $1,665 £900

Mid 19th century mahogany oblong tripod tip-up wine table. (T. Bannister & Co.) $160 £90

Late 19th century American rococo revival rosewood marble top table, 34in. wide. (Robert W. Skinner Inc.)$400 £225

French Art Nouveau mahogany table in the manner of Majorelle, 107cm. wide. (Phillips) $785 £440

George II mahogany tripod table, circa 1740, 2ft.6in. diam. (Sotheby's)
      $750 £420

French marquetry table d'accoucher of serpentine form, circa 1840, 1ft.11in. wide.(Sotheby, King & Chasemore)
      $2,885 £1,550

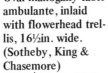

Oval mahogany table ambulante, inlaid with flowerhead trellis, 16½in. wide. (Sotheby, King & Chasemore)
      $1,395 £750

Unusual Regency mahogany tray-top table with two galleried tiers, the upper lifting off, 31¼in. wide. (Christie's) $890 £480

French table ambulante, circular top with pierced gallery, 2ft.4in. diam., circa 1900. (Sotheby, King & Chasemore) $780 £420

Set of three Regency brass inlaid rosewood quartetto tables in the manner of Louis Le Gaigneur, 18½in. to 14in. wide. (Christie's)
      $3,515 £1,900

Gilt plaster and mosaic centre table by Morant of London, 1850's, 27in. diam. (Sotheby's Belgravia) $3,330 £1,850

457

19th century Louis XV style kingwood occasional table, stamped Edwards & Roberts, 17½in. wide. (Hy. Duke & Son) $770 £400

French walnut and satinwood jardiniere table with serpentine-shaped top, 48in. wide. (Morphets) $855 £460

20th century American Chippendale style pie crust tip table, top with carved edge, 30in. diam. (Robert W. Skinner Inc.) $225 £125

Early 19th century Shaker cherry and birch candle-stand, Massachusetts, 26¾in. high. (Robert W. Skinner Inc.) $700 £370

Late George III mahogany oval occasional table on turned and ringed supports with undertier, circa 1800, 2ft. wide. (Sotheby, King & Chasemore) $1,330 £720

Chippendale pine bird cage candlestand, New England, circa 1780, 14½in. diam. (Robert W. Skinner Inc.) $1,795 £950

One of a pair of Victorian mahogany tables, carved to simulate linen folds and feathers. (Sotheby's Belgravia) $1,355 £740

19th century boulle centre table. (Christie's S. Kensington) $2,930 £1,600

Late 19th century Italian carved white marble table with round top, 37in. diam. (Robert W. Skinner Inc.) $450 £255

18th century French Louis XV provincial one-drawer table with shaped apron, 49in. wide. (Robert W. Skinner Inc.) $1,500 £815

George III mahogany reading stand with folding top, 2ft. wide, circa 1770. (Edwards, Bigwood & Bewlay) $1,115 £610

Victorian papier-mache pedestal occasional table with plate glass top, 40in. wide. (Dee & Atkinson) $670 £360

Continental rectangular top occasional table in floral marquetry, 22in. wide. (Edwards, Bigwood & Bewlay) $660 £360

Mid 19th century boulle centre table of serpentine outline, 36in. wide. (Sotheby Beresford Adams) $630 £340

19th century black lacquered pedestal table with circular top, 20in. diam. (Dee & Atkinson) $630 £340

Federal mahogany tip table, New England, circa 1790, 28¼in. high. (Robert W. Skinner Inc.) $675 £370

Rectangular marquetry table with brass stringing, on rosewood cluster column, 40in. wide. (Edwards, Bigwood & Bewlay) $2,290 £1,250

American Federal mahogany inlaid tip-top candlestand, circa 1790, 28½in. high. (Robert W. Skinner Inc.) $575 £315

459

TABLES

William and Mary style birch tavern table, circa 1930, 50in. wide. (Robert W. Skinner Inc.) $350 £185

Hepplewhite period satinwood table with banded and inlaid decoration. (J. M. Welch & Son) $985 £540

Elm kneading trough with shaped apron and trestle legs, 3ft.6in. wide. (J. M. Welch & Son) $130 £72

19th century provincial French style centre table in rosewood and walnut, 53in. wide. (Coles, Knapp & Kennedy) $715 £400

Early Victorian mahogany teapoy with sarcophagus-shaped top, 20in. wide. (Lawrence Fine Art) $440 £240

Centre table with circular top on square stem and spiral geometric quadripartite base, 104cm. diam. (Christie's) $690 £380

Victorian burr-walnut stretcher table on carved and fluted underframe, 43in. wide. (Burtenshaw Walker) $700 £390

Florentine mosaic marble top table on walnut tripod stand, 1860's, 19½in. diam.(Sotheby's Belgravia)$1,685 £902

Regency mahogany dressing table with bowed top, 44in. wide. (Christie's) $1,965 £1,080

Rare Sheraton period satinwood and mahogany lady's dressing cabinet, 34½in. high. (Edgar Horn) $1,630 £890

17th century Spanish chestnut side table on baluster legs and square stretchers, 61in. wide. (Christie's) $1,315 £720

Mid 17th century oak box table with hinged lid, on turned baluster legs, 31½in. wide. (Christie's) $880 £480

George III mahogany dressing table with divided double-flap top crossbanded in rosewood, 27in. wide, closed. (Christie's) $2,950 £1,620

Mid 18th century George III rosewood tripod table with dished snap top, 16in. diam. (Sotheby's) $845 £460

Regency rosewood four-tier occasional table on turned supports, 25in. wide. (Christie's) $2,515 £1,404

William and Mary maple and pine tavern table, circa 1750, 31in. wide. (Robert W. Skinner Inc.) $850 £465

Early George III mahogany stand, circular recess with scalloped border, 23in. high. (Christie's) $2,865 £1,500

Late 19th century rosewood and inlaid display table. (J. M. Welch & Son) $710 £390

461

George III mahogany and satinwood Pembroke table with serpentine top, 37¾in. wide, open. (Christie's) $6,060 £3,240

Late Georgian mahogany Pembroke table with kingwood crossbanding, 21½in. wide. (Lawrence Fine Art) $520 £270

George III mahogany Pembroke table, top crossbanded with satinwood and rosewood, 39½in. wide, open. (Christie's) $3,440 £1,800

One of a pair of Federal mahogany Pembroke tables, circa 1808-16, 39¾in. wide. (Robert W. Skinner Inc.) $7,000 £3,845

Small mahogany Pembroke table with rounded flaps, now on square pillar with rectangular base, 17.5cm. wide. (Lawrence Fine Art) $270 £150

Late George III mahogany Pembroke table with oval crossbanded top, circa 1790, 2ft.6in. wide. (Sotheby, King & Chasemore) $705 £380

George III satinwood Pembroke table in the manner of Ince & Mayhew, 39in. wide, top crossbanded with rosewood. (Christie's) $1,755 £950

American Federal style inlaid mahogany Pembroke table with shaped top and leaves, circa 1920, 31in. wide. (Robert W. Skinner Inc.) $225 £125

Antique oval inlaid dropleaf table on square tapering legs. (Farrant & Wightman) $395 £225

George III satinwood Pembroke table, top bordered with a broad plumwood band, 40½in. wide, open. (Christie's)$7,355 £3,850

19th century French rosewood and marquetry occasional table with four oval drop leaves, 21in. square. (Morphets)$855 £475

Sheraton period satinwood veneered oval Pembroke table with mahogany and harewood crossbanding, 31in. wide. (Woolley & Wallis) $11,815 £6,600

Small Georgian mahogany Pembroke table with inlaid top, 1ft. 4in. wide. (Dickinson, Davy & Markham) $520 £280

Late 19th century painted Pembroke table on square tapering legs, 35in. wide. (Sotheby's Belgravia) $1,130 £605

Late Georgian mahogany Pembroke table with two-flap top, 34in. wide, extended. (Lawrence Fine Art) $625 £340

George III mahogany Pembroke table, top with central shell patera and tulipwood crossbanding, 2ft. 6in. wide, circa 1785. (Sotheby's)$1,300 £700

Late Georgian mahogany Pembroke table with fluted edge, 18in. wide. (Lawrence Fine Art) $480 £250

George III mahogany Pembroke table with serpentine top crossbanded with satinwood, 41½in. wide. (Christie's) $1,965 £1,080

SIDE TABLES

18th century crossbanded mahogany serving table with serpentine front, 4ft.2in. wide. (Russell, Baldwin & Bright) $1,080 £600

George I Irish walnut tray top side table, circa 1720, 31in. wide. (Sotheby, King & Chasemore) $3,845 £2,100

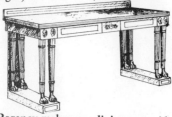

Regency mahogany diningroom side table, circa 1805, 7ft.6in. wide. (Sotheby's) $805 £450

Mid 18th century Irish beechwood side table with gadrooned border, 58½in. wide. (Christie's) $1,630 £900

George III mahogany serpentine-fronted side table, circa 1790, 36in. wide. (Sotheby, King & Chasemore)
          $590 £320

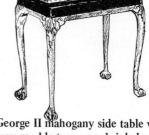

George II mahogany side table with grey marble top, on cabriole legs, 2ft.10in. wide, circa 1740.(Sotheby's)
          $1,860 £1,000

Early George III grained side table with later mahogany eared serpentine top, 54in. wide. (Christie's) $2,035 £1,100

One of a pair of George I style gilt gesso side tables, 39in. wide.(Sotheby, King & Chasemore) $3,295 £1,800

464

Late 18th century fruitwood side table with quarter mirror-figured top, 50½in. wide. (Christie's) $1,290 £700

Adam style serpentine-fronted serving table decorated with urns and husks, 60in. wide. (Edwards, Bigwood & Bewlay) $1,100 £600

Edwards & Roberts walnut and marquetry writing table, 1860's, 52in. wide. (Sotheby's Belgravia) $1,435 £780

Late 17th century oak side table on chamfered legs, 35in. long. (Andrew Grant) $855 £460

Mid 18th century Dutch walnut and marquetry side table, demi-lune top with shaped edge. (Sotheby Beresford Adams) $2,510 £1,350

French Regency style large mahogany side table of serpentine form, 6ft.1in. wide. (Dickinson, Davy & Markham) $690 £375

One of a pair of George III style giltwood side tables with marble tops, 3ft. 7in. wide. (Sotheby's) $4,835 £2,600

Painted and gilded side table in Adam style with brass-bordered top, 49¼in. wide. (Christie's) $1,355 £750

One of a pair of 'George III' satinwood side tables with D-shaped tops, circa 1880, 47in. wide. (Sotheby's Belgravia) $2,570 £1,375

Oak side table with single drawer under, 29in. wide. (J. M. Welch & Son) $175 £95

One of a pair of Edwardian mahogany side tables with decoration in coloured woods, 4ft. wide. (Russell, Baldwin & Bright) $1,620 £900

William and Mary oak side table with moulded top, circa 1690, 2ft.8in. wide. (Sotheby's) $955 £517

George II walnut side table with shaped frieze, 35½in. wide. (Christie's) $4,935 £2,640

19th century walnut and inlaid side table, 24in. wide. (J. M. Welch & Son) $420 £230

Mahogany side table with marble top, circa 1740, possibly Irish, 4ft.3in. wide. (Sotheby's) $4,090 £2,200

Late George 1 walnut side table with cross-banded top, circa 1720, 2ft.5in. wide.(Sotheby's) $4,705 £2,530

Mid 19th century giltwood pier table with marble top, 53in. wide. (Sotheby's Belgravia) $905 £484

Mahogany bow-fronted side table with drawer, on turned and stretchered legs, 34in. wide. (John Hogbin & Son) $145 £80

Sheraton style serpentine front serving table in crossbanded and inlaid mahogany, 152cm. wide. (Osmond, Tricks) $820 £450

Early 18th century oak lowboy on slender cabriole legs, 28½in. wide. (Locke & England) $545 £300

Sheraton style mahogany semi-circular side table, crossbanded in kingwood, 22in. wide. (Hy. Duke & Son) $770 £400

George III serving table with fretwork frieze, 72in. wide.(Christie's) $3,495 £1,870

One of a pair of Regency rosewood side tables in the manner of George Smith, 27¼in. wide. (Christie's) $3,290 £1,760

Mid 19th century giltwood side table, one of a pair, with serpentine marble top, 53½in. wide. (Sotheby's Belgravia) $2,570 £1,375

Tubular steel and zebrawood side table with circular drum top, 1930's, 73.5cm. high. (Sotheby's Belgravia) $840 £462

Late 18th century oak and fruitwood Continental table with carved apron, on cabriole legs. (Gilbert Baitson) $490 £260

Regency rosewood sofa table crossbanded with calamanderwood and satinwood, 57in. wide. (Christie's)
$2,470 £1,320

Late George III mahogany sofa table, crossbanded in rosewood, 5ft.1½in. wide. (Sotheby's) $2,895 £1,540

Regency padoukwood sofa table with baluster turned stretcher, on reeded sabre legs, 62in. wide. (Lawrence Fine Art) $2,025 £1,100

George IV mahogany sofa table, circa 1825, 40in. wide. (Sotheby, King & Chasemore) $1,005 £550

Regency mahogany sofa table, top crossbanded in rosewood, circa 1830, 37in. wide. (Sotheby, King & Chasemore)
$3,865 £2,100

Regency mahogany sofa table with 'plum pudding' top and kingwood crossbanding, 57in. wide, extended. (Lawrence Fine Art) $1,730 £900

Georgian mahogany sofa table with reeded edge and ebony line inlay, 5ft. 3in. wide, extended. (Lawrence Fine Art) $3,680 £2,000

Regency rosewood veneered sofa table in well-figured wood, circa 1805, 4ft. 11in. wide. (Sotheby's) $7,365 £3,960

Late Regency rosewood sofa table, inlaid with brass motifs, 58in. wide, extended. (Lawrence Fine Art)
$1,610 £900

Late George III mahogany sofa table with D-shaped ends, circa 1820, 5ft. 10½in. wide. (Sotheby's)
$5,585 £2,970

Late George III satinwood small sofa table with satinwood banding, 63cm. wide. (H. Spencer & Sons Ltd.)
$1,025 £550

George III mahogany sofa table, top crossbanded with rosewood, 57in. wide. (Christie's)
$2,055 £1,100

Small Regency rosewood sofa table, inlaid with brass lines, on trestle end supports, 42in. wide, extended. (Lawrence Fine Art)
$1,700 £950

Early 19th century Regency mahogany sofa table inlaid with ebony lines, 50in. wide. (Sotheby Beresford Adams)
$1,265 £680

Regency mahogany sofa table, top banded with satinwood and inlaid with ebony stringing, 62½in. wide, extended. (Lawrence Fine Art)
$2,235 £1,250

Regency mahogany sofa table with inlaid ebony stringing, legs joined by an arched stretcher, 148.6cm. long. (Jackson-Stops & Staff) $730 £400

469

Mid 19th century walnut combined sewing and games table with fold-over top, 30in. wide. (Sotheby Beresford Adams) $1,265 £680

Burr-walnut combined games and work table with swivel oval-ended top, 1860's, 27in. wide. (Sotheby's Belgravia) $1,115 £620

Georgian mahogany games table with shaped corners, on cabriole legs, 33in. wide. (Hall Water-idge & Owen) $1,110 £600

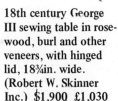

George III mahogany work table with two-flap top, circa 1800, 2ft.4in. wide. (Sotheby's) $1,345 £715

'Louis XVI' brass inlaid mahogany games table for chess and backgammon, 1880-1900, 29½in. wide. (Sotheby's Belgravia) $720 £374

18th century George III sewing table in rose-wood, burl and other veneers, with hinged lid, 18¾in. wide. (Robert W. Skinner Inc.) $1,900 £1,030

Victorian walnut games and work table on carved and baluster end standard, 27in. wide. (Hy. Duke & Son) $920 £480

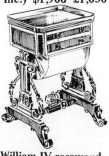

Unusual papier-mache work table with domed top, circa 1850, 19in. wide. (Sotheby's Belgravia) $1,170 £650

William IV rosewood and mahogany work table, top with solid gallery, circa 1835, 1ft.9in. wide. (Sotheby's) $775 £420

Victorian rosewood work table with marquetry inlay, 1ft.8in. wide. (Dickinson, Davy & Markham) $615 £330

19th century Regency bow-fronted sewing table in mahogany and mahogany veneer, 36in. wide. (Robert W. Skinner Inc.) $900 £490

Regency partridge-wood and mahogany work table, lid inset with satinwood oval, 1ft.1½in. wide, circa 1810. (Sotheby's)
$725 £385

Rosewood work table with hinged top on octagonal stem on concave-sided base, circa 1840, 19in. square. (Sotheby's Belgravia) $990 £550

Northern New England Federal birch work table, circa 1800, 19in. wide. (Robert W. Skinner Inc.)
$755 £400

Fine Regency walnut teapoy of tapering octagonal panelled form, 29in. high. (W. H. Lane & Son)
$505 £280

Small Georgian walnut work box on square tapering legs with X-stretcher. (Pattison Partners & Scott)
$675 £370

Regency mahogany and satinwood banded work table with inlaid motifs, circa 1810, 1ft. 10in. wide. (Sotheby, King & Chasemore) $1,445 £780

Mid Victorian sewing and games table in walnut strung with boxwood, 61cm. wide. (H. Spencer & Sons Ltd.) $965 £520

471

WORKBOXES & GAMES TABLES

German or Flemish mahogany work table, 19½in. wide, 1840's. (Sotheby's Belgravia) $515 £275

One of a pair of rare New York City Empire rosewood and grain painted games tables, 36½in. wide. (Wm. Doyle Galleries Inc.)
$10,500 £5,555

Late Regency mahogany work table with two-flap top, 28in. wide, extended. (Lawrence Fine Art)
$660 £360

George III mahogany writing and work table with hinged leather top, circa 1790, 1ft.11in. wide. (Sotheby's) $1,665 £900

19th century figured mahogany work table with satin work box, 20½in. wide. (Lawrence Fine Art)
$845 £460

Mid 19th century rosewood sewing table with fitted swing top and wool well, 20in. wide. (W. H. Lane & Son) $310 £170

George IV mahogany work table of teapoy shape, circa 1815, 1ft. 8½in. wide.(Sotheby's)
$1,025 £550

Damascus combined chess and backgammon table with hinged lid, 1920's, 33¼in. wide. (Sotheby's Belgravia) $865 £462

Georgian mahogany work table with satinwood edging, 36in. wide, extended. (Lawrence Fine Art)
$645 £350

Burr-walnut work table with tulipwood cross-banding, circa 1860, 25in. wide. (Sotheby's Belgravia) $805 £429

Anglo-Dutch mid Georgian walnut games table with sliding tray top, 35½in. wide. (Christie's) $1,560 £825

Early George II mahogany games table with double-hinged top, circa 1720, 2ft.9½in. wide. (Sotheby's) $1,810 £990

Georgian mahogany work table with reeded edge, on ring turned supports, 32in. wide, extended. (Lawrence Fine Art) $830 £450

Irish mid Georgian tea and games table with double folding top, 30½in. wide. (Christie's) $1,510 £800

Viennese mahogany and cherrywood work table with hinged top, circa 1830, 1ft.7in. wide. (Sotheby's) $780 £418

19th century Burmese hardwood and rosewood work table with carved border, 30in. wide. (Coles, Knapp & Kennedy) $285 £160

Small Victorian rosewood work table with glazed panel doors to the top. (Butler & Hatch Waterman) $400 £220

19th century rosewood games table on turned and carved legs. (J. M. Welch & Son) $945 £520

WRITING TABLES & DESKS

Pollard oak writing table with tooled leather writing surface, circa 1840, 43¼in. wide. (Sotheby's Belgravia) $3,900 £1,950

Mid 19th century giltwood centre table by C. Hindley & Son, London, 52in. wide. (Sotheby's Belgravia) $595 £330

William IV parcel gilt rosewood writing table with leather inset top, circa 1835, 60in. wide. (Sotheby's Belgravia) $1,530 £850

Edwards & Roberts walnut and marquetry writing table, 1860's, 52in. wide. (Sotheby's Belgravia) $1,435 £780

Small mahogany bonheur du jour with lion-head handles and on ring turned legs, 22in. wide. (Aldridge's)· $2,715 £1,500

Kingwood bonheur du jour with amboyna interior, 42in. wide, circa 1860. (Sotheby's Belgravia) $1,290 £700

Rosewood writing table, top inset with writing surface, circa 1860, 46in. wide. (Sotheby's Belgravia) $1,400 £748

George IV rosewood veneered library table on panelled trestle supports, circa 1820, 3ft.9in. wide. (Sotheby's) $1,075 £600

474

One of a pair of George I style gilt gessò side tables, 39in. wide. (Sotheby, King & Chasemore) $3,295 £1,800

Ormolu mounted kingwood bureau plat with leather-lined top, 56in. wide. (Christie's) $6,255 £3,400

George III mahogany library table, circa 1780, 66in. wide, with writing slope. (Sotheby, King & Chasemore) $7,685 £4,200

Unusual painted papier-mache centre table inlaid with mother-of-pearl chipping, circa 1850, 57in. wide. (Sotheby's Belgravia) $4,500 £2,600

American Art Deco sycamore and mahogany desk with V-shaped top surrounded by walnut banding, 36¼in. wide, circa 1920. (Robert W. Skinner Inc.) $600 £340

Regency mahogany writing table, top crossbanded with rosewood and on ring-turned beechwood supports, 54in. wide. (Christie's) $2,960 £1,600

Regency rosewood writing table on spindle-filled trestle ends, 41in. wide. (Christie's) $1,515 £820

George III oval mahogany library table, circa 1820, 67in. wide. (Sotheby, King & Chasemore) $27,450 £15,000

WRITING TABLES & DESKS

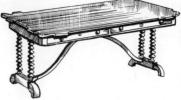

Mahogany writing desk
with hinged flap and
on trestle base, circa
1840, 22in. wide.
(Sotheby's Belgravia)
$515 £280

French Second Empire rosewood
library table on bobbin turned
pedestals, 65in. wide. (W. H.
Lane & Son) $1,120 £600

Victorian satinwood
writing desk painted
with cherubs, flowers
and portraits, 39in.
wide. (Morphets)
$1,580 £850

Edwardian lady's shaped
rosewood marquetry
kneehole desk on cabriole
legs, 36in. wide. (Burtenshaw Walker)$1,285 £680

George IV rosewood writing
table with pierced brass
gallery, 107cm. wide. (H.
Spencer & Sons Ltd.)
$780 £420

Reproduction lady's
burr-walnut writing
desk with slant front,
on cabriole legs. (T.
Bannister & Co.)
$415 £230

Mahogany library table with
rectangular top, circa 1840,
54in. wide. (Sotheby's Belgravia) $685 £380

French Art Deco
bureau de dame
painted in relief,
120cm. high.
(Christie's)
$820 £440

Regency mahogany writing
table with leather-lined top
with ebonised borders, 60½in.
wide. (Christie's)$6,660 £3,600

Satinwood Carlton House desk with fitted superstructure, circa 1910, 53in. wide. (Sotheby's Belgravia) $2,340 £1,300

Early 20th century Maple & Co. mahogany and marquetry writing desk, 48in. wide. (Sotheby Beresford Adams) $1,675 £900

Edwardian inlaid mahogany cylinder top kneehole desk on square tapering legs, 48in. wide. (Burtenshaw Walker) $2,080 £1,100

Victorian lady's small bonheur du jour with gilt metal gallery and inset leather top, 41½in. wide. (Butler & Hatch Waterman) $745 £400

Lady's Eastlake walnut and burl veneer desk with mirrored top, circa 1870, 31in. wide. (Robert W. Skinner Inc.) $625 £350

Rosewood and bone inlaid Regency Carlton House desk. (Christie's S. Kensington) $1,325 £720

Late Georgian mahogany library table with rosewood crossbanding and beaded decoration, 56in. wide. (Locke & England) $1,395 £750

George III mahogany and satinwood strung cheveret with detachable superstructure, 55cm. wide. (Phillips) $2,700 £1,450

19th century French walnut bureau plat with serpentine-shaped top crossbanded in kingwood, 4ft. wide. (Edwards, Bigwood & Bewlay) $2,470 £1,350

Late Regency rosewood library table with turned and carved stretcher, 54in. wide. (Lawrence Fine Art) $770 £420

Late Regency faded rosewood library table with moulded edge, 54in. wide. (Lawrence Fine Art) $590 £320

Late Regency rosewood writing table with leather top, 47in. wide.(Lawrence Fine Art) $770 £420

George III mahogany writing table with tooled leather top, circa 1790, 4ft. wide. (Sotheby's) $5,115 £2,750

Regency rosewood library table with rectangular top, 54in. wide. (W. H. Lane & Son) $935 £500

George III bonheur du jour with five satinwood veneered drawers, circa 1780, 2ft.6½in. wide. (Sotheby's) $9,410 £5,060

17th century Dutch oak library table with waived frieze, 64in. wide.(Lawrence Fine Art) $1,290 £700

Unusual George III mahogany double-sided library table, circa 1800, 4ft.6in. wide. (Sotheby's) $3,410 £1,815

Edwardian Sheraton inlaid mahogany Carlton House desk with shaped rising back, 4ft.5½in. wide. (Jackson-Stops & Staff) $2,390 £1,300

George IV rosewood library table on baluster column and four scroll legs, circa 1820, 5ft.6in. wide.(Sotheby's) $2,790 £1,485

Victorian walnut kidney-shaped writing table, stamped Gillow, 51½in. wide. (Lawrence Fine Art) $1,075 £560

19th century inlaid walnut writing table with leather top, 3ft.11½in. wide. (Jackson-Stops & Staff) $1,470 £800

George II mahogany writing table with tambour top, circa 1790, 3ft. wide. (Sotheby's) $1,860 £990

Mid 19th century French boulle and marquetry library table, 60in. long. (Robert W. Skinner Inc.) $2,200 £1,195

Sheraton mahogany circular library table with crossbanded top, 45in. diam. (Lawrence Fine Art) $1,840 £1,000

One of a pair of Regency style mahogany library tables in the manner of Thomas Hope, 5ft. wide. (Sotheby's) $2,590 £1,400

German mahogany com-
bined writing and dress-
ing table, inlaid with
satinwood stringing,
43¼in. wide. (Sotheby's
Belgravia) $550 £286

Regency rosewood writing
table with rounded rectangular top, on splayed trestle ends, 60in. wide.
(Christie's) $9,280 £5,184

19th century French pro-
vincial mahogany bonheur
du jour, with serpentine
fall-front, 35½in. wide.
(Coles, Knapp & Kennedy)
$895 £500

Early 20th century fruit-
wood writing desk with
shelved superstructure,
141cm. high. (Sotheby's
Belgravia) $1,045 £572

Regency mahogany architect's
table with rising top, circa
1815, 3ft.6in. wide. (Sotheby,
King & Chasemore)
$1,400 £800

Walnut writing desk,
superstructure with
pierced gallery, drawer
inset with porcelain
plaques, circa 1860,
40½in. wide.(Sotheby's
Belgravia)$2,675 £1,430

Walnut and burr-walnut
bonheur du jour with
gilt bronze mounts,
circa 1870, 35in. wide.
(Sotheby's Belgravia)
$2,335 £1,210

Rare lacquer and giltwood
kneehole table on cabriole
legs, 5ft.2½in. wide, restored. (Sotheby's)
$7,220 £3,740

Edwardian rosewood writ-
ing table with shaped
front and baluster gallery,
109cm. wide. (H. Spencer
& Sons Ltd.)$1,105 £600

Louis XV kingwood bureau plat, stamped Criaerd, 57in. wide. (Wm. Doyle Galleries Inc.) $30,000 £15,875

Mid 19th century Dutch marquetry side table with oval centre panel, 52cm. wide. (H. Spencer & Sons Ltd.) $2,430 £1,300

Late 19th century Louis XV style bureau plat in ebonised wood, 42in. long. (Robert W. Skinner Inc.) $1,000 £545

Inlaid Edwardian mahogany two-tier table with fret sides, on thimble and castor legs. (John Hogbin & Son) $430 £240

19th century mahogany folding desk of unusual design, 24in. wide. (Lawrence Fine Art) $790 £430

George I walnut side table with chamfered crossbanded and quartered top, 32in. wide. (Christie's) $2,360 £1,296

Inlaid mahogany desk with rising top and on tapered legs. (John Hogbin & Son) $635 £340

Walnut partner's desk with brass drop handles and leather inset top, 60in. wide. (John Hogbin & Son) $990 £550

Victorian pollard elm writing table, stamped Howard & Sons, with raised superstructure, 43in. wide. (Christie's) $1,935 £1,080

481

Early 18th century four-panelled coffer, inscribed A.H. 1723, 50in. long. (Andrew Grant)   **$335 £180**

Oak dower chest with three-panel front, 48in. wide. (Hall Wateridge & Owen)   **$425 £230**

16th century oak linenfold chest with rising plank lid, 52in. wide. (Boardman's)   **$890 £480**

Late 18th century pine decorated dower chest, Pennsylvania, 48in. wide. (Robert W. Skinner Inc.)   **$1,700 £900**

Mid Georgian mahogany coffer on chest with brass carrying handles, 44in. wide. (Christie's)   **$1,630 £880**

17th century oak chest with plain rising top and carved front panels, 4ft.9in. wide. (Edwards, Bigwood & Bewlay)   **$515 £280**

Small 16th century oak linenfold chest with rising panelled lid and iron hasp and hinges, 39½in. wide. (Boardman's)   **$2,035 £1,100**

Country Federal grain painted blanket chest with lift top, 44¼in. wide, circa 1810. (Robert W. Skinner Inc.)   **$350 £190**

Mid 17th century Commonwealth oak coffer with four-panel top and carved frieze rail, 50in. wide. (Sotheby's) $900 £473

Large mid 17th century oak coffer with hinged top in two parts, 74in. wide. (Sotheby's) $880 £462

Mid 17th century oak mule chest with carved frieze rail, restored. (Sotheby's) $795 £418

George I walnut coffer on stand with brass carrying handles, circa 1715, 4ft. wide. (Sotheby's) $2,480 £1,320

Small 18th century oak coffer with triple panelled top and front, 3ft.2in. wide. (Dickinson, Davy & Markham) $295 £160

Rare carved pine child's blanket box, New England, 1788, 21¼in. wide. (Robert W. Skinner Inc.) $4,300 £2,275

Mid 16th century Charles I oak coffer with triple panel front, 51in. wide. (Sotheby's) $460 £242

German stained and painted pine chest, circa 1670, 4ft.9in. wide. (Sotheby, King & Chasemore) $780 £420

15th century North Italian pine casket carved on three sides, 53cm. wide. (Sotheby's)   **$1,245 £700**

Alto Adige cedarwood chest with three-panelled front, circa 1680, 6ft.4½in. wide. (Sotheby's)   **$1,480 £792**

North Italian cedarwood 'Cyprus chest', 63in. wide. (J. M. Welch & Son)   **$365 £200**

17th century coffer, front with four arcaded panels and original lock, 50in. wide. (W. H. Lane & Son)   **$370 £200**

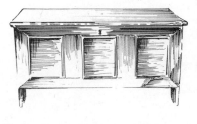

Early 18th century William and Mary oak and pine chest on frame, with lift top, 30in. wide. (Robert W. Skinner Inc.)   **$6,500 £3,530**

Plymouth pine blanket chest, circa 1700, 49½in. wide. (Robert W. Skinner Inc.)   **$2,455 £1,300**

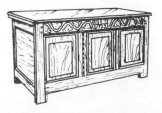

Early 18th century panelled oak chest, with carved frieze, 44in. wide. (J. M. Welch & Son)   **$400 £220**

17th century leather covered trunk, domed lid inlaid with gilt brass nailheads, 45½in. wide. (Christie's)   **$880 £480**

Breton Louis XV provincial inlaid elm-wood chest, front inlaid in light and dark wood, circa 1770, 5ft.10in. wide. (Sotheby's) $710 £400

Late 16th century Italian walnut cassone with deeply panelled top, 4ft. 2½in. wide. (Sotheby's) $925 £520

Decorated pine blanket box, New York, dated 1816, 39¾in. wide, with hinged moulded top. (Robert W. Skinner Inc.)
$4,100 £2,240

17th century Dutch or North German iron strong box with rustic landscape panels, 33in. wide. (Christie's)
$770 £420

Small 17th century steel strong box, overlaid with riveted iron strapwork, 2ft.5in. wide. (Sotheby's)$1,220 £682

Early 18th century black and gold lacquer casket on stand, 29½in. wide. (Christie's) $1,195 £638

Late 16th century North Italian painted and gilded cassone, restored, 5ft.3in. wide. (Sotheby's) $1,110 £594

18th century oak coffer with plank top and panelled front, 3ft.9in. wide.(J. M. Welch & Son) $365 £200

485

18th century Dutch walnut armoire in marquetry with double panelled doors, on ogee bracket feet, 60in. wide. (Edwards, Bigwood & Bewlay)

$7,500   £4,100

Wardrobe, designed by Marcel Breuer, in pale wood, 1920's, 186cm. wide. (Sotheby's Belgravia) $375 £210

18th century French provincial oak armoire with overhanging cornice, 4ft. 8in. wide. (Edwards, Bigwood & Bewlay)

$1,555 £850

Dutch mahogany armoire with broken pediment, circa 1780, 5ft. 9in. wide. (Sotheby's)

$2,225 £1,250

Mid 18th century Dutch walnut and marquetry wardrobe, 5ft.7½in. wide. (Sotheby's) $10,080 £5,390

Quartered mahogany wardrobe in Chippendale manner with carved key pattern cornice. (Gilbert Baitson)
$320 £170

Gentleman's mahogany wardrobe with dentil cornice and two inlaid and crossbanded doors, 4ft.3in. wide. (Butler & Hatch Waterman)
$530 £295

Mid 18th century Liegeois carved armoire on stand with serpentine top, 6ft. 7in. wide. (Sotheby's)
$2,580 £1,450

20th century oak wardrobe by JPC with carved frieze panel, 42½in. wide. (Sotheby's Belgravia) $445 £231

19th century German rosewood wardrobe, 7ft.5in. wide. (Phillips & Brooks) $3,640 £2,000

Large early oak armoire with fan and rose carving and geometric moulding. (Butler & Hatch Waterman)$1,190 £650

Flemish rosewood and ebony armoire with moulded overhanging cornice, 95½in. wide. (Christie's)$4,415 £2,400

Dutch mahogany armoire with moulded arched broken pediment centred by a vase stand, 76in. wide. (Christie's) $2,575 £1,400

17th century Dutch oak four door cupboard with scrollwork frieze, 58in. wide. (Boardman's) $7,770 £4,200

Anglo-Dutch walnut and burr-walnut armoire with crossbanded panelled doors, 67½in. wide. (Christie's) $4,785 £2,600

Late 18th/early 19th century George III mahogany breakfront wardrobe with dentil cornice, 92in. wide. (Sotheby Beresford Adams) $1,210 £650

Louis XVI provincial oak armoire with moulded cornice and carved frieze, 64½in. wide. (Christie's) $3,130 £1,700

George III inlaid mahogany breakfront wardrobe. (Sotheby Bearne) $1,795 £980

487

Georgian mahogany wash-
stand with folding top
and unusual cross stret-
cher support, in original
condition. (Gilbert Bait-
son) $150 £80

19th century mahogany
washstand on turned legs.
(Phillips) $190 £100

Georgian mahogany in-
laid corner washstand
with centre drawers,
on splay legs, 29in.
wide. (Dee & Atkinson)
                $295 £160

18th century American
painted pine water bench,
upper shelf with splash-
back, 26½in. wide.
(Robert W. Skinner Inc.)
                $400 £225

Mid 18th century George
III mahogany circular
washstand with Copeland
Spode basin, 32in. high.
(Sotheby Beresford Adams)
                $540 £290

Victorian marble topped
washstand on a walnut
veneered base.(Phillips)
                $160 £85

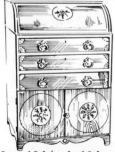

Late 18th/early 19th cen-
tury mahogany and mar-
quetry washstand with
cylinder front, 26½in.
wide. (Sotheby's)
                $535 £300

Antique mahogany cor-
ner washstand with
brass handles. (Farrant
& Wightman)$150 £85

Liberty oak washstand
with green-tiled top,
labelled, circa 1900,
141cm. high. (Sotheby's
Belgravia) $225 £130

Kingwood and parquetry etagere with three serpentine tiers, circa 1880, 14in. wide. (Sotheby's Belgravia) $425 £231

Victorian whatnot in polished rosewood with six serpentine-fronted tiers. (Aldridge's) $525 £290

Mahogany whatnot with four tiers joined by baluster turned supports, circa 1840, 48½in. high. (Sotheby's Belgravia) $940 £510

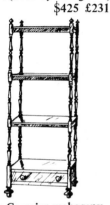

Late Georgian mahogany four-tier whatnot on turned supports with brass castors, 18in. wide. (Locke & England) $465 £260

Mid 19th century mahogany whatnot, top with adjustable book rest, 16in. wide. (Sotheby's) $770 £420

Late George III mahogany whatnot with turned and ringed spindles, 18½in. wide.(Lawrence Fine Art) $1,430 £800

Early 20th century mahogany whatnot, one of a pair, 23½in. wide. (Sotheby's Belgravia) $820 £440

19th century three-tier bird's-eye maple and rosewood whatnot, crossbanded in satinwood, 20in. wide. (W. H. Lane & Son) $435 £240

Late 19th century American Renaissance revival carved walnut whatnot, over cupboard base, 40in. wide. (Robert W. Skinner Inc.)$525 £295

Georgian brass bound mahogany wine cooler of octagonal shape and with lead liner. (Dacre, Son & Hartley)$2,640 £1,450

Late Regency sarcophagus form wine cellaret in cross-banded mahogany with lead lining. (Locke & England) $780 £420

Late 18th century mahogany and inlaid cellaret of Sheraton design, with brass carrying handles. (Locke & England) $1,075 £600

One of a pair of 'George III' mahogany wine coolers with hexagonal bodies, mid 19th century, 19in. wide. (Sotheby's Belgravia)$5,710 £3,190

Georgian oval mahogany wine cooler, with brass carrying handles and reeded base and legs. (D. M. Nesbit & Co.) $1,575 £880

George III mahogany and brass bound octagonal wine cooler, lead lined, 17½in. wide. (Burrows & Day) $990 £540

George III oval mahogany wine cooler with brass carrying handles, circa 1790, 1ft.9in. wide. (Sotheby's) $1,240 £660

Mahogany wine cellaret of canted form, with fitted lead interior, 12in. wide. (W. H. Lane & Son) $295 £160

George IV mahogany cellaret, 2ft. wide, with brass bound body. (Sotheby's)$1,035 £550

Early 19th century William IV mahogany wine cooler of tapering rectangular form, 22in. wide. (Sotheby Beresford Adams)$445 £240

William IV mahogany cellaret, circa 1820, 2ft.2in. wide. (Sotheby's) $1,795 £935

Late 18th/early 19th century George III mahogany wine cooler of hexagonal outline, 20½in. wide. (Sotheby's)$1,290 £700

George III mahogany brass bound hexagonal wine cooler, lined in lead, 45cm. diam. (Osmond, Tricks) $945 £520

Late 18th century George III mahogany wine cooler with brass handles and bands, 19in. wide. (Sotheby's)$2,300 £1,250

George III mahogany wine cooler with three brass bands, 1ft.9in. wide, circa 1790. (Sotheby's) $2,215 £1,210

George III mahogany cellaret of hexagonal form with brass handles and bands, 50cm. wide. (H. Spencer & Sons Ltd.) $1,030 £550

George III oval mahogany cellaret with brass bands, 61.5cm. wide. (Jackson-Stops & Staff) $2,655 £1,450

Mahogany cellaret with domed lid and side carrying handles, on turned legs with casters.(Alfred Mossop & Co.) $1,090 £600

491

GLASS

French opaque-opaline glass flared octagonal beaker, circa 1725, 9cm. high. (Christie's) $505 £270

.Yellowish green glass beaker with straight flaring sides, circa 3rd century A.D., 3¼in. high. (Sotheby's) $440 £225

Bohemian Zwischengold fluted dice beaker in two parts, circa 1740, 8.5cm. high. (Christie's) $970 £158

Bohemian amber-flash waisted hexagonal beaker, engraved in the manner of Hoffmann, 12.5cm. high, circa 1840. (Christie's) $1,110 £594

Transparent enamelled topographical beaker by Carl von Scheidt, circa 1815, 12cm. high. (Sotheby's) $11,740 £6,380

One of a pair of rare 'Zwischengold-und-Silberglas' beakers by Johann Mildner, 1799, 12cm. high.(Sotheby's) $9,715 £5,280

German enamelled and dated Kurfurstenhumpen, 32.7cm. high, 1620. (Phillips) $1,630 £880

German dated enamelled Reichsadler humpen, Bohemia, 1624, 28cm. high. (Christie's) $8,510 £4,600

German enamelled beaker of tapering bucket shape, inscribed Vive Mamie anne, 1743. (Phillips) $220 £120

Small late 19th century cameo glass bottle, body etched with chinoiserie scene, 5.7cm. high. (Sotheby's Belgravia) $415 £220

Etched and polished internally decorated bottle and stopper, incised Marinot, 13.2cm. high. (Christie's) $5,825 £3,200

Glass wine bottle of squat mallet shape, neck with string rim, 20cm. high. (Phillips) $40 £22

Dutch engraved bottle by Willem van Heemskerk with dark emerald green body, 1689, 33cm. high. (Sotheby's)$11,740 £6,380

19th century Indian glass hookah bottle with bell-shaped sides, 7in. high. (Sotheby's) $175 £99

17th century Dutch sealed wine bottle, shoulder applied with armorial seal, 9½in. high. (Sotheby's) $2,430 £1,320

Northern Indian rich purple glass hookah bottle, circa 1700, 7¼in. high. (Sotheby's) $395 £220

17th century Netherlandish blue-tinted glass bottle with slim tapering neck, 13.5cm. high. (Sotheby's) $1,375 £748

18th/19th century Indian blue glass hookah bottle with flaring ridged neck, 7½in. high. (Sotheby's) $435 £242

Early 20th century Tiffany Favrile blue iridescent glass bowl, New York. (Robert W. Skinner Inc.)$300 £165

Mt. Washington cameo glass bowl, late 19th century, in opaque pink on white, 9in. diam. (Robert W. Skinner Inc.)
$375 £210

Late 19th century glass bowl by Stevens & Williams, with gold and silver applied decoration, 5¾in. diam. (Robert W. Skinner Inc.)$275 £155

Iridescent blue Favrile glass flower centre by Tiffany & Co., early 20th century, 11in. diam. (Robert W. Skinner Inc.) $550 £290

Galle cameo glass bowl, marked, after 1904, 7.75cm. (Sotheby's Belgravia) $520 £286

One of a pair of early 19th century covered pedestal bowls, 31cm. high. (Sotheby's Belgravia) $380 £209

Enamelled dated Baccarat opaline bowl of thistle shape, 1867, 30.4cm. diam., on wood stand. (Sotheby's Belgravia) $1,080 £572

One of a set of six Tiffany iridescent glass bowls and saucers, circa 1900, 6cm. high. (Sotheby's Belgravia) $1,700 £935

One of a pair of early 20th century Tiffany Favrile glass finger bowls, with undertrays. (Robert W. Skinner Inc.) $425 £235

South Bohemian lithyalin flared octagonal two-handled bowl, circa 1835, Count Buquoy's Glassworks, 19cm. wide. (Christie's) $1,390 £750

Daum etched and gilded glass bowl, marked, 1890's, 8.25cm. high. (Sotheby's Belgravia) $570 £320

Amberina shade by the New England Glass Co., Massachusetts, circa 1880, 7¾in. diam. (Robert W. Skinner Inc.) $200 £105

Early 20th century European crystal, brass and enamel bowl with portrait base, 5¼in. diam. (Robert W. Skinner Inc.) $350 £195

One of a pair of cut glass bowls, covers and stands, circa 1780, stands 19.5cm. diam. (Christie's) $275 £150

One of nine Steuben Rosaline cased bowls, New York, circa 1925, signed, 5in. diam. (Robert W. Skinner Inc.) $650 £360

Golden iridescent Favrile glass rose bowl by Tiffany Studios, 25cm. diam. (Christie's) $820 £440

495

American cut-glass Mon-
teith bowl, circa 1880,
10in. diam. (Robert W.
Skinner Inc.) $225 £125

Galle etched and enamel-
led cameo glass bowl, circa
1900, 11.5cm. wide.
(Sotheby's Belgravia)
$560 £320

Opalescent glass bowl by
R. Lalique, France, 8in.
wide. (Lawrence Fine Art)
$110 £60

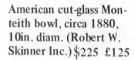

Argy Rousseau pate de
cristal bowl, moulded
with leaves and arrow-
heads, 7.75cm. wide.
(Sotheby's Belgravia)
$875 £500

Lalique opalescent glass bowl,
1920's, 30.25cm. diam., marked. (Sotheby's Belgravia)
$710 £374

Argy Rousseau pate de
cristal bowl with bell-
shaped body, 9.75cm.
high, 1920's. (Sotheby's
Belgravia)$1,670 £880

1st century A.D. dark-blue
cast glass pillar moulded
bowl with ribbed body,
19.5cm. diam.(Sotheby's)
$8,870 £4,620

Lithyalin foot bowl
in marbled glass,
Bohemian, circa 1840,
14.5cm. high.(Sothe-
by's Belgravia)
$500 £275

Lalique opalescent glass
bowl with frieze of budgerigars, 24.5cm. diam., 1930's.
(Sotheby's Belgravia)
$525 £300

Pate-de-verre rectangular box and cover by G. Argy Rousseau, 13.2cm. wide. (Christie's)
$4,730 £2,600

Frosted and opalescent glass bonbonniere and cover, by R. Lalique, 16cm. diam. (Christie's) $275 £150

Fire-polished over-lay glass bonbonniere and cover of-spherical form, 17cm. diam. (Christie's)$1,235 £660

White glass box cover, moulded by R. Lalique, 11.5cm. diam. (Christie's) $275 £150

Galle cameo glass box and cover with squat tapering body, circa 1900, 7.5cm. wide. (Sotheby's Belgravia)
$1,000 £500

17th century Venetian glass box and cover, 8in. high. (Robert W. Skinner Inc.) $100 £55

Opalescent circular glass box and cover with bluish finish, moulded by R. Lalique, 26cm. diam. (Christie's) $640 £350

Double overlay triangu-lar box and cover, sig-ned, 11.5cm. high. (Christie's)
$2,675 £1,430

Small Walter pate-de-verre box and cover with wais-ted body, 1920's, 7cm. diam. (Sotheby's Bel-gravia) $520 £286

CANDLESTICKS

One of a pair of early 20th century Tiffany Favrile glass candlesticks, New York, 7¼in. high. (Robert W. Skinner Inc.) $400 £220

One of three circular glass candle holders, marked R. Lalique, 14.4cm. diam. (Christie's) $220 £120

One of a pair of cobalt blue glass candlesticks, Massachusetts, circa 1840, 9½in. high. (Robert W. Skinner Inc.) $700 £385

Glass taperstick with slim nozzle, circa 1730, 6¾in. high. (Sotheby's) $660 £352

Airtwist taperstick with beaded knop and domed foot, circa 1750, 17.5cm. high. (Christie's) $705 £380

Silesian stemmed candlestick, nozzle set on three collars, 22.5cm. high, circa 1730. (Sotheby, King & Chasemore) $230 £130

Georgian cut glass candlestick on domed and faceted foot, circa 1780, 20cm. high. (Sotheby, King & Chasemore) $340 £190

Early 20th century Aurene candlestick, signed, 10in. high. (Robert W. Skinner Inc.) $225 £125

Unusual glass taperstick of hollow section and with pear-shaped knop, circa 1740, 4½in. high. (Sotheby's) $370 £198

498

18th century Chinese ruby glass wine cup, 7.5cm. high. (Vernons) $90 £50

17th century Facon de Venise engraved cup with shallow body, opposed auricular handles, 10cm. diam.(Sotheby's) $1,175 £638

German milchglas mug with strap handle and barrel-shaped body, 12cm. high. (Phillips) $420 £230

Mid 18th century Bohemian milchglas mug decorated with a roundel enclosing a figure. (Christie's) $875 £450

A Facon de Venise ice glass standing cup, South Netherlands, 16th century, 16.5cm. high. (Christie's) $3,300 £1,700

Gutenbrunn Mildner cylindrical mug with oval plaque, dated 1792, 9.5cm. high.(Christie's) $1,920 £1,026

A small opaque glass cylindrical mug, South Staffordshire, circa 1760, 7cm. high. (Christie's) $675 £350

Late 19th century plated amberina punch cup, ribbed, with shaped rim, 2¾in. high. (Robert W. Skinner Inc.) $1,300 £725

Pressed glass ale mug with geometric decoration, circa 1860. (Vernons) $24 £12

499

DECANTERS

GLASS

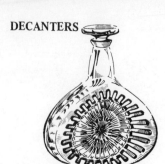

One of a pair of clear glass and brown stained decanters and stoppers, inscribed Lalique, 27.3cm. high. (Christie's) $495 £264

Cobalt blue bar bottle, cork stopper with pewter and cobalt stopper, circa 1850, 12in. high. (Robert W. Skinner Inc.) $250 £135

Burmese glass spirit decanter in the shape of a pig. (Christie's S. Kensington) $275 £150

One of a pair of cut-glass decanters and stoppers of club form, circa 1820, 26.5cm. high. (Christie's) $705 £380

Clear glass flattened spherical decanter, etched R. Lalique, France, 34cm. high. (Christie's) $550 £302

One of a rare pair of white enamelled electioneering decanters and one stopper, circa 1765-68, 22cm. high. (Christie's) $10,175 £5,500

One of a rare pair of rock crystal engraved decanters and stoppers, by Stevens & Williams, circa 1885. (Sotheby's Belgravia) $5,405 £2,860

Lalique glass decanter, bulbous body with tapering neck, 32cm. high, 1920's. (Sotheby's Belgravia) $300 £165

Overlay decanter and stopper by A. Bohm, signed, 38cm. high. (Sotheby's Belgravia) $2,495 £1,320

500

Lalique glass decanter, signed, 1920's, 25.5cm. high, sides moulded with masks. (Sotheby's Belgravia)
$340 £190

One of a pair of Regency cut-glass decanters and stoppers with concentric horizontal grooves, circa 1820, 26.5cm. high. (Sotheby, King & Chasemore)
$375 £210

One of a pair of diamond-cut crystal ship's decanters with mushroom stoppers, 24.5cm. high. (Jackson-Stops & Staff)
$290 £160

Late 19th century American two-colour green cut-glass decanter of conical shape, 16¾in. high. (Robert W. Skinner Inc.)
$200 £110

Cut-glass wine set of two decanters and stoppers and a claret jug and stopper. (Dee & Atkinson)
$410 £220

Lalique glass decanter and stopper with slender cylindrical neck, 1920, 39.5cm. high. (Sotheby's Belgravia)
$980 £550

Large cut-glass decanter and stopper, circa 1820, 11¾in. high, chipped. (Sotheby's) $385 £209

Enamelled decanter and stopper for 'Port', by Wm. and Mary Beilby, circa 1765. (Christie's)
$4,440 £2,400

German enamelled decanter jug with pewter cap, possibly Franconia, 1664, 28.5cm. high. (Sotheby's)
$2,055 £1,100

Enamelled glass dish
and cover, attributed
to Fachschule Szwiesel,
circa 1910, 17cm. high.
(Sotheby's Belgravia)
$160 £90

Galle cameo glass dish of squat
tapering form, circa 1900,
28cm. wide. (Sotheby's Belgravia)
$790 £450

Galle enamelled
glass pot and cover
with barrel-shaped
body, 1890's, 19cm.
high. (Sotheby's
Belgravia)
$1,600 £900

Opalescent circular glass
dish moulded with a sea
nymph, 36.5cm. diam.,
by R. Lalique.(Christie's)
$825 £450

17th century Facon de
Venise sweetmeat dish
with flat bowl, 13.5cm.
diam. (Sotheby's)
$405 £220

Walter pate-de-verre glass
dish, incised mark, circa
1920's, 23.5cm. diam.
(Sotheby's Belgravia)
$795 £418

Venetian footed dish of
straight-sided form, circa
1500, 26.5cm. diam.
(Sotheby's)$3,170 £1,650
502

Late 18th century Irish
canoe-shaped footed
glass dish, 30cm. high.
(Sotheby, King &
Chasemore)$315 £170

Daum cameo glass dish
and cover, circa 1900,
9.5cm. diam. (Sotheby's
Belgravia) $785 £400

Massive Daum glass dish in clear yellow glass, engraved, 1930's, 25cm. wide. (Sotheby's Belgravia) $440 £242

One of a pair of American glass compotes, circa 1845, with pointed scalloped rims, 4¾in. high. (Robert W. Skinner Inc.) $750 £415

Double overlay triangular glass dish with inverted rim, 24.5cm. wide. (Christie's)$1,030 £550

Crested amethyst circular shallow glass dish, gilt by Isaac Jacobs, circa 1800, 17.5cm. diam. (Christie's) $460 £250

Unusual sweetmeat glass with cup-shaped bowl, circa 1750, 5½in. high. (Sotheby's)$190 £104

Clear and opalescent glass dish by R. Lalique, France, 38cm. wide. (Christie's) $585 £320

Unusual Galle cameo glass dish in the form of a leaf, circa 1900, 27.75cm. long. (Sotheby's Belgravia) $835 £440

Sweetmeat dish on pedestal stem, 6in. high, circa 1730. (Sotheby's) $165 £85

Good Almeric Walter pate-de-verre dish of scallop shell-shape, signed, 19cm. wide. (Phillips)$3,400 £1,900

503

GLASS

Boxed set of six Lalique glasses, panels stained brown, 1920's, 9.8cm. high. (Sotheby's Belgravia) $1,030 £580

Part of a late 19th century Stourbridge glass table service of fifty-two pieces. (Sotheby's Belgravia) $800 £440

Three-bottle tantalus in brass bound case. (Honiton Galleries) $250 £135

Three from a set of thirty 20th century drinking glasses with enamelled bands. (Sotheby's Belgravia) $520 £275

Part of a one hundred and twenty-eight-piece gilt glass table service, circa 1900. (Sotheby's Belgravia) $830 £440

Suite of table glass by R. Lalique, France, thirty-five pieces in all. (Coles, Knapp & Kennedy) $330 £185

Unusual parquetry table decanter set with globe body, circa 1860-80, 13¼in. high. (Sotheby's Belgravia)$2,920 £1,650

Clear and amber stained glass carafe and stopper with six glasses en suite, inscribed R. Lalique, France. (Christie's) $740 £396

Etched enamelled and applied glass ewer and glasses by E. Galle, signed. (Christie's) $1,850 £990

Mid 19th century Black Forest tantalus of table cabinet form, 19in. high. (Sotheby's) $465 £260

Unusual gilt water set of eight pieces, circa 1900, jug 30.5cm. high. (Sotheby's Belgravia) $420 £231

Boulle and ebonised rosewood serpentine decanter box with glasses, 13in. wide, circa 1850. (Sotheby's Belgravia) $1,025 £572

Part of a set of seventeen Lalique glasses, 1930's, with square stems and rectangular panels. (Sotheby's Belgravia) $1,360 £748

Late Victorian blue glass decanter and six glasses with silver and gilt decoration. (Sotheby's) $585 £300

Galle enamelled glass liqueur set in smoked glass with gold foil inclusions, 1880's. (Sotheby's Belgravia) $4,025 £2,300

Oak tantalus, inscribed Betjemanns Patent, with silver plated mounts and cut glass whisky decanters, 12in. high. (Dickinson, Davy & Markham) $130 £74

505

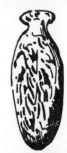

German enamelled flask of octagonal shape, 14cm. high. (Phillips) $405 £220

Aubergine translucent glass flask with ribbed decoration, circa 3rd/4th century A.D., 6¼in. high. (Christie's) $1,765 £935

Iridescent blue translucent glass date flask, 1st century A.D., 3¼in. high. (Christie's) $705 £375

German enamelled flask with pewter mounted neck, 17.5cm. high. (Phillips) $1,145 £620

Late 17th century Bohemian enamelled pewter mounted square spirit flask with pewter cover, 21.5cm. high.(Christie's) $1,110 £600

German enamelled flask of canted rectangular form, with pewter mounted neck, 18.5cm. high. (Phillips) $850 £460

Mid 18th century Central European enamelled silver mounted flask with canted corners, 14.5cm. high. (Christie's) $565 £302

Interesting German enamelled flask with pewter mounted neck and screw stopper, 14.5cm. high. (Phillips) $665 £360

Mid 18th century Armorial middle-European enamelled glass flask with pewter rim, 16.7cm. high. (Sotheby, King & Chasemore) $465 £260

Clear glass and grey stained rectangular scent flask, signed R. Lalique, 13.8cm. high.(Christie's) $730 £400

Translucent yellowish-green glass flask, circa 3rd century A.D., 3¼in. high. (Christie's) $875 £462

Aubergine translucent glass date flask, 1st century A.D., 3in. high. (Christie's)$520 £275

17th century Spanish Facon de Venise flask with hexa-lobed body, 18.5cm. high. (Sotheby's) $485 £264

Mid 18th century Armorial middle-European enamelled glass flask, with pewter rim, 16.8cm. high. (Sotheby, King & Chasemore) $360 £200

Glass flask in the form of bellows, the clear glass combed in blue and white, circa 1840, 33cm. high. (Sotheby's Belgravia) $160 £88

German enamelled glass flask of chamfered rectangular form, with pewter mounted neck. (Phillips) $310 £170

German dated locksmith's rectangular pewter mounted spirit flask, 1788, 13cm. high. (Christie's) $360 £194

German enamelled flask with pewter mounted neck, 12.5cm. high. (Phillips) $500 £270

507

One of four early 20th century Tiffany iridescent gold glass goblets, 5¾in. high. (Robert W. Skinner Inc.) $475 £260

One of a pair of engraved goblets, circa 1870, 16.4cm. high. (Sotheby's Belgravia) $190 £100

Wine goblet with rounded funnel bowl, circa 1700, 5¾in. high. (Sotheby's) $525 £286

Dutch-engraved Newcastle goblet, shoulder knop with air-thread inclusions, circa 1750, 7¾in. high. (Sotheby's) $1,275 £682

Engraved wine goblet with large ovoid bowl, circa 1780, 7in. high. (Sotheby's) $505 £275

Bohemian cut and engraved goblet on baluster knopped stem, circa 1710, 21cm. high. (Christie's) $295 £160

Baluster wine goblet with pointed funnel bowl, circa 1700, 7¾in. high. (Sotheby's) $605 £330

Early lead glass goblet in Venetian style, supported on wrythen serpentine stem, circa 1680, 9¾in. high. (Sotheby's) $1,215 £660

Bohemian ruby flashed faceted goblet of thistle shape, circa 1850, 28cm. high. (Sotheby's Belgravia) $380 £209

508

Masonic goblet with bucket-shaped bowl on knopped stem, circa 1830, 15.5cm. high. (Sotheby, King & Chasemore) $270 £150

French hyalith goblet, by Hautin & Cie, circa 1840, 11cm. high. (Christie's) $205 £110

Early 19th century glass rummer with large square bowl, etched with initials J.B., 6½in. high. (Dacre, Son & Hartley) $370 £200

Late 18th century Dutch-engraved goblet, Scandinavian or Lauenstein, 23.5cm. high.(Christie's) $335 £180

Bohemian ruby stained goblet and cover on faceted knopped stem, circa 1850, 55cm. high. (Sotheby's Belgravia) $720 £395

Engraved Paris Exhibition goblet and cover on knopped stem and stepped foot, 29cm. high, 1878. (Sotheby's Belgravia) $875 £462

One of six early 20th century American cut-glass goblets, with starburst bases, 6in. high.(Robert W. Skinner Inc.) $400 £220

Bohemian armorial goblet with funnel bowl, engraved with a coat-of-arms, circa 1700, 23cm. high. (Christie's) $405 £220

17th century Facon de Venise goblet with cup-shaped bowl, 12.8cm. high. (Sotheby's) $385 £209

509

Baluster goblet with round funnel bowl, circa 1700, 23cm. high. (Christie's) $740 £400

Baluster goblet with round funnel bowl, on domed and folded foot, circa 1720, 17cm. high. (Christie's) $315 £170

Unusual goblet with deep ribbed ovoid bowl, circa 1750, 8¼in. high. (Sotheby's) $185 £99

Mid 18th century Williamite goblet with engraved bucket bowl, circa 1760, 17cm. high. (Christie's) $2,035 £1,100

Unusually large engraved air-twist goblet, circa 1750, 12in. high. (Sotheby's) $205 £110

Thuringian engraved goblet with funnel bowl, circa 1740, 19.5cm. high. (Christie's) $645 £350

Dutch engraved goblet with funnel bowl, lower part cut on facets, circa 1760, 18cm. high. (Christie's) $425 £230

Early 18th century Bohemian engraved goblet with widely flared funnel bowl, 15cm. high. (Christie's) $295 £160

Very fine Dutch-engraved Newcastle goblet with funnel bowl, circa 1750, 8in. high. (Sotheby's) $3,290 £1,760

Baluster goblet with deep rounded funnel bowl, circa 1700, 8¼in. high. (Sotheby's) $865 £462

Engraved facet stemmed goblet, with inscribed bowl, circa 1780, 18.5cm. high. (Christie's) $370 £200

Baluster goblet with flared bowl and domed and folded foot, circa 1700, 6¾in. high. (Sotheby's)
$1,235 £660

German armorial goblet engraved with a coat-of-arms, circa 1730, 18cm. high. (Christie's)
$405 £220

Dutch engraved goblet with slightly waisted funnel bowl, stem enclosing a large tear, circa 1750, 22cm. high. (Christie's) $705 £380

Dutch-engraved wine goblet with pointed round funnel bowl, circa 1750, 8¼in. high. (Sotheby's) $945 £506

Baluster goblet with large flared bucket bowl, circa 1700, 9¼in. high. (Sotheby's) $390 £209

Rare wine goblet, funnel bowl with solid base, circa 1715, 7in. high. (Sotheby's) $615 £330

Mammoth baluster goblet with round funnel bowl, circa 1700, 29cm. high. (Christie's) $335 £180

JUGS & EWERS

GLASS

Cased wheeling peach blow pitcher, 5½in. high. (Robert W. Skinner Inc.) $650 £325

Early 19th century glass champagne jug with trefoil rim, diagonal ice funnel, 11½in. high. (Dacre, Son & Hartley) $140 £75

Daum etched and enamelled miniature jug with applied glass handle, 8.9cm. high. (Christie's) $535 £286

Lobmeyr engraved jug with strap handle, 33.6cm. high, 1870's. (Sotheby's Belgravia) $1,145 £605

18th century Spanish or Bohemian jug and cover with applied scroll handle, 31.5cm. high. (Sotheby's) $675 £352

Engraved glass claret jug with loop handle. (Christie's S. Kensington) $525 £280

One of a pair of green glass eagle claret jugs with electroplated mounts, 10¼in. high. (Christie's S. Kensington) $705 £380

Olive-green glass jug with spherical body and flaring mouth, 11cm. high, circa 3rd-4th century A.D. (Sotheby's) $200 £104

Eastern United States cut glass footed pitcher with panelled pouring spout, circa 1880, 9in. high. (Robert W. Skinner Inc.) $200 £115

512

Galle enamelled glass jug in smoked glass, 1880's, 35.5cm. high.(Sotheby's Belgravia) $1,225 £700

Late 19th century cameo glass metal mounted jug in cranberry coloured glass. (Sotheby's) $585 £320

Small Daum etched and enamelled glass jug, marked, circa 1900, 7.25cm. high. (Sotheby's Belgravia) $835 £440

Early Ravenscroft 'crizzled' decanter jug, circa 1674, 20cm. high. (Christie's) $710 £380

Heath & Middleton silver mounted jug, Birmingham, 1893, 30.25cm. high. (Sotheby's Belgravia) $1,255 £660

Ravenscroft 'crizzled' decanter jug with tapering oviform body, circa 1685, 23.5cm. high. (Christie's)$890 £480

Glass water pitcher by Hawkes, Corning, New York, circa 1900, 8½in. high. (Robert W. Skinner Inc.) $200 £110

Blown three mould glass jug with wide flaring rim and pouring spout, circa 1828, 6¼in. high. (Robert W. Skinner Inc.)$425 £230

American cut glass champagne jug, circa 1890, 13½in. high with flared rim. (Robert W. Skinner Inc.) $300 £165

513

Late 19th century amberina basket, floral decorated, 10½in. high. (Robert W. Skinner Inc.) $275 £150

Pair of ormolu mounted two-branch cut glass candelabra, 41cm. high. (Sotheby, King & Chasemore)$2,560 £1,400

Mid 19th century vaseline glass bell with diagonally ribbed body, and clear handle, 27cm. high. (Sotheby's Belgravia) $70 £38

Clear glass etched and enamelled basket with gilded metal handle, by Emile Galle, 18cm. diam. (Christie's) $2,260 £1,210

Late 19th century ruby and white cameo glass knife handle, 9.2cm. long. (Sotheby's Belgravia) $165 £88

Gilt and enamelled cut glass stemmed jar and cover, attributed to Faschule Haida, circa 1910-20, 25cm. high. (Sotheby's Belgravia)
        $240   £132

Pate-de-verre figure of a seated girl, by A. Walter, signed, 20.5cm. high. (Christie's)
        $2,455 £1,350

Lalique glass cockerel's head on wood stand, 1930's, signed, 16.5cm. high.(Sotheby's Belgravia) $390 £220

One of a pair of mid 19th century amber bells with white rims, 29.5cm. high. (Sotheby's Belgravia)
        $170 £93

One of a pair of cut glass candelabra, circa 1900, 25½in. high. (Robert W. Skinner Inc.) $450 £250

Pate-de-verre tray by A. Walter, modelled by Henri Berge, 20.8cm. wide. (Christie's) $2,185 £1,200

One of a rare pair of early 19th century Irish cut glass butter piggins, 13cm. high. (Sotheby, King & Chasemore) $395 £220

Lalique frosted glass figure of a mermaid, 10cm. high, 1920's, marked. (Sotheby's Belgravia) $265 £150

Cameo glass biscuit barrel, electroplated mounts by W. W. Harrison & Co., Sheffield, circa 1885, 17cm. high. (Sotheby's Belgravia) $830 £440

Early 20th century Burmese double-handled urn by Mt. Washington Glass Co., Massa., 13½in. high. (Robert W. Skinner Inc.) $675 £375

American Gothic revival walnut and glass terrarium with peaked top, 29½in. wide, circa 1840. (Robert W. Skinner Inc.) $200 £115

Unfinished cameo glass plaque in translucent ruby, 1880's, 30.8cm. diam. (Sotheby's Belgravia) $415 £220

Lalique glass frog moulded with angular features, 1930's, 6.25cm. high. (Sotheby's Belgravia) $1,335 £750

515

Signed St. Louis concentric millefiori weight with mauve cane, 6.3cm. diam. (Sotheby's) $1,195 £638

Daum pate-de-verre paperweight modelled as a moth, signed, 12cm. wide. (Christie's) $945 £506

Rare St. Louis colour ground weight in salmon pink, green and white, 8cm. diam. (Sotheby's) $1,030 £550

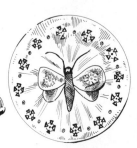

St. Louis marble weight in alternate red and white loops, 7cm. diam. (Sotheby's)$1,440 £770

Clear pale amethyst glass and grey stained paperweight by R. Lalique, 21cm. high. (Christie's)$1,645 £880

Baccarat butterfly and garland weight with star-cut base, 6.5cm. diam. (Sotheby's) $1;110 £594

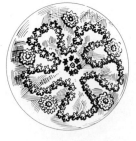

American flower weight cut with circular windows, in pink, white and green, 8.2cm. diam. (Sotheby's) $1,750 £935

Clichy patterned millefiori weight on tossed muslin ground, 7.9cm. diam. (Sotheby's) $495 £264

One of a rare pair of St. Louis doorknobs in the form of paperweights, 5cm. diam. (Sotheby's) $1,705 £935

St. Louis mushroom paper-
weight in white, blue, pink
and green, 7.3cm. diam.
(Sotheby's) $1,070 £572

Pate-de-verre paper-
weight by A. Walter,
11cm. wide.
(Christie's)$1,130 £605

St. Louis mushroom paper-
weight of concentric canes,
8cm. diam. (Sotheby's)
$535 £286

St. Louis flat-bouquet
weight of swirling latt-
cinio threads, 7.8cm.
diam. (Sotheby's)
$1,150 £616

Clear and frosted glass
paperweight by R.
Lalique, France, 20.5cm.
high. (Christie's)
$1,235 £660

St. Louis mushroom weight
on star-cut base, 7.6cm.
diam. (Sotheby's)
$1,605 £858

Rare Baccarat camomile
and garland weight with
star-cut base, 7.5cm. diam.
(Sotheby's) $1,480 £792

Venetian millefiori weight by
Bigaglia in red, white and
turquoise, 7.8cm. diam.
(Sotheby's) $700 £374

Clichy swirl weight in
green, white and pink,
7.9cm. diam. (Sotheby's)
$495 £264

517

Baccarat signed and dated carpet-ground paperweight, 1848, 7.5cm. diam. (Phillips) $1,490 £850*

Paperweight in clear and frosted glass by R. Lalique, France, 10.8cm. high. (Christie's)$985 £528

Good Baccarat dated close millefiori paperweight, dated 1848, 7.8cm. diam. (Phillips) $630 £360

Frosted glass paper-weight 'Vitesse', moul-ded R. Lalique, France, 18.8cm. high. (Christie's)$1,770 £972

Rare Baccarat snake paper-weight, sides with diamond facets, 7.5cm. diam. (Phillips) $9,100 £5,200

Clear glass paperweight 'Falcon', on circular base, by R. Lalique, France, 15.6cm. high. (Christie's)$1,475 £810

Baccarat primrose paper-weight with stardust centre and star-cut base, 6.5cm. diam. (Phillips) $440 £250

Clichy sulphide and colour-ground paperweight, set with busts of Victoria and Albert, 7.3cm. diam. (Phillips) $475 £270

Clichy miniature patter-ned paperweight, 2in. diam. (Sotheby's) $475 £250

Lalique glass perfume
bottle and stopper, for
Worth, 8.5cm. high,
marked. (Sotheby's
Belgravia) $80 £44

Circular late 19th century
cameo glass scent bottle
with silver top. (Christie's
S. Kensington)$400 £220

Lalique glass perfume
bottle and stopper of
flat spherical form,
8.5cm. high, marked.
(Sotheby's Belgravia)
        $85 £46

Lalique turquoise glass perfume bottle, moulded with
triangular leaves, circa
1925, 9cm. high. (Sotheby's
Belgravia) $900 £495

Late 19th century cameo
glass scent bottle with
silver cap. (Christie's S.
Kensington) $635 £350

Cameo glass perfume
atomiser by Ricard, with
knopped neck, 23cm.
high. (Christie's)
        $295 £162

Glass perfume bottle
and stopper, after a
design by Lalique,
1930's, 14cm. high.
(Sotheby's Belgravia)
        $180 £99

Swan's head scent bottle with
silver cap. (Christie's S. Kensington) $505 £280

Cylindrical scent bottle
of clear glass with fros-
ted top and stopper,
4¼in. high, marked R.
Lalique, France. (Law-
rence Fine Art)
        $200 £110

519

Brown stained glass scent bottle, moulded Lalique, 8.1cm. diam. (Christie's)$455 £250

Cameo glass and gilt metal mounted scent flask modelled as a curled dolphin, circa 1885, 13cm. wide. (Christie's) $2,220 £1,200

Brown glass scent bottle with dome-shaped stopper, R. Lalique, 7.6cm. high. (Christie's) $510 £280

Lalique glass perfume bottle and stopper for Worth's 'Dans la Nuit', 1920's, 10cm. high. (Sotheby's Belgravia) $250 £140

Unusual Daum cameo glass perfume bottle and stopper, signed, 13.5cm. high. (Phillips) $645 £360

Late 19th century unfinished cameo glass scent bottle, 6.5cm. (Sotheby's Belgravia) $85 £44

Double-overlay atomizer scent bottle with metal fitting, signed, 19.8cm. high. (Christie's) $290 £160

Clear glass and amber stained cologne bottle and stopper, moulded R. Lalique, 17.6cm. high. (Christie's) $245 £132

Clear and grey stained glass scent bottle and stopper, by Lalique, 11.2cm. high. (Christie's)$730 £400

Worth perfume bottle
by R. Lalique, France,
with amber glass stop-
per, 10.6cm. high.
(Christie's)$275 £150

Lalique glass perfume bottle
and stopper in original box,
1920's, 13.5cm. high.
(Sotheby's Belgravia)
$730 £410

Frosted glass globular
scent bottle and stop-
per, moulded as a
nymph, by Lalique,
9.8cm. high.
(Christie's)$545 £300

Cameo glass silver moun-
ted scent bottle of tear-
drop form, circa 1885,
11cm. long. (Christie's)
$520 £280

One of a pair of French 19th
century lime green opaline glass
square-shaped scent bottles,
4¾in. high. (Geering & Colyer)
$260 £140

Late 19th century
moulded overlay scent
bottle shaped as a per-
ching owl, 11.5cm. high.
(Sotheby's Belgravia)
$62 £33

Lalique glass perfume
bottle and stopper,
signed, 1930's, 14cm.
high. (Sotheby's Bel-
gravia) $745 £420

French 'gorge de pigeon' opaline globular scent bottle and
stopper, circa 1830, 11.5cm.
high. (Christie's)$2,220 £1,200

Lalique heart-shaped per-
fume bottle with crescent-
shaped flat stopper, 1920's,
10.5cm. high. (Sotheby's
Belgravia) $745 £420

STAINED GLASS

One of a set of nine stained glass panels with arched tops, 27in. wide. (Sotheby's Belgravia) $1,260 £700

Art Deco cameo and stained glass window, circa 1930, 49½in. long. (Robert W. Skinner Inc.) $1,300 £720

One of a set of four late 19th century stained glass panels, 16¼in. wide. (Sotheby's Belgravia) $410 £220

TANKARDS

18th century Central European enamelled milchglas tankard painted in polychrome, 14.5cm. high. (Sotheby's) $485 £264

Bohemian Hausmalerei opaque-opaline glass tankard and cover of barrel shape, circa 1750, 16.5cm. high.(Christie's) $1,515 £810

Mid 18th century Bohemian enamelled milchglas mug with convex body, 11cm. high. (Sotheby's) $485 £264

Mid 18th century Bohemian enamelled milchglas tankard, applied strap handle, 16cm. high. (Sotheby's) $605 £330

Saxon dated cylindrical tankard with engraved body, dated 1763, 13.5cm. high. (Christie's) $1,010 £540

Mid 18th century Bohemian enamelled milchglas tankard with masonic symbols, 15cm. high. (Sotheby's) $305 £165

Unusual 16th/17th century turquoise tinted tazza with wide tray, 25cm. diam. (Sotheby's) $305 £165

Mid 17th cenury Facon de Venise tazza of circular shape with upturned edge, 7in. diam. (Sotheby's) $325 £176

16th/17th century Facon de Venise tazza of amber-tinted metal on blue-tinted base, 24cm. diam. (Sotheby's) $690 £374

TUMBLERS

Early 18th century Bohemian evangelist's flared tumbler, engraved with four portraits, 10.5cm. high. (Christie's) $775 £420

North Bohemian engraved and fluted waisted tumbler with everted lower part, circa 1840, 12cm. high. (Christie's) $910 £486

French 'bleu lavende' opaline cylindrical tumbler gilt with a figure of Napoleon, circa 1825, 9cm. high. (Christie's) $335 £180

Bohemian Zwischengold fluted dice tumbler in two parts, circa 1740, 8.5cm. high. (Christie's) $970 £158

Early 18th century Bohemian glass engraved tumbler with slightly flared sides, 15.5cm. high. (Christie's) $555 £300

Bohemian engraved tumbler attributed to Franz Gottstein, circa 1825, 10.5cm. high. (Christie's) $1,515 £810

Loetz silver and iridescent glass oviform vase, signed, 11cm. high. (Christie's)
$450 £242

Early oviform locust vase in translucent opalescent glass, inscribed Lalique, France, 27cm. high. (Christie's) $1,440 £770

Two-colour cameo vase, circa 1880, in opaque white cut to blue, 10in. high. (Robert W. Skinner Inc.) $3,200 £1,695

Daum etched and enamelled slender oviform vase, signed, 36cm. high. (Christie's)$1,235 £660

One of a pair of 19th century Bohemian cranberry tinted glass vases with lustre drops, 12¼in. high. (Geering & Colyer) $795 £425

Daum double overlay cameo glass vase, signed Daum Nancy, circa 1900, 13½in. high. (Sotheby's) $705 £374

Attractive Austrian glass vase with short trumpet neck, circa 1900, 5¾in. high, sold with another. (Sotheby's) $375 £198

Daum etched and enamelled vase of rectangular section, 11.7cm. high. (Christie's) $820 £440

Early oviform locust vase in clear and frosted glass, inscribed R. Lalique, France, 27.5cm. high. (Christie's)$1,195 £638

Early 20th century Tiffany
Favrile iridescent gold vase,
New York, 5½in. high.   St. Louis shot vase on scram-
(Robert W. Skinner Inc.)   bled paperweight base, 8cm.
                    $375 £200   high. (Sotheby's)$700 £374

Wheel carved and etched
boat-shaped vase by
Emile Galle, signed, 16cm.
wide. (Christie's)
          $1,030 £550

Vase from a late
19th century cran-
berry glass garniture
of four pieces with   Pair of George Jones pate-sur-
enamelled paintings.   pate vases with white relief
(Sotheby's)   decoration, 24cm. high, circa
          $500 £264   1875. (Sotheby, King & Chase-
                                  more) $610 £330

Green glass amphora
with trailed decora-
tion, 3rd century
A.D., 11½in. high.
(Christie's)
          $1,560 £825

Loetz gourd-shaped vase   Thick-walled flared cylindrical
with dimpled neck, 16cm. vase with two broad loop handles,
high. (Christie's)   engraved R. Lalique, France.
          $225 £121   (Christie's) $1,235 £660

Handel cameo glass
vase, circa 1920,
signed Mosher,
9¾in. high.
(Robert W. Skinner
Inc.) $400 £210

Tiffany paperweight aquamarine vase, New York, circa 1910, 5in. diam. (Robert W. Skinner Inc.) $3,500 £1,935

Cameo glass vase in topaz with white overlay, 11cm. high, 1880's, slightly chipped. (Sotheby's Belgravia) $800 £440

Webb glass overlay vase, amber on clear glass, signed. (Capes, Dunn & Co.) $150 £80

Legras cameo glass vase with grey glass body, circa 1900, 25.4cm. high. (Sotheby's Belgravia) $390 £220

Galle cameo glass landscape vase with original bronze light fitment, circa 1900, 24.75cm. high. (Sotheby's Belgravia) $800 £450

Mid 19th century ruby overlay vase, 25.2cm. high. (Sotheby's Belgravia) $190 £100

Flared cylindrical vase, inscribed R. Lalique, France, 24.5cm. high. (Christie's) $825 £450

One of a pair of Loetz iridescent glass vases of baluster form, inscribed Loetz, Austria, circa 1900, 9½in. high. (Woolley & Wallis) $1,575 £880

Galle enamelled amber glass vase with squat square body, 1890's, 16.5cm. high.(Sotheby's Belgravia) $1,515 £850

One of a pair of amethyst tulip glasses with scalloped rims, circa 1845, 10in. high. (Robert W. Skinner Inc.) $725 £395

Unusually decorated cameo glass vase, circa 1880. (Sotheby's Belgravia) $2,550 £1,400

Loetz pale golden iridescent glass vase of spiralled triangular section, 20.8cm. high.(Christie's) $165 £88

Multi-coloured Peking glass brushpot of cylindrical shape, 12cm. high, on wood stand. (Sotheby, King & Chasemore)$170 £95

Galle carved and applied glass vase with spiralling grooves, 1890's, signed, 27.5cm. high.(Sotheby's Belgravia) $1,780 £1,000

Etched and polished internally decorated shaped oviform vase, incised Marinot, 13.5cm. high. (Christie's) $5,095 £2,800

Galle cameo glass vase with teardrop body, signed, circa 1900, 26cm. high. (Sotheby's Belgravia) $1,245 £700

Iridescent glass vase attributed to Loetz, circa 1900, 24.74cm. high. (Sotheby's Belgravia) $925 £520

Cameo fire-polished double baluster vase with milky amber ground, 23.2cm. high. (Christie's) $1,365 £750

527

Late 19th century minia-
ture Tiffany blue irides-
cent vase of baluster
form, 2¾in. high, signed.
(Robert W. Skinner Inc.)
$350 £195

Legras winter landscape
cameo vase of square
section, signed, 11cm.
high. (Phillips)
$535 £300

Early 20th century gold
iridescent vase by Tif-
fany, New York, 3½in.
high. (Robert W. Skin-
ner Inc.) $425 £235

Galle cameo glass 'land-
scape' vase of tapering
cylindrical form, signed,
25cm. high. (Phillips)
$1,005 £560

Loetz iridescent glass
vase with flared neck
decorated with silver
and pale blue banding,
signed, 20cm. high.
(Phillips) $715 £400

Late 19th/early 20th
century Webb cameo
glass vase in blues and
white, 13in. high.
(Robert W. Skinner
Inc.) $3,900 £2,180

Late 19th century peach-
blow vase with coral
decoration, 12in. high.
(Robert W. Skinner Inc.)
$250 £140

Lalique vivid turquoise
glass vase moulded
with budgerigars, signed,
25.5cm. high. (Phillips)
$1,970 £1,100

Galle cameo glass vase,
signed, circa 1910,
12in. high. (Robert W.
Skinner Inc.)$850 £480

Walter pate-de-verre
vase by Henri Berge,
circa 1920, 18cm.
high. (Sotheby, King
& Chasemore)
$3,050   £1,650

Loetz iridescent glass vase
of compressed form with
silver coloured metal rim,
10.5cm. high. (Phillips)
$785 £440

Moss agate vase by
Steuben, Corning,
New York, circa 1920,
10¾in. high. (Robert
W. Skinner Ltd.)
$800   £445

Large late 19th/early
20th century Galle cameo
glass vase, 23¼in. high.
(Robert W. Skinner Inc.)
$825 £460

Daum cameo glass vase of
goblet shape with three
petals at rim, signed,
15cm. high. (Phillips)
$1,215 £680

Daum cameo glass vase of
tall slender shape, applied
with white wheel-cut with
flowers, 33.5cm. high, signed. (Phillips)$1,255 £700

Early 20th century
etched and cut glass
vase with flaring top
and bottom. (Robert
W. Skinner Inc.)
$1,150 £650

Webb 'ivory' cameo glass
baluster vase in Oriental
style, circa 1890, 14cm.
high. (Christie's)
$1,200 £650

Late 19th century blue
iridescent glass vase by
Tiffany, New York,
11¾in. high. (Robert W.
Skinner Inc.)$975 £545

Unfinished cameo glass vase by J. B. Hill, signed, 1918, 11cm. high. (Sotheby's Belgravia) $290 £154

Late 19th century cameo glass vase of globular form with short clear glass neck, 5.7cm. high. (Sotheby's Belgravia) $185 £99

Yellow and black cameo vase with flared mouth, 10cm. high. (Sotheby's Belgravia) $625 £330

One of a pair of green overlay vases with ovoid bodies, circa 1850, 35.8cm. high. (Sotheby's Belgravia) $1,225 £649

Daum cameo glass vase of compressed conical shape, signed, 18.5cm. high. (Phillips) $930 £520

French cameo glass vase, signed A. Delatte Nancy, circa 1925, 15in. high. (Sotheby Beresford Adams) $775 £420

Double overlay cameo vase with flared neck, 1880's, 11.7cm. high. (Sotheby's Belgravia) $580 £308

Unusual French iron and glass lamp in the form of a flower, signed Roby, Paris, circa 1900, 60cm. high. (Sotheby, King & Chasemore) $275 £150

One of a pair of opaline enamelled vases with flared necks, circa 1880, 46cm. high. (Sotheby's Belgravia) $705 £374

Early 20th century Quezal iridescent Art Glass vase, New York, 12½in. high. (Robert W. Skinner Inc.) $550 £310

Lalique opalescent vase with flat flared rim, France, circa 1925, 9in. high. (Robert W. Skinner Inc.) $375 £210

Unusual early 20th century unfinished chinoiserie cameo glass vase in Art Nouveau style, 10cm. high. (Sotheby's Belgravia) $310 £165

Eastern United States tall cut glass vase with ruffled rim, circa 1890, 16in. high. (Robert W. Skinner Inc.) $325 £185

Daum 'Winterscape' cameo glass vase of ovoid form, 11.5cm. high, signed. (Phillips) $535 £300

Late 19th century American cranberry overlay cut glass vase with scalloped top, 10in. high. (Robert W. Skinner Inc.) $200 £110

Late 19th century cameo glass vase with pear-shaped body and flared neck, 11.7cm. high. (Sotheby's Belgravia) $580 £308

One of a pair of portrait overlay vases, covers and stands, mid 19th century, 63cm. high. (Sotheby's Belgravia) $3,015 £1,595

One of a pair of mid 19th century enamelled grey glass vases, with shouldered ovoid bodies, 41.4cm. high. (Sotheby's Belgravia) $205 £110

531

One of a set of twelve late 19th century two-colour brilliant cut champagne glasses, American, 4½in. high. (Robert W. Skinner Inc.)   **$600 £340**

Beilby Masonic firing glass, ogee bowl enamelled in white and iron-red, circa 1770, 8cm. high. (Christie's) **$1,565 £900**

One of four late 19th century two-colour cut glass wine glasses, American, 4½in. high. (Robert W. Skinner Inc.)**$850 £480**

Engraved colour twist wine glass, ogee bowl with border of fruiting vine, circa 1770, 15cm. high. (Christie's) **$275 £150**

Mixed twist wine glass with waisted bucket bowl, on conical foot, circa 1760, 17cm. high. (Christie's) **$240 £130**

Beilby opaque twist wine glass, funnel bowl enamelled in white, circa 1765, 15.5cm. high. (Christie's) **$890 £480**

Facet stemmed dated wine glass with inscribed bowl, 1752, 16cm. high. (Christie's)   **$110 £60**

Mead glass with bucket bowl having gadrooned lower part, circa 1715, 15cm. high. (Christie's) **$480 £260**

Beilby opaque twist wine glass, funnel bowl enamelled in white, circa 1765, 15cm. high. (Christie's) **$925 £500**

One of ten American cut glass wine glasses with knopped stems, circa 1910, 4in. high.(Robert W. Skinner Inc.)$75 £45

Heavy baluster toast-master's glass with thick funnel bowl, circa 1700, 13.5cm. high.(Christie's) $260 £140

One of four late 19th cen-tury American two-colour cranberry cut glass wine glasses, 5in. high.(Robert W. Skinner Inc.) $250 £140

Balustroid wine glass of drawn trumpet shape, circa 1745, 16cm. high. (Christie's) $165 £90

Opaque twist champagne glass with double ogee bowl, circa 1770, 15.5cm. high. (Christie's) $275 £150

Dutch engraved wine glass on inverted baluster stem, circa 1740, 17cm. high. (Christie's) $295 £160

One of six late 19th cen-tury American green over-lay cut glass liqueur glasses, 5¼in. high, on long stems. (Robert W. Skinner Inc.) $175 £100

Baluster wine glass with bell bowl supported on a cushion knop, circa 1720, 16cm. high. (Christie's) $370 £200

Lynn opaque twist wine glass, funnel bowl moul-ded with horizontal ribs, circa 1770, 14.5cm. high. (Christie's) $260 £140

GLASS

One of a rare set of six wine glasses with round funnel bowls, 14cm. high. (Phillips) $665 £360

One of a set of six wine glasses with bell bowls, 17cm. high. (Phillips) $1,110 £600

Baluster deceptive glass with thick trumpet bowl, circa 1710, 5in. high. (Sotheby's) $450 £242

Engraved air-twist wine glass of Jacobite significance, circa 1750, 15cm. high. (Christie's)$390 £210

Opaque twist cordial glass, funnel bowl with hammered flutes, on conical foot, circa 1765, 16cm. high.(Christie's) $185 £100

Air-twist Jacobite wine glass of drawn trumpet shape, bowl engraved with a rose, circa 1750, 16.5cm. high.(Christie's) $220 £120

Beilby enamelled wine glass with petal-moulded bowl, circa 1770, 5in. high. (Sotheby's) $825 £440

One of a rare set of six slender toasting glasses on conical feet, 19cm. high. (Phillips) $1,390 £750

Engraved cordial wine glass with small funnel bowl, circa 1750, 6¾in. high. (Sotheby's) $165 £88

Baluster wine glass of dark
brilliant metal on domed
and folded foot, circa 1700,
5¾in. high. (Sotheby's)
$780 £418

17th century Lowlands
diamond Facon de Venise,
wine glass, 14cm. high.
(Sotheby's) $185 £99

Dutch-engraved Newcastle
glass decorated in the manner of Jacob Sang, circa
1745-55, 7½in. high.
(Sotheby's)$1,440 £770

Colour-twist wine glass with
funnel bowl, on conical foot,
circa 1770, 15.5cm. high.
(Christie's) $370 £200

Jacobite wine glass with
engraved flared bowl, circa
1750, 7in. high.
(Sotheby's) $575 £308

Colour-twist wine glass
with waisted bucket
bowl, circa 1770, 5¾in.
high. (Sotheby's)
$945 £506

Wine glass with cylinder
knop, circa 1700, 6in.
high, with flared bowl.
(Sotheby's)$2,055 £1,100

Cordial glass with small
bucket bowl, circa 1770,
7in. high, with corkscrew
stem. (Sotheby's)$195 £104

Chinoiserie wine glass
with ogee bowl, on
facet-cut stem, circa
1780, 6in. high.
(Sotheby's)$245 £132

WINE GLASSES

Commemorative 'Hano-
verian' wine glass, inscribed Liberty, circa 1750,
6¾in. high. (Sotheby's)
$615 £330

Enamelled ale glass, painted with hops and barley,
circa 1760, 18.2cm. high.
(Sotheby, King & Chase-
more) $270 £150

Tartan-twist wine glass
with bell bowl, circa
1770, 17.5cm. high.
(Christie's) $890 £480

Cordial with small flared
bowl on a double-series
opaque-twist shank, 7in.
high, circa 1760.
(Sotheby's) $305 £165

Colour-twist wine glass
with ribbed funnel bowl,
circa 1770, 5¾in. high.
(Sotheby's) $905 £484

Flute with slim funnel
bowl on opaque-twist
stem, circa 1760, 7¾in.
high. (Sotheby's)
$225 £121

One of a set of four Tif-
fany Favrile glass wine
glasses, signed, 19.5cm.
high. (Phillips)$965 £540
536

Engraved Beilby wine
glass, circa 1770, 4½in.
high. (Anderson & Gar-
land) $3,130 £1,700

Late 16th/early 17th cen-
tury Venetian 'cristallo'
goblet with bell bowl,
17.5cm. high.(Christie's)
$1,295 £700

Jacobite cordial glass of drawn-trumpet type with engraved bowl, circa 1750, 6¼in. high. (Sotheby's) $535 £286

Unusual stirrup glass, early 18th century, 6¼in. high. (Sotheby's) $185 £99

Incise-twist wine glass, circa 1750, 18.5cm. high. (Sotheby, King & Chasemore)$150 £85

Cordial glass with rounded funnel bowl, 7in. high, circa 1750. (Sotheby's) $115 £60

Wine glass with ogee bowl on multi-spiral opaque-twist stem, circa 1760, 6¾in. high. (Sotheby's) $140 £77

Colour-twist wine glass with drawn-trumpet bowl, circa 1770, 6in. high. (Sotheby's) $825 £440

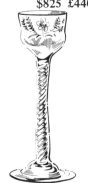

Dutch engraved wine glass, Friesia, circa 1740, 15cm. high, on folded conical foot. (Christie's) $370 £200

Tartan-twist wine glass with bell bowl and corkscrew core, on conical foot, circa 1770, 16cm. high. (Christie's) $460 £250

Engraved cordial glass with ribbed ogee bowl, circa 1760, 6¼in. high. (Sotheby's) $185 £99

537

French two-colour gold
and tortoiseshell pow-
der box, Paris, 1789-
92, 6.1cm. diam.
(Sotheby's)
$1,805 £935

18ct. gold engine-turned snuff
box by Daniel Hockly, London,
1819, 3in. long. (Christie's)
$1,480 £800

Victorian gold apple
pomander with leaf
ring lid, 1½in. high.
(Woolley & Wallis)
$595 £330

14ct. yellow gold mesh purse
with engraved frame, cabo-
chon garnet clasp and a pencil
attached to side. (Robert W.
Skinner Inc.) $800 £435

Gold mounted whip,
handle formed as a
swan's head, 19th
century, sold with
another. (Christie's)
$480 £259

18ct. French Art Deco
gold powder compact
by Chaumet, 1923, 3¼in.
long. (Christie's)
$1,415 £750

Louis XVI oval gold and enamel snuff box by Joseph
Etienne Blerzy, Paris, 1776,
3¼in. wide. (Christie's)
$20,790 £11,000

Early 19th century
French gold moun-
ted glass scent bot-
tle, 3.2cm. wide.
(Sotheby's)
$235 £121

19th century Swiss diamond
set rectangular gold snuff
box, 3½in. long. (Christie's)
$3,535 £1,870

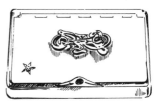

Gold buckle by Myer Myers, New York, circa 1765. (Sotheby's) $10,000 £5,375

Gold and hardstone necessaire of rectangular form, circa 1760, 5cm. high, restored. (Sotheby's) $3,395 £1,760

Gold cigarette case by Faberge, St. Petersburg, 1899-1908, 8.7cm. wide. (Sotheby's) $2,760 £1,485

9ct. gold guard chain with four girdled links, 22cm. long overall. (Sotheby Beresford Adams) $280 £150

Large gold mounted scent bottle, probably Portuguese, 5in. long, circa 1780. (Christie's) $660 £350

9ct. gold vesta case, Birmingham, 1920, and an 18ct. gold and platinum guard chain, 44mm. diam. (Sotheby Beresford Adams) $205 £110

Gold Art Nouveau brooch with rose-diamonds, in the style of Boucheron, circa 1900. (Locke & England)$1,455 £800

18ct. gold mounted ornament with pink hardstone base, 21.5cm. long, 1979. (Sotheby's Belgravia) $825 £440

Oblong gold Royal presentation cigarette case, London, 1886, 3¼in. long.(Christie's) $1,230 £650

Silver gilt and hardstone snuff box, French, circa 1740, 7.7cm. wide. (Sotheby's) $610 £330

Small English gold and hardstone vinaigrette, late 18th century, ¾in. wide. (Sotheby's) $295 £165

A solid agate silver shaped sauceboat. (Christie's) $3,500 £1,800

A striated fluorspar flattened baluster vase and cover with dragon finial, 14cm. high. (Christie's) $1,150 £600

Guangxu hardstone flowering shrub in cloisonne jardiniere, 61cm. high. (Sotheby's Belgravia) $725 £396

George III circular gold mounted grey agate toilet box and cover, circa 1800, 5in. high.(Christie's) $7,485 £3,960

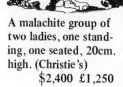

Solid agate pectin shell teapot and cover, 16cm. high. (Christie's) $1,250 £650

Early 20th century Austrian or Hungarian agate bon bon dish with gem-set mounts, 9.1cm. diam. (Sotheby's Belgravia) $745 £396

A malachite group of two ladies, one standing, one seated, 20cm. high. (Christie's) $2,400 £1,250

18th century rhinoceros horn libation cup with handle, 15.5cm. wide. (Christie's) $575 £320

Guangxu carved rhinoceros horn on rosewood stand, 55cm. wide. (Sotheby's Belgravia) $790 £440

19th century Japanese rhinoceros horn cup in the shape of a lily pad, 5¾in. long. (Robert W. Skinner Inc.) $1,400 £755

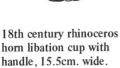

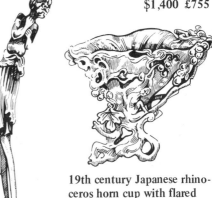

18th century rhinoceros horn bowl of honey colour, 18cm. wide. (Christie's) $810 £450

19th century Japanese rhinoceros horn cup with flared rim, 4in. high. (Robert W. Skinner Inc.) $1,550 £865

Good stagshorn sashi netsuke showing Ashinaga, signed Isshin. (Sotheby's)$605 £330

17th century rhinoceros horn libation cup carved with dragons, 17cm. wide. (Christie's) $470 £260

19th century carved horn, pierced with immortals amongst trees, on rosewood stand, 74cm. wide.(Sotheby's Belgravia) $845 £462

19th century Japanese rhinoceros horn cup with flaring top, 4in. high. (Robert W. Skinner Inc.) $800 £430

Icon of the Palekh School 'The Resurrection and Descent into Hell', circa 1800, 35.5cm. high. (Christie's) $1,310 £702

18th century Palekh School icon 'The Old Testament Trinity', 31.3cm. high. (Christie's) $1,920 £1,026

Russian icon 'Christ Pantocrator', dated 1870, 31.2cm. high.(Christie's) $1,110 £594

Late 17th century Russian icon 'The Apostles Peter and Paul', 31.2cm. high. (Christie's) $1,515 £820

Russian icon 'The Saviour', by Vladimirov, 1908-17, 32.1cm. high. (Christie's)$2,020 £1,080

17th century Central Russian icon of Saints Samon, Gury, Aviv and Simeon the Stylite, 31.3cm. high. (Christie's) $970 £518

17th century Russian icon 'Birth of the Virgin', 28.1cm. high. (Christie's) $1,415 £756

18th century Russian iconostasis panel 'The Evangelist St. Matthew', 53.5cm. high.(Christie's) $1,715 £918

18th century Central Russian icon 'The Virgin of Smolensk', 31.2cm. high. (Christie's) $1,415 £756

19th century Russian icon of St. Nicholas, 101cm. high. (Christie's) $2,625 £1,404

19th century Russian menological icon for the month of July, 41.5cm. high. (Christie's) $1,310 £702

17th century icon 'The Virgin of Kazan' on ivory ground, 33cm. high. (Christie's) $3,435 £1,836

17th century Russian icon 'St. Nicholas' shown shoulder-high, 31cm. high. (Christie's) $765 £410

19th century Palekh School icon 'The Resurrection and Descent into Hell', 34.1cm. high.(Christie's)$1,415 £756

11th/13th Byzantine steatite showing a representation of Hodegitria Virgin, 9cm. high.(Christie's) $1,615 £864

Moscow School icon 'The Metropolitan Philip' holding the Gospels, circa 1700, 32cm. high.(Christie's) $1,310 £702

17th century North Russian iconostasis panel 'The Apostle Peter', 94cm. high. (Christie's)$1,615 £864

19th century Russian icon 'The Virgin of Kazan', circa 1900, 31.5cm. high. (Christie's) $2,725 £1,458

Small 19th century inro of two cases, carved in low relief, unsigned, slightly cracked.(Sotheby's) $545 £297

Single-case inro of natural wood, decorated in coloured takamakie, signed Toshi. (Sotheby's) $530 £297

Small 18th century three-case inro decorated with butterflies among plants, unsigned. (Sotheby's) $560 £300

Small 18th century five-case inro decorated in gold and silver takamakie, chipped, unsigned. (Sotheby's) $820 £440

18th century four-case inro decorated with travellers in a boat, unsigned.(Sotheby's) $705 £380

Late 18th century small four-case inro of cylindrical form, unsigned. (Sotheby's) $370 £200

Very good five-case inro of tall shape, decorated with gold takamakie, signed Kajikawa Bunryusai. (Sotheby's) $3,640 £2,035

Small late 18th/early 19th century two-case inro decorated in pewter, unsigned. (Sotheby's)$315 £170

19th century Hirado porcelain inro of four cases, unmarked. (Sotheby's)$550 £308

19th century three-case inro of wood, carved with two panels, unsigned, sold with a wood netsuke. (Sotheby's) $325 £176

18th century single-case inro of wide oval shape, brown-ground decorated with shell-gatherers, unsigned.(Sotheby's) $590 £330

Four-case inro of dark-brown-ground with falling cherry blossoms, signed Inagawa saku. (Sotheby's)$985 £550

Late 18th century gold lacquer inro of five cases, decorated in gold takamakie, hiramakie and kirigane, unsigned. (Sotheby's) $745 £400

Unusual 18th century three-case inro of gold and black lacquer, unsigned. (Sotheby's) $630 £352

Four-case inro of roun-ded form, signed Shokosai, slight chips. (Sotheby's)$690 £374

Early 18th century four-case inro decorated with three sages, unsig-ned. (Sotheby's) $325 £176

Unusual two-case inro deco-rated with fish and waves, chipped, signed Kyukoku with kakihan. (Sotheby's) $985 £550

Four-case inro, signed Kajikawa saku with red pot seal.(Sotheby's) $590 £330

INSTRUMENTS

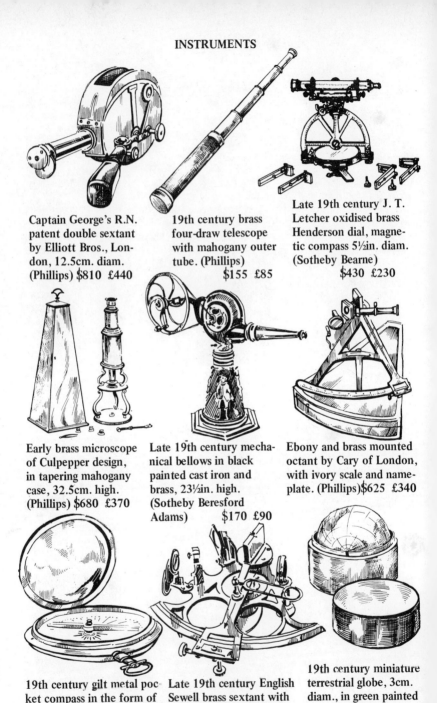

Captain George's R.N. patent double sextant by Elliott Bros., London, 12.5cm. diam. (Phillips) $810 £440

19th century brass four-draw telescope with mahogany outer tube. (Phillips) $155 £85

Late 19th century J. T. Letcher oxidised brass Henderson dial, magnetic compass 5½in. diam. (Sotheby Bearne) $430 £230

Early brass microscope of Culpepper design, in tapering mahogany case, 32.5cm. high. (Phillips) $680 £370

Late 19th century mechanical bellows in black painted cast iron and brass, 23½in. high. (Sotheby Beresford Adams) $170 £90

Ebony and brass mounted octant by Cary of London, with ivory scale and nameplate. (Phillips) $625 £340

19th century gilt metal pocket compass in the form of a watch by Webb, London, 5.5cm. diam. (Phillips) $90 £48

Late 19th century English Sewell brass sextant with silvered scale and vernier, 8½in. radius. (Sotheby Beresford Adams) $160 £85

19th century miniature terrestrial globe, 3cm. diam., in green painted cylindrical case and cover. (Phillips) $295 £160

Mid 19th century post-mortem set, inscribed Place & Co., in fitted mahogany case. (Sotheby Beresford Adams) $230 £125

19th century six-draw monocular telescope by I. Abraham, Bath, outer tube inlaid with mother-of-pearl. (Phillips) $155 £85

Brass box sextant by Elliot Bros., in drum-shaped case, 7.5cm. high. (Phillips) $165 £90

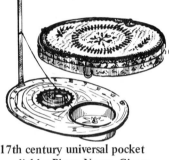

19th century Russian universal equinoctial dial by Mills of Petersberg, 9.5cm. (Phillips) $535 £290

17th century universal pocket sundial by Pierre Norry, Gisors, 7cm. long, in original tooled leather case. (Phillips) $3,130 £1,700

Mahogany terrestrial globe by E. Stanford, dated 1878, 23in. diam. (Sotheby's Belgravia) $1,655 £900

Early 19th century brass theodolite of small size, by W. & S. Jones, London. (Phillips) $1,215 £660

17th century ivory German diptych dial, dated 1650, with the trade mark of Leonhardt Mire of Nuremberg. (Phillips) $3,405 £1,850

Mid 19th century English pocket sextant by W. & S. Jones, 3in. diam. (Sotheby Beresford Adams) $215 £115

Early 20th century French brass sextant, inscribed A. J. Fortier, Havre, 9½in. radius. (Sotheby's) $355 £187

Early 19th century brass plotting protractor, signed Troughton, London, 16cm. diam. (Phillips) $390 £210

Early 19th century American scrimshaw jagging wheel in the form of a horse's head, 6in. long. (Robert W. Skinner Inc.) $550 £300

17th/18th century surgeon's iron brace with turned head, 8½in. long. (Christie's S. Kensington)$1,080 £580

Marconiphone television model 705, 1940's, 36¾in. wide, in walnut veneered cabinet with hinged lid. (Sotheby's Belgravia) $480 £260

Right hand precision bench lathe by F. Lorche on cast iron frame. (Sotheby's) $320 £170

Victorian brass monocular microscope. (Cooper Hirst) $290 £160

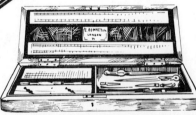

Set of brass drawing instruments by Rowney & Co., with boxwood and ivory rules, 25.5cm. wide. (Phillips) $100 £55

Rare 2¾in. 'Silex Multiplier' spinning reel, stamped D.W., with ebonite handle. (Sotheby's)$455 £242

Late 18th century microscope specimen slicer in original mahogany box, by A. Cumming, London, (H. Spencer & Sons Ltd.) $4,185 £2,300

Unusual narrow-drum 'perfect' trout reel of aluminium and brass, marked Hardy Bros. Alnwick. (Sotheby's) $415 £219

Electric fan heater, designed by Wells Coates, 1930's, 29.5cm. high. (Sotheby's Belgravia) $195 £110

Late 19th century Adco false tooth vulcanizer with cast iron shell, 24¾in. high. (Sotheby's)$145 £77

Mid 19th century monocular microscope in fitted mahogany case, 13in. high, with two boxes of slides. (Sotheby's) $185 £99

Columbian printing press with cast iron caduceus frame, eagle and dolphin counterweight, 1820, 91in. high. (Sotheby's Belgravia)$5,150 £2,800

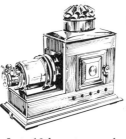

French drum microscope, inscribed Nachet, Paris, circa 1850, 9in. high. (Sotheby's) $165 £88

Late 19th century mahogany and brass magic lantern with tinplate chimney above. (Sotheby's) $270 £143

Late 19th century mechanical bellows of black painted iron construction, 20in. high. (Sotheby's) $250 £132

INSTRUMENTS

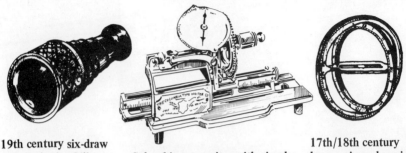

19th century six-draw monocular by Gilbert, London, with carved ivory decoration, 10cm. fully extended.(Phillips) $110 £60

Columbia typewriter with circular dial and maker's plaque at front, circa 1895, 9¾in. wide. (Sotheby's Belgravia) $1,470 £800

17th/18th century brass universal equinoctial ring dial, unsigned, 14.8cm. diam. (Phillips) $970 £520

19th century brass compound pocket microscope, unsigned, 16.3cm. wide. (Phillips) $300 £160

19th century brass Lords Patent calculator by W. Wilson, London, 32cm. square. (Phillips)$390 £210

Pocket compass by Jeremias Koglet, Danzig, 1680, 7cm. wide. (Phillips) $785 £420

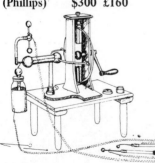

Mahogany framed plate electrical machine, unsigned, 36cm. wide. (Phillips) $505 £270

Eight-day marine chronometer by Duncan McGregor & Co., Glasgow, 145mm. diam. (Sotheby's)$3,325 £1,760

Late 19th century set of Avery scales and seven brass weights, 31in. high.(Sotheby's $270 £143

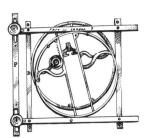

17th century brass ring dial by J. Stammer, Sacrow, 80mm. diam. (Sotheby's)
$1,560 £825

Early 19th century brass ellipsograph by Farey of London, in original case, 165mm. long.(Sotheby's)
$1,080 £572

Ferguson's terrestrial globe inscribed G. Wright, 17in. diam. (Woolley & Wallis)
$890 £480

Mid 19th century Smith & Beck brass monocular microscope, 12½in. high, in mahogany case. (Sotheby's Belgravia)
$295 £160

Columbia typewriter No. 2, circa 1885, in original wooden carrying case. (Sotheby's Belgravia)
$2,760 £1,500

Brass compound monocular microscope by Ross, London, 44.5cm. high.(Phillips)
$935 £500

8th/19th century brass Islamic celestial globe, 14mm. diam. (Sotheby's)
$2,080 £1,100

Two-day marine chronometer by Breguet & Cie, 16cm. square. (Phillips) $5,480 £2,900

Shaped ivory spy-glass with silver mounts and dust cap, 5.4cm. diam. (Phillips) $120 £65

English 2in. brass refracting telescope on stand, circa 1830, 43in. long, extended. (Sotheby's Belgravia) $250 £143

Late 19th century Swift & Son 'Paragon' binocular microscope with twin tubes. (Sotheby Bearne) $675 £360

Brass and ormolu Cupid balance on tortoiseshell and brass inlaid base, 15cm. high. (Phillips)$930 £500

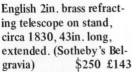

Brass monocular microscope by A. Ross, 1859, 17½in. high, in mahogany case. (Sotheby Bearne) $1,120 £600

English patent orrery by Parkes & Hadley, with papier-mache model of the earth, circa 1900, 9¾in. diam. (Sotheby's Belgravia) $220 £120

Early 20th century French oxidised brass transit theodolite by Breithaupt & Sohn, 6¾in. high.(Sotheby's Belgravia) $550 £300

Mid 19th century English telescope-microscope set in mahogany case, 7½in. long.(Sotheby's Belgravia) $405 £220

Mid 19th century Smith & Beck brass monocular microscope, 14½in. high. (Sotheby's Belgravia) $440 £240

INSTRUMENTS

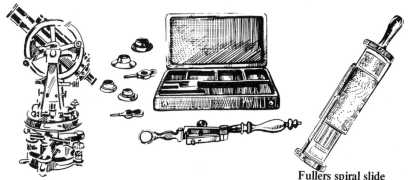

Early 20th century
Stanley oxidised brass
transit theodolite,
13¾in. high.(Sotheby's
Belgravia) $405 £220

18th century brass compass microscope with turned ivory handle, in
fishskin case, 13.5 x 9.5cm.
(Phillips) $955 £520

Fullers spiral slide
rule by W. F.
Stanley, 17in. long,
circa 1900, in
mahogany case.
(Phillips)$165 £90

Mid 19th century English amputation
set, each instrument with ivory handle,
in mahogany case, 17in. wide.
(Sotheby Beresford Adams)$315 £170

Late 19th century English mahogany
brass and steel revolution counter by
Goodbrand & Co., 31½in. wide.
(Sotheby's Belgravia) $350 £190

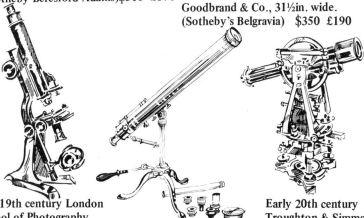

Mid 19th century London
School of Photography
brass monocular micro-
scope, 15¼in. high, in
mahogany case.(Sotheby's
Belgravia) $480 £260

Dolland 2½in. brass refracting
library telescope, mid 19th
century, 55in. long. (Sotheby,
King & Chasemore)$820 £450

Early 20th century
Troughton & Simms
oxidised brass transit
theodolite, 15in.
high. (Sotheby's
Belgravia) $440 £240

Mid 19th century Troughton & Simms brass level with 3in. diam. compass, 15in. long. (Sotheby's Belgravia) $290 £165

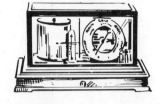

Early 20th century oak cased aneroid barometer with skeleton chapter ring, 14in. wide. (Sotheby's) $440 £231

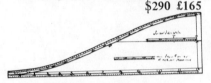

Early 19th century chart template signed James Wright, London, 13in. long. (Phillips) $1,345 £720

19th century Roth's Adding Machine, marked Wertheimber Patentee, 39cm. long. (Phillips) $485 £260

American typewriter by Merritt, No. 12095, 12¼in. wide, circa 1895, on oak base. (Sotheby's Belgravia) $1,015 £550

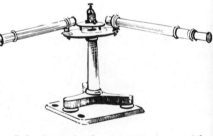

John Browning brass spectroscope with refracting prism, telescope, 15in. long. (Sotheby's Belgravia) $575 £330

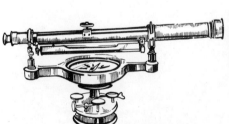

Mid 19th century brass level by F. Day, London, 19in. long, in mahogany case. (Sotheby's Belgravia) $325 £187

William's No. 2 typewriter with grass-hopper mechanism, circa 1894, 14½in. long. (Sotheby's Belgravia) $515 £280

Steelyard letter scale with brass beam, circa 1840, 13in. high overall. (Sotheby's) $335 £176

George III swan-necked beam scale with wooden overhead platform and a 19¾in. wooden yard. (Eldon E. Worrall & Co.) $330 £180

Mahogany and brass spirit level by J. Pallant, London, 2ft. long. (Phillips) $255 £140

Georgian brass camera Lucida by Watkins & Hill, London, with table screw and clamp. (Phillips)$205 £110

Early 19th century 2½in. James Watson brass Gregorian reflecting telescope on stand, 11in. long. (Sotheby's Belgravia) $810 £462

Unusual early 20th century set of four graduated brass beam scales. (Sotheby's Belgravia) $385 £220

Early 20th century brass Post Office letter scale, 10in. long, with five weights. (Sotheby's) $250 £140

Roberval type brass letter scale by S. Mordan & Co., circa 1871, 8½in. long. (Sotheby's) $110 £62

Cast iron stove finished in vitreous enamel, circa 1940, 20in. wide. (Sotheby's) $85 £44

Iron group of two horses by P. J. Mene, signed, 21in. long. (Sotheby, King & Chasemore) $1,675 £900

Late 19th century Komai iron box and cover, inlaid with gold and silver, 9cm. high. (Sotheby's Belgravia) $975 £506

Rare 17th century German miniature iron sword pommel of Hercules and the Hydra, 5.5cm. high.(Christie's) $2,110 £1,100

Komai inlaid iron incense chest with inlaid panels, circa 1900, 8cm. high. (Sotheby's Belgravia) $850 £440

One of a pair of mid 19th century cast iron garden urns of campana form, 30in. high. (Sotheby's) $1,045 £550

French cast iron stove finished in mid brown vitreous enamel, circa 1920, 20in. square. (Sotheby's) $85 £44

Early 18th century American wrought iron pipe kiln, 13½in. long. (Robert W. Skinner Inc.) $350 £190

17th century iron strong box, 30in. wide. (J. M. Welch & Son) $1,365 £750

Early 19th century steel footman, pierced with scroll and star design, 14½in. high. (Lawrence Fine Art) $165 £90

Late 19th century cast iron Victorian doll's house fencing, 6in. long, four sections. (Robert W. Skinner Inc.) $275 £155

18th century pair of French steel and brass cresset spit dogs, 28in. high. (Robert W. Skinner Inc.) $200 £110

Iron model of a pointer after Mene, 7½in. high. (Sotheby, King & Chasemore) $445 £240

One of a pair of 15th/16th century wrought iron pricket candlesticks, 19in. high. (Christie's) $840 £460

Iron group of a cow and suckling bullock, 8¾in. wide. (Sotheby, King & Chasemore) $145 £80

Salamandre cast iron stove finished in mid green vitreous enamel, circa 1900, 23½in. wide. (Sotheby's) $250 £132

Late 17th century iron 'Armada' chest with key, 3ft.7in. wide. (J. M. Welch & Son) $875 £480

Iron model of an ostrich, 3¼in. high. (Sotheby, King & Chasemore) $100 £55

Mid 19th century French ivory group of two children, on gilt metal base, 9.5cm. high. (Sotheby's Belgravia) $455 £242

Carved ivory bird catcher, Japanese, circa 1900, 10¾in. long, slightly cracked. (Robert W. Skinner Inc.) $625 £335

Japanese carved ivory figure of a peasant, 12¼in. high, unsigned, circa 1900.(Sotheby's) $1,000 £528

Mid 19th century French ivory figure of a tinker carrying a basket, 13.8cm. high. (Sotheby's Belgravia) $745 £396

Large mid 19th century French ivory group of Bacchus and two nymphs and three children, 30cm. long. (Sotheby's Belgravia) $8,270 £4,400

Mid/late 19th century German ivory standing cup and cover carved with hunting scenes, 49.5cm. high.(Sotheby's Belgravia) $4,135 £2,200

Early 19th century teak and ivory crucifix, 28½in. long. (Robert W. Skinner Inc.) $350 £190

Rare 19th century English chess set in red and natural, 4.5cm. to 10cm. high. (Sotheby's Belgravia) $745 £396

Mid 17th century Flemish ivory group of a woman and two children. (Sotheby's) $26,880 £14,000

One of a pair of 19th century Dieppe ivory candlesticks on circular bases, 9in. high. (Christie's) $890 £480

French ivory group of Venus and Cupid, 1870's, 24.7cm. long. (Sotheby's Belgravia) $660 £352

Japanese carved ivory figure of a peasant, circa 1900, 8¾in. high. (Sotheby's) $330 £176

Dieppe ivory figure of a young girl feeding doves and farmyard animals, circa 1895, 14cm. high. (Sotheby's Belgravia) $1,200 £638

Late 19th century French carved ivory figure of Cupid, 16cm. high. (Sotheby's Belgravia) $785 £418

Late 19th century carved figure of a naked nymph, 18.5cm. high. (Sotheby's Belgravia) $455 £242

Ivory tankard with silver gilt mounts, 17th century, 28.5cm. high. (Sotheby's Belgravia) $3,720 £1,980

One of a pair of late 19th century figures of Courtiers, 9.5cm. high. (Sotheby's Belgravia) $660 £352

Chinese stained ivory group of a fourteen-armed female Boddhisattva, late 19th century, 65.5cm. high. (Christie's) $2,880 £1,600

559

Good ivory figure of a
cook, signed Homin
with kakihan.
(Sotheby's) $335 £180

Late 18th/early 19th century
ivory study of a monkey
seated on a large gunsen
uchiwa, unsigned.
(Sotheby's) $780 £420

Ivory figure of a young
child by F. Preiss, in-
scribed, 9cm. high.
(Christie's) $615 £330

19th century Japanese carved ivory flowering narcis-
sus bulbs, signed, slightly
damaged, 7¾in. high.
(Robert W. Skinner Inc.)
                $260 £140

Fine 19th century French
ivory oliphant carved with
portraits of kings, 69cm.
long. (H. Spencer & Sons
Ltd.) $630   £340

Attractive ivory group of
four boys, signed, circa
1880-90, 3in. high.
(Sotheby, King & Chase-
more) $575 £310

17th century German ivory
statuette of the infant Bacchus, 16cm. high.
(Christie's) $1,585 £825

19th century Japanese carved
ivory basket vendor, with inlay decoration, 7¼in. high.
(Robert W. Skinner Inc.)
          $1,000 £545

17th century Goanese
ivory statuette of the
sleeping Christ Child on
carved base, 38.5cm.
high. (Christie's)
          $1,690 £880

18th century Austrian rococo ivory half-length statuette on boxwood base, 15cm. high. (Christie's)$1,690 £880

Ivory model 'Thoughts', carved from a model by F. Preiss, on green and black onyx base, 15.8cm. high. (Christie's) $2,675 £1,430

Good Komezawa ivory figure of Hotei, signed, 4in. high. (Sotheby, King & Chasemore) $670 £360

18th century ivory figure of Gama Sennin, of the Kyoto school, unsigned. (Sotheby's) $355 £190

One of a pair of late 19th century carved ivory figures of goddesses, 8¾in. high. (Sotheby Beresford Adams) $620 £280

One of a pair of early 20th century Chinese carved ivory goddesses, 12¼in. high. (Robert W. Skinner Inc.) $575 £315

Ivory group of Ebisu, holding a large carp, 5¼in. high, circa 1900. (Sotheby, King & Chasemore) $595 £320

Early 18th century Dutch ivory handled carving knife and fork with steel blades. (Sotheby's) $570 £308

18th century French or German ivory group of a satyr abducting a nymph, 16cm. high. (Christie's)$1,585 £825

Ivory okimono of a rat and some nuts, circa 1900, 3in. high.(Sotheby's) $250 £132

Anglo-Indian coromandel-wood workbox inlaid with ivory, circa 1830, 15in. wide. (Sotheby, King & Chasemore) $345 £190

20th century ivory figure of a horse on a rectangular base, 36cm. wide.(Sotheby's Belgravia) $680 £352

Early 18th century Northern French ivory snuff rasp carved in relief, 7½in. high. (Sotheby's) $455 £242

Flemish ivory group of the Virgin and Child and St. John, circa 1650, 12½in. high. (Sotheby's) $29,105 £15,400

17th century Flemish ivory crucifix figure, 16¼in. high. (Sotheby's) $2,600 £1,375

Early 20th century ivory figure of an Immortal with a fishing rod, 34cm. high. (Sotheby's Belgravia) $300 £154

Pair of 18th century North Italian fruitwood and ivory Commedia Dell'Arte figures, 11in. high. (Sotheby's) $2,910 £1,540

One of a set of four 17th/18th century ivory carvings of bearded Daoist immortals, 28cm. high. (Christie's)$2,015 £1,045

Small ivory group of Kanzan and Jittoku with good detail, signed Yoshitomo. (Sotheby's)
$345 £187

German ivory snuff box of cartouche shape, circa 1730, with silver mounts, 7.8cm. wide. (Sotheby's)
$1,320 £715

Small early 19th century ivory netsuke of a dog with a large ball, unsigned. (Sotheby's)
$345 £187

Ivory figure of a nude young woman, inscribed F. Preiss, 23cm. high. (Christie's)
$2,015 £1,100

Early 18th century ivory head of one of the Three Fates, inspired by Michelangelo, mounted as a seal. (Sotheby's)
$580 £308

Unusual Guangxu ivory acrobatic group of four articulated figures, 12.5cm. high. (Sotheby's Belgravia)
$320 £165

Indian ivory carving of a female divinity, circa 1900, 9in. high. (Sotheby's)
$375 £198

Early 18th century Franco-Flemish ivory river god, plinth of brass inlaid with bone. (Sotheby's)
$3,430 £1,815

19th century engraved scrimshaw whale's tooth, 7in. high.(Robert W. Skinner Inc.)
$300 £165

18th century pale celadon jade bowl with dragon head handles, 22cm. wide. (Christie's) $15,760 £8,250

18th century mottled white jade pebble carved as a deer, with wood stand, 9cm. wide. (Christie's) $3,990 £2,090

Rare Shang/Western Zhou dynasty jade deer pendant of flattened form, 4.1cm. long. (Sotheby's) $4,320 £2,310

Han dynasty jade carving of a pig of flattened cylindrical form, 11.2cm. long. (Sotheby's) $3,085 £1,650

Mottled celadon and brown jade rectangular table screen, wood stand, 21.2cm. wide. (Christie's) $945 £495

18th century pale jade cylindrical brush-holder, carved in cameo, 11.5cm. high. (Christie's) $10,085 £5,280

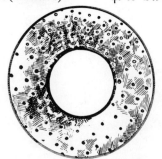

Zhou dynasty archaic celadon and brown jade disc carved on each side, 13.5cm. diam. (Christie's) $1,680 £880

Late Ming dynasty greyish celadon jade mythical beast, wood stand, 10cm. long. (Christie's) $840 £440

Small Ming dynasty mottled jade group of a horse and a monkey, 6cm. long. (Christie's) $5,885 £3,080

Pale celadon jade bowl carved with dragons, with inverted rim, 1774, 15.5cm. diam. (Christie's) $18,910 £9,900

Western Zhou dynasty green jade fish pendant with incised eyes, 4.2cm. long. (Sotheby's) $660 £352

Song dynasty pale celadon and mottled brown jade figure of a tiger, with wood stand, 6.9cm. long. (Christie's) $3,360 £1,760

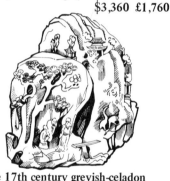

Late 18th century celadon jade chrysanthemum pierced bowl and cover, 14.5cm. wide. (Christie's) $2,100 £1,100

Large 17th century greyish-celadon jade boulder carved and pierced in high relief, 31.3cm. high. (Christie's) $14,705 £7,700

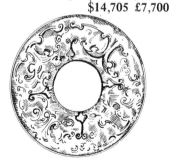

19th century yellowish celadon jade group carved and pierced as three peaches, 9cm. wide. (Christie's) $840 £440

Zhou dynasty pale celadon jade disc carved on both sides, 15.5cm. diam. (Christie's) $1,785 £935

Oval ruby and diamond cluster ring in white gold setting. (Hy. Duke & Son) $715 £370

Gold and diamond brooch/pendant of scroll form, set with six diamonds and a centre pearl. (Robert W. Skinner Inc.) $325 £175

Two row diamond set crescent brooch, in graduated sizes. (Geering & Colyer)
$1,655 £900

Victorian gold and enamel bangle bracelet, ½in. wide, 21gm. (Robert W. Skinner Inc.)
$275 £150

Diamond and platinum circle pin set with eighteen round and eighteen baguette diamonds. (Robert W. Skinner Inc.)
$1,800 £980

Arts and Crafts pendant possibly by Professor Joseph A. Hodel, 1.5cm. across. (Phillips)
$145 £80

Gold vari-coloured enamelled openwork pendant with pearl tassel fringe, by Carlo Giuliano. (Christie's S. Kensington)
$1,955 £1,050

Strand of sapphire beads with 14 carat white gold clasp, 18½in. long. (Robert W. Skinner Inc.)$525 £285

Art Nouveau silver plique-a-jour pearl pendant, French, on silver chain. (Robert W. Skinner Inc.) $800 £435

Square emerald set with diamond surrounds in 18 carat white gold. (Honiton Galleries) $5,550 £3,000

Oval sapphire and diamond cluster ring in white gold setting. (Hy. Duke & Son) $655 £340

Two-colour gold set fire opal, diamond, sapphire, emerald and ruby crested kingfisher brooch by Cartier, signed. (Geering & Colyer) $1,610 £875

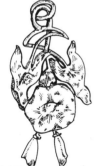

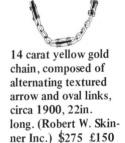

Diamond and baguette diamond openwork plaque bracelet. (Christie's S. Kensington) $4,230 £2,300

Diamond and platinum bracelet set with sixteen round diamonds. (Robert W. Skinner Inc.) $750 £405

14 carat yellow gold chain, composed of alternating textured arrow and oval links, circa 1900, 22in. long. (Robert W. Skinner Inc.) $275 £150

Art Nouveau pearl and enamel pendant, circa 1900, slightly damaged. (Robert W. Skinner Inc.) $90 £50

Snake bracelet in green and white enamel on silver. (Robert W. Skinner Inc.) $300 £165

Swiss gold and enamel brooch watch, 32mm. long. (Christie's) $5,235 £2,800

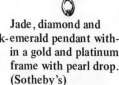

Sapphire and diamond clip of mitre shape, circa 1930, pierced and pave-set.(Sotheby's) $1,870 £990

Victorian pearl and peridot necklace on 15ct. gold chain. (Lawrence Fine Art) $520 £270

Jade, diamond and emerald pendant within a gold and platinum frame with pearl drop. (Sotheby's) $1,385 £715

Emerald and diamond bracelet designed as two tonneau-shaped panels. (Sotheby's) $20,790 £11,000

Victorian diamond tiara of scrolling form, in fitted case from Carrington & Co. (Lawrence Fine Art) $4,055 £2,100

Jade and diamond brooch of oblong shape. (Sotheby's) $2,175 £1,122

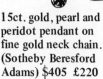

Diamond brooch designed as a posy of ribbons and flowers, one stone missing. (Sotheby's)$2,090 £1,100

15ct. gold, pearl and peridot pendant on fine gold neck chain. (Sotheby Beresford Adams) $405 £220

Diamond brooch in the form of an inverted crescent, in gold and silver setting. (Sotheby's) $1,110 £572

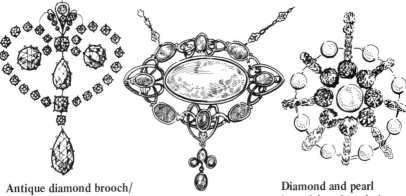

Diamond crescent brooch set with a single row of circular cut diamonds. (Sotheby's)$1,415 £748

Knife edge bar brooch set with three circular cut diamonds. (Sotheby's) $6,400 £3,300

Pair of turquoise, diamond and gold stud earrings of domed form. (Lawrence Fine Art) $145 £75

Antique diamond brooch/pendant of heart shape, mid 19th century. (Sotheby's) $5,615 £2,970

Opal pendant of Art Nouveau style. (Lawrence Fine Art) $385 £200

Diamond and pearl brooch/pendant designed as a wheel. (Sotheby's) $2,775 £1,430

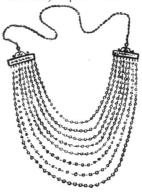

Diamond and aquamarine pendant on silver neckchain. (Sotheby's) $1,150 £594

Pearl and diamond necklace of nine strands with cannetille gold clasp. (Sotheby's) $1,705 £880

Victorian pearl pendant brooch. (Lawrence Fine Art) $290 £150

Antique oval black enamel gold memorial locket with diamond star-set front. (Christie's) $1,115 £600

Murrle Bennett & Co., gold and enamel brooch of bowed triangular form. (Christie's) $130 £70

Diamond collet star cluster circular brooch pendant with twisted fetter-and-three pattern neckchain. (Christie's) $3,350 £1,800

Diamond pendant brooch of floral stylised design, with rose-diamond surround. (Woolley & Wallis)$2,700 £1,500

One of a set of three blonde tortoiseshell hair combs with diamond and rose-diamond collets. (Christie's) $1,395 £750

Diamond and synthetic calibre sapphire arrow surete pin. (Christie's) $890 £480

Rose-diamond and fire opal scroll and collet brooch suspending twin pendants. (Christie's)$930 £500

Diamond pierced panel brooch of scroll, leaf and collet design. (Christie's) $3,350 £1,800

Antique gold coiled snake bracelet, head set with a sapphire and rose-diamonds. (Christie's) $1,955 £1,050

Diamond brooch in the form of a Celtic harp with winged angel, platinum mounted. (Woolley & Wallis) $1,050 £540

Lady's 18ct. white gold hand bracelet set with diamonds, approximately 8ct. (Gilbert Baitson) $4,535 £2,400

Silver and enamel waist clasp by Liberty & Co. (Christie's) $145 £80

Lady's ornate platinum dress watch, set with sixty-six diamonds.(Gilbert Baitson) $3,215 £1,700

Diamond tiara, composed of graduated leaves and collets enclosed in tapering ribbon frames. (Christie's) $22,320 £12,000

18ct. white gold necklet set with sixty-two graded diamonds, total weight 24ct. (Gilbert Baitson) $16,065 £8,500

Silver gilt and plique-a-jour enamel brooch, circa 1905, 4cm. wide. (Sotheby's Belgravia) $265 £150

Gold and mother-of-pearl necklace with pearl drops, circa 1900, 42cm. long. (Sotheby's Belgravia) $625 £350

Art Nouveau gold and enamelled shaped circular pendant and chain. (Christie's) $2,015 £1,100

Handel reverse painted and patinated metal table lamp, Meriden, circa 1930, 20½in. high. (Robert W. Skinner Inc.) $400 £225

Late 19th century Burmese fairy lamp by Mt. Washington Glass Co., 6in. high. (Robert W. Skinner Inc.) $150 £85

Miniature American satin glass 'Gone with the Wind' lamp, circa 1880, 8½in. high. (Robert W. Skinner Inc.) $250 £140

Galle cameo glass table lamp signed on shade and base, 52cm. high. (Phillips) $6,445 £3,600

One of a pair of late 19th century bronze and Favrile glass candlesticks with shades, by Tiffany Studios, New York, 12in. high. (Robert W. Skinner Inc.) $1,550 £865

Le Verre Francais cameo glass table lamp with conical shade, signed, 37.5cm. high. (Phillips) $1,255 £700

Miniature American cranberry glass lamp with moulded dot and panel shade and font, circa 1880, 9½in. high.(Robert W. Skinner Inc.) $325 £185

Galle cameo glass circular hanging lampshade of shallow domed form, signed, 44cm. diam. (Phillips)$3,220 £1,800

Miniature American porcelain lamp with globe-shaped opalescent white shade, circa 1880, 9¼in. high. (Robert W. Skinner Inc.) $125 £70

Miniature American 'Gone with the Wind' lamp with cranberry coin spot shade and font, circa 1880, 8¼in. high. (Robert W. Skinner Inc.) $200 £115

19th century Chinese champleve opaque enamel on bronze lamp base and shade, 20½in. high. (Robert W. Skinner Inc.) $400 £215

Miniature mauve satin glass lamp with half shade, circa 1880, 7in. high. (Robert W. Skinner Inc.) $225 £125

Galle cameo glass table lamp with domed shade, signed, 42cm. high. (Phillips) $6,445 £3,600

One of a pair of parcel gilt candelabra, circa 1850, 30½in. high. (Sotheby's Belgravia) $790 £430

Tiffany Studios 'Nautilus' gilt bronze table lamp inset with mother-of-pearl studs, 33.5cm. high. (Phillips) $2,505 £1,400

Pairpoint reverse painted glass and brass table lamp with signed shade, circa 1920, 23½in. high. (Robert W. Skinner Inc.) $1,500 £845

Daum cameo glass hanging lampshade, acid etched with branches around rim, signed, 45cm. diam. (Phillips) $1,180 £660

Early 20th century Pairpoint bronze and reverse painted table lamp, 23in. high. (Robert W. Skinner Inc.) $1,150 £640

Queen's Burmese fairy lamp by Thos. Webb & Sons, circa 1902, with domed shade, 5¼in. high. (Robert W. Skinner Inc.) $300 £160

Fulper pottery lamp, Flemington, New Jersey, circa 1900-10. (Robert W. Skinner Inc.) $550 £290

Mid 19th century Bulpitt & Sons brass lantern with cylindrical funnel and swing handle, 20in. high. (Sotheby's) $150 £79

Miniature American opaque blue lamp, shade in overlapping leaf motif, circa 1880. (Robert W. Skinner Inc.) $75 £40

Art Deco piano lamp, amber shade with floral motif supported by a bronze nude, on green marble base, circa 1925, 14½in. long. (Robert W. Skinner Inc.) $375 £210

Miniature American cranberry thumbprint lamp with half shade, circa 1880, 7½in. high.(Robert W. Skinner Inc.) $160 £90

Handel reverse painted and painted metal table lamp, no. 712, circa 1920, 23½in. high. (Robert W. Skinner Inc.) $2,400 £1,355

Tall oil lamp with brass fluted column stem, 28in. high, with glass shade. (Dickinson, Davy & Markham) $160 £85

Handel bronze and reverse painted table lamp, 24½in. high. (Robert W. Skinner Inc.) $1,900 £1,005

Acorn leaded glass and bronze table lamp by Tiffany Studios, 47cm. high. (Christie's) $1,850 £990

Austrian glass and gilt bronze lamp in the form of a peacock, circa 1920, 16in. long. (Sotheby's Belgravia) $1,050 £561

One of a pair of late 19th/early 20th century brass carriage side lamps, 15in. high. (Sotheby's) $130 £68

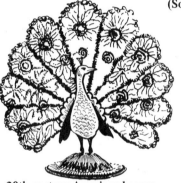

Tall oil lamp with embossed metal base, green glass reservoir, 24in. high. (Dickinson, Davy & Markham) $65 £34

20th century American bronze table lamp in the form of a peacock, 16½in. high. (Robert W. Skinner Inc.) $100 £55

Bronze and cameo glass table lamp by G. Raspellier, signed, 53cm. high. (Christie's) $4,115 £2,200

American half shade table lamp by Bradley & Hubbard, circa 1870, 20in. high. (Robert W. Skinner Inc.) $180 £100

Miniature American opalescent 'Gone with the Wind' lamp on square base, circa 1880, 8¼in. high. (Robert W. Skinner Inc.) $230 £130

Handel reverse painted glass and bronze table lamp, signed and numbered 6819, circa 1920, 23½in. high. (Robert W. Skinner Inc.) $1,800 £1,015

575

Old Sheffield plated lampstand with globe, marked Hinks/Duplex/Patent, circa 1860. (Sotheby, King & Chasemore)$510 £280

Tiffany Studios poinsettia leaded glass shade, domed, circa 1900, 40cm. diam. (Sotheby's Belgravia) $3,025 £1,700

Maltese library oil lamp in silver by Gaetano Offennaghel, circa 1800, 22½in. high, 52oz. (Christie's) $3,080 £1,620

Modernist standard lamp, 1930's, 203cm. high, on spiral glass column. (Sotheby's Belgravia) $135 £75

Tiffany Studios daffodil lamp, marked on base, circa 1900, 66cm. high. (Sotheby's Belgravia) $11,035 £6,200

Late 19th century ornate brass and copper tripod telescopic standard lamp. (T. Bannister & Co.) $140 £77

Art Deo electric table lamp in glass. (J. M. Welch & Son) $75 £40

Lacemaker's lamp with loop handle and pad foot, 23.5cm. high. (Phillips) $205 £110

Tiffany Studios gilt bronze reading lamp, 1920's, marked, 135cm. high.(Sotheby's Belgravia) $980 £550

Early 19th century American painted tin and glass whale oil hand lamp, 10¼in. high. (Robert W. Skinner Inc.) $625 £345

Desny chromed metal and glass table lamp with movable square of green tinted glass, 1920's, 12.5cm. (Sotheby's Belgravia) $675 £380

Tiffany bronze and Favrile glass three-light lily table lamp, circa 1900, 16in. high. (Robert W. Skinner Inc.) $2,300 £1,270

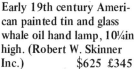

Art Deco bronze figural table lamp. (Capes, Dunn & Co.) $355 £190

Daum etched glass lamp on wrought iron base, shade engraved, 1920's, 50.5cm. high. (Sotheby's Belgravia) $855 £480

Red painted standard lamp with triangular stem and spiral geometric tripod base, 228.5cm. high. (Christie's) $165 £90

Art Deco moulded glass lamp base in the form of a nude female, 13in. high, circa 1930. (Robert W. Skinner Inc.)$300 £170

Modernist lamp with spherical green glass shade on blue glass base, 1930's, 31cm. high. (Sotheby's Belgravia) $360 £198

Tiffany leaded Favrile glass and Dore bronze bridge lamp, circa 1900, 57½in. high. (Robert W. Skinner Inc.) $3,200 £1,695

17th century Italian
marble head of a satyr,
27cm. high, with two
bases. (Christie's)
$1,265 £660

19th century Indian marble seat,
back of pointed arched form, 4ft.
3½in. wide. (Sotheby's)
$2,755 £1,540

19th century Italian
marble bust of a
lady, inscribed G.
Gambacciani Firenze,
72cm. high.(Christie's)
$1,195 £669

Mid 19th century Belgian
marble statue of the Re-
pentant Magdalen, by
Willem Geefs, 136.5cm.
high, 1841. (Christie's)
$4,060 £2,268

Pair of English white marble
busts of Queen Elizabeth I
and Robert Dudley, circa
1600, 26in. high.(Sotheby's)
$10,395 £5,500

Marble figure of a
medieval woman
carrying a book,
6ft. high. (Woolley
& Wallis)$535 £300

18th century Italian marble
bust of a matron, cracked,
66cm. high. (Christie's)
$2,325 £1,210

Late 19th century French
marble, enamel and porce-
lain pedestal with octagonal column, 112cm. high.
(H. Spencer & Sons Ltd.)
$1,870 £1,000

Roman marble portrait
head of a lady, 2nd cen-
tury A.D., 11¼in. high.
(Christie's)$2,285 £1,210

Roman marble pilaster capital, 2nd century A.D., 10½in. wide. (Christie's) $270 £143

One of a pair of ormolu models of chimerae, on marble bases, 9in. wide. (Christie's)$985 £540

North Italian marble relief of Cherubim, circa 1690, 18in. wide. (Sotheby's)$4,160 £2,200

White marble statue of Venus, circa 1880, 38in. high. (Sotheby, King & Chasemore) $985 £550

16th century Italian white marble elephant, 9¾in. wide, base damaged and restored. (Sotheby's) $5,200 £2,750

17th century Flemish marble figure of Venus, an urn at her side, 21in. high. (Sotheby's) $1,870 £990

19th century Florentine marble group of three children, inscribed F. Andreini Firenze, 75cm. high. (Christie's) $1,450 £810

Bronze and marble encrier on yellow marble base, circa 1840, 11in. wide. (Sotheby's Belgravia) $245 £132

Late 19th century American marble bust of the Greek Slave, by H. Powers, 39.5cm. high.(Christie's)$6,186 £3,456

579

A gentleman wearing a black jacket and white cravat, ebonised wood frame, 7.6cm., by Thos. Richmond, circa 1800. (Sotheby's) \$525 £270

Prince William of Orange, gouache on vellum, ebony and tortoiseshell frame, 7cm., French School, circa 1740. (Sotheby's) \$3,225 £1,655

A field officer of the 42nd Royal Highlanders The Black Watch, papiermache frame, 8.2cm., attributed to George Place, circa 1785. (Sotheby's)
\$4,960 £2,455

A young lady wearing a tall black hat and a brown jacket over a blue and white striped dress, silver gilt frame, 5.6cm., French School, circa 1785. (Sotheby's) \$405 £205

A rider approaching a crossroads with a cottage in the background, oil on copper, 6.5cm., Continental School, 18th century. (Sotheby's)
\$340 £175

A young girl with curling fair hair wearing a white dress with a pearl necklace, 5.1cm., attributed to Edward Nash, circa 1800. (Sotheby's)
\$680 £350

A young lady with her hair falling to her shoulders, wearing a white low-cut dress, gold frame, 8.2cm., by Andrew Plimer, circa 1800. (Sotheby's) \$990 £510

A lady reclining on a crimson cushion, on vellum, giltwood frame, 11.3cm., French School, circa 1680. (Sotheby's) \$745 £380

A gentleman wearing a plum coloured gown, signed with initials, oil on panel, 10.5cm., by Pieter Van Slingeland. (Sotheby's)\$5,575 £2,860

A young lady seated on a chair holding a book, gilt metal mount, 7cm., signed and dated 1789, by Jacques Anthoine Marie Lemoine. (Sotheby's) $2,605 £1,335

A battle scene, gouache on vellum, 8.3cm., signed and dated 1776 by Van Blarenberghe. (Sotheby's) $8,990 £4,610

A young man wearing a blue jacket, 6.5cm., signed and dated 1805, by Tonna. (Sotheby's) $370 £190

19th century Continental School, lady wearing lace-trimmed cap, 8.2cm., painted on card. (Sotheby's) $560 £286

Mademoiselle de Marcieux of Grenoble, giltwood frame, 9.5cm., signed and dated 1790 by Muralt. (Sotheby's) $4,650 £2,385

A young child holding a parrot, on vellum, gilt metal frame, 5.2cm., Continental School, early 17th century. (Sotheby's) $16,120 £8,265

A gentleman wearing a brown jacket and striped waistcoat, gold mount, 7cm., signed, by Le Chevalier De Chateaubourg, circa 1790. (Sotheby's) $13,360 £6,850

Marie De Medici kneeling in prayer before an altar, oil on copper, 12cm., Franco-Flemish School, 17th century. (Sotheby's) $1,490 £765

A young lady with brown hair, wearing a white dress with lace trimmings, enamel, 8.2cm., signed and dated 1826, by Wm. Essex. (Sotheby's) $2,170 £1,120

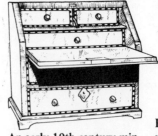

19th century miniature giltwood four-poster bed, 2ft.9in. high, with original hangings. (Christie's & Edmiston's) $635 £360

An early 19th century miniature bureau in mahogany, 1ft. wide. (Phillips) $600 £325

Edwardian mahogany miniature chest of five drawers, 16in. wide. (J. M. Welch & Son) $190 £105

Seven-piece suite of 19th century French drawingroom furniture for a doll's house. (Woolley & Wallis) $85 £48

19th century miniature walnut and floral marquetry bureau cabinet. (Christie's S. Kensington) $1,345 £700

Early Louis XVI provincial walnut miniature armoire, circa 1780, with arched top, 2ft.3in. wide. (Sotheby's) $785 £440

Early George II oak miniature bureau on separate stand, 1ft. 11in. wide, circa 1730. (Sotheby's) $1,525 £825

Late 18th century American transitional shaving mirror on stand, 11¼in. wide. (Robert W. Skinner Inc.) $550 £300

Tiffany Studios bronze and Favrile glass mirror, New York, circa 1920, 13in. high. (Robert W. Skinner Inc.) $6,000 £3,175

Early George III carved giltwood overmantel, 5ft. 10in. wide, circa 1760. (Sotheby's)$1,570 £858

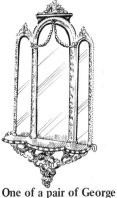

Chromed tubular steel cheval mirror on four castors, 1930's, 160cm. high. (Sotheby's Belgravia) $300 £165

Art Nouveau bronze mirror cast with the figure of a young woman, 31cm. high. (Christie's) $1,060 £580

One of a pair of George III carved and gilded gesso framed mirrors, 43½in. high. (Dacre, Son & Hartley) $365 £200

Queen Anne green and gold lacquer toilet mirror with arched plate, 15½in. wide.(Christie's) $1,080 £572

Federal mahogany and mahogany veneer shaving mirror on stand, circa 1800, 24½in. wide. (Robert W. Skinner Inc.) $1,150 £630

Early 19th century American Federal mahogany shaving mirror with shield-shaped glass, 20in. wide. (Robert W. Skinner Inc.) $350 £195

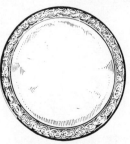

Cut glass picture frame by Hawkes, Corning, New York, circa 1900, 7in. long. (Robert W. Skinner Inc.) $150 £85

George III mahogany serpentine-fronted toilet mirror, circa 1790, 17½in. wide. (Sotheby, King & Chasemore) $625 £340

Lalique circular easel mirror, signed, 39cm. diam., with glass moulded frame. (Phillips) $895 £500

20th century American Chippendale style mahogany mirror with painted glass plates, 48in. high. (Robert W. Skinner Inc.) $275 £155

'George III' rococo giltwood wall mirror, circa 1840, with pagoda top, 78½in. high. (Sotheby's Belgravia) $1,440 £800

20th century George III style giltwood wall mirror, 73in. high.(Sotheby Beresford Adams) $560 £300

George II carved giltwood wall mirror with candle sconce, circa 1750, 60in. high. (Sotheby, King & Chasemore)$1,380 £750

One of a pair of George III giltwood mirrors with later plates, 43in. high.(Christie's) $3,330 £1,800

George III giltwood wall mirror, circa 1770, 61in. high.(Sotheby, King & Chasemore) $4,025 £2,200

584

George II giltwood mirror with arched bevelled plate, cresting centred by a pierced cartouche, 48½in. high. (Christie's) $1,850 £1,000

Early 19th century Regency mahogany toilet mirror on a bow-fronted three-drawer base, 21in. wide. (Sotheby Beresford Adams) $150 £80

Small George III oval giltwood mirror, re-gilded, circa 1760, 1ft.6½in. wide. (Sotheby's) $1,215 £680

WMF silvered pewter mirror with Art Nouveau maiden reaching upwards to branches, 37cm. high.(Phillips) $825 £460

Gilt rectangular wall mirror with ball, star and scroll fluted columns, 26in. high. (John Hogbin & Son) $90 £50

Early 20th century George III style giltwood mirror in pierced frame, 55in. high. (Sotheby Beresford Adams) $295 £160

Early 20th century George III style mahogany toilet mirror with oval swing plate, 18in. wide.(Sotheby Beresford Adams)$165 £90

Late 19th century Dresden mirror of oval form, slightly damaged, 17¼in. high. (Sotheby Beresford Adams) $315 £170

Reproduction, figured walnut toilet mirror in Queen Anne style, 14in. wide, on bracket feet. (Locke & England) $205 £115

Carved giltwood 'Sunburst' framed convex mirror. (Gilbert Baitson) $130 £70

Early George III carved giltwood overmantel mirror, circa 1760, 4ft.3½in. wide. (Sotheby's) $3,205 £1,705

Regency mahogany swing toilet mirror with brass urn-shaped finials. (Gilbert Baitson) $380 £200

George II carved giltwood looking glass, circa 1750, 2ft.3in. wide. (Sotheby's) $1,570 £850

Early 19th century Empire mahogany and gilt bronze cheval mirror, 41in. wide. (Sotheby Beresford Adams) $780 £420

Dresden bevelled oval mirror decorated with blue and white flower spray, 10½in. high. (Dee & Atkinson) $280 £150

19th century Louis XV style kingwood occasional table, stamped Edwards & Roberts, 17½in. wide. (Hy. Duke & Son) $770 £400

19th century painted wood-encased mirror, 18in. wide. (Robert W. Skinner Inc.) $250 £135

George II looking glass in carved giltwood frame with two brass candle branches. (Christie's & Edmiston's) $3,110 £1,700

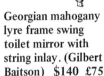

Giltwood pier glass
of Chippendale de-
sign, 31in. wide, with
gadrooned border.
(Lawrence Fine Art)
$660 £360

Regency gilt framed triple plate
overmantel mirror, circa 1810,
4ft.7½in. wide. (Sotheby, King
& Chasemore) $1,075 £580

Georgian mahogany
lyre frame swing
toilet mirror with
string inlay. (Gilbert
Baitson) $140 £75

Giltwood wall mirror
with carved frame, 2ft.
7in. wide. (Sotheby's)
$4,030 £2,145

Late 19th/early 20th century
Venetian giltwood mirror
with shaped plate, 42in. high.
(Sotheby's Belgravia)$740 £396

Empire mahogany cheval
mirror with arched cor-
nice, on scrolled legs and
paw feet, 78½in. high.
(Christie's)$1,840 £1,000

George II parcel gilt
mahogany wall mirror,
circa 1750, 1ft.6½in.
wide. (Sotheby's)
$1,595 £858

Koening & Lengsfeld ceramic
figure of a woman looking into a mirror, 70cm. high.
(Christie's) $865 £462

Early 18th century
rare giltwood pier
glass with divided
bevelled plate, 70½in.
high.(Christie's)
$3,865 £2,100

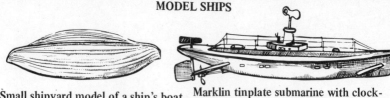

Small shipyard model of a ship's boat, with painted hull, 46cm. long. (Phillips) $275 £150

Marklin tinplate submarine with clockwork mechanism, circa 1935, 22in. long. (Sotheby's Belgravia) $1,805 £935

French prisoner-of-war bone model of a 48-gun frigate, 19½in. long. (Christie's) $2,455 £1,300

Fully rigged bone and mahogany model of a 16-gun Admiralty cutter, 16in. wide. (Christie's) $1,135 £600

Fully planked, framed and rigged wooden model of the frigate 'Endymion', by F. A. Chapman, Basildon, 53in. wide.(Christie's) $720 £380

Well-presented fully planked model of the 'Golden Hind' of 1578, built by V. Rodriguez-Bento, Bath, 42in. long. (Christie's) $795 £420

Nautical diorama of the Titanic and other vessels, circa 1915, 26½in. wide. (Sotheby's) $205 £110

Bing tinplate gunboat with clockwork mechanism, circa 1910, 15in. long. (Sotheby's) $955 £506

588

Tin Ocean liner, U.S. Zone Germany, circa 1947, 20in. long. (Robert W. Skinner Inc.) $410 £215

Shipyard model of a ship's boat with patent specification, 95cm. long. (Phillips) $570 £310

Early 19th century French bone model of a frigate, 13½in. wide, on wooden base. (Sotheby Beresford Adams) $205 £110

Early 19th century Admiralty Board Room fully rigged model of the 120-gun 'Caledonia', 70in. long. (Christie's) $4,160 £2,200

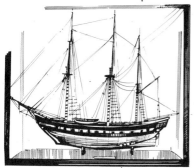

Contemporary bone, horn and boxwood fully rigged French prisoner-of-war model frigate, 13in. wide. (Christie's) $5,670 £3,000

Exhibition standard scale fully planked model of H.M.S. Victory, by J. Bright, Gosport, 40in. long. (Christie's) $2,455 £1,300

Fleischmann twin-funnelled tinplate liner with clockwork mechanism, 12in. long, circa 1950. (Sotheby's Belgravia) $235 £121

Fleischmann tinplate liner, circa 1945, 9in. long, with clockwork mechanism. (Sotheby's Belgravia) $65 £33

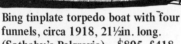

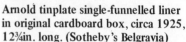

Bing tinplate torpedo boat with four funnels, circa 1918, 21½in. long. (Sotheby's Belgravia) $805 £418

Arnold tinplate single-funnelled liner in original cardboard box, circa 1925, 12¾in. long. (Sotheby's Belgravia) $180 £93

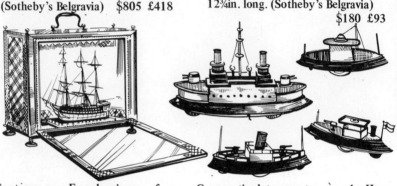

Contemporary French prisoner-of-war bone and horn model of a 112-gun man-of-war, 12in. long. (Christie's) $9,450 £5,000

German tinplate carpet convoy by Hess, circa 1915, of four ships. (Sotheby's Belgravia) $360 £187

Steam launch 'Chough', circa 1972, by Monachoram Plastics, Ltd., Plymouth, 16ft. long. (Christie's) $2,835 £1,500

Shipbuilder's detailed model of a freighter built by Wm. Doxford, Sunderland, 1947, 4ft.8in. long. (Anderson & Garland) $4,485 £2,450

Exhibition standard boxwood and pine model of a single screw steam yacht, circa 1900, by W. Morrison, Saltcoats, 43in. long. (Christie's) $7,560 £4,000

Scale radio-controlled model of the salvage tug 'Lloydsman' of Hull, built by E. R. Warwick, Sevenoaks, 56in. wide. (Christie's) $1,040 £550

Incomplete live steam model of a 3½in. gauge locomotive and tender, by Percival Marshal & Co., 3ft.10½in. long. (Phillips)　　$755 £420

Exhibition standard 5in. gauge model of a 4-6-0 locomotive and tender 'King John', by J. Perrier, Ringwood, 73in. long. (Christie's)　　$14,175 £7,500

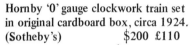

Bassett-Lowke gauge 'O' electric 4-4-0 locomotive with matching tender. (Sotheby's Belgravia)　　$320 £165

Hornby 'O' gauge clockwork train set in original cardboard box, circa 1924. (Sotheby's)　　$200 £110

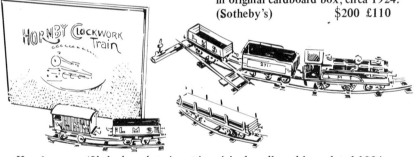

Hornby gauge 'O' clockwork train set in original cardboard box, dated 1924. (Sotheby's)　　$355 £187

7mm. scale model of a London and North Eastern Railway 1st Class sleeping car, 19in. long. (Christie's)　　$415 £220

Bassett-Lowke gauge 'O' electric 4-6-0 locomotive 'Royal Scot', with matching tender. (Sotheby's Belgravia)　　$850 £440

Gauge 'one' carette live steam spirit-fired 2-2-0 locomotive with four wheeled tender, 14¾in. long. (Sotheby Beresford Adams)$205 £110

7mm. scale electric model of a condensing side tank locomotive No. 10, by B. Miller, 8¾in. long. (Christie's) $1,605 £850

3½in. gauge model of an Ivatt Atlantic 4-4-2 locomotive and tender by A. F. Farmer, Stechford, 1967, 44½in. long. (Christie's) $1,795 £950

Hornby 4-4-2 gauge '0' clockwork engine 'Lord Nelson' and tender. (Allen & May) $140 £75

Exhibition standard 7mm. fine scale model of a 2-6-0 goods locomotive and tender, by J. S. Beeson, Ringwood, 15½in. long. (Christie's) $2,270 £1,200

Lionel tinplate gauge '0' clockwork Disney train, circa 1940, 30in. long. (Sotheby's Belgravia) $570 £308

5in. gauge model of the Welsh quarry 0-4-0 tank locomotive No. 1, by S. F. Price, Sheppey, 31½in. long.(Christie's) $4,535 £2,400

3½in. gauge display model of a Webb 2-4-0 side tank locomotive by H. A. Taylor, Bletchley, 22in. long. (Christie's) $1,700 £900

7mm. fine scale model of a Johnson
class 2P 0-4-4 side tank locomotive,
by J. S. Beeson, Ringwood, 9¾in.
long. (Christie's) $1,230 £650

7mm. fine scale electric model of a
'Jinty' class 0-6-0 side tank locomotive,
by J. S. Beeson, Ringwood, 9in. long.
(Christie's) $905 £480

7mm. scale electric model of a 4-2-2 locomotive and tender 'Lorna Doone',
by P. G. Rose, 16in. long. (Christie's) $1,795 £950

Gauge 'one' clockwork L. & N.W.R.
tank locomotive by Bassett Lowke,
16¼in. long. (Sotheby's)$375 £198

Bassett Lowke 4-6-0 railway engine
'Royal Scot', and tender. (Allen &
May) $360 £190

5in. gauge model of the Johnson 'Spinner' 4-2-2 locomotive and tender 'Princess
of Wales', 64in. long. (Christie's) $4,915 £2,600

Exhibition standard 7mm. fine scale
electric model of a Webb class 1P
2-4-2 side tank locomotive, by J. S.
Beeson, Ringwood, 9½in. long.
(Christie's) $1,890 £1,000

3½in. gauge model of the Hunslett
narrow gauge 2-6-2 side tank locomotive 'Russell', 34½in. long. (Christie's)
        $2,270 £1,200

593

2in. scale model of a coal-fired Burrell showman's engine. (Lacy Scott)
$2,785 £1,450

Fine model of an 1830's stagecoach in hardwood with brass fittings, modern, 16in. wide. (Sotheby's) $250 £132

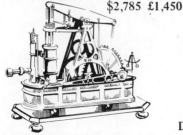

Brass and copper 1/12 scale gas-fired model of a steam plant, 36in. wide. (Christie's) $380 £200

Detailed 1/12 scale model of fishermen and equipment on Worthing beach, circa 1920, by S. Bunker, 29¼in. wide. (Christie's) $850 £450

Contemporary 4-pillar table engine, circa 1845, 25in. high. (Christie's) $755 £400

Modern replica of a 19th century fairground in fibre-glass, 10ft.10in. wide. (Sotheby Beresford Adams) $655 £350

American carved and painted stagecoach model and four-horse team, circa 1900, 53in. long. (Robert W. Skinner Inc.) $550 £300

Model of a Stuart single cylinder beam engine, 14in. wide. (Dickinson, Davy & Markham)$95 £52

1½in. scale live steam Allchin traction engine. (Phillips) $3,070 £1,600

Model single horizontal cylinder bayonet frame mill engine by A. H. Allen, Keighley, 11¼in. wide. (Christie's) $340 £180

Well-engineered coarse scale coal-fired live steam model of a traction engine, 54cm. long. (Sotheby, King & Chasemore) $890 £490

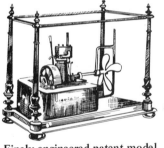

3in. scale model of a single cylinder Burrell agricultural traction engine, by K. B. Thirsk, Driffield, 1973, 45in. long. (Christie's) $6,425 £3,400

Finely engineered patent model of a twin cylinder vertical reversing steam plant, by W. Morrison, Saltcoats, circa 1900, 10½in. wide. (Christie's) $1,095 £580

1½in. scale model of a road roller, living van and water cart, by J. McW. Morrison, Thatcham. (Christie's) $1,700 £900

Detailed 1/8 scale wood and metal model of a gig of circa 1850, by A. Lee, Hendon, 17½in. long. (Christie's) $190 £100

Scale model of a steam fire engine by Shands & Mason, 1863, London. (Edwards, Bigwood & Bewlay) $4,210 £2,300

Late 19th century American cast-iron negro and shack money bank, 4¼in. long. (Sotheby's Belgravia) $300 £165

American cast-iron Tammany money bank, circa 1880. (Sotheby's Belgravia) $200 £110

19th century American cast-iron mechanical bank 'Eagle & Eaglets'. (Wm. Doyle Galleries Inc.) $150 £80

German Mickey Mouse tinplate mechanical bank, both sides having different scenes, circa 1930, 6¾in. high. (Sotheby's Belgravia) $345 £187

Late 19th century American cast-iron mechanical bank, 'Paddy and the Pig', 8in. high. (Sotheby's Belgravia) $320 £165

Late 19th century American Uncle Sam cast-iron mechanical bank by Shepard Hardware Co., 11½in. high. (Sotheby's Belgravia) $285 £154

German tinplate monkey money bank with decorated base, 6½in. high. (Sotheby's Belgravia) $100 £55

Cast iron 'Novelty Bank' money box with hinged front, 6½in. high, American, circa 1875. (Sotheby's) $215 £120

One of a pair of German electroplated Britannia metal 'porker' money boxes, 13.7cm. long. (Sotheby's Belgravia) $415 £220

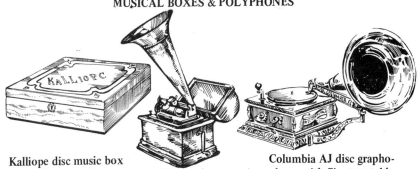

Kalliope disc music box with bells in inlaid fruitwood case, 15¾in. wide. (Robert W. Skinner Inc.) $1,600 £845

An Edison phonograph model D, American, circa 1908. (Sotheby's Belgravia) $190 £100

Columbia AJ disc graphophone with 7in. turntable, circa 1902, complete with original case. (Sotheby's Belgravia) $510 £285

Rare Francois Nicole key-wound overture cylinder musical box, No. 101, circa 1830, 18in. wide. (Sotheby's Belgravia)$7,480 £4,180

Nicole Freres Swiss musical box in rosewood veneer, 24in. wide. (Woolley & Wallis) $650 £350

Alfred Junod Alexandra 'bells and drum in sight' cylinder musical box, 21in. wide, circa 1895. (Sotheby's Belgravia) $1,280 £715

Nicole Freres key-wound cylinder musical box in fruitwood case, circa 1835. (Sotheby's Belgravia) $825 £462

Edison opera phonograph, No. 2948, with self-supporting laminated horn, circa 1912. (Sotheby's) $3,740 £2,090

Swiss Nicole Freres key-wound two-perturn cylinder musical box, circa 1858, 20in. wide. (Sotheby's Belgravia) $1,770 £990

Mira Orchestral Grand musical box, in mahogany case, 29½in. wide.(Robert W. Skinner Inc.) $5,250 £2,775

Swiss bells in sight cylinder musical box by Nicole Freres, in rosewood case, 26in. wide. (Sotheby Beresford Adams) $2,245 £1,200

Musical box with nine bells, in inlaid walnut case. (Hall Wateridge & Owen) $1,130 £600

Late 19th century walnut cased polyphon made for H. Peters & Co., London, sold with nineteen discs. (Locke & England) $2,775 £1,500

Swiss interchangeable bells in sight cylinder musical box, dated 1890, 15¼in. wide, with additional cylinders. (Sotheby Bearne) $785 £420

Late 19th century walnut cased floor standing symphonium with twenty-four discs. (Locke & England) $3,235 £1,750

Polyphon disc music box with serpentine front mahogany case, 11in. wide. (Robert W. Skinner Inc.) $500 £265

Sirion disc music box in inlaid fruitwood case, complete with ten discs, 25in. wide. (Robert W. Skinner Inc.) $3,250 £1,720

Symphonion disc musical box in maple case, with twenty-seven extra discs, 10¾in. wide. (Robert W. Skinner Inc.) $750 £395

Symphonion disc musical box in rosewood case, complete with twenty discs, 13¼in. long. (Robert W. Skinner Inc.) $650 £345

Swiss cylinder music box with butterflies and bells, in grain painted case, 18¾in. wide. (Robert W. Skinner Inc.) $800 £425

19th century Swiss musical box in rosewood with marquetry lid, 19in. wide. (Woolley & Wallis) $560 £300

Late 19th century German symphonion disc musical box with thirty-four discs, 47½in. high, in walnut veneered case. (Sotheby Beresford Adams) $2,055 £1,100

Edison fireside phonograph, circa 1909, with approximately one hundred cylinders. (Sotheby, Beresford Adams) $655 £350

Regina disc music box in cherry case with two discs, 14½in. wide. (Robert W. Skinner Inc.) $900 £475

Swiss bells and drum in sight cylinder musical box in rosewood veneered case, circa 1880.(Sotheby Beresford Adams) $935 £500

Swiss cylinder music box with drum, bells and butterflies, 27¼in. wide, in rosewood case. (Robert W. Skinner Inc.) $2,200 £1,165

Swiss bells in sight cylinder musical box in grained wood case with brass handles, 19in. wide. (Sotheby Beresford Adams) $935 £500

599

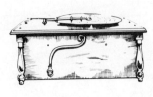

Amopette Atlas organette in black painted case, with twelve discs, 17in. wide. (Robert W. Skinner Inc.) $275 £145

Late 19th century Swiss bells in sight cylinder musical box, 19in. wide. (Sotheby's) $1,975 £1,045

Swiss cylinder music box, in inlaid rosewood case, 25in. wide, with ten tunes. (Robert W. Skinner Inc.) $1,400 £740

Kalliope panorama automat disc music box in rosewood and walnut case, 25½in. wide. (Robert W. Skinner Inc.) $5,000 £2,645

Late 19th century Swiss cylinder musical box playing eight airs, 25in. wide. (Sotheby's) $2,080 £1,100

Criterion No. 5 disc music box in mahogany case, with matching stand, 26in. wide. (Robert W. Skinner Inc.) $2,600 £1,375

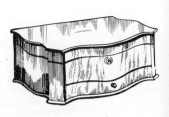

Amoretto disc organ in ebonised wood case with twelve discs, 20½in. wide. (Robert W. Skinner Inc.) $500 £265

Stella disc music box in walnut cabinet, carried on barley-twist supports, 28in. wide. (Locke & England) $1,685 £925

Polyphon disc music box with serpentine front rosewood veneer case, 11in. wide. (Robert W. Skinner Inc.) $550 £290

Swiss cylinder musical box in walnut case with boxwood stringing, circa 1880's, 23in. wide. (Sotheby's)$1,350 £715

Columbia disc phonograph with outside horn, 78 speed, 10¾in. wide. (Robert W. Skinner Inc.) $550 £290

Regina accordion top disc music box in oak case, with thirteen discs, 34½in. wide. (Robert W. Skinner Inc.) $4,500 £2,380

Regina music and gum machine in oak case with glass door, 16in. wide. (Robert W. Skinner Inc.) $2,600 £1,375

Edison home phonograph with black japanned shaped octagonal horn, patent date 1906. (Sotheby Bearne) $205 £110

Upright American symphonion in oak case, complete with ten discs, 28in. wide. (Robert W. Skinner Inc.) $3,500 £1,850

German polyphon disc musical box and fifteen discs, retailer's label Edward Dale, Chester, circa 1900, 50½in. high. (Sotheby Beresford Adams) $1,775 £950

Academy gramophone with bell-shaped tinplate horn, circa 1930, 13in. square. (Sotheby's) $455 £242

Small carved music box showing three bears, 9in. high. (Robert W. Skinner Inc.) $180 £95

601

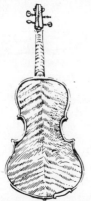

English violin by Arthur Richardson, Crediton, 1932, labelled, length of back 14in., sold with a silver mounted bow. (Sotheby's)$1,525 £825

Early 19th century English serpent, possibly by Thos. Key, London, in leather on wood. (Phillips) $770 £420

Fine French violin by Jean Baptiste Vuillaume, Paris, 1862, labelled, length of back 14in. (Sotheby's) $18,720 £10,120

18th century French ivory treble recorder, 19½in. long. (Phillips) $3,845 £2,100

Rare ivory flute by Hill, late Monzani & Co., London, with silver mounts, 23¾in. long. (Phillips) $730 £400

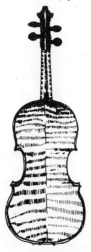

Violin by Paul Bailly, signed and dated London, 1891, length of back 14in. (Phillips) $2,070 £1,150

Italian violoncello by Giorgio Taningar, Rome, 1703, labelled, length of back 29¾in. long. (Sotheby's) $8,955 £4,840

Italian violin attributed to Carlo Ferdinando Landolfi, Milan, length of back 14in., circa 1766. (Sotheby's) $10,175 £5,500

Unlabelled violin with two-piece back 14¼in. long, circa 1860, in shaped leather case. (Sotheby's) $775 £418

Late 18th century cittern by Frederick Hintz, London. (Phillips) $950 £520

French viola by Charles Louis Buthod, labelled, with one-piece back 15¾in. long.(Sotheby's) $1,320 £715

Early 19th century flute by Monzani & Co., London, with silver mounts, 23¼in. long. (Phillips) $1,005 £550

18th century ivory treble recorder by I. B. Gahn, 20in. long. (Phillips) $8,785 £4,800

Fine violin by Joseph Hill, London, length of two-piece back 14in. (Phillips)$7,020 £3,900

Italian viola of the Amati School, circa 1700, reduced in size to 15in. (Phillips) $7,560 £4,200

Violin by Paul Bailly, signed and dated Leeds, 1898, No. 1013, length of back 14in. (Phillips) $4,140 £2,300

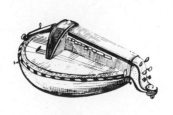

French hurdy-gurdy by Jean-Baptiste Pajot, 1795, 26¼in. long. (Christie's)
$2,705 £1,512

Violin labelled Francesco Ruggieri detto il per Cremona, 1676, length of back 14in., circa 1800. (Sotheby's)$2,035 £1,100

Unlabelled Neapolitan mandoline of fluted maple ribs, neck inlaid with mother-of-pearl, 22¾in. long. (Christie's) $345 £194

Tanzbar accordion roller organ in black case, closed width 11in. wide. (Robert W. Skinner Inc.)
$600 £315

Neapolitan mandoline by Antonio Vinaccia, 1763, 22½in. long. (Christie's)$1,450 £810

Unsigned monochord, keyboard with beech naturals and stained beech accidentals, 47½in. long. (Christie's) $540 £302

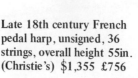

Italian violin ascribed to Gennaro Gagliano, 1773, with two-piece back, length of back 14in. (Christie's)
$13,530 £7,560

Late 18th century French pedal harp, unsigned, 36 strings, overall height 55in. (Christie's) $1,355 £756

Italian violin, labelled Antonion Mariani/ Pesaro 16—, length of back 14in. (Christie's)
$615 £345

Good netsuke group of two pups playing, signed Ittan with kakihan. (Sotheby's) $590 £330

Early 19th century ivory netsuke of a dog and a shell, unsigned, Osaka School. (Sotheby's) $355 £198

Osaka School ivory netsuke of two biwa fruit on a branch, signed Koho.(Sotheby's) $1,085 £605

Small ivory netsuke figure of a karako seated, playing with a turtle, signed Gyokuyosai. (Sotheby's) $395 £220

Small wood netsuke of Shoki seated on a sack, signed Ryukei.(Sotheby's) $375 £209

Wood netsuke of a baby boy, signed Shumin saku. (Sotheby's) $945 £528

18th century ivory netsuke of a tiger, unsigned, eyes inlaid with horn. (Sotheby's) $630 £352

Ivory netsuke of a monkey with young, signed Sadayoshi. (Sotheby's) $1,025 £572

Late 18th century netsuke study of a Tengy No Tamago, signed Tametaka. (Sotheby's) $825 £462

Wooden netsuke model of a coiled mouse with inlaid eyes, signed Masakiyo. (Sotheby's)
$1,155 £620

18th century wood netsuke group of three chestnuts, one containing an ivory maggot, unsigned. (Sotheby's)
$225 £121

Ivory netsuke of a Shishi, signed Gyokuyosai, seated with a paw on a ball. (Sotheby's) $335 £180

Early 19th century Kyoto School netsuke of a Kirin. (Sotheby's) $1,205 £660

Late ivory netsuke figure of a Sambaso dancer, stained, signed Masakazu.(Sotheby's)
$230 £126

Large wooden netsuke figure of a Raiden, signed Hokyudo Itsuminto, seated beside a drum. (Sotheby's)
$630 £340

Mid 19th century wood netsuke of a kappa on a clam. (Christie's S. Kensington)
$315 £170

Ivory netsuke Okimono style figure of a young boy kneeling on the ground, inscribed Kaigyoku. (Sotheby's)
$355 £190

Large ivory netsuke study of a wolf with human skull, signed Tomonobu. (Sotheby's) $485 £264

18th century ivory netsuke model of a rat beside a large overturned mushroom, unsigned. (Sotheby's) $280 £150

Wooden netsuke group of Jurojin with two Karako seated in a boat, signed Ikkosai.(Sotheby's) $445 £240

Unusual wooden netsuke study of a rat on a rice bale, signed Ryukei. (Sotheby's) $240 £132

Wood and ivory netsuke of a young boy holding some fruit, signed on red lacquer Hideyuki. (Sotheby's) $565 £308

18th century ivory netsuke of a Nio holding a club, unsigned. (Sotheby's) $390 £220

Late ivory netsuke figure of Saishi, signed Kotnsai Kosen. (Sotheby's) $385 £209

Small ivory netsuke model of a skeleton beating a mokugyo, signed Tomochika. (Sotheby's) $160 £88

Late 18th century ivory netsuke model of a dragon, unsigned. (Sotheby's) $835 £450

Attractive early 19th century ivory netsuke of a snail on a mushroom, signed Kogyoku. (Sotheby's) $385 £209

Commonwealth pewter tankard, circa 1650, 5¾in. high. (Sotheby's) $2,790 £1,485

15th century pewter spoon with latten 'sceptre' knop, possibly unique, 5¾in. long. (Sotheby's) $650 £352

Mid 17th century bossed pewter dish, 15¾in. diam. (Sotheby's) $975 £528

Mid 18th century Bernese stegkanne with hexagonal spout, 34.5cm. high. (Sotheby's) $1,445 £770

William and Mary pewter candlestick, 6in. high, circa 1690-96. (Sotheby's) $2,135 £1,155

18th century German Peterskirchen stoneware handled jug with pewter lid, 18in. high.(Robert W. Skinner Inc.) $250 £135

One of a pair of painted pewter mantel ornaments, circa 1790, 12¼in. high. (Robert W. Skinner Inc.) $750 £405

Broad-rimmed 'Mount Edgecumbe' pewter plate by ND, circa 1660-80, 10in. diam. (Sotheby's) $530 £286

19th century European pewter communion flagon with double domed hinged lid, 14in. high. (Robert W. Skinner Inc.) $200 £105

German or Bohemian pewter passover plate, circa 1803, 34.3cm. diam. (Sotheby's) $1,755 £935

'Diamond-point' pewter spoon with stem and terminal of pentagonal section, 6½in. long. (Sotheby's) $185 £99

One of a pair of WMF silvered pewter and brass two-branch candelabra, 25cm. high. (Christie's) $2,250 £1,210

Early 18th century North Country pewter baluster measure with flat cover, 6½in. high. (Sotheby's) $1,425 £770

18th century German pewter mounted stoneware flagon with applied white decoration, 13½in. high. (Robert W. Skinner Inc.) $1,000 £545

19th century South German hexagonal pewter cannister, 13in. high. (Sotheby's) $600 £325

One of a pair of rare Georgian pewter candlesticks, circa 1720, 6¾in. and 6½in. high. (Sotheby's) $915 £495

Early 18th century pewter wrigglework plate with single reeded border, 8½in. diam. (Sotheby's) $470 £253

18th century Swiss pewter covered flagon with domed hinged cover, 12½in. high. (Robert W. Skinner Inc.) $1,200 £650

Dutch pewter beaker, Amsterdam, circa 1760. (Sotheby's) $290 £160

One of a pair of late 18th century oval pewter dishes, 18in. wide. (Woolley & Wallis) $595 £320

One of a pair of Scottish pewter flagons, circa 1786, 13in. high. (Sotheby's) $950 £506

One of a fine pair of Charles I pewter flagons, circa 1635, 11in. high. (Sotheby's)$6,615 £3,520

WMF Art Nouveau wafer barrel and lid. (Capes, Dunn & Co.) $150 £80

Charles I pewter flagon with plain 'muffin' cover, circa 1630-40, 11½in. high.(Sotheby's) $1,220 £660

Rare pewter Stuart lidless tavern pot by James Donne, London, 6½in. high, circa 1685-90. (Sotheby's)$1,525 £825

Decorated pewter Charles II charger, circa 1670, 20½in. diam. (Sotheby's)$1,015 £550

Small 'York' acorn flagon in pewter, circa 1725-50, 8¾in. high. (Sotheby's) $1,525 £825

18th century Swiss pewter covered glockencanne with fixed ring carrying handle, 12in. high. (Robert W. Skinner Inc.) $500 £270

Bavarian pewter dish, rim embossed with flower petals, circa 1800, 41.7cm. diam. (Sotheby's) $435 £231

Stuart pewter flat-lid tankard by W. W., circa 1690, 6½in. high. (Sotheby's) $2,135 £1,155

Norwich Friendly Society flagon in pewter, by Gerardin & Watson, circa 1819, 13½in. high. (Sotheby's) $2,950 £1,595

Large North German pewter flagon by CTN, Stade, circa 1823, 64.5cm. high.(Sotheby's) $1,075 £572

Rare mid 17th century Saxon spouted flagon in pewter, with double-domed cover, 33cm. high. (Sotheby's) $1,965 £1,045

Rare Stuart pewter flat-lid flagon or tall tankard, circa 1690, 8¾in. high. (Sotheby's)$1,015 £550

Dutch wriggleworked Corporation dish in pewter, circa 1661. (Sotheby's) $1,640 £900

18th century pewter flagon, inscribed on drum, 12½in. high, with spray thumbpiece. (Sotheby's) $775 £418

18th century tapering cylindrical pewter flagon, by Graham & Wardrop, Glasgow, 14¼in. high. (Sotheby's) $420 £220

Liberty & Co. pewter muffin dish and cover by Archibald Knox, circa 1905, 29cm. wide. (Sotheby's Belgravia) $300 £165

WMF pewter mounted green glass decanter, circa 1900, 42cm. high. (Sotheby's Belgravia) $390 £220

One of a pair of mid 19th century pewter table candlesticks with fixed nozzles, 11in. high. (Sotheby's) $145 £77

Liberty & Co. 'Tudric' pewter tea service by Archibald Knox. (Christie's) $400 £220

Late 16th century 'horse-hoof' knop spoon, 6½in. long. (Sotheby's) $650 £352

18th century pewter tapered cylindrical flagon by Graham & Wardrop, 10½in. high. (Sotheby's) $460 £242

Art Nouveau pewter framed mirror from a model by Charles Jonchery, 72cm. wide. (Christie's) $1,455 £800

WMF green glass and pewter claret jug of trumpet form, 40.5cm. high. (Christie's)$475 £260

Late 17th century German or Dutch pewter beaker engraved with wrigglework panels, 6¾in. high. (Christie's) $475 £260

18th century pewter barber's bowl of oval outline, 11¾in. wide. (Christie's) $675 £370

18th century German pewter wasserbehalter by Georg Ludwig Ruepprecht, Memmingen, 12½in. high. (Christie's) $1,465 £800

WMF pewter mounted green glass decanter with pierced and cast stopper, circa 1900, 38cm. high. (Sotheby's Belgravia) $500 £275

Liberty & Co. pewter tea service by Archibald Knox, circa 1905. (Sotheby's Belgravia) $520 £286

Pewter spouted flagon of spreading cylindrical shape, 15¼in. high, spout with hinged cover. (Lawrence Fine Art) $150 £85

Urania pewter bucket and cover with fixed arched handle, stamped, 28.5cm. high, circa 1900. (Sotheby's Belgravia) $170 £95

Early 18th century circular pewter charger with broad rim, 18in. diam. (Sotheby's) $210 £110

Early 18th century lidded baluster measure of half-pint capacity, 4¾in. high. (Sotheby's) $260 £137

Boy seated on a bench, by J. Whistler, Salt Print, 259 x 217mm., c. 1855.(Sotheby's Belgravia) $320 £175

Virginia Dalrymple by O. G. Rejlander, Albumen Print, c. 1860.(Sotheby's Belgravia) $80 £44

Setting up the bow nets, by P. H. Emerson, platinum print, 120 x 174mm., 1886. (Sotheby's Belgravia) $440 £242

One from a series of sixteen portraits of Sporting Celebrities, 1890.(Sotheby's Belgravia)$120 £66

Sir Henry Taylor, Albumen Print, 252 x 202mm., circa 1865.(Sotheby's Belgravia) $1,395 £770

One from an album of eight views in the Yosemite, by C. E. Watkins, approx. 400 x 520mm. (Sotheby's Belgravia $5,975 £3,300

Undine by H. Lambert, Toned Silver Print, 200 x 157mm. (Sotheby's Belgravia) $65 £35

'Hypatia' Portrait of Marie Spartali, Albumen Print, 300 x 345mm., c. 1870.(Sotheby's Belgravia) $1,400 £770

Maid at the Well Dimbo Freshwater, Isle of Wigh Albumen Print, c. 1860 (Sotheby's Belgravia) $45 £2

Portrait of Sir. T. Phillips, 277 x 234mm., Albumen Print, c.1865.(Sotheby's Belgravia) $400 £220

Portrait of Mrs. Duckworth, by J. M. Cameron, Albumen Print, 320 x 220mm., c. 1872.(Sotheby's Belgravia) $360 £198

One from a collection of approx. 135 nude studies, 140 x 100mm., 1880's. (Sotheby's Belgravia) $995 £550

Portrait of a Woman, by O. G. Rejlander, Albumen Print, 208 x 145mm., c. 1860.(Sotheby's Belgravia) $260 £143

A Claudet half-plate daguerreotype portrait of A. Hewat, after 1851.(Sotheby's Belgravia) $220 £121

One from an album of 35 Neapolitan Portraits, attributed to G. Sommer, 245 x 175mm., 1880's.(Sotheby's Belgravia) $995 £550

Newhaven Fisherman, Calotype, by R. Adamson & D. O. Hill, 155 x 116mm., circa 1845.(Sotheby's Belgravia) $755 £418

Girl at a window by Lady C. Hawarden, Albumen Print, 84 x 65mm., early 1860's.(Sotheby's Belgravia) $6,770 £3,740

Naked wrestlers by O. G. Rejlander, Albumen Print, c. 1860.(Sotheby's Belgravia) $90 £49

One of a rare group of Seven Stereoscopic studies of Polynesian Natives, dated 1860. (Sotheby's Belgravia) $360 £198

One from a group of twenty-four Japanese portraits by Sohutamarko, each approx. 90 x 135mm., 1870's.(Sotheby's Belgravia) $320 £176

Sleep by John Whistler, Salt Print, 205 x 160mm., c. 1855. (Sotheby's Belgravia) $560 £308

Xie Kitchin lying on a sofa with open book, Albumen Print by Lewis Carroll, 141 x 185mm., c. 1870. (Sotheby's Belgravia) $895 £495

A half-plate daguerreotype portrait of three ladies with photographer J. G. Eynard-Lullin, passe partout, c. 1845-50.(Sotheby's Belgravia) $1,155 £638

One from an album of 100 studies from Japan, each approx. 200 x 250mm. c. 1870.(Sotheby's Belgravia)$440 £242

Still Life with a basket, bottles, flask, bonnet hat and dog, Albumen Print, 112 x 156mm., 1850's. (Sotheby's Belgravia) $260 £143

The Paddle Steamer 'Princess' on the New Orleans Waterfront, 156 x 206mm., 1850's, by J. D. Edwards. (Sotheby's Belgravia) $1,600 £880

Exterior of The Colosseum by Robert McPherson, 237 x 403mm. (Sotheby's Belgravia) $240 £132

A stereoscopic daguerreotype portrait of a middle-aged lady, by T. R. Williams, c. 1855. (Sotheby's Belgravia) $520 £286

Marilyn Monroe, Silver Print, by Weegee, 277 x 355mm., 1953. (Sotheby's Belgravia) $260 £143

St. Mark's Venice, Calotype, 169 x 217mm., c. 1850. (Sotheby's Belgravia) $150 £82

'Jackson R. R. Engine Shop', 154 x 205mm., 1850's. (Sotheby's Belgravia) $1,300 £715

Paris, The Banks of the Seine, Salt Print by Ferrier, 229 x 302mm., signed and dated 1852. (Sotheby's Belgravia) $2,590 £1,430

The Mosque of Kaitbey by Frances Frith, signed and dated 1858, 391 x 465mm. (Sotheby's Belgravia) $360 £198

Notre Dame, Salt Print by Ferrier, 172 x 240mm., c. 1852. (Sotheby's Belgravia) $745 £412

Eavestaff 'minipiano pianette' with matching stool, 86cm. wide, 1930's. (Sotheby's Belgravia) $535 £300

Baby grand piano by Carl Meverstein, in floral lacquered satinwood case. (John Hogbin & Son) $3,180 £1,700

Broadwood square piano, crossbanded in rosewood and with ebony stringing, circa 1813. (Cooper Hirst) $605 £325

Late 19th century French 20-key barrel organ with pinned wooden cylinder, 27in. wide. (Sotheby's Belgravia) $2,165 £1,210

Late 18th century George III clavichord by Schoene & Insen, London, 66in. long. (Robert W. Skinner Inc.) $125 £70

Keith Prowse 'pennyano cafe barrel piano in stained wood case, circa 1900, 40in. wide. (Sotheby's Belgravia) $1,475 £825

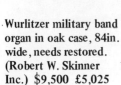

Wurlitzer military band organ in oak case, 84in. wide, needs restored. (Robert W. Skinner Inc.) $9,500 £5,025

Steinway & Sons ebonised wood upright piano, New York, circa 1903, 62in. wide. (Robert W. Skinner Inc.) $300 £165

Boudoir grand piano in polished case, by C. Bechstein, Berlin, no. 74474. (John Hogbin & Son) $3,105 £1,725

Hurdy-Gurdy monkey organ in mahogany case, 18½in. wide. (Robert W. Skinner Inc.) $2,300 £1,215

Small organ grinder in grain painted case, 12½in. wide. (Robert W. Skinner Inc.) $170 £90

Haines Bros. player piano with ampico action, complete with thirty-six rolls, 63in. wide. (Robert W. Skinner Inc.) $700 £370

Satinwood grand piano by Bluthner, top with crossbanded border, 74in. wide. (Sotheby's Belgravia)$3,610 £1,870

Coin operated barrel organ by Cannon A. O. Wintle. (Lacy Scott) $1,885 £1,020

Broadwood marquetry oak boudoir grand piano with iron frame, circa 1880. (Sotheby's Belgravia) $1,850 £990

Jazz band barrel organ in beech case, with automatic barrel, 32in. wide. (Robert W. Skinner Inc.) $550 £290

Baillie Scott Manxman upright pianoforte by John Broadwood & Sons, London, in oak case, 144cm. wide. (H. Spencer & Sons Ltd.) $740 £420

Street automatic piano in beech case, slightly damaged, 40in. wide. (Robert W. Skinner Inc.) $250 £130

Late 19th/early 20th century Austrian Meerschaum cheroot holder, 12.2cm. long. (Sotheby's Belgravia) $50 £27

Late 19th century Meerschaum pipe with metal collar and amber mouthpiece, 6¼in. long. (Sotheby Beresford Adams) $230 £125

Late 19th century Meerschaum pipe in fitted case. (Sotheby Beresford Adams) $175 £95

Late 19th/early 20th century Austrian Meerschaum cheroot holder, 12.8cm. long. (Sotheby's Belgravia) $230 £121

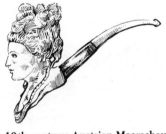

German Meerschaum pipe, bowl of plain form, with pierced silvery metal cover and mounts. (Burrows & Day) $75 £40

Late 19th century Austrian Meerschaum pipe, bowl carved as a young lady, 14.5cm. long. (Sotheby's Belgravia) $245 £132

Early 20th century Austrian Meerschaum pipe, head carved as a roaring tiger, 14.5cm. long. (Sotheby's Belgravia) $170 £88

Late 19th/early 20th century Austrian Meerschaum pipe, 16.5cm. long. (Sotheby's Belgravia) $550 £286

Late 19th century Austrian Meerschaum pipe with carved bowl, 15.5cm. long. (Sotheby's Belgravia) $185 £99

Well carved Meerschaum pipe, front with nude mermaid, with silver mounted amber stem and mouthpiece, 7in. long. (Burrows & Day) $165 £88

Late 19th/early 20th century Austrian Meerschaum cheroot holder, 17cm. long. (Sotheby's Belgravia) $230 £121

Late 19th century Austrian Meerschaum pipe, bowl carved as a hatching egg, 14.5cm. long. (Sotheby's Belgravia)
$305 £165

Well carved Meerschaum pipe, bowl in the shape of an Irishman's head, 6in. long. (Burrows & Day) $165 £90

One of two Continental pipes with decorated porcelain bowls and horn mounted cherrywood stems. (Burrows & Day)
$22.£12

Late 19th/early 20th century Meerschaum pipe with carved bowl, 16cm. long. (Sotheby's Belgravia)$360 £187

Late 19th century Meerschaum pipe with metal collar and amber mouthpiece, 6½in. long. (Sotheby Beresford Adams) $165 £90

621

Late 19th/early 20th century Meerschaum cheroot holder, 11.3cm. long. (Sotheby's Belgravia) $125 £66

Late 19th century Austrian Meerschaum pipe carved as the head of a negro boy, 17cm. long. (Sotheby's Belgravia) $580 £308

Mid 19th century blue glass pipe with long curved stem, 70.5cm. long. (Sotheby's Belgravia) $150 £82

Well carved Meerschaum cigar holder in the form of a head of a Kaiser, 3¼in. (Burrows & Day) $110 £60

One of two late 19th century German Meerschaum pipes, 9½in. long. (Robert W. Skinner Inc.) $150 £80

Austrian Meerschaum pipe, bowl carved as a young woman carrying a parasol, 20.3cm. long, circa 1880. (Sotheby's Belgravia) $660 £352

Mid 19th century three-colour glass pipe with knopped stem, 48.2cm. long. (Sotheby's Belgravia) $320 £176

Meerschaum cigar holder in the form of a young boy in a skittle alley, 4in. long. (Burrows & Day) $90 £50

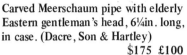

Carved Meerschaum pipe with elderly
Eastern gentleman's head, 6¼in. long,
in case. (Dacre, Son & Hartley)
$175 £100

Austrian Meerschaum pipe with carved
bowl, circa 1905, 16.4cm. long, with
case. (Sotheby's Belgravia) $350 £187

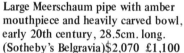

Large Meerschaum pipe with amber
mouthpiece and heavily carved bowl,
early 20th century, 28.5cm. long.
(Sotheby's Belgravia)$2,070 £1,100

Austrian silver mounted Meerschaum
pipe with hinged cover, Vienna, 1824,
5in. long. (Sotheby's) $450 £253

Austrian Meerschaum cheroot holder,
elaborately carved, 28.5cm. long,
1880's. (Sotheby's Belgravia)
$2,480 £1,320

Large Viennese Meerschaum bowl with
silver mount, circa 1870, 20.3cm. long,
in case. (Sotheby's Belgravia)
$4,550 £2,420

Late 19th century Meerschaum pipe
carved as a skull, with silver collar and
amber mouthpiece, 6¼in. long.
(Sotheby's) $155 £88

Meerschaum pipe, bowl carved as
woman with a fur collar, circa 1900,
15.5cm. long, probably Austrian.
(Sotheby's Belgravia) $160 £88

'Princenza Wilhelmina' lithographic poster by Paul Berthon, signed, circa 1900, 39 x 36cm. (Sotheby's Belgravia) $150 £82

'Art et Decoration', lithographic poster by G. Lorin, signed and dated '98, 65.5 x 44.75cm. (Sotheby's Belgravia) $420 £220

'Young Woman with Flowers', lithographic poster by Paul Berthon, circa 1900, 44 x 42cm. (Sotheby's Belgravia) $170 £93

'Course de Cote Chavigny Nancy', lithographic poster by Polbor, signed and dated '32, 78 x 119cm. (Sotheby's Belgravia) $85 £46

'Flirt', lithographic poster, signed, framed and glazed, 1890, 25 x 58.5cm. (Sotheby's Belgravia) $940 £495

Lazenby's Specialities, framed showcard with large selection of food products, 28½ x 36½in. (Sotheby's Belgravia) $130 £71

One from a collection of fifty-nine lithographic posters by Conrad E. Leigh, 31 x 47in.(Sotheby's Belgravia)$360 £198

Le Courrier Francais, French lithographic poster, signed Cheret, 31¼ x 45in. (Sotheby's Belgravia) $150 £82

'Sarah Bernhardt' lithographic poster by Paul Berthon, circa 1900, signed, 36 x 50cm. (Sotheby's Belgravia) $525 £300

'Sables D'Or les Pins', large lithographic poster by C. Loupot, 1925, signed, 102 x 72.5cm. (Sotheby's Belgravia) $500 £264

Fap'anis poster by Delval, depicting colourful girl holding glass of liqueur, 62½ x 47in., circa 1920's. (Sotheby's Belgravia) $100 £55

'Au Quartier Latin', small lithographic poster, 26.5 x 36cm., signed and dated '98, framed and glazed. (Sotheby's Belgravia) $625 £330

H. Russell Flint, Chester, G. W. R. poster, 38 x 48in. (Sotheby's Belgravia) $190 £99

Yvette Guilbert, French lithographic poster, signed Bac 1895, 29¾ x 77½in. (Sotheby's Belgravia) $100 £55

Warwick Goble, Charming Chepstow, The New Racecourse, G. W. R. poster, 38 x 48in. (Sotheby's Belgravia) $276 £143

'Paris 1937 Exposition Internationale', lithographic poster by Paul Colin, 59.5 x 39.5cm. (Sotheby's Belgravia) $145 £77

Italian School, design for a poster announcing a street Carnival, circa 1873. (Sotheby's Belgravia) $100 £55

'Austin Reed's of Regent Street', lithographic poster by Tom Purvis, signed, late 1920's, 74.3 x 49.6cm. (Sotheby's Belgravia) $210 £110

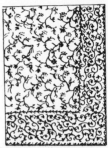

Silk patchwork bed-cover lined with Paisley pattern cotton, circa 1830, 89in. square. (Lawrence Fine Art) $335 £180

One of a pair of early 20th century cotton and lace bedcovers with filet-work panels, 82 x 90in. (Sotheby's Belgravia) $595 £319

Mid 18th century embroidered cotton bedcover with white ground and green threads, 92 x 85in. (Sotheby's Belgravia) $850 £451

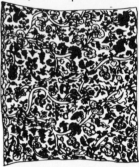

Sino-Portuguese brocade bedcover, mid 18th century, with crimson ground, 115 x 120in. (Sotheby's Belgravia) $2,310 £1,320

Embroidered silk bed-cover with pheasant on a tree, circa 1900, 92 x 74½in. (Sotheby's Belgravia) $695 £396

One of a pair of early 18th century crewel-work bed-hangings or curtains, sold with a pelmet. (Sotheby's Belgravia) $3,220 £1,705

20th century tapework bedcover with central flower, 113in. square. (Sotheby's Belgravia) $305 £165

19th century American appliqued and patchwork quilt, 88 x 94in. (Robert W. Skinner Inc.) $400 £225

Civil War patriotic quilt, 68 x 88in., dated 1864.(Robert W. Skinner Inc.) $450 £245

Striking patchwork quilt of tiny hexagons using late 18th/early 19th century chintzes. (Christie's S. Kensington)$660 £360

Mid 18th century Indo-Portuguese silk embroidered quilted bedcover, 72 x 56in. (Sotheby's Belgravia) $390 £209

Pennsylvania pieced quilt of 'Spider's Web' pattern in multi-coloured cottons, 84in. square, 1860-70. (Sotheby's Belgravia) $730 £385

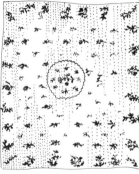

Early 19th century embroidered satin bedcover with central medallion, 91½ x 84in. (Sotheby's Belgravia)$1,540 £880

Indian silk-embroidered bedcover with white satin ground, circa 1700, 91 x 85in. (Sotheby's Belgravia) $2,310 £1,320

Brocade bedcover of gold thread on crimson ground, circa 1900, 102 x 71¾in. (Sotheby's) $3,150 £1,760

19th century pieced and appliqued quilt, slightly faded, 84in. square. (Robert W. Skinner Inc.) $450 £245

White American Marseilles-type quilt with cotton face, circa 1820, 80 x 66in. (Robert W. Skinner Inc.)$350 £190

19th century American pieced appliqued quilt with white cotton field, 102 x 82in.(Robert W. Skinner Inc.)$600 £325

Abbey Road, The Borough of St. Marylebone, enamelled street sign, 30 x 18in. (Sotheby's Belgravia) $640 £352

Mitch Mitchell's twelve-piece drum kit with accessories and spares.(Sotheby's Belgravia) $440 £242

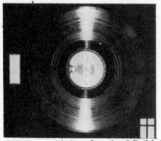

Dire Straits, gold disc for the LP 'Making Movies', with presentation, 16 x 14in., 1981.(Sotheby's Belgravia) $835 £462

Cliff Richard in 1958, contemplating his rise to top of the bill at Chiswick Empire.(Sotheby's Belgravia) $140 £77

An A.M.I. Continental Jukebox, 45-rpm, 64in. high.(Sotheby's Belgravia) $600 £330

Buddy Holly and the Crickets, photographed in England during 1958. (Sotheby's Belgravia) $160 £88

The Coset Pop Award 1970, bronze 10in. (Sotheby's Belgravia) $1,235 £682

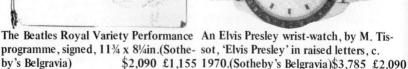

The Beatles Royal Variety Performance programme, signed, 11¾ x 8¼in.(Sotheby's Belgravia) $2,090 £1,155

An Elvis Presley wrist-watch, by M. Tissot, 'Elvis Presley' in raised letters, c. 1970.(Sotheby's Belgravia)$3,785 £2,090

A Raleigh Super 50 Moped once owned by John Lennon, complete with registration book, 69in. long, c. 1965.(Sotheby's Belgravia)　　　　$5,175　£2,860

Eddie Cochrane and Gene Vincent photographed in 1960 on a British tour.(Sotheby's Belgravia)　　　　$180　£99

A pair of Beatle woven nylon stockings printed with caricatures of the Beatles, c. 1965.(Sotheby's Belgravia)$280 £154

John Lennon, pen and ink self-portrait seated within a circle, 3¾in. (Sotheby's Belgravia)　　　　$15,930　£8,800

A bronzed bust of Elvis Presley by J. Douglas, 8½in. high, English 1976. (Sotheby's Belgravia)　　　　$110　£60

Paul McCartney's Chappell & Co. Ltd. upright piano, 50 x 50 x 24½in., English c. 1902. (Sotheby's Belgravia) $17,920 £9,900

A Seeburg symphonia jukebox, 58½in. high, American, c. 1946. (Sotheby's Belgravia)　　　$2,190　£1,210

Introducing Elvis Presley in 'Love Me Tender' Film Poster, 30 x 40in. (Sotheby's Belgravia)　　　$60　£35

The Beatles for their fans — a handout leaflet — 6 x 9in., c. 1961. (Sotheby's Belgravia)　$440　£242

South Caucasian/Talish prayer rug with dark blue field, 2ft.11in. x 4ft.11in. (Robert W. Skinner Inc.)
$850 £465

20th century American Santa Claus hooked rug, 31¾ x 39in. (Robert W. Skinner Inc.)$450 £245

Esfahan rug with ivory field, circa 1930, condition, fair, 6ft.11in. x 4ft.11in. (Sotheby's)
$2,025 £1,078

Kashan prayer rug in fair condition, circa 1930, 6ft.10in. x 4ft.7in. (Sotheby's)$1,965 £1,045

Shirvan rug with pattern of medallions, octagons and rosettes with border stripes. (Sotheby, King & Chasemore)
$2,885 £1,550

Fine Tabriz rug, field with indigo and ivory pole medallion, circa 1900, 5ft.7in. x 4ft.1in. (Sotheby's)
$4,030 £2,145

Teheran rug with ivory field, circa 1900, in fair condition, 6ft.10in. x 4ft.7in. (Sotheby's)
$1,860 £990

Kazak Fachralo rug, border of stylised design, 55 x 41in. (Sotheby, King & Chasemore)
$3,220 £1,800

One of a pair of Tabriz prayer rugs with madder border, circa 1930, 6ft. 3in. x 4ft.7in.(Sotheby's)
$1,755 £935

Orduj rug with triple medallion, circa 1880, 4ft.5in. x 3ft., in fair condition. (Sotheby's) $1,325 £704

Metropolitan Persian portrait rug depicting two women, 32 x 42in. (W. H. Lane & Son) $360 £200

Shirvan rug in fair condition, circa 1920, 4ft.8in. x 3ft.9in. (Sotheby's) $1,035 £550

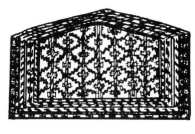

East Caucasian/Shirvan rug with narrow dark blue field, 3ft. 8in. x 8ft.10in. (Robert W. Skinner Inc.) $1,600 £980

Yomut Asmalyk, woven in the serrated lozenge trellis field design, 4ft.1in. x 2ft.4in. (Robert W. Skinner Inc.) $625 £345

Hamadan runner with dark blue field, 13ft. 3in. x 2ft.11½in. (Robert W. Skinner Inc.) $450 £240

Sarouk carpet with green field, 6ft.11in. x 10ft.1in. (Wm. Doyle Galleries Inc.) $6,000 £3,175

Veramin Soumak panel with dark blue field, 1ft. 3in. x 2ft.7in. (Robert W. Skinner Inc.) $750 £415

Nurata Susani panel with ivory field, circa 1900, 7 x 5ft., condition worn. (Sotheby's) $455 £242

Ispahan rug with all-over floral design on dark blue field, 6ft.9½in. x 4ft.5in. (Geering & Colyer) $1,755 £950

Kuba rug with deep blue field within a main border of white, 3ft.5in. x 5ft.7in. (Robert W. Skinner Inc.) $2,900 £1,585

Turkoman chuval rug with liver red field, 3ft.3in. x 2ft.2in. (Robert W. Skinner Inc.) $450 £245

Yoruk rug, large panels of blue, green and red filled with medallions, 3ft.6in. x 7ft.4in. (Robert W. Skinner Inc.) $800 £435

Sarouk rug with mulberry red field and pendanted blue medallion, 4ft.4in. x 7ft. (Robert W. Skinner Inc.) $400 £225

Kerman mat, ivory field with central medallion depicting a lady, circa 1930, in fair condition, 1ft.8in. x 1ft.2in. (Sotheby's) $250 £132

Moghan runner with blue field and ivory border, 3ft.8in. x 7ft.3in. (Robert W. Skinner Inc.) $1,900 £1,040

Interesting multi-bordered Oriental rug, 35 x 47in. (John Hogbin & Son) $75 £41

Trans Caucasian rug with rich blue field and geometric motifs, 3ft.2in. x 5ft. (Robert W. Skinner Inc.) $900 £490

Kuba rug, white field filled with rows of geometric motifs, 4ft. x 5ft.3in. (Robert W. Skinner Inc.) $2,500 £1,365

Soumak carpet, field with three medallions, 7ft.8in. x 8ft.7in. (Robert W. Skinner Inc.) $425 £230

Shiraz rug with triple lozenge pole medallion on magenta ground, 5ft.9in. x 4ft.2½in.(Geering & Colyer) $460 £250

Kuba rug, field of grey-blue with five medallions, dated 1347. (Robert W. Skinner Inc.) $2,300 £1,255

20th century Persian/ Lillihan mat with magenta red field, 2ft.3in. x 3ft.7in. (Robert W. Skinner Inc.)$200 £110

Persian/Lur rug with midnight blue field and five white medallions, 4ft.2in. x 9ft.6in. (Robert W. Skinner Inc.)$1,500 £815

Bidjar mat with cherry red field and blue central medallion, 2ft.6in. x 4ft.3in. (Robert W. Skinner Inc.)$350 £200

Caucasian/Sileh rug with four rows of four 'Z' motifs, 3ft. 4in. x 8ft.7in.(Robert W. Skinner Inc.) $3,700 £2,010

20th century Shiraz area rug with blue field, 2ft. 9in. x 4ft.5in. (Robert W. Skinner Inc.) $200 £115

633

Kayseri Anatolian rug with stylised cyprus trees and arches, 6ft. 6in. x 4ft. (Smith-Woolley & Perry) $590 £320

Kirman pictorial mat depict-ing a seated royal figure, 2ft. 2in. x 2ft.10in. (Robert W. Skinner Inc.) $325 £170

Small Isphahan carpet with ivory field and two floral borders, 10ft.2in. x 7ft.1in. (Richard Baker & Thomson) $1,870 £1,050

Kirman rug in good condition with deep blue field and red border, 6ft.9in. x 4ft.3½in. (Lawrence Fine Art) $1,120 £600

Tibetan saddle cover with pastel blue field, 2ft.4in. x 3ft.7in. (Robert W. Skinner Inc.) $550 £300

Turkish embroidered prayer rug with tree-of-life design, 72 x 48½in. (Lawrence Fine Art) $785 £420

Kurdish rug with in-digo field, 8ft. x 4ft. 5in. (Sotheby, King & Chasemore) $890 £480

Bahktiari carpet with midnight blue field, 10ft. x 6ft.6in. (Robert W. Skinner Inc.) $2,000 £1,085

Shirvan rug, indigo field with stepped medallions and two guls, 7ft.7in. x 3ft.11in. (Sotheby, King & Chasemore) $1,480 £800

Kashan rug with all-over diapered tile pattern, 6ft.11in. x 4ft.5½in. (Lawrence Fine Art)
$1,400 £750

Soumak bagface, central panel containing one Lesghi star, 2ft.2in. x 1ft.10in. (Robert W. Skinner Inc.)
$200 £105

Kashan rug with blue field woven with a navette medallion, 6ft.7½in. x 4ft.3in. (Lawrence Fine Art)
$2,055 £1,100

Caucasian runner woven with six panels, 11ft.2in. x 3ft.7in. (Lawrence Fine Art)
$485 £260

North West Persian Kelim saddlebags of trellis design, 2ft. x 4ft.6in. (Robert W. Skinner Inc.) $850 £460

One of a pair of good Kashan rugs with blue fields strewn with floral sprays, 6ft.11in. x 4ft.5in. (Lawrence Fine Art)
$4,115 £2,200

Persian tribal rug, possibly Lur of Kurd, with dark blue field, 3ft.11in. x 7ft.3in. (Robert W. Skinner Inc.)$350 £190

Kazak rug with red field of medallion, leaf and bar design, 4ft. x 6ft.11in. (Robert W. Skinner Inc.)
$900 £490

Bokhara Susanni panel worked in coloured silks, 98 x 57in. (Lawrence Fine Art)
$1,010 £540

Early 19th century sampler 'On Easter Day'. (Edwards, Bigwood & Bewlay) $200 £110

Linen worked sampler with central inscription, 19½in. wide, sold with another. (Sotheby's) $165 £93

William IV linen worked sampler by Fanney Wood, April, 1831, 17½in. square. (Sotheby's) $175 £99

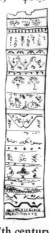

An early needlework sampler dated 1677. (Phillips) $675 £350

Needlework sampler in circular reserve on linen ground, 1817, 20½ x 19½in. (Robert W. Skinner Inc.) $1,300 £705

Early 17th century needlework sampler worked in cross stitch and running stitch, 86 x 16.5cm. (Phillips) $500 £270

American needlework sampler with wide floral border, circa 1825, 18in. square. (Robert W. Skinner Inc.) $350 £190

Silk worked picture of a map of England and Wales, by Elizabeth Foley, 1819, 21½in. wide. (Sotheby's) $315 £176

Early 19th century sampler by Emma Toogood, framed, 16 x 12in. (Sotheby's Belgravia) $270 £143

SAMPLERS

Early 19th century needle-work sampler by Selina Doughty, 1835, framed and glazed, 38 x 32cm. (Phillips) $260 £140

18th century needlework sampler 'A Trusty Servant', bearing arms and initials W.W. (Edwards, Bigwood & Bewlay) $345 £190

Sampler by Sarah Ann Hunt, aged 12, 1839, in rosewood frame, 24½ x 20in. (Sotheby's Belgravia) $270 £143

Spot-motif sampler with geometric panels outlined with silver thread, circa 1630, framed, 20 x 8in. (Sotheby's Belgravia) $1,635 £880

Mid 19th century needlework sampler by Ann Rebecca Willingham, 1842, 63 x 56cm. (Phillips) $275 £150

Embroidered border band sampler by Elizabeth Woodworth, 1758, 17¾ x 8½in. (Sotheby's Belgravia) $695 £374

'Stone' family register by Anna Stone, 1810, 21½ x 15½in. (Robert W. Skinner Inc.) $400 £220

Fine spot-motif sampler on ivory linen ground, 20 x 6½in., circa 1630, framed. (Sotheby's Belgravia) $1,840 £990

Late 18th century needle-work sampler, altered, framed and glazed, 31.5cm. square. (Phillips)$335 £180

SEALS

Regency three-sided engraved crystal swivel seal in gold serpent handle. (Woolley & Wallis)
$450 £250

Late 18th/early 19th century Italian lavastone desk seal with gold eyes, 11.5cm. high. (Sotheby's) $1,380 £715

Regency gold seal, inset with a milky stone and chased gold ring. (Woolley & Wallis)$200 £110

French gold mounted rock crystal desk seal, 5.4cm. high, circa 1910. (Sotheby's Belgravia) $825 £440

SHIBAYAMA

Ivory seal carved with a squirrel on a grapevine, circa 1900, 7.5cm. high. (Sotheby's Belgravia) $75 £38

Mid 19th century Italian gold and hardstone desk seal, 8.3cm. high. (Sotheby's)$1,205 £682

One of a pair of Minko enamelled silver shibayama vases, circa 1900, 17.5cm. high, on wood stands. (Sotheby's Belgravia) $2,125 £1,100

Late 19th century Masahura shibayama elephant, inlaid with coloured stones, 5cm. high. (Sotheby's Belgravia) $340 £176

Shibayama and ivory basket and cover with loop handle, circa 1900, 20cm. high. (Sotheby's Belgravia) $805 £418

Sunlight Soap, enamel sign of boy holding bars of Sunlight soap, 33½ x 32½in., circa 1905. (Sotheby's Belgravia) $320 £176

American bicycle shop sign, circa 1900, with applied moulding, 77in. wide. (Robert W. Skinner Inc.) $600 £340

Hodges Inn sign with oval shield, Vermont, circa 1790, 31¾in. wide. (Robert W. Skinner Inc.) $5,000 £2,715

Morse's Distemper, enamel sign by Hassall, 60 x 40in. (Sotheby's Belgravia) $695 £385

18th century tobacco figure of 'The Black Boy', on ebonised column, 42in. high. (Sotheby's) $3,445 £1,925

'Selo Film' enamel sign in yellow, red and black, 14in. wide. (Sotheby's Belgravia) $355 £198

A Barringer, Wallis & Manners Ltd. printed sign, 14in. high, circa 1910. (Sotheby's Belgravia) $40 £22

Ogden's St. Julien Tobacco, enamel sign showing two blends of tobacco against green brick background, 18 x 60in., circa 1900. (Sotheby's Belgravia) $120 £66

A decorative enamel sign, for 'Pullars of Perth', Cleaners and Dyers, 24in. high, circa 1920. (Sotheby's Belgravia) $80 £44

639

One of a matched pair of silver gilt two-handled baskets. (H. Spencer & Sons Ltd.) $1,280 £680

George II shaped oval basket by Edward Aldridge, London, 1748, 40oz.4dwt., 12½in. wide. (Sotheby's) $2,180 £1,155

George III silver cake basket by Philip Batchelor, London, 1793, 14½in. diam.(Sotheby, King & Chasemore) $855 £450

William IV cake basket by E., E., J. & W. Barnard, London, 1832, 44oz. 15dwt., 13in. diam. (Sotheby's) $1,630 £858

Shaped oval fruit basket, pierced and embossed, by James Dixon & Sons, Sheffield, 1898, 27.1oz., 36cm. long. (Sotheby's Belgravia) $550 £300

18th century George II reticulated silver basket with gadrooned edge, by Edward Wakelin, London, 12½in. long. (Robert W. Skinner Inc.) $1,500 £815

George III shaped oval cake basket by Michael Plummer, 1793, 15in. long, 26oz. (Christie's) $2,055 £1,100

George III shaped oblong sweetmeat basket by John Robins, London, 1796, 10oz.7dwt., 6½in. wide. (Sotheby's) $1,255 £660

George III shaped oval cake basket by William Plummer London, 1775, 13¼in. long 27oz.5dwt. (Sotheby's) $2,195 £1,155

George III cake basket by Peter Archambo, London, 1736, 54oz., 12¼in. wide. (Sotheby, King & Chasemore) $18,300 £10,000

Shaped circular cake basket by Henry Wilkinson & Co., Sheffield, 1844, 18.4oz., 25.5cm. wide. (Sotheby's Belgravia) $550 £286

George IV shaped circular cake basket by Emes & Barnard, 1827, 44oz. 16dwt., 13¾in. diam. (Sotheby's) $1,065 £550

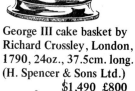

George IV plain shaped oval cake basket by Paul Storr, 1823, 13in. long, 35oz. (Christie's) $2,590 £1,400

George III boat-shaped sweetmeat basket by Peter and Ann Bateman, London, 1799, 8oz.1dwt., 6½in. wide. (Sotheby's) $665 £352

George III cake basket by Richard Crossley, London, 1790, 24oz., 37.5cm. long. (H. Spencer & Sons Ltd.) $1,490 £800

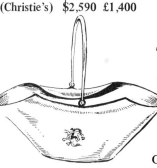

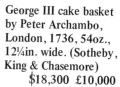

Hukin & Heath silver sugar basket with incurved rim and hinged handle, 6oz., London, 1881, 17cm. wide. (Phillips) $360 £200

George III sugar basket, with vase-shaped body, London, 1820, 7¾in. high, 7.3oz. (Lawrence Fine Art) $540 £280

Early George III shaped oval cake basket by Elizabeth Godfrey, London, 1760, 21oz.9dwt., 12in. wide. (Sotheby's) $1,145 £605

641

George III silver gilt metal oval sweetmeat basket, 6¾in. wide, by Vere & Lutwyche, London, 1767, 6oz.5dwt. (Sotheby's) $772 £400

William IV circular cake basket by Henry Wilkinson & Co., Sheffield, 1835, 22oz.1dwt., 10in. diam. (Sotheby's) $735 £400

One of a pair of George III oval basket salts by Fras. Spilsbury, London, 1769, 5oz. (Dickinson, Davy & Markham)$280 £155

Early George III oval sweetmeat basket by William Plummer, London, 1761, 6½in. wide, 4oz.10dwt. (Sotheby's)$515 £280

George III oval cake basket by Hester Bateman, London, 1787, 29oz.8dwt., 14½in. wide. (Sotheby's) $1,810 £990

George III shaped oval cake basket, London, 1771, 30oz.9dwt., 13in. wide.(Sotheby's) $885 £480

George III oval cake basket by Hester Bateman, London, 1780, 14in. wide, 22oz. 8dwt. (Sotheby's) $1,720 £935

George III sweetmeat basket by Alexander Field, London, 1793, 6oz., 5¼in. wide. (Sotheby's)$495 £270

George III oval cake basket by William Plummer, 1778, 13¾in. long, 34oz. (Christie's) $4,060 £2,268

Regency rectangular cake basket, London, 1810, 37.5oz., with gadroon borders. (Woolley & Wallis) $595   £330

Shaped oval pierced and chased fruit basket by Sibray, Hall & Co., Sheffield, 1890, 16.5oz., 29.8cm. wide. (Sotheby's Belgravia) $515   £275

One of a pair of oval baskets by D. & J. Wellby, 1910, 9¾in. wide, 26oz. (Lawrence Fine Art)
$885   £490

George II shaped oval cake basket by George Methuen, London, 1748, 14½in. long, 60oz.13dwt. (Sotheby's) $5,525   £2,970

George V oval dessert basket by Manoah Rhodes, Bradford, 46oz., 44cm. wide. (H. Spencer & Sons Ltd.) $645   £350

Shaped oval cake basket with rococo scrolls, 34.7cm. long, by Brasted & Co., London, 1898, 44oz. (Sotheby's Belgravia) $1,445   £770

George III oblong vase-shaped sweetmeat basket by Peter and Ann Bateman, London, 1793, 8oz.4dwt. (Sotheby's)
$645   £352

George IV shaped circular cake basket by Stephen Bergin, Dublin, 1822, 40oz.8dwt., 13½in. diam. (Sotheby's) $1,330   £715

Late 19th century/early 20th century enamelled silver mounted agate sweetmeat dish, 15.5cm. long. (Sotheby's Belgravia) $870   £462

Tapering cylindrical beaker by Niels Svendsen, Copenhagen, 1689, 11cm. high, 7oz.2dwt. (Sotheby's)
$2,125 £1,100

Parcel gilt and niello beaker with everted rim, Moscow, 1848, 7.7cm. high. (Sotheby's) $615 £330

Russian silver gilt beaker by Grigory Lakomkin, Moscow, circa 1750, 3½in. high. (Christie's)
$460 £250

Silver beaker of tapering form by V. Nikitin, Moscow, 1740, 14.3cm. high. (Sotheby's) $735 £396

George III plain beaker by James McEwen, Glasgow, circa 1780, 4oz.16dwt. (Christie's) $345 £190

Swedish tapering beaker by Johan Hamargren, Pitea, 1780, 6¼in. high, 8oz.11dwt. (Christie's)
$940 £520

Mid 17th century Batavian silver beaker, 8oz.15dwt., 15.3cm. high. (Sotheby's)
$1,805 £935

Cylindrical silver beaker by A.B. & F.G., Moscow, 1792, 8.4cm. high. (Sotheby's)
$450 £242

Swedish parcel gilt beaker on fluted foot, by Nils Reetz, Umea, 1764, 6½in. high, 8oz. 14dwt. (Christie's)
$1,190 £626

German parcel gilt beaker with strapwork band, Dresden, circa 1725, 5oz. 10dwt., 14.7cm. high. (Sotheby's) $1,700 £880

Early 18th century silver beaker of flared cylindrical form, 6oz.8dwt., 2½in. high. (Sotheby's) $1,255 £660

German silver beaker by Moritz Krelle, Augsburg, circa 1730, 3½in. high. (Christie's) $1,295 £700

Cylindrical silver beaker by Savelev, Moscow, 1796, 8.7cm. high. (Sotheby's) $530 £286

Finnish parcel gilt beaker by Anders Tidstrom, Vasa, 1772, 6½in. high, 9oz. 2dwt. (Christie's) $2,445 £1,350

German silver beaker with spiral fluting, by Thomas Kuntze, Breslau, circa 1700, 3¼in. high. (Christie's) $1,015 £550

Silver beaker of tapering cylindrical form, possibly by Gergori Serebryanikov, Moscow, 1758, 7.9cm. high. (Sotheby's) $490 £264

Large Danish silver beaker by Johann Henrich Mundt, Copenhagen, 1706, 4¾in. high, 7oz.5dwt. (Christie's) $2,160 £1,155

Early George II flared cylindrical beaker by William Darker, London, 1727, 3oz., 3¼in. high. (Sotheby's) $725 £396

Early 20th century circular two-handled fruit bowl, 31cm. wide, 21.4oz. (Sotheby's Belgravia) $305 £165

Circular sugar bowl with embossed edge, London, 1890, 3oz.(Dickinson, Davy & Markham) $85 £45

Lobed circular fruit bowl by Manoah Rhodes & Sons Ltd., London, 1908, 64.1oz., 34.5cm. diam. (Sotheby's Belgravia) $995 £528

Modern silver and gem-encrusted punch bowl with ladle, by Deirdre Peterson, Birmingham, 1970. (Alfred Mossop & Co.) $985 £510

Large pierced rose bowl with engraved inscription, by James Deakin & Sons, Sheffield, 1904, 54.1oz., 20.1cm. diam. (Sotheby's Belgravia) $1,345 £715

Silver gilt Cellini pattern rose bowl by Charles Boyton, London, 1891, 61.3oz., 27.5cm. diam. (Sotheby's Belgravia) $2,110 £1,100

Pedestal rose bowl by R. & S. Garrard, London, 1878, 31.6cm. diam., 69.9oz. (Sotheby's Belgravia) $1,760 £935

Boat-shaped bowl by Viners Ltd., Sheffield, 1934, 49cm. long, 81.3oz. (Sotheby's Belgravia) $1,585 £825

Silver gilt shallow circular bowl by Edward Barnard & Sons Ltd., London, 1937, 35oz., 35cm. wide. (Sotheby's Belgravia) $350 £187

Early 20th century boat-shaped fruit bowl with chased and pierced sides, 45.2oz., 39cm. long. (Sotheby's Belgravia) $950 £495

Early George II punch bowl by Humphrey Payne, 1727, sold with a ladle, 61oz.11dwt., 11in. diam. (Sotheby's) $6,270 £3,300

Mid 18th century French silver sucrier, 4¾in. high, 12 troy oz. (Robert W. Skinner Inc.) $150 £80

George III hemispherical punch bowl, London, 1810, 9¾in. diam., 37oz.12dwt. (Sotheby's) $1,740 £935

Late 19th century Indian presentation rose bowl, 108.8oz., 46cm. wide. (Sotheby's Belgravia) $1,265 £660

Oval openwork fruit bowl by Elkington & Co. Ltd., London, 1900, 39.5oz., 31cm. long. (Sotheby's Belgravia) $1,445 £770

George II circular bowl by Samuel Walker, Dublin, circa 1745, 7in. diam., 18oz.14dwt. (Sotheby's) $4,090 £2,200

Dutch parcel gilt two-handled brandy bowl, Rotterdam, 1689, 6in. diam., 6oz. (Christie's) $2,990 £1,600

Late 19th century Dutch parcel gilt oval brandy bowl, 24.7cm. wide, 8.8oz. (Sotheby's Belgravia) $240 £130

George IV fruit bowl, Sheffield, 1827, 10¼in. diam. (Sotheby, King & Chasemore) $420 £220

George IV silver punch bowl by Benjamin Smith, London, 1827-28, 5¾in. high, 40 troy oz. (Robert W. Skinner Inc.) $1,000 £545

Two-handled circular rose bowl by Sibray, Hall & Co., London, 1890, 88.1oz., 44.5cm. wide. (Sotheby's Belgravia) $1,555 £850

William IV small shaped circular silver bowl by John Tapley, 1836, 6½in. diam., 16oz. (Christie's)$2,220 £1,200

Mid 18th century two-handled silver bowl, 4in. diam., 3oz.7dwt. (Christie's) $875 £462

Circular silver rose bowl by T. Wilkinson & Sons, Birmingham, 1905, 25.3cm. diam., 33.8oz. (Sotheby's Belgravia) $550 £300

Modern silver fruit bowl by Lee & Wigfull, Sheffield, 1931, 24oz., 10¼in. wide. (Lawrence Fine Art) $250 £130

Dutch oval invalid feeding bowl and cover, Rotterdam, 1671, 5in. long, 6oz. 1dwt. (Christie's) $3,555 £1,900

Late 19th century Dutch chased oval brandy bowl, 25.7cm. long, 6.6oz. (Sotheby's Belgravia) $240 £130

Circular flower bowl by C. S. Harris & Sons Ltd., London, 1898, 25cm. diam., 29.7oz. (Sotheby's Belgravia)
$935 £506

George II plain circular bowl by Christopher Locks, 6in. diam., 10oz., Dublin, 1732. (Christie's) $1,090 £1,100

Victorian silver footed compote with scalloped rim, Sheffield, 1886-87, 6in. high. (Robert W. Skinner Inc.)
$275 £150

One of a set of six rare George III finger bowls by Rebecca Emes and Edward Barnard, London, 1815, 46oz. (H. Spencer & Sons Ltd.)
$4,465 £2,400

Pair of boat-shaped fruit bowls, pierced with slats, by the Goldsmiths & Silversmiths Co. Ltd., London, 1897, 52.1oz. (Sotheby's Belgravia) $2,340 £1,265

Oval brandy bowl by Obbe Ydema, Sneek, 1770, 25cm. wide, 6oz.4dwt. (Sotheby's) $955 £495

Charles II plain circular bleeding bowl, 1682, 7oz.5dwt. (Christie's)
$2,900 £1,620

Dutch oval brandy bowl by Jan Papinck, Groningen, 1716, 9oz.10dwt., 23.3cm. wide. (Sotheby's) $1,870 £968

Silver compote by S. Kirk & Son, with removable rim and embossed decoration, 42oz. (Wm. Doyle Galleries Inc.)
$1,100 £580

Keswick School of Industrial Arts silver bowl, Birmingham, 1899, 7cm. wide. (Sotheby's Belgravia) $160 £88

Liberty & Co. two-handled silver bowl, Birmingham, 1913, 4¼oz., 14.6cm. wide. (Christie's) $275 £150

George III oval sugar basin by Heron, Edinburgh, 1818, 8in. wide, 10oz.2dwt. (Sotheby's) $290 £154

George II circular bowl by William Townsend, Dublin, circa 1747, 6in. diam., 12oz.4dwt. (Sotheby's)
$2,215 £1,210

20th century sterling silver handled bowl of oval form, 15¼in. long, 37.8 troy oz. (Robert W. Skinner Inc.) $325 £185

Plain circular bowl by William Sutton, Dublin, 1729, 6¼in. diam., 13oz.5dwt. (Christie's) $3,215 £1,650

Oval Russian silver sugar box by A. Afanasiev, Moscow, 1777, 6oz.15dwt., 12.2cm. wide. (Sotheby's) $1,445 £748

Sterling silver fruit bowl, Connecticut, early 20th century, 4½in. high, 46 troy oz. (Robert W. Skinner Inc.) $450 £250

Circular rose bowl in Burmese style by Carrington & Co., London, 1887, 23.7oz., 23.3cm. diam. (Sotheby's Belgravia) $535 £286

Boat-shaped pedestal fruit bowl by Edward Barnard & Sons, London, 1894, 46cm. high, 114.4oz. (Sotheby's Belgravia) $4,135 £2,200

18th century hemispherical punch bowl, circa 1750, 42oz.16dwt., 10½in. diam. (Sotheby's) $1,145 £605

George I hemispherical bowl, London, 1718, by Samuel Lea, 5in. diam., 5oz. 18dwt. (Sotheby's) $3,590 £1,950

SILVER

Reeded oval biscuit box, cover inset with shell cameo, circa 1880, 14.7cm. long, London, 1921. (Sotheby's Belgravia) $580 £308

Parcel gilt casket with cedar lining, by Leslie G. Durbin, London, 1961, 17cm. long. (Sotheby's Belgravia) $495 £264

Oblong silver box by Alfred Taylor, Birmingham, 1861, 15oz., 15.2cm. long. (Sotheby's Belgravia)$805 £429

One of a pair of rare and unusual George III silver gilt oval-shaped spice boxes by Thomas Heming, 28oz., 5½in. wide. (Sotheby, King & Chasemore) $9,515 £5,200

Rectangular silver cigarette box by Walker & Hall, Sheffield, 1903, 18.4cm. long. (Sotheby's Belgravia) $760 £396

19th century Viennese jewellery casket, urn containing a watch, 12¾in. high. (Christie's) $8,880 £4,800

Freedom casket and cover by V. & S., Birmingham, 1912, 28.8cm. long. (Sotheby's Belgravia) $1,550 £825

Engraved gilt metal jewel casket with corded borders, 21.2cm. long, circa 1860. (Sotheby's Belgravia)$660 £352

Silver enamelled box showing King Cole and his fiddlers, by Omar Ramsden. (Graves, Son & Pilcher)
$1,335 £750

Silver pill box with inset hinged cover, Birmingham, 1893, 1¾in. wide. (Dickinson, Davy & Markham)$85 £46

Unusual George III freedom box, circa 1795, 3in. wide. (Sotheby's)
$6,060 £3,190

Circular silver gilt and enamel box, stamped 'Made for Tiffany & Co.', Moscow, 1887, 5cm. diam. (Sotheby's)
$820 £440

Electroplated beehive biscuit box on stand, by Martin, Hall & Co. Ltd., circa 1875, 23.5cm. high. (Sotheby's Belgravia)
$620 £330

Continental silver gilt oblong marriage casket, circa 1660, 5¾in. long, 10oz. 6dwt. (Christie's) $4,600 £2,420

Late 19th century Austrian pill box by J. C. Klinkosch, Vienna, 4.2cm. long. (Sotheby's Belgravia) $455 £242

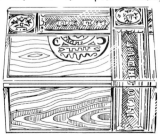

Rectangular silver cigarette box, Moscow, 1892, 10.1cm. wide. (Sotheby's)
$980 £528

BOXES

One of two octagonal
baluster toilet boxes,
London, circa 1685,
2½in. high, 6oz.19dwt.
(Sotheby's) $665 £360

Omar Ramsden silver and enamel
cigar box, inscribed, 1936, 21cm.
wide. (Sotheby's Belgravia)
$675 £380

George III taper box
by Hester Bateman,
London, 1783, 3in.
high, 4oz.13dwt.
(Sotheby's)$955 £520

18th century German sha-
ped silver gilt pill box,
Augsburg, circa 1775,
2½in. wide. (Woolley &
Wallis) $815 £420

Oblong spice box
by D. S., circa 1680,
1¾in. wide.
(Sotheby's)$590 £320

Colonial circular bowl
and cover with bud
finial, 8¾in. diam.
(Sotheby's)
$1,005 £550

BRANDY SAUCEPANS

George III brandy sauce-
pan and cover by Thos.
Death, London, 1818,
3½in. high, 5.9oz. (Law-
rence Fine Art)
$615 £320

George II baluster brandy
saucepan by Paul de
Lamerie, London, 1741,
11oz.17dwt., 3¼in. high.
(Sotheby's)$5,015 £2,640

George I baluster brandy
saucepan by Benjamin
Pemberton, Chester,
1724, 2oz.2dwt., 1¾in.
high. (Sotheby's)
$550 £300

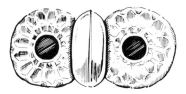

Liberty & Co. silver and enamel belt buckle in the form of two flowers, Birmingham, 1909, 8.25cm. wide. (Sotheby's Belgravia) $70 £40

Liberty & Co. 'Cymric' silver and enamel belt buckle of butterfly shape, Birmingham, 1902, 9.25cm. wide. (Sotheby's Belgravia) $300 £170

Liberty & Co. silver and enamel belt buckle, Birmingham, 1903, 8cm. wide. (Sotheby's Belgravia) $140 £80

William Hutton & Son Ltd., silver and green hardstone waist clasp of openwork design, Birmingham, 1902. (Christie's) $165 £90

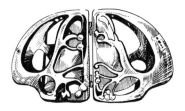

Theodor Fahrner silver and stone buckle, London, 1902, 6.75cm. wide.(Sotheby's Belgravia) $300 £165

Late 19th century lava belt buckle in gold plate, set with carved round and navette-shaped heads. (Robert W. Skinner Inc.) $150 £80

Unusual belt buckle by H. Hobson & Sons, Birmingham, 1910, 7cm. wide. (Phillips) $125 £70

Art Nouveau silver buckle by William Comyns, London, 1898, 13cm. wide. (Phillips) $230 £130

SILVER

Victorian candelabrum centrepiece by E. & J. Barnard, 1855, 30¼in. high, 196oz. (Christie's) $4,440 £2,400

One of a pair of 20th century Georg Jensen silver candelabra, Copenhagen, 8½in. high, 70 troy oz. (Robert W. Skinner Inc.) $3,700 £2,045

One of a pair of George V four-branch table candelabra, London, 1917, 88oz., 45cm. high. (H. Spencer & Sons Ltd.) $2,205 £1,180

One of a pair of George III four-light candelabra by Digby Scott and Benjamin Smith, 1804, 419oz. (Christie's) $68,640 £35,200

One of a pair of Ramsden & Carr three-light candelabra, 1905, 104oz., 22½in. high. (Christie's) $18,300 £10,000

One of a pair of Victorian four-light candelabra, maker's mark AM, 1873, 198oz., 23¼in. high. (Christie's) $8,140 £4,400

Five-light candelabrum by C. Boyton & Son, London, 1899, 62cm. high. (Sotheby's Belgravia) $1,280 £682

Electroplated four-light candelabrum, stamped C. Kay, 1930's, 55cm. high. (Sotheby's Belgravia) $1,245 £700

One of a pair of Regency candlesticks by J. Cradock and W. Reid, 1817, 18in. high, 101oz. (Christie's) $4,810 £2,600

One of a pair of Victorian Corinthian column table candelabra by H. Wilkinson and J. Batt, 53cm. high. (H. Spencer & Sons Ltd.)
$1,460 £780

German five-light candelabrum in silver coloured metal, 1937, 15cm. high. (Sotheby's Belgravia)
$300 £165

One of a superb pair of silver gilt candlesticks in rococo style, London, 1967, 85oz., 30cm. high. (H. Spencer & Sons Ltd.)
$1,590 £850

Edward VII silver Corinthian column five-light candelabrum, Sheffield, 1903-04, 19in. high, 45oz.6dwt. (Geering & Colyer) $1,710 £925

One of a pair of silver plated on copper three-light candelabra, 20in. high. (Sotheby, King & Chasemore) $360 £190

Victorian five-light candelabrum centrepiece by Martin Hall & Co., 1862, 32¾in. high, 290oz. (Christie's)
$6,105 £3,300

One of a pair of five-light candelabra with shaped square bases, 21¼in. high. (Sotheby Beresford Adams)
$480 £260

One of a pair of George III three-light candelabra by John Parsons & Co., Sheffield, 1791, 17¾in. high. (Lawrence Fine Art)
$4,055 £2,100

Large six-light candelabrum in silver plate, by Elkington & Co., 1884, 29½in. high. (Sotheby's)$660 £341

One of a pair of George III Ionic column candlesticks by John Carter, 1773, 13in. high. (Christie's)$1,955 £1,045

One of a pair of George II table candlesticks by John Priest, 1748, 8in. high, 36oz. (Hy. Duke & Son) $2,590 £1,350

One of a pair of silver table candlesticks by Hawkesworth, Eyre & Co. Ltd., Sheffield, 1916, 28.2cm. high. (Sotheby's Belgravia) $770   £420

One of a pair of large George IV candlesticks by Robt. Garrard, 1829, 12½in. high, 99oz. (Christie's)$4,625 £2,500

One of a pair of silver and enamel candlesticks of dwarf column form, late 18th century, 5¾in. high. (Christie's) $720 £380

One of a pair of 18th century George III table candlesticks by D. Smith and R. Sharp, London, 1762-3, 10½in. high. (Robert W. Skinner Inc.)$3,300 £1,795

One of a set of four table candlesticks by Goldsmiths & Silversmiths Co. Ltd., London, 1897, 27.5cm. high. (Sotheby's Belgravia)$1,935 £1,045

George II taperstick by James Gould, London, 1733, 3oz.14dwt., 4½in. high. (Sotheby Beresford Adams) $610 £330

One of a set of four silver candlesticks by Matthew Boulton & Co circa 1830, 11¼in. high. (Sotheby Beresford Adams) $775 £420

One of a pair of table candlesticks, Sheffield, 1900, 11½in. high. (Hy. Duke & Son) $490 £255

One of a pair of George II table candlesticks by John Priest, London, 1752, 6in. high, 26oz.12dwt.(Sotheby's) $1,515 £850

One of a pair of George III cluster columns candlesticks by Peter Werritzer, 1767, 11½in. high. (Christie's) $1,590 £850

One of four George III candlesticks by George Hill, Dublin, 1770, 96oz., 11¼in. high. (Christie's) $5,430 £3,000

One of a pair of George IV silver candlesticks by Wm. Burwash, 1820, 8in. high, 34oz. (Christie's) $1,755 £950

One of a pair of Regency silver gilt tapersticks by R. Emes & E. Barnard, 1819, 5½in. high, 12oz. 12dwt. (Christie's) $2,035 £1,100

One of a pair of early George II tapersticks, London, 1727, 7oz. 4dwt., 4¼in. high. (Sotheby Beresford Adams) $1,295 £700

One of a pair of table candlesticks by J. Dixon & Sons, Sheffield, 1900, 34.5cm. high. (Sotheby's Belgravia) $815 £440

George II taperstick by James Gould, London, 1730, 4oz., 4½in. high. (Sotheby Beresford Adams) $610 £330

SILVER

One of a set of four shaped-oval table candlesticks by Walker & Hall, Sheffield, 1920, 24cm. high.(Sotheby's Belgravia) $1,055 £550

One of a pair of candlesticks by William Hutton & Sons Ltd., London, 1909, 30cm. high. (Sotheby's Belgravia)
$590 £308

One of a pair of table candlesticks by Martin, Hall & Co., Sheffield, 1891, 29.5cm. high. (Sotheby's Belgravia) $845 £440

One of a pair of George II table candlesticks by William Cafe, London, 1757, 34oz.3dwt., 9½in. high. (Sotheby's) $2,180   £1,155

One of a pair of George I candlesticks by Thomas Sutton, Dublin, 1717, 6¼in. high, 18oz.17dwt. (Christie's) $2,925 £1,540

One of four George II table candlesticks by John Cafe, London, 1756, 82oz.16dwt., 10in. high. (Sotheby's) $4,600 £2,420

One of a pair of George III table candlesticks by John Smith II, London, 1771, 12¾in. high. (Sotheby's)
$3,030 £1,595

One of a set of four George II candlesticks by John Cafe, 1746, 7¼in. high, 61oz. (Christie's)
$6,280 £3,300

One of a pair of George II bedroom candlesticks, London, 1759, 8¼in. high. (Lawrence Fine Art
$1,060 £55(

One of a pair of early George III table candlesticks by John Carter, London, 1768, 12¼in. high. (Lawrence Fine Art) $850 £440

One of four George III candlesticks by John Younge & Sons, Sheffield, 1791, 12¼in. high. (Christie's) $5,435 £2,860

One of a set of four George III table candlesticks by Edmund Vincent, London, 1769, 13in. high. (Sotheby's) $4,600 £2,420

One of a set of four George III table candlesticks by John Carter, London, 1774, 10¾in. high, 92oz. (Sotheby's) $18,390 £9,680

One of a pair of George II candlesticks, Dublin, circa 1745, 8¼in. high, 31oz.8dwt. (Christie's) $3,555 £1,870

One of a set of four George III table candlesticks by David Bell, London, 1763, 94oz. 15dwt., 10in. high. (Sotheby's) $6,235 £3,300

One of a pair of George III table candlesticks by Ebenezer Coker, London, 1763, 27oz.16dwt., 8¾in. high. (Sotheby's) $2,080 £1,100

One of two matching George III table candlesticks, 8½in. high, 21oz.4dwt. (Sotheby's) $1,560 £825

One of a pair of George II table candlesticks by John Cafe, London, 1749, 37oz.7dwt., 8½in. high. (Sotheby's) $2,715 £1,430

One of a set of four George II table candlesticks by Thomas Heming, London, 1759, 111oz.5dwt., 11in. high. (Sotheby's) $5,115   £2,750

One of a pair of Liberty & Co. 'Cymric' silver and enamel candlesticks, Birmingham, 1901, 15.25cm. high. (Sotheby's Belgravia) $800 £450

One of a pair of George III table candlesticks by John Watson, Sheffield, 1808, 10in. high. (Sotheby's)$1,665 £858

One of a set of four Victorian Sheffield silver candlesticks by Hawksworth, Eyre & Co. Ltd., 1875, 13¼in. high.(Wm. Doyle Galleries Inc.) $1,600   £845

One of a pair of William and Mary table candlesticks, London, 1690, 7½in. high, 16oz.18dwt. (Sotheby's) $4,295 £2,310

One of a pair of table candlesticks, mid 18th century, possibly Irish, 11¾in. high, 66oz.14dwt. (Sotheby's)$1,410 £770

One of a pair of George III table candlesticks by Younge, Greaves & Hoyland, Sheffield, 1784, 10¾in. high.(Sotheby's) $1,150 £594

One of a pair of Italian neoclassical silver candlesticks, 11in. high, 21 troy oz. (Robert W. Skinner Inc.) $950 £515

One of a pair of George I candlesticks by Anthony Nelme, 1722, 6¾in. high, 30oz. (Christie's) $5,335 £2,808

One of a pair of table candlesticks by T. J. & N. Creswick, Sheffield, 1840, 29.5cm. high. (Sotheby's Belgravia) $1,075 £572

One of a pair of chromed metal candlesticks, 1930's, 55.75cm. high. (Sotheby's Belgravia) $265 £150

One of a pair of George III table candlesticks, sold with plated three-light candelabra branches, 1782, 16½in. high. (Sotheby's) $1,840 £990

One of a pair of Queen Anne candlesticks by Wm. Denny, 1703, 8in. high, 21oz. (Christie's) $4,925 £2,592

One of a set of four George II candlesticks, Dublin, circa 1750, 10in. high, 78oz. (Christie's) $6,280 £3,300

One of a set of four George III table candlesticks by John Parsons & Co., Sheffield, 1788, 11in. high. (Sotheby's) $3,630 £1,870

One of a set of four cast table candlesticks, 110.4oz., 30cm. high, London, 1919.(Sotheby's Belgravia) $1,860 £990

One of two matching silver gilt tapersticks by David Green, circa 1718-22, 5½in. high, 6oz.16dwt.(Christie's) $2,460 £1,296

One of a pair of George II candlesticks by Robt. Calderwood, Dublin, circa 1750, 40oz., 9¼in. high. (Christie's) $4,720 £2,420

Rectangular card case with a view of Newstead Abbey, by Taylor & Perry, Birmingham, 1836, 9.5cm. high. (Sotheby's Belgravia) $385 £209

Rare shaped rectangular card case by A. & S., Birmingham, 1858, 10cm. long. (Sotheby's Belgravia) $285 £154

Shaped rectangular card case by Nathaniel Mills, Birmingham, 1844, 10.1cm. high.(Sotheby's Belgravia) $345 £187

Silver card case by Gervase Wheeler, Birmingham, 1839, 3¾in. long. (Sotheby's) $415 £220

Austrian silver and enamel rectangular cigarette and card case, stamped. (Christie's) $275 £150

William IV silver gilt rectangular card case by Joseph Willmore, Birmingham, 1834, 3¾in. long. (Sotheby's) $280 £148

Parcel gilt card case by Edward Smith, Birmingham, 1850. (Sotheby's Belgravia) $480 £250

Shaped rectangular card case by Joseph Taylor, Birmingham, 1844, 10cm. high.(Sotheby's Belgravia) $455 £247

Silver card case by Taylor & Perry, Birmingham, 1842, 9.2cm. high, stamped with views.(Sotheby's Belgravia) $265 £143

Baluster-shaped silver caster with pierced cover, London, 1751, by John Berthelot, 9oz. (Lacy Scott) $750 £400

George I vase-shaped caster by Samuel Welder, London, 1725, 5¾in. high, 6oz.1dwt. (Sotheby's) $835 £440

Silver caster by Henricus de Potter, Brussels, 1778, 8oz.9dwt., 19.5cm. high. (Sotheby's)$1,020 £528

George I plain caster of inverted baluster form, by Augustine Courtauld, 1719, 8¼in. high, 13oz. 9dwt. (Christie's)
    $4,935   £2,530

One of a pair of Queen Anne lighthouse casters by Joseph Ward, London, 1702, 11oz. 13dwt., 6½in. high. (Sotheby's) $3,450 £1,815

George II vase-shaped caster, London, 1734, 7¼in. high, 9oz.7dwt. (Sotheby's) $940 £495

One of a set of three George II vase-shaped casters by Charles Martin. London, 1730, 21oz.1dwt., 7in. high. (Sotheby's) $1,665 £880

Large silver sugar caster with pierced cover, Sheffield, 1899, 6½in. high, 5¼oz. (Dickinson, Davy & Markham)
    $150 £80

George II silver muffin-eer by Simon Pantin, London, 1725-26, 6¼in. high, 11 troy oz. (Robert W. Skinner Inc.)
    $600 £325

665

SILVER

Epergne by William Comyns & Sons, London, 1898, 48cm. long, 114.8oz. (Sotheby's Belgravia) $2,585 £1,375

Early 19th century Italian parcel gilt model of the Virgin Immaculata, 22.9cm. high, 19oz. (Sotheby's) $550 £286

George II epergne pierced scroll feet, by William Cripps, circa 1755-56, 20½in. high, 193oz. (Christie's) $11,285 £5,940

Victorian table centrepiece by S. Smith and W. Nicholson, 1853, 27in. high, 158oz. (Christie's) $3,885 £2,100

Set of three silver dessert dish stands, German, circa 1870, 61.6oz. (Sotheby's Belgravia) $1,370 £715

English electroplated centrepiece with glass nautilus shell, 1860's, 36.4cm. high.(Sotheby's Belgravia) $310 £165

Epergne by Henry Wilkinson & Co., London, 1900, 17¼in. high, 70oz.18dwt. (Sotheby Beresford Adams) $1,480 £800

Large silver plated table candelabrum cum centrepiece by Padley, Parkin & Co., circa 1860, 34in. high. (Sotheby's) $1,920 £990

Large electroplated dessert stand with ivory stem, 1890's, 55.4cm. high. (Sotheby's Belgravia) $390 £209

Electroplated table centrepiece by W. & G. Sissons,
Sheffield, circa 1860,
60.5cm. high. (Sotheby's
Belgravia) $730 £396

Silver epergne with cut glass
dishes, by Walker & Hall,
Sheffield, 1900, 65.6oz.,
53.5cm. wide. (Sotheby's
Belgravia) $1,005 £550

Electroplated table centrepiece by Elkington & Co.,
30cm. high, 1898.
(Sotheby's Belgravia)
              $370 £198

Silver centrepiece by
Edward Barnard &
Sons, London, 1860,
38cm. high, 61oz.
(Sotheby's Belgravia)
      $1,315 £720

Elkington & Co. three-piece
garniture, Birmingham, 1890,
115oz. (Sotheby, King & Chasemore) $1,520 £800

Table ornament of a
man holding a shell
on his head, by Bar-
nard & Co., 1910,
15¾in. high, 71oz.
(Christie's)
      $1,260 £680

Victorian centrepiece by
S. Smith and W. Nichol-
son, 1862, 20¼in. high,
52oz. (Christie's)
          $1,295 £700

Silver and glass epergne and
condiment set by Christopher
Haines, Dublin, 1786, 14½in.
high. (Robert W. Skinner Inc.)
          $2,600 £1,415

Victorian table centre-
piece by S. Smith and
W. Nicholson, London,
1862, 39oz., 16¼in. high.
(Lawrence Fine Art)
          $850 £440

French shaped circular chamber candle-stick, Paris, 1722-26, 5oz.4dwt. (Christie's) $3,075 £1,700

Maltese silver chamberstick with ribbed and fluted plan, circa 1760, 6oz.12dwt. (Sotheby's) $1,380 £715

George III chamber candlestick by William Stroud, London, 1815, 5in. diam., 8oz.5dwt. (Sotheby's) $665 £352

French chamber candlestick on rim foot with reeded border, 1787, 7oz. 15dwt. (Christie's) $2,535 £1,400

French plain circular chamber candle-stick, Marseilles, 1741, 5oz.13dwt. (Christie's) $3,440 £1,900

One of a pair of William IV chamber candlesticks by T. J. & N. Creswick, Sheffield, 1834, 19oz.1dwt., 6in. diam. (Sotheby's) $1,565 £850

One of a pair of George IV shaped cir-cular chamber candlesticks by Matthew Boulton, Birmingham, 1827, 23oz. (Christie's) $2,220 £1,200

Mid 18th century French plain chamber candlestick by Jean Vieuseux, Albi, 10oz.18dwt. (Christie's) $2,355 £1,300

Mid 18th century French plain pear-shaped chocolate pot with wood handle, 7½in. high, 15oz. 14dwt. (Christie's)
$2,995   £1,620

Continental white metal chocolate pot with turned wood handle. (J. M. Welch & Son)
$530   £290

George II pear-shaped chocolate pot by Charles Kandler, circa 1745, 11in. high, 41oz. (Christie's)
$17,160   £8,800

CIGARETTE CASES

German enamelled cigarette case on silver coloured metal, circa 1910, 9.4cm. high.(Sotheby's Belgravia) $1,445 £770

Rectangular cigar box by Horace Woodward & Co. Ltd., London, 1896, 25cm. long. (Sotheby's Belgravia) $785 £418

Oval black lacquer cigarette box, stamped Charlton & Co., 1920's, 7cm. high. (Sotheby's Belgravia) $550 £285

Plain oblong enamel cigarette case, Birmingham, 1905, 9.1cm. high. (Sotheby's Belgravia)
$1,135 £605

Austrian rounded rectangular silver cigarette case designed by Georg Anton Scheidt, 8.8cm. wide. (Christie's) $235 £129

Engine-turned oblong cigarette case, with secret compartment, London, 1922, 3¾in. wide. (Sotheby's) $895 £495

CLARET JUGS

Plated metal and glass claret jug designed by Christopher Dresser, with hinged cover, 23.5cm. high. (Phillips) $145 £80

Late 19th century decorative claret jug, 15in. high. (Sotheby's) $895 £462

One of a pair of silver gilt mounted clear glass claret jugs by W. & G. Sissons, Sheffield, 1866, 24.5cm. high. (Sotheby's Belgravia) $1,555 £850

Victorian silver and glass claret jug by George Fox, 1889, 12¼in. high. (Christie's) $1,755 £950

Bulbous glass claret jug with ribbed body, silver mounted neck and lip, Sheffield, 1904, 8in. high. (Burrows & Day) $330 £180

One of a pair of German gilt metal mounted cut glass claret jugs, circa 1890, 31cm. high. (Sotheby's Belgravia) $1,075 £572

Victorian urn-shaped claret jug with plain glass body and silver fittings, Sheffield, 1883, 10in. high. (Burrows & Day) $335 £185

Glass claret jug with bulbous body and silver mounts, London, 1896, 7¾in. high. (Burrows & Day) $330 £180

One of a pair of silver gilt mounted Victorian claret jugs by J. W. Figg, London, 1865, 16¼in. high. (Sotheby's) $6,615 £3,410

Fine late 19th century cameo glass claret jug with Continental silver mounts, 9½in. high. (Locke & England) $485 £260

Silver mounted clear glass claret jug by C. E. Nixon, Sheffield, 1894, 30.5cm. high. (Sotheby's Belgravia) $990 £495

Silver mounted clear glass claret jug by Charles Boyton, London, 1874, 26.4cm. high.(Sotheby's Belgravia) $660 £352

German silver mounted etched glass claret jug, Bremen, circa 1879, 36.5cm. high.(Sotheby's Belgravia) $665 £363

Plated metal and glass lemonade jug, engraved, 22cm. high, with ebonised wooden handle. (Phillips) $145 £80

Victorian silver mounted glass claret jug, Birmingham, 1872, 10½in. high. (Sotheby's) $980 £506

Late Victorian claret jug by Dixon & Sons, Sheffield, 1890, 33cm. high, 29oz. (H. Spencer & Sons Ltd.) $645 £360

Silver mounted clear glass claret jug by J. Grinsell & Sons, Ltd., London, 1898, 27.5cm. high. (Sotheby's Belgravia) $650 £352

Silver mounted cut glass claret jug by S. Drew & Sons, London, 1899, 28.7cm. high.(Sotheby's Belgravia) $730 £400

One of a set of four George III decanter coasters by R. & S. Hennell, London, 1808, 14cm. diam. (H. Spencer & Sons Ltd.) $2,695 £1,450

One of a pair of George IV wine coasters, by John and James Settle, Sheffield, 1822, 6in. diam. (Sotheby's) $1,535 £792

One of a pair of early Victorian wine coasters by Joseph and John Angell, London, 1838, 5¼in. diam. (Sotheby's) $915 £506

One of a pair of George IV wine coasters by John Bridge, London, 1826, 5¾in. diam. (Sotheby's) $3,980 £2,200

Set of four silver wine coasters by John and Thomas Settle, Sheffield, 1818. (Phillips) $1,810 £1,000

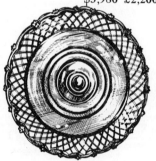

One of a pair of Victorian plated shallow shaped circular coasters, circa 1860, 20cm. diam. (Phillips) $235 £130

One of a set of four George III silver gilt wine coasters by Jonathan Alleine, London, 1771, 5in. diam.(Sotheby's) $6,695 £3,740

One of a set of four George III circular coasters by Robert Hennell, London, 1776, 5in. diam. (Sotheby's) $3,970 £2,090

George I tapered cylindrical coffee pot by Edward Vincent, London, 1725, 16oz.16dwt., 7¾in. high.(Sotheby's) $2,965 £1,595

Early George II cylindrical coffee pot by John le Sage, London, 1728, 8½in. high, 23oz.16dwt. (Sotheby's) $5,320 £2,860

George II tapered cylindrical coffee pot by Thos. Tearle, London, 1732, 23oz.9dwt., 9¼in. high. (Sotheby's)$4,025 £2,200

George II baluster coffee pot by John Payne, London, 1757, 23oz.9dwt., 9½in. high. (Sotheby's) $2,715 £1,430

Mid 18th century Irish provincial coffee pot, by Samuel Johns, Limerick, circa 1770, 34oz.15dwt., 10½in. high. (Sotheby's) $4,225 £2,310

George II coffee pot by Thomas Whipham, London, 1744, 30oz., 35.5cm. high. (H. Spencer & Sons Ltd.) $2,850 £1,550

Belgian pear-shaped coffee pot with domed cover, Brussels, 1759, 8¾in. high, 14oz.10dwt. (Christie's)$3,285 £1,728

George II plain pear-shaped coffee pot on gadrooned foot, by D. Smith and R. Sharp, 1766, 9¾in. high, 25oz. (Christie's) $2,665 £1,404

Plain tapering circular coffee pot by Mappin & Webb Ltd., London, 1965, 27.8oz.(Sotheby's Belgravia) $675 £352

673

COFFEE POTS

Silver coffee pot by Thos. Bradbury, Sheffield, 1903, 22oz., 10½in. high. (Lawrence Fine Art)
$540 £280

George III coffee pot on stand by Paul Storr, London, 1802, 12¾in. high, 55oz. (Lawrence Fine Art) $3,860 £2,000

Victorian silver coffee pot by Hands & Son, London, 1858, 10in. high, 30oz. (Lawrence Fine Art)
$985 £510

George III pear-shaped coffee pot by Tudor & Leader, Sheffield, 1774, 12in. high, 23oz. (Christie's)$2,055 £1,100

Early George III pear-shaped coffee pot, London, 1764, 27oz. (H. Spencer & Sons Ltd.) $1,505 £800

George II coffee pot with ivory handle, London, 1747, 25oz. (H. Spencer & Sons Ltd.)
$1,090 £580

George II tapered cylindrical coffee pot by Edward Feline, London, 1743, 24oz.2dwt., 8¾in. high. (Sotheby's)
$2,910 £1,540

Victorian silver coffee pot by E. & J. Barnard, London, 1862, 31oz., 10in. high. (Lawrence Fine Art)
$1,060 £550

George III pear-shaped coffee pot by Benjamin Gignac, 1767, 11¼in. high, 32oz. (Christie's)
$2,355 £1,300

George III coffee pot by William Cripps, London, 1775, 10in. high. (Sotheby, King & Chasemore) $720 £380

George III pear-shaped coffee pot by D. Whyte and W. Holmes, 1762, 12in. high, 32oz. (Christie's) $2,195 £1,155

George II pear-shaped coffee pot by Robert Calderwood, Dublin, circa 1760, 9¼in. high, 27oz. (Christie's) $2,880 £1,540

George II plain tapering pot by Samuel Wilmott, Plymouth, 9½in. high, 24oz.18dwt.(Christie's) $3,260 £1,800

George III vase-shaped coffee jug by Fogelberg & Gilbert, London, 1784, 24oz.17dwt., 12¾in. high.(Sotheby's) $2,910 £1,540

George II vase-shaped coffee pot by James Gould, 1743, 9in. high, 30oz. (Christie's) $2,510 £1,420

Tapering circular coffee ug by Tessiers Ltd., London, 1928, 14.3oz., 9cm. high. (Sotheby's Belgravia) $590 £308

George II pear-shaped coffee pot by Lothian & Robertson, Edinburgh, 1759, 12in. high, 36oz. (Christie's) $3,345 £1,760

Tapering cylindrical coffee pot by Tessiers Ltd., London, 1927, 17.8oz., 21.5cm. high. (Sotheby's Belgravia) $530 £275

COFFEE POTS

Heavy silver octagonal-shaped coffee pot with domed lid and wooden handle. (Butler & Hatch Waterman) $235 £130

Compressed circular coffee pot with reeded girdle, by J. & H. Lias, London, 1838, 26oz., 20cm. high.(Sotheby's Belgravia) $890 £480

George II pear-shaped coffee pot by John Swift, 1756, 35oz., 10¾in. high. (Christie's)$3,860 £1,980

George II tapered cylindrical coffee pot by Gabriel Sleath, London, 1744, 20oz., 8¼in. high. (Sotheby's)$2,615 £1,430

George III baluster coffee jug, by John Edwards·III, London, 1806, 27oz. 13dwt., 8in. high. (Sotheby's) $735 £396

One of a pair of tapering circular jugs for coffee and hot milk by Tessiers Ltd., London, 1928, 51.2oz., 23cm. high. (Sotheby's Belgravia) $1,240 £660

One of a pair of tapering circular pots by Collingwood & Co. Ltd., London, 1966, 49.6oz., 24.5cm. high. (Sotheby's Belgravia) $1,200 £638

Victorian oval tapering coffee pot by J. Whipple & Co., Exeter, 1877, 27oz., 9¼in. high. (Christie's) $1,130 £594

George II plain tapering cylindrical coffee pot by Humphrey Payne, 1736, 8¾in. high, 17oz.13dwt. (Christie's)$3,430 £1,760

Small silver cream jug decorated in Art Nouveau style, by Walker & Hall, Sheffield, 2¾oz. (Butler & Hatch Waterman) $100 £55

George IV compressed circular milk jug by William Eaton, London, 1822, 16oz. 1dwt., 4in. high. (Sotheby's) $565 £297

George III milk jug, London, 1812, with reeded handle.(Lawrence Fine Art) $185 £95

George III helmet-shaped milk jug by John Emes, London, 1805, 7oz.14dwt., 6¼in. high. (Sotheby's) $580 £308

American silver footed cream jug with high pouring spout by John Allen, Boston, 3in. high, 3 troy oz. (Robert W. Skinner Inc.) $1,700 £930

Silver gilt milk jug by R. & S. Garrard & Co., London, 1869, 13.5oz., 18.5cm. high.(Sotheby's Belgravia) $1,445 £770

Silver cream jug by Stokes & Ireland, London, 1900, 4½in. high.(Lawrence Fine Art) $115 £60

George II cream pail, maker's mark WM, London, 1751, 3oz.3dwt., 2¼in. high. (Sotheby's) $715 £385

George III fluted helmet-shaped milk jug by H. Chawner, London, 1792, 7oz., 5½in. high. (Sotheby's) $580 £308

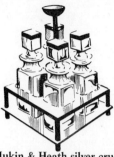

George III seven-bottle cruet by William Barrett II, London, 1817-18. (Sotheby, King & Chasemore) $815 £430

George III cruet stand of oblong shape, by I. E. Terry, circa 1819-20, 27.5oz. (Phillips) $490 £270

Hukin & Heath silver cruet in carrying frame, 1881, designed by Christopher Dresser, 14.25cm. high. (Sotheby's Belgravia) $1,240 £682

Regency rectangular egg cruet by Rebecca Emes and Edward Barnard, London, 1814, 27.5oz. (Woolley & Wallis) $680 £350

George IV four-bottle cruet frame by Philip Rundell, London, 1820, 43oz.15dwt., 11in. high. (Sotheby's) $3,220 £1,705

Electroplated eight-bottle cruet frame, mounts by Elkington & Co., 1867, 32.7cm. long.(Sotheby's Belgravia) $435 £231

One of a pair of Victorian cruet frames, by Robert Harper, London, 1875, 11oz.7dwt., 4¾in. high. (Sotheby's) $1,385 £715

George II Warwick cruet frame, Edinburgh, 1736-7, 32oz.9dwt., 8½in. high. (Sotheby's)$2,080 £1,100

George III Warwick frame, complete with casters and bottles, by Thomas Daniel, London, 1776, 37oz.7dwt., 9¾in. high. (Sotheby's) $2,380 £1,320

Parcel gilt egg cruet of six, by R. Hennell & Sons, London, 1850, 27.9oz. (Sotheby's Belgravia) $1,135 £605

George IV silver cruet stand with glass bottles. (May, Whetter & Grose) $400 £220

George IV egg cruet by J. E. Terry & Co., London, 1829, 64oz. (H. Spencer & Sons Ltd.) $810 £430

George III navette-shaped seven-bottle cruet frame by Henry Greenway, London, 1795, 38oz.11dwt., 16¾in. wide. (Sotheby's) $1,710 £935

George III three-bottle decanter stand, London, 1818, 30oz. (H. Spencer & Sons Ltd.) $940 £500

George III cruet frame with pierced gallery sides, by John Delmester, 1764, 16.25oz. (Phillips) $615 £340

George II composite Warwick frame by Samuel Wood, circa 1755, London, 35oz.17dwt. (Sotheby's) $510 £280

Two-handled bell-shaped cup by West & Son, Dublin, 1893, 58.6oz., 27.5cm. high. (Sotheby's Belgravia) $550 £300

George II two-handled cup and cover by Edward Vincent, circa 1730, 10¾in. high, 46oz.7dwt.(Christie's) $1,775 £935

Arts & Crafts two-handled silver cup by C. R. Ashbee, London, 1903, 17½oz., 6¼in. high. (Woolley & Wallis) $700 £375

One of a pair of silver gilt cups and covers by R. & S. Garrard, London, 26¼in. high, 217oz. (Christie's)$9,250 £5,000

One of two matching George III two-handled cups and covers, London, 1771, 66oz. 8dwt., 10¾in. high.(Sotheby's) $3,030 £1,595

Circular standing cup and cover by Chas. Boyton & Sons Ltd., London, 1935 38.1oz., 34.5cm. high. (Sotheby's Belgravia) $740 £385

George I two-handled cup by J. Hamilton, Dublin, 1714, 33oz.18dwt., 7¾in. high. (Sotheby's) $1,455 £770

Two-handled presentation cup by Edward Barnard & Sons, London, 1863, 90.4oz., 43.5cm. high. (Sotheby's Belgravia) $1,160 £605

One of a pair of George two-handled cups, Dublin circa 1750, 27oz.7dwt., 5½in. high. (Sotheby's) $1,415 £748

George III two-handled silver loving cup, London, 1775-76, 6¼in. high, 19 troy oz. (Robert W. Skinner Inc.) $400 £215

Late 19th century Continental three-handled cylindrical cup and cover, 14¾in. high, 100oz. (Christie's) $2,405 £1,300

Victorian christening cup by Richard Hennell, 1865, 4in. high. (Lawrence Fine Art) $185 £95

George III silver gilt two-handled cup and cover by Solomon Hougham, London, 1801, 51oz.1dwt.(Sotheby's) $1,150 £605

Two-handled lidded silver cup, Sheffield, 1907, 149oz. (Honiton Galleries) $1,355 £730

George III two-handled cup and cover by Wakelin & Taylor, circa 1777, 34oz.5dwt. (Sotheby's) $525 £275

One of a pair of large two-handled cups and covers by Elkington & Co., Birmingham, 1909, 30in. high, 87oz. (Christie's) $16,650 £9,000

George I two-handled cup by Philip Kinnersley, Dublin, 1724, 32oz.14dwt., 7½in. high. (Sotheby's) $1,415 £748

George III silver gilt two-handled cup and cover by Gustavus Byrne, Dublin, 1802, 13in. high, 86oz. (Christie's) $3,430 £1,760

SILVER

Beaten silver three-handled cup, Sheffield, 1910, 20oz. (J. M. Welch & Son)
$380 £210

William III two-handled cup and cover by Thomas Bolton, Dublin, 1696, 6in. high, 11oz.11dwt. (Christie's) $2,255 £1,188

One of a pair of George III bell-shaped two-handled cups by Bergin & Macklin, Dublin, 1817, 7½in. high, 32oz. (Sotheby's) $845 £462

Two-handled cup and cover by E. C. Purdee, London, 1896, 65.6oz., 40cm. high. (Sotheby's Belgravia) $1,035 £550

Replica of a steeple cup by Goldsmiths & Silversmiths Co. Ltd., London, 1921-29, 24oz., 41.5cm. high. (Sotheby's Belgravia) $385 £210

George III coconut cup and cover by Phipps & Robinson, London, 1794, 6¾in. high. (Sotheby's) $830 £429

George III two-handled silver gilt cup and cover by W. Burwash and R. Sibley, 1810, 17in. high, 109oz. (Christie's) $3,695 £1,944

George III vase-shaped two-handled cup and cover by John Scofield, 1796, 16½in. high, 78oz. (Christie's) $3,900 £2,052

George III two-handled silver gilt cup and cover by W. Burwash and R. Sibley, 1808, 18in. high, 96oz. (Christie's) $2,870 £1,512

Circular presentation cup and cover, by Horace Woodward & Co. Ltd., 1890, 173.7oz., 68.5cm. high. (Sotheby's Belgravia) $2,480 £1,320

Sterling silver and agate three-handled loving cup, circa 1900, 4½in. diam. (Robert W. Skinner Inc.) $200 £105

Large two-handled bell-shaped cup by Elkington & Co., Birmingham, 1868, 81.9oz., 40cm. high. (Sotheby's Belgravia) $730 £396

One of a pair of Dutch ornamental standing cups, London, 1911, 76oz., 34cm. high. (H. Spencer & Sons Ltd.) $2,945 £1,600

One of a pair of George III silver gilt mounted ostrich cups and covers, by Thos. Robins, 1808, 11¼in. high. (Christie's) $5,800 £3,240

German parcel gilt beaker-shaped cup and cover, circa 1880, 39.5cm. high, 60.3oz. (Sotheby's Belgravia) $1,240 £660

Queen Anne two-handled cup with bell-shaped body, Dublin, 1708, 33oz.1dwt., 7¾in. high. (Sotheby's) $820 £440

One of a pair of German parcel gilt cups by B. Neresheimer & Sohne, Chester, 1902, 9oz.5dwt., 7in. high. (Sotheby's) $450 £231

George II two-handled cup by Joseph Jones, Limerick, circa 1730, 8½in. high, 36oz. (Christie's) $3,080 £1,620

One of a pair of George III Irish two-handled cups, Dublin, 1770, 6in. high, 29oz.15dwt. (Sotheby's) $810 £440

Guild of Handicrafts Ltd. silver cup by C. R. Ashbee, London, 1901, 28.5cm. wide.(Christie's) $1,375 £750

Swiss parcel gilt cup and cover by Bossard & Son, Lucern, circa 1880, 21½in. high, 82oz.(Christie's) $2,000 £1,080

Early 17th century Dutch miniature wine cup with hexagonal bowl engraved with figures, 2¼in. high. (Sotheby's) $810 £451

William III silver gilt two-handled cup and cover by John Smith I, 1699, 9¼in. high, 30oz. (Christie's) $11,600 £6,480

Early 20th century sterling silver cup, Towle Silversmiths, Massachusetts, 18in. high, 215.6 troy oz. (Robert W. Skinner Inc.} $1,950 £1,115

DECANTERS

Attractive decanter with pierced silver vine pattern. (Biddle & Webb) $170 £90

Late 19th century Viennese enamelled and gemset silver gilt wine-wagon, 14¼in. long. (Christie's) $3,885 £2,100

Glass decanter and stopper with Liberty & Co., silver and enamel mounted neck, 1905, 52.5cm. high. (Sotheby's Belgravia) $500 £275

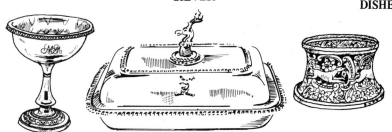

Sterling silver compote by Duhme Co., Ohio, circa 1900, 9½in. high, 18 troy oz. (Robert W. Skinner Inc.)$150 £85

One of a set of four Regency plain oblong entree dishes and covers by Joseph Angell, 1817, 237oz. (Christie's)$6,380 £3,564

Dish ring in Irish style, Birmingham, 1910, 7in. diam., with blue glass liner.(Lawrence Fine Art) $305 £170

Mid 18th century Central American dish, by Gueixa, Guatemala, 36cm. diam., 19oz:6dwt. (Sotheby's) $2,975 £1,540

WMF electroplated dish cast with a young woman, 23.5cm. wide, circa 1900. (Sotheby's Belgravia) $300 £165

George III circular dish by Paul Storr, London, 1815, 28oz.8dwt., 10¼in. diam. (Sotheby's) $1,535 £825

George I circular strawberry dish by Henry Daniell, Dublin, 1724, 9in. diam., 12oz.18dwt. (Christie's) $5,150 £2,640

One of a pair of George III butter shells by Turner & Fox, London, 1802, 6oz. 5dwt., 5¾in. long. (Sotheby's) $660 £360

Early 18th century Italian parcel gilt circular dish with domed centre, 48cm. diam., 54oz.4dwt. (Sotheby's)$7,645 £3,960

685

One of a pair of George III oblong entree dishes and covers, London, 1809, 127oz. 2dwt., 11½in. wide. (Sotheby's)
$3,970 £2,090

One of a pair of George III silver entree dishes and covers by John Edwards III, London, 1795, 75oz., 14¼in. wide. (Lawrence Fine Art) $1,660 £860

One of a pair of silver William IV octagonal meat dish covers, London, 1831-34, 15in. wide. (Sotheby's)
$2,135 £1,100

One of a pair of George III shaped oblong entree dishes and covers by W. Burwash and R. Sibley, 1808, 110oz., 11in. long. (Christie's) $3,260 £1,800

Victorian oval revolving breakfast dish with plain hinged cover, by Fenton Bros., Sheffield, 54oz.8dwt. (Sotheby Beresford Adams) $1,110 £600

William IV parcel gilt large shaped circular sideboard dish by Benjamin Preston, 1833, 25¾in. diam., 77oz. (Christie's) $2,590 £1,400

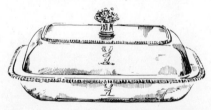

One of four George III plain oblong entree dishes and covers by John Edwards III, 1808, 11¼in. long, 208oz.(Christie's)
$9,460 £5,060

George III Irish dish ring by Thomas Jones, Dublin, 1787, 9oz.15dwt., 7½in. diam. (Sotheby's)
$2,345 £1,210

One of a pair of Sheffield plated entree dishes, covers and stands, 15in. wide. (Lawrence Fine Art) $500 £260

One of a pair of presentation shaped oval entree dishes, covers and handles, 103.4oz., 35cm. long. (Sotheby's Belgravia) $2,470 £1,350

One of four plain George III octagonal entree dishes and covers by D. Scott and B. Smith, 1803, 234oz., 11¾in. long. (Christie's) $9,955 £5,500

One of a pair of George III oblong entree dishes and covers by T. & J. Guest and J. Cradock, London, 1811, 120oz.9dwt. (Sotheby's) $3,450 £1,815

One of a pair of George IV silver gilt shaped circular sideboard dishes by Edward Farrell, 1822, 18in. diam., 108oz. (Christie's) $8,325 £4,500

Irish sterling silver dish ring, Dublin, 1796, 8in. diam., 13 troy oz. (Robert W. Skinner Inc.) $950 £510

Victorian melon pattern silver dish cover by Robert Garrard, London, 1841, 30oz.18dwt., 11½in. wide. (Sotheby Beresford Adams) $760 £410

One of a pair of George III plain oblong entree dishes and covers by Paul Storr, 1809, 155oz., 12½in. long. (Christie's) $11,765 £6,500

687

Circular silver dish with embossed rim, standing on four feet. (Biddle & Webb) $270 £140

One of a set of four George III entree dishes and covers by P. & W. Bateman, 1807, 11in. long, 229oz. (Christie's) $8,150 £4,180

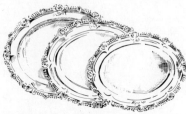

Set of three George III shaped oval meat dishes in sizes, by Paul Storr, London, 1811, 266oz. (Sotheby's) $15,960 £8,580

George III silver gilt shaped circular dish by William Pitts, 1809, 15½in. diam., 51oz. (Christie's) $4,625 £2,500

Early 20th century decorative hardstone dish with silver gilt mounts, 14.5cm. long. (Sotheby's Belgravia) $725 £385

Plain oval breakfast dish and liner, Sheffield, 1926, 75oz., 34.4cm. wide. (Sotheby's Belgravia) $1,240 £660

Deep silver dish with embossed rim, standing on three feet. (Biddle & Webb) $270 £140

One of a pair of silver gilt oval sweetmeat dishes by Henry William Curry, London, 1887, 17.6oz. (Sotheby's Belgravia) $370 £198

One of a set of four George III oblong entree dishes and covers by Benjamin Smith II, 12in. long, 285oz. (Christie's) $12,000 £6,050

Novelty trinket dish in the form of a walnut and a rat, 11.4cm. long, 5.2oz. (Sotheby's Belgravia) $270 £143

One of a pair of George IV butter shells, by William Eley, London, 1825, 7oz. 12dwt., 4¾in. long. (Sotheby's) $1,165 £638

Georgian oval silver gilt dish, by Richard Williams, Dublin, circa 1770, 16oz. 10dwt., 11¾in. wide. (Sotheby's) $775 £418

Georg Jensen silver compote, Copenhagen, 20th century, 9½in. diam., 28 troy oz. (Robert W. Skinner Inc.) $1,000 £550

One of a set of five pedestal dessert stands by H. & Co., London, 71.7oz., 1919. (Sotheby's Belgravia) $1,935 £1,045

Circular vegetable dish and cover on Sheffield Plate base, 47.6oz., 26.5cm. diam., circa 1849. (Sotheby's Belgravia) $970 £528

One of a pair of shaped circular open-work salt dishes by C. T. & G. Fox, London, 1841, 11.8cm. diam. (Sotheby's Belgravia) $370 £198

689

EWERS

George III inverted pear-shaped cream ewer by Nathaniel Appleton and Ann Smith, London, 1780. (Woolley & Wallis) $340 £190

Helmet-shaped ewer by Giuseppe Palmentiero, Naples, circa 1720, 25oz. 10dwt., 23.5cm. high. (Sotheby's)$7,430 £3,850

20th century American silver presentation ewer of helmet shape, 14in. high, 32 troy oz. (Robert W. Skinner Inc.) $300 £165

Armada pattern ewer richly chased, 59.3oz., 46.5cm. high. (Sotheby's Belgravia) $2,275 £1,210

Pompeian Ascos shaped wine ewer by Paul Storr, London, 1838, 8¾in. high, 35oz.18dwt. (Sotheby's) $7,525 £3,960

George III inverted pear-shaped ewer by Fred. Vonham, London, 1767, 51oz.7dwt., 16¾in. high. (Sotheby's)$4,630 £2,530

One of a pair of late 19th century Austro-Hungarian decorative ewers, 18.4cm. high. (Sotheby's Belgravia) $530 £286

American silver ewer by J. & I. Cox, New York, circa 1835, 34oz.10dwt., 12¼in. high. (Sotheby's) $965 £528

Lobed circular wine ewer with rustic handle, by Edward Barnard & Sons, London, 1860, 30.6oz., 33cm. high. (Sotheby's Belgravia) $975 £528

Austrian ewer with sterling silver overlay, by Loetz, circa 1900, 5¼in. high. (Robert W. Skinner Inc.) $1,050 £585

William IV large ewer by Morris and Michael Emanuel, London, 1835, 218oz., 27½in. high. (Sotheby's)$5,705 £3,100

19th century decorative gilt metal ewer with pentafoil foot, 13in. high.(Sotheby's) $1,080 £572

FLASKS

Victorian brandy flask by James Dixon & Sons, Sheffield, 1875, 3oz.11dwt., 6¼in. high. (Sotheby's) $460 £242

Oval spirit flask with detachable base, by Elkington & Co., London, 1872, 13.9oz., 18cm. high. (Sotheby's Belgravia) $540 £286

17th century silver flask, circa 1675, 2oz.13dwt. (Sotheby's)$800 £400

FRAMES

Victorian rectangular dressing glass with silver frame, by William Comyns, 1885, 15¾in. high. (Lawrence Fine Art) $655 £340

WMF mirror frame cast with a young girl, circa 1900, 34cm. high. (Sotheby's Belgravia) $800 £450

Art Nouveau silver photograph frame by W.N., Chester, 1903, 31cm. high.(Christie's) $765 £420

691

Part of a set of twelve George II three-pronged table forks, London, 1737, 26oz. (H. Spencer & Sons Ltd.)
$1,210 £650

Fine shagreen cased St. Cloud cutlery set, 19cm. wide, circa 1720. (Sotheby, King & Chasemore) $560 £300

One of twelve silver tablespoons by Geo. Timberlake, circa 1756, 26oz (Woolley & Wallis) $395 £220

One of a set of six unusual silver and enamelled coffee spoons with Mickey Mouse terminals, 11cm. high, Birmingham, 1929. (Phillips) $500 £280

Victorian presentation trowel by Martin Hall & Co., Sheffield, 1879, 13¼in. long. (Sotheby's)$385 £198

Sheffield plate pie server with turned wooden grip, 1777, 15in. long. (Robert W. Skinner Inc.) $70 £40

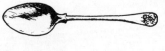

One of twelve dessert spoons, maker R.R., London, 1770-74, 13oz. (Woolley & Wallis) $305 £170

16th century seal top spoon probably by John Quycke, Barnstaple, circa 1590. (Sotheby's) $625 £330

Old English and bead pattern cutlery canteen, London, 1884, fifty pieces in all. (Locke & England) $2,640 £1,450

Cased set of cutlery by Vintner's of Sheffield, 1930, in bow-fronted mahogany case. (Phillips) $3,660 £2,000

Part of a set of twelve fruit knives and forks by Atkin Brothers, Sheffield, 1937, in wood case. (Sotheby's Belgravia) $515 £275

One of a set of twelve three-prong table forks, by Wm. Wooler, London, 1764, 28oz. (Woolley & Wallis) $595 £330

Gibson patent-type caster-oil spoon by Henry Flavelle, Dublin, circa 1835, 5½in. long. (Sotheby's) $1,870 £1,000

One of six Hanoverian pattern table-spoons, circa 1750, by Hugh Ross, Tain, 14oz.13dwt. (Sotheby's) $1,665 £880

Twelve-setting canteen of cutlery in mahogany box, marked Jayes, Oxford Street, London. (Allen & May) $1,415 £750

Electroplated dessert spoon, designed by Charles Rennie Mackintosh, circa 1903, 15.5cm. long. (Sotheby's Belgravia) $1,515 £850

George III travelling apple corer by Joseph Willmore, Birmingham, 1814, 4in. long. (Sotheby's) $545 £285

Charles I apostle spoon by Ralph Herman, Exeter, circa 1630. (Sotheby's) $1,880 £990

Late 19th century fiddle and thread composite suite of ninety-three-pieces of cutlery, 158oz. (Lacy Scott) $4,070 £2,200

Part of a set of twelve fruit knives and forks with green hardstone handles, by Atkin Brothers, Sheffield, 1900. (Sotheby's Belgravia) $310 £170

SILVER

Gibson-patent type castor oil spoon, circa 1800, 2oz., 5¼in. long. (Sotheby's) $325 £176

One of a set of twelve Elkington & Co. silver teaspoons, designed by Charles Rennie Mackintosh, circa 1907, 13.5cm. long. (Sotheby's Belgravia) $710 £400

Part of a Georg Jensen table service of eighty-four pieces, 1939, 106oz. (Christie's) $5,305 £2,916

Part of a George I Hanoverian table service, engraved with Prince of Wales' feathers, 92oz. (Christie's) $7,295 £3,740

Composite canteen of fiddle pattern table cutlery, 130oz. in all. (Lacy Scott) $1,850 £1,000

Part of a late 19th/early 20th century Austrian canteen of cutlery, by J. C. Klinkosch, Vienna, in fitted case. (Sotheby's Belgravia) $2,955 £1,650

Electroplated spoon and two forks designed by Charles Rennie Mackintosh, circa 1903, 18.5cm. long. (Sotheby's Belgravia) $360 £198

Large punch ladle by Wood & Hughes, New York, circa 1870, 15¾in. long, 8 troy oz. (Robert W. Skinner Inc.) $475 £265

Silver soup ladle by Hester Bateman, 1782. (Christie's) $360 £185

George III jockey cap caddy spoon by Joseph Taylor, Birmingham, 1798. (Woolley & Wallis) $295 £165

Pair of William IV silver gilt grape scissors, by William Traies, London, 1833, 4oz.14dwt. (Sotheby's) $750 £396

Part of a Hanoverian silver gilt dessert service by Lewis Mettayer, 1709, 72oz.(Christie's) $8,580 £4,400

Part of a set of six Victorian silver gilt dessert knives, forks and spoons, London, 1857, 38oz. (H. Spencer & Sons Ltd.) $1,140 £610

Part of a set of twelve fiddle pattern teaspoons and a pair of sugar tongs, 12.8oz. (Sotheby's Belgravia) $155 £85

Arts & Crafts silver caddy spoon, Birmingham, 1919, 9.5cm. long, handle set in mother-of-pearl. (Phillips) $135 £75

Part of a canteen of table silver by James Dixon & Sons, Sheffield, contained in brass bound oak box. (Sotheby's Belgravia) $4,330 £2,420

Pair of French parcel gilt salad servers, Paris, circa 1880, 9oz. 15dwt.(Christie's) $260 £140

Pair of late 19th century vine pattern grape scissors, 18cm. long, 3.8oz. (Sotheby's Belgravia) $175 £93

Guild of Handicrafts Ltd. silver teaspoon by C. R. Ashbee, London, 1907. (Christie's) $440 £240

SILVER

Victorian engraved silver goblet, 19½oz. (Phillips) $255 £140

Gorham sterling silver chalice in Renaissance revival style, Rhode Island, circa 1864, 9½in. high, 14½ troy oz. (Robert W. Skinner Inc.) $275 £155

George II vase-shaped goblet by Henry Chawner, London, 1792, 10oz.8dwt., 6¾in. high. (Sotheby's)$450 £231

One of a pair of George III wine goblets by Walter Brind, London, 1774, 16oz.4dwt., 6½in. high. (Sotheby's) $1,290 £700

One of six George IV silver gilt goblets by Joseph Angell, 1826, 6¾in. high, 55oz. (Christie's) $4,440 £2,400

One of a pair of Victorian goblets by George Fox, 1869, 8in. high, 23oz. (Christie's) $1,200 £650

One of a pair of George III wine goblets by Walter Brind, London, 1774, 13oz. 18dwt., 6in. high. (Sotheby's) $3,555 £1,870

William IV chalice by Joseph and John Angell, London, 1835. (Sotheby's) $340 £175

One of a pair of George III bell-shaped goblets by Robert and David Hennell, London, 1796, 14oz.4dwt., 6½in. high. (Sotheby's)$1,165 £638

One of a rare set of eight
George III silver goblets
by Rebecca Emes and
Edward Barnard, London,
1816, 32oz., 12.5cm. high.
(H. Spencer & Sons Ltd.)
$5,580 £3,000

Silver gilt recusant chalice
on spreading hexafoil foot,
circa 1630, 8¼in. high,
14oz.7dwt. (Christie's)
$10,725 £5,500

One of a set of six gob-
lets on pedestal feet, by
Gladwin Ltd., Sheffield,
1946, 55.1oz., 16.9cm.
high. (Sotheby's Belgra-
via) $550 £300

Goblet formed as an oak
tree on hexagonal base,
1902, 6¾in. high, 24oz.
(Christie's)$1,385 £750

One of a set of four William
IV silver goblets by Charles
Price, London, 1832-33,
27oz.9dwt., 6in. high.
(Sotheby's)$3,760 £1,980

19th century lacquered
silver goblet decorated
in enamel and gold hira-
mahie, 15cm. high.
(Sotheby's Belgravia)
$1,400 £726

Silver goblet by Omar
Ramsden, 4½in. high.
(Graves, Son & Pilcher)
$675 £380

German silver gilt chalice
with hexagonal stem,
circa 1500, 8oz.3dwt.,
15.8cm. high. (Sotheby's)
$2,015 £1,045

Fireman's coin silver chalice by John Curry, Phila-
delphia, 17½ troy oz.,
9½in. high. (Robert W.
Skinner Inc.)$400 £220

William IV shaped oval inkstand by Thomas Wimbush and Henry Hyde, London, 1833, 86oz.13dwt. (Sotheby's) $3,740 £1,980

American Kutani and sterling silver inkstand, circa 1900, 12¼in. long, by John Wanamaker. (Robert W. Skinner Inc.) $550 £305

Shaped oblong double well inkstand by Pearce & Sons, London, 1912, 33oz., 31cm. long. (Sotheby's Belgravia) $650 £352

Late 19th/early 20th century white metal novelty inkstand, 43cm. wide. (Sotheby's Belgravia) $660 £352

Two-bottle inkstand with pierced gallery border, by R. & S. Garrard & Co., London, 1853, 46oz., 29.1cm. long. (Sotheby's Belgravia) $1,135 £605

Silver shaped double well inkstand by Henry Wilkinson & Co., Sheffield, 1869, 9¾in. long, 26oz.8dwt. (Sotheby's) $625 £330

Shaped oval double well inkstand by Edward Barnard & Sons, London, 1853, 28.4oz., 35.5cm. long. (Sotheby's Belgravia) $825 £440

Shaped rectangular two-bottle inkstand by James Dixon & Sons, Sheffield, 1837, 39.8oz., 28cm. long. (Sotheby's Belgravia) $970 £528

Continental silver coloured metal ink-stand in the shape of two shells. (H. Spencer & Sons Ltd.) $745 £400

Shell-shaped single well inkstand by D. & C. Houle, London, 1875, 28.5cm. wide, 19.6oz. (Sotheby's Belgravia) $455 £250

Shaped oval two-bottle inkstand by Henry Wilkinson & Co., Sheffield, 1853, 30.9oz., 35cm. long. (Sotheby's Belgravia) $850 £462

Spanish shaped oval inkstand on claw and ball feet, Madrid, 1786, 11in. long, 62oz. (Christie's)$3,980 £2,200

Victorian inkstand by Charles T. and George Fox, London, 1847, 10in. wide, 23oz. (Lawrence Fine Art) $850 £440

Rectangular two-bottle inkstand by Charles Stuart Harris & Sons Ltd., London, 1903, 24oz.11dwt., 9¼in. long. (Sotheby's) $540 £286

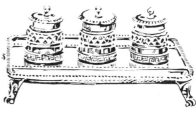

Oval two-bottle inkstand on four panel feet, by Edward Barnard & Sons, London, 1873, 14.6oz. (Sotheby's Belgravia) $850 £462

George III oblong three-bottle inkstand by T. & G. Guest & Cradock, London, 1809, 19oz.8dwt., 8½in. wide. (Sotheby's) $1,075 £577

19th century rosewood inkstand, inlaid with brass scrolls, and with brass handle, 14in. wide. (Edwards, Bigwood & Bewlay) $330 £180

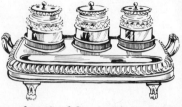

One of a pair of George III oblong inkstands by T. & J. Guest and J. Cradock, 1808, 66oz. (Christie's) $4,290 £2,200

Victorian granite and antler mounted oblong silver inkstand and letter knife, mid 19th century, 14in. wide. (Sotheby's) $1,080 £572

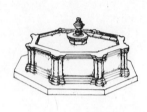

Silver gilt inkstand by Charles & Richard Comyns, 1920, 12½in. wide, 137oz. (Lawrence Fine Art) $1,540 £850

Rectangular two-bottle inkstand by Charles Stuart Harris & Sons Ltd., London, 1903, 24oz.11dwt., 9¼in. long. (Sotheby's) $540 £286

George III unusual silver gilt inkstand by Robert & Samuel Hennell, London, 1805, 16oz.1dwt., 5½in. high. (Sotheby's) $1,850 £1,012

George I oblong inkstand by Paul de Lamerie, London, 1721, 9¾in. wide, 30oz. (Sotheby's) $13,165 £6,930

George II oblong silver gilt inkstand by Paul de Lamerie, 1731, 9in. long, 23oz. (Christie's) $11,600 £6,480

Silver mounted cut-glass claret jug with leaf-capped scroll handle, Sheffield, 1895, 10in. high. (Sotheby, King & Chasemore) $435 £240

Louis XVI pear-shaped hot milk jug, Paris, circa 1786-87, 6¾in. high, 10oz.12dwt. (Christie's) $2,000 £1,080

Liberty & Co. 'Cymric' silver hot water jug designed by Archibald Knox, 1904, 10oz., 20cm. high. (Phillips) $550 £300

George I baluster beer jug by Thomas Morse, London, 1721, 7½in. high, 29oz.3dwt. (Sotheby's) $6,300 £3,520

George III silver gilt covered jug by Paul Storr, London, 1799, 47oz.6dwt., 13¼in. high. (Sotheby's) $41,350 £23,100

Large early 19th century German pear-shaped wine jug, Luneburg, 15in. high, 47oz. (Christie's) $1,435 £810

Jensen silver jug, designed by Johan Rohde, 1920, 22.75cm. high. (Sotheby's Belgravia) $1,045 £550

Silver mounted glass jug of flattened circular body, by Heath & Middleton, Birmingham, 1907, 16.5cm. high. (Sotheby's Belgravia) $165 £88

North Italian baluster covered jug, body fluted and ribbed, circa 1775, 15.5cm. high. (Sotheby's) $850 £440

701

George II pear-shaped hot water jug by John Hamilton, Dublin, circa 1740, 11in. high, 43oz. (Christie's) $1,465 £770

George II plain pear-shaped beer jug by W. Shaw and W. Preist, 1759, 9¾in. high, 35oz. (Christie's) $5,575 £2,860

George II pear-shaped hot water jug on reeded rim foot, by Peze Pilleau, 1730, 8½in. high, 29oz. (Christie's) $11,155 £5,720

William IV vase-shaped jug by C. Reily and G. Storer, 1831, 11¼in. high, 38oz. (Christie's) $1,755 £950

George II plain pear-shaped beer jug by Charles Leslie, Dublin, circa 1730, 7¾in. high, 33oz. (Christie's) $3,800 £2,100

George II baluster covered jug by Erasmus Cope, Dublin, 1736, 33oz.9dwt., 11in. high. (Sotheby's) $5,435 £2,860

Circular silver jug, chased round foot and shoulder, by C.T. & G. Fox, London, 1845, 37.5oz., 23cm. high. (Sotheby's Belgravia) $970 £506

Mid 19th century silver water pitcher with shaped rim and pouring spout, 11in. high, 23 troy oz. (Robert W. Skinner Inc.) $250 £140

George II pear-shaped jug and cover by John Hamilton, Dublin, circa 1745, 42oz., 9¾in. high. (Christie's) $1,900 £1,050

Silver George II beer jug
by R. A. Cox, London,
1759, 16oz., 7½in. high.
(Sotheby, King & Chase-
more) $1,599 £820

Liberty & Co. 'Cymric' silver jug, Birmingham, 1901,
4½oz., 11cm. wide.
(Christie's) $510 £280

Regency style Victo-
rian hot water jug,
1898, 25oz., 9in. high.
(Hy. Duke & Son)
          $480 £250

Gorham sterling silver
pitcher in Renaissance
revival style, Rhode
Island, circa 1864,
15½in. high. (Robert
W. Skinner Inc.)
  $500   £280

German silver baluster jug,
circa 1890, 20.4cm. high,
19.1oz. (Sotheby's
Belgravia) $870 £462

George III vase-shaped
hot water jug with
domed lid by Wakelin
& Taylor, London,
1777, 12¼in. high.
(Sotheby's) $1,880 £990

Hungarian pear-shaped
hot water jug by Joh-
annes Georgius Puskail-
ler, circa 1720, 14oz.
(Christie's) $2,470 £1,320

George II plain pear-sha-
ped beer jug by Wm.
Grundy, 1750, 7¾in.
high, 28oz. (Christie's)
        $6,865 £3,520

Silver hot water pot
by Thomas Bradbury,
Sheffield, 1903, 10½in.
high, 21oz. (Lawrence
Fine Art) $335 £175

703

SILVER

One of a pair of silver plated plant troughs, 13½in. diam., with lion mask and ring handles. (Gilbert Baitson)
$285 £150

Guild of Handicrafts Ltd., mace head in silver coloured metal, circa 1900, 17.5cm. high. (Sotheby's Belgravia) $240 £135

Liberty & Co. silver stopper by Archibald Knox, Birmingham, 1906, 6.5cm. high. (Sotheby's Belgravia) $260 £143

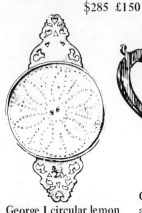

George I circular lemon strainer with pierced handles, by John Albright, 1724, 1oz. 18dwt. (Christie's)
$965 £495

George III vase-shaped argyle by John Scofield, 1786, 7in. high, 12oz. 8dwt. (Christie's)
$2,260 £1,250

George IV beehive honey pot by Rebecca Emes and Edward Barnard, London, 1828, 16oz., 14.5cm. high. (H. Spencer & Sons Ltd.)
$4,370 £2,350

Silver plated egg coddler on spirit stand with lid, on circular base. (Butler & Hatch Waterman)
$35 £20

Silver table lighter on black marble base, by E. H. Stockwell, London, 1879, 15.5cm. long. (Sotheby's Belgravia)
$505 £264

George III silver wax jack by J. Langford and J. Sebille, London, 1764, 5½in. high, 8¼oz. (Christie's S. Kensington)
$1,080 £580

Late 19th/early 20th century silver bell in the form of a lady, German, 4.4oz., 10.5cm. high. (Sotheby's Belgravia) $590 £319

Pair of George III military spurs by J. Aldous, London, 1815, 5oz. (H. Spencer & Sons Ltd.) $560 £300

One of two 19th century silver mounted snuff mulls, 3½in. long. (Sotheby's) $375 £198

Silver plated wax jack with reeded base and nozzle, 6¾in. high. (Lawrence Fine Art) $230 £120

George III vase-shaped argyle by Henry Green, London, 1793, 13oz., 7in. high. (Sotheby's) $920 £495

Silver gilt and cloisonne enamel tea glass holder by Maria Semyonova, Moscow, 1908-17, 8cm. high. (Sotheby's) $1,225 £660

Silver mounted shagreen triple spectacle case, early 19th century, 13cm. high, complete with spectacles. (Sotheby's) $855 £462

Rare early 18th century solid gilt winepot, cover and cup, 14.6cm. and 8.6cm. high. (Sotheby's) $925 £495

One of a pair of silver replicas of 17th century ginger jars and covers by Searle & Co., London, 1911, 40.8oz., 24.5cm. high. (Sotheby's Belgravia) $1,550 £825

705

George IV table bell by
William Eaton, London,
1821, 3in. high, 4oz.
7dwt. (Sotheby's)
$830 £450

Unusual set of silver gilt
letter scales, complete
with a set of brass weights,
London, 1903. (Sotheby,
King & Chasemore)
$435 £240

George III table bell by
Abraham Portal, Lon-
don, 1764, 6oz.11dwt.,
4¾in. high. (Sotheby's)
$775 £420

Oval vesta case in the form
of a creel, by Thomas
Johnson, London, 1883,
5.7cm. long. (Sotheby's
Belgravia) $1,445 £770

Table ornament in the
form of an elephant,
28cm. long, by B.
Neresheimer & Sohne,
Hanau, 63.6oz.
(Sótheby's Belgravia)
$1,280 £682

Late 19th/early 20th cen-
tury electroplated copper
wall sconce, one of a
pair, 38.4cm. high.
(Sotheby's Belgravia)
$550 £300

Small Puiforcat beaker
with gently flared body,
1920's, 7.75cm. high.
(Sotheby's Belgravia)
$220 £121

Silver plated Victorian triple shell biscuit warmer.
(Christie's S. Kensington)
$310 £170

One of two silver Race
Tickets, for Doncaster
racecourse, 1777. (H.
Spencer & Sons Ltd.)
$4,460 £2,450

19th century Continental silver model of a fox with detachable head, 12½in. long, 18oz. (Geering & Colyer) $670 £380

German model of a stag, circa 1770, 10oz.17dwt., 28.3cm. high. (Sotheby's) $2,125 £1,100

Cast model of a running fox by F. B. Thomas & Co., London, 1930, 50oz., 42cm. long. (Sotheby's Belgravia) $1,415 £770

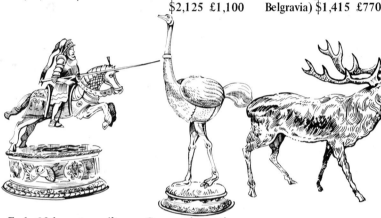

Early 20th century gilt metal figure of an equestrian knight, 32.5cm. high. (Sotheby's Belgravia) $930 £495

German decorative model of an ostrich with damaged body, circa 1880, 50.5cm. high. (Sotheby's Belgravia) $1,450 £770

Continental cast silver model of a stag, 78oz. (Christie's S. Kensington) $2,560 £1,400

Cast silver model of a racehorse by Roberts & Belk, Sheffield, 1967, 55oz. (H. Spencer & Sons Ltd.) $805 £430

Pair of late 19th century German silver hand raised pheasants with articulated wings, 12½ and 15½in. long. (Robert W. Skinner Inc.) $725 £395

Full-sized silver model of a hare by Asprey & Co., London, 1963, 184oz., 14½in. high. (Sotheby, King & Chasemore) $4,915 £2,700

SILVER

Cylindrical mug by Atkin Brothers, Sheffield, 1887, 5.3oz., 9.8cm. high. (Sotheby's Belgravia) $125 £66

Queen Anne mug on reeded foot, by John Elston, Exeter, 1712, 3½in. high, 5oz.10dwt. (Christie's) $1,115 £572

George I baluster mug by Nathaniel Gulliver, London, 1725, 4½in. high, 14oz.6dwt. (Sotheby's) $1,390 £748

Octagonal spool-shaped christening can by John Evans, London, 1846, 5.2oz., 10.3cm. high. (Sotheby's Belgravia) $280 £148

George III tapered cylindrical mug by Charles Wright, London, 1778, 16oz.12dwt., 5in. high. (Sotheby's) $925 £506

Fluted baluster mug by W., London, 1837, 4.4oz., 9.8cm. high. (Sotheby's Belgravia) $205 £110

American silver cann with moulded lip and pedestal foot, 5½in. high, 14 troy oz. (Robert W. Skinner Inc.) $2,750 £1,500

Victorian child's christening mug by Martin Hall & Co., London, 1880, 3oz.13dwt., 3¼in. high. (Sotheby's) $255 £132

George II baluster-shaped mug with scroll handle, by Richard Zouch, 1737, 4¾in. high, 12oz.16dwt. (Christie's) $1,640 £864

Victorian silver pint mug of barrel form, London, 1863, 10oz., 4½in. high. (Sotheby's) $335 £176

Rare dated silver mounted saltglaze mug, 1721, 9¼in. high, chipped. (Sotheby's)$1,000 £528

Early George I quart mug by Gabriel Sleath, London, 1727, 25oz., 6¼in. high. (Lawrence Fine Art) $870 £450

Faceted mug of waisted form by Henry Wilkinson & Co., Sheffield, 1854, 4.6oz., 9.5cm. high. (Sotheby's Belgravia) $205 £110

Queen Anne tapering cylindrical mug by Alice Sheene, 1708, 4¾in. high, 11oz.14dwt. (Christie's) $1,640 £864

Campana-shaped mug by E., E., J. & W. Barnard, London, 1836, 5.7oz., 10cm. high. (Sotheby's Belgravia) $310 £165

George III baluster mug by Thomas Evans, London, 1774, 4¾in. high, 9oz. (Sotheby, King & Chasemore) $370 £210

Victorian silver octagonal mug on bracket feet, 1847, 4in. high, 7oz. 15dwt. (Christie's)
          $1,110 £600

Tapering cylindrical mug engraved and flat-chased, by Alfred Ivory, London, 1880, 5.7oz., 10.4cm. high. (Sotheby's Belgravia) $225 £121

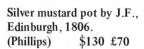

Silver mustard pot by J.F., Edinburgh, 1806. (Phillips) $130 £70

Victorian mustard pot in George III style, Birmingham, 1889. (Hy. Duke & Son) $55 £30

William IV cylindrical mustard pot by J. McKay, Edinburgh, 1834, 2¾in. high, 4oz.17dwt. (Sotheby's) $250 £132

Kangaroo pepperette by GB & Co., London, 1908, 3.6oz., 10cm. high. (Sotheby's Belgravia) $370 £198

One of a pair of silver mounted tooth owlet pepperettes, 7.8cm. high, in novelty box. (Sotheby's Belgravia) $705 £374

William IV bell-shaped pepperette by Charles Fox, London, 1832, 2oz.8dwt., 3in. high. (Sotheby's) $295 £160

Silver gilt mustard pot and spoon, London and Birmingham, 1838, 5.2oz. (Sotheby's Belgravia) $890 £473

Dutch pepper caster in the form of a quail, Chester, 1917, 3¾in. high. (Lawrence Fine Art) $290 £150

Unusual early Victorian mustard pot by Richard Sibley, London, 1841, 4¾in. diam., 12oz. (Sotheby's) $915 £506

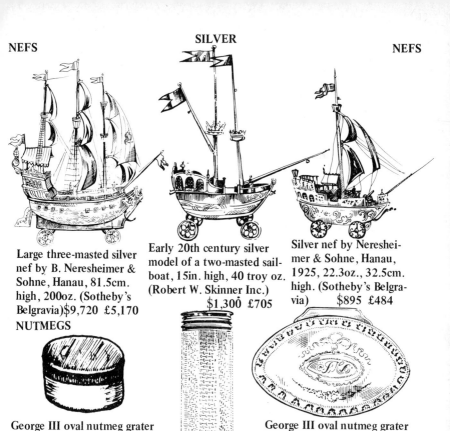

Large three-masted silver nef by B. Neresheimer & Sohne, Hanau, 81.5cm. high, 200oz. (Sotheby's Belgravia)$9,720 £5,170

Early 20th century silver model of a two-masted sailboat, 15in. high, 40 troy oz. (Robert W. Skinner Inc.)
$1,300 £705

Silver nef by Neresheimer & Sohne, Hanau, 1925, 22.3oz., 32.5cm. high. (Sotheby's Belgravia) $895 £484

NUTMEGS

George III oval nutmeg grater by Samuel Pemberton, Birmingham, 1798, 2½in. wide. (Dickinson, Davy & Markham)
$140 £75

George III oval nutmeg grater by Roger Biggs, London, 1795, 2in. wide. (Sotheby's)
$495 £275

William IV tube nutmeg grater by Rawlings & Sumner, London, 1835, 2½in. long. (Sotheby's) $635 £352

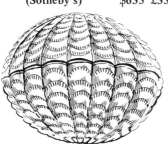

Vase-shaped nutmeg grater, unmarked, circa 1800, 3½in. high. (Sotheby's)
$575 £319

Unusual clam-shaped nutmeg grater by Hilliard & Thomason, Birmingham, 1853, 4.7cm. wide. (Sotheby's Belgravia)
$745 £396

George III oblong hanging nutmeg grater by J. Reily, London, 1818, 4in. long.(Sotheby's)
$655 £352

PORRINGERS

Charles II porringer, maker's mark TC, London, 1681, 3¼in. high, 7oz.3dwt. (Sotheby's) $885 £495

Charles II porringer, London, 1674, 9oz. 4dwt., 4in. high. (Sotheby's)
$2,610 £1,375

William III porringer by Robert Peake, London, 1699, 10oz., 4in. high. (Sotheby's) $1,790 £962

James I bleeding bowl or porringer, London, 1686, 8oz.10dwt., 20cm. long. (H. Spencer & Sons Ltd.) $1,840 £1,000

William and Mary porringer with everted rim, London, 1691, 6oz., 8.5cm. high. (H. Spencer & Sons Ltd.)
$1,065 £580

Charles II porringer by DG, London, 1679, 3in. high, 5oz.9dwt.,(Sotheby's)
$1,205 £660

QUAICH

Large two-handled circular quaich, unmarked, circa 1680, 7in. diam., 10oz. (Christie's) $3,860 £1,980

Two-handled silver quaich of ornate design by JD/WD, Chester, 1894, 7in. wide, 2½oz. (Dickinson, Davy & Markham) $60 £34

One of a set of four compressed circular salt cellars by Charles Stuart Harris, London, 1894, 33oz., sold with spoons. (Sotheby's Belgravia) $885 £495

One of two salt cellars by Robert and Samuel Hennell, 1803-04, sold with two spoons, London, 7oz. 4dwt. (Sotheby's)
$495 £270

One of a set of four salt cellars by Robert Hennell, London, 1783, 10oz.2dwt., 3¼in. wide. (Sotheby's)
$1,195 £650

One of a pair of William and Mary capstan form trencher salts, London, 1698, 2oz.15dwt., 2¼in. high. (Sotheby's)
$1,720 £935

One of a pair of pedestal salt cellars with coiled dolphin stems, by Smith Nicholson & Co., London, 1852. (Sotheby's Belgravia)
$790 £440

One of a set of four circular salt cellars by Paul de Lamerie, 1730, 23oz. (Christie's)
$19,855 £10,450

One of two George III oval salt cellar stands by Wm. Abdy, London, 1802, 4oz. 17dwt., 4¾in. wide. (Sotheby's) $275 £150

One of a pair of oval boat-shaped salt cellars by H. Chawner, London, 1791, 6oz.10dwt., 5¾in. wide. (Sotheby's) $440 £242

Charles II octagonal trencher salt, London, 1680, 1oz.14dwt., 3in. diam. (Sotheby's) $625 £340

713

SALTS

One of a set of four
George III oval salt
cellars by D. & R.
Hennell, 1765, 8oz.
16dwt. (Christie's)
$600 £308

One of a pair of George
III compressed salt cellars
and spoons, Glasgow &
London, 8oz., 3in. diam.
(Sotheby's) $460 £242

One of a set of four George
III circular fluted two-
handled salt cellars, by D.
Pontifex, 1806, 21oz.
(Christie's) $1,610 £825

One of a set of six circular
salt cellars by Joseph and
John Angell, London, 1838,
39.6oz., 8.6cm. diam.
(Sotheby's Belgravia)
$2,070 £1,100

One of a pair of salt cellars in 16th century
taste, by S. Garrard,
1902, 10½in. high.
(Christie's)
$2,960 £1,600

One of a pair of circular
salt cellars by Joseph and
John Angell, London,
1844, 13.3oz., 8.6cm.
diam. (Sotheby's Bel-
gravia) $455 £242

One of a set of four George
II salt cellars by Edward
Wood, London, 1731, 11oz.
14dwt., 3in. diam. (Sotheby's)
$3,345 £1,760

George III cauldron
salt by Chas. Hougham,
London, 1783, 2½in.
diam., with blue glass
liner. (Dickinson, Davy
& Markham) $75 £40

One of a set of six George
III salt cellars, by John
Emes, London, 1801,
(Sotheby, King & Chase-
more) $945 £520

One of a pair of George III oval salts by J. Weldring, London, 1771, 3in. wide., 4oz. (Dickinson, Davy & Markham)
$175 £95

One of a set of four George III salts by I.G., 1801, 12oz. (Hy. Duke & Son)
$575 £300

One of a pair of George III oval salts by Robt. Hennell, 1782, 3in. high, 3.6oz. (Hy. Duke & Son)
$180 £95

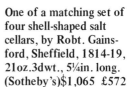

One of a set of three George III oval salt cellars by Robt. Hennell, London, 1777, 5¼in. wide, 13oz.10dwt. (Sotheby's)$960 £506

One of a pair of silver table salts by R. & S. Garrard & Co., London, 1857, 57.2oz., 14.5cm. high. (Sotheby's Belgravia) $8,270 £4,400

One of a matching set of four shell-shaped salt cellars, by Robt. Gainsford, Sheffield, 1814-19, 21oz.3dwt., 5¼in. long. (Sotheby's)$1,065 £572

One of a pair of George I octagonal trencher salts by Edward Wood, London, 1722, 3oz.1dwt., 3in. wide. (Sotheby's) $625 £330

One of a set of six oval salt cellars by Peter Desvignes, London, 1777, 7oz.15dwt., 3½in. long. (Sotheby's)$1,045 £550

One of three Regency oval salt cellars with gadrooned borders, by Paul Storr, 1817, 19oz. 10dwt. (Christie's)
$1,825 £935

SAUCEBOATS

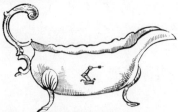

One of a pair of George II oval sauce-boats by George Hodder, Cork, circa 1745, 7¾in. wide, 19oz.9dwt. (Sotheby's) $3,745 £2,035

One of a pair of George II oval sauce-boats by Peze Pilleau, London, 1732, 28oz.19dwt., 8¼in. wide. (Sotheby's) $6,480 £3,410

Tiffany silver sauceboat, New York, circa 1860, with scrolled handle, 9 troy oz., 6in. high. (Robert W. Skinner Inc.) $200 £110

One of a pair of oval sauceboats by Fordham & Faulkner, Sheffield, 1900, 29.2oz., 21.5cm. long. (Sotheby's Belgravia) $870 £462

George III oval sauceboat by Matthew West, Dublin, 1790, 10oz., 8in. wide. (Sotheby's) $645 £352

One of a pair of shell-shaped sauceboats by C. S. Harris & Sons Ltd., London, 1900, 34.7oz., 19cm. long. (Sotheby's Belgravia) $1,135 £605

One of a pair of George II oval sauce-boats by John Kincaid, London, 1745, 27oz.14dwt., 8in. wide. (Sotheby's) $2,090 £1,100

One of a pair of rare early George II circular sauceboats by Isaac Cookson, Newcastle, 1728, 15oz.11dwt., 6½in. wide. (Sotheby's) $3,240 £1,705

One of a pair of George IV shell-shaped sauceboats, 1828, 31oz. (Christie's)
$2,405 £1,300

One of a pair of George II cast silver sauceboats, London, 1747, 7¾in. wide, 36oz. (Wm. Doyle Galleries Inc.)
$5,500 £2,910

George II shaped oval creamboat by Isaac Cookson, Newcastle, 1745, 4oz. 12dwt. (Christie's) $1,025 £540

George II oval sauceboat by Peze Pilleau, London, 1758, 18oz.10dwt., 9in. wide. (Sotheby's) $1,595 £858

George III oval sauceboat by Thomas Daniell, London, 1783, 8oz.1dwt., 7in. wide. (Sotheby's) $665 £352

George II sauceboat by Richard Kersill, London, 1743, 7oz.10dwt., 14.5cm. long. (H. Spencer & Sons Ltd.)
$625 £340

Oval creamboat by Melchior Faust, Goteborg, 1768, 18.8cm. wide, 8oz. 17dwt. (Sotheby's) $4,245 £2,200

One of a pair of silver sauceboats, London, 1911, 24oz. (J. M. Welch & Son)
$545 £300

SILVER

English gold and hardstone scent bottle with agate stopper, 8.7cm. high, circa 1765. (Sotheby's)
$2,550 £1,320

Early 19th century gold mounted glass scent bottle, 2¼in. high. (Christie's) $665 £360

Silver gilt mounted double overlay scent bottle, interior stamped S. Mordan & Co., London, 1850's, 9.2cm. high. (Sotheby's Belgravia) $190 £104

Unusual silver gilt mounted enamel scent flask in the form of an egg, 8.6cm. high, London, 1882. (Sotheby's Belgravia) $1,035 £550

Late 18th century gold and glass scent bottle and stopper, 12.5cm. long. (Sotheby's)
$190 £104

Mid 19th century Palais Royale gilt metal mounted engraved glass scent stand, 29.5cm. high. (Sotheby's Belgravia) $445 £242

Wiener Werkstatte cut glass globular bottle with electroplated bottle top, circa 1910. (Sotheby's Belgravia) $1,780 £1,000

French parcel gilt silver mounted clear glass scent flask, circa 1844, 11.4cm. high. (Sotheby's Belgravia) $660 £352

Silver mounted and tortoiseshell veneered scent bottle case complete with silver mounted scent bottle, London, 1910. (Sotheby's Belgravia) $445 £242

William IV oblong snuff box by Reily & Storer, London, 1834, 3¼in. wide. (Sotheby's) $350 £190

Rectangular silver snuff box, lid inset with an unusual medal, by Norbert Roettier. (Woolley & Wallis) $465 £240

George III Irish oval snuff box by Alexander Ticknell, Dublin, 1795, 3¼in. long. (Sotheby's) $735 £400

Silver and tortoiseshell pique snuff box, lid decorated with a figure, circa 1710, 8.5cm. long. (Sotheby's) $730 £396

Late 17th/early 18th century French silver and tortoiseshell pique snuff box, 7.2cm. wide. (Sotheby's) $490 £264

Circular silver snuff box, hinged lid set with tortoiseshell portrait of Charles I, 2½in. diam. (Woolley & Wallis) $505 £260

Silver and Neapolitan pique snuff box of oval form, 7cm. wide, circa 1730. (Sotheby's) $320 £165

Oval silver gilt snuff box by Lawrence Oliphant, Edinburgh, circa 1740, 2½in. long. (Sotheby's) $270 £143

Shaped silver snuff box, inset with tortoiseshell, lid with bust of George II, 3½in. wide.(Woolley & Wallis) $545 £280

Presentation snuff box, London, 1812, 7.4cm. wide, in red leather case. (Sotheby's) $1,380 £715

Carved coquilla nut snuff box of boat shape, circa 1800, 2¾in. long. (Christie's) $370 £200

Early 19th century silver gilt snuff box with gold rims, 3½in. long.(Christie's) $555 £300

Rectangular silver gilt and shaded cloisonne enamel snuff box, Moscow, 1899-1908, 6.3cm. wide. (Sotheby's) $735 £396

German oval silver and tortoiseshell snuff box, 1750, 7.7cm. wide. (Sotheby's) $325 £176

Rectangular silver and elephant's tooth snuff box by Joseph Willmore, Birmingham, 1834, 9cm. wide.(Sotheby's) $405 £220

Silver and niello snuff box by I.K., Moscow, 1829, 7.5cm. wide.(Sotheby's) $940 £506

Russian silver snuff box, Moscow, 1838, 3in. long, 2.5 troy oz. (Robert W. Skinner Inc.) $300 £160

Silver gilt mounted horn snuff box with hinged lid, London, 1880. (Sotheby's Belgravia) $265 £143

Oval silver and tortoiseshell pique snuff box, circa 1720, 8.3cm. wide. (Sotheby's) $550 £297

Silver gilt and mother-of-pearl snuff box of kidney form, circa 1835, 7cm. wide. (Sotheby's) $385 £209

Early 19th century coquilla nut snuff box of boat form and with silver gilt thumbpiece, 3½in. long. (Christie's) $295 £160

Silver gilt and hardstone snuff box by Nathaniel Mills, Birmingham, 1828, 6.8cm. wide. (Sotheby's)$305 £165

Nathaniel Mills rectangular silver snuff box with a castle view, Birmingham, 1837, 2½in. long. (Christie's)$460 £250

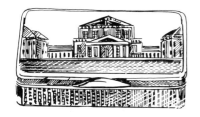

Rectangular silver and niello snuff box, Moscow, 1880, 7.5cm. wide. (Sotheby's) $570 £308

Parcel gilt and niello snuff box, by O.B., Moscow, 1842, 7.5cm. wide.(Sotheby's) $775 £418

STANDS

Early George I oval wine bottle stand by Anthony Nelme, London, 1715. (Sotheby's)$8,230 £4,400

One of a pair of shaped circular fruit stands by Reily & Storer, London, 1837, 50.1oz. (Sotheby's Belgravia) $825 £440

One of a pair of circular tazzas by C. T. & G. Fox, London, 1853, 43.8oz., 25.5cm. diam. (Sotheby's Belgravia)
$1,550 £825

One of a set of three George III oval dessert stands, by Pitts & Preedy, London, 1795, 4¾in. wide, 25oz.3dwt. (Sotheby's)$1,455 £770

Art Deco silver plated tazza with lobed dish. (J. M. Welch & Son)
$225 £125

One of a set of four George III silver gilt oval sweetmeat stands, by Pitts & Preedy, 1792, 31oz.10dwt. (Sotheby's)
$1,695 £920

Circular fruit stand by R. H. Halford & Sons, London, 1900, 22.8cm. high, 28.5oz.(Sotheby's Belgravia) $510 £280

George III oval teapot stand by Peter and Ann Bateman, London, 1792, 4oz.18dwt., 8in. wide. (Sotheby's)
$310 £165

One of a pair of Tiffany & Co. enamelled silver comports, 14cm. high, 22oz. (Phillips)
$610 £340

Charles II plain cylindrical tankard by E. G., 1684, 8in. high, 36oz. (Christie's)
$4,805 £2,530

Cylindrical tankard by Claus Sulsen Hamburgensis, Hamburg, circa 1645, 29oz.11dwt., 20.2cm. high.(Sotheby's)
$8,915 £4,620

George I plain cylindrical tankard by Thomas Mason, 1722, 7in. high, 24oz. (Christie's)
$2,925 £1,540

Silver tankard by David King, Dublin, 1704-06, 8in. high, 30oz. (Christie's)$2,895 £1,465

Reeded tapering cylindrical mug by William Knight, London, 1837, 11.3oz., 10.7cm. high. (Sotheby's Belgravia) $495 £264

George I plain cylindrical tankard by Augustine Courtauld, 1719, 8in. high, 51oz. (Christie's)
$4,105 £2,160

George I tapering cylindrical tankard on moulded foot, by Richard Bayley, 1723, 7¼in. high, 27oz. (Christie's)$1,845 £972

George I plain tapering cylindrical tankard on rim foot, by Edmund Pearce, 1715, 8in. high, 36oz. (Christie's) $3,860 £1,980

George I tapering cylindrical tankard by Thos. Bolton, Dublin, 1718, 9in. high, 35oz. (Christie's)
$4,290 £2,200

George I plain tapering cylindrical tankard, Exeter, 1718, 7¾in. high, 29oz. (Christie's) $3,135 £1,650

Mid 17th century silver gilt mounted serpentine tankard, 4¾in. high. (Christie's) $2,715 £1,500

Large Continental silver tankard, hinged cover inset with lapis lazuli, 38oz., 7½in. high. (Dickinson, Davy & Markham) $665 £360

George III plain cylindrical tankard by John Langlands, Newcastle, 1795, 8in. high, 28oz. (Christie's) $1,720 £950

George III tapering cylindrical tankard by Hester Bateman, London, 1785, 26oz.5dwt., 6¾in. high. (Sotheby's) $1,620 £858

Early George II baluster tankard by James Manners, London, 1735, 7¾in. high, 29oz.4dwt. (Sotheby's) $3,135 £1,650

Mid 18th century Danish plain cylindrical peg tankard by Knud Rasmussen Brandt, 7¼in. high, 22oz.(Christie's) $3,800 £2,100

Charles II cylindrical tankard, London, 1675, with later engraving, 6¾in. high, 24oz.15dwt. (Sotheby's) $3,680 £1,980

George I tapering cylindrical tankard by James Smith I, London, 1720, 7¼in. high, 24oz.16dwt. (Sotheby's) $2,455 £1,320

Queen Anne tapering cylindrical tankard by Augustine Courtauld, 1707, 6¾in. high, 28oz. (Christie's) $4,180 £2,200

Lidded silver tankard by William Shaw, London, 1765, now converted to a jug. (H. Spencer & Sons Ltd.) $1,250 £680

George I plain cylindrical tankard by George Boothby, 1718, 8in. high, 34oz. (Christie's)
$3,345 £1,760

George I tapering cylindrical tankard by Michael Boult, London, 1723, 7¼in. high, 30oz.11dwt. (Sotheby's) $4,390 £2,310

Presentation silver tankard by Smith, Nicholson & Co., London, 1858, 35.7oz., 27.5cm. high. (Sotheby's Belgravia) $750 £407

George III baluster tankard by Thomas Wallis, London, 1781, 23oz. 12dwt., 8in. high. (Sotheby's)
$1,880 £968

William III cylindrical tankard by Anthony Nelme, London, 1699, 39oz.9dwt., 8½in. high. (Sotheby's)
$4,705 £2,530

George III baluster tankard by Jacob Marsh or John Moore, London, 1766, 24oz. 4dwt., 7¾in. high.(Sotheby's)
$1,920 £990

William III tapered cylindrical tankard by Robert Peake, London, 23oz. 3dwt., 6¾in. high. (Sotheby's)
$6,690 £3,520

James II cylindrical tankard, 1686, 8¾in. high, 43oz. (Christie's)
$6,005   £3,080

Charles II cylindrical tankard by E.G., 1679, 7¼in. high, 29oz. (Christie's)
$6,280 £3,300

One of a pair of George III cylindrical tankards by Robert Gaze, 1796, 7¼in. high, 58oz. (Christie's)
$3,675 £2,052

Continental parcel gilt tankard with mermaid thumbpiece, circa 1600, 8¼in. high, 26oz. (Christie's)
$4,795 £2,592

George II tapered cylindrical quart tankard by Benjamin Godfrey, London, 1737, 44oz.5dwt., 9¾in. high. (Sotheby's)
$3,945 £2,145

George III cylindrical tankard with reeded girdle and skirt foot, by Langlands & Robertson, Newcastle, 25oz.17dwt. (Sotheby's)$1,930 £1,050

George III tapered cylindrical tankard with flat cover, by E. Fernell, London, 1787, 35oz. 15dwt., 8in. high. (Sotheby's)$1,415 £770

Large silver tankard by J. H. Rawlings, London, 1893, 30cm. high, 95.1oz. (Sotheby's Belgravia)
$2,380 £1,265

Early George II quart tankard by Wm. Darker, London, 1733, 7½in. high, 26oz.10dwt.(Woolley & Wallis) $1,710 £950

Four-piece tea and coffee service of squat melon form, Sheffield, 1966, 86oz. (Sotheby, King & Chasemore) $1,275 £700

Gorham sterling silver teaset, Rhode Island, 1960, 60 troy oz. (Robert W. Skinner Inc.) $1,250 £690

Four-piece tea and coffee set by Hayne & Cater, London, 1840, 73.1oz. (Sotheby's Belgravia) $2,365 £1,320

Five-piece tea and coffee set by Goldsmiths & Silversmiths Co. Ltd., London, 1909/10, 56oz. (Sotheby's Belgravia) $1,280 £715

Continental silver tea and coffee service and tray. (Sotheby, King & Chasemore) $1,640 £900

Silver three-piece tea service designed by Kate Harris, 1901, teapot 11cm. high.
(Sotheby's Belgravia) $800 £450

Late 18th century New York silver three-piece teaset by Joel Sayre, 45oz. (Wm.
Doyle Galleries Inc.) $2,500 £1,325

German silver four-piece teaset, marked '950 Wilh. Giese', 67oz. (Sotheby,
King & Chasemore) $1,235 £680

Victorian three-piece inverted pear-shaped teaset, by Mackay & Chisholm,
Edinburgh, 1842, 44oz.1dwt. (Sotheby's) $1,120 £594

Hukin & Heath silver travelling teaset, London, 1880, designed by Christopher Dresser. (Sotheby's Belgravia) $855 £480

Regency oblong tea service in three pieces, by George Fenwick, Edinburgh, 1811, 73oz. (Christie's) $2,510 £1,320

George III silver tea service by John Robins, 1806, 71oz. (Christie's) $5,335 £2,808

Victorian circular three-piece teaset by J. McKay, Edinburgh, 1844-45, 47oz. 18dwt. (Sotheby's) $1,245 £660

729

William IV tea service of three pieces, by R. W. Atkins and W. N. Somersall, 1834, 58oz. (Christie's) $1,850 £990

Four-piece silver plated tea service by Elkington & Co. (Lawrence Fine Art) $580 £300

Four-piece silver teaset in embossed design, 19th century, 75oz., sold with tray. (Honiton Galleries) $4,930 £2,650

Five-piece silver tea and coffee service by Barker Brothers & Son Ltd., Birmingham, 1929-30, 96oz. (Lawrence Fine Art) $905 £470

Early Victorian silver three-piece teaset, London, 1841, 45.5oz. (Dee & Atkinson) $1,025 £550

George IV tea and coffee service by J. Wrangham and W. Moulson, 1825, 100oz. (Christie's) $3,700 £2,000

Four-piece tea and coffee set by C. S. Harris, London, 1897, 54.9oz. (Sotheby's Belgravia) $1,055 £550

Four-piece silver tea service by Elkington & Co., Birmingham, 1920, 41oz. (Lawrence Fine Art) $635 £330

George IV three-piece teaset by John Angel, 1829, 56oz. (Hy. Duke & Son)
$1,115 £580

Four-piece tea service with reeded girdles, Sheffield, 1911-12, 25oz. (Lawrence Fine Art) $490 £255

Seven-piece tea and coffee set with two-handled tray, by Tiffany & Co., 239oz. (Sotheby Beresford Adams) $3,235 £1,750

Three-piece teaset in Art Nouveau style, Chester 1906, 29oz. (Gilbert Baitson)
$555 £295

Three-piece teaset by C. S. Harris & Sons, Ltd., London, 1900-01, 50.8oz.
(Sotheby's Belgravia) $1,015 £528

George V four-piece tea service by Walker & Hall, Sheffield, circa 1918-21,
73oz. (H. Spencer & Sons Ltd.) $1,010 £540

Four-piece silver plated tea service and tray, stamped Maple & Co. (Lawrence
Fine Art) $300 £155

Three-piece silver teaset and tray by William Davie, Edinburgh, 1783.
(Sotheby, King & Chasemore) $1,655 £900

733

Aesthetic movement three-piece parcel gilt teaset, London, 1880-82, 32oz.4dwt. (Sotheby Beresford Adams) $850 £460

Four-piece tea and coffee set by Mappin & Webb, Sheffield, 1877, 66oz. (Sotheby's Belgravia) $2,220 £1,200

Six-piece sterling silver teaset by Shreve, Crump & Low Co., Boston, circa 1875, 118½ troy oz. (Robert W. Skinner Inc.) $1,200 £680

Oval three-piece teaset by C. S. Harris & Sons Ltd., London, 1894-95, 26.7oz. (Sotheby's Belgravia) $520 £280

Three-piece tea service by GR, London, 1850, 46oz. (Dickinson, Davy & Markham) $965 £525

Victorian four-piece matching teaset by Barnard & Sons, London, 1838-39, 77oz. 18dwt. (Sotheby Beresford Adams) $3,700 £2,000

Four-piece electroplated tea and coffee set and a matching tea kettle, stand and burner, circa 1860. (Sotheby's Belgravia) $515 £280

William IV composite three-piece tea service by E., E., J. & W. Barnard, London, 1832, 46oz. (H. Spencer & Sons Ltd.) $780 £420

SILVER

George III three-piece teaset, London, 1818-19, 46oz.8dwt. (Sotheby
Beresford Adams) $960 £520

George IV four-piece teaset by Henry and Charles Lias, London, 1823, 93oz.
10dwt. (Sotheby Beresford Adams) $2,405 £1,300

Late 19th century five-piece English sterling silver teaset, 86 troy oz. (Robert W.
Skinner Inc.) $850 £480

Four-piece tea and coffee set by Martin, Hall & Co. Ltd., London, 1880, 62.3oz.
(Sotheby's Belgravia) $1,110 £600

Large George III three-piece tea service with gadrooned edges, by Thos. Wallace and Jonathan Hayne, London, 1813, 38½oz. (Dickinson, Davy & Markham)

$920 £500

Electroplated four-piece tea and coffee set, circa 1855, stamped Waterhouse/Dublin. (Sotheby's Belgravia)

$335 £180

Seven-piece tea and coffee service by W. & J. Barnard, 1889-90, 145.6oz. (Sotheby's Belgravia)

$3,145 £1,700

Four-piece tea and coffee set by Joseph Angell, London, 1855, 77.3oz. (Sotheby's Belgravia)

$2,745 £1,500

TEA & COFFEE SETS

Four-piece teaset and tea tray by Elkington & Co. Ltd., Birmingham, 1947, 190.6oz., 67.7cm. wide. (Sotheby's Belgravia) $2,480 £1,320

Three-piece teaset with fluted circular bodies by A. B. Savory & Sons, London, 1858. (Sotheby's Belgravia) $1,050 £572

William IV three-piece teaset by Charles Fox, London, 1836, 56oz.8dwt. (Sotheby's) $1,840 £990

Silver plated four-piece teaset with vase-shaped bodies, circa 1900, by WMF. (Sotheby's) $310 £159

Matching six-piece tea and coffee set, 1907-30, 147.4oz. (Sotheby's Belgravia) $2,070 £1,100

Three-piece teaset with vase-shaped bodies, by Martin, Hall & Co. Ltd., London, 1879, 48.4oz. (Sotheby's Belgravia) $990 £528

Teapot and milk jug by William Hunter, London, 1851, 31.8oz. (Sotheby's Belgravia) $935 £506

Five-piece tea and coffee set by Edward Barnard & Sons, London, 1896-97, 141.7oz. (Sotheby's Belgravia) $2,895 £1,540

Four-piece tea and coffee set and two-handled tray, circa 1910, 178.1oz. (Sotheby's Belgravia) $2,935 £1,595

Four-piece tea and coffee set by Martin, Hall & Co. and M. Rhodes & Sons Ltd., 73.5oz. (Sotheby's Belgravia) $1,550 £825

William IV three-piece compressed circular teaset by Hawksworth, Eyre & Co., Sheffield, 1836, 42oz.8dwt. (Sotheby's) $1,210 £638

William IV four-piece tea and coffee set by Richard Smith, Dublin, 1836, sold with sugar tongs, 96oz.8dwt. (Sotheby's) $4,295 £2,310

Three-piece teaset by Reily & Storer, London, 1841, 47.5oz. (Sotheby's Belgravia) $970 £528

Victorian four-piece tea service by E. & J. Barnard, London, 1863, 62oz.16dwt. (Sotheby's) $1,750 £902

Silver tea service by P. Ovchinnikov, Moscow, 1887-1893. (Sotheby's)
$4,090 £2,200

Three-piece silver and enamel coffee set by P. Ovchinnikov, Moscow, 1887.
(Sotheby's) $1,840 £990

Victorian three-piece teaset by Barnard Bros., London, 1868, 40oz.4dwt.
(Sotheby's) $1,150 £594

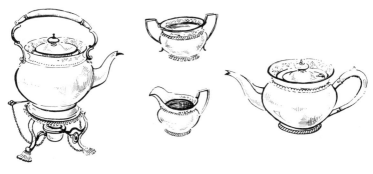

Four-piece teaset by C. S. Harris, London, 1912-15, 81oz.10dwt.(Sotheby's)
$1,410 £726

TEA CADDIES

Silver tea caddy, Bergen, 1713, 12.5cm. high, 5oz. 11dwt. (Sotheby's)
$2,865 £1,485

Guild of Handicrafts Ltd. silver tea caddy, London, 1906, 7cm. high, on four ball feet. (Sotheby's Belgravia) $220 £121

George II oval bombe tea caddy, by Samuel Taylor, London, 1745, 12oz.6dwt., 5in. high. (Sotheby's)
$1,535 £825

George III rectangular tea caddy by J. E. Terrey, London, 1818, 4½in. high, 12oz.6dwt. (Sotheby's)
$970   £528

George III tea caddy and sugar basin by Wm. Plummer, 1773, in silver mounted wood case, 12oz. 16dwt. (Christie's)
$1,810 £1,000

George III oblong tea caddy by Elizabeth Godfrey, London, 1765, 6in. high, 12oz.1dwt. (Sotheby's)$1,140 £638

One of a pair of early George III bombe tea caddies by J. Langford II and J. Sebille, London, 1763, 24oz.9dwt. (Sotheby's) $2,610 £1,375
742

George III oval tea caddy by A. Lestourgeon, London, 1777, 4½in. high, 11oz.6dwt. (Sotheby's)
$2,820 £1,485

One of a set of two George II oblong tea caddies and a sugar box by D. Smith and R. Sharp, 1761, 25oz. (Christie's) $5,605 £3,13

George III oval tea caddy by Fogelberg & Gilbert, London, 1783, 4½in. high, 12oz.6dwt. (Sotheby's) $2,180 £1,155

George III shaped oval tea caddy by Aldridge & Green, London, 1783, 4¾in. high, 12oz.13dwt. (Sotheby's)$3,310 £1,800

George III oval tea caddy and cover by H. Chawner, London, 1786, 12oz. (H. Spencer & Sons Ltd.) $765 £410

George II octagonal tea caddy by Simon Pantin, London, 1738, 7oz. 5dwt., 4in. high. (Sotheby's)$1,620 £880

Pair of George III rectangular tea caddies and covers of bombe form, by Wm. Vincent, 21oz. (Neales) $1,570 £850

One of a pair of sterling silver tea caddies, London, 1732, 15 troy oz., 5in. high. (Robert W. Skinner Inc.)

$1,600 £860

One of two George II bombe tea caddies in sizes, by Emick Romer, London, 1762, 5¼in. high, 19oz.5dwt. (Sotheby's) $1,750 £950

George III cylindrical tea caddy by Parker & Wakelin, London, 1763, 14oz. 1dwt., 4¼in. high. (Sotheby's)$3,275 £1,760

One of a set of three George II oval caddies by John Newton, circa 1730, 31oz. (Christie's) $2,445 £1,350

George III plain oval tea kettle, stand and lamp, by William Fountain, 1799, 75oz.(Christie's) $2,175 £1,188

Electroplated teapot, designed by Christopher Dresser, on triangular stand with burner, 19.5cm. high. (Phillips) $215 £120

Victorian circular plated tea kettle on stand with hardwood handle, 12in. high.(Dickinson, Davy & Markham) $85 £45

Late William IV silver water kettle on stand by J. & J. Aldous, London, 1837, 14in. high, 78oz. (Wm. Doyle Galleries Inc.) $1,800 £955

Large pear-shaped tea kettle, stand and lamp by R. Smith, Dublin, 1843, 15¼in. high, 119oz. (Christie's) $2,900 £1,620

George II inverted pear-shaped tea kettle and stand by P. Archambo, 1742, 68oz.(Christie's) $3,085 £1,650

George II melon-shaped tea kettle, lamp and stand, by Paul de Lamerie, 1734, 61oz. (Christie's) $4,475 £2,500

Silver tea kettle on lamp-stand, with detachable burner, by Robert Stocker, London, 1907, 33cm. high, 57.5oz. (Sotheby's Belgravia) $695 £380

George II inverted pear-shaped tea kettle and lampstand by Charles Woodward, London, 1747, 55oz.12dwt., 15in. high.(Sotheby's) $2,515 £1,375

Late 19th century baluster hexagonal tea kettle on stand, Dutch, 70.6oz., 32cm. high. (Sotheby's Belgravia) $1,435 £748

Victorian plated tea kettle on lampstand with turned wood handle, 12in. high. (Dickinson, Davy & Markham) $95 £50

George III tea kettle with stand and burner by R. Crossley, London, 1799, 42oz. (H. Spencer & Sons Ltd.) $820 £440

Oblong tea kettle, stand and burner by William Hutton & Sons Ltd., London, 1894, 51oz., 12¾in. high.(Sotheby's) $475 £260

Swiss spherical tea kettle and stand with burner, circa 1800, 38.3cm. high, 1,970gm. (Sotheby's) $4,605 £2,462

Early George III tea kettle on lampstand by T. Whipham and C. Wright, London, 1760, 47oz.19dwt., 14¼in. high. (Sotheby's) $1,985 £1,045

George II circular tea kettle, stand and lamp by Richard Bayley, 1738, 56oz. (Christie's) $4,165 £2,300

George V tea kettle, stand and lamp by Goldsmiths & Silversmiths Co. Ltd., 48oz. (H. Spencer & Sons Ltd.) $590 £320

Large Russian tea kettle on stand with lobed body, 1887, 15¼in. high, 107oz. (Lawrence Fine Art) $1,450 £800

SILVER

Circular teapot by J. & G. Angell, London, 1847, 22.5oz. (Sotheby's Belgravia) $490 £264

Electroplated teapot and cover designed by Christopher Dresser, 1880, 18cm. wide. (Christie's) $925 £495

Victorian teapot by Joseph and Albert Savory, London, 1839, 20oz. (Lawrence Fine Art) $385 £200

Circular teapot by Edward Barnard & Sons, London, 1852, 18.1oz., 13cm. high. (Sotheby's Belgravia) $400 £220

George I plain bullet-shaped teapot by Anthony Nelme, 1718, 14oz.10dwt. (Christie's) $3,495 £1,870

Plain circular teapot, hinged cover with strawberry button, by J. J. Keith, London, 1841, 22oz. (Sotheby's Belgravia) $425 £231

Dutch pear-shaped teapot Groningen, 1740, 10oz.15dwt. (Christie's) $1,685 £902

Tapering circular teapot by Martin, Hall & Co. Ltd., Sheffield, 1879, 26.2oz. (Sotheby's Belgravia) $505 £264

Late George III silver teapot by Wm. Bruce, London, 1819. (Sotheby, King & Chasemore) **$380 £200**

Oval silver teapot with engraved decoration, London, 1804, 16½oz. (Lacy Scott) **$480 £250**

William IV teapot by E. & J. Barnard, London, 1830, 25.5oz., 5¾in. high. (Lawrence Fine Art) **$520 £270**

George III oval teapot by William Plummer, London, 1787, 16oz.11dwt., 5in. high. (Sotheby's) **$830 £440**

George III shaped oval teapot by Hester Bateman, 1785, 13oz.4dwt. (Christie's) **$1,450 £800**

Walker & Hall silver tea kettle, London, 1886, 13cm. high, 17oz. (Phillips) **$270 £150**

George III shaped oval teapot and stand by Henry Chawner, 1788, 18oz.3dwt. (Christie's) **$1,085 £600**

Georgian teapot and stand with domed lid and wood handle, London, 1786. (Hall Wateridge & Owen) **$660 £350**

Compressed silver teapot with silver
handle, by William Moulson, London,
1841, 26.6oz., 13.7cm. high.
(Sotheby's Belgravia) $455 £242

Rare 18th century Scottish provincial
bullet teapot, by IS., Banff, circa
1740, 14oz.8dwt., 4½in. high.
(Sotheby's) $13,515 £7,150

Pear-shaped teapot on moulded foot,
The Hague, 1739, 9oz.5dwt., 10.6cm.
high. (Sotheby's) $1,380 £715

George III compressed circular teapot
by William Burwash, London, 1817,
26oz.13dwt., 5¼in. high. (Sotheby's)
          $725 £396

George II bullet-shaped teapot by John
Main, Edinburgh, 1742, 19oz., 5¾in.
high. (Sotheby's) $1,215 £660

Shaped oblong teapot by Frederick
Brasted, London, 1883, 19oz., 13.2cm.
high. (Sotheby's Belgravia) $620 £330

George III pear-shaped teapot by W. &
J. Priest, London, 1770, 6¾in. high,
16oz.2dwt. (Sotheby's) $1,025 £550

George III inverted pear-shaped teapot
by Ebenezer Oliphant, Edinburgh,
21oz., 6½in. high. (Sotheby's)
          $905 £495

George III teapot and stand by Wm. Plummer, London, 1786, 15oz.5dwt., 5¾in. high. (Sotheby's) $770 £396

Compressed circular teapot with silver handle and button, by Richard Wm. Elliott, London, 1842, 20.4oz. (Sotheby's Belgravia) $390 £209

George II bullet-shaped teapot by I.F., London, 1734, 15½oz., with shaped fruitwood handle. (D. M. Nesbit & Co.) $2,685 £1,500

George III octagonal teapot and stand by Henry Chawner, London, 1790, 19oz. (Sotheby's) $1,535 £825

Pear-shaped teapot by Tessiers Ltd., London, 1927, 30.1oz. (Sotheby's Belgravia) $660 £352

Victorian silver teapot by Squire & Brother Co., New York, circa 1850, 19.5 troy oz., 7in. high. (Robert W. Skinner Inc.) $275 £145

Victorian teapot in 'aesthetic' movement taste, by Francis Elkington, 1880, 21oz. (Lawrence Fine Art) $470 £260

Pear-shaped teapot with floral decoration, by Francis Crump, London, 1769, 16oz. (Woolley & Wallis) $790 £440

TOAST RACKS

SILVER

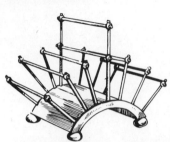

Hukin & Heath electroplated toast rack designed by Christopher Dresser, 1881, 12.5cm. high. (Phillips) $360 £200

One of a pair of lyre-shaped toast racks by A., F. & A., Pairpoint, London, 1929, 15.1oz., 20.5cm. high. (Sotheby's Belgravia) $420 £220

One of a pair of seven-bar toasters by Samuel Whitford, London, 1874, 17.7cm. long, 17.6oz. (Sotheby's Belgravia) $870 £462

TOILET REQUISITES

Fitted rosewood vanity case with cut glass bottles, London, 1849. (Sotheby, King & Chasemore) $665 £350

Early 20th century seven-piece 14 carat gold dresser set, Massachusetts. (Robert W. Skinner Inc.) $2,000 £1,115

Silver gilt and tortoise-shell manicure box and fittings, by C. H. Dumenile Ltd., London, 1919, 21.7cm. wide.(Sotheby's Belgravia) $325 £176

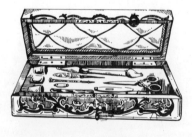

French lacquered etui of tapering form, circa 1760, 9.6cm. high. (Sotheby's) $265 £143

Rectangular necessaire, wood body veneered in mother-of-pearl, 1854, fully fitted. (Sotheby's Belgravia) $490 £264

English gilt metal necessaire in the manner of James Cox, 14.5cm. high, circa 1770. (Sotheby's)$850 £440

Rectangular papier-mache necessaire with hinged lid inlaid with mother-of-pearl, circa 1850, 14.4cm. long. (Sotheby's Belgravia) $315 £170

Gilt metal beehive necessaire applied with honey bees, circa 1875, 18.5cm. high.(Sotheby's Belgravia) $425 £231

Fitted coromandelwood travelling toilet case, London, 1850, with silver-topped glass bottles. (Sotheby, King & Chasemore) $510 £280

Mid 18th century etui, oval tapered body, fully fitted. (Sotheby's) $525 £286

Reproduction Queen Anne eighteen-piece dressing table set of gilt Britannia silver, London, 1915-16. (Sotheby, King & Chasemore) $17,290 £9,500

English silver mounted shagreen lancet case, circa 1800, 7.7cm. high. (Sotheby's) $405 £220

Gentleman's travelling dressing case of brass bound hardwood, by Francis Diller, London, 1845. (Sotheby's Belgravia) $610 £330

George III silver and tortoiseshell folding comb by George Hall, London, 1804, 6in. long.(Sotheby's) $585 £308

George IV dressing case by John and Archibald Douglas, London, 1822. (Sotheby's) $875 £451

751

George III circular salver by John Hutson, London, 1791, 66oz.14dwt., 17½in. diam. (Sotheby's) $2,025 £1,045

One of a pair of George III shaped circular salvers by Thomas Heming, London, 1756, 7½in. diam., 20oz.12dwt. (Sotheby's)$1,595 £858

George III circular salver by P. & A. Bateman, London, 1792, 9oz.5dwt., 8in. diam. (Sotheby's) $600 £319

Shaped circular salver with inscription, by Benjamin Smith, London, 1847, 18.1oz., 28cm. diam. (Sotheby's Belgravia) $325 £176

George III circular salver by Solomon Hougham, London, 1816, 160oz., 23¼in. diam.(Sotheby's) $4,705 £2,530

George III shaped circular salver by John Carter, London, 1771, 47oz.4dwt., 14¾in. diam. (Sotheby's) $1,600 £825

George II shaped circular salver by William Peaston, London, 1750, 17oz. 10dwt., 9¾in. diam. (Sotheby's) $995 £528

George III circular salver by John Hutson, London, 1785, 43oz.12dwt., 14½in. diam. (Sotheby's Belgravia) $1,675 £902

George I octofoil salver by John Bache, London, 1723, 40oz.19dwt., 12¾in. diam. (Sotheby's) $6,235 £3,300

George III shaped circular salver by John Carter, London, 1775, 29oz., 12in. diam.(Sotheby's) $1,150 £594

George III circular salver by P. & A. Bateman, London, 1792, 9oz.5dwt., 8in. diam. (Sotheby's) $600 £319

One of a pair of Victorian shaped circular salvers by J. Garrard, 1895, 15in. diam., 108oz. (Christie's)$4,070 £2,200

One of ten George II shaped circular dinner plates by Paul Crespin, 1749, 9½in. diam. (Sotheby's) $7,485 £3,960

Early George I circular salver on foot by Alice Sheene, London, 1714, 5oz.19dwt., 6in. diam. (Sotheby's)$1,255 £660

George II shaped circular salver by R. Rugg or Rew, London, 1755, 10¼in. diam., 20oz.2dwt. (Sotheby's)$1,210 £638

George II shaped circular salver by Robert Abercromby, London, 1735, 13½in. diam., 41oz.19dwt. (Sotheby's) $3,970 £2,090

William and Mary circular salver on foot, London, 1690, 8oz.7dwt., 8¼in. diam. (Sotheby's) $1,225 £660

One of a pair of George III hexafoil salvers by Ebenezer Coker, London, 1768, 7in. diam., 18.3oz. (Lawrence Fine Art) $1,700 £880

George III snuffers tray by Joseph Creswell, London, 1774, 9oz.8dwt., 7¾in. long. (Sotheby's) $605 £319

One of a pair of George III oval salvers by John Scofield, London, 1777, 25oz. 15dwt., 9in. long. (Sotheby's) $3,450 £1,815

George III oval salver by Solomon Hougham, London, 1806, 10in. wide, 16oz.8dwt. (Sotheby's) $665 £352

Shaped rectangular two-handled tray by William Aitken, Birmingham, 1903, 141.9oz., 74cm. long. (Sotheby's Belgravia) $1,660 £902

Oval two-handled tea tray by Edward Barnard & Sons, London, 1865, 80.2cm. wide, 153.7oz. (Sotheby's Belgravia) $3,205 £1,705

Large electroplated tea tray by Elkington & Co., 1871, 69cm. long. (Sotheby's Belgravia) $350 £187

George III shaped oblong snuffers tray by Cradock & Reid, London, 1818, 8oz.12dwt., 9¾in. wide. (Sotheby's) $470 £253

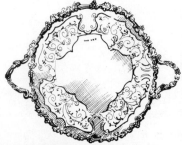

Two-handled shaped circular fruit stand with pierced body, 41.5cm. wide, 43.5oz. (Sotheby's Belgravia) $785 £418

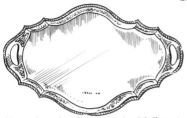

Shaped oval gallery tray by Walker & Hall, Sheffield, 1920, 101oz., 60.7cm. wide. (Sotheby's Belgravia) $2,070 £1,100

One of a pair of crested shaped circular dishes by Hunt & Roskell, London, 1845, 43cm. long, 108.6oz.(Sotheby's Belgravia) $1,965 £1,045

Large rectangular tea tray with lobed border by Cooper Brothers, Sheffield, 1896, 116.5oz., 69.5cm. wide. (Sotheby's Belgravia) $1,550 £825

One of eleven shaped circular dinner plates, late 19th/early 20th century, 217oz., 25.7cm. diam. (Sotheby's Belgravia) $3,100 £1,650

William and Mary circular salver on foot by Jonah Kirk, London, 1691, 16oz.19dwt., 10¾in. diam.(Sotheby's) $3,220 £1,760

George III oval tea tray by Hannam & Crouch, London, 1803, 104oz.14dwt., 26½in. wide. (Sotheby's) $4,830 £2,640

Large presentation two-handled tea tray by Henry Wilkinson & Co., Sheffield, 1845, 167oz., 76.5cm. wide. (Sotheby's Belgravia)$3,720 £1,980

George III small circular salver by Hester Bateman, 1783, 6in. diam. (Lawrence Fine Art) $540 £280

755

Silver diamond-shaped pin tray with embossed centre, London, 1884, 4½in. wide. (Dickinson, Davy & Markham) $35 £20

Set of three George III plain oval salvers by J. Wakelin and W. Taylor, 1786, 100oz., 18¾in. and 9in. long. (Christie's) $5,790 £3,200

George II plain circular salver by William Williamson, Dublin, 1727, 12¼in. diam., 30oz. (Christie's) $3,600 £1,925

George II circular waiter with pie crust and shell edge, J. Morrison, London, 1750, 5¾oz., 6¼in. diam. (Dickinson, Davy & Markham) $310 £170

Sheffield sterling silver tray by J. E. Caldwell & Co., Sheffield, circa 1930, 171 troy oz., 31in. long. (Robert W. Skinner Inc.) $2,000 £1,130

Large shaped circular salver by West & Son, Dublin, 138.9oz., 60.5cm. diam. (Sotheby's Belgravia) $1,610 £880

Victorian silver gilt shaped circular salver, 11in. diam., 27oz. (Christie's) $1,075 £580

One of a set of four Regency shaped oval meat dishes by William Stroud, 1814, 17in. long, 210oz. (Christie's) $6,660 £3,600

George III salver by John Mewburn,
London, 1812, 78oz., 18½in. diam.
(Sotheby, King & Chasemore)
$1,440 £750

Large and heavy two-handled silver
tray by Walker & Hall, Sheffield, 1920,
132oz., 2ft.5½in. wide. (Dickinson,
Davy & Markham) $1,455 £790

Good pair of George IV candle snuf-
fers and tray by Rebecca Emes and
Edward Barnard, London, 1825, 14oz.
(H. Spencer & Sons Ltd.)$910 £490

Shaped circular salver by Edward
Barnard & Sons, London, 1888,
25.5cm. diam., 16.2oz. (Sotheby's
Belgravia) $255 £140

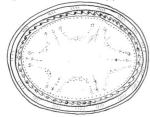

One of a pair of George III stands by
Thomas Wallis, London, 1787.
(Sotheby, King & Chasemore)
$815 £430

Shaped rectangular two-handled tray
by Joseph Rodgers & Sons Ltd.,
Sheffield, 1901, 157oz., 72cm. wide.
(Sotheby's Belgravia) $1,575 £860

Fine George IV silver two-handled
rectangular tray by S. C. Younge & Co.,
Sheffield, 1820, 142oz. (Geering &
Colyer) $2,775 £1,500

One of a pair of George IV shaped
circular entree dishes by J. C. Edington,
1829, 9½in. diam., 50oz. (Christie's)
$2,260 £1,250

Large silver tea tray by James Deakin & Sons, Sheffield, 1902, 26in. wide, 147oz. (Lawrence Fine Art) $1,485 £820

Novelty ash tray cast as a frog, by R. Hennell & Sons, London, 1884, 10.1cm. diam., 2.2oz. (Sotheby's Belgravia) $475 £253

19th century Kate Greenaway silver plated tray of pentagonal shape, 6in. high. (Robert W. Skinner Inc.) $125 £70

Victorian silver plated oval tea tray with beaded scroll handles, 28½in. wide. (Lawrence Fine Art) $200 £110

Chinese silver tea tray and teapot, stamped mark Guangxu, 1,538gm. (Sotheby's Belgravia) $545 £297

George II silver gilt shaped circular salver by Wm. Cripps, 1754, 14¼in. diam., 53oz. (Christie's) $3,430 £1,760

George III oval coffee tray by Smith & Hayter, London, 1794, 22¾in. wide, 78oz.18dwt. (Sotheby's) $3,240 £1,760

One of a pair of George III stands by Thomas Heming, London, 1776, 17½in. wide, 105oz.17dwt. (Sotheby's) $2,760 £1,500

One of a set of four George III faceted navette-shaped sauce tureens and covers by Henry Chawner, London, 65oz.6dwt. (Sotheby's) $4,430 £2,420

One of a pair of Regency rectangular Sheffield plate sauce tureens, with gadrooned edges, 7½in. wide. (Woolley & Wallis) $650 £360

Sheffield plate lobed oval soup tureen and cover, 41cm. wide, circa 1840. (Sotheby's Belgravia) $1,760 £935

One of a pair of two-handled boat-shaped sauce tureens and covers, 23.5cm. wide, 24.3oz. (Sotheby's Belgravia) $735 £418

One of a set of four George III two-handled oval sauce tureens and covers, by J. Wakelin and W. Taylor, 1776, 66oz. (Christie's) $2,445 £1,350

One of a set of four oval sauce tureens and covers by Charles Wright, London, 1778, 77oz.10dwt., 9½in. wide. (Sotheby's) $8,780 £4,620

One of a pair of George III boat-shaped sauce tureens and covers, by Charles Hougham, London, 1791, 28oz.11dwt., 9½in. wide. (Sotheby's) $2,455 £1,320

George III oblong sauce tureen and cover by J. Angell, London, 1816, 8in. wide, 25oz.7dwt. (Sotheby's) $820 £440

One of a pair of George III plain oval sauce tureens and covers by John Robins, 1798, 33oz. (Christie's)
$3,700 £1,980

Peruvian oval two-handled soup tureen and cover, mid 20th century, 44cm. long, 54.6oz. (Sotheby's Belgravia)
$695 £380

Victorian octagonal two-handled soup tureen, cover and stand by Robert Garrard, 1843, 20¼in. long, 201oz. (Christie's) $8,325 £4,500

One of a pair of George III sauce tureens by Samuel Whitford, London, 1814, 8½in. long, 65oz. (Phillips & Jolly's) $2,930 £1,600

One of four George III two-handled oval sauce tureens and covers by D. Smith and R. Sharp, 1780, 80oz. (Christie's) $3,980 £2,200

Two-handled fluted boat-shaped soup tureen and cover, London, 1897, 39cm. wide, 51.8oz. (Sotheby's Belgravia) $1,795 £935

Georgian sauce tureen in Adam style, London, 1782. (Hall Wateridge & Owen) $525 £280

One of a pair of George IV compressed oblong sauce tureens and covers, 37oz. 6dwt., 8½in. wide. (Sotheby's)
$1,495 £792

George III sauce tureen by Robert Hennell, II, London, 1810. (Sotheby, King & Chasemore) $930 £490

Lobed oval two-handled soup tureen and cover by Gorham Manufacturing Co., America, 36.7oz., circa 1910, 32cm. wide. (Sotheby's Belgravia)
$620 £340

George III oval sauce tureen and cover by William Burwash, 1818, 28oz.3dwt., 8¼in. wide. (Sotheby's) $1,415 £748

Silver plated on copper tureen and cover, on stand, 13in. high. (Sotheby, King & Chasemore) $475 £250

Hukin & Heath electroplated soup tureen supported on three spike feet, 20.5cm. high. (Phillips) $1,165 £650

One of four George III two-handled oval sauce tureens by John Gibson Leadbetter, 55oz. (Christie's)
$2,535 £1,400

Lobed oblong two-handled sauce tureen and cover by Walker & Hall, Sheffield, 1894, 42.2oz., 24cm. wide. (Sotheby's Belgravia) $1,100 £572

George IV shaped oval two-handled soup tureen and cover by William Eaton, 1824, 12¾in. long, 181oz. (Christie's)
$9,250 £5,000

One of a pair of George III oval sauce tureens by W. Holmes and N. Dumee, 1774, 26oz. (Christie's) $1,930 £990

Silver plated soup tureen in the form of a turtle, circa 1860, 21in. long. (J. M. Welch & Son) $1,820 £1,000

One of a pair of George III sauce tureens and covers by Robert & Samuel Hennell, London, 1804, 13oz.10dwt., 5in. high. (Sotheby's) $1,965 £1,012

Large shaped oval soup tureen and cover by Reily & Storer, London, 1838, 176.2oz., 44cm. wide. (Sotheby's Belgravia) $6,620 £3,520

George III oval soup tureen and cover by Thomas Holland II, London, 1809, 14¾in. wide, 94oz.15dwt. (Sotheby's) $4,295 £2,310

Electroplated tureen and cover in the form of a broody hen, by G. R. Collins & Co., 1850's, 22cm. wide. (Sotheby's Belgravia) $705 £374

One of a pair of George III oval sauce tureens, covers and stands by Thomas Heming, London, 1769, 9in. wide. (Sotheby's) $5,320 £2,860

Hukin & Heath sauce tureen, designed by Christopher Dresser, 1880, 13.5cm. high. (Phillips) $930 £520

George II tea urn by Wm. Holmes, 1776, 94oz. (Louis Taylor & Sons) $1,805 £1,025

Large Victorian Sheffield plate tea urn with curving handles, 14in. high. (Dickinson, Davy & Markham) $225 £130

George III tea urn by Francis Crump, London, 1768, 71oz.17dwt., 19in. high. (Sotheby's) $1,380 £780

Silver tea urn of neo-classical design with vase-shaped body on square base, dated 1771. (W. H. Lane & Son) $1,910 £1,040

Regency two-handled circular vase-shaped tea urn by B. & J. Smith, 1810, 15½in. high, 157oz. (Christie's) $5,350 £2,820

George III two-handled vase-shaped tea urn by Henry Chawner and John Emes, 1796, 17½in. high, 133oz. (Christie's) $3,060 £1,728

George III vase-shaped tea urn by John Robins, London, 1786, 100oz. 3dwt., 20½in. high. (Sotheby's) $1,680 £950

George III tea urn by Daniel Smith and Robert Sharp, London, 1770, 102oz., 19½in. high. (Sotheby's) $2,560 £1,430

George III partly fluted tea urn by Richard Cooke, 1804, 19¾in. high, 198oz.(Christie's) $4,525 £2,420

Liberty & Co. 'Cymric'
silver and lapis lazuli
vase, Birmingham, 1910,
2½oz., 7cm. high.
(Christie's) $330 £180

Art Nouveau Russian sil-
ver flared vase with clear
glass liner, 20.5cm. wide.
(Christie's) $535 £285

Georg Jensen trumpet-
shaped silver vase, 1929,
15.5cm. high, 6¾oz.
(Christie's) $510 £280

One of a pair of late
19th/early 20th cen-
tury German ampho-
ra-shaped vases, 28cm.
high, 34.4oz. (Sothe-
by's Belgravia)
$565 £310

Set of three George III two-
handled sugar vases and
covers by John Scofield,
1787, 46oz. (Christie's)
$2,790 £1,430

Late 19th century
Japanese silver and
shibayama vase de-
corated in mother-
of-pearl, 29cm. high.
(Geering & Colyer)
$660 £360

Liberty & Co. 'Cymric'
silver bullet-shaped
vase, Birmingham,
1903, 2¾oz., 11.2cm.
high. (Christie's)
$345 £190

Late 19th century cloisonne
enamelled silver vase, with
urn-shaped body, 9¼in. high.
(Robert W. Skinner Inc.)
$1,600 £895

Guild of Handicrafts Ltd.
silver vase, London,
1905, 8½oz., 13cm. high.
(Christie's) $310 £170

Victorian silver vase with two side handles, 15in. diam., 80oz., London, 1852. (Sotheby, King & Chasemore) $1,420 £780

Late 19th century Faberge silver vase in Art Nouveau style, 6in. high. (Christie's) $3,330 £1,800

One of a set of three German die-stamped slipper vases, late 19th/early 20th century, 20oz., 21cm. long. (Sotheby's Belgravia)$1,345 £715

Omar Ramsden silver vase on short knopped stem, London, 1936, 10½oz., 15.6cm. high. (Christie's) $655 £360

Set of three Charles II oviform vases and covers of different sizes, 1669, 107oz. (Christie's) $14,500 £8,100

Victorian posy holder by E. H. Stockwell, London, 1877, 3oz.12dwt., 5in. high. (Sotheby's) $750 £407

Sterling silver vase by Arthur Stone, Gardner, Massachusetts, circa 1920's, 10 troy oz., 6¾in. high. (Robert W. Skinner Inc.) $120 £70

Victorian silver gilt replica of the Warwick vase, by Barnard & Co., 1901, 11½in. high, 243oz. (Christie's)$6,475 £3,500

Large Art Deco electroplated vase, urn-shaped on pedestal foot, 1920's, 47cm. high. (Sotheby's Belgravia) $285 £160

Small shaped oblong vinaigrette with engraved initials, Birmingham, 1855, 3.7cm. long. (Sotheby's Belgravia) $150 £82

19th century silver mounted horn vinaigrette, 2in. wide, lid set with agates. (Sotheby's)$290 £154

Silver vinaigrette in the form of a seated cow, by Henry Wilkinson, Sheffield, circa 1838, 2½in. long. (Christie's)
$555 £300

George III oval shaped silver vinaigrette, circa 1810. (Sotheby's)
$390 £200

Mid Victorian hallmarked vinaigrette with pierced floral grille, by Joseph Turner. (Locke & England)
$380 £210

George IV silver gilt vinaigrette, by W.S., Birmingham, 1825, 1½in. wide. (Lawrence Fine Art) $230 £120

Large rectangular vinaigrette by Francis Clark, Birmingham, 1845, 5.1cm. long. (Sotheby's Belgravia)
$1,075 £572

Early 19th century Scottish silver gilt mounted hardstone vinaigrette, 2in. high. (Christie's)$760 £410

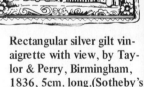

Rectangular silver gilt vinaigrette with view, by Taylor & Perry, Birmingham, 1836, 5cm. long.(Sotheby's Belgravia) $870 £462

George IV oblong vinaigrette by T. & W.S., Birmingham, 1824, 1¾in. wide. (Sotheby's)
$330 £180

George III oblong vinaigrette by Joseph Willmore, Birmingham, 1815. (Sotheby's)
$360 £185

Large rectangular silver gilt vinaigrette by Nathaniel Mills, Birmingham, 1838, 2½in. long. (Christie's)
$1,295 £700

William IV silver gilt vinaigrette of oblong form, by Nathaniel Mills, Birmingham, 1835, 2in. long. (Sotheby's) $345 £187

19th century Scottish gold mounted citrine vinaigrette with faceted sides, 1¾in. high. (Christie's) $600 £324

George III oblong vinaigrette decorated with lobes, Birmingham, 1806, 1½in. wide.(Sotheby's) $165 £90

George IV silver gilt vinaigrette by Nathaniel Mills, Birmingham, 1827, 1½in. long. (Sotheby's) $285 £154

Purse-shaped vinaigrette by L. & C., Birmingham, 1817. (Sotheby's) $485 £250

Shaped rectangular vinaigrette with detached grille, by Frederick Marson, Birmingham, 1857, 4.4cm. long. (Sotheby's Belgravia) $170 £93

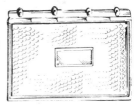

George IV vinaigrette in the form of a flower-filled basket, by John Shaw, Birmingham, 1820, 1in. long. (Sotheby's) $770 £418

Silver gilt vinaigrette in the form of a lamp, by H. W. & L. Dee, London, 1870, 3.4cm. high. (Sotheby's Belgravia) $870 £462

Early Victorian vinaigrette in the form of a book, by Joseph Willmore, Birmingham, 1838, 1¼in. long. (Sotheby's) $325 £176

Rectangular silver gilt vinaigrette by Nathaniel Mills, Birmingham, 1837, 1¾in. long. (Christie's) $705 £380

Victorian shaped rectangular vinaigrette by Yapp & Woodward, Birmingham, 1845, 1¾in. wide.(Lawrence Fine Art) $155 £80

Shaped rectangular vinaigrette by Nathaniel Mills, Birmingham, 1842, 4.4cm. long. (Sotheby's Belgravia) $305 £165

One of a pair of Sheffield
plated campana-shaped
wine coolers. (J. M. Welch
& Son) $820 £450

One of a pair of Sheffield
plate wine coolers of
campana shape, 10¾in.
high. (Lawrence Fine Art)
     $1,400 £775

One of a pair of cam-
pana-shaped wine
coolers, circa 1825,
10¼in. high, in silver
plate. (Sotheby's)
     $2,300 £1,210

One of a pair of campana-
shaped wine coolers, in
silver plate, circa 1810,
10in. high. (Sotheby's)
     $1,470 £800

Silver two-handled wine
cooler on square base,
Sheffield, 1906, 10½in.
high. (Gilbert Baitson)
     $1,585 £840

One of a pair of silver
plated wine coolers,
circa 1835, 10¼in. high.
(Sotheby's)$1,880 £990

One of a pair of mid 19th
century twin-handled
plate mounted wine cool-
ers, 11in. high. (Christie's)
     $2,035 £1,100

One of a pair of plate
mounted bell-shaped
glass wine coolers,
12in. circa 1820.
(Sotheby's)
     $1,560 £825

One of a pair of mid 19th
century two-handled
plate mounted wine cool-
ers and liners, 11in. high.
(Christie's)$1,940 £1,050

SILVER

Large wine funnel with applied reeding to stem, 6in. high, London, 1838, 3¼oz. (Dickinson, Davy & Markham) $160 £90

George III wine funnel of plain design, by John Emes, London, 1801, 2½oz., 5½in. long. (Dickinson, Davy & Markham) $130 £75

Silver wine funnel, London, 1785, 3oz. (Phillips) $145 £80

WINE LABELS

George III wine label for Port, by John Whittingham, London, 1792. (Lawrence Fine Art) $65 £35

Pair of Victorian vine leaf wine labels by George Unite, Birmingham, 1859. (Lawrence Fine Art) $105 £55

George III wine label of navette form, by W. S., circa 1790. (Lawrence Fine Art) $75 £40

George III embossed decanter label, Sherry, Sheffield, 1808. (Dickinson, Davy & Markham) $75 £40

Pair of George III plain crescent shape wine labels, circa 1790. (Lawrence Fine Art) $195 £100

George III wine label for Brandy, by Wm. Snooke Hall, 1817. (Lawrence Fine Art) $105 £55

Agate snuff bottle and stopper with raised panels, 2¼in. high. (Sotheby's) $20 £11

Chinese green jade snuff bottle, circa 1900, with jade stopper, 2¼in. high. (Robert W. Skinner Inc.) $50 £26

Double overlay glass snuff bottle of flattened globular form, carved with hawks, 2¼in. high. (Sotheby's) $40 £22

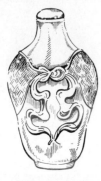

Rare 18th century Imperial yellow glass snuff bottle with stopper, in rich tone. (Sotheby's) $1,205 £638

Mid 19th century ivory snuff bottle and cover carved with the Eight Immortals, 10cm. high. (Sotheby's Belgravia) $255 £132

Reticulated porcelain snuff bottle carved in relief and decorated in famille rose, 2½in. high. (Sotheby's) $60 £33

Pekin glass snuff bottle of faceted hexagonal shape in rich ruby tone, 1800/1860, with stopper. (Sotheby's) $165 £88

Rare double overlay glass snuff bottle of disc shape, white ground overlaid in red and black. (Sotheby's) $1,040 £550

Chinese moss agate snuff bottle, circa 1900, with carnelian top, 2¼in. high. (Robert W. Skinner Inc.) $50 £26

STONE

14th century Belgian sandstone relief of Two Apostles, one with missing head, 36cm. wide. (Christie's)$3,170 £1,650

One of a pair of early 19th century stone Talbot hounds on sandstone plinths, 50in. wide.(Sotheby's)$1,255 £660

One of a pair of late 17th century Italian limestone statues of the Annunciation, 75cm. high. (Christie's)$6,970 £3,630

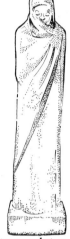

Khmer sandstone head of Buddha, on wood stand, circa 12th century, 7¾in. high.(Sotheby's) $790 £440

Tall stone sculpture of a figure in a cloak, 72cm. high. (Phillips) $395 £220

Khmer sandstone head of Buddha, carved in low relief, circa 12th century, 6¾in. high. (Sotheby's) $435 £242

One of a pair of Ilminster stone garden urn ornaments on pedestals. (David Symonds) $395 £225

10th/12th century buff sandstone male head with pointed beard, 12½in. long.(Sotheby's) $885 £495

10th/12th century Central Indian buff sandstone female figure with jewelled girdle, 22¼in. high. (Sotheby's) $4,725 £2,640

Early 18th century Dutch armorial tapestry cushion cover, 22 x 26in. (Sotheby, King & Chasemore) $1,115 £600

One of two early 17th century Flemish tapestry border fragments, 62 x 12in. (Sotheby's Belgravia) $625 £330

Brussels tapestry woven with a scene from Roman history, 9ft.4in. x 7ft. 11in. (Christie's) $1,920 £1,000

Aubusson verdure tapestry depicting a landscape, 4ft.4in. x 9ft.10in. (Robert W. Skinner Inc.) $700 £380

19th century Brussels 'Art of War' tapestry by Gaspar van der Borcht, 86 x 94in. (Sotheby, King & Chasemore) $1,490 £800

One of a pair of Aubusson tapestry portiers, 43in. wide, circa 1840. (Sotheby's Belgravia) $1,140 £638

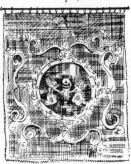

Arts & Crafts style carpet, designed by C. F. A. Voysey. (Sotheby's Belgravia) $3,020 £1,650

Early 20th century Persian wall-hanging, 167 x 104in. (Sotheby's Belgravia) $205 £110

Early 17th century Florentine red velvet altar hanging embroidered in silks, 75 x 63in. (Sotheby, King & Chasemore) $1,115 £600

TAPESTRIES

17th century Brussels armorial tapestry with arms of the Contreras family, 13ft.3in. x 9ft. (Christie's)$6,530 £3,400

Early 18th century Gobelins tapestry in muted colours, 15ft.2in. x 11ft.3in. (Christie's) $9,600 £5,000

Late 19th century Indo-portuguese embroidered wall-hanging from Goa, 129 x 105in.(Sotheby's Belgravia) $4,575 £2,420

19th century Japanese wall-hanging worked in ivory silk and grey and blue thread, 2.32 x 1.07m. (Phillips) $1,200 £650

19th century wall-hanging in gold and grey thread, 2.20 x 1.52m. (Phillips)$1,145 £620

Early 19th century American embroidered picture on a silk ground, 15 x 18½in. (Robert W. Skinner Inc.) $400 £220

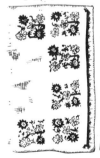

17th century silk work picture, mainly in tent stitch, framed and glazed, 22 x 23cm. (Phillips)$350 £190

Balkan-Middle Eastern embroidery panel in pink, red and blue, 3ft. 9in. x 6ft.6in. (Robert W. Skinner Inc.)$100 £55

Flemish biblical tapestry from the story of Esther, circa 1600, 10ft.10in. wide. (Sotheby's) $4,990 £2,640

773

German tinplate ambulance, probably by Fischer, 10½in. long, circa 1918. (Sotheby's Belgravia) $1,165 £638

19th century papier-mache games box by Jennens & Bettridge's, 11¼in. wide.. (W. H. Lane & Son) $450 £250

Unusual Bing tinplate horse-drawn fire engine, hand-enamelled, circa 1903, 12in. long. (Sotheby's Belgravia)
                                $6,040 £3,300

French tinplate child's cooking stove complete with utensils, circa 1900, 17½in. wide. (Sotheby's Belgravia)
                                $300 £165

German mechanical boxers 'Pit and Fox', early 1930's, by Gebruder Einfalt, 6½in. long. (Robert W. Skinner Inc.)
                                $300 £165

Ham and Sam 'The Minstrel Team', by Ferdinand Strauss Corporation, New York, 1921, 7½in. high. (Robert W. Skinner Inc.) $230 £120

French 'walking griffon' automaton, circa 1920, 14in. long. (Sotheby's Belgravia) $325 £176

Late 19th century English carved wood rocking horse with horsehair mane and leather saddlery, 54in. long. (Sotheby's Belgravia) $525 £286

Dinky toy, A.E.C. double-decker bus with Dunlop Tyres slogan, circa 1938. (Sotheby's) $90 £48

English horse-drawn road cleaners cart, circa 1880, 32in. long. (Sotheby's Belgravia) $565 £308

Spic and Span 'The Hams What Am', by Louis Marx & Co., New York, circa 1925, 10in. high. (Robert W. Skinner Inc.) $575 £305

Cast iron 'Old Dutch' pull toy, America, circa 1925, 9in. long. (Robert W. Skinner Inc.) $725 £385

German wind-up beetle by Lehmann, 1895, in excellent condition, 3¾in. long. (Robert W. Skinner Inc.) $100 £55

Early 20th century English fairground galloper with flowing mane and glass eyes, 64in. long. (Sotheby's Belgravia) $765 £418

French child's 'galloper' tricycle with applied mane, tail and saddlery, circa 1880, 29in. long. (Sotheby's Belgravia) $965 £528

Early 20th century horse-drawn pantechnicon removal van, 28½in. wide overall. (Sotheby's) $25 £13

German tin auto by Whitan Co.,
circa 1925, 13½in. long. (Robert W.
Skinner Inc.) $175 £95

'Buddy L Model T' pickup truck, East
Moline Illinois, circa 1925, 12in. long.
(Robert W. Skinner Inc.) $525 £275

One of six tin wind-up toys, circa
1925-50, 3¾in. to 8¾in. high.
(Robert W. Skinner Inc.)
                          $190 £100

Six T.T. Bury fantascope discs in original
folder, circa 1833, 9½in. diam.
(Sotheby's Belgravia) $480 £260

Bing tinplate tram with clockwork
mechanism, circa 1920, 7in. long,
slightly rusted. (Sotheby's Belgravia)
                          $530 £275

French tinplate peacock with clockwork
mechanism, circa 1905, 10in. long.
(Sotheby's Belgravia) $255 £132

Late 19th century American tin
kitchen with stove, cupboard and
pump, 19in. wide. (Robert W.
Skinner Inc.) $320 £170

Hubley two-seated brake drawn by a
pair of horses, 16½in. long. (Robert
W. Skinner Inc.) $4,000 £2,115

Schoenhut 'Barney Goggle' and 'Spark Plug', Pennsylvania, circa 1924, 6in. and 7in. high. (Robert W. Skinner Inc.) $675 £355

German EPL I tinplate Zeppelin, by Lehmann, circa 1910, 7½in. long. (Sotheby's Belgravia) $340 £176

Early 20th century Steiff ride-on donkey and two-wheel cart, 47in. long. (Robert W. Skinner Inc.) $575 £305

American child's pedal car, circa 1925, by Steelcraft, 36in. long. (Robert W. Skinner Inc.) $350 £185

Late 19th century American rocking horse with horsehair mane and tail, 47in. long. (Robert W. Skinner Inc.) $400 £210

Wolverine 'Sunny Andy Kiddie Kampers', Pittsburgh, 1928, 14in. long. (Robert W. Skinner Inc.) $190 £100

French chamois-covered pig automaton, probably by Decamps, circa 1910, 10¼in. long. (Sotheby's Belgravia) $160 £88

Early 20th century toy vehicles in excellent condition, 18¾in. and 23½in. wide. (Robert W. Skinner Inc.) $80 £42

French P2 Alpha Romeo, probably by CIJ, circa 1925-30, 21in. long. (Sotheby Beresford Adams) $245 £130

French tinplate 'collision' racing car in yellow and gold, circa 1910, 8in. long. (Sotheby Beresford Adams) $205 £110

Large hand-enamelled tinplate limousine, probably by Carette, circa 1911, 16½in. long. (Sotheby's Belgravia) $1,295 £700

French 'walking pussy cat' toy with white fur covering, circa 1930, 30cm. long. (Sotheby, King & Chasemore) $240 £130

German hand-enamelled tinplate duck in original cardboard box, circa 1905, 7in. long. (Sotheby's Belgravia) $85 £45

Bing tinplate limousine with clockwork mechanism, circa 1910, 7½in. long. (Sotheby's Belgravia) $480 £260

Tinplate limousine by Carette, circa 1912, 14in. long, with clockwork mechanism. (Sotheby's Belgravia) $700 £380

Bing gauge 'one' electric tram, circa 1909, finished in red and cream, 9in. long. (Sotheby Beresford Adams) $505 £270

Britain's civilian model of a motorcycle and sidecar, circa 1939. (Phillips) $1,685 £920

Lineol tinplate Krupp Prime Mover truck. (Christie's S. Kensington) $705 £380

German tinplate steam-fired automobile, probably by Doll & Cie, circa 1910, 18in. long. (Sotheby's Belgravia) $700 £380

Late 19th century pull-along carved wooden horse and cart in poor condition, 23in. long. (Sotheby Beresford Adams) $85 £45

Lehmann Li-La tinplate carriage, no. 520, circa 1915, 5½in. long. (Sotheby's Belgravia) $405 £220

Victorian dark polished and gilt painted softwood miniature gypsy van, circa 1900, 21in. wide. (Sotheby Beresford Adams) $85 £45

German tinplate novelty toy of a man and a trolley with two geese, circa 1935, 7½in. long. (Sotheby Beresford Adams) $300 £160

Philip Vielmetter tinplate drawing clown, 5in. wide, circa 1905, with six metal cams. (Sotheby's Belgravia) $645 £350

Printed tinplate dancing couple with clockwork motor, probably French, circa 1905, 8in. high. (Christie's S. Kensington) $370 £200

Bing tinplate monoplane, 1930's. (Christie's S, Kensington) $180 £100

Trooper of the Camel-Mounted Detachments, 1910. (Phillips) $475 £260

Early American hand-enamelled tinplate horse and carriage, circa 1880, 15½in. long.(Sotheby's Belgravia) $1,105 £572

Chad Valley tinplate van with opening rear door, circa 1935, 10¼in. long. (Sotheby's Belgravia) $340 £176

Large plush-covered cartoon figure 'Felix the Cat', English, circa 1830, 28½in. high.(Sotheby's Belgravia) $1,060 £550

Lane's telescopic view of the Great Exhibition within printed cardboard envelope, circa 1851. (Sotheby's Belgravia) $370 £200

German 'Oh-My' tin-, plate dancer by Lehmann, 10in. high, circa 1925, in original box. (Sotheby's Belgravia)$425 £220

French Cinematograph-Toy viewer with eight paper bands, circa 1900. (Sotheby's Belgravia) $515 £280

Special mounted commission of Henry V, signed R. Courtney, and accompanied by an historical note. (Phillips)$240 £130

Two Fun-e-Flex painted wooden toys, Mickey & Minnie Mouse, circa 1931, American, 6¾in. high. (Sotheby's Belgravia) $205 £110

Rare Lehmann 'zig-zag' rocking vehicle with two figures, circa 1910, 5in. wide. (Sotheby's Belgravia) $850 £440

Early 20th century set of Britain's Spanish dragoons. (Phillips) $1,375 £750

Unusual painted lead and papier-mache tea-drinking toy, probably French, circa 1880, 12in. high. (Sotheby's Belgravia) $710 £385

Czechoslovakian Gaiety Cinema viewer, 1920, 8¼in. high. (Sotheby's Belgravia)$200 £110

Stuffed toy 'Minnie Mouse' by Dean's Rag Book Ltd., circa 1930, 7in. high. (Sotheby's Belgravia) $135 £71

Meccano Dinky toy with metal wheels, circa 1935, rear doors repaired. (Sotheby's) **\$310 £165**

Modern cast plaster figure of a negro entertainer, 70in. high. (Sotheby's Belgravia) **\$300 £165**

Scale model of a timbered Tudor house with oak beams and red brickwork, 21in. wide. (Boardman's) **\$445 £250**

Marx lithographed tin wind-up 'Donald Duck Duet', New York, 1946, in good condition, 9in. high. (Robert W. Skinner Inc.) **\$325 £185**

Marx tin wind-up 'Tidy Tim', New York, 1933, in excellent condition, 9in. long. (Robert W. Skinner Inc.) **\$160 £90**

Early German hand-enamelled tinplate carousel, 15¼in. high, circa 1895. (Sotheby's Belgravia) **\$905 £495**

Marx lithographed tin wind-up 'Popeye Express', New York, 1935, in original box, 9in. diam. (Robert W. Skinner Inc.) **\$250 £145**

Papier-mache figure of 'Nipper', the R.C.A. trademark dog, 17½in. high. (Robert W. Skinner Inc.) **\$300 £160**

Stevens & Brown tin mechanical Champion velocipede, patented 1870, 9¼in. high. (Robert W. Skinner Inc.) **\$1,000 £570**

Early 20th century French child's hippo tricycle with black painted chassis. (Sotheby's) $165 £88

1926 Jewett two-door sedan, 6 cylinder, blue and white body, restored. (Robert W. Skinner Inc.) $3,500 £1,955

Mid 18th century Italian giltwood and black leather sedan chair with brass studded canopy, 32in. wide. (Christie's) $1,655 £900

20th century English stagecoach designed to harness ponies, 7ft. wide, damaged. (Sotheby's) $935 £495

1960 Mercedes 220 S.E. convertible with dark green exterior, mileage 73,563. (Robert W. Skinner Inc.) $20,000 £11,175

Early 20th century American wicker baby carriage with parasol, 56½in. high. (Robert W. Skinner Inc.) $225 £125

Mid Victorian velocipede with cast iron frame and iron rimmed wooden wheels. (Samuel Rains & Son) $1,180 £620

Cadillac, 1979, blue Biarritz coupe with many extras. (Robert W. Skinner Inc.) $10,300 £5,819

Early 20th century Edwardian mahogany tray with boxwood and mahogany gallery, 24in. wide. (Sotheby's) $140 £74

Papier-mache desk folder, front inlaid with mother-of-pearl, circa 1860, 12in. high. (Sotheby's Belgravia) $115 £65

Early 19th century toleware tray, probably Connecticut, 12½in. long. (Robert W. Skinner Inc.) $150 £85

Emile Galle marquetry octagonal tray inlaid with a landscape, 49.3cm. wide. (Christie's) $885 £486

Mid 19th century Williams' Burton papier-mache King Gothic tea tray, 32in. wide. (Sotheby's) $210 £110

Tole bread tray, probably New York, early 19th century, 13in. long. (Robert W. Skinner Inc.)$370 £210

Small rectangular tray with incurved sides, decorated with coloured takamakie, 19.5cm. long. (Sotheby's) $2,360 £1,320

Papier-mache tray with moulded serpentine border, painted in gilt, circa 1850, 30½in. long. (Sotheby's Belgravia) $450 £250

Sukashi tsuba of oval form, details in gold nunome and copper, 7.9cm. high, unsigned. (Sotheby's) $205 £110

Kinai school tsuba of mokko form, pierced with a rain dragon, eye in gold, 8.1cm. high, signed Echizen ju Kinai saku. (Sotheby's)　$120 £66

Soten school tsuba of circular form, pierced within the rim, unsigned, 8.3cm. high. (Sotheby's)　$240 £132

Higo school tsuba of circular form, 7.3cm. high, unsigned. (Sotheby's)　$110 £60

Oval tsuba applied in silver, gold and coloured enamels, unsigned, 7.9cm. long. (Sotheby's)　$670 £374

Circular tsuba, pierced and applied in relief, 8.2cm. long, signed Tetsugendo. (Sotheby's)　$570 £319

One of three 19th century Japanese cut-out iron tsubas of round shape, signed. (Robert W. Skinner Inc.)　$175 £95

Tsuba of mokko form applied with two spiders, details in silver and gold nunome, 7.9cm. high, signed Chikatoshi. (Sotheby's) $345 £187

One of three 19th century Japanese cut-out iron tsubas, signed. (Robert W. Skinner Inc.) $170 £90

INDEX